THE LEGAL PROFESSION:

Responsibility and Regulation

THIRD EDITION

By

GEOFFREY C. HAZARD, JR.
Sterling Professor of Law, Yale Law School

DEBORAH L. RHODE
Professor of Law, Stanford Law School
Director, Institute for Research on Women and Gender
Stanford University

Westbury, New York
THE FOUNDATION PRESS, INC.
1994

Library of Congress Cataloging-in-Publication Data

The Legal profession : responsibility and regulation / [edited] by
  Geoffrey C. Hazard, Jr. and Deborah L. Rhode. — 3rd ed.

    p.   cm.

  Includes bibliographical references.

ISBN 1–56662–128–3

  1. Legal ethics—United States. I. Hazard, Geoffrey C.

II. Rhode, Deborah L.

KF306.A4L44   1994

174'.3'0973—dc20   93–36631

H. & R. Legal Profession 3rd Ed.

TABLE OF CONTENTS

TABLE OF CONTENTS

PART II. PROFESSIONAL ROLES

TABLE OF CONTENTS

TABLE OF CONTENTS

*

THE LEGAL PROFESSION:

Responsibility and Regulation

*

INTRODUCTION

Interest in the legal profession as a serious academic subject is a relatively recent phenomenon. Until the last quarter century, the subject generally held a peripheral position on the academic agenda. Courses on professional responsibility, if taught at all, tended to be perfunctory. Most were short on content and long on platitudes. Coverage was generally too theoretical or not theoretical enough; too removed from the actual context of practice and too uninformed by interdisciplinary frameworks. Rarely did serious scholarship focus on the bar's organization or the premises underlying its regulatory efforts.

Over the last two decades, issues of professional roles and responsibilities have started to come under more searching scrutiny. Critics, courts, and educators have begun to give greater attention to the social, economic, and ideological underpinnings of professional governance. This volume is designed to present various dimensions in which such analysis has proceeded.

The readings and references collected here are neither exclusive nor exhaustive. Rather, they identify topics that can form the core of a basic course on the legal profession or serve as background for a more focused scholarly agenda. The organizing premise is that inquiry into attorneys' individual and collective responsibilities should be informed by a variety of intellectual disciplines. The following excerpts survey historical, sociological, economic, and philosophical perspectives that should illumine contemporary debates over the legal profession's ideals and institutions.*

* The authors gratefully acknowledge the assistance of Mirah James, Ruth E. Roth and Isabel Traugott in preparing this manuscript.

Almost all of the material appearing in this collection has been edited. The deletion of sentences and paragraphs is indicated by ellipses. Most footnotes and citations have been omitted. The remaining footnotes retain their original numbers.

1

Part I

HISTORICAL AND SOCIOLOGICAL PERSPECTIVES ON PROFESSIONAL REGULATION

I. THE ATTRIBUTES OF A PROFESSION: THREE VIEWS OF THE CATHEDRAL

INTRODUCTION

In a book focussing on the legal "profession," it is appropriate to begin with certain fundamental questions about what that term implies. On a descriptive level, what are the social meanings and consequences of professional status? How do particular occupations achieve it and how does the process vary across time and culture? On a normative level, how can concepts of professionalism serve useful purposes as theoretical tools, aspirational ideals, or regulatory frameworks?

Occupations that we now consider "professional" have been in existence for well over 2,000 years, although the term itself and the distinctive features of these vocational groups did not begin to emerge until the sixteenth century. "Profession" comes from the Latin, *professionem,* meaning to make a public declaration. The term evolved to describe occupations that required new entrants to take an oath professing their dedication to the ideals and practices associated with a learned calling.

Most contemporary theories of professionalism have taken a functionalist approach. Analysis has focused on explaining the professions' societal role and status in terms of the functions they perform. Emphasis generally centers on professionals' claim to special expertise and ethical responsibilities, which in turn give rise to other defining attributes such as regulatory autonomy, economic monopoly, codes of conduct, associational structures, and a common vocabulary, education, and sense of purpose.[1]

---

1. *See* A. Carr-Saunders and P. Wilson, *The Professions* (1933); W. Moore, *The Professions: Roles and Rules* 5–6 (1970); Hughes, "Professions" in *The Professions in America* 1–14 (K. Lynn ed. 1965); Greenwood, "The Attributes of a Profession" in *Professionalization* (H. Vollmer & D. Mills eds. 1966); Goode, "Community Within a Community: The Professions," 22 *Am. Soc. Rev.* 194 (1957).

This analytic framework builds on various sociological traditions. The focus on professional ethics draws force from Emile Durkheim's concept of normative occupational communities, which were to occupy the void left by breakdowns in other secular and religious institutions.[2] The significance of professional expertise is consistent with Max Weber's theories of specialization and technical rationality.[3] Such characteristics also occupy a central place in Talcott Parsons' analysis of the legal profession. For Parsons, the central distinction between professions and other vocations arises from their functional characteristics rather than the personal objectives of their membership. While professionals, like businessmen, are motivated by the same central desires, "objective achievement and recognition," the accepted means of attaining and realizing those ends vary in accordance with occupational roles.[4] In Parsons' view, the bar acts as a "mechanism of social control," both by providing assistance and forestalling deviance; the lawyer's function is

> often to resist [clients'] pressures and get them to realize some of the hard facts of their situations .... In this sense then, the lawyer stands as a kind of buffer between the illegitimate desires of his clients and the social interest. Here he 'represents' the law rather than the client.[5]

These functional accounts of the profession have drawn increasing criticism from both the left and right. The more radical critiques proceed on several levels. The ahistorical focus of conventional paradigms, and their assumption of a monolithic occupational community, ignore the variation across time, place, and professional subcultures. The attempt to construct catalogues of vocational characteristics has been denounced as mindless "definition mongering." [6]

To rank occupations in terms of simple dichotomies—*i.e.*, profession/non-profession—is elitist and reductive; it obscures the richness and variation among organizational cultures and reflects undefended value judgments about the relative worth of certain forms of labor. From many critics' perspectives, the claims of expertise and service orientations that professionals advance are

2. *See* Emile Durkheim, *Professional Ethics and Civil Morals* (1940 ed.), *infra* at 80.

3. Max Weber, "On Law," in *Economy and Society* (M. Rheinstein ed. 1922).

4. Talcott Parsons, "The Professions and Social Structure," in *Essays in Sociological Theory* 43–46 (rev. ed. 1954).

5. "A Sociologist Looks at the Legal Profession" in Parsons, *supra* note 4, at 384.

6. Terence Johnson, *Professions and Power* 31 (1972); *see also* E. Freidson, "The Theory of Professions: The State of the Art in the Sociology of the Professions" (R. Dingwell & P. Lewis, 1983).

not different in kind from those of other groups that are thought to lack professional status (*compare e.g.*, midwives and journalists).[7]

Moreover, functionalist explanations have been thought to leave all the interesting questions unanswered. Thus, Terence Johnson argues that such accounts border on the tautological: theorists like Parsons simply hypothesize objectives, such as "achievement and recognition," on such an abstract level that no one can disagree, and then asserts with some confidence that professionals seek those goals.[8] What such analyses leave out is how those general objectives are pursued in particular social settings and whether that pursuit is consistent with broader societal interests.

As to those questions, theorists such as Richard Abel, Magali Larson, and Milton Friedman have provided different perspectives. Abel and Larson's approach, which borrows heavily from contemporary Marxist scholarship, emphasizes both the professions' role in creating a market for their claimed expertise, and their reliance on that claim to legitimate professional power and prerogatives.[9] Neo-classical economic analysis interprets professionalism as an elaborate form of market restraint.[10] Other critics have focused less on professions' collective interests than on their client relationships. While Parsons stressed the positive functions of professionals in mediating public and private concerns, theorists such as Maureen Cain and Ivan Illich have emphasized the preemptive and disabling consequences of such mediation.[11] In their analysis, professions are more than trades with pretensions. Rather, professional practitioners occupy a position of dominance that enables them unilaterally to define, assess, and mystify the terms of their assistance.[12] A more moderate critical position, the one most characteristic among lawyers themselves, accepts the

7. *See e.g.* Frye v. Commissioner of Finance, 466 N.Y.S.2d 3 (1983) (holding that journalism does not have the "hallmarks" of a profession within the meaning of New York City's unincorporated business tax provision since journalists need not complete an advanced course of specialized study and are not subject to the authority of a licensing agency, disciplinary body, or binding code of ethics).

8. Johnson, supra note 6 at 33–34.

9. M. Larson, *The Rise of Professionalism: A Sociological Analysis* (1977), *supra* at 20; R. Abel, "Delegalization," in *Alternative Rechtsformen und Alter-* *nativen zum Recht: 6 Jahrbuch für Rechtssoziologie und Rechtstheorie* (E. Blankenburg, E. Klausa & H. Rottleuthner eds. 1979); "The Rise of Professionalism, R. Abel," 6 *Brit. J. Law & Soc'y* 82 (1979).

10. *See, e.g.*, M. Friedman, *Capitalism and Freedom* (1962).

11. I. Illich, *Disabling Professions* 86–87 (1977); Cain, "The General Practice Lawyer and the Client: Towards a Radical Conception," 7 *Int'l J. Soc. & Law* 331 (1979). *See also* J. Lieberman, *Tyranny of the Experts* 55–68 (1970).

12. *See* sources cited *supra* note 10.

basic role and value of the profession, but criticizes some members for failing to live up to professional ideals. The following readings offer a sample of these competing accounts.

Louis D. Brandeis, "The Opportunity in the Law," in Business: A Profession
(1913).[1]

I assume that in asking me to talk to you on the Ethics of the Legal Profession, you do not wish me to enter upon a discussion of the relation of law to morals, or to attempt to acquaint you with those detailed rules of ethics which lawyers have occasion to apply from day to day in their practice. What you want is this: Standing not far from the threshold of active life, feeling the generous impulse for service which the University fosters, you wish to know whether the legal profession would afford you special opportunities for usefulness to your fellow-men, and, if so, what the obligations and limitations are which it imposes. I say special opportunities, because every legitimate occupation, be it profession or business or trade, furnishes abundant opportunities for usefulness, if pursued in what Matthew Arnold called "the grand manner." It is, as a rule, far more important *how* men pursue their occupation than *what* the occupation is which they select.

But the legal profession does afford in America unusual opportunities for usefulness. That this has been so in the past, no one acquainted with the history of our institutions can for a moment doubt. The great achievement of the English-speaking people is the attainment of liberty through law. It is natural, therefore, that those who have been trained in the law should have borne an important part in that struggle for liberty and in the government which resulted. Accordingly, we find that in America the lawyer was in the earlier period almost omnipresent in the State. Nearly every great lawyer was then a statesman; and nearly every statesman, great or small, was a lawyer. De-Tocqueville, the first important foreign observer of American political institutions, said of the United States seventy-five years ago:

"In America there are no nobles or literary men, and the people are apt to mistrust the wealthy; lawyers, consequently, form the highest political class. ... As the lawyers form the only enlightened class whom the people do not mistrust, they are naturally called upon to occupy most of the public stations. They

---

1. An address delivered May 4, 1905,   Harvard Ethical Society.
at Phillips Brooks House, before the

fill the legislative assemblies and are at the head of the administration; they consequently exercise a powerful influence upon the formation of the law and upon its execution."

For centuries before the American Revolution the lawyer had played an important part in England. His importance in the State became much greater in America. One reason for this, as DeTocqueville indicated, was the fact that we possessed no class like the nobles, which took part in government through privilege. A more potent reason was that with the introduction of a written constitution the law became with us a far more important factor in the ordinary conduct of political life than it did in England. Legal questions were constantly arising and the lawyer was necessary to settle them. But I take it the paramount reason why the lawyer has played so large a part in our political life is that his training fits him especially to grapple with the questions which are presented in a democracy.

The whole training of the lawyer leads to the development of judgment. His early training—his work with books in the study of legal rules—teaches him patient research and develops both the memory and the reasoning faculties. He becomes practised in logic; and yet the use of the reasoning faculties in the study of law is very different from their use, say, in metaphysics. The lawyer's processes of reasoning, his logical conclusions, are being constantly tested by experience. He is running up against facts at every point. Indeed it is a maxim of the law: Out of the facts grows the law; that is, propositions are not considered abstractly, but always with reference to facts.

Furthermore, in the investigation of the facts the lawyer differs very materially from the scientist or the scholar. The lawyer's investigations into the facts are limited by time and space. His investigations have reference always to some practical end. Unlike the scientist, he ordinarily cannot refuse to reach a conclusion on the ground that he lacks the facts sufficient to enable one to form an opinion. He must form an opinion from those facts which he has gathered; he must reason from the facts within his grasp.

If the lawyer's practice is a general one, his field of observation extends, in course of time, into almost every sphere of business and of life. The facts so gathered ripen his judgment. His memory is trained to retentiveness. His mind becomes practised in discrimination as well as in generalization. He is an observer of men even more than of things. He not only sees men of all kinds, but knows their deepest secrets; sees them in situations which "try men's souls." He is apt to become a good judge of men.

Then, contrary to what might seem to be the habit of the lawyer's mind, the practice of law tends to make the lawyer judicial in attitude and extremely tolerant. His profession rests upon the postulate that no contested question can be properly decided until both sides are heard. His experience teaches him that nearly every question has two sides; and very often he finds—after decision of judge or jury—that both he and his opponent were in the wrong. The practice of law creates thus a habit of mind, and leads to attainments which are distinctly different from those developed in most professions or outside of the professions. These are the reasons why the lawyer has acquired a position materially different from that of other men. It is the position of the adviser of men.

. . .

The ordinary man thinks of the Bar as a body of men who are trying cases, perhaps even trying criminal cases. Of course there is an immense amount of litigation going on; and a great deal of the time of many lawyers is devoted to litigation. But by far the greater part of the work done by lawyers is done not in court, but in advising men on important matters, and mainly in business affairs. In guiding these affairs industrial and financial, lawyers are needed, not only because of the legal questions involved, but because the particular mental attributes and attainments which the legal profession develops are demanded in the proper handling of these large financial or industrial affairs. The magnitude and scope of these operations remove them almost wholly from the realm of "petty trafficking" which people formerly used to associate with trade. The questions which arise are more nearly questions of statesmanship. The relations created call in many instances for the exercise of the highest diplomacy. The magnitude, difficulty and importance of the problems involved are often as great as in the matters of state with which lawyers were formerly frequently associated. The questions appear in a different guise; but they are similar. The relations between rival railroad systems are like the relations between neighboring kingdoms. The relations of the great trusts to the consumers or to their employees is like that of feudal lords to commoners or dependents. The relations of public-service corporations to the people raise questions not unlike those presented by the monopolies of old.

. . .

It is true that at the present time the lawyer does not hold as high a position with the people as he held seventy-five or indeed fifty years ago; but the reason is not lack of opportunity. It is this: Instead of holding a position of independence, between the wealthy and the people, prepared to curb the excesses of either, able lawyers have, to a large extent, allowed themselves to become adjuncts of great corporations and have neglected the obligation to use their powers for the protection of the people. We hear much of the "corporation lawyer," and far too little of the "people's lawyer." The great opportunity of the American Bar is and will be to stand again as it did in the past, ready to protect also the interests of the people.

. . .

The leading lawyers of the United States have been engaged mainly in supporting the claims of the corporations; often in endeavoring to evade or nullify the extremely crude laws by which legislators sought to regulate the power or curb the excesses of corporations.

Such questions as the regulation of trusts, the fixing of railway rates, the municipalization of public utilities, the relation between capital and labor, call for the exercise of legal ability of the highest order. Up to the present time the legal ability of a high order which has been expended on those questions has been almost wholly in opposition to the contentions of the people. The leaders of the Bar, without any preconceived intent on their part, and rather as an incident to their professional standing, have, with rare exceptions, been ranged on the side of the corporations, and the people have been represented, in the main, by men of very meagre legal ability.

If these problems are to be settled right, this condition cannot continue. Our country is, after all, not a country of dollars, but of ballots. The immense corporate wealth will necessarily develop a hostility from which much trouble will come to us unless the excesses of capital are curbed, through the respect for law, as the excesses of democracy were curbed seventy-five years ago. There will come a revolt of the people against the capitalists, unless the aspirations of the people are given some adequate legal expression; and to this end coöperation of the abler lawyers is essential.

For nearly a generation the leaders of the Bar have, with few exceptions, not only failed to take part in constructive legislation designed to solve in the public interest our great social, economic and industrial problems; but they have failed likewise to oppose legislation prompted by selfish interests. They have often gone further in disregard of common weal. They have often advocated, as lawyers, legislative measures which as citizens they could not approve, and have endeavored to justify themselves by a false analogy. They have erroneously assumed that the rule of ethics to be applied to a lawyer's advocacy is the same where he acts for private interests against the public, as it is in litigation between private individuals.

The ethical question which laymen most frequently ask about the legal profession is this: How can a lawyer take a case which he does not believe in? The profession is regarded as necessarily somewhat immoral, because its members are supposed to be habitually taking cases of that character. As a practical matter, the lawyer is not often harassed by this problem; partly because he is apt to believe, at the time, in most of the cases that he actually tries; and partly because he either abandons or settles a large number of those he does not believe in. But the lawyer recognizes that in trying a case his prime duty is to present his side to the tribunal fairly and as well as he can, relying upon his adversary to present the other side fairly and as well as he can. Since the lawyers on the two sides are usually reasonably well matched, the judge or jury may ordinarily be trusted to make such a decision as justice demands.

But when lawyers act upon the same principle in supporting the attempts of their private clients to secure or to oppose legislation, a very different condition is presented. In the first place, the counsel selected to represent important private interests possesses usually ability of a high order, while the public is often inadequately represented or wholly unrepresented. Great unfairness to the public is apt to result from this fact. Many bills pass in our legislatures which would not have become law, if the public interest had been fairly represented; and many good bills are defeated which if supported by able lawyers would have been enacted. Lawyers have, as a rule, failed to consider this distinction between practice in courts involving only private interests, and practice before the legislature or city council involving public interests. Some men of high professional standing have even endeavored to justify their course in advocating professionally legislation which in their character as citizens they would have voted against.

Furthermore, lawyers of high standing have often failed to apply in connection with professional work before the legislature or city council a rule of ethics which they would deem imperative in practice before the court. Lawyers who would indignantly retire from a court case in the justice of which they believed, if they had reason to think that a juror had been bribed or a witness had been suborned by their client, are content to serve their client by honest arguments before a legislative committee, although they have as great reason to believe that their client has bribed members of the legislature or corrupted public opinion. This confusion of ethical ideas is an important reason why the Bar does not now hold the position which it formerly did as a brake upon democracy, and which I believe it must take again if the serious questions now before us are to be properly solved.

Here, consequently, is the great opportunity in the law. The next generation must witness a continuing and ever-increasing contest between those who have and those who have not. The industrial world is in a state of ferment. The ferment is in the main peaceful, and, to a considerable extent, silent; but there is felt to-day very widely the inconsistency in this condition of political democracy and industrial absolutism. The people are beginning to doubt whether in the long run democracy and absolutism can co-exist in the same community; beginning to doubt whether there is a justification for the great inequalities in the distribution of wealth, for the rapid creation of fortunes, more mysterious than the deeds of Aladdin's lamp. The people have begun to think; and they show evidences on all sides of a tendency to act. ... The people's thought will take shape in action; and it lies with us, with you to whom in part the future belongs, to say on what lines the action is to be expressed; whether it is to be expressed wisely and temperately, or wildly and intemperately; whether it is to be expressed on lines of evolution or on lines of revolution. Nothing can better fit you for taking part in the solution of these problems, than the study and preeminently the practice of law. Those of you who feel drawn to that profession may rest assured that you will find in it an opportunity for usefulness which is probably unequalled. There is a call upon the legal profession to do a great work for this country.

Magali Larson, The Rise of Professionalism

12–15, 54–55, 56 (1977).*

The Constitution of Professional Markets

.... There had been great progress in higher education and the importation of British professional models in the eighteenth

* Magali S. Larson: *The Rise to Pro-*   (1977); used by permission.
fessionalism: A Sociological Analysis

century, but the colonies remained poor, provincial, and sparsely populated. In a decentralized setting, the nine American colleges that existed before the Revolution could not hold the same consecrating power that Oxford and Cambridge held, despite their intellectual and political liveliness. These colleges gave a gentlemanly seal to those many graduates who did not enter the professions: the more numerous graduates who entered the ministry, most especially, or the law, or lastly medicine, constituted an elite among professionals. In the two secular callings, those practitioners who had studied abroad were an elite of the elite. The bar, in particular, had risen to great power and prestige during the eighteenth century: from being an occupation of "mostly pettifoggers and minor court officers ... who stirred up litigation for the sake of the petty court fees," it had become in urban centers a social and political elite which matched the clergy in importance and tended toward closure. The Revolution purged the bar of its best practitioners, democratizing it, on the whole, but also setting back the general standards of a profession based on apprenticeship and creating a wide gap between the urban legal elites, who shaped the new republic's institutions, and the mass of a growing profession.

But the existence of urban and Eastern professional elites did not mean that they constituted the apex of a recognized professional hierarchy. The difference between cities that looked to Europe and hinterland communities created almost unbridgeable chasms in all professions and trades. In remote frontier areas, geographic isolation assured a de facto monopoly to the lone attorney or physician; it must, however, have been a short-lived advantage, since isolation and decentralization also made self-appointment easy and thus made competition keener. Moreover, professional practice in eighteenth-century America most often was a part-time avocation, except for clergymen, one of whom each township was legally required to support in the old settlements, and who often doubled as part-time lawyers or healers. ...

... To insure their livelihood, the rising professionals had to unify the corresponding areas of the social division of labor around homogeneous guarantees of competence. The unifying principles could be homogeneous only to the extent that they were universalistic—that is, autonomously defined by the professionals and independent, at least in appearance, from the traditional and external guarantees of status stratification. Thus, the modern reorganization of professional work and professional markets tended to found credibility on a different, and much enlarged, monopolistic base—the claim to sole control of superior expertise.

The Organizational Task

. . .

First, for a professional market to exist in a modern sense, a distinctive "commodity" had to be produced. Now professional work, like any other form of labor, is only a *fictitious* commodity: it "cannot be detached from the rest of life, be stored or mobilized," and it is not produced for sale. Unlike craft or industrial labor, however, most professions produce intangible goods: their product, in other words, is only formally alienable and is inextricably bound to the person and the personality of the producer. It follows, therefore, that *the producers themselves have to be produced* if their products or commodities are to be given a distinctive form. In other words, the professionals must be adequately trained and socialized so as to provide recognizably distinct services for exchange on the professional market.

Second, in the formative period, most of the markets for professional services had to be created, for the existing markets were unstable and far from unified; common standards of what this unique commodity—intangible services—meant, and even of what needs it served, were lacking. For a secure market to arise, the superiority of one kind of services had to be clearly established with regard to competing "products." The various professional services, therefore, had to be *standardized* in order to clearly differentiate their identity and connect them, in the minds of consumers, with stable criteria of evaluation. A tendency to monopoly by *elimination* of competing "products" was inherent in this process of standardization; for if other standards of evaluation were allowed to prevail, the preference of the public could not easily be reclaimed away from older "consumer loyalties." Professional entrepreneurs, not unlike their counterparts in industry, were therefore bound to solicit state protection and state-enforced penalties against unlicensed competitors—that is to say, those producers of services whose training and entry into the market they had not controlled. However, no amount of coercion could force a clientele to switch allegiances and seek professional services which it did not even know it needed—at least not in the form that the leaders of professional reform were giving to those professional services. To establish in the public at large common bases for an evaluation of both need and professional competence was, therefore, an ideological task to which the rising professions actively contributed; but obviously, its magnitude was such that it could not be advanced by their efforts alone—ideological persuasion ultimately depended on the completion of the general social shift to a new "symbolic universe." In consequence, the road that the professional reformers had mapped in the liberal phase of capitalism could not be traveled to the end with the "social technology" they had available.

Third, because the standardization of professional services is bound to the production of producers—that is to say, to education—it depends upon inducing new recruits to accept the economic and social sacrifices of training. Hence, at least a moderate guarantee that the recruits' educational investment would be protected had to be sought from the beginning. In a market situation, the guarantee against risks incurred tends to take the form of monopoly, or at least of special protection by the public authorities. In this case, the nature of the products and the state of their markets were such that only the state, as the supreme legitimizing and enforcing institution, could sanction the modern professions' monopolistic claims of superiority for their "commodities." The attitude of the state toward education and toward monopolies of competence is thus a crucial variable in the development of the professional project.

. . .

Professions and the Ideal of Community

... The regulation and organization of market-oriented practice in the professions that consolidated toward the turn of the century stood in contrast to the anarchy of the commodity markets and of capitalist production. Therefore, Emile Durkheim could see in the organization of the professions not only the modern expression of the medieval corporation, but also the social model that would produce the ethics and rules needed by a complex division of labor, and thus save modern society from the chronic anomie rooted in its economy.

If the professions appeared to Durkheim as capable of generating organic solidarity, it is because they possessed some of the characteristics of community which, in their traditional form, were declining in the larger society. William Goode describes the special community of profession by the following traits:

(1) Its members are bound by a sense of identity. (2) Once in it, few leave, so that it is a terminal or continuing status for the most part. (3) Its members share values in common. (4) Its role definitions vis-à-vis both members and non-members are agreed upon and are the same for all members. (5) Within the areas of communal action there is a common language, which is understood only partially by outsiders. (6) The community has power over its members. (7) Its limits are reasonably clear, though they are not physical

and geographical, but social. (8) Though it does not produce the next generation biologically, it does so socially, through its control over the selection of professional trainees, and through its training processes it sends these recruits through an adult socialization process.

. . .

What gave the solidarity of professional producers its typical significance in this early phase, then, was that they were *autonomous*. In a market society where labor is a commodity, these associations of free producers had arisen, in fact, in order to *constitute and control* a new type of market. This fundamental aspect modifies the "anti-market" potential of their corporate solidarity. The atypical "community of profession" did not extend its nomic functions beyond the boundaries of its own market position: the solidarity of the professional producers was seldom, if ever, mobilized to advocate or help the organization of their own consumers. Thus, on the consumer side, the ideal professional market closely approximates the atomistic liberal model, while on the producers' side, with all due qualifications, it presents an analogy with the rise of corporate capitalism against the consequences of anarchic competition. If it is true, besides, that "the professions sought to use the state to achieve greater autonomy for themselves vis-à-vis nongovernmental pressures, and sometimes they even used government to protect themselves from government," then the goal was clearly laissez-faire for the producers, although on the model of liberal pluralism. Thus although the professional community, based on solidarity and on a shared set of cognitive and normative rules, may be seen as part of the reaction against the market, its aims were formulated within a market orientation: the professions' appeal to non-contractual social relations was aimed, in fact, at promoting certain kinds of contractual transactions.

———

NOTES

During the 1980s, such critiques of professionalism, together with widespread concerns about lawyers' public image, prompted increasing attention. The American Bar Association formed a Commission on Professionalism, which reported that only 6% of surveyed corporate legal clients believed attorneys deserved to be called professionals; over two-thirds of these clients, and over half of interviewed judges believed that professionalism had declined within the bar.[1]   While recent surveys have not generally reflected substantial changes in public attitudes toward lawyers, neither have their results been especially encouraging. For example, Gallup polls have indicated that over one-quarter of surveyed Americans rate lawyers "low" or "very low" in honesty and ethical standards, while only four to six percent rate them very high.[2]

In many respects, the ABA Commission on Professionalism follows in the tradition exemplified by Brandeis' earlier observations. For at least a century, much of the bar's rhetoric on professionalism has identified a significant decline in lawyers' public reputation and ethical standards. What is the significance of this persistent longing for some presumptively more "professional" era? Does it suggest that the bar too often looks backward rather than forward in defining its ideal? How does the ideology of professionalism shape lawyers' sense of collective identity and strategies for reform?[3]

American Bar Association, Commission on Professionalism, "In the Spirit of a Public Service: A Blueprint for the Rekindling of Lawyer Professionalism"
(1986), 1–2, 4, 17, 95–96.

"Professionalism" is an elastic concept[,] the meaning and application of which are hard to pin down. That is perhaps as it should be. The term has a rich, long-standing heritage, and any single definition runs the risk of being too confining.

Yet the term is so important to lawyers that at least a working definition seems essential. Lawyers are proud of being part of one of the "historic" or "learned" professions, along with medicine and the clergy, which have been seen as professions through many centuries.

When he was asked to define a profession, Dean Roscoe Pound of Harvard Law School said:

1. American Bar Association, Commission on Professionalism, *In the Spirit of a Public Service* (1986). For comparable concerns, see Moore, "Review Essay: Professionalism Reconsidered," 1987 *A.B.F. Res. J.* 773.

2. Oliver, "Lawyers Losing the Verdict in the Court of Public Opinion," *L.A. Times*, Oct. 19, 1983, p. 3; Stieb-

man, "Bar Study Finds Public Sees Lawyers as Greedy, Unethical," *San Francisco Bar Daily Journal*, December 24, 1987, pp. 1, 20.

3. See Gordon, "The Independence of Lawyers," *Boston College L.Rev.* (1988).

The term refers to a group ... pursuing a learned art as a common calling in the spirit of public service—no less a public service because it may incidentally be a means of livelihood. Pursuit of the learned art in the spirit of a public service is the primary purpose.[*]

The rhetoric may be dated, but the Commission believes the spirit of Dean Pound's definition stands the test of time. The practice of law "in the spirit of a public service" can and ought to be the hallmark of the legal profession.

... Has our profession abandoned principle for profit, professionalism for commercialism?

The answer cannot be a simple yes or no. The legal profession is more diverse and provides more legal services to more people today than ever before. These are not inconsiderable achievements. Further, most lawyers, the Commission believes, are conscientious, fair, and able. They serve their clients well and are a credit to the profession. Yet the practices of some lawyers cry out for correction. Without denigrating the Bar generally, this report proposes some needed changes in the practices of law schools, practicing lawyers and judges. We believe the future of the legal profession will be bright if all elements of the profession resolve to confront their problems and deal with them forthrightly.

. . .

The public views lawyers, at best, as being of uneven character and quality. ...

The primary question for this Commission thus becomes what, if anything, can be done to improve both the reality and the perception of lawyer professionalism.

Perhaps the golden age of professionalism has always been a few years before the time that the living can remember. Legend tends to seem clearer than reality. Still, it is proper—indeed it is essential—for a profession periodically to pause to assess where it is going and out of what traditions it has come.

Clearly, the legal profession is in a process of evolution. This is inevitable. The challenge for individual lawyers and the organized Bar is to understand these changes and to preserve those principles of professionalism which endure despite the changing legal landscape.

[*] Citing R. Pound, *The Lawyer from*   at p. 95.
Antiquity to Modern Times (1953), *infra*

Even with our shortcomings, all is far from bleak on the legal horizon. Examples abound—even in this anti-heroic age—of lawyers who have given of themselves unselfishly and at considerable personal sacrifice to provide their services to the public at large.

. . .

NOTES

To meet the contemporary challenges to professionalism, the Commission proposed various strategies, including increased legal ethics education, greater efforts to promote civility in litigation, improvements in bar disciplinary procedures, and more pro bono service. Following release of the ABA report, most states and many local bar associations convened their own committees on professionalism, which generally expressed views similar to those of the national commission.

Underlying these reports is a widespread disaffection about the increasing pressures and competitiveness of contemporary practice—its higher billable hour requirements, lower partner-associate ratios, less stable law firm relationships, and more adversarial tactics. Yet how lawyers can remedy such trends is by no means obvious. As Robert Nelson and David Trubeck argue:

> To be sure, many within the legal profession might ... prefe[r] stable markets and stable relationships guided by 'professional' rather than commercial values. But this option ... has never really been available in recent history. The bar is too fragmented to agree on what relationships and values should be fostered. It has been too tolerant of entrepreneurship and too leery of effective professional association or governmental control to develop truly powerful regulatory mechanisms. ... or do anything significant about the trends [bar leaders have decried]. The result [has been] a vague and general invocation of 'shared' values that really aren't shared and a symbolic and nostalgic crusade in the name of an ideology almost no one really believes in fully and which has little to do with the everyday working visions of American lawyers.[1]

Do you agree? If so, what follows from this diagnosis? How are "professions" different from other occupational groups? What would it mean for lawyers truly to "put professionalism first," as the ABA Commission recommends? Consider that issue in light of

1. Nelson and Trubeck, "New Problems and New Paradigms in the Studies of the Legal Profession," in *Lawyers' Ideals/Lawyers' Practices: Transformation in the American Legal Profession* 1 (R. Nelson, D. Trubeck & R. Solomon eds., 1992).

the materials on professional codes, discipline, and regulation of competition that follow.

REFERENCES

For further historical and sociological perspectives on the professions in general and the legal profession in particular, see sources cited in Introduction and Notes, *supra, and*

Abel, "Comparative Sociology of Legal Professions: An Exploratory Essay," 1985 *A.B.F. Res. J.* 1.

R. Abel, *American Lawyers* (1990).

Abel, "United States: The Contradictions of Professionalism," in 1 *Lawyers in Society: The Common Law World* 186 (R. Abel and P. Lewis, eds., 1988).

Abbott, "Jurisdictional Conflict: A New Approach to the Development of the Legal Profession," 1986 *A.B.F. Res. J.* 187.

Auerbach, "Control and Responsibility in the Powerful Professions," 93 *Political Science Quarterly* 4 (1978).

Barber, "Control and Responsibility in the Powerful Professions," 93 *Political Science Quarterly,* 512 (1978).

Barker, "What is a Profession?," 1 *Professional Ethics* 73 (1992).

B. Bledstein, *The Culture of Professionalism* (1976).

Bucher and Strauss. "Professions in Process," 66 *American Journal of Sociology* (1961).

R. Dingwall & P. Lewis, ed. *The Sociology of the Professions, Doctors, Lawyers and Others* (1983).

E. Freidson, *Profession of Medicine* (1970).

E. Freidson, *Professional Powers: A Study of the Institutionalization of Formal Knowledge* (1986).

Freidson, "The Changing Nature of Professional Control," 10 *American Review of Sociology* 20 (1984).

G. Geisen, ed. *Professions and Professional Ideologies in America* (1983).

Gordon and Simon, "The Redemption of Professionalism," in *Lawyers' Ideals/Lawyers' Practices: Transformation in the American Legal Profession* 230 (R. Nelson, D. Trubeck & R. Solomon eds., 1992).

R. Hall, *Occupations and the Social Structure* (2d ed.) 72–77 (1975).

Haug and Sussman, "Professional Autonomy and the Revolt of the Client," 17 *Social Problems* 153 (1969).

Luban, "The Noblesse Oblige Tradition in the Practice of Law," 41 *Vand.L.Rev.* 717 (1988).

Morgan, "The Rise and Fall of Professionalism," 19 *U. Richmond L. Rev.* 451 (1985).

Nonet & Carlin, "The Legal Profession," 9 *International Encyclopedia of the Social Sciences* 66–72 (1968).

Richards, "Moral Theory, The Developmental Psychology of Ethical Autonomy and Professionalism," 31 *J. Legal Educ.* 351 (1981).

W. Robison, M. Pritchard & J. Ellin eds., *Profits and Professions* (1983).

Rueschemeyer, "Doctors and Lawyers: A Comment on the Theory of the Professions," *Canadian Rev.Soc. & Anthropology* 17 (1964).

Rueschemeyer, "Comparing Legal Professions Cross Nationally: From a Profession-Centered to a State-Centered Approach," 1987 *A.B.F. Res. J.* 415.

Simon, "Babbit v. Brandeis: The Decline of the Professional Ideal," 37 *Stan.L.Rev.* 565 (1985).

P. Starr, *The Social Transformation of American Medicine* (1982).

Stone, "The Public Influence of the Bar," 48 *Harv.L.Rev.* 1 (1934).

Wilensky, "The Professionalization of Everyone?" 70 *Am. J.Soc.* 136 (1964).

II. THE GROWTH OF THE
LEGAL PROFESSION

A. THE ORIGINS OF THE PROFESSION

INTRODUCTION

The legal profession's historical pedigree spans at least two millenia. By the mid-fourth century B.C., advocates appeared before Greek tribunals and legal counselors handled commercial matters and drafted legislative proposals. However these individuals did not constitute a "professional" community in the contemporary sense of the term. Ethical standards were lax, and systematic education and discipline were lacking.[1]

By contrast, Roman traditions gave rise to a somewhat more professionalized culture of advocates and advisors. Between the first and third centuries A.D., associations of advocates with formal training and disciplinary standards emerged around the courts of major cities. However, with the fall of the Holy Roman Empire, this professional tradition also declined.[2]

In England, the development of a legal community proceeded more slowly. Prior to the Norman invasion, disputes were settled informally through communal adjustment or, more formally, through ordeal or trial by compurgation. Ordeals were a form of adjudication based on divine intervention, in which the accused was generally at a considerable disadvantage. In ordeals by water, for example, defendants who sank were presumed innocent. Under the alternative trial procedure, a critical issue was the credibility of the accused, which was established through oaths by a specified number of compurgators. In order for their oaths to be valid, compurgators had to complete their recitation without any verbal slips. Tradition has it that the earliest Anglo-American analogues to our current advocates were those who could be counted on to deliver their oaths without a sneeze or a stumble.[3]

---

1. *See generally* T. Holton, *Preface to Law: The Professional Milieu* 2–4 (1980) (discussing *inter alia* bribery, breaches of confidentiality, incompetence). *See also* G. Calhoun, *Introduction to Greek Legal Science* 44–48 (1944); R. Bonner, *Lawyers and Litigants in Ancient Athens* 200–213, 218–243 (1927).

2. *See* W. Kunkel, *An Introduction to Roman Legal and Constitutional History* 105–116 (J. Kelly trans. 1973); H. Wolff, *Roman Law* 95–117 (1951).

3. S. Milsom, *Historical Foundations of the Common Law* 28 (1969); Neef and Nagel, "The Adversary Nature of the American Legal System: A Historical

The Normans who invaded England brought with them traditions of both trial by combat and trial by jury. As the latter form of adjudication gradually took hold, a role for advocates developed. Precursors of the British barrister began to appear as "narratores" who essentially "told the [plaintiff's] tale for him." [4] From these antecedents emerged a stratified professional class.

At the top of the hierarchy were sergeants appointed by the Crown after a substantial period of experience; they enjoyed a monopoly over practice in certain courts and provided the ranks from which judges were appointed. Under the sergeants were the barristers, who provided trial representation. These advocates prepared for their role by attending one of four Inns of Court and then serving as apprentices to a practicing barrister. The educational requirements of the Inns varied over time, but during the American bar's formative era, they were anything but rigorous.

Other legal professionals had even less training. They included attorneys, who functioned as intermediaries between solicitors and clients and who did the bulk of pleading and conveyancing; solicitors, who began as business agents performing quasi-legal functions and who ultimately merged with attorneys; and notaries and scriveners, who prepared documents of legal significance. Various subspecialties also arose, along with complicated traditions about who could perform what services in which courts.

Over time, much of this formal stratification broke down and the English legal profession divided into two groups: barristers, subject to regulation by autonomous Inns of Court; and solicitors, governed by professional associations and rules of court, supplemented by legislative enactment. By contrast, the American bar began without such formal stratification and gradually developed into more specialized groups. The following excerpts from Friedman and de Tocqueville indicate the course of that evolution.

Perspective," in *Lawyers Ethics* 73, 76, 80 (A. Gerson ed. 1980). For accounts of contemporary usage of trials by ordeals to legitimate a tribunal's conclusion see Roberts, "Oaths, Autonomic Ordeals, and Power," 67 *Amer. Anthrop.* 187.

4. T. Plucknett, *A Concise History of the Common Law* 217 (5th ed. 1956). *See also* H. Cohen, *History of the English Bar and Attornatus to 1450* 18–35 (1929); R. Pound, *The Lawyer from Antiquity to Modern Times* (1953).

B. LAWYERS IN 18TH AND 19TH CENTURY AMERICA

Lawrence Friedman, A History of American Law
94–98, 633–635, 638–639 (2d ed. 1985).

THE LEGAL PROFESSION

The early colonial years were not friendly years for lawyers. There were few lawyers among the settlers. In some colonies, lawyers were distinctly unwelcome. In Massachusetts Bay, the *Body of Liberties* (1641) prohibited pleading for hire. The "attorneys" of early Virginia records were not trained lawyers, but attorneys-in-fact, laymen helping out their friends in court. In 1645, Virginia excluded lawyers from the courts; there had been a ban in Connecticut too. The Fundamental Constitutions of the Carolinas (1669) was also hostile; it was considered "a base and vile thing to plead for money or reward." Apparently, no lawyers practiced law in South Carolina until Nicholas Trott arrived in 1699. The Quaker colony at Burlington, West New Jersey, made do with a single lawyer until the end of the seventeenth century. In Pennsylvania, it was said, "They have no lawyers. Everyone is to tell his own case, or some friend for him . . . 'Tis a happy country."

There is some evidence, then, to back Daniel Boorstin's comment that "ancient English prejudice against lawyers secured new strength in America . . . [D]istrust of lawyers became an institution." [148] Thomas Morton, who arrived in Plymouth about 1624 or 1625, has been called the first Massachusetts lawyer. He was jailed and expelled for scandalous behavior. Thomas Lechford, who had some legal training, arrived in 1638. He practiced in the colony as a courtroom attorney, and as a draftsman of documents. Lechford had unorthodox religious views, which won him no friends among the magistrates, nor did the fact that he meddled with a jury by "pleading with them out of the Court." It was an uncomfortable, hostile environment; Lechford eventually sailed back to England.

Distrust of lawyers arose from various sources. The Puritan leaders of Massachusetts Bay had an image of the ideal state. Revolutionary or Utopian regimes tend to be hostile to lawyers, at least at first. Lawyers of the old regime have to be controlled or removed; a new, revolutionary commonwealth must start with new law and new habits. Some colonists, oppressed in England, carried with them a strong dislike for all servants of government. Merchants and planters wished to run their affairs, without intermediaries. The theocratic colonies believed in a certain kind of social order, closely directed from the top. The legal profession, with its special privileges and principles, its private, esoteric

---

148. Daniel J. Boorstin, *The Americans: The Colonial Experience* (1958), p. 197.

language, seemed an obstacle to efficient or godly government. The Quakers of the Middle Atlantic were opposed to the adversary system in principle. They wanted harmony and peace. Their ideal was the "Common Peacemaker," and simple, nontechnical justice. They looked on lawyers as sharp, contentious—and unnecessary—people. For all these reasons, the lawyer was unloved in the 17th century.

In the 18th century, too, there was sentiment against lawyers. The lower classes came to identify lawyers with the upper class. Governors and their royal parties, on the other hand, were not sure of the loyalty of lawyers, and were sometimes afraid of their influence and power. In 1765, Cadwallader Colden, lieutenant governor of New York, told the Board of Trade in England that the "Gentlemen of the Law" had grown overmighty. They ranked just below the large landowners, and just above the merchants in society. Lawyers and judges, said Colden, had such power that "every Man is affraid of offending them"; their "domination" was "carried on by the same wicked artifices that the Domination of Priests formerly was in the times of ignorance." Lay judges, too, may have resented the lawyers' threats to their competence and prestige. And as law became more "rational" and "professional," it became more confusing and remote to merchants and businessmen.

How strong the resentment against lawyers was, how deep it went, is hard to say. The evidence is partly literary; pamphlets and speeches are notoriously unreliable as measures of actual feeling among a diverse population. Some hatred was surely there; there is hard evidence of riots and disorders against lawyers and judges. Lawyers, like shopkeepers, moneylenders, and lower bureaucrats, are social middlemen; they are lightning rods that draw rage during storms in the polity. In 18th–century New Jersey, the "table of the Assembly groaned beneath the weight of petitions ... invoking vengeance on the heads of the attorneys." The "Regulators," in late colonial North Carolina—a kind of vigilante group—rose up to smash corrupt and incompetent government. Lawyers were in the camp of the enemy. They perverted justice; they were "cursed hungry Caterpillars," whose fees "eat out the very Bowels of our Common-wealth." In Monmouth and Essex counties (New Jersey), in 1769 and 1770, mobs rioted against the lawyers.

But the lawyers were, in the end, a necessary evil. In the end, no colony could even try to make do without lawyers. In the very beginning, to be sure, there were makeshift alternatives.

Lay judges knew enough English law to run their local courts; and a few practical books of English law circulated in the colonies.

. . .

As soon as a settled society posed problems for which lawyers had an answer or at least a skill, lawyers began to thrive, despite the hostility. Courts were in session; merchants were drawn into litigation; land documents had to be written, and the more skill the better. Men trained in law who came from England found a market for their services; so did laymen with a smattering of law; there were semiprofessionals, too, with experience for sale. In the late 17th century, justices of the peace, sheriffs, and clerks, acted as attorneys in New Jersey. In the literature, there are constant complaints against unauthorized lawyers, pettifoggers, shysters, and lowlifes—unprincipled men stirring up unprincipled litigation. These complaints, like the outcry against ambulance chasers more than a century later, sometimes had a curiously inconsistent quality. Lawyers were criticized both for incompetence and for wrongful competence. And an unauthorized or underground bar has been common in many societies; it crops up when the need for legal services outstrips the supply of legitimate lawyers. At any rate, there was a competent, professional bar, dominated by brilliant and successful lawyers—Daniel Dulany of Maryland, Benjamin Chew of Philadelphia, and many others—in all major communities by 1750, despite all bias and opposition.

No law schools in the colonies trained these men. Particularly in the South, where there were no colleges, some young men went to England for training, and attended the Inns of Court, in London. The Inns were not law schools as such; they had "ceased to perform educational functions of a serious nature," and were little more than living and eating clubs. Theoretically, a man could become a counselor-at-law in England without reading "a single page of any law book." But the Inns were part of English legal culture; Americans could absorb the atmosphere of English law there; they read law on their own, and observed English practice.

The road to the bar, for all lawyers, was through some form of clerkship or apprenticeship. The aspiring lawyer usually entered into a contract with an established lawyer. The student paid a fee; in exchange, the lawyer promised to train him in the law; sometimes, too, the lawyer would provide food and lodging. Apprenticeship was a control device as well as a way of learning the trade. It kept the bar small; and older lawyers were in firm command. How much the apprentice learned depended greatly on his master. At worst, an apprentice went through a haphazard course of drudgery and copywork, with a few glances, catch-as-catch-can, at the law books. William Livingstone, who was clerking in the office of a New York lawyer, denounced the system in a letter to the *New York Weekly Post–Boy* (Aug. 19, 1745). The system was an "Outrage upon common Honesty ... scandalous, horrid, base, and infamous to the last degree!" No one could "attain to a competent Knowledge in the Law ... by gazing on a Number of Books, which he has neither Time nor Opportunity to read; or ... be metamorphos'd into an Attorney by virtue of a *Hocus–Pocus.*" A young clerk "trifle[d] away the Bloom of his Age ... in a servile Drudgery nothing to the Purpose, and fit only for a Slave." Other young men found clerkship valuable experience. Some senior lawyers were good teachers and good men. Some famous lawyers trained or attracted clerks, who themselves became famous. Thomas Jefferson was a student of George Wythe. James Wilson studied with John Dickinson, paying Dickinson a fee from the sale of a farm. The first law schools ... grew out of law offices which became so good at teaching that they gave up practice entirely.

. . .

THE NIMBLE PROFESSION

In 1850 there were, according to one estimate, 21,979 lawyers in the country. As we have seen, the number of lawyers grew very rapidly after the Revolution. In the last half of the century, there was even greater increase. The transformation of the American economy after the Civil War profoundly affected the demand for lawyers, and hence the supply. By 1880, there were perhaps 60,000 lawyers; by 1900, about 114,000.

The functions of the profession changed along with its numbers. The New York Code of Civil Procedure, of 1848, symbolized one kind of change. The code did not end the lawyer's monopoly of courtroom work. It did not abolish the bag of jargon and artifice that was as much a part of his equipment as the doctor's black bag with stethoscope and tools. But the code symbolized, in a way, the end of the hegemony of the courtroom. One reason why procedural codes had become necessary in the first place was because lawyers were less talented in the art of pleading, less oriented toward procedure and litigation. The codes in turn dethroned the ancient pleading arts. The slow estrangement of the lawyer from his old and natural haunt, the court, was an outstanding fact of the practice in the second half of the century. Most lawyers still went to court; but the Wall Street lawyer, who perhaps never spoke to a judge except socially, made more money and had more prestige than any courtroom lawyer could.

The change of function reflected changes in the law itself. Life and the economy were more complicated; there was more, then, to be done, in the business world especially; and the lawyers proved able to do it. There was nothing inevitable in the process. It did not happen, for example, in Japan. The legal profession might have become smaller and narrower, restricted like the English barrister, or the brain surgeon, to a few rare, complex, and lucrative tasks. Automation and technological change posed dangers to lawyers, just as they posed dangers to other occupations. Social invention constantly threatened to displace them. It was adapt or die. For example, lawyers in the first half of the century had a good thing going in title searches and related work. After the Civil War, title companies and trust companies proved to be efficient competitors. By 1900, well-organized, efficient companies nibbled away at other staples of the practice, too: debt collection and estate work, for example.

Nevertheless the lawyers prospered. The truth was that the profession was exceedingly nimble at finding new kinds of work and new ways to do it. Its nimbleness was no doubt due to the character of the bar: open-ended, unrestricted, uninhibited, attractive to sharp, ambitious men. In so amorphous a profession, lawyers drifted in and out; many went into business or politics because they could not earn a living at their trade. Others reached out for new sorts of practice. At any rate, the profession did not shrink to (or rise to) the status of a small, exclusive elite. Even in 1860, the profession was bigger, wider, more diverse than it had been in years gone by. In 1800, lawyers in Philadelphia came "predominantly from families of wealth, status, and importance." In 1860, a much higher percentage came from the middle class—sons of shopkeepers, clerks, small businessmen. In Massachusetts, too, in the period 1870–1900, there was an increase in the percentage of lawyers who were recruited from business and white-collar backgrounds, rather than professional or elite backgrounds, compared to the prewar period.

The external relations of the bar were always vitally important. After 1870, there was another line of defense against competition: the lawyers' unions (never called by that name), which fought vigorously to protect the boundaries of the calling. The organized profession raised (or tried to raise) its "standards"; tried to limit entry into the field, and (above all) tried to resist conversion of the profession into a "mere" business or trade. In fact, lawyers did not incorporate and did not become fully bureaucratized. The bar was able to prevent the corporate practice of law. Large private law firms were able to compete with captive legal departments and house counsel staffs of large corporations. For the time being, at least, the private lawyer kept his independent status as a middle-class craftsman and entrepreneur. The lawyer's role in American life had never been too clearly defined. The practice of law was what lawyers did. This was a truth as well as a tautology. The upper echelons of the profession never quite succeeded in closing the doors against newcomers and outsiders. They dreamt of a close-knit, guildlike bar. They longed for the honor and security of the barrister. But because it was easy to pass in and out of the profession, their dream could never be fulfilled.

The corporation lawyer, on Wall Street and its sister streets in other cities, was a dramatic new figure at the bar. But he did not chase the other kinds of lawyer out of business. He merely supplemented them; he superimposed another layer on the profession, which was already made up of many layers and strata.

. . .

By and large, the leading lawyers of the big Wall Street firms were solid Republican, conservative in outlook, standard Protestant in faith, old English in heritage. But the firms were never wholly monolithic. Morawetz was a southern Democrat. Guthrie, Seward's most militant and reactionary partner, was Roman Catholic; he began his career as an office boy. Da Costa, another partner, was descended from West Indian Jews. Charles O'Conor (1804–84), a dominant figure in the New York trial bar, was born in New York, of Irish parents. There were many others at the bar of Irish descent, like Charles P. Daly (1816–99), author, lawyer, and chief judge of the New York court of common pleas. Good background and cultural compatibility were, however, helpful to the rising young lawyer. Old-line lawyers were never too happy about the influx of "Celts," Jews, and other undesirables. George T. Strong, writing in his diary in 1874, hailed the idea of a test for admission at the Columbia Law School: "either a college diploma, or an *examination including Latin.* This will keep out the little scrubs (German Jew boys mostly) whom the School now promotes from the grocery-counters ... to be 'gentlemen of the Bar.' " Meritorious outsiders sometimes reached the celestial heights of Wall Street or the equivalent—Louis Dembitz Brandeis, from a Jewish family of Louisville, Kentucky, was an extremely prominent Boston lawyer in the 1890s. But such people generally succeeded by adopting, to a greater or lesser extent, the protective coloration of the dominant culture.

**Joseph G. Baldwin, The Flush Times
of Alabama and Mississippi**
47–55 (1957) (1st ed. 1858).*

THE BENCH AND THE BAR

In the month of March, A.D., 1836, the writer of these faithful
chronicles of law-doings in the South West, duly equipped for
forensic warfare, having perused nearly the whole of Sir William
Blackstone's Commentaries on the Laws of England, left behind
him the red hills of his native village, in the valley of the
Shenandoah, to seek his fortune.

. . .

To the South West he started because magnificent accounts
came from that sunny land of most cheering and exhilarating
prospects of fussing, quarrelling, murdering, violation of contracts,
and the whole catalogue of *crimen falsi*—in fine, of a flush tide of
litigation in all of its departments, civil and criminal. It was
extolled as a legal Utopia, peopled by a race of eager litigants, only
waiting for the lawyers to come on and divide out to them the
shells of a bountiful system of squabbling: a California of Law,
whose surface strife only indicated the vast *placers* of legal dispute
waiting in untold profusion, the presence of a few craftsmen to
bring out the crude suits to some forum, or into chancery for trial
or essay.

. . .

Alabama and East Mississippi was something marked. It was
somewhat like a sudden change from "Sleepy Hollow" to the
Strand. A man, retailing onions by the dozen in Weathersfield,
and the same man suddenly turned into a real estate broker in
San Francisco, would realize the contrast between the picayune
standard of the one region, and the wild spendthriftism, the
impetuous rush and the magnificent scale of operations in the
other.

The writer pitched his tabernacle on the thither side of the
state line of Alabama, in the charming village of P., one of the
loveliest hamlets of the plain, or rather it would be, did it not
stand on a hill. Gamblers, then a numerous class, included, the
village boasted a population of some five hundred souls; about a
third of whom were single gentlemen who had come out on the

* Reprinted by permission of Peter
Smith Publishers, Inc.

vague errand of seeking their fortune, or the more definite one of seeking somebody else's. ...

A shed for an office procured, the next thing was a license; and this a Circuit Judge was authorized to grant, which service was rendered by the Hon. J.F.T. in a manner which shall ever inspire gratitude—he asking not a single legal question; an eloquent silence which can never be appreciated except by those who are unable to stand an examination.

. . .

Those were jolly times. Imagine thirty or forty young men collected together in a new country, armed with fresh licenses which they had got gratuitously, and a plentiful stock of brass which they had got in the natural way; and standing ready to supply any distressed citizen who wanted law, with their wares counterfeiting the article.

. . .

There was one consolation: the clients were generally as sham as the counsellors. For the most part, they were either broke or in a rapid decline. They usually paid us the compliment of retaining us, but they usually retained the fee too, a double retainer we did not much fancy. However, we got as much as we were entitled to and something over, *videlicet*, as much over as we got at all. The most that we made was experience. We learned before long, how every possible sort of case could be successfully lost; there was no way of getting out of court that we had not tested. The last way we learned was *via* a verdict: it was a considerable triumph to get *to* the jury, though it seemed a sufficiently easy matter to get away from one again. But the perils of the road from the writ to an issue or issues—for there were generally several of them—were great indeed. The way was infested and ambushed, with all imaginable points of practice, quirks and quibbles, that had strayed off from the litigation of every sort of foreign judicature,—that had been successfully tried in, or been driven out of, regularly organized forums, besides a smart sprinkling of indigenous growth. Nothing was settled. Chaos had come again, or rather, had never gone away. Order, Heaven's first law, seemed unwilling to remain where there was no other law to keep it company.

Robert W. Gordon, "The Ideal and the Actual in the Law:
Fantasies and Practices of New York City Lawyers,
1870–1970," in G. Gawalt, ed., The New High Priests:
Lawyers in Post-Civil War America
52–53, 56–59, 65–66 (1984).*

... There were various projects through which New York's
late 19th century elite lawyers sought to make good their commitment to what they liked to call the Ideal: the development of a
legal "science" consisting of general "principles" derived from
philosophical reflection and historical scholarship; the application
of the principles to training law students, proposing changes in
procedure or substantive law, settling international disputes
through arbitration, and above all to arguing or deciding cases;
and the sponsorship of "reform"—meaning the purification of
legislation, judicial decisions and appointments to office of corrupt
influence; and the displacement of politics in some fields altogether by expert professional (or nonpartisan amateur) administration.

Disenchantment with some of the results of all this busy
activity has given us a historical literature that is quick to spot
the motives of interest that got it started and made it work.
Reform in the name of scientific professionalism was among things
an ideology of middle-class native-born whites. They could invoke
it to impose training or certification requirements to exclude
riffraff; or to create and control new markets for their services; or
to assert that it gave them title to cultural dominance over
immigrant groups, since only scientists could know the "one best
system" for running cities or schools. Scientific reform could also
be and often was, a convenient slogan for advancing the interests
of business clients: "legal science" was deployed to attack labor
unions or protective labor laws, scientific public administration of
rates or service to restrict competition.

Without disputing the validity of these critical insights, I still
think it will be helpful to look at the lawyers' version of the
general late 19th century elite ideology of scientific reform from a
different angle, one that tries to see what they were thinking and
doing more or less as they themselves saw it. This means to see
them as having "ideal interests" as well as material ones, and as
struggling to work out a relationship between their beliefs and
their practices—the Ideal and the Actual—with which they could
live in comfort. Lawyers are perhaps especially interesting objects of this kind of study because they are double agents. They
have obligations to a universal scheme of order, "the law," under-

stood as some fairly coherent system of rules and procedures that are supposed to regulate social life in accordance with prevailing political conceptions of the good. The law, to put this another way, is an artificial utopia of social harmony, a kind of collectively maintained fantasy of what society would look like if everyone played by the rules. But lawyers are also supposed to be loyal toward and advance the interests of clients pursuing particular ends. The lawyer's job is thus to mediate between the universal vision of legal order and the concrete desires of his clients, to show how what the client wants can be accommodated to the utopian scheme. The lawyer thus has to find ways of squeezing the client's plan of action into the legally recognized categories of approved conduct. ... As leaders of the bar they belonged to a tradition, communicated through endless reiteration in formal speeches, of patrician Whig aspirations to play a distinctive role in American society as a Third Force in politics (in fact the role of the Few in classical republican theory), mediating between Capital and Labor, between private acquisitiveness and democratic redistributive follies; and thus kept looking for social stages on which to enact the role of Tocqueville's lawyer-aristocrats. If anything, their ambition for roles of public virtue was intensified by the fact that they were not really aristocrats at all by background; but the sons of the Protestant, back-country gentry, the ministers, doctors, and lawyers of small New England and upstate New York towns. Their picture of the Ideal tended to call on images of the communities they had left; and they themselves were often men of high, not to say rigid personal rectitude, with a mission to reform a world ensnared in sin. Moreover the means for reformation were at hand in the techniques of science; and there was as yet no reason not to be as confident as the rest of the American intelligentsia at this time that science would not fail them.

There was a special urgency to realizing the Ideal in the fact that most of the reform lawyers were not set apart from the Actual, but were deeply implicated in it, that is to say, in the very practices that they wanted to reform. One of the motives behind the formation of the City Bar Association was concern over some leading lawyers' roles in the efforts of Fisk and Gould to keep control of the Erie Railroad from Vanderbilt and to corner the market in gold. ... The lawyers involved were all lions of the New York bar: ... It is clear that legislative favors, municipal franchises, and judicial decisions could sometimes be bought; and in the case of municipal franchises may have only been available if bought. Eminent lawyers often acted as counsel for the corporate favorseeker. They may have done the buying; more likely they just knew about it. ...

II. Lawyers help undermine their own ideal, 1885–1910

The 1870–90 legal elite's vision of the Ideal was an integrated whole, in the sense that if all of its projects could have been carried through, they would all have *fit together:* Lawyers in their public roles would perfect the system for defining rights that lawyers in private roles would apply to the affairs of clients. What is irretrievably lost in the late 19th century is the wholeness of the vision, the possibility of seeing an effective synthesis of all its parts. Lawyers were far from passive spectators of this process of disintegration. Though they usually attributed it to evolutionary forces beyond their control, they were truly zealous servants of those forces. ... Perhaps the most dramatic evidence of the inadequacy of the old Ideal was its increasing irrelevance to the principal preoccupations of corporate practice. ... Right after the Civil War the elite's collective hope was to reconstitute the professions' virtue on the foundation of legal science, made effective through reform. But that conception of the Ideal had worn thin.

. . .

In default of a new unifying ideology, the bar leadership split along (roughly) three divergent paths. (1) One was simply reactionary, reverting to the now discredited and irrelevant principles of classical legal science, incongruously combining an insistence upon the inevitability of corporate concentration with the old rhetoric of individualism and the inviolable rights of property. James Beck and William D. Guthrie were probably the best-known lawyers who took this position. (2) A second was what might be called institutionalized schizophrenia: the position that lawyers should take some time off from private practice to engage in public service, but that the two roles were antagonistic: so that it was appropriate for lawyers in one role to do the utmost to undo their accomplishments in the other. This perspective, which is of course familiar to us today, represents an uneasy compromise between the Progressive notion of law as a tool for the efficient management of the social order in the public interest, and the classical notion that the structure of the legal-regulatory framework as a whole automatically guarantees ultimate harmony through agonistic contest. Some notable representatives of this approach were lawyers like Elihu Root, George Wickersham, and Samuel Untermyer. (3) The third was probably the most common of all: This was the path of withdrawal from issues of public concern altogether, and retreat into the role of apolitical technician with no ideology save that of craftsmanlike client service. This sort of lawyer treats both client desires and the framework of legal regulation as wholly exogenous givens for which he has no responsibility: his is merely the technical role of maximizing the one in view of the constraints dictated by the other. Although in fact the corporate lawyer has a major part in framing the client's desires—by translating them into the legal categories that constitute important forms of public discourse, ways of specifying what it's legitimate to want; and also a major part, through thousands of discrete acts of interpretation, application, manipulation, and resistance, in specifying the day-to-day practical operational content of legal rules; he avoids responsibility for the profession's impact on its clients or the state of the law simply by denying, in the teeth of ordinary experience, that it has any impact.

Alexis de Tocqueville, Democracy in America

Vol. I, 283–90 (H. Reeve trans., P. Bradley ed., F. Bowen rev., 1973) (1st ed. 1835).

In visiting the Americans and studying their laws, we perceive that the authority they have entrusted to members of the legal profession, and the influence that these individuals exercise in the government, are the most powerful existing security against the excesses of democracy. This effect seems to me to result from a general cause, which it is useful to investigate, as it may be reproduced elsewhere ....

Men who have made a special study of the laws derive from this occupation certain habits of order, a taste for formalities, and a kind of instinctive regard for the regular connection of ideas, which naturally render them very hostile to the revolutionary spirit and the unreflecting passions of the multitude.

The special information that lawyers derive from their studies ensures them a separate rank in society, and they constitute a sort of privileged body in the scale of intellect. This notion of their superiority perpetually recurs to them in the practice of their profession: they are the masters of a science which is necessary, but which is not very generally known; they serve as arbiters between the citizens; and the habit of directing to their purpose the blind passions of parties in litigation inspires them with a certain contempt for the judgment of the multitude. Add to this that they naturally constitute *a body;* not by any previous understanding, or by an agreement that directs them to a common end; but the analogy of their studies and the uniformity of their methods connect their minds as a common interest might unite their endeavors.

Some of the tastes and the habits of the aristocracy may consequently be discovered in the characters of lawyers. They participate in the same instinctive love of order and formalities; and they entertain the same repugnance to the actions of the multitude, and the same secret contempt of the government of the people. I do not mean to say that the natural propensities of lawyers are sufficiently strong to sway them irresistibly; for they, like most other men, are governed by their private interests, and especially by the interests of the moment.

In a state of society in which the members of the legal profession cannot hold that rank in the political world which they enjoy in private life, we may rest assured that they will be the foremost agents of revolution. ...

I am in like manner inclined to believe that a monarch will always be able to convert legal practitioners into the most serviceable instruments of his authority. There is a far greater affinity between this class of persons and the executive power than there is between them and the people, though they have often aided to overturn the former; just as there is a greater natural affinity between the nobles and the monarch than between the nobles and the people, although the higher orders of society have often, in concert with the lower classes, resisted the prerogative of the crown.

Lawyers are attached to public order beyond every other consideration, and the best security of public order is authority. It must not be forgotten, also, that if they prize freedom much, they generally value legality still more: they are less afraid of tyranny than of arbitrary power; and, provided the legislature undertakes of itself to deprive men of their independence, they are not dissatisfied.

I am therefore convinced that the prince who, in presence of an encroaching democracy, should endeavor to impair the judicial authority in his dominions, and to diminish the political influence of lawyers, would commit a great mistake: he would let slip the substance of authority to grasp the shadow. He would act more wisely in introducing lawyers into the government; and if he entrusted despotism to them under the form of violence, perhaps he would find it again in their hands under the external features of justice and law.

The government of democracy is favorable to the political power of lawyers; for when the wealthy, the noble, and the prince are excluded from the government, the lawyers take possession of it, in their own right, as it were, since they are the only men of information and sagacity, beyond the sphere of the people, who can be the object of the popular choice. If, then, they are led by their tastes towards the aristocracy and the prince, they are brought in contact with the people by their interests. They like the government of democracy without participating in its propensities and without imitating its weaknesses; whence they derive a two-fold authority from it and over it. The people in democratic states do not mistrust the members of the legal profession, because it is known that they are interested to serve the popular cause; and the people listen to them without irritation, because they do not attribute to them any sinister designs. The lawyers do not, indeed, wish to overthrow the institutions of democracy, but they constantly endeavor to turn it away from its real direction by means that are foreign to its nature. Lawyers belong to the people by birth and interest, and to the aristocracy by habit and taste; they may be looked upon as the connecting link between the two great classes of society.

The profession of the law is the only aristocratic element that can be amalgamated without violence with the natural elements of democracy and be advantageously and permanently combined with them. I am not ignorant of the defects inherent in the character of this body of men; but without this admixture of lawyer-like sobriety with the democratic principle, I question whether democratic institutions could long be maintained; and I cannot believe that a republic could hope to exist at the present time if the influence of lawyers in public business did not increase in proportion to the power of the people.

This aristocratic character, which I hold to be common to the legal profession, is much more distinctly marked in the United States and in England than in any other country. This proceeds not only from the legal studies of the English and American lawyers, but from the nature of the law and the position which these interpreters of it occupy in the two countries. The English and the Americans have retained the law of precedents; that is to say, they continue to found their legal opinions and the decisions of their courts upon the opinions and decisions of their predecessors. In the mind of an English or American lawyer a taste and a reverence for what is old is almost always united with a love of regular and lawful proceedings.

This predisposition has another effect upon the character of the legal profession and upon the general course of society. The English and American lawyers investigate what has been done;

the French advocate inquires what should have been done; the former produce precedents, the latter reasons. A French observer is surprised to hear how often an English or an American lawyer quotes the opinions of others and how little he alludes to his own, while the reverse occurs in France. There the most trifling litigation is never conducted without the introduction of an entire system of ideas peculiar to the counsel employed; and the fundamental principles of law are discussed in order to obtain a rod of land by the decision of the court. This abnegation of his own opinion and this implicit deference to the opinion of his forefathers, which are common to the English and American lawyer, this servitude of thought which he is obliged to profess, necessarily gives him more timid habits and more conservative inclinations in England and America than in France.

The French codes are often difficult to comprehend, but they can be read by everyone; nothing, on the other hand, can be more obscure and strange to the uninitiated than a legislation founded upon precedents. The absolute need of legal aid that is felt in England and the United States, and the high opinion that is entertained of the ability of the legal profession, tend to separate it more and more from the people and to erect it into a distinct class. The French lawyer is simply a man extensively acquainted with the statutes of his country; but the English or American lawyer resembles the hierophants of Egypt, for like them he is the sole interpreter of an occult science. ...

In America there are no nobles or literary men, and the people are apt to mistrust the wealthy; lawyers consequently form the highest political class and the most cultivated portion of society. They have therefore nothing to gain by innovation, which adds a conservative interest to their natural taste for public order. If I were asked where I place the American aristocracy, I should reply without hesitation that it is not among the rich, who are united by no common tie, but that it occupies the judicial bench and the bar.

The more we reflect upon all that occurs in the United States, the more we shall be persuaded that the lawyers, as a body, form the most powerful, if not the only, counterpoise to the democratic element. In that country we easily perceive how the legal profession is qualified by its attributes, and even by its faults, to neutralize the vices inherent in popular government. When the American people are intoxicated by passion or carried away by the impetuosity of their ideas, they are checked and stopped by the almost invisible influence of their legal counselors. These secretly oppose their aristocratic propensities to the nation's democratic instincts, their superstitious attachment to what is old to its love of novelty, their narrow views to its immense designs, and their habitual procrastination to its ardent impatience. ...

The influence of legal habits extends beyond the precise limits I have pointed out. Scarcely any political question arises in the United States that is not resolved, sooner or later, into a judicial question. Hence all parties are obliged to borrow, in their daily controversies, the ideas, and even the language, peculiar to judicial proceedings. As most public men are or have been legal practitioners, they introduce the customs and technicalities of their profession into the management of public affairs. The jury extends this habit to all classes. The language of the law thus becomes, in some measure, a vulgar tongue; the spirit of the law, which is produced in the schools and courts of justice, gradually penetrates beyond their walls into the bosom of society, where it descends to the lowest classes, so that at last the whole people contract the habits and the tastes of the judicial magistrate. The lawyers of the United States form a party which is but little feared and scarcely perceived, which has no badge peculiar to itself, which adapts itself with great flexibility to the exigencies of the time and accommodates itself without resistance to all the movements of the social body. But this party extends over the whole community and penetrates into all the classes which compose it; it acts upon the country imperceptibly, but finally fashions it to suit its own purposes.

Geoffrey C. Hazard, Jr., "The Future of Legal Ethics"
100 *Yale L.J.* 1239 (1991).

. . .

A POLITICAL THEORY OF THE LEGAL PROFESSION'S ROLE

... A century ago, lawyers were predominantly engaged in the representation of business and property interests, interests with which they were politically sympathetic. Today's lawyers are still predominantly engaged in such representation, and generally have corresponding political sympathies. But modern courts, at least from the 1960's through the mid–1980's, have not been as congenial to those interests. The change in the courts' orientation becomes quite clear if we compare the general outlook of the Supreme Court under Chief Justice White in 1908, when the Canons were promulgated, with that of the Supreme Court under Chief Justices Warren and Burger, when the Code and the Rules were adopted. The courts simply do not make the same parallel

they once did between the legal protection of life and liberty
interests and the legal protection of property interests. This
implicit rejection of the lawyer's traditional role has called into
question the profession's conception of its place in American
society.

[T]he legal profession's traditional ideal viewed the lawyer as
the protector of life, liberty, and property through due process....
Legal practice primarily involves the protection of property, specifically business property. The profession's legitimacy in performing this function rests on the continual reaffirmation, under
the rubric of due process, of the parity between property on the
one hand and life and liberty on the other.

. . .

Although such a conception of the function of lawyers may be
unfashionable today, it accords very well with the history of the
American legal profession. I draw here on the seminal work of
Alexis de Tocqueville ....

Tocqueville's analysis shows a clear-eyed awareness of social
class and its relationship to politics. Although he regarded American devotion to the idea of equality as profound and pervasively
shared, he also thought the egalitarian ideal masked two fundamental realities with which it was incompatible. One was race;
the other was class. The latter is directly related to Tocqueville's
conception of the role of law and lawyers in America.

. . .

It is well known that Tocqueville described the American
legal profession as aristocratic. However, little attention has been
paid to what he meant by "aristocracy." A careful reading, with
an eye to Tocqueville's own background, suggests that he meant to
denote an elite political force that in his view was necessary to
maintain stable, nontyrannical government, which in turn was
essential to achieving a prosperous commonwealth. Tocqueville's
point of departure is the proposition that the American polity
contained two basic affinities or "parties":

America has had great parties; now they no longer exist....
When the War of Independence came to an end ... the nation
was divided between two opinions. Those opinions were as
old as the world itself.... One party wanted to restrict
popular power and the other to extend it indefinitely.

. . .

Tocqueville then identifies the legal profession with the "aristocratic" party, which is the antipode of the democratic tendency:

"Study and specialized knowledge of the law give a man a rank apart in society and make of lawyers a somewhat privileged intellectual class.... [H]idden at the bottom of a lawyer's soul one finds some of the tastes and habits of an aristocracy." These tastes and habits are "habits of order, something of a taste for formalities, and an instinctive love for a regular concatenation of ideas ... strongly opposed to ... the ill-considered passions of democracy."

. . .

The profession's mentality and its functions give it a critical strategic position in American democracy, since "[t]he legal body is the only aristocratic element which can unforcedly mingle with elements natural to democracy and combine with them...."

A key element in Tocqueville's definition of this legal aristocracy is that it includes both judges and lawyers. He sees the professional bond between these two groups as the foundation of the profession's political identity and function. By implication, the fact that some members of the legal profession are on the bench and some are practitioners at the bar is a secondary differentiation:

> It is at the bar or the bench that the American aristocracy is found. [T]he legal body forms the most powerful and, so to say, the only counterbalance to democracy....
>
> The courts are the most obvious organs through which the legal body influences democracy.

. . .

Tocqueville discerns a special language understood only by judges and lawyers, employed not only in court but in political discourse at large. Although the language is constituted from words familiar in American English, it involves special nuances and connotations: It is "Mandarin" English. Another specific legal link between the bench and the bar is the exclusive right of members of the bar to have audience before the courts. That is, only lawyers "working in secret" participate when "a political question ... sooner or later turn[s] into a judicial one."

As Tocqueville described it, the legal profession's other basic linkage—to property interests—derives from its services to the "wealthy classes." The "wealthy classes" in a democracy are people who have turned to industry: "When ... men are no longer distinguished, or hardly distinguished, by birth, standing, or profession; there is ... hardly anything left but money.... Distinction based on wealth is increased by the disappearance or diminution of all other distinctions.... [L]ove of money chiefly turns men to industry."

Tocqueville does not develop the implications for political economy that might follow from this definition. However, some are fairly clear. The wealthy class Tocqueville discusses is engaged in the pursuit of enrichment through wealth-producing business ventures—not, for example, in pursuit of wealth through family alliances, military domination, or imperial adventures. It is a group whose members are actively engaged in business, not a class of rentiers or beneficiaries of inherited wealth. In an early capitalist economy this class consisted of business owner-operators; in a fully industrialized economy it includes the managerial element.

. . .

It is important to contrast Tocqueville's view of aristocracy with what seems to be a widely shared contemporary misinterpretation of that concept. In present-day American usage, "aristocracy" signifies a class constituted by inheritance, endowed with unearned wealth and income, and privileged to remain in idleness. Its members enjoy their status by an accident of history and interject themselves in serious matters only occasionally and then merely as a matter of personal choice. This concept of an aristocracy calls up images of the English country house dilettantes of the Victorian era.

Tocqueville knew that aristocracy in the classical sense had been abolished in America. He recognized that there was no established church here, certainly not in the European form, and that the professional military was relatively insignificant. He remarked upon the virtual absence of a state bureaucracy. These constituents—the church, the army, and the state bureaucracy— were the core of the "aristocratic element" in the European *Ancien Regime,* which was Tocqueville's frame of reference. Yet Tocqueville assumes that an "aristocratic element" must exist even in a democracy, and finds it in the legal profession and in "those who have turned to industry." In Jeffersonian terms— perhaps compatible with democratic ideology—members of the legal profession would be a "natural aristocracy," as distinct from an inherited one.

In discerning an "aristocratic element" in America, it seems evident that Tocqueville had in mind the governing class of provincial France of which he was a descendant. That class was intimately involved in local and regional government, agriculture, industry, preservation of the peace, and political and administrative relationships with authorities in central government and adjoining communities. It was not a politically monolithic group, but was aligned in regional, religious, and political alliances and antagonisms. Nor was the aristocracy itself homogeneous: it was divided into gradations of position, place, and power. However, its members shared a concern with management of authority and property, and it had a functional interest in the stability of the community as a whole—an interest in perpetuating its overall position as "arbiters between citizens" through "the habit of directing."

This is not far off as a description of the American legal profession, then and now.

. . .

A Theory of the Legal Profession's "Crisis"

American political and constitutional theory has not dealt directly with the question of the legal profession's aristocratic role in our system of government. And clearly, political and constitutional theory that does not acknowledge the existence of a legitimate "aristocratic" element cannot address constitutional constraints on such an element. Our constitutional theory does address the problem of constraints on oppressive majoritarianism, but it does not identify the element which exercises that counter-majoritarian control. According to Tocqueville, that element is the legal profession.

. . .

Since the adoption of the Constitution, the basic function of the legal profession in the United States has been to reconcile the constitutional necessities of an economic system devoted to the production of wealth through business enterprise with a political system that is predominantly democratic. A related function is to reconcile majoritarian politics with protection of the rights of religious and other minorities. The lawyer's "practice" of bringing about these accommodations embodies the legal profession's primary set of skills and expresses its primary role in the American social system. This role was actualized in our society by linking the legal profession to the courts, on one end, and to business enterprise on the other end.

Until the last generation or so public opinion did not successfully challenge the profession's mediating function. This conception of its role gave the legal profession a useful place in society and gave lawyers a sense of meaning and common identity.

Over the last half century, however, the legitimacy of the business enterprise system itself has been severely undercut by that system's apparent economic failure in the Great Depression, by the Watergate scandals, and by cumulative and intensified attack on capitalism in the name of democratic politics. Over the same period the courts, particularly the Supreme Court, moved away from their long-established practice of using constitutional law to constrain democratic politics for the protection of business. Under the aegis of the equal protection clause the Supreme Court affirmatively pursued a program of democratic reform going well beyond democratic sentiment as expressed in legislatures. The Rehnquist Court has terminated this program, out of deference to democratic politics. As a result, attacks on the "elitism" which the Warren Court personified are now coming from the right, based on antipathy to judicial activism, as well as from the left, based on antipathy toward business.

These political and economic cleavages have weakened the legal profession's place in the American political system and have affected the profession's legitimacy. The effect has been no less demoralizing for not being acknowledged. The legal profession no longer enjoys an unchallenged sense of purpose and worth in its traditional practice of mediating through the courts between business enterprise and popular politics. The practice of the profession is no longer intelligible in the terms that prevailed in the century and three quarters between Marbury v. Madison in 1803 and Roe v. Wade. By the same token, the profession no longer presupposes its own identity as the aristocratic element in such a constitutional structure. Its governing norms no longer represent the shared understandings of a substantially cohesive group. They are simply rules of public law regulating a widely pursued technical vocation whose constitutional position is now in doubt.

What do these transformations imply for the future of legal ethics? "Legalized" regulation will undoubtedly continue to dominate the normative structure of the legal profession, through court-promulgated rules, increasingly intrusive common law, and public statutes and regulations. As a consequence, the dominant normative institution for the legal profession will no longer be "the bar," meaning the profession as a substantially inclusive fraternal group. The bar has become too large, diverse, and balkanized in its practice specialties for the old informal system to be effective as an institution of governance. In the emergent "legalized" era, increasingly dominant power reposes in government regulatory authorities, including courts, legislatures, and disciplinary agencies.

This is not to say that leadership in the profession will disappear. But leadership goes where the action is. As an inclusive fraternal relationship plays a decreasing role in the profession at large, organization and leadership will emerge in other professional settings. It seems evident that the most effective nonlegal governance in the profession of the future will be through the law firm and subspecialty practice fields. Most lawyers now practice in multilawyer work groups, including independent law firms and the law departments of governments and private organizations. Specialized practice now predominates, including tribunal practice before courts and agencies with specific regulatory jurisdiction. For better or worse, the law firm and specific tribunals, not "the bench and the bar," have become the centers of professional relationships among the lawyers. Whether "the bar" as such can remain a coherent entity seems increasingly doubtful.

However, at a more fundamental level, the courts will continue to be an indispensable instrument for ordering and clarifying norms.

. . .

It is another question whether (to use Tocqueville's terms) the legal profession will remain a key "aristocratic" influence—one that tries to contemplate the past while acting in the present, and to take account of democratic desires while protecting minority rights. If Tocqueville's assumptions about political economy are correct, exercise of that influence requires cohesiveness built upon political strength combined with constitutional legitimacy. It is not clear that the legal profession still has these qualities.

NOTES

Women and Minorities

Like other elite professions, the organized bar has been unreceptive to women and minorities for much of its history. Early English efforts to establish law as a "gentlemen's" profession resulted in restrictive entry practices. For a substantial period, barristers excluded certain presumptively unfit groups including Catholics, tradesmen, journalists, and women. Class also served as a filtering device, since the costs of obtaining an education and establishing a practice limited access to those with substantial means. Although solicitors were less exclusive in their entrance standards, lengthy apprenticeship requirements and selective referral networks discouraged applicants from socially or economically marginal groups.[1]

In the United States, formal admission mandates were fairly lax until the late nineteenth century. However, informal screening occurred through educational, apprenticeship, hiring, and client patronage practices. Such practices were strongly colored by class, race, ethnic and religious prejudices.

Although the first black graduated from law school in 1869, and a number of predominantly black institutions formed graduate programs in law around this same period, few of the programs survived after the Reconstruction era. Estimates suggest that blacks constituted less than .5% of the profession at the turn of the century, and that they remained under 2% until the '60s. Other racial minorities were similarly underrepresented. Beginning in the 1930s, a series of legal actions began challenging educational systems that were racially segregated by law. Such litigation initially forced establishment of "separate but equal" minority law schools, and eventually helped integrate all-white institutions. However, even after changes in formal policies, the absence of financial aid, affirmative action, active recruitment, or supportive academic environments worked against minority admissions. Discrimination by employers, clients, and bar associations had comparable effects.[2]

Bias against religious and ethnic minorities was also apparent in employment, law school admissions, and bar character screening practices. During the late nineteenth and early twentieth centuries, some universities maintained quotas on Jewish applicants. Certain leaders of the bar also spearheaded campaigns to upgrade entry requirements in the hope of screening out those with immigrant and lower class backgrounds.[3] Antisemitic and nativist attitudes were also apparent among some state bar moral

1. M. Birks, *Gentlemen of the Law,* (1960); W. Reader, *Professional Men; The Rise of the Professional Classes in Nineteenth Century England* (1966); Rhode, "Moral Character as a Professional Credential," 94 *Yale L.J.* 491, 494–95 (1981).

2. G. Segal, *Blacks in the Law* (1983); Leonard, "The Development of the Black Bar," 407 *Annals of the Amer. Acad. Of Pol. and Soc. Science,* 134, 136–44; Parker and Stebman, "Legal Education for Blacks," 407 *Annals of the American Acad. Of Pol. and Soc. Science* 146 (1973). See J. Auerbach, *Unequal Justice: Lawyers and Social Change in Modern America* (1976), excerpted in chapter 3 *infra.*

3. For example, Columbia Law School was urged to require that applicants have a college diploma or pass an examination including Latin in order to "keep out the little scrubs whom the school now promotes from grocery counters...." *See* sources cited in Weisberg, "Barred from the Bar: Women and Legal Education in the United States, 1870–1890," 2 *Women and the Law 231,* 252 (D. Weisberg, ed. 1982); R. Stevens, *Law School: Legal Education in America From the 1850s to the 1980s* 100–01 (1983).

character committees and established law firms during this period.[4]

Discrimination against women was more overt and more persistent. Until the 1960s, gender defined much of the geography of occupational life. The conventional view was that women's primary responsibility was in the domestic rather than professional sphere. There were, however, certain exceptions to this general pattern. In the Colonial period, when labor was relatively scarce and licensing practices lax, some women participated in legal transactions by acting as their husbands' representatives or obtaining powers of attorney. Yet it was rare for any woman to perform advocacy functions on a regular basis. The first female lawyer in America was reported to be an "honorary male" in more than a figurative sense; she was often addressed in person and in court records as Gentleman Margaret Brent.[5]

The gradual formalization of bar entrance criteria in the late 18th century made it increasingly difficult for women to act as agents in legal matters. However, after the Civil War, the rise in female education, political consciousness, and reform activity sparked increasing challenges to sex-based admission standards. In 1867, Iowa became the first state to license a woman attorney, and in 1872, Howard University conferred the first law school degree on a female graduate.

However, the reception for women generally was less enthusiastic. In a celebrated 1873 decision, the United States Supreme Court affirmed Myra Bradwell's exclusion from the Illinois bar. The concurring opinions by Justice Bradley summarized prevailing assumptions about the sexes' "separate spheres." Speaking for himself and two colleagues, Bradley noted:

> [T]he natural and proper timidity and delicacy which belongs to the female sex evidently unfi[t] it for many of the occupations of civil life.... The paramount destiny and mission of woman is to fulfill the noble and benign office of wife and mother. This is the law of the Creator.[6]

Similar divine inspiration revealed itself to other decision makers as well. To many constituencies, the "peculiar qualities of

4. *See* J. Auerbach, *supra* note 2; Rhode, *supra* note 1, at 500–502.

5. K. Morrello, *The Invisible Bar: The Woman Lawyer in America 1638 to the Present* (1986); D. Rhode, *Justice and Gender* 20–24 (1989); Rhode, "Perspectives on Professional Women," 40 Stan. L.Rev. 1163 (1988). See generally, B. Harris, *Beyond Her Sphere; Women and the Professions in American History* (1978): Salmon, "The Legal Status of Women in Early America: A Reappraisal," *Law and Hist. Rev.* 129 (1985).

6. Bradwell v. State, 83 U.S. 130, 141 (1872) (Bradley, J., concurring).

womanhood" seemed ill-suited for "forensic strife."[7]

Although by the turn of the century, sustained political and legal challenges had secured women's formal right to admission in most states, informal barriers remained substantial. Some prominent law schools resisted the "clack of these possible Portias" for prolonged intervals; not until 1972 did all-ABA accredited institutions admit female applicants.[8] Throughout the first half of the century, women constituted less than three percent of the profession and women of color were even more underrepresented. Biases in salary, hiring, promotion, and placement were also pronounced, and until the last two decades, females rarely attained the most prestigious professional positions.[9]

However, by the late 1960s, the demographics of the profession began reflecting substantial changes, as the following chapter indicates.

HISTORY: REFERENCES

R. Abel, *American Lawyers* (1989).

M. Bloomfield, *American Lawyers in a Changing Society 1776–1876* (1976).

Bloomfield, "Lawyers and Public Criticism: Challenge and Response in Nineteenth Century America," 15 *Am.J.Legal Hist.* 269 (1971).

D. Boorstin, *The Americans: The Colonial Experience* (1958).

A. Chroust, *The Rise of the Legal Profession in America* (1965).

R. Ferguson, *Law and Letters in American Culture* (1984).

G. Gawalt, *The Promise of Power: The Emergence of the Legal Profession in Massachusetts 1760–1840* (1979).

W. Gawalt (ed.), *The New High Priests: Lawyers in Post–Civil War America* (1984).

S. Haber, *The Quest for Authority and Honor in the American Professions, 1750–1900* (1991).

M. Horowitz, *The Transformation of American Law: 1780–1860* (1977).

---

7. In the Matter of Goodell, 39 Wis. 232, 245 (1875); Rhode, *supra* note 5.

8. Lazarou, "Fettered Portias: Obstacles Facing Nineteenth Century Women Lawyers," 64 *Woman Lawyer's Journal* 21, 22 (1978); Barnes, "Women and Entrance to the Legal Profession", 23 *J. of Legal Education* 283 (1970); Stevens, *supra* note 3 at 83 n. 86; Fossum, "Law and the Sexual Integration of Institutions: The Case of American Law Schools," VII *ALSA Forum* 22 (1983). See Part IV, I *infra*.

9. G. Segal, *supra* note 2; C. Epstein, *Women in Law* (1986); Rhode, *supra* note 5; White, "Women in the Law," 65 *Mich.L.Rev.* 105 (1967).

P. Miller, *The Legal Mind in America: From Independence to the Civil War* (1962).

D. Nolan, *Readings in the History of the American Legal Profession* (1980).

R. Pound, *The Lawyer from Antiquity to Modern Times* (1953).

C. Warren, *A History of the American Bar* (1911).

III. THE STRUCTURE OF THE AMERICAN LEGAL PROFESSION

A. A DEMOGRAPHIC PROFILE

Barbara A. Curran and Clara N. Carson, Supplement
to the Lawyer Statistical Report: The United
States Legal Profession in 1988
1–14 (1992).

In 1971, the U.S. lawyer population was one-third of a million; by 1980, it had grown to half a million; in early 1988, it had reached almost three-quarters of a million; and, by the turn of the century, will probably exceed a million. The rate of lawyer population growth has surpassed that of the general population as reflected in the progressive decline of population/lawyer ratios from 1 lawyer for each 695 persons in 1951 to 1 lawyer per 340 persons in 1988.

. . .

During the 1970s, growth rate accelerated. Fueled by rising law school enrollments, bar admissions increased from less than 15,000 in 1970 to almost 30,000 by 1980. Since then, the number of yearly admissions has stabilized at or near the 1980 level.

. . .

THE CHANGING SEX COMPOSITION OF THE PROFESSION.

Starting in the early 1970s, the number of women entering the profession began to rise. Five percent of lawyers admitted in 1971 were women. Each year thereafter, a successively greater proportion of new entrants were women. By 1987, women comprised 36% of new admissions.

. . .

Female lawyer population growth rate has far exceeded that of the male population. While the number of male lawyers has almost doubled since 1971, that of females has increased ten-fold. The dramatic growth in the number of female lawyers, a phenomenon of the 1970s and 1980s, was preceded by a history of limited entry of women into the profession. As a result, change in the male/female composition of the lawyer population has proceeded at a slower rate than the recent statistics on new bar admissions might imply. The reason is that the overall representation of women in the profession at any given time depends not only on the size of recent admission cohorts and the number of women in them but also on representation of women from earlier admission years. In 1988, women admitted prior to 1971 made up only 1% of the total lawyer population and only 3% of all lawyers admitted before 1971. In contrast, women admitted thereafter made up 15% of all lawyers in 1988 and 24% of all lawyers admitted post–1970.

. . .

THE AGE COMPOSITION OF THE LAWYER POPULATION.

The median age at which individuals are admitted to the bar has for many years been 26 and the modal age has been 25. The age composition of the profession at any given time is therefore a reflection of the history of bar admissions over several generations of lawyers. In 1980, the median age of the lawyer population was 39. This was far lower than the median age of 45 for lawyers in 1971 and was directly attributable to the sharp rise in bar admissions during the 1970s. By 1988, the median age had risen to 40 as new entries of the previous decade moved into their middle years and bar admissions of the 1980s stabilized at late 1970 levels.

. . .

Figure 3 displays not only the difference in the age distributions of the male and female lawyer populations in 1988 but also underlines the disparate size of the two populations, particularly among the older age cohorts. Representation of women is substantially higher among younger lawyers. Almost one third (32%) of lawyers under 30 are female. The proportions drop to slightly over one quarter (27%) among 30–34–year–olds, to one fifth (20%) among 35–39–year–olds, to 13% among 40–44–year–olds, to 8% among 45–54–year–olds and to 4% among those lawyers 55 years of age and older.

DISPOSITION OF LAWYERS BY EMPLOYMENT.

Private practice remains the principal professional activity of lawyers. There were 40% more lawyers in private practice in 1988 than in 1980, compared with an increase of 22% in private industry and 15% in government employment. Employment in the judiciary, private associations, legal aid, public defender, and education increased only marginally, if at all.

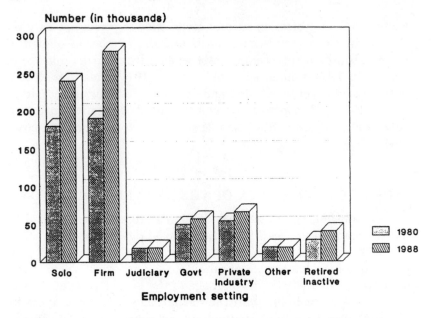

Fig. 4. Distributions of 1980 and 1988 Lawyer Populations by Employment

. . .

EMPLOYMENT IN THE PRIVATE PRACTICE SECTOR

In 1980, there were 370,111 lawyers in private practice repre-senting 68% of the 1980 lawyer population. By 1988, the number of private practitioners had increased to 519,941 or 72% of the 1988 lawyer population. The population/lawyer ratio declined from 1 lawyer per 612 persons in 1980 to 1 lawyer per 473 persons in 1988. As shown by Fig. 7, the number of lawyers in every private practice setting was greater in 1988 than in 1980. The rate of increase was largest among lawyers in firm settings of more than 10 lawyers and smallest in firms of 2–5 lawyers.

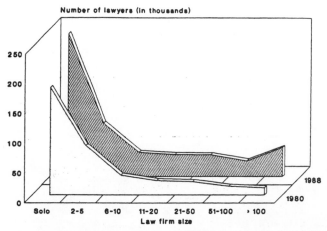

Net Increase in number in each setting.
Solo:34%   2-5:8%   6-10:22%   11-20:53%
21-50:62%   51-100:77%   Over 100:302%

Fig. 7. Distributions of Private Practitioner Populations by Practice Setting in 1980 and 1988

In spite of significant increase in the number of solo practitioners over the last eight years, their representation among private practitioners has declined from 49% of all lawyers in private practice to 46%. The proportion of lawyers practicing in firm settings has correspondingly increased from 51% to 54%. An important element in this shift is the rise in the number of firm practitioners holding associate status.

Table 4.   Distributions of 1980 and 1988 Private Practitioner Populations by Practice Status

	1980 N = 370,111	1988 N = 519,941
Solo	49%	46%
Firm: partner	38	35
Firm: Of Counsel	1	2
Firm: Associate	12	16
Total	100%	100%

. . .

EMPLOYMENT OF FEMALE LAWYERS

In 1988, a higher proportion of the male lawyer population was employed in private practice than was the case for the female

lawyer population. While almost three-quarters of men were in
private practice, about two-thirds of women were private practitioners. Male lawyers dominated in all employment settings.
However, female lawyers were more highly represented in government employment, private associations, legal aid, public defender,
and education.

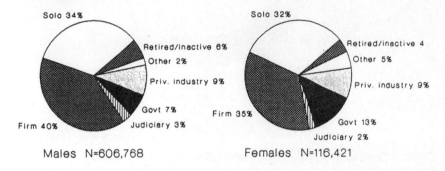

Males N=606,768   Females N=116,421

Fig. 9. Distributions of Male and Female Lawyer Populations by Employment, 1988

· · ·

In each age group, the only setting in which women were
neither overrepresented nor underrepresented was solo practice.
They were underrepresented among partners in law firms and
progressively more so within each older age group. They were
reasonably well represented as firm associates in the two younger
age groups, but were significantly overrepresented among associates 35 years of age or older. In all age groups, women were
overrepresented in most nonpractice settings.

· · ·

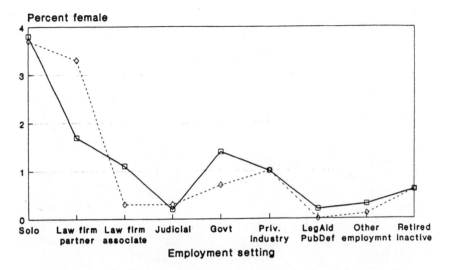

Percent female

N=520,217 total lawyer population 35
years of age or older in 1988

Fig. 14. 1988 Lawyer Population Age 35 or Older:
Expected and Actual Percent Female by Employment Setting

· · ·

RETIRED AND INACTIVE LAWYERS

The number of retired/inactive lawyers increased by 43%
between 1980 and 1988. Because of the significant growth of the
general lawyer population during the intervening years, however,
the proportion of lawyers represented by retirees/inactives rose
only moderately. While 53 out every 1,000 lawyers in 1980 were
retired/inactive, the ratio rose to 56 per 1,000 in 1988. The
median age of retirees was 69 in 1980 and remained so in 1988.

· · ·

LAW FIRMS

The total number of law firms in 1988 was 42,649, representing a net increase of about 4,000 firms since 1980.

· · ·

The number of law firms in every size group grew, but the
rate of increase in the number of large firms substantially exceeded that of smaller firms. While law firms with ten or fewer
lawyers increased by 7% over the last eight years, the number of
firms with more than 100 lawyers almost tripled in number.

Table 7.   Net Increase in Number of Law
Firms by Firm Size, 1980–88

Firm Size	1980 No. of Firms	1988 No. of Firms	Net Increase (%)
2 lawyers	16,859	17,501	4
3 lawyers	7,894	8,028	2
4 lawyers	4,141	4,460	8
5 lawyers	2,424	2,740	13
6–10 lawyers	4,482	5,497	23
11–20 lawyers	1,678	2,583	64
21–50 lawyers	717	1,201	68
51–100 lawyers	200	381	91
Over 100 lawyers	87	258	196
All firms	38,482	42,649	11

Of the 279,800 lawyers practicing in law firms in 1988, 84,824 were associates. Only one-third of law firms, however, had associate members. As expected, the larger the firm, the more likely it included associates in its roster.

. . .

Table 8.   Firms with One or More Associates: Median
Associate/Partner Ratio by Firm Size (1988)

Firm size	Associate/Partner Ratio
2 lawyers	1/1
3 lawyers	1/2
4 lawyers	1/3
5 lawyers	2/3
6–10 lawyers	1/2
11–20 lawyers	3/4
21–50 lawyers	4/5
51–100 lawyers	4/5
Over 100 lawyers	1.1/1

. . .

The larger the firm, the more likely that at least one of the partners was a woman. Fig. 18 shows the percent of firms within each firm size category that had female partners in 1988.

Law firm size

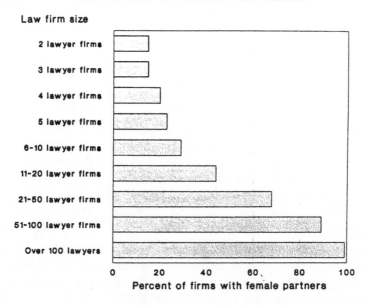

Fig. 18. Percent of Law Firms with Female Partners by Law Firm Size, 1988

B. PROFESSIONAL OPPORTUNITIES

1. WOMEN

NOTES*

During the late 1960s, the gender composition of most elite professions, including law, began to change dramatically. Between 1960 and 1990, women's representation in law school classes grew from 3 to 40%, and their representation among practicing lawyers grew from 3 to 14%.

That increase reflected a complicated set of social, economic and ideological factors. Over the last quarter century, traditional assumptions about gender roles fell increasingly out of step with demographic patterns. After the post-war baby boom, the development of effective oral contraceptives contributed to a decline in birth rates. This decline, coupled with increases in life expectancy, meant that the average mother could anticipate spending about two-thirds of her adult years with no children under eigh-

* This material is adapted from D.   88 (1992).
Rhode and D. Luban, *Legal Ethics* 86–

teen.[1] A rising divorce rate also meant that a marriage was becoming a less stable foundation on which to build an entire life.[2] The pressures of inflation and aspirations for a higher living standard also propelled more women into the workforce for longer periods.[3] These structural forces both reflected and reinforced ideological trends. During the 1960s and 1970s, the growth in progressive political movements and the discrimination experienced by women within them fueled demands for greater equality.[4] The frustrations of many middle-class homemakers, trapped in menial tasks and vicarious roles, found expression in feminist publications and political activity. An increasing array of antidiscrimination initiatives responded to these forces and helped pave the way for greater equality in professional opportunities.

Other factors made the bar an especially attractive channel for women's increasing aspirations. The demand for corporate legal services was increasing, as was the market for low-cost, middle-income consumer services. Particularly during the Vietnam era, women provided the additional law school applicants that could eventually meet this demand.

Women's equal access has not, however, ensured their equal acceptance, a fact that has gained increasing attention. As late as 1980, only one article on the entire subject of gender bias in the courts had appeared in mainstream legal literature.[5] A decade later, 30 states had gender bias commissions and the National Judicial Education Association had an active program to promote equality for women and men in the courts.[6] In the late 1980s, the

---

1. . See D. Rhode, *Justice and Gender* 53–56 (1989); M. Ryan, *Womanhood in America: From Colonial Times to the Present* 401 (1975); E. Klein, *Gender Politics: From Consciousness to Mass Politics* 66–67 (1984).

2. At the turn of the century, one in five hundred marriages ended in divorce; current estimates are one in two. *See* J. Bardwick, *supra* note 1, at 100; A. Cherlin, *Marriage, Divorce, and Remarriage* 21–25 (1981); G. Masnick & M. Bane, *The Nation's Families: 1960–1990* 29–34 (1980); J. Bernard, *The Future of Marriage* (1982).

3. This trend was not unprecedented. A high percentage of women of color had always worked and World War II had brought a substantial percentage of white women into the workforce. *See* J. Jones, *Labor of Love, Labor of Sorrow: Black Women, Work and the Family, From Slavery to the Present*

(1985); A. Kessler–Harris, *Out to Work* (1982). But the influx of female employees beginning in the 1960s was more widespread and sustained.

4. *See generally* S. Evans, *Personal Politics: The Roots of Women's Liberation in the Civil Rights Movement and the New Left* (1979); J. Hole & E. Levine, *Rebirth of Feminism* (1971); Freeman, "The Origins of the Women's Liberation Movement," 78 *Am.J.Soc.* 792 (1973); D. Rhode, *supra* note 1, at 53–61.

5. Wikler, "Water on Stone: A Perspective on the Movement to Eliminate Gender Bias in the Courts," Proceedings of the National Conference on Gender Bias in the Courts, May 18, 1989 at 6.

6. Schafran, "Gender and Justice: Florida and the Nation," 42 *Fla.L.Rev.* 181, 186 (1990). New Jersey issued the

American Bar Association's Commission on Women in the Professions issued a major report excerpted below, and the subject was generating a substantial body of legal scholarship.

That scholarship, together with state commission reports, has documented sex discrimination in areas including:

(1) women's opportunities for professional advancement;

(2) the treatment of female lawyers, litigants and witnesses;

(3) substantive standards on gender-related issues such as divorce, custody, and domestic violence; and

(4) the allocation of judicial resources for dealing with these issues.[7]

Research on women's status in the profession reveals that they are significantly overrepresented in the least prestigious and least remunerative areas of practice, and significantly underrepresented among law firm partners, tenured law school faculty, federal judges and bar association leaders.[8] Female lawyers have also earned substantially less and expressed greater dissatisfaction with practice than male lawyers.[9] Although these disparities are often attributed to women's recent entrance into the profession, empirical studies reflect that in law, as in other elite professions, female members advance less far and less quickly than male colleagues with comparable qualifications, and that women of

first report in 1984 and by the close of the decade, eight other states had published reports. *Id.* The National Judicial Education Association programs have been launched through assistance from the National Association of Women Judges and the National Organization for Women's Legal Defense and Education Fund. *See id.;* Wikler, *supra* note 5.

7. Czapanskiy, "Gender Bias in the Courts," 4 *Geo. J. Legal Ethics* 1, 2–6 (1990); Schafran, "The Obligation to Intervene: New Directions from the American Bar Association's Code of Judicial Conduct," 4 *Geo. J. Legal Ethics* 55 (1990); "How Gender Bias Creeps into Courts," L.A. Times, November 27, 1990 (describing one prominent California judge's account of spending ten days in civil trial court presiding over a $100,000 dispute between two corporations and then being asked in family court to resolve 30 to 40 cases of abuse and custody per day involving an average of 2.5 children).

8. See Maclanahan & Jensen, "Progress Glacial for Women, Minorities," *Nat'l L.J.*, Jan. 27, 1992, at 1; Nelson, "The Futures of American Lawyers: A Demographic Profile of a Changing Profession," *Case Western L.Rev.* (1993); Merrit, Reskin, & Fordell, "Families, Place, and Career: The Gender Paradox in Law School Hiring," 1993 *Wisc. L.Rev.* 305; *Ninth Circuit Gender Bias Task Force Report: Discussion Draft* (1992).

9. C. Menkel-Meadow, "Feminization of the Legal Profession: The Comparative Sociology of Women Lawyers," in *Lawyers in Society: Comparative Theories* 196, 226 (R. Abel & P. Lewis eds. 1989); "Lawyers Give Thumbs Up," Nat.L.J., May 28, 1990, at 52 (principal sources of dissatisfaction include boredom, long hours, work/family conflicts, frustration with firm management and gender bias); see Caplow and Scheindlin, " 'Portrait of a Lady': The Woman Lawyer in the 1980s," 35 *N.Y.L.Sch. L.Rev.* 391, 408 (1990).

color are especially disadvantaged.[10]

The following readings describe some of the barriers still confronting women in the bar. Rhode's research identifies three sources of gender inequality. The first involves sex-based socialization patterns that encourage women to form somewhat lower aspirations for vocational achievement, to assume a greater share of family responsibilities, and to develop feminine personality traits that are not associated with career success under current cultural norms. A second set of barriers involves institutional structures that make it difficult for individuals to accommodate significant work and family commitments. A third category of problems arise from gender stereotypes and unconscious biases analogous to those that Charles Lawrence describes regarding race in the excerpt below.

Deborah L. Rhode, "Perspectives on Professional Women"

40 Stan.L.Rev. 1163 (1988).

Socialization Patterns

[Any adequate account of gender inequality must begin by acknowledging the different cues that society sends to men and women about appropriate occupations, traits, behaviors and values. Children respond to signals about desirable masculine and feminine roles at very early ages....]

In a variety of studies, female students have also expressed lower expectations for occupational success than males and have attached greater priority to relational aspects of employment such as opportunities for helping others than to opportunities for money, status and power. Family and peer pressure can also skew vocational choices and discourage career decisions that would compete with domestic responsibilities, require geographic mobility, or bring wives greater prestige and income than their husbands. Such pressures can be particularly intense within certain class, race, and ethnic groups.

---

10. See studies cited in Rhode, "Missing Questions: Feminist Perspectives on Legal Education," 45 *Stan. L.Rev.* 1547, 1550 (1993); Merrit & Reskin, "The Double Minority: Empirical Evidence of a Double Standard in Law School Hiring of Minority Women," 65 *S.Cal.L.Rev.* 2299, 2301 (1992); American Bar Association Commission on Women in the Profession, Report to the House of Delegates (1988); Menkel-Meadow, *supra* note 10; Rhode, "The No–Problem: Feminist Challenges and Cultural Change," 100 *Yale L.J.* 1731 (1991). For discussion of other managerial and professional contexts, *see e.g.,* G. Powell, *Women and Men in Management* (1988); A. Morrison, R. White & E. Van Velsor, *Breaking the Glass Ceiling* (1987); Eisenberg, "Medicine is No Longer a Man's Profession," 321 *New Eng.J.Med.* 1542 (1989).

Disparities between traits associated with femininity and traits associated with vocational achievement further reinforce these gender socialization processes. A wide array of experimental and clinical evidence indicates that profiles of successful professionals conflict with profiles of normal or ideal women. The aggressiveness, competitiveness, dedication, and emotional detachment traditionally presumed necessary for advancement in the most prestigious and well-paid occupations are incompatible with traits commonly viewed as attractive in women: cooperativeness, deference, sensitivity, and self-sacrifice. Despite substantial progress toward gender equality over the last several decades, these gender stereotypes remain remarkably resilient. Females aspiring to nontraditional or high-status positions remain subject to a familiar double bind. Those conforming to traditional characteristics of femininity are often thought lacking in the requisite assertiveness and initiative, yet those conforming to a masculine model of success may be ostracized in work settings as bitchy, aggressive, and uncooperative. As long as aspiring women are found wanting either as professionals or as women, they face substantial disincentives to aspire....

Of particular significance are the sexes' different priorities concerning family responsibilities. Although cultural commitments to equal opportunity in vocational spheres have steadily increased, these sentiments have not translated into equal obligations in domestic spheres. Most studies have indicated that women still perform about 70 percent of the family tasks in an average household. Employed wives spend about twice as much time on homemaking demands as employed husbands; men married to women with full-time jobs devote only 1.4 hours a week more to domestic duties than other husbands. When time spent in paid labor and domestic labor is combined, employed males average two hours less per day than employed females, and a disproportionate amount of male homemaking contributions involve relatively enjoyable activities such as playing with the children.... Women, particularly racial and ethnic minorities, are also far more likely to become single parents, with all the associated demands. In the late 1980s, females headed 90 percent of the nation's single-parent households, and women of color were disproportionately likely to have such responsibilities....

Institutional Constraints

Not only do women bear the vast majority of family obligations, they do so in occupational environments designed by and for men. As a result, career success has often meant compromise of caretaking values. Female employees unwilling to make that sacrifice have paid a demanding professional price....

... Elite professions also tend to impose longer and more unpredictable working hours, and are particularly resistant to extended leaves, part-time or flexible-time shifts, and home work. That resistance springs from a variety of sources. Many clients and colleagues object to the inconveniences and the apparent lack of commitment among employees working nonconventional hours. Although no professional can be accessible at all times for particular needs, inaccessibility related to family needs has often carried special stigma.... Individuals who make work the central priority in their own lives are often unwilling to accommodate those with divided loyalties. Even temporary suspension of normal working hours can create permanent professional risks.

Moreover, what passes for normal working hours in many professional and business contexts poses special problems for women. A Puritan ethic run amok often makes life unmanageable for those with significant family commitments. Extended hours, unpredictable schedules, and frequent travel mesh poorly with child-rearing responsibilities.

Gender Stereotypes and Unconscious Bias

... As the preceding discussion suggests, traditional understanding of sexual roles continue to constrain women's occupational choices. Such stereotypes also affect a variety of other attitudes and practices that translate into gender disadvantages.

Part of the difficulty stems from lingering skepticism about female competence, a problem compounded for women of color. Although such doubts are no longer generally aired in polite company, they still emerge in studies of unconscious bias. For example, surveys involving managers, students, and chairs of university departments have revealed that the same resume receives a significantly lower rating if the applicant is a woman rather than a man. In analogous studies, both male and female subjects have given less favorable evaluations to identical scholarly articles and artistic endeavors when the author or artist is thought to be a woman. Other evidence suggests that college students evaluate male professors more favorably than females, and that supervisors are more likely to promote or provide training opportunities for male managers than for their equally qualified female counterparts....

Unconscious gender bias can operate on three levels: (1) prototypes, the images associated with members of a particular occupation; (2) schema, the personal characteristics and situational factors that are used to explain conduct; and (3) scripts, definitions of appropriate behavior in a given situation. Thus, when a female applicant for a given position (e.g., litigator) does not fit the evaluator's prototype (e.g., aggressive male), her credentials will be judged with greater skepticism. Many explanatory schema embody similar stereotypes: Men's success is more likely to be explained in terms of ability and their failure in terms of luck, while women's achievement is more often attributed to luck or effort and their failures ascribed to inability. Since evaluations of ability are most crucial in hiring and promotion decisions, these attribution biases entrench gender hierarchies. So too, the scripts defining appropriate social behavior often reflect patterns of gender dominance, deference, and accommodation. For example, in group conversation, male participants tend to speak and interrupt more often, and to hold the floor for longer periods than females. Women are expected not only to talk less but also to allow more interruptions, and those who deviate from their accustomed role provoke negative evaluations. Once again, these perceptual prejudices create a double bind: Women who conform to accepted stereotypes will appear to have less to contribute and less leadership potential than their male colleagues, while women who take a more assertive stance risk appearing arrogant, aggressive, and abrasive. How to seem "demure but tough" is particularly difficult when standards vary among those whose opinions are most critical. In male-dominated cultures, women are subject to criticism for being "too feminine" and not "feminine enough."

Unconscious gender prejudices affect not only the evaluation of individual performance, they also affect the performance itself. As both experimental and longitudinal studies have repeatedly demonstrated, low expectations of achievement frequently become self-fulfilling prophecies. Individuals often signal their assumptions in subtle or not so subtle ways. These forms of negative feedback, including lower salaries and less demanding assignments, can adversely affect self-confidence and job performance. Such consequences then reinforce the initial expectations, and a self-perpetuating cycle continues ...

... More overt, although often unintentional, forms of gender bias have comparable consequences. Women in male-dominated occupations face continuing problems of "fitting in" and forming the client and collegial relationships necessary for advancement. Female professionals often lack access to the informal networks of advice, collaboration, and contacts on which successful careers depend....

Women of color face particular difficulties ...   The same biases in evaluation and collegial support that disadvantage women also operate against minorities.   Women of color thus face unconscious discrimination on two fronts and their small numbers amplify problems such as high visibility, few mentors and role models, and additional counseling and committee responsibilities. . . .

Given these biases, women, particularly minorities, must work harder than men to succeed.   When they are in fact successful, they must deal with the envy and anxiety that such achievement arouses.   Those who do not advance under such circumstances, or who become frustrated and opt for different employment, confirm the adverse stereotypes that worked against their advancement in the first instance.   The perception remains that women cannot succeed by conventional standards, or are less committed to doing so than men.   In either event, female professionals do not warrant the same investment in training, assistance, and other opportunities as their male counterparts.   Women employees disproportionately drift off the occupational fast track, leaving the most powerful sectors of the professions insulated from alternative values. Again, the result is a subtle but self-perpetuating cycle in which individual choices are constrained by gender biases.   Those biases are not adequately addressed by traditional equal opportunity mandates.

American Bar Association, Commission on Women in the Profession Report to the House of Delegates
7, 9, 15 (1988).

The statistics demonstrate that women are not rising to "upper" levels of the profession in appropriate numbers and dispel any sense of complacency that the sheer numbers of women entering the profession will eliminate barriers to their advancement.   Indeed, witnesses observed that women often reach a level above which they seem unable to rise.   Some commentators describe this phenomenon as the "glass ceiling."

For the few women who do "make it" beyond the "glass ceiling," the consequences are often a lack of support networks and the stresses that accompany living life as a constant token, with the extra demands and scrutiny that status attracts.   These women partners or judges are not regarded as just partners or judges, but as *women* partners and judges, supposed representatives of how all women will do in such positions.   In addition, as many witnesses observed, women who "made it," often did so at the great expense of not having a spouse and children. As one successful witness testified, she found herself to be, "43, single, childless and typical."

II. OVERT BARRIERS TO WOMEN'S ADVANCEMENT IN THE LEGAL PROFESSION

C. *Discrimination in the Courts*

... Supreme Court Task Forces on gender bias ... have documented the variety of disparate and demeaning behavior women often encounter. Women are often addressed by terms of endearment ("sweetheart" or "honey") rather than professional titles. Judges and opposing attorneys make comments about women's physical appearance, clothing, sexual attractiveness and availability. The studies report that women's arguments and courtroom demeanor are likely to draw far more comments, including reprimands for being too aggressive, when more aggravated conduct by male attorneys goes unmentioned....

One example involved a Texas judge, who asked a 5′2″ lawyer to turn around and face the courtroom and, when she did, said, "Ladies and gentlemen, can you believe this pretty little thing is an Assistant Attorney General?" These examples are not atypical.

This type of conduct results in more than personal embarrassment. It undercuts credibility and professionalism. How does an attorney establish authority when the judge has just described her to the entire courtroom as a "pretty little thing?" Even the most subtle conduct cannot help but have an impact on a client when that client's lawyer is perceived to be treated with less dignity than her male adversary.

The woman attorney is caught in a double bind. If she objects to the conduct, she is a "women's libber." If she lets it go, she is weak. Such comments shift the woman's attention away from the case at hand to an evaluation process about how to respond to these incidents. The New York Task Force on Women in the Court concludes that, "The added pressures engendered by a climate of disrespect or hostility distract the attention of the judge, the jury, and attorneys from the merits of the particular proceeding and thereby reduce the quality of justice received by all."

D. *Discrimination in Law Firms and Corporate Counsel Offices*

Witnesses also report biased treatment within law firms and corporate counsel offices. Recurring testimony was received on the topic of mentoring—women's difficulty in establishing mentoring relationships with senior male attorneys. A shortage of mentors is particularly acute for minority women who rarely have any role models and face additional sources of discrimination from other lawyers. Some senior male attorneys' discomfort in establishing mentor relationships with women may be due to fear of sexual overtones or unfamiliarity with working with women.

Absence of mentor relationships results in problems with case assignments, a failure to consider women for various positions of responsibility that might lead to business development or referrals and an absence of a guide through the labyrinth of firm politics and advancement, a path which is already strewn with additional obstacles for women. If members of the profession make a conscious effort to give equal mentoring consideration to women, the talents of women will become more widely known....

Some women also report being frozen out of firm discussions and professional socialization. The exclusion may stem from discomfort or uncertainty about how to engage in camaraderie with a woman but acquiescing in this behavior only perpetuates the unfamiliarity and discomfort. Women lawyers are often not included when colleagues go out for lunch or drinks after work where business is going to be discussed. Male colleagues may conduct work discussions or professional meetings in settings that are likely to exclude women, such as clubs that do not accept women as members. These settings often provide the starting point for development of business contacts, professional trust and collegiality. The problems of professional exclusion appear to be especially acute in small firms in smaller towns where women are often among the first women lawyers in the area. Indeed, several witnesses from smaller town practice settings insisted on confidentiality, because they feared the repercussions from candor.

Witnesses also testified that there is a perception that women will not be successful rainmakers. It should be noted, however, that women are often excluded from social environments where business contacts can be established and nurtured. The use of rainmaking as an evaluation standard seems to be a yardstick more commonly applied to women than men. Few lawyers in firms are star rainmakers; thus holding all potential women partners up to excessive scrutiny on this score, when not all men are expected to serve principal rainmaking functions for a firm, is a form of gender bias.

III. THE SUBTLE BARRIERS TO WOMEN'S ADVANCEMENT IN THE PROFESSION

One subtle but significant form of bias women experience concerns the greater degree of scrutiny given to their work and their work styles. Many women who testified before the Commission reported that they still have to work harder, do better and make fewer mistakes in order to receive even the same degree of professional respect received by men of average skill, competence and diligence.

Women report that they are often treated with a presumption of incompetence, to be overcome only by flawless performance, whereas they see men attorneys treated with a presumption of competence overcome only after numerous significant mistakes. Minority women testified that adverse presumptions are even more likely to be made about their competence.

This differential scrutiny imposed on women also relates to their styles of lawyering. Men are often perceived to be aggressive and combative lawyers while women are seen as less competitive and more soft-spoken. When women employ a different style from that of men, it is often assumed that the different style is attributable to the lawyer's femaleness and is therefore less valid or successful.... Yet, women who do act with assertive confidence risk being perceived as *too* aggressive. Although this type of behavior is rewarded when engaged in by men, women's competency may sometimes be questioned simply because they do things differently.

The profession must become more open to a wide variety of lawyering styles for both men and women in order to provide all lawyers full professional opportunities, unconstrained by gender stereotypes.

The profession's traditional response to many of the subtle barriers identified by women has been to deny that bias exists or deny that the profession is responsible. The implication is that women themselves are to blame. Women are told they are not aggressive enough in promoting themselves or seeking out business while simultaneously being criticized as too pushy or discouraged from working in certain areas. Women are told they are humorless or too sensitive when they do not accept sexist jokes or demeaning forms of address with grace. Women's career commitments are questioned when they ask for some recognition of their family responsibilities.

Women's reaction to the subtle barriers they encounter is often a hard to articulate perception that they are at a disadvantage because they are operating in an alien culture. Some women express this as a sense that they and the men they work with are from different worlds. Others express it as a realization that a woman will never be one of the boys no matter how hard she tries.

Often, women can share their feelings with other women but cannot articulate these perceptions convincingly to men. Men, in return, frequently do not see these barriers as anything other than the normal requirements of the profession.

IV. THE PROFESSIONAL CULTURE—HOW IT DEVELOPED AND HOW IT HAS CHANGED

The structures and attitudes of the legal profession were originally developed by men in an era when the workforce was predominantly male and the dual career family was an anomaly. The work expectations and definitions of career commitment were created at a time when the prototypic lawyer was one whose wife, in most instances, devoted full time to raising their children and providing him with a well-organized home life. Lawyers were seen as breadwinners and professionals with little or no responsibility for child care. Numerous witnesses testified that the structure of the profession is still largely based on this, now outmoded, model.

Today, the structures and attitudes of the legal profession—developed in an era that no longer is representative of American society—pose great problems for women lawyers. These cultural norms are not often thought about by the group that has defined and most often fits them, but for women lawyers, these norms represent the subtle attitudinal and structural barriers encountered on a daily basis discussed throughout this report. They are the problems that have no name, yet most men do not even understand the description of them as "problems," but rather perceive them as the inevitable and necessary norms of the profession to which all members must adapt.

However, for lawyers who bear children and have primary responsibility for childrearing, the clash between the professional culture and these life circumstances operates as a barrier to full and equal participation. Thus, it is not surprising that the problem drawing the most concern and attention at the Commission hearings focused on how legal employers respond to family responsibilities.

V. FAMILY AND WORKPLACE ISSUES: NOT FOR WOMEN ONLY

Numerous witnesses stressed that family and workplace issues are not simply women's issues but are issues of crucial importance to both men and women in the profession. These issues include the need to develop parental leave, child care and part-time work arrangements.

All of these issues undeniably have a greater impact on women because women continue to bear a disproportionate share of the responsibility for child care and family duties. However, the Commission also heard evidence that more male lawyers are starting to yearn for greater opportunities to be more actively involved with their families. Several witnesses indicated that men are starting to evaluate practice settings based on their accommodation to family responsibilities. Today, both men and women are struggling to establish a more healthy balance between work and other aspects of their lives.

One barrier encountered by lawyers who try to juggle their family responsibilities with work demands is the assumption that family responsibilities are not an acceptable reason to ask for professional scheduling adjustments. The assumption is that lawyers who ask for an extended leave or part-time work arrangement display a reduced professional commitment and want to receive "special treatment." This "special treatment" subjects these lawyers to resentment from both male and female co-workers.

Men and women reported that their career commitment was sometimes called into question when they sought a part-time work arrangement. Members of the profession should recognize that men or women who seek to balance family responsibilities with work demands are demonstrating the depth of their career commitment because they are trying to find a way to remain actively engaged in their career while still meeting family needs.

Witnesses pointed out that it should also be universally recognized that having children is personally and societally important and warrants flexible work arrangements just like other responsibilities the profession has always accommodated, such as political involvement, military reserve duty and government service. Members of the profession need to examine the wide range of activities they have frequently accommodated and ask why having children should not assume a place alongside other valued activities. The profession should reevaluate the current situation where men who have families suffer little or no adverse consequences to their careers while women who have families often must sacrifice career advancement, remuneration and respect of colleagues.

Witnesses who worked part-time and firm representatives who helped fashion part-time policies, stressed that such arrangements can make good economic sense for firms by enhancing productivity and lawyer satisfaction. The policies help firms retain experienced lawyers and often give firms a recruiting edge.

According to the testimony of several large-firm senior partners, in today's competitive marketplace, part-time policies can, in the long run, inure to the economic benefit of the firm. Witnesses cautioned, however, that part-time arrangements must be structured so that they do not become another source of professional disadvantage to women, relegating them to lower-paid, lower-status jobs within the profession.

2. RACIAL AND ETHNIC MINORITIES

NOTES *

Beginning in the late 1960s, minority representation in the legal profession began to increase substantially, but progress remained limited. By the late 1980s, when blacks, Hispanics, Native Americans and Asian Americans accounted for almost a quarter of the American population, they constituted only about 12% of the nation's law students, less than 8% of its lawyers, and 6% of its law professors. According to a comprehensive survey by the ABA Task Force on Minorities, more than half of all law firms employed no minority lawyers and over three quarters had no minority partners. Minorities also remained underrepresented in the most prestigious firms and specialties. A 1990 survey of the nation's 250 largest firms found that minorities constituted less than 2% of the partners (blacks, .9%; Hispanics, .48%; Asian American or American Indian, .53%). The partnerships at sixty-nine of those firms were all white and less than ⅕ had more than one black or one Hispanic lawyer. Attorneys of color are also more likely to be unemployed and to express dissatisfaction with their current job.[1]

Part of the problem stems from the unconscious racial biases that Lawrence describes in the following excerpt. Such biases diminish minorities' aspirations and opportunities to enter law school, and constrain their performance and advancement once they graduate. Some of the problems are comparable to those confronting women: the devaluation of competence; the special scrutiny that accompanies token status; the exclusion from informal networks of advice and assistance, and the absence of mentors

---

* This material is adapted from D. Rhode and D. Luban, *Legal Ethics* 97–99 (1992).

1. American Bar Association Task Force on Minorities in the Legal Profession, *Report With Recommendations*

(1986); and Task Force on Minorities and the Justice System, Achieving Justice in a Diverse America (July, 1992). Jensen, "Minorities Didn't Share in Firm Growth," *Nat'l L.J.*, Feb. 19, 1990 at 1, 28; Fisk, "Lawyers Give Thumbs Up," *Nat'l L.J.*, May 28, 1990 at S–2.

and role models.[2]   In addition, barriers of race and ethnicity intersect with barriers of class. As the materials in Chapter XVII reflect, minorities' underrepresentation in the law school applicant pool is partly attributable to inadequate financial resources and inferior educational preparation. These factors, together with pressures resulting from isolation and bias, contribute to minorities' disproportionate attrition rate during law school.[3]

Theories of racial prejudice proceed on several levels. Some research, based on psychoanalytic approaches, suggests that groups with highly visible differences become targets for rejection and displaced hostility. Individuals who experience frustration in their relationships with authority figures, or who cannot live up to their own aspirations, often subconsciously project their conflicts into racial stereotypes. In the process, they attribute undesirable characteristics, such as ignorance, weakness, laziness, or aggression to subordinate groups.[4]

A second framework stresses the historical, socioeconomic and political forces that help determine when and which groups become targets of subordination. According to some theorists, social and economic dislocation that generates widespread anxiety often triggers a search for scapegoats. So too, groups that have achieved dominance generally seek to legitimize their position by magnifying group differences.[5]

A final approach, informed by cognitive psychology, stresses the role of social categorization in perpetrating racial stereotypes. Individuals' needs to simplify experience and to maintain group affiliations can reinforce hierarchical arrangements. So too, the desire to believe in a "just world" often results in assigning subordinate groups responsibility for their own subordination. Individuals generally want to assume that life follows orderly, predictable, and equitable patterns in which everyone gets what

2. Jensen, *supra* note 1. *See also* Keeva, "Unequal Partners," *ABA J.* Feb. 1993 at 541; Chused, "The Hiring and Retention of Minorities and Women as American Law School Faculties," 137 *U.Pa.L.Rev.* 537, 539 (1988).

3. *See* American Bar Association Task Force, *supra* note 1; G. Segal, *Blacks in the Law* (1983); Diamond, "A Trace Element in the Law," 73 *A.B.A.J.* 46 (1987); Impellizzeri, "Women, Minorities Made Gains at City Firms," *Manhattan Law.*, March, 1990, at 4.

4. See G. Allport, *The Nature of Prejudice* (1979); T. Adorno, E. Frenk-el-Brunswik, D. Levinson, & R. Sanford, *The Authoritarian Personality* (1969); Harding, Proshansky, Kutner, and Chein, "Prejudice and Ethnic Relations," 5 *Handbook of Social Psychology* 1, 38 (G. Lindsey and E. Aronson ed. 1968); Delgado, Dunn, Brown, Lee & Hubbert, "Fairness and Formality: Minimizing the Risk of Prejudice in Alternative Dispute Resolution," 1985 *Wisc.L.Rev.* 1359.

5. Id., J. Kovel, *White Racism: A Psychohistory* 44 (1984); Handlin, "Prejudice and Capitalist Exploitation," 6 *Commentary* 79 (1948).

they deserve and deserves what they get. To sustain this view, people will often adjust their evaluations of merit to justify existing social arrangements.[6]

In the excerpt that follows, Charles Lawrence explores the unconscious underpinnings of racial bias and in cultural practices that sustain them.

Charles Lawrence, "The Id, the Ego, and Equal Protection: Reckoning with Unconscious Racism"
39 Stanford Law Review, 317, 335–339 (1987).

How is the unconscious involved when racial prejudice is less apparent—when racial bias is hidden from the prejudiced individual as well as from others? Increasingly, as our culture has rejected racism as immoral and unproductive, this hidden prejudice has become the more prevalent form of racism. The individual's Ego must adapt to a cultural order that views overtly racist attitudes and behavior as unsophisticated, uninformed, and immoral. It must repress or disguise racist ideas when they seek expression.

Joel Kovel refers to the resulting personality type as the "aversive racist" and contrasts this type with the "dominative racist," the true bigot who openly seeks to keep blacks in a subordinate position and will resort to force to do so. The aversive racist believes in white superiority, but her conscience seeks to repudiate this belief or, at least, to prevent her from acting on it. She often resolves this inner conflict by not acting at all. She tries to avoid the issue by ignoring the existence of blacks, avoiding contact with them, or at most being polite, correct, and cold whenever she must deal with them. Aversive racists range from individuals who lapse into demonstrative racism when threatened—as when blacks get "too close"—to those who consider themselves liberals and, despite their sense of aversion to blacks (of which they are often unaware), do their best within the confines of the existing societal structure to ameliorate blacks' condition. . . .

Cognitivists see the process of "categorization" as one common source of racial and other stereotypes. All humans tend to categorize in order to make sense of experience. Too many events occur daily for us to deal successfully with each one on an

---

6. I. Katz, *Stigma—A Social Psychological Analysis* 121 (1981); Snyder, "On the Self–Perpetuating Nature of Social Stereotypes," *Cognitive Processes* in Stereotyping and Intergroup Behavior 183 (D. Hamilton ed. 1981); M. Lerner, *The Belief in a Just World: A Fundamental Delusion* vii–viii (1980).

individual basis; we must categorize in order to cope. When a category—for example, the category of black person or white person—correlates with a continuous dimension—for example, the range of human intelligence or the propensity to violence—there is a tendency to exaggerate the differences between categories on that dimension and to minimize the differences within each category.

The more important a particular classification of people into groups is to an individual, the more likely she is to distinguish sharply the characteristics of people who belong to the different groups. Here, cognitivists integrate the observations of personality theorists and social psychologists with their own. If an individual is hostile toward a group of people, she has an emotional investment in preserving the differentiations between her own group and the "others." Thus, the preservation of inaccurate judgments about the out-group is self-rewarding. This is particularly so when prejudiced judgments are made in a social context that accepts and encourages negative attitudes toward the out-group. In these cases, the group judgment reinforces and helps maintain the individual judgment about the out-group's lack of worth.

The content of the social categories to which people are assigned is generated over a long period of time within a culture and transmitted to individual members of society by a process cognitivists call "assimilation." Assimilation entails learning and internalizing preferences and evaluations. Individuals learn cultural attitudes and beliefs about race very early in life, at a time when it is difficult to separate the perceptions of one's teacher (usually a parent) from one's own. In other words, one learns about race at a time when one is highly sensitive to the social contexts in which one lives.... Conditions, when the child remains in awe of the source of truth, tend to be precisely the conditions under which children learn socially sanctioned truths about race. Lessons learned at this early developmental stage are not questioned: They are learned as facts rather than as points of view.

Furthermore, because children learn lessons about race at this early stage, most of the lessons are tacit rather than explicit. Children learn not so much through an intellectual understanding of what their parents tell them about race as through an emotional identification with who their parents are and what they see and feel their parents do. Small children will adopt their parents' beliefs because they experience them as their own. If we do learn lessons about race in this way, we are not likely to be aware that the lessons have even taken place. If we are unaware that we have been taught to be afraid of blacks or to think of them as lazy or stupid, then we may not be conscious of our internalization of those feelings and beliefs.

All of these processes, most of which occur outside the actor's consciousness, are mutually reinforcing. Furthermore, there is little in our environment to counteract them; indeed, our culture often supports and rewards individuals for making hostile misjudgments that exaggerate the differences between themselves and members of a racial out-group. Cultural prejudice also removes the possibility of checking judgments against outside reality, further inhibiting the chance that the holder of a prejudiced belief will perceive his mistake and correct it. Thus, through personal and cultural experience the individual comes to associate characteristics such as "intelligence," "laziness," "honesty," or "dirtiness" with classifications of people. In ambiguous social situations, it will always be easier to find evidence supporting an individual's assumed group characteristics than to find contradictory evidence. Furthermore, whenever one is confronted with the need to interpret the behavior of members of a particular group en masse, there will be little opportunity to observe behavior that conflicts with the group's assumed characteristics.

Case studies have demonstrated that an individual who holds stereotyped beliefs about a "target" will remember and interpret past events in the target's life history in ways that bolster and support his stereotyped beliefs and will perceive the target's actual behavior as reconfirming and validating the stereotyped beliefs. While the individual may be aware of the selectively perceived facts that support his categorization or simplified understanding, he will not be aware of the process that has caused him to deselect the facts that do not conform with his rationalization. Thus, racially prejudiced behavior that is actually the product of learned cultural preferences is experienced as a reflection of rational deduction from objective observation, which is nonprejudicial behavior. The decisionmaker who is unaware of the selective perception that has produced her stereotype will not view it as a stereotype. She will believe that her actions are motivated not by racial prejudice but by her attraction or aversion to the attributes she has "observed" in the groups she has favored or disfavored.

NOTES *

In 1986, the American Bar Association's Task Force on Minorities in the Legal Profession issued a broad set of recommenda-

* This material is adapted from D.   02 (1992).
Rhode and D. Luban, *Legal Ethics* 101–

tions. First, it urged the bar to induce employers to intensify their efforts in hiring, retaining, and promoting minority law school graduates. In particular, employers should reassess recruitment procedures and evaluation criteria that have a disproportional racial impact. Recruiters should be encouraged to make greater contact with law schools that have substantial minority enrollments; where on site interviews are impractical, letters of inquiry could be sent to minority student associations, and visits could be made to regional minority placement conferences. Hiring standards should avoid excessive reliance on first year grades, LSAT scores, and law review experience, which disproportionately exclude students of color and do not measure the full range of skills that are necessary for successful practice. Promotion criteria such as collegiality and ability to attract client business need to take into account the special obstacles facing minorities. Employers should also be encouraged to create a favorable working environment for underrepresented groups. Providing mentoring programs and opportunities for challenging assignments, supervisory experiences, and client contact should be key priorities.

The Task Force also urged bar organizations to promote relations between minority and non-minority lawyers and to improve continuing legal education programs that might enhance practice and office management capabilities among minorities. For example, the bar should encourage federal, state and local governments as well as large corporate legal departments to give preference to minority lawyers or to law firms that employ minority lawyers. In referring legal business, attorneys should exercise similar preferences.

Finally, the Task Force recommended various efforts to expand minority access to the bar. Such steps should include increased recruitment of talented minority high school and college students, greater financial assistance for disadvantaged students, more support for educational preparation programs by the Council on Legal Educational Opportunities, and additional programs that assist minority graduates to pass the bar.

What other strategies would you add to this agenda? What are the major barriers to its implementation, and how can they be addressed? Several years after this Task Force report, several groups had launched initiatives along the lines it recommended. For example, the California Minority Counsel Program began in 1989 under the auspices of the Bar Association of San Francisco. By the end of its first two years, the program included approximately 50 California corporations, 100 minority-owned law firms and 50 non-minority firms. Each participating corporation agrees to hire and promote more lawyers of color, to use more minority-owned firms for outside legal work, and to encourage other firms that it employs to assign lawyers of color to its work. Among other things, participating non-minority firms must: accept the affirmative action goals approved by the bar; indicate whether lawyers of color worked on a particular matter; and specify what percentage of the bill those lawyers accounted for.

Observers of the program give it mixed reviews. Some report increased billings for lawyers of color; others maintain that the percentage of corporations and the type of volume of business involved in the initiative is "nothing to write home about." [4] What would be your response to such criticism? Are there alternative strategies that would be more promising or complementary initiatives that deserve greater attention?

C. THE ORGANIZATION OF PRACTICE

INTRODUCTION

The term "legal practice" is an abstraction that covers a wide range of professional activities whose only common denominator is that lawyers engage in them. Indeed, the variety of what attorneys do makes it difficult to identify shared experiences, besides the facts that almost all practitioners have gone to law school and that all those who are in active practice are members of a bar somewhere. However, similarity of educational background and equality in formal status make for important resemblances and social ties. These affinities also contribute to, and are in turn supported by, many shared beliefs, ideals, and professional mythologies.

Lawyers' work varies along several dimensions: core functions, substantive fields, and practice contexts. A lawyer's minimal function, viewed analytically, is providing advice and advocacy concerning legal rights. It seems more accurate to think of the function of legal counselor as prior to that of legal advocate, for advice may not result in litigation but will almost assuredly precede it. From these core functions derive further specializations, cutting across substantive areas. The menu of skills required includes knowledge of substantive and procedural law,

---

4. "The Minority Report," *Calif.Law.* June 1991, at 22 (quoting Carolyn Yee, and noting other criticisms that the retainers to many minority-owned firms are extremely small).

understanding of legal institutions such as courts and government agencies, and various interpersonal capabilities. It is conventional to classify lawyers according to which of these skills or substantive fields predominate in their professional repertoire. Thus, we speak of litigators and labor negotiators, or of tax and securities specialists.

Another classification, more often used by sociologists of the profession than by lawyers themselves, is "situation in practice." This concept can include locality (small town, metropolitan area, etc.), work context (solo practitioner, small firm lawyer, large firm lawyer, etc.) or variables such as professional experience and status. A different form of sociological classification is premised on the attorney's primary clientele. Such distinctions depend on the proportion of professional assistance that involves indigents, individuals of modest means, small businesses, large corporations, governmental institutions, etc.

When considered in all these terms, the American legal profession appears to be quite heterogeneous. Lawyers perform a range of diverse functions that encompasses counseling ordinary citizens about ordinary legal problems, orchestrating "megalaw" litigation for transnational corporations,[1] and representing various client interests before governmental institutions. Over time, lawyers tend to specialize and, while they may move around in the system, most do not stray far from where they started.

The aggregate effect of specialization along the foregoing lines is a pronounced stratification within the profession. In broad terms, that stratification corresponds to types of practice and, more particularly, to types of clientele.[2] Yet there remain localities in which such distinctions are less apparent. The legal profession's self-image tends to emphasize a common identity and solidarity within the bar. Sociological and economic analysis tends to emphasize differentiation and stratification. Reality involves some of both, in mixtures that reflect the degrees of heterogeneity in American society itself.

---

1. Galanter, "Mega-Law and Mega-Lawyering in the Contemporary United States", in R. Dingwell and P. Lewis eds., *The Sociology of the Professions: Lawyers, Doctors, and Others* (1983).

2. Heinz and Laumann, "The Legal Profession: Client Interests, Professional Roles and Social Hierarchies," 76 *Mich.L.Rev.* 1111 (1978); Heinz and Laumann, "The Organization of Lawyers' Work," 1979 *Am.Bar Found. Research J.* 217.

John H. Heinz and Edward O. Laumann, Chicago
Lawyers: The Social Structure of the Bar

3–5, 319–21, 327–32 (1982).

It has been apparent for some time that the simple view of the bar as a single, unified profession no longer fits the facts. First of all, lawyers, of course, are not merely lawyers. They are advisors to businessmen and are businessmen themselves; they are politicians, lobbyists, and judges or potential judges; they are real estate and insurance salesmen, claims adjustors, facilitators of zoning variances, scholars, and rich lie-abouts. But even those roles that are usually thought of as lawyers' work, more narrowly defined, display considerable variety.

The division of labor has proceeded in the law as it has in most other fields of endeavor, and a number of distinct types of lawyers are now clearly identifiable. A form of the old general practitioner survives in small towns and in some city neighborhoods, but these are a minority of the profession—in 1970, about 62 percent of American lawyers lived in cities of over 100,000 population, and relatively few of these city lawyers probably served primarily a neighborhood clientele. In large cities like Chicago, the focus of this book, the differences among the several sorts of lawyers are dramatic. The lawyer who commutes to Brussels and Tokyo and who spends his time negotiating the rights to distribute Colonel Sanders throughout the world will have little in common with the lawyer who haunts the corridors of the criminal courts hoping that a bailiff will, in return for a consideration, commend his services to some poor wretch charged with a barroom assault. Both of those private practitioners will differ from the government-employed lawyers who prosecute criminal cases or who practice public international law in the employ of the State Department, as the two sorts of government-employed lawyers differ from one another. And all of those types will be distinguishable from the partner of the large law firm who devotes his days to advising corporations on the probable tax consequences of several alternative real estate acquisition strategies, who in turn will differ from another sort of tax lawyer, the sort who fills out individual income tax forms as April 15 approaches. Then there are the patent lawyers, many of whom prepared for law school not with the traditional liberal arts, prelaw courses but with training in engineering or some other scientific discipline and who may spend much of their time analyzing mechanical drawings; and the divorce lawyers, who may choose to process their cases quickly or to become family counselors or semiprofessional psychotherapists; and the personal injury plaintiffs' lawyers, who devote their ingenuity to devising dramatic ways of making clear to juries what it means to be paralyzed from the waist down; and the personal injury defense lawyers, who are retained by insurance companies to make the same juries understand that insurance rates will go up if they allow themselves to be overwhelmed by emotion. ... One could posit a great many legal professions, perhaps dozens, and to some degree there are perceptible distinctions among all of these types of lawyers.

... As the analysis presented in this book has unfolded, we have advanced the thesis that much of the differentiation within the legal profession is secondary to one fundamental distinction— the distinction between lawyers who represent large organizations (corporations, labor unions, or government) and those who represent individuals. The two kinds of law practice are the two hemispheres of the profession. Most lawyers reside entirely in one hemisphere or the other and seldom, if ever, cross the equator.

Lawyers who serve major corporations and other large organizations differ systematically from those who work for individuals and small businesses whether we look at the social origins of the lawyers, the prestige of the law schools they attended, their career histories and mobility, their social or political values, their networks of friends and professional associates, or several other social variables. Though there certainly are distinctions among lawyers that cut across the line between the two broad classes of clients, this fundamental difference in the nature of the client served appears to be the principal factor that structures the social differentiation of the profession.

... [O]ur attempts at generalization here are just that; we do not mean to assert that there are no exceptions to the rule. And it would, of course, be a mistake to overdraw the precision of the cleavage between the corporate and personal client hemispheres of the Chicago bar. The client type distinction is too crude and too simple to account for the full complexity of the social structure of the profession. Any scholar who had the temerity to suggest that such a large bundle of social phenomena was anything less than polycrystalline and polymorphic would very likely be sent to stand in the corner with the journalists. One who wishes to look for variability, imprecision, or ambiguity in the structure of the legal profession would surely find it. It is there. There are, in some respects, larger differences within the hemispheres than between them. The greatest difference in the social values of lawyers in different fields is, for example, not that between the corporate and personal client hemispheres but the difference between lawyers who practice in the personal plight fields and those in the business or wealth-oriented fields of the personal client sector. And ... the different roles of litigators and office lawyers may create a systematic difference in the distribution of power between lawyer and client that cuts across the distinction between types of clients. Nonetheless, the distinction between corporate and individual clients is a very important one, and that distinction is probably key to an understanding of the social structure of the legal profession and of that structure's consequences for the distribution of power and influence.

Like other persons, lawyers have private causes. They may act as "moral entrepreneurs," and this may bring them into conflict with other lawyers who have opposing moral principles. But their principles may also be influenced by their areas of practice. The corporate lawyers who dominate the Association of the Bar of the City of New York advocate "no fault" systems of automobile accident compensation. They never touch a personal injury case. And they are vigorously opposed by the personal injury plaintiffs' lawyers, whose voice is the American Trial Lawyers Association. The personal injury lawyers complain that the corporate lawyers "don't understand our problems." It is certainly true that one of the consequences of specialization is that the different roles may come to exist in separate social worlds and that, as they lose contact with one another, the lawyers may also lose their sensitivity to one another's problems, thus diminishing consensus on the profession's goals. ...

[T]he types of clients represented, the mechanisms by which lawyers obtain business, the sorts of tasks performed, the organizational setting of the practice, the type of law school attended, and the religion of the practitioners—appear to create an overall structure that is strongly associated with the extent to which Chicago lawyers perceive that each of the fields has a claim to deference within the profession. Further analysis persuaded us that the nature of prestige within the profession largely reflected the types of clients served by the fields. An alternative hypothesis that we considered is that prestige might be determined by the extent to which the field presents intellectual challenge—that the profession might value intelligence, high levels of professional skill in legal research, and creativity in devising original arguments or theories, and might therefore accord prestige to fields that present greater opportunity for the display of such talents. Because there will be fewer such opportunities in the sort of law practice that processes a large volume of cases for relatively impecunious clients than in the practice of law for clients who are able to pay for the hours consumed in creativity and introspection, prestige accorded to creative, intellectually satisfying work will *ipso facto* be accorded to work done for clients with deep pockets. The wealth and intellectual challenge variables are, thus, closely interrelated, and it is therefore difficult to determine whether the prestige of the fields is to be attributed more to client type or to the differential opportunities that the fields present for the exercise of intellectual skills. But comparison of the prestige of the two sides of doctrinal areas of the law that the adversary system divides into opposing fields—criminal prosecution versus criminal defense, labor law work for unions versus labor work for management, personal injury plaintiffs' work versus personal injury defense, environmental plaintiffs versus environmental defense, antitrust plaintiffs versus antitrust defense, and consumer law work for debtors versus consumer work for creditors—discloses that the side of the case that characteristically represents corporate clients is consistently assigned higher prestige than is the side that more often represents individuals. ...

It may be that the greater wealth of the corporate clients means that their lawyers are regularly able to devote greater resources to the issues and thus that the opportunities for creativity are consistently higher in the corporate fields even when the general doctrinal area of the law is held constant. We believe, however, that our findings provide strong support for the inference that the prestige accorded by the legal profession to the fields of law, constituting a set of distinct lawyers' roles, is determined in large measure by the types of clients served by the fields. Fields that serve corporate, wealthier, more "establishment" clients are accorded more deference within the profession than are those that serve individual, poorer clients. This suggests the thesis that prestige within law is acquired by association, that it is "reflected glory" derived from the power possessed by the lawyers' clients.

We also found a strong relationship between the types of work that lawyers do and their social background characteristics, including ethnoreligious origins (see chaps. 3 and 6). Lawyers from less prestigious social origins were overrepresented among those practicing in the less prestigious fields. A Catholic respondent was three times more likely than either a Protestant or a Jew to be working as a prosecutor. A respondent who was affiliated with a high status Protestant denomination (that is, a Type I Protestant—Episcopalian, Presbyterian, Congregationalist, etc.) was five times more likely than either a Catholic or a Jewish respondent to be found doing securities or antitrust defense work. Jews were more than twice as likely as were Catholics to do divorce work, and they were incalculably more likely to do so than were Type I Protestants—in our sample, we found no one of high status Protestant origin who did a substantial amount of divorce work. Other fields with particularly high concentrations of Type I Protestants were banking, patents, municipal, and personal tax; Jews were disproportionately represented in labor law, both on the union and on the management side, in business tax, commercial work, criminal defense, and personal injury plaintiffs' work; and Catholics were greatly overrepresented in personal injury work, on both the plaintiffs' and the defendants' sides, and in both business litigation and general litigation. Generally, WASPs were more likely to be found in the corporate hemisphere, Jews in the personal client hemisphere, and Catholics in the litigation fields. Thus, the kinds of tasks that a lawyer performs and the kinds of clients for whom he does those tasks are strongly associated with the lawyer's social origins.

Jerome E. Carlin, Lawyers on Their Own

1, 6, 8, 17–18, 41–42 (1962).*

THE ROAD TO INDIVIDUAL PRACTICE

The individual practitioner of law in Chicago is a self-made man who came up the hard way from poor, immigrant surroundings. ... [He] has in most cases received his professional training in one of the "proprietary" or Catholic night law schools. ...

In general, the individual practitioner works for another lawyer as a kind of apprentice during his first few years out of law school. These are usually temporary positions—rarely lasting more than a year or two—paying little or, in the case of the space-for-service arrangement, no salary, the assumption being that the young lawyer will be building up his own practice on the side. ...

The practice of most metropolitan individual practitioners is consequently confined to those residual matters (and clients) that the large firms have not pre-empted: (1) matters not large enough or remunerative enough for the large firms to handle—most general work for small to medium-sized businesses and corporations, the smaller real estate transactions (for individuals or small businesses), and estate matters for middle-income families; (2) the undesirable cases, the dirty work, those areas of practice that have associated with them an aura of influencing and fixing and that involve arrangements with clients and others that are felt by the large firms to be professionally damaging. The latter category includes local tax, municipal, personal injury, divorce, and criminal matters. ...

The Work of the Individual Practitioner

A Loop law office occupied on a rent-sharing basis with two or three other lawyers is the principal work setting of most individual practitioners in Chicago. The individual lawyer is in his office an average of four to five hours a day conferring with clients and handling office paper work. A little over an hour a day will be spent in court, generally in the clerk's office of one of the county or municipal courts filing documents or answering court calls. Another hour a day is spent in the administrative agencies of government, and here again it is the city and county agencies that claim the largest share of the lawyer's time. The remainder of his day may be occupied with a visit to a title company, a client's place of business, a law library, the office of a bank or trust company, insurance or real estate agent, or a savings and loan association. ...

Donald D. Landon, Country Lawyers: The Impact of Context on Professional Practice
9–11, 16–17, 142–145 (1990).

[In this study, sociologist Donald Landon explored the importance of practice context by collecting data on lawyers in two settings: small Missouri towns, and one medium size Missouri city (Springfield, population 155,000). He then compared his findings with Heinz and Laumann's data on the Chicago bar. In essence, Landon found that differences in economic and population scale translated into substantial differences in legal practice.]

Given the more modest economic scale of the rural, small-town environment, it seems logical to assume that law practice there would contrast with urban practice in several respects. Such contrast would include the following dimensions:

1. *Client mix.* While metropolitan practice is "corporate-intensive" practice, small town practice will likely be "person-intensive" practice. The bulk of small town clients will probably be individuals, and small town lawyers would derive the greatest proportion of their income from representing persons.

2. *Cases and issues.* If small town practice is person-intensive practice, then the bulk of legal effort will tend to be devoted to

issues important to individuals. This will include such matters as family law and divorce, criminal defense, personal
injury, and real estate. One would expect the small town
attorney's typical practice to consist of a large volume of small
matters while the typical metropolitan lawyer will have a
small volume of relatively large matters.

3. *Practice style.* Whereas the scale and complexity of economic
   activity in metropolitan settings tends to produce specialized
   law practice focused in large law firms, the norm in small
   settings will likely be general practice carried out in an
   entrepreneurial (solo or small firm) mode. While the growing
   complexities of law practice may press country lawyers to
   restrict their practice, the economic realities would make it
   only rarely feasible to specialize.

4. *Structure of the bar.* The scale and complexity of the metropolitan setting produces a fragmented and highly stratified
   bar. The hierarchy is dictated by clientele differences and is
   reflected in differentials in lawyer income, status, and power.
   Because the range of client differences is greatly reduced in
   smaller towns, we would expect a relatively less stratified bar.
   The opportunity to serve an exclusive clientele in the country
   is reduced by the reduced scale of the economy and the
   population. Thus, we would anticipate that rural attorneys
   will have remarkably similar clienteles with quite similar
   problems. The "moral division of labor" seen in metropolitan
   settings is not likely to be experienced in smaller settings.

5. *Accountability.* If the core clients of country practitioners
   come from individuals in the community rather than from
   corporate or business entities, it appears that country lawyers
   would experience a higher level of accountability in their
   practice. The necessity to serve a large number of small
   clients means enhanced exposure to criticism. Such criticism
   coupled with small-town communication systems would appear
   to constitute a significant threat to practitioners' reputations
   and thus to their business.

6. *Lawyer autonomy.* Research in metropolitan settings suggests
   that lawyers serving elite corporate clientele tend to have less
   professional autonomy (Heinz and Laumann, 1982:359–60).
   Because of the immense volume of business from a single
   client, the firm sacrifices some of its independence to retain
   the lucrative business. We would presume that, in smaller
   settings where lawyers depend on a high volume of business
   from a variety of relatively infrequent players in the system,

attorneys would retain considerable autonomy over their practice and escape the dilemma of large client dependence.

. . .

We have argued that the legal profession is an externally determined social system. It derives its structure not only from the common socialization the profession receives in law school, but more importantly from the context in which practice occurs. As a profession, the bar is thus likely to reflect the variations of context more visibly than many other forms of professional practice. Part of the reason for this extreme sensitivity to context lies in the fact that the practice of law is not a science rooted in principles and structures that are essentially invariant in nature, as—for example—is the practice of medicine. Rather, the practice of law is rooted in the varied and changing character of human institutions. Its roots are imbedded in the character of a local economy. Its issues represent the social and political preferences of a discrete population. Its procedures are invented and altered under the dictates of immediate situations. Thus even within a single large metropolitan area there are multiple professions of law, depending on which segment of the population is being addressed.

. . .

[More specifically, Landon found that 88 percent of small town lawyers practiced alone or in two to three-person firms, compared with 47 percent in Springfield and 21 percent in Chicago. The average number of clients ranged from 350 for country practitioners to 35 for Chicago attorneys. Unlike metropolitan lawyers, who generally served either businesses or individuals, the small town attorneys did not fall into two stratified groups. On average, 90 percent of the clients in country settings were individuals rather than businesses. Over half of the total legal effort of small-town lawyers centered on five fields: domestic relations, estates, negligence (plaintiff), residential real estate and criminal defense. A relatively small percentage involved corporate matters, which occupied over half the efforts of the Chicago bar. Only 8 percent of country lawyers found their work so specialized that they needed to concentrate exclusively in one area. By contrast, 45 percent of Chicago and 34 percent of Springfield lawyers found a need for specialization.

The small town bar was also much more homogenous in background and conservative in ideology than the metropolitan bar. Missouri country lawyers were overwhelmingly white, male and Christian, and 90% had gone to law school within the state. Chicago had a substantially higher representation of women, ra-

cial and religious minorities, and practitioners educated out of
state. Unlike the metropolitan bar, where status depended on the
relative wealth and power of the lawyer's clients, prestige in
small-town practice depended on the lawyer's own income level.
Many country attorneys pursued business interests in addition to
their law work, and generally held more conservative views on
economic issues than their metropolitan counterparts. The difference is apparent in responses to the statement that "economic
profits by and large are justly distributed in the United States."
Forty-two percent of small town practitioners agreed, compared
with only 26 percent of the Chicago bar.

From the standpoint of lawyers' ethics, two aspects of small
town practice stand out. One is the "discipline of continuing
relationships." Lawyers who know that they will be "working
with and against each other for years" make a "considerable effort
to get along."]

The precise content of the current local understandings
among small town lawyers is summarized in a description given by
a lawyer in a town of 15,000.

> You don't have to notice-up for hearings here. Attorneys
> trust each other—at least until they find they can't.

> You don't lay twenty pages of interrogatories on each
> other out here or run up the bill with depositions. Piling up
> paper work does not make for good relations in the country.
> You don't file a five day motion on Charley Jones while he's
> on a two week vacation, or try to take advantage of him. If
> he's forgot to file an answer, you don't ask the judge for
> default. You call him. You pass the case yourself because
> fairness is more important than winning.

> Practice here is on the honor system. The telephone is
> used instead of paper. We tend to work things out because we
> trust each other. You soon learn who you can't trust.

The unwritten rules of country courtesy are not left unen-
forced, though. They are sufficiently important to the professional community that discipline to protect their integrity is swift and
explicit. An older attorney in a town of 2,500 said, "If an attorney
messes me up, I'll sing like a canary at coffee the next morning."
An attorney in a larger community added,

> When an attorney here violates those understandings, the
> word is quickly passed around. We begin dragging out the
> interrogatories and imposing the technical rules until the guy

gets the message that that's not the way we do things around here.

. . .

Then, too, the attorney representing the other side in a dispute can complicate matters enormously for a fellow practitioner. Rural attorneys work in a high-volume setting where a host of smaller matters occupy their time; consequently, their economic viability depends on the expeditious handling of matters. As noted by the lawyer who was quoted earlier, much of their work is handled by phone instead of paper. They depend on colleagues to cooperate in expediting matters by not demanding a shower of paperwork or showing an unreasonable stubbornness that would require additional hours of time with little prospect of being able to charge the client for them. In this sense, cooperation from colleagues is vital to the well-being of the small town attorney. A practitioner for 25 years said,

> Lawyers protect each other in the country. They will need each others' support over the years since in small town practice the shoe changes foot frequently. If you take advantage of a lawyer's lapses or exploit something that reflects on him, he will get you the next time.

This informality and courtesy characteristic of country practice is essentially professional interaction based on the norm of reciprocity. It expects attorneys to be cooperative, rather than contentious; trustworthy, not tricky; reasonable, not radical. The constant interaction among a relatively small group of private practitioners who can greatly complicate each another's work appears to transform professional relationships. In place of the strong, zealous, partisan relationship of opposing counsel implied in the professional code and governed by a host of technical rules, country practice involves a more person-to-person collegial relationship that is guided by sentiment—not written rules—and that accommodates the self-interests unique to practitioners in small settings. The essential identity among colleagues is personal, rather than formally professional. The country practitioner claims that this results in efficiency: Less gets litigated; more gets solved. And the professional community remains intact.

. . .

[A less positive aspect of the "need to get along" involves constraints on small town attorneys' choice of cases. Country lawyers were significantly less likely than metropolitan lawyers to feel that they had "wide latitude" in selecting clients (39 percent versus 55 percent). The limitations assumed particular force

when it came to representing unpopular causes, or opposing individuals who had personal ties with the lawyer].

Generally, the risky cases, as far as community reaction is
concerned, involve matters that either impinge on the community
generally or offend traditional community standards. An attorney in a town of just over 3,500 said,

> I represented a family in a civil rights matter against the
> school district. It was the worst mistake of my career! The
> community held that against me for ten years!

Another attorney in a town of less than 10,000 said,

> Recently, I took on a medical malpractice suit against a local
> doctor. It was a bad mistake. I think I'm finished in this
> community.

Most of the attorneys agreed that there are clear-cut costs
involved in taking on cases the community will resist. A lawyer
who grew up where he was practicing said,

> I'll never take on a sexual abuse case in this town. It's one of
> these matters you quickly refer to an outside attorney.

. . .

Reconciling the dual claims of desire for community respect
and admiration—on the one hand—and the realistic demands of
law practice—on the other—is particularly acute for the attorney
who returns to his hometown to hang out his shingle. A young
attorney in a town of 5,000 confessed,

> The adversarial nature of law practice is perhaps the biggest
> problem of the rural practitioner, especially when you have
> lived here all your life. My family has lived here for four
> generations. Everybody in town knows us, and I know them.
> They can't imagine my taking action against them. I have
> had difficulty myself. I found it hard to file a suit. I had to
> get calloused up before I could accept a lot of work. I had
> reservations about whether I could be zealous against people I
> went to church with or had been school chums with. One of
> my first cases was taking the other side of a matter against a
> fellow I went to school with and whose mother was a school
> chum of my mother. They both belong to the same garden
> club. We all belong to the same church. The family doesn't
> speak to us anymore and that's hard. Some folks don't care
> what other people think about them, but I do. I don't know

how thick the callouses have to get before you can do this work without cringing.

.   .   .

The unique thing about accountability in the country is its multifaceted character and its evenness in salience. Accountability to the client is predicated on the fiduciary relationship and strengthened by the multiple ties that frequently bind client to practitioner. The practitioner is clearly aware that he cannot afford to have a client bad-mouthing him in a small town. Accountability to colleagues is raised to a very salient level by their ability to facilitate or frustrate a high-volume practice. Dependent on them in some instances for referrals—and in all instances for not obstructing reasonable solutions to clients' problems—the country practitioner cannot afford to conduct his practice as if he may never encounter a particular colleague again. Accountability to the community is raised to a very salient level because reputation is the individual entrepreneur's chief business-getting tool. This tool is forged in the community. And the smaller community—with its intense scrutiny and discussion of its members' conduct, and its greater ability to mobilize consensus about controversial matters (including clients and cases)—becomes a formidable source of sanctioning. In combination, these varying centers of appraisal and accountability constitute a substantial reference system for legal practice.

What becomes apparent is that the expectations of the local setting—clients', colleagues', and community's—are relatively well articulated together, at least in regard to the issue of partisan zeal. Clients in the country (with some exceptions) tend to prefer solutions, not confrontations; they prefer low-key advocacy, not the clash and clang of combat. Colleagues certainly expect balance and reasonableness from opposing counsel, an absence of sharp practices and advantage-taking, and partisanship but not contentiousness. The community expects the avoidance of divisive and offensive issues. While individual interests are important, they are not to be pursued at the expense of the community or its valued amiability.

The convergence of these expectations at the community level impinge on the execution of the lawyer's role at the professional level. Excessive zeal becomes deviance. Thus, while the rural lawyer's conduct may be informed by the professional code, it is ultimately shaped by the day-to-day necessities implicit within the containing community.

**Robert L. Nelson, "Practice and Privilege: Social Change
and the Structure of Large Law Firms"**

1981 American Bar Foundation Research Journal, 97–98, 110–11, 117, 118.

The large law firm is an apparent contradiction. It represents the most modern, sophisticated form of the practice of law. Its members are drawn from elite law schools and account for a significant segment of the leadership in the bar; its clientele consists of major corporations and wealthy individuals; and its practice is highly specialized and rapidly changing. And the large law firm is a growth industry. When Erwin Smigel wrote the epilog to *The Wall Street Lawyer* in 1969, he counted 20 firms in the nation with more than 100 lawyers. A 1980 survey found more than 100 firms with that many lawyers. The growth in size has been accompanied by steady differentiation into additional fields of practice, branching into other cities, the introduction of computerized research and word processing, and the deployment of substantial paralegal staffs. Yet, in many respects, the large law firm has changed very little. When its organizational structure is compared to that of the upper tiers of the modern corporation or even of the leading organizations of other professions, such as the university, the hospital, or the accounting firm, the law firm appears remarkably unsophisticated. It has undergone no significant structural transformation that would parallel the emergence of professional management in the corporation or the hospital. And despite the long-standing charge that the law firm is a law factory, the large firm does not fit the conventional model of a bureaucracy.

This seemingly contradictory record is the basis of the central inquiry for this article: How has the large law firm accommodated tremendously rapid change in the law, in the legal profession, and in the size and complexity of its organization, while maintaining relatively stable structural arrangements within the firm?

. . .

B. Two Paths to Growth: Expansion by General Service and by
Special Representation

. . .

In the era of traditional practice, the strategy of law firms was simple, if unarticulated: add enough good men to handle client demands. Some economies of scale could be realized by small increases in size, and there was little need for internal organizational control beyond the observance of professional ethics and a loose set of master-apprentice relationships among partners and associates. But with the proliferation in legal complexity, growth by volume alone was no longer feasible. Growth and specialization became interdependent. To grow, a firm faced two paths. First, it could develop a "stable of clients" for whom the firm provided a full range of general counseling and specialized services, expansion through a concept of general service to existing clients. Second, it could develop a stable network for getting referrals, with the firm providing specialized services to differing clients on a case-by-case basis or providing continuing service to some clients but only for one, particular function (such as labor law). This is expansion through a concept of special representation, which aims at serving the needs of a specialized market rather than the general needs of regular clients. Most firms rotated between these two modes of growth to a certain extent, with efforts to expand in a particular specialized field followed by efforts to consolidate the remainder of the client's legal business. The converse took place as well, when firms attempted to capitalize on specialties developed for regular clients by offering services in those specialties to other clients on a case-by-case basis. Such a strategy was often limited, however, by potential conflicts of interest with existing clients.

The uncertainties of the large-firm marketplace contributed to the "push-me-pull-me" character of growth. While steady clients could provide a steady flow of work to a firm, there was no guaranteed flow. There was always the possibility of losing a client, either through its acquisition by a corporation with its own counsel or as a consequence of the death, retirement, or departure of the lawyer chiefly responsible for the client. More recently, the development of corporate house counsel has eaten into much of the old bread and butter of corporate practice. The same has been true of other fields that have become sufficiently routine to allow deployment of in-house counsel in the area. And even stable clients have unexpected shifts in the demands they make of firms: Clients (and, therefore, their attorneys) frequently face unusual or unexpected litigation or new developments in the law (such as the imposition of wage-price controls). Firms relying more on client referrals to their specialty fields than on providing general service to a stable clientele have the mixed blessing of "certain uncertainty." They may staff in a way that is more sensitive to fluctuations in the demand for their specialized services, a demand which may be more predictable in the aggregate than is the demand of any one client. But they lack the steady flow of business to make up

for fluctuations in the market for their special services and constantly face competition from the expansion of general service
firms into their specialty fields. Also as specialty firms grow
larger, they may find it more difficult to sustain growth.

. . .

Because most firms have attempted to grow through both
general service and special representation, there are few pure
types of general service and specialty firms. Still, one mode of
growth appears to dominate in most firms. The dominance of one
style of growth over the other has consequences internal to the
firm. I already suggested how the careers of lawyers may differ
according to the firm's pattern of development. It follows that
activities will be rewarded differently depending on the style of
growth: in firms oriented to special representation there will be a
premium on external visibility and client-drawing ability, while in
firms oriented to general service there may be greater rewards for
client maintenance. Competition for leadership in the firms may
rotate on similar axes, with marketability being more significant
as a ladder to leadership in specialty firms than it is in general
service firms.

There may also be consequences external to the firm. The
rise and rapid growth of specialty firms may be an indication of a
change in the traditional lawyer-client relationship, away from
the role of lawyer as general counselor to lawyer as special agent.
The orthodox view of the legal profession suggests that lawyers
exert a positive moral force in society by modifying the extremes
of their client's self-interest, thereby minimizing conflict.[42] If the
trend in the market for large-firm services favors isolated, highly
specialized relationships between lawyer and client, however, lawyers may be less effective in their role as social mediators. Indeed, if more lawyers are being employed as "hired guns," it may
lead to more shooting (higher rates of litigiousness, etc.) than in
the past. Furthermore, it suggests a level of differentiation
among large law firms that was not recognized before. Lawyers
for the most powerful sectors of society are usually thought to be
rather uniformly interested in the stability of law, legal institutions, and the relationships among lawyers and clients. I am
suggesting that there is an active and growing sector in the legal
community who are interested in changes in law and in the
relationships among lawyers and clients because it may give them
entrée to practice on an expanded scale. It is not clear what

---

42. Talcott Parsons, A Sociologist
Looks at the Legal Profession, *in* Tal-
cott Parsons, Essays on Sociological
Theory 370 (rev.ed. New York: Free
Press of Glencoe, 1954).

directions these changes might take in terms of the substance or procedure of law. Much less is it possible to say whether such change is for better or worse according to some normative standard. Still it may be significant if some lawyers are committed to change for the sake of change.

. . .

III.   The Structure of the Firm

A.   The Roles: Finders, Minders, and Grinders

. . .

... As the following exchange with a senior partner in a large firm indicates, lawyers in firms are aware of different roles played in the firm.

Q.   There are so many different lawyers here. ... [S]ome people have suggested that now there are really different kinds of partners in a firm of this size.

A.   There is what we call, and you have probably heard this, the finders, the minders, and the grinders.

Q.   That's an interesting set of distinctions.

A.   Well, they mean there are lawyers who seem to bring in substantial clients, there are lawyers who take care of the clients who are already here, and there are the grinders who do the work. And there's some truth to the saying.

Q.   How would you consider yourself in that?

A.   I guess I'm something of a minder. I am pretty much concerned with answering the questions and problems of clients we already have.

Finders, minders, and grinders. These terms define the roles traditionally played in the large firm and provide a useful key to the hierarchy of lawyers within firms. These roles roughly correspond to the roles Chandler defines in his study of the historical construction of the multidivisional corporation. Because Chandler's terms are already used in the organizations literature and are defined in terms of a theory of structure and social change in organizations, they are adopted here. Finders, minders, and grinders become entrepreneurs, managers, and workers.

———

REFERENCES

In addition to the materials previously cited, see;

American Bar Association Task Force on the Role of the Lawyer in the 1980s, *Report on the Role of the Lawyer in the 1980s* (1981).

C. Epstein, *Women in Law* (1981).

Erlanger, "The Allocation of Status Within Occupations: The Case of the Legal Profession," 58 *Soc. Forces* 882 (1980).

M. Galanter and T. Palay, *Tournament of Lawyers: The Transformation of the Big Law Firm* (1991).

M. Goldman, *A Portrait of the Black Attorney in Chicago* (1972).

R. Jack and D. Jack, *Moral Vision and Professional Decisions: The Changing Values of Women and Men Lawyers* (1989).

Holley and Kleven, "Minorities and the Legal Profession: Current Platitudes, Current Barriers," 12 *T. Marshall L.Rev.* 299 (1987).

Landon, "Lawyers and Localities: The Interaction of Community Context and Professionalism," 1982 *Am. Bar Found. Research J.* 459.

Littlejohn and Hobson, "Black Lawyers, Law Practice, and Bar Associations—1844 to 1970: A Michigan History," 33 *Wayne Law Review 1625* (1987).

O. Maru, *Research on the Legal Profession: A Review of Work Done* (1972).

K. Morello, *The Invisible Bar: The Woman Lawyer in America, 1638 to the Present* (1986).

Pashigian, "The Market for Lawyers: The Determinants of the Demand for and Supply of Lawyers," 20 *J.L. & Econ.* 53 (1977).

Schneyer, "Professionalism as Politics: The Making of a Modern Legal Ethics Code," in *Lawyers' Ideals/Lawyers' Practices: Transformations in the American Legal Profession* 95 (R. Nelson, D. Trubek, R. Solomon, eds., 1992).

Siegfried, "The Effect of Firm Size on the Economics of Legal Practice," *Legal Econ.*, Fall 1976, at 23.

R. Tomasic, Lawyers and the Community (1978).

For an excellent general bibliography on the sociology of the profession *see*

Abel, "The Sociology of American Lawyers: A Bibliographic Guide," *L. & Pol.Q.* 335 (1980).

For an overview essay on social science research relevant to the legal profession *see*

> Sarat, "Studying American Legal Culture: An Assessment of Survey Evidence," 11 *Law & Soc'y Rev.* 427 (1977).

NOTES

Government Lawyers

The preceding excerpts dealt with various private practice situations. From a historical perspective, it is somewhat ironic that private practice is the primary professional model. When the English legal profession first developed, the bar's elite were experts for the crown. Even today, many lawyers at some point in their careers obtain formative experience in state and federal agencies. Currently, about 9% of all practicing attorneys are government employees.

There are almost as many types of public as private law practice. Roughly the same system of classification applies to both sectors. Legal functions of government lawyers include counseling, litigating civil and criminal cases, and drafting legislative and administrative regulations. These tasks cut across a variety of substantive areas encompassing most private law specialities.

All government lawyers have the same formal "situation in practice" in that they are public employees. Behind this resemblance lie many significant variations. For example, district attorneys in sparsely populated rural jurisdictions may handle all the public legal work in the area, often on a part-time basis, including criminal prosecutions, indigent child support claims, and representation of county commissioners. On the other hand, the district attorney's office in a large metropolitan center will have dozens or even hundreds of lawyers, diversified across many specialties. In addition to such variations at the state and local level of government, thousands of federal employees perform virtually all kinds of legal tasks.

Although the government lawyer's client is usually the agency for which he or she works, this is not always the case; public defenders and civil legal aid attorneys owe traditional duties of loyalty to the individuals they assist. However, where lawyers represent "the government," their relationship with the client ordinarily is not the same as in a private context. A governmental legal department may often have independent authority over matters within its jurisdiction. Thus, a district attorney has discretion as to whom to prosecute, without being answerable to any other public official. Prosecutors have no clients except in the metaphorical sense. Or, to put it differently, they have the authority of both client and lawyer in the representation. Even where government attorneys do not enjoy such complete discretion, they usually have substantially greater power in relation to the agency official for whom they act than do their counterparts in private law practice. The agency client has authority only by virtue of the law creating his office, and that law itself is subject to interpretation by government counsel.*

Corporate Law Departments

A growing area of private practice involves lawyers employed as "in-house counsel" in corporate law departments. Over the last two decades such departments have increased substantially in size and status, a trend largely fueled by the lower costs of employing internal rather than outside counsel for certain basic legal work.[1] Corporate law departments range in size from one to 900 attorneys, and provide a wide variety of services including advice, negotiation, document preparation, implementation of government regulations, and advocacy in nonjudicial forums such as legislative committees or administrative agencies. Corporate counsel's substantive areas of practice are determined by the corporation's scope of business. The needs of small real estate businesses may rarely extend beyond routine property, contracts, and taxation issues; a multinational corporation will encounter practically every kind of legal problem at one time or another.

Corporate counsel is the client's employee. In that sense, the attorney's role appears to lack the autonomy that is a defining feature of professionalism. But in practice, the degree of independence exercised by in-house counsel can vary widely. If the organization is itself complex—a multidivision multinational corporation, for example—its lawyer-client relationships can be as diverse as those of an outside law firm. Given the diffusion of power and competing interests within many corporate structures, one of the lawyer's most critical tasks may be determining who speaks for the organization.[2] This fragmentation of authority often gives in-house counsel considerable flexibility and bargaining leverage. Moreover, while he lacks some of the autonomy of

---

* For references on government lawyers, see Part II, IV *infra*.

1. Chayes & Chayes, *Corporate Counsel and the Elite Law Firms*, 37 *Stan.L.Rev.* 277 (1985) (citing survey).

2. *See, e.g.,* Forrow, "Corporate Law Department Lawyer: Counsel to the Entity", 34 *Bus.Law.* 1797 (1979); Rosen, "The Inside Counsel Movement Professional Judgement and Organizational Responsibility," 64 *Ind.L.J.* 479 (1989); Schneyer, "Professionalism and Public Policy: The Case of House Counsel," 2 *Geo.J. Leg. Ethics* 449 (1988).

outside counsel, his greater intimacy with the client often expands opportunities for influence.

———

REFERENCES:

J. Carlin, *Lawyers' Ethics: A Survey of the New York City Bar* (1964).

J. Donnell, *The Corporate Counsel: A Role Study* (1970).

———, "Reflections of Corporate Counsel in a Two Way Mirror," 22 *Bus.Law.* 991 (1967).

Hand & Gang, "The Practice of Law in a Corporation," in J. Fishman & A. Kaufmann eds., *Practicing Law in New York City* (1975).

R. Rosen, *Corporate Counsel: Corporate Attorney: The Dynamics of Freedom and Independence in the Practice of Business Law* (unpublished dissertation 1984).

Slovak, "Giving and Getting Respect: Prestige and Stratification in a Legal Elite," 1980 *Am. Bar Found. Research J.* 31.

E. Smigel, *The Wall Street Lawyer* (1964).

E. Spangler, *Lawyers for Hire* (1986).

R. Swaine, 1 *The Cravath Firm and Its Predecessors, 1819–1948* Vol. 2 (1948).

Public Interest Law and Legal Services Organizations

As the preceding demographic survey indicated, approximately 2% of the bar work for legal aid, public defender, and non-profit associations. Some of these associations have been defined as public interest organizations, *i.e.*, "tax exempt non-profit groups devoting at least 30% of their resources to representing previously unrepresented interests on matters of public policy."[1] By that standard, the Council for Public Interest Law has identified some 200 centers employing slightly over a thousand attorneys.[2]

Most of these organizations formed during the last two decades, funded by a mix of foundation grants, membership fees, and private contributions. Their work spans a broad array of substantive fields, including environmental, consumer, poverty, civil rights, and civil liberties issues. Despite their modest numbers,

1. N. Aron, *Liberty and Justice for All: Public Interest in the 1980's and Beyond* (1989).

2. *Id.*

public interest lawyers have had a considerable social impact, in part through careful marshalling of resources, and in part by enlisting assistance from the private bar as well as various non-legal organizations and coalitions.

Government-subsidized legal aid programs also grew dramatically during the 1960s and 1970s, although recent budget cutbacks have forced a significant reduction in services.[3] Like public interest lawyers, civil legal aid attorneys confront a highly expandable universe of legal needs, and often exercise considerable discretion in allocating their assistance. As the materials in Part III reflect, the appropriate exercise of that discretion remains a subject of continuing professional debate.

REFERENCES:

Bellow and Kettleson, "The Mirror of Public Interest Ethics: Problems and Paradoxes in Professional Responsibility. A Guide for Attorneys" 219 (A.B.A., 1978).

Cahn & Cahn, "Power to the People or to the Profession?— The Public Interest in Public Interest Law," 79 *Yale L.J.* 1005 (1970).

Council for Public Interest Law, *Balancing the Scales of Justice: Financing Public Interest Law in America* (1976).

"Developments in the Law—Class Actions," 89 *Harv.L.Rev.* 1318 (1976).

Garth, Nagel, and Plager, "The Institution of the Private Attorney General; Perspectives from an Empirical Study of Class Action Litigation," 61 *U.S.C. Law Rev.* 353 (1988).

Halpern & Cunningham, "Reflections on the New Public Interest Law: Theory and Practice at the Center for Law and Social Policy," 59 *Geo.L.J.* 1095 (1971).

G. Harrison & S. Jaffe, *The Public Interest Law Firm: New Voices for New Constituencies* (The Ford Foundation 1973).

Hegland, "Beyond Enthusiasm and Commitment," 13 *Ariz. L.Rev.* 805 (1971).

---

3. See the discussion in Part II, IV *infra*. In 1981, the Reagan administration persuaded Congress to reduce federal funding for civil legal assistance 25%, from $321 million to $241 million. Subsequent surveys reported a 30% staff reduction in response to that cutback. Loren Siegel, David Landau, American Civil Liberties Union, *No Justice for the Poor*: How Cutbacks Are Destroying the Legal Services Program (1983).

Houck, *"With Charity for All,"* 93 *Yale L.J.* 1415 (1984).

Rabin, "Lawyers for Social Change: Perspectives on Public Interest Law," 28 *Stan.L.Rev.* 207 (1976).

Stewart, "The Reformation of American Administrative Law," 88 *Harv.L.Rev.* 1669, 1763–72 (1975).

Trubek & Trubek, "Civic Justice Through Civil Justice: A New Approach to Public Interest Advocacy in the United States," in *Access to Justice and the Welfare State* 119 (M. Cappelletti ed. 1981).

B. Weisbrod, J. Handler & N. Komesar, *Public Interest Law: An Economic and Institutional Analysis* (1978).

IV. PROFESSIONAL ASSOCIATIONS AND PROFESSIONAL AUTONOMY

A. AN HISTORICAL FRAMEWORK

James W. Hurst, The Growth of American Law
285–89, 290–92 (1950).

During most of the years after the American Revolution, in the local communities, in the states, and in the nation, there was no bar in any but a courtesy use of the title. A "bar" implies internal organization and cohesion, and on the whole lawyers in the United States were among the most unthinkingly and stubbornly individualistic members of the loosely organized American society. In the late eighteenth century the more populous places had local bar associations, which the lawyers formed for social, library, or disciplinary purposes, or for a combination of these ends. In the Northern states some local bar associations—for example, the Suffolk County bar in Massachusetts—attained a high degree of guild organization, and for a generation firmly controlled admissions and professional conduct. In the first two generations after independence the popular temper demanded relaxation of bar standards, and most of these local associations disappeared, or became wholly social. ...

Planned bar organization revived first in the great cities. It marked a reaction against the corruption in local government. In 1870 a number of leading lawyers organized the Association of the Bar of the City of New York, primarily to fight the Tweed ring. The activities of a notorious fringe of unlicensed practitioners gave impetus to the formation of the Chicago Bar Association, in 1874. Between 1870 and 1878 eight city and eight state bar associations, in twelve states, were formed largely under the motive of reform of municipal government and of conditions within the bar. ...

By 1890 there were 20 state or territorial bar associations in the United States. By 1900 there were 40; by 1916 there were 48; by 1925 all the states and territories could claim some sort of association. It was hard to get reliable counts of city or county bar organizations, either of those which claimed formal existence or of those which in fact functioned. Estimates put the total at 159 in 36 jurisdictions in 1890, at 623 in 41 jurisdictions in 1916, and at above 1100 by 1930. The great growth in numbers in both cases came after the turn of the century. However, like the

American Bar Association, most state and local associations originated primarily for social reasons; and, like the national organization, most of them held to this character until the 1920s. With such rare local exceptions as the Association of the Bar of the City of New York, on the record of functional achievement it is fair to take the American Bar Association as the strongest representative of the organized bar as it grew after the 1870s. ...

Structurally, the organized bar was weak because of the ill-considered adoption of the practice of a select instead of an all-inclusive membership; it was weak, also, because it failed to solve the characteristically American problem of federalism. The stronger local bar groups of the late eighteenth century won so complete a control of admissions and professional discipline that they grew to include almost all lawyers in their areas. The 1870s brought revived efforts at formal organization of lawyers in local, state, and national associations. But by then the bar had been too long without standards, and in this condition it was too formless and varied in character, to make practicable or desirable any effort at organization embracing all licensed lawyers. Quite naturally, therefore, those who started the new bar organizations invited only selected lawyers to join. For fifty years thereafter the firm tradition was that the individual lawyer had neither the right nor the duty to join a bar association; membership was a privilege, conferred by election of the existing membership.

The defect was not in the original adoption of the practice of selective membership, but in the failure to turn the practice into a principle. The new associations did not fix reasonably objective, uniform, and defensible criteria for the selection of their members. Hence they weakened their authority to speak either to laymen or to lawyers, as representatives of the profession. ... As late as 1915 the total membership of all state bar associations in the country was reckoned as but 20 percent of the lawyers; and even when membership in local associations was estimated in addition, only about 30 percent of the country's lawyers in 1915 belonged to some bar organization. ...

After 1910 state and local associations ... sought broader membership. Some of them went from the extreme of restriction to an extreme in which they emphasized merely quantitative growth. By 1935 it was estimated that 60 percent of lawyers in the United States belonged to some professional association.

There were large claims in behalf of the representative character of associations. But the claims were unsupported by proof regarding the distribution of members according to area, income, class, or types of law business. There was some evidence that not all lawyers would concede the representative character of the established associations. ...

At Saratoga, New York, in August, 1878, seventy-five lawyers from twenty-one jurisdictions organized the American Bar Association. They responded to a proposal made earlier that year by a small group which owned no authority beyond its conviction that such a national organization was desirable.

. . .

... The Association was organized in the vacation month of August at the best known, if not the most fashionable, summer resort of the country, and the annual meeting was held only at Saratoga Springs until 1889. A convivial group of Southern lawyers, accustomed to vacation every year at the Springs, formed the largest single element in the original membership. For many years election was a highly selective, personalized matter; for at least twenty years the atmosphere of the Association was mainly social. The objective evidence of this was the fact that there was almost no effective formulation or execution of policy in the name of the Association until in the years 1911–1919 the Association campaigned to rouse public opinion against the Progressive movement for adoption of the recall of judges and of judicial decisions.
. . .

After the first decade the apparent clique leadership of the Association was reinforced for years by an unplanned development which grew out of the Association's main field of public policy work. Though the Association early began discussion of reforms in legal education, its outstanding field of action during its first generation was in the preparation and recommendation of uniform laws for adoption by the states. The Association took the initiative in forming, and chiefly financed the operations of, the Conference of Commissioners on Uniform State Laws. The "commissioners" were in form appointed by their respective state governments. In practice they were self-selected from among those members of the Association who were willing and able to give time and effort to considerable uncompensated work. For over twenty years the Conference was the one branch of the Association in which work was always going forward. It regularly met during the week before the annual meetings of the Association, and out of the cohesion of its membership came the political direction of the succeeding meeting. About one third of the Association's presidents over a twenty year span came from the Conference group, and the election of scores of Executive Committeemen and other officers was there determined.

This evolution of affairs was without sinister cast. But it did not tend to build up the representative title of the organization as a whole. As part of a general reorganization of structure in 1936, the policy-making authority for the Association was taken from the Executive Committee and vested in a representative House of Delegates. The step reflected the reality of the problem of wider participation in the shaping of the Association's programs.

Jerold Auerbach, Unequal Justice: Lawyers and Social Change in Modern America

62–67 (1976).

The bar association movement was a characteristic feature of the decades surrounding 1900. Lawyers, in common with doctors, social workers, teachers, and engineers, flocked into professional associations, whose growth—the number of bar associations jumped from 16 in 1880 to more than 600 by 1916—expressed the impulse for professional cohesion in a fragmented society undergoing rapid change. Their local revival after the Civil War was attributable to unease over urban corruption. Nationally, the American Bar Association, organized in 1878, had more diffuse purposes: to promote the administration of justice, to advance jurisprudence, to uphold professional honor, and to encourage social intercourse among lawyers. But the ABA exuded the genial tone of a social club, set by its predominantly Southern members who came to Saratoga Springs each year to escape the summer heat. The "benefit of the waters," one member declared, rivaled in importance the professional business of the association. Simeon Baldwin, the moving spirit behind the association, labored to confine membership "to leading men or those of high promise. ..." Local associations often were similarly exclusive. The Boston Bar Association seemed to exist solely for the benefit of State Street and Federal Street lawyers. The Chicago Bar Association, founded (in the words of one of its presidents) to bring "the better and the best elements of the profession together," charged high admission fees and annual dues to achieve its purpose. The strongest pillars of the Association of the Bar of the City of New York were Yale, Harvard, and Protestantism.

Bar associations were not the exclusive preserve of corporate lawyers, but lawyers whose practices provided them with a sufficient margin of wealth and leisure to pay fees, attend conventions, and participate in committee work were bound to predominate. Leadership patterns within the American Bar Association measured the ascent of the corporate lawyer. During the 1890's

association members still looked for leadership to prominent courtroom advocates like James C. Carter and Joseph Choate. Between
1899 and 1905, a transition period, more specialized railroad
lawyers were elected president. In 1909 the "lawyer as businessman" reached the ABA pinnacle. State associations were more
diversified; even in the most heavily urbanized and industrialized
states general practitioners retained a strong voice. In fact, in
states like New York, Massachusetts, and Illinois, metropolitan
and state associations, representing respectively the urban and
rural wings of the profession, engaged in constant internecine
sniping. Whether corporate or country lawyers predominated,
however, the "best men" used bar associations as a lever of control
over professional ethics, educational qualifications, and bar admission. Claiming the right to represent and to police the entire
profession, they discriminated against an increasingly substantial
number of urban practitioners from ethnic minority groups.

Understandably, bar associations defended stability, order,
and control. Confronting social turmoil endemic to a society
undergoing rapid change, lawyers sought firm bedrock. They
found it in natural law, Adam Smith economics, Tocquevillian
assurances of high status, social Darwinism, and constitutional
certitudes defended by a judiciary that would stand as Gibraltar
against regulatory legislation. In 1915 the president of the American Bar Association asserted that law was "as omniscient and
omnipotent as God because it is an attribute of God, and its home
is the bosom of God." But a younger lawyer, less certain of legal
divinity, accused his professional colleagues of using bar associations "as a broom to sweep back the waters of ... modernism."
Lawyers, he suggested, should not permit their "rapt contempla-
tion of the past" to cripple their ability to cope with the present.
Janus-like, professional associations plunged into the twentieth
century beset by nineteenth-century yearnings.

Bar associations did venture timidly into the shallower waters
of law reform, but they usually skirted the dangerous shoals of
substantive charge. In 1912 ABA president Stephen Gregory
declared that professional associations were "the chief instrumen-
tality of constructive legal reform." Rarely, however, did their
concern extend to such problems as the provision of legal services.
At best, they preoccupied themselves with the most technical,
professional aspects of legal issues—for example, the ethical pro-
prieties of contingent fees rather than the social and individual
costs of lives broken in industrial accidents. The result was that
law reform served as "a banner of rectitude waved in the public
eye," a shield to deflect public criticism. The law reform move-

ment, sponsored by bar associations after the turn of the century, became the plaything of the legal specialist, whose job "was not to turn society on its head, but to refine and embroider his own special product. ... Law was supposed to be socially relevant; but the areas chosen for reform were not the areas of law most socially relevant."

During the second decade of the twentieth century the American Bar Association began to assert itself aggressively as a professional protective organization. Its purpose was twofold: to preserve its own exclusiveness (and the status that accompanied its preservation) and to exert professional leverage upon the political process. Two prewar episodes provided a test of its strength and scope: the admission of black lawyers and the nomination of Louis D. Brandeis to the Supreme Court.

In 1912 the executive committee of the American Bar Association unknowingly admitted three black lawyers to membership. Informed of its carelessness, it quickly passed a resolution rescinding the admission and—"since the settled practice of the Association has been to elect only white men as members"—referring the matter for determination by the entire association. Attorney General George W. Wickersham protested (one of the contested members, a Harvard Law School graduate, was his assistant in the Department of Justice)—not from any commitment to racial equality but from disgust with procedural irregularities that violated association by-laws. He was assured by the association's secretary that the recision resolution had been adopted only with "a sincere purpose to do what seemed ... to be right and just. ..." And he was sternly chastised for his "discourteous and dogmatic" criticism, a display of pique unbecoming an association member. But Moorfield Storey, a past president of the bar association and the first president of the National Association for the Advancement of Colored People, was incensed. "It is a monstrous thing," he complained, "that we should undertake to draw a color line in the Bar Association." Storey repudiated the notion that blacks were excluded by association policy, although he conceded that none had ever been admitted. The association was in a quandary. Claiming to be a national organization, it functioned as a restricted social club. The admission of blacks, in the words of its membership chairman, posed "a question of keeping pure the Anglo-Saxon race." A compromise resolution precluded future associational miscegenation. Prodded by Storey, members permitted the three duly elected black lawyers to remain but provided that all future applicants must identify themselves by race. The association thereby committed itself to lily-white membership for

the next half-century. It had elevated racism above professionalism.

Professionalism converged with politics in the Brandeis don-
nybrook. The first of several dramatic twentieth-century Court
nomination controversies, it brought into sharp focus the public
implications of professional parochialism. More was at stake than
a judicial seat, although a place on the Supreme Court was hardly
inconsequential at a time when the judiciary was praised or
blamed as the most reliable defender of vested property interests
against public regulation. On the surface the division seemed
clear. Brandeis' opponents, drawn largely from State Street law
firms and from the American Bar Association, could plausibly
view the Boston people's attorney as a threat to their restricted
professional world. They spoke of law as a bulwark of private
property; Brandeis, who would not have disagreed, had often used
it as an instrument of social change to make property owners
more responsible to the public. They devoted their careers to
counseling private interests; Brandeis committed much of his to
public service. Their law was a "brooding omnipresence"; his was
shaped by contemporary social needs. They defined themselves as
counselors to corporations; Brandeis, an opponent claimed, "acts
the part of a judge toward his clients instead of being his clients'
lawyer." They were Protestant; he was the first Jewish nominee
to the Supreme Court.

These differences masked some striking similarities between
Brandeis and his critics: his commitment to efficiency and order;
his application of business values to the operation of his law firm;
his admiration for the great New York firms; his fear of radical
challenges to American institutions; and his insistence that only
lawyers were competent to criticize and remedy defects in the
administration of law and justice. But the differences were crucial. They determined that the challenge to Brandeis would cut
across every major professional concern of the day: ethnicity; the
social function of law; the role of lawyers; and standards of
professional character, conduct, and ethics. As "an outsider,
successful, and a Jew," Brandeis was suspect. His confirmation
fight was a symbolic crusade, pitting the newest defenders of the
established professional order against the outsider who was especially dangerous because he shared so many of their attributes yet
put them to such different use. It was precisely because Brandeis'
credentials were so impeccable—a brilliant record at Harvard Law
School and a lucrative corporate practice—that the opposition to
his appointment was so revealing. Even the most qualified of
outsiders—qualified according to professional terms set by the

insiders—encountered a wall of antipathy from the elite. Their resistance, and their defeat, exposed both the sources of their professional power and its limits.

. . .

Emile Durkheim, Professional Ethics and Civil Morals
3–9, 12–13 (1957).

Now rules are of two kinds. The first apply to all men alike. They are those relating to mankind in general, that is, to each one of us as to our neighbor. All rules that set out the way in which men must be respected and their progress advanced—whether it be ourselves or our fellow-men—are equally valid for all mankind without exception. These rules of universal moral application are again divided into two groups: those concerning the relation of each one of us to his own self, that is, those that make up the moral code called individual; and those concerning the relations we maintain with other people, with the exception of any particular grouping. The obligations laid upon us by both the one and the other arise solely from our intrinsic human nature or from the intrinsic human nature of those with whom we find ourselves in relation.

. . .

But between these two extremes lie duties of a different kind. They depend not on our intrinsic human nature in general but on particular qualities not exhibited by all men. ... As professors, we have duties which are not those of merchants. Those of the industrialist are quite different from those of the soldier, those of the soldier from those of the priest, and so on.

. . .

We shall only touch on them briefly, for it is obviously impossible to describe the code of morals proper to each calling and to expound them—their description alone would be a vast undertaking. It only remains to make a few comments on the more important aspects of the subject. We may reduce these to two: (1) what is the general nature of professional ethics compared with any other province of ethics? (2) what are the general conditions necessary for establishing any professional ethics and for their normal working? ... A system of morals is always the affair of a group and can operate only if this group protects them by its authority. It is made up of rules which govern individuals, which compel them to act in such and such a way, and which impose limits to their inclinations and forbid them to go beyond.

Now there is only one moral power—moral, and hence common to all—which stands above the individual and which can legitimately make laws for him, and that is collective power. To the extent the individual is left to his own devices and freed from all social constraint, he is unfettered too by all moral constraint. It is not possible for professional ethics to escape this fundamental condition of any system of morals. Since, then, the society as a whole feels no concern in professional ethics, it is imperative that there be special groups in the society, within which these morals may be evolved, and whose business it is to see they be observed. ...

From this proposition another follows at once by way of corollary. Each branch of professional ethics being the product of the professional group, its nature will be that of the group. In general, all things being equal, the greater the strength of the group structure, the more numerous are the moral rules appropriate to it and the greater the authority they have over their members. For the more closely the group coheres, the closer and more frequent the contact of the individuals, and, the more frequent and intimate these contacts and the more exchange there is of ideas and sentiments, the more does a public opinion spread to cover a greater number of things. This is precisely because a greater number of things is placed at the disposal of all. Imagine, on the other hand, a population scattered over a vast area, without the different elements being able to communicate easily; each man would live for himself alone and public opinion would develop only in rare cases entailing a laborious calling together of these scattered sections. But when the group is strong, its authority communicates itself to the moral discipline it establishes and this, it follows, is respected to the same degree. On the other hand, a society lacking in stability, whose discipline it is easy to escape and whose existence is not always felt, can communicate only a very feeble influence to the precepts it lays down. Accordingly, it can be said that professional ethics will be the more developed, and the more advanced in their operation, the greater the stability and the better the organization of the professional groups themselves.

· · ·

[The] amoral character of economic life amounts to a public danger. The functions of this order to-day absorb the energies of the greater part of the nation. The lives of a host of individuals are passed in the industrial and commercial sphere. Hence, it follows that, as those in this *milieu* have only a faint impress of morality, the greater part of their existence is passed divorced from any moral influence. How could such a state of affairs fail to be a source of demoralization? If a sense of duty is to take strong root in us, the very circumstances of our life must serve to keep it always active. There must be a group about us to call it to mind all the time and, as often happens, when we are tempted to turn a deaf ear. A way of behaviour, no matter what it be, is set on a steady course only through habit and exercise. If we live amorally for a good part of the day, how can we keep the springs of morality from going slack in us? We are not naturally inclined to put ourselves out or to use self-restraint; if we are not encouraged at every step to exercise the restraint upon which all morals depend, how should we get the habit of it? If we follow no rule except that of a clear self-interest, in the occupations that take up nearly the whole of our time, how should we acquire a taste for any disinterestedness, or selflessness or sacrifice? Let us see, then, how the unleashing of economic interests has been accompanied by a debasing of public morality. We find that the manufacturer, the merchant, the workman, the employee, in carrying on his occupation, is aware of no influence set above him to check his egotism; he is subject to no moral discipline whatever and so he scouts any discipline at all of this kind.

It is therefore extremely important that economic life should be regulated, should have its moral standards raised, so that the conflicts that disturb it have an end, and further, that individuals should cease to live thus within a moral vacuum where the life-blood drains away even from individual morality. For in this order of social functions there is need for professional ethics to be established, nearer the concrete, closer to the facts, with a wider scope than anything existing today. There should be rules telling each of the workers his rights and his duties, not vaguely in general terms but in precise detail, having in view the most ordinary day-to-day occurrences. All these various inter-relations cannot remain for ever in a state of fluctuating balance. A system of ethics, however, is not to be improvised. It is the task of the very group to which they are to apply. When they fail, it is because the cohesion of the group is at fault, because as a group its existence is too shadowy and the rudimentary state of its ethics goes to show its lack of integration. Therefore, the true cure for the evil is to give the professional groups in the economic order a stability they so far do not possess. Whilst the craft union or corporate body is nowadays only a collection of individuals who have no lasting ties one with another, it must become or return to being a well-defined and organized association. Any notion of this kind, however, comes up against historical prejudices that make it still repugnant to most, and on that account it is necessary to dispel them.

B. THE RATIONALE FOR CODES OF CONDUCT AND REGULATORY AUTONOMY: THE STATED PURPOSE AND THE REVISIONIST RESPONSES

INTRODUCTION

Prior to the twentieth century, the American bar's ethical governance remained largely a matter of professional traditions and community norms, punctuated by an occasional judicial disciplinary action.   In 1836, David Hoffman, a University of Maryland professor, published the first systematic attempt to reduce some of those traditions to writing in his *Fifty Resolutions in Regard to Professional Deportment*. As the title suggests, Hoffman was as much concerned with etiquette as ethics, and his prescribed standards tended to be uncompromising in both respects. His view was that lawyers should refrain from all activity that might compromise professional dignity or personal honor; no involvement in self-promotion, unjust causes, or disingenuous tactics could be countenanced.

The other leading nineteenth century work on professional responsibility took a somewhat different tack. In 1854, a Pennsylvania judge, George Sharswood, published an *Essay on Professional Ethics*, which heavily influenced the first state bar association's ethical code (Alabama, 1887) and the American Bar Association's *Canons of Ethics* (1908). Although echoing Hoffman's distaste for any form of commercial rivalry, Sharswood articulated a more complex notion of lawyers' normative obligations. In essence, Sharswood posited certain distinctions between personal and professional morality that remain at the core of much contemporary debate concerning legal ethics.

The contours of that debate will be explored more fully in Part II. The readings that follow here seek to place the bar's regulatory enterprise in a broader social perspective. In particular, they raise certain fundamental questions about the rationale for professional codes and their adequacy as mechanisms of social governance.

In the following excerpt from *The Lawyer from Antiquity to Modern Times*, Roscoe Pound maintains that "it must not be supposed that an organized profession is the same sort of thing as a retail grocer's association."[1]   In fact, the degree of difference remains a matter of considerable public and scholarly controversy. Thus, for example, sociologist Eliot Freidson argues that, when defining their terms of work, "professionals differ from trade unions only in their sanctimoniousness."[2] The latter perspective does not necessarily imply a crude materialist account of professional motivation. It does, however, suggest the risk of allocating exclusive control over regulatory standards to the group subject to regulation.

A related issue involves the form that such standards should assume. As Murray Schwartz has suggested, the American bar's history of codification reflects diminishing interest in ethical aspirations and a greater reliance on minimum prohibitions.[3] That progression has been both lauded and lamented. Defenders of the regulatory approach see its primary virtue as clarifying credible, enforceable requirements, unconfused by cant and exhortation; accordingly, the proposed Model Rules are defended as a code of legal standards, not of ethics.[4] A countervailing concern, however, is that such a code

> "will pass for ethics. In that respect, the bar's insistence on minimal, enforceable standards may have missed the mark. No such code, however well drafted, can definitively respond to the complexities of professional practice. Where a threat of formal sanctions is remote, as is generally the case in professional contexts, the most significant, function of official codes will be symbolic and pedagogic. To the extent that codified precepts can affect behavior, an exclusively minimalist approach could prove misguided. The result may be socialization to the lowest common denominator of conduct that a highly self-interested constituency will publicly brand as deviant. ...
>
> To be sure, a codified catechism that aspires beyond the capacity of 'ordinary men on ordinary occasions' may seem irrelevant to the resolution of practical problems. ... But it by no means follows that a less platitudinous document, expressing certain core notions of honest and equitable conduct, would generate comparable cynicism simply because many practitioners would occasionally stray from the pre-

1. R. Pound, *infra*, at 110.

2. E. Freidson, *Profession of Medicine* 369 (1970). *See also* Green, "ABA as Trade Association" in *Verdicts on Lawyers* 3 (R. Nader & M. Green eds. 1976).

3. Schwartz, "The Death and Regeneration of Ethics," 1980 *Am.Bar Found.Research J.* 953.

4. G. Hazard, "Rules of Ethics: The Drafting Task," 36 *The Record* 77 (1981).

scribed path. ... [Moreover, the] difficulty with the current code manque—and the cases, commentary, and course instruction that parse it—is that together they may fortify the illusion that the profession's moral responsibilities have been adequately identified.[5] "

The extent to which codes can express or exhaust the profession's moral energies remains a subject of continuing debate.[6] The following excerpts reflect certain differing conceptions of ethical codes, and may illumine subsequent discussion of the substantive content of professional standards.

Roscoe Pound, The Lawyer From Antiquity to Modern Times
4–8 (1953).[*]

What Is a Bar Association?

2. What is a Profession—the Elements of a Profession. We may start with the proposition that a bar association is an association of persons practicing the profession of law formed and maintained to promote the administration of justice according to law and to promote and uphold the purposes and spirit of that profession. This requires us to ask what we mean by a profession, what elements go to make up a profession, and what are the purposes and what is the spirit of a profession in distinction from other callings, and, in particular, from a trade. Unhappily the term "professional" has obtained a bad connotation in general understanding from the absorbing public interest in sport. There the distinction between the amateur and the professional has led to thinking of "professional" and "profession" as referring to a money-making calling. Undoubtedly the exigencies of the economic order require most persons to gain a livelihood and the gaining of a livelihood must be a purpose to which they are constrained to direct their activities. But while in all walks of life men must bear this in mind, in business and trade it is the primary purpose. In a profession, on the other hand, it is an incidental purpose, pursuit of which is held down by traditions of a chief purpose to which the organized activities of those pursuing

---

5. Rhode, "Ethical Perspectives on Legal Practice," 37 *Stan.L.Rev.* 589, 647 (1985).

6. Compare Schneyer, "The Model Rules and Problems of Code Interpretation and Enforcement," 1980 *Am.B.Found.Research J.* 939; with Kutak, "The Rules of Professional Conduct in an Era of Change," 29 *Emory L.J.* 889 (1980); and Patterson, "The Function of a Legal Code of Ethics," 35 *U.Miami L.Rev.* 695 (1981).

[*] A history of the profession prepared under ABA sponsorship.

the calling are to be directed primarily, and by which the individual activities of the practitioner are to be restrained and guided.

. . .

Historically there are three ideas involved in a profession: organization, learning, *i.e.,* pursuit of a learned art, and a spirit of public service. These are essential. A further idea, that of gaining a livelihood is involved in all callings. It is the main if not the only purpose in the purely money-making callings. In a profession it is incidental.

. . .

It must not be supposed, however, that an organized profession of lawyers or of physicians is the same sort of thing as a retail grocers' association or that there is no essential difference between an organized bar and plumbers' or lumber dealers' associations. The conditions of an unorganized body of lawyers, with no differentiation between advocates and agents for litigation, which obtained in the United States in the last century, gave to bar associations in the decadence of professional organizations something of the look of trade associations or else of dinner clubs. But this condition, as it existed in the last third of the century, was the lingering effect of a general movement to deprofessionalize the traditionally professional callings and put all callings in one category of money-making activities, which was characteristic of frontier modes of thought in the formative era of American institutions. Fortunately, after formal organization for the most part lapsed or disappeared, the legal profession had inherited a tradition of solidarity and traditional incidents of professional organization which survived and were of real value for our administration of justice. But the ideal of the profession involves an inclusive and responsible organization toward which we have been moving back steadily since the revival of bar associations in the last third of the nineteenth century and more rapidly since the first quarter of the present century.

American Bar Association "Report of the Committee on [the] Code of Professional Ethics"
1906 American Bar Association Reports 600, 600–04.*

To the American Bar Association:

Your instructions direct us to report upon the "advisability and practicability" of the adoption of such a code [of professional ethics].

First, *as to advisability.*

We are of opinion that the adoption of such a code is not only advisable, but under existing conditions of very great importance. There are several considerations moving us to this conclusion:

1. With Wilson, Webster and others, we believe that "justice is the great interest of man on earth." And here in America, where justice reigns only by and through the people under forms of law, the lawyer is and must ever be the high priest at the shrine of justice. Under our form of government, unless the system for establishing and dispensing justice is so developed and maintained that there shall be continued confidence on the part of the public in the fairness, integrity and impartiality of its administration, there can be no lasting permanence to our republican institutions. Our profession is necessarily the keystone of the republican arch of government. Weaken this keystone by allowing it to be increasingly subject to the corroding and demoralizing influence of those who are controlled by graft, greed and gain, or other unworthy motive, and sooner or later the arch must fall. It follows that the future of the republic depends upon our maintenance of the shrine of justice pure and unsullied. We know it cannot be so maintained unless the conduct and motives of the members of our profession, of those who are the high-priests of justice, are what they ought to be. It therefore becomes our plain and simple duty, our patriotic duty, to use our influence in every legitimate way to help make the American Bar what it ought to be. A code of ethics, adopted after due deliberation and promulgated by the American Bar Association, is one method in furtherance of this end.

2. With the marvelous growth and development of our country and its resources, with the ranks of our profession ever extending, its fields of activities ever widening, the lawyer's opportunities for good and evil are correspondingly enlarged, and the limits have not been reached. We cannot be blind to the fact that, however high may be the motives of some, the trend of many is away from the ideals of the past and the tendency more and more to reduce our high calling to the level of a trade, to a mere means of livelihood or of personal aggrandizement. With the influx of increasing numbers, who seek admission to the profession mainly for its emoluments, have come new and changed conditions. Once

possible ostracism by professional brethren was sufficient to keep from serious error the practitioner with no fixed ideals of ethical conduct; but now the shyster, the barratrously inclined, the ambulance chaser, the member of the Bar with a system of runners, pursue their nefarious methods with no check save the rope of sand of moral suasion so long as they stop short of actual fraud and violate no criminal law. These men believe themselves immune, the good or bad esteem of their co-laborers is nothing to them provided their itching fingers are not thereby stayed in their eager quest for lucre. Much as we regret to acknowledge it, we know such men are in our midst. Never having realized or grasped that indefinable ethical something which is the soul and spirit of law and justice, they not only lower the *morale* within the profession, but they debase our high calling in the eyes of the public. They hamper the administration and even at times subvert the ends of justice. Such men are enemies of the republic; not true ministers of her courts of justice robed in the priestly garments of truth, honor and integrity. All such are unworthy of a place upon the rolls of the great and noble profession of the law.

3. Members of the Bar, like judges, are officers of the courts, and like judges should hold office only during good behavior. "Good behavior" should not be a vague, meaningless or shadowy term devoid of practical application save in flagrant cases. It should be defined and measured by such ethical standards, however high, as are necessary to keep the administration of justice pure and unsullied. Such standards may be crystallized into a written code of professional ethics, and a lawyer failing to conform thereto should not be permitted to practice or retain membership in professional organizations, local or national, formed, as is the American Bar Association, to promote the administration of justice and uphold the honor of the profession. Such a code in time will doubtless become of very great practical value by leading to action through the judiciary, for the courts may, as conditions warrant, require all candidates for the Bar to subscribe to suitable and reasonable canons of ethics as a condition precedent to admission. If this be done, the courts will be in an indisputable position to enforce, through suspension or disbarment, the observance of proper ethical conduct on the part of members of the Bar so admitted. Indeed, eventually the people, for the welfare of the community and to further the administration of justice, may, either by constitutional provisions or legislative enactments, demand that all, before being granted by the state the valuable franchise to practice, shall take an oath to support not only the Constitution, but such canons of ethics as may be established by

law. One state already, Alabama, to its credit be it said, has by statute made it a misdemeanor for an attorney to employ runners to solicit practice, and the public prosecutor is required to institute proceedings upon complaint of the council of the State Bar Association. But whatever measures may in time be developed to preserve the judicial department of the government, of which the Bar forms so important a part, from the taint of unworthy motives and conduct, we believe that, viewed from almost any standpoint, the adoption and promulgation of a series of reasonable canons of professional ethics in the form of a code by the American Bar Association cannot but have a salutary effect upon the administration of justice and upon the conduct of lawyers generally, whether on the Bench or at the Bar. Action by the national Association will also tend to develop uniformity between the various states, not only in form and method of statement, but also in application, and this we deem of practical importance. Indeed, the ultimate measure of success of this movement to keep the Bar true to its pristine glory will be largely enhanced by harmony between the different states and by the moral support given not only by the Bars of the various jurisdictions to each other, but by the courts of the sovereign states one to the other.

4. A further reason why we report the advisability of canons of ethics being authoritatively promulgated arises from the fact that many men depart from honorable and accepted standards of practice early in their careers as the result of actual ignorance of the ethical requirements of the situation. Habits acquired when professional character is forming are lasting in their effects. The "thus it is written" of an American Bar Association code of ethics should prove a beacon light on the mountain of high resolve to lead the young practitioner safely through the snares and pitfalls of his early practice up to and along the straight and narrow path of high and honorable professional achievement.

Second, *as to practicability.*

We report that the adoption and promulgation of a code of ethics by the American Bar Association is entirely practicable.

1. It is in keeping with the objects for which our Association was organized, among which the following are declared by the constitution:

> "To advance the science of jurisprudence, promote the administration of justice and ... uphold the honor of the profession of the law."

2. It is not impossible or indeed difficult to crystallize abstract ethical principles into a series of canons applicable to the

usual concrete ethical problems which confront the lawyer in the routine of practice. Several State Bar Associations have already done so.

Canons of ethics for promulgation by the American Bar Association should be drafted with care and deliberation by a body thoroughly representative of the profession in America. We recommend the appointment of such a committee of nine from Bench and Bar to report, for consideration and action at the 1907 meeting, a series of canons of professional ethics in the form of a code suitable for adoption and promulgation by the Association.

Jethro K. Lieberman, The Tyranny of the Experts: How Professionals Are Closing the Open Society
14–17 (1980).

Licensing is the imprimatur of status; it serves to label specialists. A complex, interdependent society requires that the method of determining how good or skilled a specialist is be quick, easy, available, and reliable. When it is impossible for the nonspecialist to evaluate the particular expert, he must depend on ratings by other specialists in the same field; the specialist must obtain professional recognition. The evaluation undertaken, the specialist approved, his skill is set forth for all to see in the status which he occupies.[5]

To forestall governmental regulation of their affairs, a few professions introduced *self-regulation* in the last third of the nineteenth century. Even when state legislatures began to enact licensing legislation at the turn of the century, the impetus came from professionals, not the public. The bulk of existing professional licensing laws was passed at the behest of the professional groups; almost invariably these groups have been given a share of the regulatory power.

At a session of the Wisconsin legislature some two decades ago, caterers, canopy and awning installers, cider makers, coal dealers, dancing school instructors, egg breakers, frog dealers, labor organizers, meat cutters, music teachers, and beer coil cleaners tried unsuccessfully to get themselves regulated. This same state in 1939 did enact legislation requiring examination for house painters; on the strength of this law, friendly citizens who helped

---

5. "Licensing can be expected when the variance in the quality of the service furnished by the practitioner is high, when the importance of that variance is great, when the amount of training necessary to evaluate the service is large, and when the degree of exposure of the consumer to the practitioner is small." Moore, "The Purpose of Licensing," 4 *J. of L. and Econ.* 93 (1961).

relatives and neighbors paint their houses were arrested and fined for failure to possess the requisite license. Unfortunately for the professional painters, the Wisconsin Supreme Court was moved to find a touch of unconstitutionality in the scheme in 1941.

Occupations which currently require licensing are so numerous as to defy classification. Even their listing is tedious in the extreme. A sampling of forty-five occupations controlled by state licensing boards in one state alone gives a fair idea of the magnitude of the licensed estate. By 1938 in North Carolina, these "professionals," among others, were licensed: lawyers, physicians, dentists, dental hygienists, pharmacists, optometrists, osteopaths, chiropractors, nurses, midwives, veterinarians, chiropodists, embalmers, pilots, pawnbrokers, photographers, public accountants, real estate brokers and salesmen, contractors, electrical contractors, mattress manufacturers, dry cleaners, burial association managers, dealers in scrap tobacco, correspondence and commercial school operators and their solicitors, liquor wholesalers, slaughterers, architects, auctioneers, barbers, threshers, collectors, plumbing and heating contractors, cosmetologists, engineers and land surveyors, insurance agents and adjusters, fidelity and fiduciary companies, dealers and companies in insurance bonding, investment, dividend, guarantee, registry, title guarantee, debentures and the like; and, of course, tile layers (and others).

By 1952, in addition to the obvious professions, at least one state and usually many more could claim the licensing of the following professions: abstracters, boiler inspectors, private detectives, egg graders, electricians, electrologists, elevator inspectors, guide-dog trainers, hoisting engineers, homeopaths, horseshoers, librarians, manicurists, masseurs, mechano-therapists, milk certifiers, mine inspectors, motor vehicle dealers and salesmen, motion picture operators, naturopaths, oculists, pest controllers, physical therapists, drugless physicians, plumbers, psychologists, certified shorthand reporters, sanitarians, social workers, watchmakers, well drillers, and yacht and ship brokers and salesmen.

Although state laws constitute the largest part of the American licensing structure, the federal government plays its limited role in precisely the same manner: at last count, the Coast Guard administered ninety-eight different licensing examinations for merchant marine masters, mates, pilots, and engineers.

There is probably no organized occupational group in the United States which has not tried at one time or another to break into the ranks of licensed professionals.[10] In 1955 a bill was

10. A collection of additional professions, businesses, trades, and other occupations in which licensing has been upheld by the courts includes: automo-

introduced in the California Assembly requiring the licensing of grass cutters as "maintenance gardeners." Mowing a lawn for pay without a license could cause the criminal to pay a fine of $500 and to stay in the local jailhouse for up to six months. A state board would administer the profession in order to prevent "gross incompetence," negligence, and "misrepresentation." The bill did not pass. A cousin of the maintenance gardener is the "tree expert," who is licensed in several states. In testimony before the Illinois State Legislature in 1959, the chairman of the Illinois State Tree Expert Examining Board calmly noted that "the intent of tree expert law was primarily to protect the public against tree quacks, shysters, and inexperienced persons."

NOTE

Following the ABA Committee Report excerpted above, the Association adopted 32 *Canons of Ethics*, with little controversy or debate. By 1920, courts or legislatures in all but 13 states and the District of Columbia had adopted the *Canons*, in some instances with local modifications. In the minority of states that never formally adopted the *Canons*, they were treated as a source of guidance to practitioners, courts, and disciplinary tribunals. However, substantial problems in enforcement persisted, in part because of the standards' brevity, generality, and attempt to combine moral exhortation and disciplinary mandates. The addition of *Canons* did not reduce these difficulties. By the late 1960s, there were 47 *Canons*, and some 1400 formal and informal ABA Committee opinions interpreting them. Despite the proliferation of texts, many significant ethical problems remained unacknowledged and unaddressed. Moreover, the reliance on ad hoc committee decision making led to considerable confusion and inconsistency.[1]

This unwieldly structure helped prompt the formation of an ABA Committee on Evaluation of Ethical Standards. In 1969,

bile dealers, bail bondsmen, bottle club operators, brick masons, chattel mortgage and salary loan brokers, cigar and cigarette dealers, coal dealers, commission merchants, creamery station owners or operators, dealers in citrus fruits, dealers in skins and hides of wild fur-bearing animals or alligators, garage operators, itinerant venders, junk dealers, labor union organizers, transportation agents, nonresident fishermen, parking lot attendants, public dance hall operators, stationary engineers, sugar refiners, travel bureau agents,

linen and towel rental service operators or solicitors, theater ticket hawkers, stevedores, and automobile towers. The cases are collected in 16A *Corpus Juris Secundum*, "Constitutional Law," Sec. 659, pp. 1013–15. For some of these occupations, the issuance of a license is admittedly far more routine than for others.

1. For a general history, *see e.g.*, H. Drinker, *Legal Ethics*, pp. 23–26 (1953); *see e.g.*, Armstrong, "A Century of Legal Ethics," 64 *A.B.A. Journal* 1063 (1978).

that Committee recommended a new *Code of Professional Responsibility*, divided into mandatory disciplinary rules and aspirational ethical considerations. Again, the proposed standards generated relatively little controversy. After approval by the ABA House of Delegates, the *Code* was ultimately adopted by every state except California, which enacted a similar body of rules, and Illinois, which passed a modified version.

Soon after the *Code's* adoption, its content and structure began to provoke increasing criticisms. According to some observers, the disparity between what its Ethical Considerations exhorted and what its Disciplinary Rules required was fostering cynicism about the bar's aspirational norms and creating confusion in enforcement efforts. Other critics identified further problems with the *Code*, including its ambiguities, its failure to distinguish among various functions that lawyers performed (*e.g.*, advocate, counselor, intermediary); and its lack of attention to certain crucial issues (such as conflicts of interest involving former clients or lawyers in organizational settings). In addition, a series of Supreme Court decisions in the 1970s on advertising, solicitation, fees, and group legal services forced reconsideration of *Code* provisions concerning professional competition. Within a decade after the *Code's* adoption, a special ABA Commission was already recommending an alternative set of standards, the *Model Rules of Professional Conduct.*

Unlike their predecessors, these *Rules* inspired considerable dispute within the profession. After heated debates over a series of preliminary drafts, the ABA in 1983 approved a final text and controversy then shifted to the states. By the early 1990s, most states had adopted the *Model Rules* in large part, although with changes in certain substantive provisions. In other jurisdictions, the *Code* remained in force, pending review of the *Model Rules* by the relevant judicial or legislative bodies.[2]

This section's focus on codes of conduct by no means implies that they are the only source of authority regulating lawyers. Other important sources include criminal prohibitions, civil procedural rules, ethics committee opinions, administrative agency rulings, and common law doctrine governing malpractice, fraud, and fiduciary relationships.[3] However, codes frequently affect, as well as reflect, these other sources of authority and provide the most

---

2. For an overview of the code provisions applicable in different jurisdictions, see G. Hazard and W. Hodes, *The Law of Lawyering* (2d ed. 1990).

3. Geoffrey Hazard, "Lawyers and Client Fraud: They Still Don't Get It," 6 *Geo.J.Leg. Ethics* 701 (1992) (discussing the different sources of regulatory authority).

comprehensive guidance for the practicing bar. Thus, their capacities and limitations warrant particular scrutiny. The readings that follow put their role into broader perspective.

American Bar Association, Model Rules of Professional Conduct, Preamble
(1983).**

PREAMBLE: A LAWYER'S RESPONSIBILITIES

A lawyer is a representative of clients, an officer of the legal system and a public citizen having special responsibility for the quality of justice.

As a representative of clients, a lawyer performs various functions. As advisor, a lawyer provides a client with an informed understanding of the client's legal rights and obligations and explains their practical implications. As advocate, a lawyer zealously asserts the client's position under the rules of the adversary system. As negotiator, a lawyer seeks a result advantageous to the client but consistent with requirements of honest dealing with others. As intermediary between clients, a lawyer seeks to reconcile their divergent interests as an advisor and, to a limited extent, as a spokesperson for each client. A lawyer acts as evaluator by examining a client's legal affairs and reporting about them to the client or to others.

In all professional functions a lawyer should be competent, prompt and diligent. A lawyer should maintain communication with a client concerning the representation. A lawyer should keep in confidence information relating to representation of a client except so far as disclosure is required or permitted by the Rules of Professional Conduct or other law.

A lawyer's conduct should conform to the requirements of the law, both in professional service to clients and in the lawyer's business and personal affairs. A lawyer should use the law's procedures only for legitimate purposes and not to harass or intimidate others. A lawyer should demonstrate respect for the legal system and for those who serve it, including judges, other lawyers and public officials. While it is a lawyer's duty, when necessary, to challenge the rectitude of official action, it is also a lawyer's duty to uphold legal process.

As a public citizen, a lawyer should seek improvement of the law, the administration of justice and the quality of service rendered by the legal profession. As a member of a learned profession, a lawyer should cultivate knowledge of the law beyond its use for clients, employ that knowledge in reform of the law and work to strengthen legal education. A lawyer should be mindful of deficiencies in the administration of justice and of the fact that the poor, and sometimes persons who are not poor, cannot afford adequate legal assistance, and should therefore devote professional time and civic influence in their behalf. A lawyer should aid the legal profession in pursuing these objectives and should help the bar regulate itself in the public interest.

Many of a lawyer's professional responsibilities are prescribed in the Rules of Professional Conduct, as well as substantive and procedural law. However, a lawyer is also guided by personal conscience and the approbation of professional peers. A lawyer should strive to attain the highest level of skill, to improve the law and the legal profession and to exemplify the legal profession's ideals of public service.

A lawyer's responsibilities as a representative of clients, an officer of the legal system and a public citizen are usually harmonious. Thus, when an opposing party is well represented, a lawyer can be a zealous advocate on behalf of a client and at the same time assume that justice is being done. So also, a lawyer can be sure that preserving client confidences ordinarily serves the public interest because people are more likely to seek legal advice, and thereby heed their legal obligations, when they know their communications will be private.

In the nature of law practice, however, conflicting responsibilities are encountered. Virtually all difficult ethical problems arise from conflict between a lawyer's responsibilities to clients, to the legal system and to the lawyer's own interest in remaining an upright person while earning a satisfactory living. The Rules of Professional Conduct prescribe terms for resolving such conflicts. Within the framework of these Rules many difficult issues of professional discretion can arise. Such issues must be resolved through the exercise of sensitive professional and moral judgment guided by the basic principles underlying the Rules.

The legal profession is largely self-governing. Although other professions also have been granted powers of self-government, the legal profession is unique in this respect because of the close relationship between the profession and the processes of government and law enforcement. This connection is manifested in the fact that ultimate authority over the legal profession is vested largely in the courts.

To the extent that lawyers meet the obligations of their professional calling, the occasion for government regulation is obviated. Self-regulation also helps maintain the legal profession's independence from government domination. An independent legal profession is an important force in preserving government under law, for abuse of legal authority is more readily challenged by a profession whose members are not dependent on government for the right to practice.

The legal profession's relative autonomy carries with it special responsibilities of self-government. The profession has a responsibility to assure that its regulations are conceived in the public interest and not in furtherance of parochial or self-interested concerns of the bar. Every lawyer is responsible for observance of the Rules of Professional Conduct. A lawyer should also aid in securing their observance by other lawyers. Neglect of these responsibilities compromises the independence of the profession and the public interest which it serves.

Lawyers play a vital role in the preservation of society. The fulfillment of this role requires an understanding by lawyers of their relationship to our legal system. The Rules of Professional Conduct, when properly applied, serve to define that relationship.

American Bar Association *Commission on Professionalism, "In the Spirit of a Public Service," A Blueprint for the Rekindling of Lawyer Professionalism* (1986)
Preamble (1982), pp. 25–26.

D. In General

All segments of the Bar should:

1. Preserve and develop within the profession integrity, competence, fairness, independence, courage and a devotion to the public interest.

2. Resolve to abide by higher standards of conduct than the minimum required by the Code of Professional Responsibility and the Model Rules of Professional Conduct.

3. Increase the participation of lawyers in *pro bono* activities and help lawyers recognize their obligation to participate.

4. Resist the temptation to make the acquisition of wealth a primary goal of law practice.

5. Encourage innovative methods which simplify and make less expensive the rendering of legal services.

6. Educate the public about legal processes and the legal system.

7. Resolve to employ all the organizational resources necessary in order to assure that the legal profession is effectively self-regulating.

Similarly, it behooves the legal profession to work voluntarily toward the implementation of these and other reforms that will make us more a profession "in the spirit of a public service." If such action is not taken, far more extensive and perhaps less-considered proposals may arise from governmental and quasi-governmental entities attempting to regulate the profession. The challenge remains. It is up to us to seize the opportunity while it is ours.

John Ladd, "The Quest for a Code of Professional Ethics: An Intellectual and Moral Confusion," in R. Chalk, M. Frankel and S. Chafer, Professional Ethics Activities in the Scientific and Engineering Societies

(AAAS Professional Ethics Projects, December 1980).

... My theme is stated in the title: it is that the whole notion of an organized professional ethics is an absurdity—intellectual and moral. ...

1. To begin with, ethics itself is basically an open-ended, reflective and critical intellectual activity. It is essentially problematic and controversial, both as far as its principles are concerned and in its application. Ethics consists of issues to be examined, explored, discussed, deliberated, and argued. Ethical principles can be established only as a result of deliberation and argumentation. These principles are not the kind of thing that can be settled by fiat, by agreement or by authority. To assume that they can be is to confuse ethics with law-making, rule-making, policy-making and other kinds of decision-making. It follows that, ethical principles, as such, cannot be established by associations, organizations, or by a consensus of their members. To speak of codifying ethics, therefore, makes no more sense than to speak of codifying medicine, anthropology or architecture.

2. Even if substantial agreement could be reached on ethical principles and they could be set out in a code, the attempt to impose such principles on others in the guise of ethics contradicts the notion of ethics itself, which presumes that persons are auton-

omous moral agents.   In Kant's terms, such an attempt makes ethics heteronomous;   it confuses ethics with some kind of externally imposed set of rules such as a code of law.   To put the point in more popular language: ethics must, by its very nature, be self-directed rather than other-directed.

3.   Thus, in attaching disciplinary procedures, methods of adjudication and sanctions, formal and informal, to the principles that one calls "ethical" one automatically converts them into legal rules or some other kind of authoritative rules of conduct such as the bylaws of an organization, regulations promulgated by an official, club rules, rules of etiquette, or other sorts of social standards of conduct.   To label such conventions, rules and standards "ethical" simply reflects an intellectual confusion about the status and function of these conventions, rules and standards. Historically, it should be noted that the term "ethical" was introduced merely to indicate that the code of the Royal College of Physicians was not to be construed as a criminal code (i.e. a legal code).   Here "ethical" means simply non-legal.

4.   That is not to say that ethics has no relevance for projects involving the creation, certification and enforcement of rules of conduct for members of certain groups.   But logically it has the same kind of relevance that it has for the law.   As with law, its role in connection with these projects is to appraise, criticize and perhaps even defend (or condemn) the projects themselves, the rules, regulations and procedures they prescribe, and the social and political goals and institutions they represent.   But although ethics can be used to judge or evaluate a disciplinary code, penal code, code of honor or what goes by the name of a "code of ethics," it cannot be identified with any of these, for the reasons that have already been mentioned.

. . .

8.   In discussing specific ethical issues relating to the professions, it is convenient to divide them into issues of *macro-ethics* and *micro-ethics*.   The former comprise what might be called collective or social problems, that is, problems confronting members of a profession as a group in their relation to society; the latter, issues of micro-ethics, are concerned with moral aspects of personal relationships between individual professionals and other individuals who are their clients, their colleagues and their employers.   Clearly the particulars in both kinds of ethics vary considerably from one profession to another.   I shall make only two general comments.

9. Micro-ethical issues concern the personal relationships between individuals. Many of these issues simply involve the application of ordinary notions of honesty, decency, civility, humanity, considerateness, respect and responsibility. Therefore, it should not be necessary to devise a special code to tell professionals that they ought to refrain from cheating and lying, or to make them treat their clients (and patients) with respect, or to tell them that they ought to ask for informed consent for invasive actions. It is a common mistake to assume that *all* the extra-legal norms and conventions governing professional relationships have a moral status, for every profession has norms and conventions that have as little to do with morality as the ceremonial dress and titles that are customarily associated with the older professions.

10. The macro-ethical problems in professionalism are more problematic and controversial. What are the social responsibilities of professionals as a group? What can and should they do to influence social policy? Here, I submit, the issue is not one of professional roles, but of *professional power*.

. . .

11. So-called "codes of professional ethics" have nothing to contribute either to micro-ethics or to macro-ethics as just outlined. It should also be obvious that they do not fit under either of these two categories. Any association, including a professional association, can, of course, adopt a code of conduct for its members and lay down disciplinary procedures and sanctions to enforce conformity with its rules. But to call such a disciplinary code a code of *ethics* is at once pretentious and sanctimonious. Even worse, it is to make a false and misleading claim, namely, that the profession in question has the authority or special competence to create an ethics, that it is able authoritatively to set forth what the principles of ethics are, and that it has its own brand of ethics that it can impose on its members and on society.

. . .

First, the objective of a professional code might be "inspirational," that is, it might be used to inspire members to be more "ethical" in their conduct. The assumption on which this objective is premised is that professionals are somehow likely to be amoral or submoral, perhaps, as the result of becoming professionals, and so it is necessary to exhort them to be moral, e.g. to be honest. I suppose there is nothing objectionable to having a code for this reason; it would be something like the Boy Scout's Code of Honor, something to frame and hang in one's office. I have severe reservations, however, about whether a code is really needed for this purpose and whether it will do any good; for those to whom it is addressed and who need it the most will not adhere to it anyway, and the rest of the good people in the profession will not need it because they already know what they ought to do. For this reason, many respectable members of a profession regard its code as a joke and as something not to be taken seriously. (Incidentally, for much the same kind of reasons as those just given, there are no professional codes in the academic or clerical professions.)

A second objective might be to alert professionals to the moral aspects of their work that they might have overlooked. In jargon, it might serve to sensitize them or to raise their consciousness. This, of course, is a worthy goal—it is the goal of moral education. Morality, after all, is not just a matter of doing or not doing, but also a matter of feeling and thinking. But, here again, it is doubtful that it is possible to make people have the right feelings or think rightly through enacting a code. A code is hardly the best means for teaching morality.

Thirdly, a code might, as it was traditionally, be a disciplinary code or a "penal" code used to enforce certain rules of the profession on its members in order to defend the integrity of the professional and to protect its professional standards. This kind of function is often referred to as "self-policing." It is unlikely, however, that the kind of disciplining that is in question here could be handled in a code of ethics, a code that would set forth in detail criteria for determining malpractice. On the contrary, the "ethical" code of a profession is usually used to discipline its members for other sorts of "unethical conduct," such as stealing a client away from a colleague, for making disparaging remarks about a colleague in public, or for departing from some other sort of norm of the profession. (In the original code of the Royal College of Physicians, members who failed to attend the funeral of a colleague were subject to a fine!) ...

Mischievous Side-Effects of Codes of Ethics

I now want to call attention to some of the mischievous side-effects of adopting a code of ethics:

The first and most obvious bit of mischief, is that having a code will give a sense of complacency to professionals about their conduct. "We have a code of ethics," they will say, "So everything we do is ethical." Inasmuch as a code, of necessity, prescribes what is minimal, a professional may be encouraged by the code to deliver what is minimal rather than the best that he can do. "I did everything that the code requires ..."

Even more mischievous than complacency and the consequent self-congratulation, is the fact that a code of ethics can be used as a cover-up for what might be called basically "unethical" or "irresponsible" conduct.

Perhaps the most mischievous side-effect of codes of ethics is that they tend to divert attention from the macro-ethical problems of a profession to its micro-ethical problems. There is a lot of talk about whistle-blowing. But it concerns individuals almost exclusively. What is really needed is a thorough scrutiny of professions as collective bodies, of their role in society and their effect on the public interest. What role should the professions play in determining the use of technology, its development and expansion, and the distribution of the costs (*e.g.* disposition of toxic wastes) as well as the benefits of technology? What is the significance of professionalism from the moral point of view for democracy, social equality, liberty and justice? There are lots of ethical problems to be dealt with. To concentrate on codes of ethics as if they represented the real ethical problems connected with professionalism is to capitulate to *struthianism* (from the Greek word *struthos-* ostrich). ...

Geoffrey C. Hazard, Jr., "Personal Values and Professional Ethics"

40 Cleveland State Law Review 133, 133–134, 139–141 (1992).

My purpose on this occasion is to urge reexamination of personal values as a fundamental resource of professional ethics. The essential point is that rules of ethics, such as those embodied in the profession's ethical codes, are insufficient guides to making the choices of action that a professional must make in practice. I will suggest that the same is true of professional tradition and conventional ways of practice. This is not to say that rules of ethics and traditions are irrelevant. Rules of professional ethics frame the ethical problems that are encountered in a lawyer's life throughout practice. Moreover, professional tradition provides an idealized portrait of a professional that serves as a model for action in real world situations. However, framing an ethical problem is one thing, resolving such a problem is something else. Oliver Wendell Holmes remarked about the judicial function that "[g]eneral propositions do not decide concrete cases." The same point supports ethical choices that must be made by lawyers in conducting their practice. So also an idealized conception of what a professional should be, as portrayed in professional tradition, does not determine what a professional should do in the nonideal world of actual practice.

I.   Professional Ethics

The term "professional ethics" can be understood to refer to at least three different but related normative sources: first, the profession's rules of ethics; second, ethical tradition including professional myths, lore and narrative; and, third, the standards of conduct that an observing anthropologist would describe as the profession's conventions of actual practice. The last source may also be captured by the term "habit" which at one time was used to describe a group's regular pattern of conduct. The term "professional" simply denotes that these normative sources function within a specific subgroup in society, in our case the American legal profession.

II.   Rules, Traditions and Practice

The rules of ethics of the American legal profession are constituted in the Rules of Professional Conduct, previously in the Code of Professional Responsibility and before that in the American Bar Association Canons of Professional Ethics. Various subsections of these codes incorporate rules of general law that govern the citizenry at large. For example, the profession's ethical codes require a lawyer to refrain from violating the general criminal law and from committing civil fraud in his own conduct. The codes also permit a lawyer to use the process of the courts only for lawful purposes.

Our professional tradition is another source of ethical guidance. That tradition includes such articles of faith as "equal justice under law," "a lawyer knows no duty other than to his client," "every client with a just cause has a right to a lawyer's assistance," and "due process of law is a fundamental right." In contemporary discourse about the legal profession, the profession's espoused tradition or mythology (I use the term in the anthropological sense) is often referred to as its narrative.

The legal profession's practice conventions or "habits"—its ways of actually doing things as observable by an anthropologist— are what we learn after we get out of law school. One example ... consists of putting off any less urgent matter in favor of a more urgent matter. In general, this is a sensible scheduling principle in our work, which mostly consists of dealing with one emergency after another. However, in practice this habit often translates into doing all tasks at the last minute.

The relationship among these normative sources—rules, traditions and "habits of practice" is dynamic and complex. Lawyers are ever mindful of the central principles in the rules of ethics even if most lawyers do not know the letter of the ethical codes, let alone follow the rules to the letter. Our profession's traditions hover in the back of every lawyer's mind, helping us to interpret, justify and give higher meaning to our work. The idealized conception of the lawyer's vocation is that we are in the service of justice and the protection of the oppressed, including oppressed corporate clients. Without such an idealization the work often would be too tedious and frustrating.

The habits of lawyers' work, as observed by an anthropologist, tend to contradict the idealized version expressed in professional narrative. Moreover, some conventions of practice violate the rules prescribed in the ethical codes. Lawyers violate the rules and fail to fulfill their own professional ideals because, like everyone else, they are subject to the constraints of economics, politics and human frailty. The contradiction between the ideal and the legal, on the one hand, and actual practice, on the other, does not prove that lawyers are indifferent to their ethical obligations. It proves only that practicing law according to the rules, let alone according to idealization, is not easy.

. . .

[In the subjective world of practice, where the lawyer is required to call the shots in resolving ethical dilemmas, neither formal rules nor standard techniques of interpretation are much assistance. The rules say that evidence may not be offered if the lawyer knows it is fabricated or that nondisclosure of a material fact in a financial transaction may constitute fraud. However, the rules do not and cannot say whether specific evidence is fabricated or whether certain financial information is fraudulent. Professional techniques in interpreting rules do not help in telling whether the factual conditions that bring the rules into play have been met.]

Likewise, professional narrative and tradition do not provide means of resolving issues of this kind. Professional narrative speaks in terms of concrete cases, not in the abstract generalizations of the ethical codes. However, the concrete cases incorporated in professional tradition are either historical or apocryphal. Either way, they do not replicate the concrete case that the lawyer must resolve. An example is the story of Abe Lincoln's successful use of the Farmer's Almanac to demolish the testimony of a lying witness. Such a concrete case presents a model for action in a present ethical dilemma, but only if the facts of the present dilemma correspond to those in the model case. If there are differences in the facts, the model indeed can be misleading. For example, a lawyer who supposes that his only duty is to his client is in for an unpleasant surprise if the client is seeking help in concealing the evidence of a crime.

The limited utility of professional narrative resembles the limited utility of the case method of judicial reasoning. A prior case that is on point may indeed be a binding authority. However, it is always an open question whether a prior case is on point. A prior decision becomes binding when we conclude that it is on point, but there is nothing about a prior decision that binds us to first test the prior case on point.

Conventions of practice have similar limited utility in the lawyer's subject realm. Studying what lawyers do in their practice does not tell us what is going on in their minds. As to that we can only make educated guesses. Indeed, on this matter Yogi Berra may have further wisdom from which we can benefit. He said that "You can't think and hit at the same time." A successful batter is in some sense unconscious in the moment of choice when he swings the bat. I also believe that a lawyer is in some sense unconscious in the moment of choice when he resolves an ethical dilemma.

In the literature of professional ethics, remarkably little attention is given to this matter. The rules of professional ethics differentiate various states of mind as the predicates of various kinds of ethical decisions. Thus, the rules differentiate between "believing," "knowing" and "reasonably believing." However, these rules are designed to guide decision-makers such as grievance committees in resolving issues of circumstantial evidence as to a particular lawyer's state of mind on a particular occasion. By extension, these rules also tell a lawyer how a tribunal may be inclined to assess the lawyer's conduct after the fact. At most, therefore, these rules inform the lawyer how others in the future will think about what the lawyer is now thinking. The rules governing others in assessing a lawyer's state of mind do not provide insight to the lawyer about his own state of mind.

VI. CONCLUSION

There is of course more to be said on this problem. When all has been said, however, the fact will remain that a lawyer's ethical deliberations are a process of personal thought and action. That process is guided by the rules of the ethical codes, by professional tradition, and by prevailing standards of practice.

. . .

The practical judgments necessary to these tasks are essentially the same as those made by people in ordinary life. They are personal judgments. As such, they incorporate an unavoidable element of personal value, just as an element of value is incorporated in how we treat our friends, members of our family, professional colleagues, rivals, and the people who live across the street. Thus, it is not true—no matter what they say—that in becoming a lawyer one ceases to be a person.

The question remains of what kind of person one wants to be.

Deborah L. Rhode, "Why the ABA Bothers: A Functional Perspective on Professional Codes"

59 Texas Law Review 689, 689–92 (1981).*

I. Introduction

In January 1980, just ten years after the American Bar Association adopted the Model Code of Professional Responsibility, a special ABA commission chaired by Robert Kutak recommended "comprehensive reformulation" of that document. The Kutak Commission's suggested replacement, the Model Rules of Professional Conduct, has generated considerable controversy within the profession, culminating in a large volume of comment and two counterproposals. So heated a debate invites the question suggested by the titles of this and Professor Abel's articles.** Of course, at one level of generality, the answer seems self-evident. As both the history and content of ABA codifications make plain, the bar bothers because its interests so dictate. Like any other occupational group, the ABA formulates and fulminates for its health, collectively speaking. What is less obvious, and what this Article will explore, is the range of concerns at stake in the codification enterprise and the wisdom of placing that endeavor under bar control.

From the profession's standpoint, codes of ethics are a primary instrument for attaining what Talcott Parsons posited as the dominant goals for any occupation: objective achievement and recognition. Codified standards can generate monetary and psychic benefits by enhancing occupational status and self-image; constraining competition; preserving autonomy; and reconciling

* Published originally in 59 Texas L.Rev. 689 (1981) (symposium on the Model Rules of Professional Conduct). Copyright © 1981 by the Texas Law Review. Reprinted by permission.

** Abel, "Why Does the ABA Promulgate Ethical Rules?," 59 *Tex.L.Rev.* 639 (1981).

client, colleague, and institutional interests. From a societal perspective, however, professional codes are desirable only insofar as they serve common goals to a greater extent than other forms of control, namely market forces or government regulation. For the legal profession, such goals presumably would include promoting the impartial and efficient administration of justice and ensuring competent legal assistance at the lowest possible price.

As the Kutak Commission acknowledges, the regulatory interests of the public and the profession are not always coextensive. Rather, "difficult ethical problems arise from conflict between a lawyer's responsibilities to clients, to the legal system and to the lawyer's own interest in remaining an upright person while earning a satisfactory living." Given this concession, it is striking that so little effort is made to justify the bar's arrogation of exclusive authority to resolve such conflicts. In marked contrast to the recently appointed British Royal Commission on Legal Services, which has a majority of laymen, only one of the Kutak Commission's thirteen members is not an attorney. This imbalance between professional and public representation in the drafting phase is exacerbated by a ratification process in which only the views of professionals are systematically solicited, and in which they alone cast the decisive vote.

Such a process is hardly conducive to an unbiased accommodation of the diverging interests at stake. Without impugning the good faith of those involved in the enterprise, it is legitimate to inquire whether the bar as a whole can rise above parochial concerns on issues that place its income or status at risk. Pure altruism may be possible, but the architects of our regulatory processes generally have proceeded on a contrary assumption. Few, if any, occupational groups have equaled lawyers in their determination to expunge both the fact and appearance of partiality from decisions implicating significant legal rights. Attorneys repeatedly have argued, and the Supreme Court has agreed, that the due process clause bars decisionmaking by individuals in cases that could substantially affect their personal interests or those of an organization to which they belong. Yet potential conflicts of interest become somehow less salient when it is the bar that "sits in judgment in [its] own cause."

Neither the Code nor the Model Rules indicate why the bar should proceed as if it were exempt from the natural human tendency to prefer private over public ends. Confronted with conflict between their self-interest and their perception of societal interests, many individuals will attempt to discount or reconstrue the less immediate concern so as to reduce internal tension.

Simply through normal processes of cognitive dissonance—reduction and acculturation—professionals may lose sensitivity to interests at odds with their own. Nothing in the bar's extended history of self-governance suggests it to be an exception. As has been convincingly demonstrated elsewhere, both the Code of Professional Responsibility and the Canons of Ethics it replaced consistently resolved conflicts between professional and societal objectives in favor of those doing the resolving. So too, given the political constraints under which the Kutak Commission is operating, one would expect the Model Rules to serve first and foremost the interests of the bar.

Of course, this observation, without more, is neither startling nor especially damning. By choice or inertia, we often delegate responsibility for monitoring professional conduct to private organizations or member-dominated licensing boards. Whether such delegations are prudent depends in large measure on the degree to which public and professional objectives converge. Thus, ... a functional overview of the bar's objectives [should help] lodge them in the context of broader social concerns.

Concededly, such a conceptual framework shares the limitations of any functionalist approach that analyzes heterogeneous occupational groups as discrete entities. Like other such groups, the bar is not a monolithic organization whose members share a single view on regulatory issues. Rather, the legal profession is a stratified body with cross-cutting interests and allegiances. Even so, the very concept of a professional code presupposes a common core of functions and concerns. Only by exploring those concerns can we understand why the ABA codifies and, more importantly, whether it should enjoy that prerogative.

. . .

In a celebrated history of the profession prepared under ABA auspices, Roscoe Pound reassured his sponsor that it was not, after all, "the same sort of thing as a retail grocers' association." If he was right, it was almost certainly for the wrong reasons. Lawyers no less than grocers are animated by parochial concerns. What distinguishes professionals is their relative success in packaging occupational interests as societal imperatives. In that regard, codes of ethics have proved highly useful. Seldom, of course, are such documents baldly self-serving; it is not to a profession's long-term advantage that it appear insensitive to the common good. But neither are any profession's own encyclicals likely to incorporate public policies that might significantly compromise members' status, monopoly, working relationships, or autonomy.

In part, the problem is one of tunnel vision. Without doubt, most lawyers—including those on the Kutak Commission—are committed to improving the legal system in which they work. What *is* open to doubt is whether a body of rules drafted, approved, and administered solely by attorneys is the most effective way of realizing that commitment. No matter how well-intentioned and well-informed, lawyers regulating lawyers cannot escape the economic, psychological, and political constraints of their position. If, as one Commission member readily acknowledges, the bar's past regulatory endeavors have foundered on self-interest and self-deception, what justifies attorneys' continued resistance to any external oversight? By abjuring outside interference, professionals can readily become victims of their own insularity, losing perspective on the points at which fraternal and societal objectives diverge. No ethical code formulated under such hermetic constraints can be expected to make an enduring social contribution. The Model Rules are no exception.

To effect significant improvements in the quality, cost, and delivery of legal services, the bar must accept fundamental changes in its regulatory structure. Anointing a few laymen to serve on drafting commissions or disciplinary committees will not suffice. As experience with token representation in other contexts makes clear, such cosmetic gestures serve more to legitimate than to affect the decisions of professionally controlled regulatory systems. Rather, structural deficiencies in the bar's present governance system mandate reforms offering nonprofessionals more than a supporting role. Lacking a constituency intent on such reforms, the Kutak Commission has proposed none. This is not, of course, to suggest that the recodification enterprise was meaningless from the profession's point of view. Quite the contrary, it is obvious why the ABA bothers. What remains is to convince the public to do likewise.

REFERENCES

H. Drinker, *Legal Ethics* 23–25 (1953).

Frankel, Book Review, 43 *U.Chi.L.Rev.* 874 (1976) (reviewing ABA, *Code of Professional Responsibility* (1975)).

G. Hazard, Jr. *Ethics in the Practice of Law* (1978).

Kernaghan, "Codes of Ethics and Administrative Responsibility," 17 Canadian Public Administration 527 (1974).

Kultgen, "The Ideological Use of Professional Codes," in *Ethical Issues in Professional Life* (J. Callahan ed., 1988).

Kutak, "The Rules of Professional Conduct in an Era of Change," 29 *Emory L.J.* 889 (1980).

McKean, "Some Economic Aspects of Ethical Behavior Codes," 27 *Pol.Stud.* 251 (1979).

Morgan, "The Evolving Concept of Professional Responsibility", 90 *Harv.L.Rev.* 702 (1977).

Patterson, "The Function of a Legal Code of Ethics," 35 *U.Miami L.Rev.* 695 (1981).

Powell, "Developments in the Regulation of Lawyers: Competing Segments and Market, Client and Government Controls," (1984).

M. Powell, *From Patrician to Professional Elite: The Transformation of the New York City Bar Association* (1988).

Powell, "Anatomy of a Counter Bar Association: The Chicago Council of Lawyers," 1979 *Am. B. Found. Res. J.* 501.

Schnapper, "The Myth of Legal Ethics", 64 *A.B.A. J.* 202 (1978).

Schneyer, "The Model Rules and Problems of Code Interpretation and Enforcement," 1980 *Am. B. Found. Research J.* 939.

Schneyer, "Professionalism as Politics: The Making of a Modern Legal Ethics Code," in *Lawyers' Ideals/Lawyers' Practices: Transformations in the American Legal Profession,* 95 (R. Nelson, D. Trubek and R. Solomon eds., 1992).

Schuchman, "Ethics and Legal Ethics: The Propriety of the Canons as a Group Moral Code," 37 *Geo.Wash.L.Rev.* 244 (1968).

Part II

PROFESSIONAL ROLES

I. INTRODUCTION: THE PREMISES OF PARTISANSHIP

INTRODUCTION

Implicit in all theories of professionalism is some concept of an occupational role that entails distinctive duties and expectations. In that respect, such theories build on broader sociological and philosophical traditions that give cultural content to role behavior. The concept of role has both factual and moral dimensions. Social scientists use the term to describe a status carrying a distinct set of cultural expectations and obligations. According to sociologist Erving Goffman, there is no self outside of roles: in all our daily interactions we are playing some part, as parent, student, friend, employee, customer.[1] Generalizing from such patterns, some philosophers have maintained that ethical behavior requires adherence to the particular norms that are appropriate to particular roles. Thus, lawyers may appropriately take certain actions in their professional capacity, such as holding information confidential or obfuscating facts, that would be ethically indefensible in other contexts.

Critiques of role morality take several forms. One school of thought, following lines set out by Richard Wasserstrom below, and Gerald Postema in Section III, stresses the corrosive aspects of role identification for the individual. The detachment of personal and professional ethics may alienate lawyers from their own values and cut off deliberation from its necessary sources in ordinary moral experience.

A second line of criticism stresses the costs to society and innocent third parties from decisions that are narrowly focused on professional obligations to clients. This critique of role morality is analogous to the critique of rule utilitarianism discussed by

---

1. E. Goffman, *Encounters* 85–110, 132–52 (1961); ___, *The Presentation of Self In Everyday Life* (rev. ed. 1959). For a seminal anthropological account of the distinction between self and status, see R. Linton, *The Study of Man* (1936).

Frankena in the excerpt below. Rule utilitarianism assumes that the greatest good for the greatest number comes from adhering to general rules even if it results in occasional injustice, just as role morality assumes that conformity with roles is good even when it produces unjust outcomes in particular cases. Yet as critics note, "whatever the general validity of having a certain rule [or role], if one has actually reached the point of seeing that the utility of breaking it on a certain occasion is greater than that of following it . . . then surely it would be pure irrationality not to break it." [2] Thus, individuals should make decisions about professional conduct not by deferring to some fixed notion of role. Rather they must determine what the role should entail based on the standard forms of ethical analysis that Frankena describes below.

A third line of criticism emphasizes not the costs of role morality, but the possibility of distinguishing it from "ordinary" moral decision making. As contemporary philosophers have often noted, "no one is ever an abstract moral agent." [3] From this perspective, developed by Geoffrey Hazard in the excerpt that follows, "ordinary" morality and role-differentiated approaches are not significantly different; rather, both assume that "persons in different circumstances and with different abilities have different obligations." [4]

Much of the debate over legal ethics is rooted in debates over role morality. Particular attention has focused on the degree to which a lawyer's duties to clients displace other moral responsibilities.

In a celebrated 1820 divorce trial of England's Queen Caroline on charges of adultery, her defense counsel Lord Brougham offered a classic definition of the advocate's role:

> An advocate, in the discharge of his duty, knows but one person in all the world, and that person is his client. To save that client by all means and expedients, and at all hazards and costs to other persons, and, amongst them, to himself, is his first and only duty; and in performing this duty he must

---

2. Bernard Williams, *Morality: An Introduction to Ethics* 102 (1972).

3. Alisdair MacIntyre, "What Has Ethics to Learn From Medical Ethics," 2 *Phil.Exchange* 37, 46 (1978); Jack L. Sammons, Jr., "Professing: Some Thoughts on Professionalism and Classroom Teaching," 3 *Geo.J.Legal Ethics* 609, 616 n. 15 (1990).

4. Virginia Held, "The Division of Moral Labor and the Role of the Lawyer, *in The Good Lawyer: Lawyers' Roles and Lawyers' Ethics*, 60, 67 (David Luban, ed., 1984). *See also* Joram Graf Haber and Bernard H. Baumrin, "The Moral Obligations of Lawyers," 1 *Can.J.L. and Jurisprudence*, Jan. 1988, at 105.

not regard the alarm, the torments, the destruction which he may bring upon others.[5]

Bougham's definition encompasses two central principles, often referred to as the "standard conception of the advocate's role." These are what William Simon describes as the principles of neutrality and partisanship. The first principle, that of neutrality,

> prescribes that the lawyer remain detached from his client's ends. The lawyer is expected to represent people who seek his help regardless of his opinion of the justice of their ends. In some cases, he may have a duty to do so; in others, he may have the personal privilege to refuse. But whenever he takes a case, he is not considered responsible for his client's purposes. . . .
>
> The second principle of conduct is partisanship. This principle prescribes that the lawyer work aggressively to advance his client's ends. The lawyer will employ means on behalf of his client which he would not consider proper in a non-professional context even to advance his own ends. These means may involve deception, obfuscation, or delay. . . . [although they are qualified by certain minimum responsibilities of lawyers] as officers of the Court.[6]

Yet American legal traditions have always included other conceptions of the advocate's role. As a matter of professional ideals, lawyers often have viewed themselves not only as neutral partisans but also as public servants and moral activists, with civic as well as client obligations. And as a matter of professional practice, attorneys frequently have found it prudent to qualify their partisanship in order to preserve their reputations and relationships with other participants in the legal process and with other potential sources of legal business.[7]

Alternative models of advocacy have deep historical roots. Many leaders of the eighteenth and nineteenth century bar viewed the attorney's role as mediating "between the universal [vision] of [the] legal order and the concrete desires of his

---

5. For competing views on the historical context and contemporary significance of Lord Brougham's statement, see Deborah L. Rhode, *An Adversarial Exchange on Adversarial Ethics: Text, Subtext, and Context,* in 41 J.Legal Educ. 29 (1991).

6. William H. Simon, *The Ideology of Advocacy: Procedural Justice and Professional Ethics,* 1978 Wis.L.Rev. 30, 36 (1978).

7. Ted Schneyer, *Moral Philosophy's Standard Misconception of Legal Ethics,* 1984 Wis.L.Rev. 529; and Schneyer,

clients." [8]   This understanding of the lawyer as civic statesman helped inspire de Tocqueville's vision of the legal profession as America's natural aristocracy, capable of checking popular passions and self-interest.[9] Similarly, many progressive era leaders echoed Louis Brandeis's assumption that attorneys should take advantage of "opportunity in law" to promote justice through reform activity and client counseling.[10]

These competing visions of the advocacy role have long coexisted in debates over legal ethics. In the first American treatise on the subject, Maryland law professor David Hoffman argued for principles of direct moral accountability rather than neutral partisanship. According to Hoffman, "[m]y client's conscience, and my own, are distinct entities ... it would be dishonorable folly in me to endeavor to incorporate [any unmeritorious claim] in the jurisprudence of the country." [11]   For George Sharswood, the other major nineteenth century theorist, the issue was more complicated. In tones reminiscent of prominent British commentators, Sharswood emphasized that the advocate was

> not morally responsible for the act of his client in maintaining an unjust cause, nor for the error of the court ...
> in deciding it in his favor. ... The lawyer, who refuses his professional assistance because in his judgment the claim is unjust and indefensible, usurps the function of both judge and jury.[12]

Yet somewhat inconsistently, Sharswood also believed that counsel "have an undoubted right, and are in duty bound" to refuse assistance to a plaintiff aiming to "perpetrate a wrong, through some means of advantage the law may allow." [13]   And, when defending an "unrighteous" action, the advocate "ought to refuse to act under instructions from his client to defeat what he believes to be an honest and just claim, by insisting upon the slips of the opposite party, by sharp practice, or special pleading. ..." [14]

Since Sharswood, the trend has been toward an ever more pronounced distinction between personal and professional ethics,

Some Sympathy for the Hired Gun, 41 J.Legal Educ. 11 (1991).

8. Robert W. Gordon, *The Ideal and the Actual in the Law: Fantasies and Practices of New York City Lawyers 1870–1910, in The New High Priests: Lawyers in Post Civil War America* (Gerard W. Gawalt ed., 1984).

9. Alexis de Tocqueville, *Democracy in America*, Vol. I (H. Reeve–Trans; P. Bradley, ed. 1973) (1st ed. 1835).

10. Louis D. Brandeis, *The Opportunity in the Law, in Business: A Profession* 329 (1933).

11. D. Hoffman, *A Course of Legal Study* 755 (2d ed. 1836).

12. G. Sharswood, *An Essay on Professional Ethics* 84–85 (3d ed. 1869).

13. *Id.* at 97–98.

14. *Id.* at 100.

and an ever greater emphasis on client allegiance. That progression has been explained on a variety of grounds. Historical accounts have linked the appeal of a neutral technician's role to the growth of a market economy, a decline in civic ideals, and the reconceptualization of law as a science.[15] Other theories have emphasized the financial underpinnings of private practice and the competitive ethos of a capitalist social order, which place a premium on client allegiance and zealous partisanship.[16] Various psychological pressures have been thought to work in similar directions. Natural human tendencies to reduce cognitive dissonance and moral complexity may filter out competing normative claims.[17] In contexts of bounded rationality and ethical uncertainty, the neutral partisanship role has particular appeal.

Such accounts, of course, help more to explain than justify that role. The most common justifications, explored at some length in the materials that follow, rest on certain perceived demands of an adversarial legal structure and a democratic social order. Zealous advocacy is thought to be essential in maintaining a competitive system of dispute resolution, preserving individual rights, and keeping governmental power within proper procedural and substantive bounds. How adequately these interests justify prevailing partisanship norms remains open to debate. As philosopher David Luban has noted, the adversary system rationale is only as good as the adversary system, and assessments of that system vary widely.[18] While conceding the virtues of zealous advocacy in some contexts, critics have challenged both the wholesale extension of partisan norms to all circumstances of legal practice, and the moral disengagement that such an extension may entail.

As the materials in Part I made evident, lawyers perform a broad array of services in a broad variety of social settings. A recurring question, to which much of the following material speaks, is the extent to which lawyers' ethical responsibilities vary across different practice contexts. Under what circumstances is

---

15. *See, e.g., Shudson,* "Public, Private and Professional Lives: The Correspondence of David Dudley Field and Samuel Bowles," 21 *Am. J. Legal Hist.* 191 (1977). Gordon, "The Independence of Lawyers, 68 *B.U.L.Rev.* 1 (1988). For a more general analysis of the erosion of secular ideals *see* R. Sennett, *The Fall of Public Man* (1977), and A. MacIntyre, *After Virtue* (1981).

16. *See* Abel, "Why Does the ABA Promulgate Ethical Rules?" 59 *Tex. L.Rev.* 639 (1981); Simon, "The Ideology of Advocacy," 1978 *Wis.L.Rev.* 29; Rhode, "Ethical Perspectives on Legal Practice" 37 *Stan.L.Rev.* 589 (1985).

17. *See* L. Festinger, *A Theory of Cognitive Dissonance (1957), discussed infra at 179–181; Wasserstrom,* Lawyers as Professionals: Some Moral Issues, 5 *Human Rights 1 (1975)* infra.

18. Luban, "The Adversary System Excuse," in *The Good Lawyer* (D. Luban ed. 1983).

conformity to established roles necessary to preserve legitimate client expectations and fundamental social values? At what point does such conformity become a substitute for more reflective moral assessments? What would such assessments entail?

William K. Frankena, Ethics

14–23 (2d ed. 1973).*

Teleological Theories

Having agreed on one ground or another that the standard of right and wrong cannot be simply the prevailing set of moral rules, moral philosophers have offered us a variety of alternative standards. In general their views have been of two sorts: (1) *deontological* theories and (2) *teleological* ones. A teleological theory says that the basic or ultimate criterion or standard of what is morally right, wrong, obligatory, etc., is the nonmoral value that is brought into being. The final appeal, directly or indirectly, must be to the comparative amount of good produced, or rather to the comparative balance of good over evil produced. Thus, an act is *right* if and only if it or the rule under which it falls produces, will probably produce, or is intended to produce *at least as great a balance of good over evil* as any available alternative; an act is *wrong* if and only if it does not do so. An act *ought to be done* if and only if it or the rule under which it falls produces, will probably produce, or is intended to produce *a greater balance of good over evil* than any available alternative.

It is important to notice here that, for a teleologist, the moral quality or value of actions, persons, or traits of character is dependent on the comparative nonmoral value of what they bring about or try to bring about. For the moral quality or value of something to depend on the moral value of whatever it promotes would be circular. Teleological theories, then, make the right, the obligatory, and the morally good dependent on the nonmorally good. Accordingly, they also make the theory of moral obligation and moral value dependent, in a sense, on the theory of nonmoral value. In order to know whether something is right, ought to be done, or is morally good, one must first know what is good in the nonmoral sense *and* whether the thing in question promotes or is intended to promote what is good in this sense.

It should also be noticed, however, that teleologists may hold various views about what is good in the nonmoral sense. Teleolo-

* William K. Frankena, ETHICS, 2nd Ed., © 1973, pp. 14–23. Reprinted by permission of Prentice-Hall, Inc., Englewood Cliffs, N.J.

gists have often been hedonists, identifying the good with pleasure and evil with pain, and concluding that the right course or rule of action is that which produces at least as great a balance of pleasure over pain as any alternative would. But they may be and have sometimes been non-hedonists, identifying the good with power, knowledge, self-realization, perfection, etc. This fact must not be forgotten when we are evaluating the teleological theory of obligation. All that is necessary is that the teleologist have *some* view about what is good or bad, and that he determine what is right or obligatory by asking what is conducive to the greatest balance of good over evil.

Deontological theories deny what teleological theories affirm. They deny that the right, the obligatory, and the morally good are wholly, whether directly or indirectly, a function of what is nonmorally good or of what promotes the greatest balance of good over evil for self, one's society, or the world as a whole. They assert that there are other considerations that may make an action or rule right or obligatory besides the goodness or badness of its consequences—certain features of the act itself other than the *value* it brings into existence, for example, the fact that it keeps a promise, is just, or is commanded by God or by the state. Teleologists believe that there is one and only one basic or ultimate right-making characteristic, namely, the comparative value (nonmoral) of what is, probably will be, or is intended to be brought into being. Deontologists either deny that this characteristic is right-making at all or they insist that there are other basic or ultimate right-making characteristics as well. For them the principle of maximizing the balance of good over evil, no matter for whom, is either not a moral criterion or standard at all, or, at least, it is not the only basic or ultimate one.

To put the matter in yet another way: a deontologist contends that it is possible for an action or rule of action to be the morally right or obligatory one even if it does not promote the greatest possible balance of good over evil for self, society, or universe. It may be right or obligatory simply because of some other fact about it or because of its own nature. It follows that a deontologist may also adopt any kind of a view about what is good or bad in the nonmoral sense.

Teleologists differ on the question of whose good it is that one ought to try to promote. *Ethical egoism* holds that one is always to do what will promote his own greatest good—that an act or rule of action is right if and only if it promotes at least as great a balance of good over evil for him in the long run as any alternative would, and wrong if it does not. This view was held by

Epicurus, Hobbes, and Nietzsche, among others. *Ethical univer-salism,* or what is usually called *utilitarianism,* takes the position that the ultimate end is the greatest general good—that an act or rule of action is right if and only if it is, or probably is, conducive to at least as great a balance of good over evil in the universe as a whole as any alternative would be, wrong if it is not, and obligato-ry if it is or probably is conducive to the greatest possible balance of good over evil in the universe. The so-called utilitarians, for example, Jeremy Bentham and John Stuart Mill, have usually been hedonists in their view about what is good, asserting that the moral end is the greatest balance of pleasure over pain. But some utilitarians are not hedonists, for example, G.E. Moore and Has-tings Rashdall, and so have been called "Ideal" utilitarians. That is, utilitarianism is a certain kind of teleological theory of obli-gation and does not entail any particular theory of value, although a utilitarian must accept some particular theory of value.

It would also be possible, of course, to adopt teleological theories intermediate between ethical egoism and utilitarianism, for example, theories that say the right act or rule is one condu-cive to the greatest balance of good over evil for a certain group—one's nation, class, family, or race. A pure *ethical altruist* might even contend that the right act or rule is the one that most promotes the good of *other* people. We shall, however, limit our coming discussion to egoism and universalism.

Deontological Theories

Deontological theories are also of different kinds, depending on the role they give to general rules. *Act-deontological theories* maintain that the basic judgments of obligation are all purely particular ones like "In this situation I should do so and so," and that general ones like "We ought always to keep our promises" are unavailable, useless, or at best derivative from particular judgments. Extreme act-deontologists maintain that we can and must see or somehow decide separately in each particular situa-tion what is the right or obligatory thing to do, without appealing to any rules and also without looking to see what will promote the greatest balance of good over evil for oneself or the world. Such a view was held by E.F. Carritt (in *Theory of Morals*) and possibly by II. A. Prichard; and was at least suggested by Aristotle when he said that in determining what the golden mean is "the decision rests with perception," and by Butler when he wrote that if:

> ... any plain honest man, before he engages in any course of action, ask himself, Is this I am going about right, or is it wrong? ... I do not in the least doubt but that this question

would be answered agreeably to truth and virtue, by almost any fair man in almost any circumstance [without any general rule].

Today, with an emphasis on "decision" rather than "intuition" and with an admission of difficulty and anxiety, this is the view of most existentialists.   In a less extreme form, act-deontologism allows that general rules can be built up on the basis of particular cases and may then be useful in determining what should be done on later occasions.   But it cannot allow that a general rule may ever supersede a well-taken particular judgment as to what should be done.   What is called "situation ethics" today includes both of these forms of act-deontologism.

Rule-deontologists hold that the standard of right and wrong consists of one or more rules—either fairly concrete ones like "We ought always to tell the truth" or very abstract ones like Henry Sidgwick's Principle of Justice: "It cannot be right for A to treat B in a manner in which it would be wrong for B to treat A, merely on the ground that they are two different individuals, and without there being any difference between the natures or circumstances of the two which can be stated as a reasonable ground for difference of treatment."   Against the teleologists, they insist, of course, that these rules are valid independently of whether or not they promote the good.   Against act-deontologists, they contend that these rules are basic, and are not derived by induction from particular cases.   In fact, they assert that judgments about what to do in particular cases are always to be determined in the light of these rules, as they were by Socrates in the *Apology* and *Crito*. The following writers are or were rule-deontologists: Samuel Clarke, Richard Price, Thomas Reid, W.D. Ross, Immanuel Kant, and perhaps Butler.   People who take "conscience" to be our guide or standard in morality are usually either rule-deontologists or act-deontologists, depending on whether they think of conscience primarily as providing us with general rules or as making particular judgments in particular situations.

We may illustrate these different theories to some extent by using the example of Socrates in the *Crito*.   If he had tried to decide his problem wholly by asking what would be for his own good, he would have been an ethical egoist.   If he had asked merely whether his escaping or not escaping would have the best results for society in general, he would have been a kind of utilitarian—what will later be called an act-utilitarian.   Actually, his procedure is that of a rule-deontologist, since he simply appeals to certain rules.   But, if he were to go on to defend those rules on the ground that having such rules and always acting on them is for the greatest general good, then he would be a kind of utilitarian after all—what will later be called a rule-utilitarian.

Ethical Egoism

We must now discuss these various normative theories, beginning with ethical egoism, which represents one rather extreme kind of reaction to the ethics of traditional rules. This is the ethics of what Butler calls self-love and of what Freudians call the ego . . . .

Psychological Egoism

The main argument that has been used as a basis for ethical egoism is a psychological one, an argument from human nature. We are all so constituted, it is said, that one always seeks one's own advantage or welfare, or always does what he thinks will give him the greatest balance of good over evil. In Butler's terms, this means that "self-love" is the only basic "principle" in human nature; in one set of contemporary terms, it means that "ego-satisfaction" is the final aim of all activity or that "the pleasure principle" is the basic "drive" in every individual. If this is so, the argument continues, we must recognize this fact in our moral theory and infer that our basic ethical principle must be that of self-love, albeit cool self-love. To hold anything else is to fly in the face of the facts.

It is usual here to object that one cannot logically infer an ethical conclusion from a psychological premise in this way. This objection has some force, as we shall see in Chapter 6. But the egoist may not be doing this. He may only be contending that, if human nature is as he describes it, it is simply unrealistic and even unreasonable to propose that we ought basically to do anything but what is for our own greatest good. For, in a sense, we cannot do anything but this, except by mistake, and, as a famous dictum has it, "Ought implies can." Thus understood, the psychological argument for ethical egoism is at least reasonable, even if it is not logically compelling.

Thus, ethical egoism has generally presupposed what is called *psychological egoism*—that each of us is always seeking his own greatest good, whether this is conceived of as pleasure, happiness, knowledge, power, self-realization, or a mixed life. But must we regard psychological egoism (not to be confused with *psychological hedonism*, which we shall discuss in Chapter 5) as true? That it is true is by no means agreed on by recent psychologists, though it is asserted by some Freudians. The question is not whether egoism is strong in human nature but whether we ever have any concern or desire for the welfare of others except as a means to our own, any concern for or interest in their welfare for its own sake, which is not derived from our concern for our own welfare. In dealing with this question, I shall borrow largely from Butler, whose discussion of psychological egoism is justly famous. (1) He maintains that the desire for one's own good presupposes or builds upon the existence of more basic desires for food, fame, sex, etc. If we did not have any of these "primary appetites," we would not have any good to be concerned about; our welfare consists of the satisfaction of such desires. (2) It follows, he says, that the object of these basic desires is not one's own welfare; it is food, fame, sex, etc., as the case may be. One's own good is not the object of all of one's desires but only of one of them, self-love. (3) He adds that in some cases the object of a basic desire is something for oneself, for example, food or the eating of food. But there is no necessity about this; the object may be something for someone else, for example, that he enjoy the sight of the ocean. In other words, there may be altruistic impulses. There may also be a desire to do the right as such. Whether there are such desires or not is a question of empirical fact. (4) As a matter of fact, he goes on, there are such altruistic interests in the welfare or illfare of others (sheer malevolence, if it exists, is a desire that another experience pain for its own sake), as well as a desire to do the right as such. Our experience shows this. (5) Butler also reminds us that primary appetites such as sexual desire may even rebel against self-love, that is, may demand and obtain satisfaction even when we know this is not for our own greatest good. This is true even of altruistic impulses, for example, in cases of self-sacrifice.

At this point it is usual for the psychological egoist to say, "Yes, we do things for others, but we get satisfaction out of doing them, and this satisfaction is our end in doing them. Doing them is only a means to this satisfaction. Hence, even in doing 'altruistic' things for others, like taking them to see the ocean, we are seeking our own good." To this Butler replies (6) that, of course, we get satisfaction out of doing such things, but we do not want to do them because of the satisfaction we expect to get out of them, we get satisfaction out of doing them because we wanted to do them. The psychological egoist is putting the cart before the horse. He confuses the *object* of B's desire (A's enjoying the ocean) with the *satisfaction* that results for B when this object is attained. Suppose B fails to get A to the ocean or that A does not enjoy seeing it. Then B will experience frustration, but it will not follow that this frustration is his goal; he experiences frustration because his goal is to have A enjoy himself.

The egoist may come back by saying, "Still, I always do what I want to do, even when I do something for someone else. And the satisfaction that results is *my* satisfaction. So I am the center of it all. Egoism is still true." But if this is all that psychological egoism is claiming, the altruist has nothing to fear. For what he means by saying that there is altruism in human nature is merely that we sometimes want to do something for others and that we are so constituted as to get satisfaction out of doing so. So long as the egoist grants this, the altruist has all he is contending for, namely, that, in David Hume's words,

> ... there is some benevolence, however small, ... some particle of the dove kneaded into our frame, along with the elements of the wolf and serpent.

Already in Butler's day, John Clarke had an answer of sorts to Butler's kind of argument. He admitted that we get pleasure out of doing things for others and out of seeing them enjoy themselves, just as we get pleasure out of eating. He insisted, however, that we get these pleasures just because of the way we are made, not because we have some prior desire for food or for the happiness of others, and that we come to desire food and the happiness of others only because we have found pleasure in these things and wish to enjoy such pleasures again. In short, one's only *object* of desire and action is pleasure for oneself. This position does sidestep Butler's argument in a way, for Butler assumes that we must first desire food or the happiness of others if we are to derive enjoyment from them, or, in other words, that pleasure comes to us only via the satisfaction of desires for other things. On the other hand, Clarke allows that we are so built as to enjoy promoting or observing the happiness of other people, and to allow this is to recognize that there is a real altruism in human beings of a kind that psychological egoists seem to wish to deny. ...

Two Kinds of Utilitarianism

We must distinguish two kinds of utilitarianism: *act-utilitarianism* and *rule-utilitarianism*. Act-utilitarians hold that in general or at least where it is practicable one is to tell what is right or obligatory by appealing directly to the principle of utility or, in other words, by trying to see which of the actions open to him will or is likely to produce the greatest balance of good over evil in the universe. One must ask "What effect will *my* doing *this* act in *this* situation have on the general balance of good over evil?", not "What effect will *everyone's* doing this *kind* of act in this *kind* of situation have on the general balance of good over evil?" Generalizations like "Telling the truth is probably always for the greatest general good" or "Telling the truth is generally for the greatest general good" may be useful as guides based on past experience; but the crucial question is always whether telling the truth in *this* case is for the greatest general good or not. It can never be right to act on the rule of telling the truth if we have good independent grounds for thinking that it would be for the greatest general good not to tell the truth in a particular case, any more than it can be correct to say that all crows are black in the presence of one that is not. Bentham and G.E. Moore may have held such a view, perhaps even Mill.

Rule-utilitarianism is a rather different view which has also been attributed to Mill and which has been finding favor recently. Like rule-deontologism, it emphasizes the centrality of rules in morality and insists that we are generally, if not always, to tell what to do in particular situations by appeal to a rule like that of truth-telling rather than by asking what particular action will have the best consequences in the situation in question. But, unlike deontologism, it adds that we are always to determine our rules by asking which rules will promote the greatest general good for everyone. That is, the question is not which *action* has the greatest utility, but which *rule* has. We should ask, when we are proposing to do something, not "What will happen if I do that in this case?" but "What would happen if everyone were to do that in such cases?"—a question we do, in fact, often ask in moral deliberations. The principle of utility comes in, normally at least, not in determining what particular action to perform (this is normally determined by the rules), but in determining what the rules shall be. Rules must be selected, maintained, revised, and replaced on the basis of their utility and not on any other basis. The principle of utility is still the ultimate standard, but it is to be appealed to at the level of rules rather than at the level of particular judgments.

The act-utilitarian may allow rules to be used; but if he does, he must conceive of a rule like "Tell the truth" as follows: "Telling the truth is *generally* for the greatest general good." By contrast, the rule-utilitarian must conceive of it thus: "Our *always* telling the truth is for the greatest general good." Or, "It is for the greatest good if we *always* tell the truth."

"Professional Responsibility: Report of the Joint Conference"

44 American Bar Association Journal, 1159–62 (1958).*

[Preface]

The Joint Conference on Professional Responsibility was established in 1952 by the American Bar Association and the Association of American Law Schools. At the first meeting of the Conference the general problem discussed was that of bringing home to the law student, the lawyer and the public an understanding of the nature of the lawyer's professional responsibilities. All present considered that the chief obstacle to the success of this undertaking lay in "the adversary system." Those who had attempted to arrange conferences on professional ethics between lawyers, on the one side, and philosophers and theologians, on the other, observed that communication broke down at this point. Similarly, those who had attempted to teach ethical principles to law students found that the students were uneasy about the adversary system, some thinking of it as an unwholesome compromise with the combativeness of human nature, others vaguely approving of it but disturbed by their inability to articulate its proper limits. Finally, it was observed that the legal profession is itself generally not very philosophic about this issue. Confronted by the layman's charge that he is nothing but a hired brain and voice, the lawyer often finds it difficult to convey an insight into the value of the adversary system or an understanding of the tacit restraints with which it is infused.

Accordingly, it was decided that the first need was for a reasoned statement of the lawyer's responsibilities, set in the context of the adversary system. The statement printed below is intended to meet that need. It is not expected that all lawyers will agree with every detail of the statement, particularly in matters of emphasis. It was considered, however, that the statement would largely fail of its purpose if it were confined to generalities too broad to elicit dissent, but, by the same token, too broad to sharpen insight or to stimulate useful discussion.

. . .

II

The lawyer appearing as an advocate before a tribunal presents, as persuasively as he can, the facts and the law of the case as seen from the standpoint of his client's interest. It is essential that both the lawyer and the public understand clearly the nature

* Reprinted with permission from the
American Bar Association Journal.

of the role thus discharged. Such an understanding is required not only to appreciate the need for an adversary presentation of issues, but also in order to perceive truly the limits partisan advocacy must impose on itself if it is to remain wholesome and useful.

In a very real sense it may be said that the integrity of the adjudicative process itself depends upon the participation of the advocate. This becomes apparent when we contemplate the nature of the task assumed by any arbiter who attempts to decide a dispute without the aid of partisan advocacy.

Such an arbiter must undertake, not only the role of judge, but that of representative for both of the litigants. Each of these roles must be played to the full without being muted by qualifications derived from the others. When he is developing for each side the most effective statement of its case, the arbiter must put aside his neutrality and permit himself to be moved by a sympathetic identification sufficiently intense to draw from his mind all that it is capable of giving,—in analysis, patience and creative power. When he resumes his neutral position, he must be able to view with distrust the fruits of this identification and be ready to reject the products of his own best mental efforts. The difficulties of this undertaking are obvious. If it is true that a man in his time must play many parts, it is scarcely given to him to play them all at once.

It is small wonder, then, that failure generally attends the attempt to dispense with the distinct roles traditionally implied in adjudication. What generally occurs in practice is that at some early point a familiar pattern will seem to emerge from the evidence; an accustomed label is waiting for the case and, without awaiting further proofs, this label is promptly assigned to it. It is a mistake to suppose that this premature cataloguing must necessarily result from impatience, prejudice or mental sloth. Often it proceeds from a very understandable desire to bring the hearing into some order and coherence, for without some tentative theory of the case there is no standard of relevance by which testimony may be measured. But what starts as a preliminary diagnosis designed to direct the inquiry tends, quickly and imperceptibly, to become a fixed conclusion, as all that confirms the diagnosis makes a strong imprint on the mind, while all that runs counter to it is received with diverted attention.

An adversary presentation seems the only effective means for combatting this natural human tendency to judge too swiftly in terms of the familiar that which is not yet fully known. The arguments of counsel hold the case, as it were, in suspension between two opposing interpretations of it. While the proper classification of the case is thus kept unresolved, there is time to explore all of its peculiarities and nuances.

These are the contributions made by partisan advocacy during the public hearing of the cause. When we take into account the preparations that must precede the hearing, the essential quality of the advocate's contribution becomes even more apparent. Preceding the hearing, inquiries must be instituted to determine what facts can be proved or seem sufficiently established to warrant a formal test of their truth during the hearing. There must also be a preliminary analysis of the issues, so that the hearing may have form and direction. These preparatory measures are indispensable whether or not the parties involved in the controversy are represented by advocates.

Where that representation is present there is an obvious advantage in the fact that the area of dispute may be greatly reduced by an exchange of written pleadings or by stipulations of counsel. Without the participation of someone who can act responsibly for each of the parties, this essential narrowing of the issues becomes impossible. But here again the true significance of partisan advocacy lies deeper, touching once more the integrity of the adjudicative process itself. It is only through the advocate's participation that the hearing may remain in fact what it purports to be in theory: a public trial of the facts and issues. Each advocate comes to the hearing prepared to present his proofs and arguments, knowing at the same time that his arguments may fail to persuade and that his proofs may be rejected as inadequate. It is a part of his role to absorb these possible disappointments. The deciding tribunal, on the other hand, comes to the hearing uncommitted. It has not represented to the public that any fact can be proved, that any argument is sound, or that any particular way of stating a litigant's case is the most effective expression of its merits.

The matter assumes a very different aspect when the deciding tribunal is compelled to take into its own hands the preparations that must precede the public hearing. In such a case the tribunal cannot truly be said to come to the hearing uncommitted, for it has itself appointed the channels along which the public inquiry is to run. If an unexpected turn in the testimony reveals a miscalculation in the design of these channels, there is no advocate to absorb the blame. The deciding tribunal is under a strong temptation to keep the hearing moving within the boundaries originally set for it. The result may be that the hearing loses its character as an open trial of the facts and issues, and becomes instead a ritual designed to provide public confirmation for what the tribunal considers it has already established in private. When this occurs adjudication acquires the taint affecting all institutions that become subject to manipulation, presenting one aspect to the public, another to knowing participants.

These, then, are the reasons for believing that partisan advocacy plays a vital and essential role in one of the most fundamental procedures of a democratic society. But if we were to put all of these detailed considerations to one side, we should still be confronted by the fact that, in whatever form adjudication may appear, the experienced judge or arbitrator desires and actively seeks to obtain an adversary presentation of the issues. Only when he has had the benefit of intelligent and vigorous advocacy on both sides can he feel fully confident of his decision.

Viewed in this light, the role of the lawyer as a partisan advocate appears not as a regrettable necessity, but as an indispensable part of a larger ordering of affairs. The institution of advocacy is not a concession to the frailties of human nature, but an expression of human insight in the design of a social framework within which man's capacity for impartial judgment can attain its fullest realization.

When advocacy is thus viewed, it becomes clear by what principle limits must be set to partisanship. The advocate plays his role well when zeal for his client's cause promotes a wise and informed decision of the case. He plays his role badly, and trespasses against the obligations of professional responsibilities, when his desire to win leads him to muddy the headwaters of decision, when, instead of lending a needed perspective to the controversy, he distorts and obscures its true nature. ...

Thus, partisan advocacy is a form of public service so long as it aids the process of adjudication; it ceases to be when it hinders that process, when it misleads, distorts and obfuscates, when it renders the task of the deciding tribunal not easier, but more difficult. Judges are inevitably the mirrors of the Bar practicing before them; they can with difficulty rise above the sources on which they must depend in reaching their decision. The primary responsibility for preserving adjudication as a meaningful and useful social institution rests ultimately with the practicing legal profession.

. . .

**Richard Wasserstrom, "Lawyers as Professionals:
Some Moral Issues"**

5 Human Rights, 1–15 (1975).

In this paper I examine two moral criticisms of lawyers which, if well-founded, are fundamental. Neither is new but each appears to apply with particular force today. Both tend to be made by those not in the mainstream of the legal profession and to be rejected by those who are in it. Both in some sense concern the lawyer-client relationship.

The first criticism centers around the lawyer's stance toward the world at large. The accusation is that the lawyer-client relationship renders the lawyer at best systematically amoral and at worst more than occasionally immoral in his or her dealings with the rest of mankind.

The second criticism focuses upon the relationship between the lawyer and the client. Here the charge is that it is the lawyer-client relationship which is morally objectionable because it is a relationship in which the lawyer dominates and in which the lawyer typically, and perhaps inevitably, treats the client in both an impersonal and a paternalistic fashion.

. . .

[The first] issue I propose to examine concerns the ways the professional-client relationship affects the professional's stance toward the world at large. The primary question that is presented is whether there is adequate justification for the kind of moral universe that comes to be inhabited by the lawyer as he or she goes through professional life. For at best the lawyer's world is a simplified moral world; often it is an amoral one; and more than occasionally, perhaps, an overtly immoral one.

. . .

As I have already noted, one central feature of the professions in general and of law in particular is that there is a special, complicated relationship between the professional, and the client or patient. For each of the parties in this relationship, but especially for the professional, the behavior that is involved is to a very significant degree, what I call, role-differentiated behavior. And this is significant because it is the nature of role-differentiated behavior that it often makes it both appropriate and desirable for the person in a particular role to put to one side considerations of various sorts—and especially various moral considerations—that would otherwise be relevant if not decisive. . . .

.[For example, to be a parent is,] in probably every human culture, to be involved in role-differentiated behavior. In our own culture, and once again in most, if not all, human cultures, as a parent one is entitled, if not obligated, to prefer the interests of one's own children over those of children generally. That is to say, it is regarded as appropriate for a parent to allocate excessive goods to his or her own children, even though other children may have substantially more pressing and genuine needs for these same items. ...

In the role of a parent, the claims of other children vis-à-vis one's own are, if not rendered morally irrelevant, certainly rendered less morally significant. In short, the role-differentiated character of the situation alters the relevant moral point of view enormously. ... It is, of course, conceivable that plausible and even thoroughly convincing arguments exist for the desirability of the role-differentiated behavior and its attendant neglect of what would otherwise be morally relevant considerations. Nonetheless, it is, I believe, also the case that the burden of proof, so to speak, is always upon the proponent of the desirability of this kind of role-differentiated behavior. ...

Consider, more specifically, the role-differentiated behavior of the lawyer. Conventional wisdom has it that where the attorney-client relationship exists, the point of view of the attorney is properly different—and appreciably so—from that which would be appropriate in the absence of the attorney-client relationship. For where the attorney-client relationship exists, it is often appropriate and many times even obligatory for the attorney to do things that, all other things being equal, an ordinary person need not, and should not do. What is characteristic of this role of a lawyer is the lawyer's required indifference to a wide variety of ends and consequences that in other contexts would be of undeniable moral significance. Once a lawyer represents a client, the lawyer has a duty to make his or her expertise fully available in the realization of the end sought by the client, irrespective, for the most part, of the moral worth to which the end will be put or the character of the client who seeks to utilize it. Provided that the end sought is not illegal, the lawyer is, in essence, an amoral technician whose peculiar skills and knowledge in respect to the law are available to those with whom the relationship of client is established. The question, as I have indicated, is whether this particular and pervasive feature of professionalism is itself justifiable. At a minimum, I do not think any of the typical, simple answers will suffice.

One such answer focuses upon and generalizes from the criminal defense lawyer. For what is probably the most familiar aspect of this role-differentiated character of the lawyer's activity is that of the defense of a client charged with a crime. The received view within the profession (and to a lesser degree within the society at large) is that having once agreed to represent the client, the lawyer is under an obligation to do his or her best to defend that person at trial, irrespective, for instance, even of the lawyer's belief in the client's innocence. ... I suspect that many persons find this an attractive and admirable feature of the life of a legal professional. I know that often I do. The justifications are varied and, as I shall argue below, probably convincing.

But part of the difficulty is that the irrelevance of the guilt or innocence of an accused client by no means exhausts the altered perspective of the lawyer's conscience, even in criminal cases. For in the course of defending an accused, an attorney may have, as a part of his or her duty of representation, the obligation to invoke procedures and practices which are themselves morally objectionable and of which the lawyer in other contexts might thoroughly disapprove. And these situations, I think, are somewhat less comfortable to confront. For example, in California, the case law permits a defendant in a rape case to secure in some circumstances an order from the court requiring the complaining witness, that is the rape victim, to submit to a psychiatric examination before trial. For no other crime is such a pretrial remedy available. In no other case can the victim of a crime be required to undergo psychiatric examination at the request of the defendant on the ground that the results of the examination may help the defendant prove that the offense did not take place. I think such a rule is wrong and is reflective of the sexist bias of the law in respect to rape. I certainly do not think it right that rape victims should be singled out by the law for this kind of special pretrial treatment, and I am skeptical about the morality of any involuntary psychiatric examination of witnesses. Nonetheless, it appears to be a part of the role-differentiated obligation of a lawyer for a defendant charged with rape to seek to take advantage of this particular rule of law—irrespective of the independent moral view he or she may have of the rightness or wrongness of such a rule.

Nor, it is important to point out, is this peculiar, strikingly amoral behavior limited to the lawyer involved with the workings of the criminal law. Most clients come to lawyers to get the lawyers to help them do things that they could not easily do

without the assistance provided by the lawyer's special competence. ...

And in each case, the role-differentiated character of the
lawyer's way of being tends to render irrelevant what would
otherwise be morally relevant considerations. Suppose that a
client desires to make a will disinheriting her children because
they opposed the war in Vietnam. Should the lawyer refuse to
draft the will because the lawyer thinks this is a bad reason to
disinherit one's children? Suppose a client can avoid the payment
of taxes through a loophole only available to a few wealthy
taxpayers. Should the lawyer refuse to tell the client of a loophole because the lawyer thinks it an unfair advantage for the
rich? Suppose a client wants to start a corporation that will
manufacture, distribute and promote a harmful but not illegal
substance, *e.g.,* cigarettes. Should the lawyer refuse to prepare
the articles of incorporation for the corporation? In each case, the
accepted view within the profession is that these matters are just
of no concern to the lawyer *qua* lawyer. The lawyer need not of
course agree to represent the client (and that is equally true for
the unpopular client accused of a heinous crime), but there is
nothing wrong with representing a client whose aims and purposes are quite immoral. And having agreed to do so, the lawyer
is required to provide the best possible assistance, without regard
to his or her disapproval of the objective that is sought.

The lesson, on this view, is clear. The job of the lawyer, so
the argument typically concludes, is not to approve or disapprove
of the character of his or her client, the cause for which the client
seeks the lawyer's assistance, or the avenues provided by the law
to achieve that which the client wants to accomplish. ... And
the difficulty I have with all of this is that the arguments for such
a way of life seem to be not quite so convincing to me as they do to
many lawyers. I am, that is, at best uncertain that it is a good
thing for lawyers to be so professional—for them to embrace so
completely this role-differentiated way of approaching matters.

More specifically, if it is correct that this is the perspective of
lawyers in particular and professionals in general, is it right that
this should be their perspective? Is it right that the lawyer should
be able so easily to put to one side otherwise difficult problems
with the answer: but these are not and cannot be my concern as a
lawyer? What do we gain and what do we lose from having a
social universe in which there are professionals such as lawyers,
who, as such, inhabit a universe of the sort I have been trying to
describe?

One difficulty in even thinking about all of this is that lawyers may not be very objective or detached in their attempts to work the problem through. For one feature of this simplified, intellectual world is that it is often a very comfortable one to inhabit.

To be sure, on occasion, a lawyer may find it uncomfortable to represent an extremely unpopular client. On occasion, too, a lawyer may feel ill at ease invoking a rule of law or practice which he or she thinks to be an unfair or undesirable one. Nonetheless, for most lawyers, most of the time, pursuing the interests of one's clients is an attractive and satisfying way to live in part just because the moral world of the lawyer is a simpler, less complicated, and less ambiguous world than the moral world of ordinary life. There is, I think, something quite seductive about being able to turn aside so many ostensibly difficult moral dilemmas and decisions with the reply: but that is not my concern; my job as a lawyer is not to judge the rights and wrongs of the client or the cause; it is to defend as best I can my client's interests. ...

But there is, of course, also an argument which seeks to demonstrate that it is good and not merely comfortable for lawyers to behave this way.

It is good, so the argument goes, that the lawyer's behavior and concomitant point of view are role-differentiated because the lawyer *qua* lawyer participates in a complex institution which functions well only if the individuals adhere to their institutional roles.

For example, when there is a conflict between individuals, or between the state and an individual, there is a well-established institutional mechanism by which to get that dispute resolved. That mechanism is the trial in which each side is represented by a lawyer whose job it is both to present his or her client's case in the most attractive, forceful light and to seek to expose the weaknesses and defects in the case of the opponent.

When an individual is charged with having committed a crime, the trial is the mechanism by which we determine in our society whether or not the person is in fact guilty. Just imagine what would happen if lawyers were to refuse, for instance, to represent persons whom they thought to be guilty. In a case where the guilt of a person seemed clear, it might turn out that some individuals would be deprived completely of the opportunity to have the system determine whether or not they are in fact guilty. The private judgment of individual lawyers would in effect be substituted for the public, institutional judgment of the judge and jury. The amorality of lawyers helps to guarantee that every criminal defendant will have his or her day in court.

In addition, of course, appearances can be deceiving. Persons who appear before trial to be clearly guilty do sometimes turn out to be innocent. Even persons who confess their guilt to their attorney occasionally turn out to have lied or to have been mistaken.

. . .

Nor is the amorality of the institutional role of the lawyer restricted to the defense of those accused of crimes. As was indicated earlier, when the lawyer functions in his most usual role, he or she functions as a counselor, as a professional whose task it is to help people realize those objectives and ends that the law permits them to obtain and which cannot be obtained without the attorney's special competence in the law. The attorney may think it wrong to disinherit one's children because of their views about the Vietnam war, but here the attorney's complaint is really with the laws of inheritance and not with his or her client. The attorney may think the tax provision an unfair, unjustifiable loophole, but once more the complaint is really with the Internal Revenue Code and not with the client who seeks to take advantage of it. And these matters, too, lie beyond the ambit of the lawyer's moral point of view as institutional counselor and facilitator. If lawyers were to substitute their own private views of what ought to be legally permissible and impermissible for those of the legislature, this would constitute a surreptitious and undesirable shift from a democracy to an oligarchy of lawyers. For given the fact that lawyers are needed to effectuate the wishes of clients, the lawyer ought to make his or her skills available to those who seek them without regard for the particular objectives of the client.

Now, all of this certainly makes some sense. These arguments are neither specious nor without force. ...

As I indicated earlier, I do believe that the amoral behavior of the *criminal* defense lawyer is justifiable. But I think that jurisdiction depends at least as much upon the special needs of an accused as upon any more general defense of a lawyer's role-differentiated behavior. As a matter of fact I think it likely that many persons such as myself have been misled by the special features of the criminal case. Because a deprivation of liberty is so serious, because the prosecutorial resources of the state are so vast, and because, perhaps, of a serious skepticism about the rightness of punishment even where wrongdoing has occurred, it is easy to accept the view that it makes sense to charge the defense counsel with the job of making the best possible case for the accused—without regard, so to speak, for the merits. This coupled with the fact that it is an adversarial proceeding succeeds, I think, in justifying the amorality of the criminal defense counsel. But this does not, however, justify a comparable perspective on the part of lawyers generally. Once we leave the peculiar situation of the criminal defense lawyer, I think it quite likely that the role-differentiated amorality of the lawyer is almost certainly excessive and at times inappropriate. That is to say, this special case to one side, I am inclined to think that we might all be better served if lawyers were to see themselves less as subject to role-differentiated behavior and more as subject to the demands of the moral point of view. In this sense it may be that we need a good deal less rather than more professionalism in our society generally and among lawyers in particular.

Moreover, even if I am wrong about all this, four things do seem to me to be true and important.

First, all of the arguments that support the role-differentiated amorality of the lawyer on institutional grounds can succeed only if the enormous degree of trust and confidence in the institutions themselves is itself justified. If the institutions work well and fairly, there may be good sense to deferring important moral concerns and criticisms to another time and place, to the level of institutional criticism and assessment. But the less certain we are entitled to be of either the rightness or the self-corrective nature of the larger institutions of which the professional is a part, the less apparent it is that we should encourage the professional to avoid direct engagement with the moral issues as they arise. And we are, today, I believe, certainly entitled to be quite skeptical both of the fairness and of the capacity for self-correction of our larger institutional mechanisms, including the legal system. To the degree to which the institutional rules and practices are unjust, unwise or undesirable, to that same degree is the case for the role-differentiated behavior of the lawyer weakened if not destroyed.

Second, it is clear that there are definite character traits that the professional such as the lawyer must take on if the system is to work. What is less clear is that they are admirable ones. Even if the role-differentiated amorality of the professional lawyer is justified by the virtues of the adversary system, this also means that the lawyer *qua* lawyer will be encouraged to be competitive rather than cooperative; aggressive rather than accommodating; ruthless rather than compassionate; and pragmatic rather than principled. ... It is surely neither accidental nor unimportant that these are the same character traits that are emphasized and valued by the capitalist ethic—and on precisely analogous grounds. Because the ideals of professionalism and capitalism are the dominant ones within our culture, it is harder than most of us suspect even to take seriously the suggestion that radically different styles of living, kinds of occupational outlooks, and types of social institutions might be possible, let alone preferable.

Third, there is a special feature of the role-differentiated behavior of the lawyer that distinguishes it from the comparable behavior of other professionals. What I have in mind can be brought out through the following question: Why is it that it seems far less plausible to talk critically about the amorality of the doctor, for instance, who treats all patients irrespective of their moral character than it does to talk critically about the comparable amorality of the lawyer?

. . .

The answer, I think, is twofold. To begin with (and this I think is the less interesting point) it is, so to speak, intrinsically good to try to cure disease, but in no comparable way is it intrinsically good to try to win every lawsuit or help every client realize his or her objective. In addition (and this I take to be the truly interesting point), the lawyer's behavior is different in kind from the doctor's. The lawyer—and especially the lawyer as advocate—directly says and affirms things. The lawyer makes the case for the client. He or she tries to explain, persuade and convince others that the client's cause should prevail. The lawyer lives with and within a dilemma that is not shared by other professionals. If the lawyer actually believes everything that he or she asserts on behalf of the client, then it appears to be proper to regard the lawyer as in fact embracing and endorsing the points of view that he or she articulates. If the lawyer does not in fact believe what is urged by way of argument, if the lawyer is only playing a role, then it appears to be proper to tax the lawyer with hypocrisy and insincerity. To be sure, actors in a play take on roles and say things that the characters, not the actors, believe. But we know it is a play and that they are actors. The law courts are not, however, theaters, and the lawyers both talk about justice and they genuinely seek to persuade. The fact that the lawyer's words, thoughts, and convictions are, apparently, for sale and at the service of the client helps us, I think, to understand the peculiar hostility which is more than occasionally uniquely directed by lay persons toward lawyers. The verbal, role-differentiated behavior of the lawyer *qua* advocate puts the lawyer's integrity into question in a way that distinguishes the lawyer from the other professionals.

Fourth, and related closely to the three points just discussed, even if on balance the role-differentiated character of the lawyer's way of thinking and acting is ultimately deemed to be justifiable within the system on systemic instrumental grounds, it still remains the case that we do pay a social price for that way of thought and action. For to become and to be a professional, such as a lawyer, is to incorporate within oneself ways of behaving and ways of thinking that shape the whole person. It is especially hard, if not impossible, because of the nature of the professions, for one's professional way of thinking not to dominate one's entire adult life.   ...   In important respects, one's professional role becomes and is one's dominant role, so that for many persons at least they become their professional being. This is at a minimum a heavy price to pay for the professions as we know them in our culture, and especially so for lawyers. Whether it is an inevitable price is, I think, an open question, largely because the problem has not begun to be fully perceived as such by the professionals in general, the legal profession in particular, or by the educational institutions that train professionals.

Geoffrey C. Hazard, Jr., "Doing the Right Thing"
70 Washington Univ.Law Quarterly 3, 691–701 (1992).

A lawyer representing a client should try to "do the right thing." Stated in simplest terms, this is the ideal that inspires the recurrent call for lawyers to be more ethical. In the most recent decade, the call has been expressed in terms of "professionalism." In earlier years, the call was expressed as a demand that lawyers dedicate themselves to "serving the public interest" and in Victorian times it was expressed in terms of the "honor of the legal profession." However expressed, the quest is for greater virtue on the part of lawyers, both individually and as a profession.

· · ·

Within this framework ..., various premises are established about what is involved in "doing the right thing" in ordinary life. These commonly held premises are the basis on which comparison is made with professional ethics, including legal ethics. By a series of small and often unnoticed steps, therefore, the question of lawyers' ethics—and whether lawyers can ever do the right thing—is compared with the ethics of people in ordinary life. In this comparison lawyers' ethics usually come out poorly. Lawyers appear partisan rather than disinterested, guileful rather than open, grasping rather than generous, and duplicitous rather than truthful. The conclusion follows that lawyers do things as a matter of course—indeed do them as the essence of their vocation—that no right-thinking ordinary person would do under any circumstance.

This conclusion is often put in question form: Can one be a good lawyer and still be a good person?

Stating the conclusion in this manner begs an important underlying question, which concerns the definition of a "good person" in comparison with a "good lawyer." I suggest that the problem lies not with the lawyer's vocation as such, but with the terms of the metaethic of conventionally professed American morality. Simply, that metaethic is simplistic, utterly unrealistic and predicated upon misconceptions about ethical choice. Implicit in the comparison in which the lawyer looks bad is an idealized ordinary person who does not exist. This idealized person has no personal history and therefore acts in problematic situations without constraining commitments to others; she confronts stipulated facts that are perfectly comprehensible at the point of fateful decision; her ethical repertoire is clearly apparent to her and she is readily able to determine the relative priority of her values in whatever circumstances may be presented; and her ethical choices are never subject to being second-guessed.

Such people exist only in the minds of some metaethicists, although by no means all of them. The comparison that is invited is not between a good "person" and a good "lawyer," but between an imaginary good person and a real lawyer, good or otherwise. Such a comparison is inevitably invidious to lawyers, even relatively good ones. The imaginary good person is essentially an angel; no one's ethics compare well with those of an angel.

A sober consideration of the ethics of a good lawyer should begin with a metaethic that contemplates the real world. Unlike angels, people in the real world have personal histories which, among other things, determine their positions in life at any moment of ethical choice. Having a position in life limits one's options in taking action, and therefore one's ethical options. People in the real world operate in a cat's cradle of commitments to others. Having commitments to others makes one a partisan, whether willingly or otherwise. People in the real world have to deal with fragmentary and often contradictory information that arrives disjointed. Having fragmentary information means that ethical choices are often based on factual assumptions that turn out to be false. This uncertainty often requires decisions modulated by concern that one should, as Oliver Cromwell said, "think it possible that you may be mistaken."

. . .

As a practical matter, in these real-world circumstances the values that we affirm as fundamental in the abstract often turn out to be incompatible in concrete application. The incommensurability of values has been tellingly expounded by Sir Isaiah Berlin in his many writings. In his most recently published book, *The Crooked Timber of Humanity,* he says:

> [S]cientifically minded rationalists declared that conflict and tragedy arose only from ignorance of fact [and] inadequacies of method ... so that, in principle, at least ... a harmonious, rationally organized society [can be] established.... But if it is the case that not all ultimate human ends are necessarily compatible, there may be no escape from choices governed by no overriding principle, some of them painful, both to the agent and to others.

. . .

The point is that in both ordinary life and in the practice of law, the problem of doing the right thing is often deeply difficult, and sometimes anguishing.

To develop the point, I would like to consider three cases drawn from ordinary life that parallel three classic "hard cases" in legal ethics. The first is defending a person that the lawyer knows is guilty. Another classic hard case is pleading the statute of limitations against a person who has a good claim. A third is interjecting the lawyer's own moral and prudential values into advice given to a client.

In these situations, the governing rules of legal ethics are very clear. With regard to defending a person who is guilty, if the client wishes to defend the case, it is the lawyer's ethical duty to defend the client. This duty holds even though the lawyer would conclude, if the matter were left to him, that the client is indeed guilty. With respect to asserting the defense of the statute of limitations, if the client wishes to assert the defense, it is the lawyer's ethical duty to interpose the statute. This duty holds even if the lawyer would not have asserted the defense if the claim had been against the lawyer himself. With regard to interjection of personal, moral and prudential values, under the governing rules of professional ethics the lawyer has authority and at times the duty to be assertive.

I propose three parallel cases drawn from ordinary life. The hypothetical facts involve only slight transformations from real cases that I have experienced. A case from ordinary life paralleling the defense of the guilty client is that in which a parent is confronted by a neighbor who says that his window was broken by a rock thrown by the parent's child. A case from ordinary life paralleling the statute of limitations defense is where one person says to another concerning an old grievance: "Can't we just forget about that?" This type of plea is often invoked in friendships, business relations and marriages. A case from ordinary life paralleling that of the lawyer as moral and prudential adviser is where business or family advice is sought and received. My general thesis is that in confronting such ethical problems in real life, ordinary people have difficulty doing the right thing. Why should it be any easier in legal practice?

Let us begin with the case of the parent confronted with an accusation against her child. This case is something of a standard in discussions of personal ethics, where the question is put: Would you lie to protect your child? The standard alternatives in answering this question usually are "Yes, I would" and "No, I wouldn't." These alternatives usually are posed as though additional circumstances are irrelevant: either one is willing to lie or one is not. However, in real life, the decision is likely to depend on considerations that include the historical background of the situation and the way in which the problem is presented to the parent. I know, believe me, for I have had several sons with better strength than aim and was involved in similar transactions when I was a child.

Under some circumstances, a reasonable parent would support the child in a denial, even when the parent is convinced that the child had in fact thrown the guilty rock. Most parents would be influenced one way or the other by such facts as the following: the child denied the accusation and was usually truthful in such statements; the child was often untruthful when confronted with accepting responsibility for bad acts; the neighbor was a mean spirited complainer who also was chronically messy with his own garbage; the neighbor was an old friend who had always been nice to the children; the basis for the accusation was wholly circumstantial; the child was going through a terrible period of maladjustment in school and would have difficulty dealing with a new crisis; there was a racial or religious difference involved that has given an ugly subtext to the incident; or, the parent was a minister, judge or policeman.

One could multiply the possibilities indefinitely. The point is that among the possibilities are ones in which sustaining the child in the denial would seem the right thing to do, or so it would seem to most people. Equally, there would be circumstances where it would be the right thing for the parent to insist that the child acknowledge responsibility, or to accept responsibility on behalf of the child if the child adamantly refused to do so. Putting the problem in conclusory terms, the choice would depend on whether, under the circumstances, the right role for the parent was that of protective advocate for the child as a "client," on the one hand, or, on the other hand, that of judge of the child and mediator with the neighbor.

Thus, we can readily visualize circumstances in which a "good person" in ordinary life would defend a "client" that he believed was guilty. Such circumstances arise not only with parent and child, but in other relationships as well. An employer will defend an employee in a conflict with someone outside the firm, for example, and then administer a severe reprimand in private. Fellow employees will protect one of their number against the boss's accusation of foul-up, but berate the misfeasor when the boss has left. These things happen even among members of law firms. And they happen all the time in marriage and everyday friendship.

The special thing about lawyers is that undertaking the task of defending the guilty is part of their vocation in life. Unless such a specialization of social function is itself evil, the fact that lawyers specialize in defending the guilty is not evil.

As we know it today, the lawyer's vocation derives from a complex political-economic history and is a practical necessity in a modern constitutional regime. Very briefly, the felt necessity for having professional defenders of the guilty results from the fact that constitutional government entails the rule of law; that the rule of law entails exercise of coercion through legal sanctions; that legal sanctions must be administered on the basis of unavoidably uncertain evidence and abstract, ambiguous laws; that the task of dealing with uncertain evidence and ambiguous laws requires special skills; and that a constitutional regime is not prepared to entrust determination of guilt to judges acting as inquisitors. That is to say, the function of an advocate has been found indispensable to the rule of law.

Similarly, acting as a partisan advocate for a person known to be guilty is also an unavoidable incident, although a morally troublesome one, of the ordinary life of a "good person." Briefly again, the felt necessity for an amateur advocate to defend the guilty, as in the case of parent for a child, results from the fact that ordinary life is governed by general norms such as that against throwing stones at neighbors' homes or lying to customers; that enforcement of these norms entails exercise of coercion in the form of such sanctions as disapproval, bad-mouthing and boycott; that such social sanctions are administered and defended on the basis of unavoidably uncertain facts and ambiguous norms; and that life does not cast us in equal relationship with all of our fellow human beings. My child is my child, whatever he or she has done. My fellow worker is my fellow worker, and my friend is my friend.

We have to face the fact that in real life a good person, in many circumstances, would defend someone he knows to be guilty. Hence, according to a realistic metaethic, defending the guilty is not intrinsically wrong. Why, then, should it be wrong for a lawyer to do so?

Defending the guilty could be wrong for a lawyer only because the lawyer takes on this unpleasant responsibility as a way of making a living. Yet it is not clear why partisanship pursued as a vocation incident to a constitutional government is morally more troublesome than when it is an incident of ordinary life.

Analysis of another classic hard case, that of pleading the statute of limitations, proceeds along essentially similar lines. The rationale for statutes of limitation in the law has often been expressed. A notable exposition is in *United States v. Kubrick,* where the United States Supreme Court said: "These enactments are statutes of repose ... affording plaintiffs ... a reasonable time to present their claims [while protecting] defendants and the courts from having to deal with cases in which the search for truth may be seriously impaired ... whether by fading memories ... or otherwise."

. . .

These same considerations apply in disputes in ordinary life. Their relevance is brought to mind by such folk sayings as "let bygones be bygones" and "forgive and forget." In common experience we recognize that someone who remembers old injuries is a nuisance and that someone who cannot forget old injuries is usually destructive and perhaps paranoid. As Matthew Arnold stated: "We forget because we must, and not because we will."

Thus, it is a recognized norm of ordinary human relationships that old grievances should be subject to expiration. That being so, it is unclear why the same norm is considered illegitimate when it is transformed into law and given enforcement through lawyers.

Of course, the principle of repose as administered through a statute of limitations often results in arbitrary distinctions. Under a statute of limitations, a legal claim fully valid on one day can become totally worthless the next day. It is also anomalous that one kind of legal claim has a life of twenty years under the statutes of limitation and another kind of legal claim has a life of only one year. However, the law, which acts as the ultimate norm for resolving controversy, requires a formality that is unnecessary in ordinary social relationships. At the margin, formality inevitably involves technicality and technicality inevitably yields arbitrary results. Everyone knows that there is no fundamental difference between parking for an hour and parking for sixty-one minutes, except in the eyes of the parking laws and the officials who enforce them. But similar anomalies occur in everyday life. Everyone who has missed an airplane flight knows that similarly technical chronology determines the difference, in everyday life, between making it and not making it.

My third example is that of giving advice shaped by one's own moral and prudential values. Until recently, lawyers assumed that giving strong advice was an important part of what they were retained to provide. As Elihu Root remarked: "About half the practice of a decent lawyer insists in telling would-be clients that they are damned fools and should stop."

Thinking of a client as a "damned fool" is not exactly formal legal analysis. To the contrary, it involves unashamed interjection of personal and prudential considerations into giving legal advice. The rules of professional ethics recognize the propriety of doing so. As stated in the Rules of Professional Conduct concerning moral factors: "[I]t is proper for a lawyer to refer to relevant moral and ethical considerations in giving advice." The same Comment concerning prudential factors states: "Legal advice often involves unpleasant facts and alternatives that a client may be disinclined to accept."

In recent years, however, attack has been made on the propriety of interjecting the lawyer's own moral and prudential sense into the lawyer-client relationship. It is charged that this puts the lawyer in a parental role that is fraught with potential for exploitation. Implicit in the charge is an assumption that a parental role is inconsistent with ethical principles prevailing in the community at large. The community at large supposedly is committed to a kind of ethical democracy in which interjection of the adviser's moral self is inconsistent with the self-hood and moral autonomy of the person to whom advice is given.

Again, I submit that this ignores experience and practice in everyday life. Most obviously, advice of a parental kind is ubiquitously given by parents themselves. Such advice is often overtly rejected but, if given in sincere concern for the child, is rarely ignored.

. . .

More fundamentally, the notion that advice can be given unshaped by the adviser's own ethical values is absurd in fact and pernicious in consequences. It is absurd in fact because it is impossible to give purely technical advice; it is pernicious in consequences because it requires the very alienation that the notion of democratic ethics seeks to avoid. When someone undertakes to give advice, whether as a lawyer or in ordinary life, it is an act of commitment and affiliation, for better or for worse. What the advice should be in specific circumstances is another question. Anyone who has been engaged as a parent, mentor or spouse knows that the appropriate response is often unclear.

Many other examples beyond these could illustrate the parallel between ethical dilemmas in legal practice and ethical dilemmas in ordinary life. I ask acceptance for the proposition that other examples would reinforce the basic point: the ethical dilemmas regularly encountered in legal practice are simply counterparts of similar dilemmas encountered in ordinary life. People who think otherwise are, in my opinion, taking a rose-colored view of ethics in ordinary life.

The only qualification of this proposition is the fact that lawyers involve themselves in these ethical dilemmas as a vocation, while others do so as an unavoidable incident of ordinary life.

. . .

Everyone who takes time to work through the problem of constitutional government reaches the conclusion that defending the guilty is simply a price of maintaining the benefits of a constitutional order. Everyone who takes time to work through the problem of statutes of limitation reaches the conclusion that refusing to examine the merits of many grievances is necessary to maintaining the capacity to examine the merits of some of them. Everyone who has given advice knows the difficulties involved in putting one's heart into another person's affairs. The work of lawyers simply embodies these paradoxes and the frustration of idealism that they reflect. The lawyer's vocation is living testimony to the discrepancy between the community's ethical aspirations and its merely human condition. It may also be that the availability of lawyers to deal with some of these discrepancies permits other members of the community to imagine themselves above such unpleasantness and allows them to live in an imaginary world.

Defending the guilty, pleading the statute of limitations, and giving hard advice, are often the right things to do, even if they involve conflicts in values. Trying to do the right thing, when it is impossible to do so without conflicts in values, is one of society's dirty jobs. However, no one is compelled to become a lawyer, and many who have originally chosen the profession find it repugnant and leave. Many people in ordinary life go about confronting adulthood in the same way.

————

REFERENCES

For general accounts of role morality *see, e.g.:*

M. Bayles, *Professional Ethics* (1981).

B. Biddle & E. Thomas, *Role Theory: Concepts and Research* (1966).

Bradley, "My Station and Its Duties" in *Ethical Studies* 160–206 (2d ed. 1927).

J. Callahan, ed., *Ethical Issues in Professional Life* (1988).

D. Emmet, *Rules, Roles, and Relations* (1966).

C. Fried, *Right and Wrong* (1978).

A. Goldman, *The Moral Foundations of Professional Ethics* (1980).

R. Unger, *Knowledge and Politics* 25 (1975).

B. Williams, *Morality: An Introduction to Ethics* 51–58 (1972).

Analysis of the ethical content of lawyers' roles includes, in addition to the materials cited above or excerpted below:

Alschuler, "The Preservation of a Client's Confidences," 52 *U.Colo.L.Rev.* 349 (1981).

Auerbach, "Book Review of *Lawyer's Lawyer*," 87 *Harv.L.Rev.* 1100 (1974).

Burger, "Standards of Conduct for Prosecution and Defense Personnel: A Judge's Viewpoint," 5 *Am.Crim.L.Q.* 11, 12–13 (1966).

Curtis, "The Ethics of Advocacy," 4 *Stan.L.Rev.* 3 (1951).

Drinker, "Some Remarks on Mr. Curtis' 'The Ethics of Advocacy,'" 4 *Stan.L.Rev.* 349 (1952).

Freedman, "Judge Frankel's Search for the Truth," 123 *U.Pa. L.Rev.* 1060 (1975).

M. Freedman, *Lawyers' Ethics in an Adversary System* (1975).

Gaetke, "Lawyers as Officers of the Court," 42 *Vand.L.Rev.* 39 (1989).

Greenbaum, "Attorney's Problems in Making Ethical Decisions," 52 *Ind.L.J.* 627 (1977).

W. Harbaugh, *Lawyer's Lawyer: The Life of John W. Davis* (1973).

R. Keeton, *Trial Tactics and Methods* (2d ed. 1973).

Krash, "Professional Responsibility to Clients and the Public Interest: Is There a Conflict?" 55 *Chi.B.Rec.* 31 (special centennial issue 1973).

Langevoort, "Where Were the Lawyers? A Behavioral Inquiry into Lawyers' Responsibility for Clients' Fraud," 46 *Vanderbilt L.Rev.* 76 (1993).

Lehman, "The Pursuit of a Client's Interest," 77 *Mich.L.Rev.* 1078 (1979).

H. Lesnick, *Being a Lawyer* (1991).

D. Luban, *Lawyers and Justice: An Ethical Study* (1988).

Maute, "Sporting Theory of Justice: Taming Adversary Zeal With a Logical Sanctions Doctrine," 20 *Conn.L.Rev.* 7, (1987).

D. Mellinkoff, *The Conscience of a Lawyer* (1973).

Menkel–Meadow, "Is Altruism Possible in Lawyering?", 8 *Ga.St.L.Rev.* 385 (1992).

Nader, "Serving Self, Not Others" (Book Review) 89 *Yale L.J.* 1442 (1980) (reviewing G. Hazard, *Ethics in the Practice of Law* (1978).

Newman, "Rethinking Fairness: Perspectives on the Litigation Process," 94 *Yale L.J.* 1643 (1985).

Patterson, "Legal Ethics and the Lawyer's Duty of Loyalty," 29 *Emory L.J.* 909 (1980).

Pepper, "The Lawyer's Amoral Ethical Role: A Defense, A Problem, and Some Possibilities," 1986 *Am.B.Found. Res.J.* 613.

Pizzi, "Judge Frankel and the Adversary System," 52 *U.Colo. L.Rev.* 357 (1981).

Redlich, "Lawyers, the Temple and the Market Place," 30 *Bus.Law.* 65 (1975).

Uviller, "The Advocate, the Truth, and Judge Hackles," 123 *U.Pa.L.Rev.* 1067 (1975).

Wolfram, "The Duty to Represent Clients, Repugnant and Otherwise, in D. Luban ed. *The Good Lawyer*" 214 (1984).

The problems of politicians in balancing immoral means and moral ends provides an interesting analogue to the tensions confronting lawyers. *See, e.g.,*

Nagel, "Ruthlessness in Public Life," in *Public and Private Morality* (S. Hampshire ed. 1978).

Walzer, "Political Action and the Problem of Dirty Hands," 2 *Phil. & Pub. Aff.* 160 (1973).

M. Weber, "Politics as a Vocation" in *From Max Weber: Essays in Sociology* (H. Gerth & C. Mills eds. 1946).

Williams, "Politics and Moral Character," in *Public and Private Morality, supra.*

II. THE CRIMINAL DEFENSE PARADIGM

Monroe H. Freedman, "Professional Responsibility of the Criminal Defense Lawyer: The Three Hardest Questions"

64 Michigan Law Review 1469–1482 (1966).[a]

In almost any area of legal counseling and advocacy, the lawyer may be faced with the dilemma of either betraying the confidential communications of his client or participating to some extent in the purposeful deception of the court. This problem is nowhere more acute than in the practice of criminal law, particularly in the representation of the indigent accused. The purpose of this article is to analyze and attempt to resolve three of the most difficult issues in this general area:

1. Is it proper to cross-examine for the purpose of discrediting the reliability or credibility of an adverse witness whom you know to be telling the truth?

2. Is it proper to put a witness on the stand when you know he will commit perjury?

3. Is it proper to give your client legal advice when you have reason to believe that the knowledge you give him will tempt him to commit perjury?

These questions present serious difficulties with respect to a lawyer's ethical responsibilities. Moreover, if one admits the possibility of an affirmative answer, it is difficult even to discuss them without appearing to some to be unethical.[1] It is not surprising, therefore, that reasonable, rational discussion of these issues has been uncommon and that the problems have for so long remained unresolved. In this regard it should be recognized that the Canons of Ethics, which were promulgated in 1908 "as a

a. Professor Freedman has expanded his analysis, and modified his conclusions somewhat, in his book, *Lawyers' Ethics in an Adversary System* (1975).

1. The substance of this paper was recently presented to a Criminal Trial Institute attended by forty-five members of the District of Columbia Bar. As a consequence, several judges (none of whom had either heard the lecture or read it) complained to the Committee on Admissions and Grievances of the District Court for the District of Columbia, urging the author's disbarment or suspension. Only after four months of proceedings, including a hearing, two meetings, and a *de novo* review by eleven federal district court judges, did the Committee announce its decision to "proceed no further in the matter."

general guide," [2] are both inadequate and self-contradictory.

I. The Adversary System and the Necessity for Confidentiality

At the outset, we should dispose of some common question-begging responses. The attorney is indeed an officer of the court, and he does participate in a search for truth. These two propositions, however, merely serve to state the problem in different words: As an officer of the court, participating in a search for truth, what is the attorney's special responsibility, and how does that responsibility affect his resolution of the questions posed above?

The attorney functions in an adversary system based upon the presupposition that the most effective means of determining truth is to present to a judge and jury a clash between proponents of conflicting views. It is essential to the effective functioning of this system that each adversary have, in the words of Canon 15, "entire devotion to the interest of the client, warm zeal in the maintenance and defense of his rights and the exertion of his utmost learning and ability." It is also essential to maintain the fullest uninhibited communication between the client and his attorney, so that the attorney can most effectively counsel his client and advocate the latter's cause. This policy is safeguarded by the requirement that the lawyer must, in the words of Canon 37, "preserve his client's confidences." Canon 15 does, of course, qualify these obligations by stating that "the office of attorney does not permit, much less does it demand of him for any client, violations of law or any manner of fraud or chicane." In addition, Canon 22 requires candor toward the court.

The problem presented by these salutary generalities of the Canons in the context of particular litigation is illustrated by the personal experience of Samuel Williston, which was related in his autobiography.[3] Because of his examination of a client's correspondence file, Williston learned of a fact extremely damaging to his client's case. When the judge announced his decision, it was apparent that a critical factor in the favorable judgment for Williston's client was the judge's ignorance of this fact. Williston remained silent and did not thereafter inform the judge of what he knew. He was convinced, and Charles Curtis [4] agrees with him, that it was his duty to remain silent.

---

2. American Bar Association, Canons of Professional Ethics, Preamble (1908).

3. Williston, Life and Law 271 (1940).

4. Curtis, It's Your Law 17–21 (1954). See also Curtis, *The Ethics of Advocacy,* 4 Stan.L.Rev. 3, 9–10 (1951); Drinker, *Some Remarks on Mr. Curtis'*

In an opinion by the American Bar Association Committee on Professional Ethics and Grievances, an eminent panel headed by Henry Drinker held that a lawyer should remain silent when his client lies to the judge by saying that he has no prior record, despite the attorney's knowledge to the contrary. The majority of the panel distinguished the situation in which the attorney has learned of the client's prior record from a source other than the client himself. William B. Jones, a distinguished trial lawyer and now a judge in the United States District Court for the District of Columbia, wrote a separate opinion in which he asserted that in neither event should the lawyer expose his client's lie. If these two cases do not constitute "fraud or chicane" or lack of candor within the meaning of the Canons (and I agree with the authorities cited that they do not), it is clear that the meaning of the Canons is ambiguous.

The adversary system has further ramifications in a criminal case. The defendant is presumed to be innocent. The burden is on the prosecution to prove beyond a reasonable doubt that the defendant is guilty. The plea of not guilty does not necessarily mean "not guilty in fact," for the defendant may mean "not legally guilty." Even the accused who knows that he committed the crime is entitled to put the government to its proof. Indeed, the accused who knows that he is guilty has an absolute constitutional right to remain silent. The moralist might quite reasonably understand this to mean that, under these circumstances, the defendant and his lawyer are privileged to "lie" to the court in pleading not guilty. In my judgment, the moralist is right. However, our adversary system and related notions of the proper administration of criminal justice sanction the lie.

Some derive solace from the sophistry of calling the lie a "legal fiction," but this is hardly an adequate answer to the moralist. Moreover, this answer has no particular appeal for the practicing attorney, who knows that the plea of not guilty commits him to the most effective advocacy of which he is capable. Criminal defense lawyers do not win their cases by arguing reasonable doubt. Effective trial advocacy requires that the attorney's every word, action, and attitude be consistent with the conclusion that his client is innocent. As every trial lawyer knows, the jury is certain that the defense attorney knows whether his client is guilty. The jury is therefore alert to, and will be enormously affected by, any indication by the attorney that he believes the defendant to be guilty. Thus, the plea of not guilty commits the

"The Ethics of Advocacy," 4 Stan.L.Rev.
349, 350–51 (1952).

advocate to a trial, including a closing argument, in which he must argue that "not guilty" means "not guilty in fact."

There is, of course, a simple way to evade the dilemma raised by the not guilty plea. Some attorneys rationalize the problem by insisting that a lawyer never knows for sure whether his client is guilty. The client who insists upon his guilt may in fact be protecting his wife, or may know that he pulled the trigger and that the victim was killed, but not that his gun was loaded with blanks and that the fatal shot was fired from across the street. For anyone who finds this reasoning satisfactory, there is, of course, no need to think further about the issue.

It is also argued that a defense attorney can remain selectively ignorant. He can insist in his first interview with his client that, if his client is guilty, he simply does not want to know. It is inconceivable, however, that an attorney could give adequate counsel under such circumstances. How is the client to know, for example, precisely which relevant circumstances his lawyer does not want to be told? The lawyer might ask whether his client has a prior record. The client, assuming that this is the kind of knowledge that might present ethical problems for his lawyer, might respond that he has no record. The lawyer would then put the defendant on the stand and, on cross-examination, be appalled to learn that his client has two prior convictions for offenses identical to that for which he is being tried.

Of course, an attorney can guard against this specific problem by telling his client that he must know about the client's past record. However, a lawyer can never anticipate all of the innumerable and potentially critical factors that his client, once cautioned, may decide not to reveal. In one instance, for example, the defendant assumed that his lawyer would prefer to be ignorant of the fact that the client had been having sexual relations with the chief defense witness. The client was innocent of the robbery with which he was charged, but was found guilty by the jury— probably because he was guilty of fornication, a far less serious offense for which he had not even been charged.

The problem is compounded by the practice of plea bargaining. It is considered improper for a defendant to plead guilty to a lesser offense unless he is in fact guilty. Nevertheless, it is common knowledge that plea bargaining frequently results in improper guilty pleas by innocent people. For example, a defendant falsely accused of robbery may plead guilty to simple assault, rather than risk a robbery conviction and a substantial prison term. If an attorney is to be scrupulous in bargaining pleas, however, he must know in advance that his client is guilty, since the guilty plea is improper if the defendant is innocent. Of course, if the attempt to bargain for a lesser offense should fail, the lawyer would know the truth and thereafter be unable to rationalize that he was uncertain of his client's guilt.

If one recognizes that professional responsibility requires that an advocate have full knowledge of every pertinent fact, it follows that he must seek the truth from his client, not shun it. This means that he will have to dig and pry and cajole, and, even then, he will not be successful unless he can convince the client that full and confidential disclosure to his lawyer will never result in prejudice to the client by any word or action of the lawyer. This is, perhaps, particularly true in the case of the indigent defendant, who meets his lawyer for the first time in the cell block or the rotunda. He did not choose the lawyer, nor does he know him. The lawyer has been sent by the judge and is part of the system that is attempting to punish the defendant. It is no easy task to persuade this client that he can talk freely without fear of prejudice. However, the inclination to mislead one's lawyer is not restricted to the indigent or even to the criminal defendant. Randolph Paul has observed a similar phenomenon among a wealthier class in a far more congenial atmosphere:

> The tax adviser will sometimes have to dynamite the facts of his case out of the unwilling witnesses on his own side— witnesses who are nervous, witnesses who are confused about their own interest, witnesses who try to be too smart for their own good, and witnesses who subconsciously do not want to understand what has happened despite the fact that they must if they are to testify coherently.

Paul goes on to explain that the truth can be obtained only by persuading the client that it would be a violation of a sacred obligation for the lawyer ever to reveal a client's confidence. Beyond any question, once a lawyer has persuaded his client of the obligation of confidentiality, he must respect that obligation scrupulously.

II. The Specific Questions

The first of the difficult problems posed above will now be considered: Is it proper to cross-examine for the purpose of discrediting the reliability or the credibility of a witness whom you know to be telling the truth? Assume the following situation. Your client has been falsely accused of a robbery committed at 16th and P Streets at 11:00 p.m. He tells you at first that at no time on the evening of the crime was he within six blocks of that location. However, you are able to persuade him that he must tell you the truth and that doing so will in no way prejudice him. He then reveals to you that he was at 15th and P Streets at 10:55 that evening, but that he was walking east, away from the scene of the crime, and that, by 11:00 p.m., he was six blocks away. At the trial, there are two prosecution witnesses. The first mistakenly, but with some degree of persuasion, identifies your client as the criminal. At that point, the prosecution's case depends on this single witness, who might or might not be believed. Since your client has a prior record, you do not want to put him on the stand, but you feel that there is at least a chance for acquittal. The second prosecution witness is an elderly woman who is somewhat nervous and who wears glasses. She testifies truthfully and accurately that she saw your client at 15th and P Streets at 10:55 p.m. She has corroborated the erroneous testimony of the first witness and made conviction virtually certain. However, if you destroy her reliability through cross-examination designed to show that she is easily confused and has poor eyesight, you may not only eliminate the corroboration, but also cast doubt in the jury's mind on the prosecution's entire case. On the other hand, if you should refuse to cross-examine her because she is telling the truth, your client may well feel betrayed, since you knew of the witness's veracity only because your client confided in you, under your assurance that his truthfulness would not prejudice him.

The client would be right. Viewed strictly, the attorney's failure to cross-examine would not be violative of the client's confidence because it would not constitute a disclosure. However, the same policy that supports the obligation of confidentiality precludes the attorney from prejudicing his client's interest in any other way because of knowledge gained in his professional capacity. When a lawyer fails to cross-examine only because his client, placing confidence in the lawyer, has been candid with him, the basis for such confidence and candor collapses. Our legal system cannot tolerate such a result.

> The purposes and necessities of the relation between a client and his attorney require, in many cases, on the part of the client, the fullest and freest disclosures to the attorney of the client's objects, motives and acts .... To permit the attorney to reveal to others what is so disclosed, would be not only a gross violation of a sacred trust upon his part, but it would utterly destroy and prevent the usefulness and benefits to be derived from professional assistance.

The client's confidences must "upon all occasions be inviolable," to avoid the "greater mischiefs" that would probably result if a client could not feel free "to repose [confidence] in the attorney to whom he resorts for legal advice and assistance." Destroy that confidence, and "a man would not venture to consult any skillful person, or would only dare to tell his counsellor half his case."

Therefore, one must conclude that the attorney is obligated to attack, if he can, the reliability or credibility of an opposing witness whom he knows to be truthful. The contrary result would inevitably impair the "perfect freedom of consultation by client with attorney," which is "essential to the administration of justice."

The second question is generally considered to be the hardest of all: Is it proper to put a witness on the stand when you know he will commit perjury? Assume, for example, that the witness in question is the accused himself, and that he has admitted to you, in response to your assurances of confidentiality, that he is guilty. However, he insists upon taking the stand to protest his innocence. There is a clear consensus among prosecutors and defense attorneys that the likelihood of conviction is increased enormously when the defendant does not take the stand. Consequently, the attorney who prevents his client from testifying only because the client has confided his guilt to him is violating that confidence by acting upon the information in a way that will seriously prejudice his client's interests.

Perhaps the most common method for avoiding the ethical problem just posed is for the lawyer to withdraw from the case, at least if there is sufficient time before trial for the client to retain another attorney. The client will then go to the nearest law office, realizing that the obligation of confidentiality is not what it has been represented to be, and withhold incriminating information or the fact of his guilt from his new attorney. On ethical grounds, the practice of withdrawing from a case under such circumstances is indefensible, since the identical perjured testimony will ultimately be presented. More important, perhaps, is the practical consideration that the new attorney will be ignorant of the perjury and therefore will be in no position to attempt to discourage the client from presenting it. Only the original attorney, who knows the truth, has that opportunity, but he loses it in the very act of evading the ethical problem.

The problem is all the more difficult when the client is indigent. He cannot retain other counsel, and in many jurisdictions, including the District of Columbia, it is impossible for appointed counsel to withdraw from a case except for extraordinary reasons. Thus, appointed counsel, unless he lies to the judge, can successfully withdraw only by revealing to the judge that the attorney has received knowledge of his client's guilt. Such a revelation in itself would seem to be a sufficiently serious violation of the obligation of confidentiality to merit severe condemnation. In fact, however, the situation is far worse, since it is entirely possible that the same judge who permits the attorney to withdraw will subsequently hear the case and sentence the defendant. When he does so, of course, he will have had personal knowledge of the defendant's guilt before the trial began. Moreover, this will be knowledge of which the newly appointed counsel for the defendant will probably be ignorant.

The difficulty is further aggravated when the client informs the lawyer for the first time during trial that he intends to take the stand and commit perjury. The perjury in question may not necessarily be a protestation of innocence by a guilty man. Referring to the earlier hypothetical of the defendant wrongly accused of a robbery at 16th and P, the only perjury may be his denial of the truthful, but highly damaging, testimony of the corroborating witness who placed him one block away from the intersection five minutes prior to the crime. Of course, if he tells the truth and thus verifies the corroborating witness, the jury will be far more inclined to accept the inaccurate testimony of the principal witness, who specifically identified him as the criminal.

If a lawyer has discovered his client's intent to perjure himself, one possible solution to this problem is for the lawyer to approach the bench, explain his ethical difficulty to the judge, and ask to be relieved, thereby causing a mistrial. This request is certain to be denied, if only because it would empower the defendant to cause a series of mistrials in the same fashion. At this point, some feel that the lawyer has avoided the ethical problem and can put the defendant on the stand. However, one objection to this solution, apart from the violation of confidentiality, is that the lawyer's ethical problem has not been solved, but has only been transferred to the judge. Moreover, the client in such a case might well have grounds for appeal on the basis of deprivation of due process and denial of the right to counsel, since he will have been tried before, and sentenced by, a judge who has been informed of the client's guilt by his own attorney.

A solution even less satisfactory than informing the judge of the defendant's guilt would be to let the client take the stand without the attorney's participation and to omit reference to the client's testimony in closing argument. The latter solution, of course, would be as damaging as to fail entirely to argue the case to the jury, and failing to argue the case is "as improper as though the attorney had told the jury that his client had uttered a falsehood in making the statement."

. . .

Of course, before the client testifies perjuriously, the lawyer has a duty to attempt to dissuade him on grounds of both law and morality. In addition, the client should be impressed with the fact that his untruthful alibi is tactically dangerous. There is always a strong possibility that the prosecutor will expose the perjury on cross-examination. However, for the reasons already given, the final decision must necessarily be the client's. The lawyer's best course thereafter would be to avoid any further professional relationship with a client whom he knew to have perjured himself.

The third question is whether it is proper to give your client legal advice when you have reason to believe that the knowledge you give him will tempt him to commit perjury. This may indeed be the most difficult problem of all, because giving such advice creates the appearance that the attorney is encouraging and condoning perjury.

If the lawyer is not certain what the facts are when he gives the advice, the problem is substantially minimized, if not eliminated. It is not the lawyer's function to prejudge his client as a perjurer. He cannot presume that the client will make unlawful use of his advice. Apart from this, there is a natural predisposition in most people to recollect facts, entirely honestly, in a way most favorable to their own interest. As Randolph Paul has observed, some witnesses are nervous, some are confused about their own interests, some try to be too smart for their own good, and some subconsciously do not want to understand what has happened to them. Before he begins to remember essential facts, the client is entitled to know what his own interests are.

. . .

Essentially no different from the problem discussed above, but apparently more difficult, is the so-called *Anatomy of a Murder* situation. The lawyer, who has received from his client an incriminating story of murder in the first degree, says, "If the facts are as you have stated them so far, you have no defense, and you will probably be electrocuted. On the other hand, if you acted in a blind rage, there is a possibility of saving your life. Think it over, and we will talk about it tomorrow." As in the tax case, and as in the case of the plea of guilty to a lesser offense, the lawyer has given his client a legal opinion that might induce the client to lie. This is information which the lawyer himself would have, without advice, were he in the client's position. It is submitted that the client is entitled to have this information about the law and to make his own decision as to whether to act upon it. To decide otherwise would not only penalize the less well-educated defendant, but would also prejudice the client because of his initial truthfulness in telling his story in confidence to the attorney.

III. Conclusion

The lawyer is an officer of the court, participating in a search for truth. Yet no lawyer would consider that he had acted unethically in pleading the statute of frauds or the statute of limitations as a bar to a just claim. Similarly, no lawyer would consider it unethical to prevent the introduction of evidence such as a murder weapon seized in violation of the fourth amendment or a truthful but involuntary confession, or to defend a guilty man on grounds of denial of a speedy trial. Such actions are permissible because there are policy considerations that at times justify frustrating the search for truth and the prosecution of a just claim. Similarly, there are policies that justify an affirmative answer to the three questions that have been posed in this article. These policies include the maintenance of an adversary system, the presumption of innocence, the prosecution's burden to prove guilt beyond a reasonable doubt, the right to counsel, and the obligation of confidentiality between lawyer and client.

Lon L. Fuller, "The Adversary System," in H. Berman, ed., Talks on American Law
32–37 (1961).

Let me begin with that aspect of the adversary philosophy which is most puzzling—not to say, most offensive—to the layman. The ethical standards of the legal profession make it perfectly proper for a lawyer to undertake in a criminal case the defense of a man whom he knows to be guilty. Because all ... inferences of guilt are so often mistaken, it is argued that the lawyer has no right to judge the guilt or innocence of his client before the case is tried. If he refuses to defend a client because he thinks he is guilty, the lawyer is wrongfully usurping the office of judge and jury. ... [But] [i]t may be answered that all human judgments are subject to error. One must calculate probabilities. We may concede that there is some chance that an experienced lawyer, with a knowledge of human nature and access to the most intimate facts, may erroneously conclude that his client is guilty when in fact he is innocent. But the chance is so slight that it may be argued it should be neglected in the actual conduct of affairs.

We may attempt to answer this argument in turn by saying that where the guilt or innocence of a human being is in issue, a calculation of mere probabilities is out of place. But the true answer goes deeper. The reason lies in considerations of an order different from those I have so far been discussing. The purpose of the rule is not merely to protect the innocent person against the possibility of an unjust conviction, precious as that objective is. The purpose of the rule is to preserve the integrity of society itself. It aims at keeping sound and wholesome the procedures by which society visits its condemnation on an erring member. ... If he is denied this representation the processes of public trial become suspect and tainted. It is for this reason that I say that the integrity of society itself demands that the accused be represented by counsel. ... [This representation] marks society's determination to keep unsoiled and beyond suspicion the procedures by which men are condemned for a violation of its laws.

Harry I. Subin, "The Criminal Defense Lawyer's 'Different Mission' "; Reflections on the 'Right' to Present a False Case"

1 *Georgetown J.L. Ethics* 125 (1987).

In United States v. Wade, Justice White defined the obligations of defense counsel as follows:

Law enforcement officers have the obligation to convict the guilty and to make sure they do not convict the innocent. They must be dedicated to making the criminal trial a procedure for the ascertainment of the true facts surrounding the commission of the crime. ... [Unlike prosecuting attorneys] defense counsel has no comparable obligation to ascertain or present the truth. Our system assigns him a different mission. He must be and is interested in preventing the conviction of the innocent, but...we also insist that he defend his client whether he is innocent or guilty. The State has the obligation to present evidence. Defense counsel need present nothing, even if he knows what the truth is. He need not furnish any witnesses to the police, or reveal any confidences of his client, or furnish any other information to help the prosecution's case. If he can confuse a witness, even a truthful one, or make him appear at a disadvantage, unsure or indecisive, that will be his normal course. Our interest in not convicting the innocent permits counsel to put the State to its proof, to put the State's case in the worst possible light, regardless of what he thinks or knows to be the truth. Undoubtedly there are some limits which defense counsel must observe but more often than not, defense counsel will cross-examine a prosecution witness, and impeach him if he can, even if he thinks the witness is telling the truth, just as he will attempt to destroy a witness who he thinks is lying. In this respect, as part of our modified adversary system and as part of the duty imposed on the most honorable defense counsel, we countenance or require conduct which in many instances has little if any, relation to the search for truth.[17]

Emanating from such an impeccable source, the concept of the defense attorney's special relation to the truth seeking process may well have a self-evident status. I suspect that it did for me when I first read it twenty years ago. Now it strikes me as excessive. It is true that in our system the prosecution has the burden of proving guilt, and the defense the corresponding right to remain completely passive in the presentation of facts to the jury. It is true that the defense attorney has the right, and the obligation, to challenge the government's proof to assure its accuracy. The question is whether it should also be the "duty" of the "most honorable" defense attorney to take affirmative steps to subvert the government's case when he or she knows it is accurate. I shall argue that the attorney can perform his or her duty fully even if not permitted to act in this way, and that if stricter limits on truth-subversion were instituted, the rights of persons accused of crimes generally would be enhanced.

The article begins with a description of a case I handled some years ago, one that I believe is a good illustration of the false defense problem. I next address the threshold question of the attorney's knowledge. It has been argued that the attorney cannot "know" what the truth is, and therefore is free to present any available defense theory. I attempt to demonstrate that the attorney can, in fact, know the truth, and I propose a process to determine when the truth is known.

I then analyze the arguments that have been advanced in support of the "different mission" theory: that the defense attorney, even if he or she knows the truth, remains free to disregard it in presenting a defense. I argue that neither the right to a defense nor the needs of the adversary system justify the presentation of a false defense. Finally, I describe a new standard that explicitly prohibits the defense attorney from asserting a false defense. I conclude with some thoughts as to why this rule would produce a generally more just system.

---

17. [388 U.S. 218, 250, 81 S.Ct. 1926, 18 L.Ed.2d 1149 (1967) (White J., joined by Harlan & Stewart, JJ., dissenting in part and concurring in part)].

II. Truth Subversion in Action: The Problem Illustrated

A. The Accusation

About fifteen years ago I represented a man charged with rape and robbery. The victim's account was as follows: Returning from work in the early morning hours, she was accosted by a man who pointed a gun at her and took a watch from her wrist. He told her to go with him to a nearby lot, where he ordered her to lie down on the ground and disrobe. When she complained that the ground was hurting her, he took her to his apartment, located across the street. During the next hour there, he had intercourse with her. Ultimately, he said that they had to leave to avoid being discovered by the woman with whom he lived. The complainant responded that since he had gotten what he wanted, he should give her back her watch. He said that he would.

As the two left the apartment, he said he was going to get a car. Before leaving the building, however, he went to the apartment next door, leaving her to wait in the hallway. When asked why she waited, she said that she was still hoping for the return of her watch, which was a valued gift, apparently from her boyfriend.

She never did get the watch. When they left the building, the man told her to wait on the street while he got the car. At that point she went to a nearby police precinct and reported the incident. She gave a full description of the assailant that matched my client. She also accurately described the inside of his apartment. Later, in response to a note left at his apartment by the police, my client came to the precinct, and the complainant identified him. My client was released at that time but was arrested soon thereafter at his apartment, where a gun was found. No watch was recovered.

My client was formally charged, at which point I entered the case. At our initial interview and those that followed it, he insisted that he had nothing whatever to do with the crime and had never even seen the woman before. He stated that he had been in several places during the night in question: visiting his aunt earlier in the evening, then traveling to a bar in New Jersey, where he was during the critical hours. He gave the name of a man there who would corroborate this. He said that he arrived home early the next morning and met a friend. He stated that he had no idea how this woman had come to know things about him such as what the apartment looked like, that he lived with a woman, and that he was a musician, or how she could identify him. He said that he had no reason to rape anyone, since he already had a woman, and that in any event he was recovering from surgery for an old gun shot wound and could not engage in intercourse. He said he would not be so stupid as to bring a woman he had robbed and was going to rape into his own apartment.

I felt that there was some strength to these arguments, and that there were questionable aspects to the complainant's story. In particular, it seemed strange that a man intending rape would be as solicitous of the victim's comfort as the woman said her assailant was at the playground. It also seemed that a person who had just been raped would flee when she had the chance to, and in any case would not be primarily concerned with the return of her watch. On balance, however, I suspected that my client was not telling me the truth. I thought the complaining witness could not possibly have known what she knew about him and his apartment, if she had not had any contact with him. True, someone else could have posed as him, and used his apartment. My client, however, could suggest no one who could have done so. Moreover, that hypothesis did not explain the complainant's accurate description of him to the police. Although the identification procedure used by the police, a one person "show up," was suggestive, the woman had ample opportunity to observe her assailant during the extended incident. I could not believe that the complainant had selected my client randomly to accuse falsely of rape. By both her and my client's admission, the two had not had any previous association.

That my client was probably lying to me had two possible explanations. First, he might have been lying because he was guilty and did not see any particular advantage to himself in admitting it to me. It is embarrassing to admit that one has committed a crime, particularly one of this nature. Moreover, my client might well have feared to tell me the truth. He might have believed that I would tell others what he said, or, at the very least, that I might not be enthusiastic about representing him.

He also might have lied not because he was guilty of the offense, but because he thought the concocted story was the best one under the circumstances. The sexual encounter may have taken place voluntarily, but the woman complained to the police because she was angry at my client for refusing to return the valued wrist watch, perhaps not stolen, but left, in my client's apartment. My client may not have been able to admit this, because he had other needs that took precedence over the particular legal one that brought him to me. For example, the client might have felt compelled to deny any involvement in the incident because to admit to having had a sexual encounter might have jeopardized his relationship with the woman with whom he lived. Likewise, he might have decided to "play lawyer," and put forward what he believed to be his best defense. Not understanding the heavy burden of proof on the state in criminal cases, he might have thought that any version of the facts that showed that he had contact with the woman would be fatal because it would simply be a case of her word against his.

I discussed all of these matters with the client on several occasions. Judging him a man of intelligence, with no signs of mental abnormality, I became convinced that he understood both the seriousness of his situation, and that his exculpation did not depend upon maintaining his initial story. In ensuring that he did understand that, in fact, I came close enough to suggesting the "right" answers to make me a little nervous about the line between subornation of perjury and careful witness preparation, known in the trade as "horseshedding." [31] In the end, however, he held to his original account.

. . .

I [later] explained to my client that we had failed to corroborate his alibi, and that the complainant appeared to be a credible witness. I said that in my view the jury would not believe the alibi, and that if we could not obtain any other information, it might be appropriate to think about a guilty plea, which would at least limit his exposure to punishment. The case, then in the middle of the aimless drift towards resolution that typifies New York's criminal justice system, was left at that.

Some time later, however, my client called me and told me that he had new evidence; his aunt, he said, would testify that he had been with her at the time in question. I was incredulous. I reminded him that at no time during our earlier conversations had he indicated what was plainly a crucial piece of information, despite my not too subtle explanation of the elements of an alibi defense. I told him that when the aunt was initially interviewed with great care on this point, she stated that he was not with her at the time of the crime. Ultimately, I told him that I thought he was lying, and that in my view even if the jury heard the aunt's testimony, they would not believe it.

---

31. The dilemma faced by the lawyer is whether, in explaining to the client the legal implications of conduct, he or she is shaping the client's version of the facts. The issue was put dramatically in R. Traver, Anatomy of a Murder (1958), in which the attorney explained the facts needed to establish an insanity defense to an apparently normal person accused of murder. *Id.* at 44–47. Whether I was quite as blatant I frankly cannot remember . . . .

Whether it was during that session or later that the client admitted his guilt I do not recall. I do recall wondering whether, now that I knew the truth, that should make a difference in the way in which the case was handled. I certainly wished that I did not know it and began to understand, psychologically if not ethically, lawyers who do not want to know their clients' stories.[34]

I did not pause very long to ponder the problem, however, because I concluded that knowing the truth in fact did not make a difference to my defense strategy, other than to put me on notice as to when I might be suborning perjury. Because the mission of the defense attorney was to defeat the prosecution's case, what I knew actually happened was not important otherwise. What did matter was whether a version of the "facts" could be presented that would make a jury doubt the client's guilt.

Viewed in this way, my problem was not that my client's story was false, but that it was not credible, and could not be made to appear so by legal means. To win, we would therefore have to come up with a better theory than the alibi, avoiding perjury in the process. Thus, the defense would have to be made out without the client testifying, since it would be a crime for him to assert a fabricated exculpatory theory under oath. This was not a serious problem, however, because it would not only be possible to prevail without the defendant's testimony, but it would probably be easier to do so. Not everyone is capable of lying successfully on the witness stand, and I did not have the sense that my client would be very good at it.

There were two possible defenses that could be fabricated. The first was mistaken identity. ... [However], given that the complainant had spent considerable time with the assailant and had led the police back to the defendant's apartment, it seemed doubtful that the mistaken identification ploy would be successful.

The second alternative, consent, was clearly preferable. It would negate the charge of rape and undermine the robbery case. To prevail, all we would have to do would be to raise a reasonable doubt as to whether he had compelled the woman to have sex with him. The doubt would be based on the scenario that the woman and the defendant met, and she voluntarily returned to his apartment. Her watch, the object of the alleged robbery, was either left there by mistake or, perhaps better, was never there at all.

---

34. *See* Mitchell, *The Ethics of the Criminal Defense Attorney—New Answers to Old Questions,* 32 Stan.L.Rev. 293, 296 n. 12 (1980) (author properly analogizes lawyer's preference not to know of the client's guilt to the doctrine of "conscious avoidance," which constitutes "knowledge" under criminal law).

The consent defense could be made out entirely through cross-examination of the complainant, coupled with argument to the jury about her lack of credibility on the issue of force. I could emphasize the parts of her story that sounded the most curious, such as the defendant's solicitude in taking his victim back to his apartment, and her waiting for her watch when she could have gone immediately to the nearby precinct that she went to later. I could point to her inability to identify the gun she claimed was used (although it was the one actually used), that the allegedly stolen watch was never found, there was no sign of physical violence, and no one heard screaming or any other signs of a struggle. I could also argue as my client had that even if he were reckless enough to rob and rape a woman across the street from his apartment, he would not be so foolish as to bring the victim there. I considered investigating the complainant's background, to take advantage of the right, unencumbered at the time, to impeach her on the basis of her prior unchastity. I did not pursue this, however, because to me this device, although lawful, was fundamentally wrong. No doubt in that respect I lacked zeal, perhaps punishably so.

Even without assassinating this woman's character, however, I could argue that this was simply a case of a casual tryst that went awry. The defendant would not have to prove whether the complainant made the false charge to account for her whereabouts that evening, or to explain what happened to her missing watch. If the jury had reason to doubt the complainant's charges it would be bound to acquit the defendant.

How all of this would have played out at trial cannot be known. Predictably, the case dragged on so long that the prosecutor was forced to offer the unrefusable plea of possession of a gun. As I look back, however, I wonder how I could justify doing what I was planning to do had the case been tried. I was prepared to stand before the jury posing as an officer of the court in search of the truth, while trying to fool the jurors into believing a wholly fabricated story, *i.e.,* that the woman had consented, when in fact she had been forced at gunpoint to have sex with the defendant. I was also prepared to demand an acquittal because the state had not met its burden of proof when, if it had not, it would have been because I made the truth look like a lie. If there is any redeeming social value in permitting an attorney to do such things, I frankly cannot discern it.

Others have discerned it, however, and while they have been criticized, they seem clearly to represent the majority view. They rely on either of two theories. The first is that the lawyer cannot

possibly be sufficiently certain of the truth to impose his or her
view of it on the client's case. The second is that the defense
attorney need not be concerned with the truth even if he or she
does know it. Both are misguided.

III. Can Lawyers "Know" The Truth?

A. "The Adversary System" Excuse

. . .

..., it does not seem to me that permitting the attorney to
achieve the client's ends by subverting the truth advances the
cause of individual autonomy. The legitimate concern of those
who advance the autonomy argument is that the government must
be prevented from interfering wrongfully or unnecessarily with
individual freedom, not that there should be no interference with
individual liberty at all. Here we are positing that the government has behaved reasonably, and the lawyer knows it. In my
view, permitting such a case to be undermined by false evidence
glorifies winning, but has very little to do with assuring justice.

2. A false defense may be necessary to preserve the rigorous
    process by which guilt is determined.

Those taking this view see the criminal process not as a truth-
seeking one, but a "screening system" designed to assure the
utmost certainty before the criminal sanction is imposed. Only by
permitting the defense attorney to use all of the tools which we
have described here can we be certain that the prosecution will be
put to its proof in all cases. The argument seems to be that if the
prosecutor knows that the defense attorney will attempt to demolish the government's case, the prosecutor will in a sense be kept
on his or her toes, and will seek the strongest evidence possible.

This position is difficult to understand. In the situation
under discussion here the prosecution has presented the strongest
case possible, i.e., the truthful testimony of the victim of a crime.
In any case, it is one thing to attack a weak government case by
pointing out its weakness. It is another to attack a strong
government case by confusing the jury with falsehoods. ...
[Accordingly] I would limit my representation at that stage to
putting forth the strongest argument I could that the facts presented by the state did not sustain its burden. In these ways, the
defendant would receive the services of an attorney in subjecting
the state's case to the final stage of the screening process provided
by the system to insure against unjust convictions. That, however, would be all that the defense attorney could do.

There are several commonly raised questions concerning the procedure proposed here that I have yet to address. The first is whether interposing the attorney as a judge of the client's guilt creates an unacceptable risk that defendants deserving a fuller day in court will be deprived of it. I do not think that would be so, for several reasons. First, the presumption in favor of the defendant on the question of the truth of his or her story is a heavy one, and will permit the attorney to proceed with that story in most cases. It is necessary to emphasize this point: I am concerned here with a class of cases which is at the edge, not the core of the defense attorney's world, the case where the facts are clear and not where legitimately held doubts exist. It is in these clear cases that the attorney would not be permitted to do what I had planned to do, which was to substitute the defendant's story for a better one.

Second, the attorney need not act on what he or she concludes is the truth before explaining the situation to the client,[114] and giving the client the opportunity to seek, as it were, a "second opinion." If the second attorney, knowing what the first attorney knows, in good faith reaches a different conclusion, he or she is free to present the defense.[115]

Geoffrey C. Hazard, Jr., "Quis custodiet ipsas custodes?" Review of Kenneth Mann, *Defending White Collar Crime*
95 *Yale L.J.* 1923 (1986).

Kenneth Mann's *Defending White Collar Crime* treats an aspect of law practice that every lawyer knows about, but many may fear to question—the concealing and distorting of facts so that a client avoids his just deserts under the law. This important book puts this issue in the complex context of actual practice, where such misconduct cannot be clearly distinguished, empirically or morally, from lawful tactics of the advocate. Anyone who has supposed that the solution to this problem is easy will have to think again in the light of Dr. Mann's fascinating study.

---

114. Several people have asked me whether I would give my client *Miranda* warnings given that I might take steps adverse to their interests. I would, just as I would try under the profession's present "protective" rules to advise clients of the dangers of speaking freely to their attorney. *See* Subin, *supra* note 2 at 1165–66, where I discuss the exceptions that all but swallow the rule of confidentiality.

115. The question whether present rules of confidentiality would permit disclosure by the first attorney to the second of the client's communications is a complex one, full exposition of which is beyond the scope of this article. Suffice it to say that if either the profession's ethical rules or the attorney-client privilege did preclude disclosure, they could, and should, be modified.

Dr. Kenneth Mann is a sociologist and a lawyer. As a sociologist he is trained in observation of human group behavior; as a lawyer he is trained in law and in the legal ethics of the adversary system of trial. His study addresses how lawyers represent persons accused of white-collar crime, a task which often involves severe moral conflict. Dr. Mann's findings suggest that, in general, lawyers do an honorable job, but that in marginal situations they sometimes resort to deception—sometimes of others, sometimes of themselves.

. . .

II. Innocent Ignorance

The morality of a seriously moral person includes concern for the truth of the matter in things of consequence. The advocate, however, must be concerned with presentation to others of evidence that will be taken as the equivalent of truth. Every trial advocate who is a seriously moral person has to be concerned with this ambiguity.

As Dr. Mann says: "The second goal, which can exist only in conjunction with the first, is to keep the client from communicating too much information to the attorney, information that would interfere with his building a strong defense." Lawyers do not commonly acknowledge that they do not wish always to gather all relevant information concerning a client's matter. To acknowledge that avoiding certain information may be a goal in the attorney-client relationship contradicts the premises of the adversary system and the conventional theory of the attorney-client privilege. Whoever heard of the attorney-client privilege being justified on the ground that it allows the lawyer merely to gather some information about the client? Dr. Mann describes the deeper reason why the lawyer may want to avoid certain information:

> Some attorneys, for instance, discourage the disclosure of facts that would negate a defense of lack of knowledge. They would not want to find out that a client actually had knowledge of a fact that would prove criminal intent.... The attorney can then more forcefully argue that the client did not know of the report or action.... The deeper moral dilemma ... is the question of what it means to devote oneself to defending persons who commit white-collar crimes.... [12]

. . .

12. Pp. 103–04.

Dr. Mann suggests that many defense counsel are people often morally troubled in their vocation, who seek refuge from torturing knowledge in the soothing folds of cognitive dissonance. This assessment corresponds to my own observation. The retreat from awareness and the moral responsibility that goes with it may merit the scorn often heaped upon lawyers. But what are the alternatives in the real and imperfect world? To have defense counsel so cognitively obtuse that they cannot recognize guilt-proving evidence when they see it? To have defense counsel so morally obtuse that they are not troubled by their work, and need no refuge? To build a system around the appointment of amateurs who are innocent of what they are doing because they do not know what they are doing? To abolish the right to counsel in any criminal case where the prosecution has evidence that any sensible person would recognize as convincing?

. . .

[A common resolution of this dilemma is for the lawyer to avoid] knowing the facts in their full implication except when it is unavoidably necessary. That comforting ignorance allows the lawyer better to play his role—"to forcefully argue that the client did not know." It also allows the *client* to believe that the lawyer does not know of his guilt. That belief in turn gives the client confidence that the lawyer will be able effectively to play the role of advocate. Why should a client, any more than any other lay person, suppose that a lawyer could effectively defend someone the lawyer knows to be guilty? The lawyer's cognitive dissonance thus serves to strengthen the lawyer-client relationship in both directions.

At this point, of course, serious moralists often protest that the whole criminal justice process is a charade. In some part of his mind, the client knows whether or not he is guilty—at least if he himself is not in a deep state of cognitive dissonance (as clients often are concerning their crimes and misdemeanors). In some part of the lawyer's mind—the part he would use, for example, in selecting a guardian for his own children—he also knows that the client is guilty. The prosecutor knows the client is guilty, for she would not want to waste the taxpayer's money and her own time on a weak case. The judge knows that most of those who are accused are guilty, and has no reason to think that this particular case is exceptional.

But the law as a system does not possess any of this knowledge. The law in a constitutional regime treats the accused as guilty only when guilt is made out beyond a reasonable doubt by lawful evidence adduced by lawful procedure. The law in such a regime limits itself to working on the basis of public knowledge of a special kind—a species of "official knowledge"—and cannot resort to the private knowledge of the prosecutor, the defense lawyer, or anyone else. The law proceeds on what is made to appear according to the rules of the game, not on what "really is." Compared with the process by which we apprehend reality in ordinary life, the law's procedure is literally a "charade": a guessing game in which each syllable of a word to be found ["guilty"] is "represented in riddling verse or by picture, tableau or dramatic action." [13] Using "dramatic action" to determine the matter "to be found" is the essence of due process.

The defense lawyer's avoidance of knowledge that incriminates his client provides an escape from the contradiction between the cognitive and normative reality of personal knowledge, and the cognitive and normative tableaus that the law uses as the basis for adjudication. Whatever moral sins the criminal defense lawyer may commit in living this contradiction, they are committed for the sake of due process and therefore for the sake of all of us.

III. Guilty Knowledge

The same cannot be said of another goal that criminal defense lawyers sometimes pursue. In any given case, the criminal defense lawyer would very much prefer that the prosecutor not obtain certain relevant documents and testimony from the client or any other source, that is, documents that incriminate and testimony that is adverse. Criminal defense counsel in "ordinary" crimes may hope that opportunities for loss of such evidence will eventuate, but the prosecution's case has usually been made before the defense lawyer becomes involved. For lawyers who defend white-collar crimes, however, opportunities often exist by which to facilitate the suppression of incriminating evidence.

These opportunities are familiar in the lore of advocacy. ... The chapter in *Anatomy of a Murder* [14] on "the lecture" is the classic explanation of how this is done. Dr. Mann's findings show that "the lecture" is not fictional:

> The attorney accepts that there are certain things he cannot and should not do—such as tell a client to alter his story—but if he explains to a client the legal significance of a particular story, manifestly a legitimate form of counsel, it is permissible even if he could foresee that given the particular client this explanation may result in client improprieties. While the

13. *Webster's New Collegiate Dictionary* 227 (9th ed. 1983).

14. J. Voelker, *Anatomy of a Murder* (1958).

immediate objective is to prevent the client from disclosing information to the attorney, the broader objective is to keep the client from disclosing inculpatory information to the government.

A second means of facilitating the suppression of incriminating evidence is to suggest to the client or witness what his testimony should *not* be. The crucial factual element in many cases does not concern those facts of which the client has affirmative recollection, but rather those of which he may lack clear memory. This is particularly true in cases involving mental states such as intention, awareness, or purpose—elements in virtually all white-collar crimes. Wouldn't it be convenient if the client could not remember such and such a conversation? Or could not recall seeing such and such a document? Or could not recollect whether or not so and so was present at a specified meeting? Most white collar defendants can figure out what is convenient not to remember. The defense lawyer must decide whether he should, through probing and memory-stimulating questions, disturb the client's emergent failure to recall.

As the problem was viewed by one of the lawyers:

'... I never ask anybody to tell me anything except what they want to tell me. I am not interested in fairy tales, and I am certainly interested in knowing at least what [the clients] have told the investigators. But I think it is absolutely ridiculous for a lawyer to say I can't help you unless I know everything. If a fellow wants to conceal something, that is because if you probe unnecessarily, he is going to tell you what you don't want to hear and it is going to be devastating. Most clients, I think, have enough brains not to tell everything.'

A third means is to eliminate discrepancies between the client's testimony and that of others. Up to a certain point, this is a standard and legitimate trial preparation technique. But in any given situation it is often not clear where that stopping point is. Should the lawyer acquiesce when the client is invoking ties of kinship or friendship to a witness in order to eliminate inconsistencies in testimony? Relationships are drawn on in this way every day in ordinary life. What parent will not remember or forget according to the interest of a child caught in the toils of the law? But what about relationships in a business or corporate setting? As one of the lawyers in Dr. Mann's study said:

In some cases ... you can represent a corporation and its president.... This gave me a great deal of leverage over most of the managerial staff in the company. They couldn't very well refuse to interview when their boss was telling them to cooperate.

. . .

Still another means of effecting the suppression of evidence is to indicate to the client the evidentiary significance of potentially incriminating documents. This is a particularly delicate matter. Suggesting the destruction of evidentiary documents is as illegal and unethical as counseling perjury. Moreover, in this era in which any piece of paper may have been photocopied, destruction of documents can be much easier to prove than perjury. For the same reasons that lawyers do not want to be taken as counseling perjury, they do not want to be taken as counseling destruction of documents. The line between opportunity and inhibition is indeed thin.

Dr. Mann summarizes how some lawyers viewed the problem:

The person faced with the tragedy of a criminal prosecution should not be told by an attorney how to handle the evidence that can lead to a conviction. As long as the attorney does not involve himself directly, it is the client's choice ....

Another lawyer viewed it as follows:

My job is to keep the client out of jail. Some of my clients have ended up in jail not because of the crime for which they were being investigated, but because they lied, or burned documents, or altered them in the course of the investigation. So I tell them right off the bat that if they want to stay out of jail, let me know what's there, and keep hands off.

It is viewed yet differently by others:

There are many cases in which one would surmise that documents summoned from the client existed at the time the summons was issued. My function in this procedure is a very limited one. I, of course, do not want the client convicted of [an] obstruction of justice charge, and I do warn him of the dire consequences of such a happening. But in the end it is the client's choice. I have no doubt that clients destroy documents. Have I ever "known" of such an occurrence? No. But you put two and two together. You couldn't convict anyone on such circumstantial evidence, but you can draw your own conclusion.

. . .

Lawyers know that the suppression of evidence through the techniques revealed by Dr. Mann is not confined to defense of criminal cases. Quite the contrary, it is common experience within the trial bar that the same thing is often done in civil cases, and that some lawyers go further by lying to cover up. As in criminal cases, these occurrences cannot legally be proved except in rare instances; they simply are facts.

Suppression of evidence is morally obnoxious. It corrupts the due process of law and perverts the defense counsel's function. As a contagion it corrupts the bar, perverts our profession, and subverts the rule of law. It is no more tolerable in the judicial function than ballot fraud is tolerable in the legislative function. It is time we stopped mincing words about the nature of the evil. Dr. Mann's study helps us to that extent.

. . .

Lawyers cannot pretend that their duty as advocates to stay "within the bounds of the law" extends only as far as a violation of that duty can be proved in court. For if that were taken as the normative and evidentiary standard of determining compliance with the advocate's duty, the lawyer's answerability to the law would be no greater than that of a white collar criminal. The notion of "officer of the court" must have more to it than that.

Deborah L. Rhode, *Ethics by the Pervasive Method*
(1994).

In 25 years, Martin Erdmann has defended more than 100,000 criminals. He has saved them tens of thousands of years in prison and in those years they have robbed, raped, burglarized and murdered tens upon tens of thousands of people. The idea of having had a very personal and direct hand in all that mayhem strikes him as boring and irrelevant. "I have nothing to do with justice," he says. "Justice is not even part of the equation. If you say I have no moral reaction to what I do, you are right."

And *he* is right. As right as our adversary judicial system, as right as jury trials, as right as the presumption of innocence and the Fifth Amendment. If there is a fault in Erdmann's eagerness to free defendants, it is not with Erdmann himself, but with the system. Criminal law to the defense lawyer does not mean equity or fairness or proper punishment or vengeance. It means get-

ting everything he can for his client. And in perhaps
98% of his cases, the clients *are* guilty. Justice is a
luxury enjoyed by the district attorney. He alone is
sworn "to see that justice is done." The defense lawyer
does not bask in the grandeur of any such noble oath. He
finds himself most often working for the guilty and for a
judicial system based upon the sound but paradoxical
principle that the guilty must be freed to protect the
innocent.[1]

No issue is more central to the American legal system and
more controversial among the American public than the criminal
defense lawyer's obligations in defending the guilty. As an abstract proposition, most individuals agree that persons accused of
a crime should be presumed innocent, and should be entitled to
force the government to make its case. But when that presumption becomes concrete, and the lawyer's role in freeing guilty,
often dangerous, offenders becomes explicit, popular sentiment
shifts.

The moral boundaries of defense lawyers' obligations are
troubling to many individuals within the profession as well as
outside it. Longstanding debates have centered on whether counsel in criminal cases should have "something to do with justice" in
particular cases as well as in the system as a whole. While
virtually all commentators agree that a defendant has, and should
have, a constitutional right to put the government to its proof,
they disagree about what that right entails for defense counsel.
Does a defendant whom counsel believes is guilty deserve what the
lawyer believes is a misleading defense? If so, may the lawyer use
techniques that do not technically violate disciplinary rules but
are likely to mislead the jury, such as impeaching truthful witnesses, and presenting evidence that is probably, but not certainly,
false?

The two most common justifications for zealous representation
on behalf of guilty defendants parallel the arguments on behalf of
the adversary system and the advocate's role more generally. One
rationale involves the pursuit of truth and the other involves the
defense of rights.[2] Many commentators who reject these argu-

---

1. Mills, "I Have Nothing to Do
With Justice," *Life*, March 12, 1971, at
56, 57.

2. The commentary on criminal defense lawyers' ethical obligations to
guilty clients is extensive. For representative selections, see Goldman, *The*

*Moral Foundations of Professional Eth-
ics* 90–155 (1980); Babcock, "Defending
the Guilty," 32 *Clev.St.L.Rev.* 175
(1983); Gillers, "Can a Good Lawyer Be
a Bad Person?", 84 *Mich.L.Rev.* 1011
(1986); Pepper, "The Lawyer's Amoral
Ethical Role: A Defense, a Problem,

ments for unqualified neutral partisanship in the civil context accept them in criminal cases because of certain distinctive procedural features and practical consequences of the penal system.

Truth

The first justification for zealous representation of clients whom an attorney believes to be factually guilty is that it is necessary to protect those who are factually, or legally innocent. Attorneys may be wrong in their assessments, particularly since defendants seldom have reason to confess their culpability to an attorney.[3] From this perspective, as Barbara Babcock notes,

> truth cannot be known. Facts are indeterminate, contingent, and in criminal cases, often evanescent. A finding of guilt is not necessarily the truth, but a legal conclusion arrived at after the role of the defense lawyer has been fully played....
> there is [often] a difference between legal and moral guilt...."[4]

Accordingly, our system proceeds on the assumption that guilt is generally best determined "not in the privacy of one lawyer's office but in open court under due process."[5]

The risks of allowing lawyers to curtail their efforts in accordance with their own perceptions of guilt are particularly great under a system in which the vast majority of all defendants never go to trial and reimbursement for pretrial preparation is usually quite limited.[6] As John Mitchell argues, without the prospect of a zealous defense in those cases, prosecutors and police have far fewer incentives to investigate the facts thoroughly, to corroborate a complainant's story, and to ensure, in short, that they are not trying the wrong person.[7] The risks of an unjust conviction are especially great where the crime is heinous or the accused is a member of an unpopular group. To take only the most obvious example, for most of this nation's history, southern blacks accused

---

and Some Possibilities," 1986 *A.B.F.Res.J.* 613; Pye, "The Role of Counsel in the Suppression of Truth," 4 *Duke L.J.* 921 (1978).

3. For discussion of defendants' unwillingness to fully trust court-appointed counsel, see Casper, *American Criminal Justice: The Defendant's Perspective* (1972); and "Did you Have a Lawyer When You Went to Court? No, I Had a Public Defender," 7 *Yale Rev.L. & Soc. Act.* (1971).

4. *See* Babcock, *supra* note 2, at 177.

5. Rhode, "An Adversarial Exchange on Adversarial Ethics: Text, Subtext, and Context," 41 *J. of Leg. Ed.* 29, 32 (1991).

6. For discussion of the inadequacy of resources, see Luban, "Are Criminal Lawyers Different?", 91 *Mich.L.Rev.* 1729 (1993).

7. Mitchell, "The Ethics of the Criminal Defense Lawyer: New Answers to Old Questions," 32 *Stan.L.Rev.* 293 (1980).

of raping a white woman stood little chance of anything approximating a fair trial.[8]

Critics of this rationale for unqualified partisanship make several responses. In William Simon's view, arguments that the fact-finding role rest properly with judges or jurors, not lawyers, are convincing only to the extent that those triers of fact have all relevant information. The difficult ethical issue, however, arises where that is not the case—where, for example, only the attorney knows that the defendant offered four other alibis before settling on the current version. We need not attribute "cosmic certainty" to the lawyer to believe that she is sometimes better able to make a judgment about guilt than a judge or juror.[9] According to Simon, lawyers should decide whether to mount an "aggressive defense" on a contextual, not categorical, basis. They should not engage in obfuscating tactics unless it would serve some important value in the particular case, such as preventing an unjust conviction or a grossly disproportionate sentence.[10]

Where defense counsel lack the resources or inclination to provide effective representation, many commentators argue that the appropriate response is to address those problems directly, not to inculcate an ideology oblivious to truth. Thus, greater resources could be available for appointed counsel to make adequate investigations, and more effective oversight of lawyers' performance could be institutionalized through civil and disciplinary liability, as well as through reversals on appeal. While none of these strategies may be wholly successful in insuring adequate representation of poor and unpopular defendants, neither is the current system.[11] Unqualified partisanship in the small percentage of cases that go to trial, and few adversarial checks in the 90 percent resolved through plea bargains, may not be the best way of securing just results overall.[12]

Rights

The second principal justification for zealous representation of the guilty involves the protection of rights. Where individuals' lives, liberty and reputation are so directly at risk, they deserve one advocate without competing loyalties to the state. That is

---

8. For representative examples, *see* Carter, *Scottsboro: A Tragedy of the American South* (1969); Kluger, *Simple Justice* (1976); Pollitt, "Counsel for the Unpopular Cause: The Hazard of Being Undone," 43 *N.C.L.Rev.* 9 (1964).

9. Simon, "The Ethics of Criminal Defense," 91 *Mich.L.Rev.* 1703 (1993).

10. *Id.*

11. Goodpaster, "The Adversary System, Advocacy, and Effective Assistance of Counsel in Criminal Cases," 14 *N.Y.U.Rev.L. & Soc. Change* 59 (1986).

12. Rhode and Luban, *Legal Ethics* 35 (1992); Luban, *supra* note 6.

particularly the case when as Babcock notes, those who commit crimes are "themselves the victims of horrible injustice." [13] The force of this argument is strengthened by the conditions of confinement in most of this nation's prisons, the inadequacy of alternatives to incarceration, and the disabling consequences of a criminal record, particularly for poor, low-skilled, and minority defendants. These distinctive features of penal sanctions, coupled with the potential for governmental repression, justify many of the special protections of the criminal process, including the Sixth Amendment rights to effective assistance of counsel and the Fifth Amendment privilege against self-incrimination. For many commentators, such protections also entail a commitment of unqualified partisanship beyond that justifiable in civil proceedings.[14] To penalize clients for making disclosures to their lawyers that suggest guilt would effectively force an impermissible choice between Fifth and Sixth Amendment guarantees.

These justifications for partisanship have been subject to several lines of challenge. One obvious response to concerns about self-incrimination is that voluntary disclosures to a lawyer do not involve the same risk of abuses and inaccuracies associated with custodial confessions to law enforcement officials. While acknowledging the uniquely disabling features of penal sanctions, some commentators argue that it would be preferable to address these concerns directly. In William Simon's view, lawyers should press for changes in the sanctioning process and dispositional alternatives rather than legitimate an ideology of zealous advocacy that is both under- and over-inclusive.[15] Misleading the judge and jury in the few cases that go to trial does nothing to address the problem of disproportionate sentences, inhuman prison conditions, and inadequate opportunities for ex-offenders. Moreover, a categorical distinction between civil and criminal proceedings fails to take account of relevant factors. In some civil cases, the potential for abuse of private power and the consequences for the parties are far more substantial than in some routine criminal cases involving petty offenses and offenders for whom one additional conviction will have relatively little practical significance. To the extent that our concern is with protecting individual rights, Simon, Subin, and other commentators argue that the rights of victims deserve some consideration in defense counsel's moral universe.

---

13. Babcock, *supra* note 2, at 178.

14. *See* Luban, *Lawyers and Justice* (1988); Wasserstrom, "Lawyers as Professionals: Some Moral Issues," 5 *Human Rights* 1 (1975).

15. Simon, *supra* note 9.

In responding to these commentators, David Luban suggests that the debate over ethics in criminal defense involves two different world views. One presents a system in which aggressive defense significantly impairs law enforcement, diminishes public safety, and undervalues victims' injury. An alternative vision sees aggressive defense as the exception rather than the norm, and emphasizes that for the vast majority of defendants, investigative resources are virtually nonexistent. From this second perspective, the aspiration to provide zealous representation is at least some counterweight to the institutional pressures toward quick pleas and "assembly line" justice.[16]

How would you evaluate these arguments? Where would you draw the line on representing defendants whom you believe to be guilty and dangerous?

REFERENCES

Bress, "Professional Ethics in Criminal Trials: A View of Defense Counsel's Responsibility," 64 *Mich.L.Rev.* 1493 (1966).

J. Casper, *American Criminal Justice: The Defendant's Perspective* (1972).

Casper, "Did You Have a Lawyer When You Went to Court? No, I Had a Public Defender," *Yale Rev.L. & Soc. Action* (Spring 1971).

Fleming, "Client Games: Defense Attorney Perspectives on Their Relations with Criminal Clients," 1986 *Am. B.Found.Res.J.* 253.

Goodpaster, "The Adversary System, Advocacy, and Effective Assistance of Counsel in Criminal Cases," 14 *N.Y.U.L.Rev. & Soc. Change* 59 (1986).

Lefstein, "Client Perjury in Criminal Cases: Still in Search of an Answer," 1 *Georgetown J. of Legal Ethics* 521 (1987).

Lefstein, "The Criminal Defendant Who Proposes Perjury: Rethinking the Defense Lawyer's Dilemma," 6 *Hofstra L.Rev.* 665 (1978).

Mitchell, "Reasonable Doubts Are Where You Find Them: A Response to Professor Subin's Position on Criminal De-

16. Luban, *supra* note 6; Rhode, *supra note 5.*

fense Lawyer's Different Mission," *Georgetown J. of Legal Ethics* 339 (1987).

Noonan, "The Purposes of Advocacy and the Limits of Confidentiality," 64 *Mich.L.Rev.* 1485 (1966).

Pye, "The Role of Counsel in the Suppression of Truth," 1978 *Duke L.J.* 921.

Rotunda, Book Review, 89 *Harv.L.Rev.* 622 (1976) (reviewing M. Freedman, *Lawyers' Ethics in an Adversary System* (1975)).

Schulhofer, "Effective Assistance on the Assembly Line," 14 *N.Y.U.Rev.L. & Soc.Change* 137 (1986).

Schulhofer, "Plea Bargaining as Disaster," 101 *Yale L.J.* 1979 (1992).

Selinger, "The Perry Mason Perspective and Others," 6 *Hofstra L.Rev.* 631 (1978).

Simon, "The Ethics of Criminal Defense," *Mich.L.Rev.* (forthcoming).

R. Spangenberg and P. Smith, *American Bar Association, An Introduction to Indigent Defense Systems* (1986).

Wolfram, "Client Perjury," 50 *S.Cal.L.Rev.* 809 (1977).

Zacharias, "Rethinking Confidentiality," 74 *Iowa L.Rev.* 351 (1989).

III. THE PARADIGM EXTENDED: ADVOCACY IN CIVIL CONTEXTS

A. ROLE–DIFFERENTIATED MORALITY

Deborah L. Rhode, "Institutionalizing Ethics"

Case Western Law Review (1993).

Law, as Rheinhold Niebuhr once noted, is a "compromise between moral ideals and practical possibilities." The same is true of lawyers' ethics. This essay explores the terms of our current compromise by focusing on its institutional context. The aim is to survey changes in regulatory, market, and socialization structures that might respond to chronic problems of professionalism. . . .

Discussion begins by summarizing the most frequently perceived problems of professional responsibility, those that involve overrepresentation, underrepresentation, and nonrepresentation of potential client interests. The first set of problems arises where pressures to pursue client concerns compromise broader societal values. Other difficulties result from pressures to subordinate client interests to lawyers' own needs. A final, but related group of problems involves issues of distribution: the lack of representation for a broad range of constituencies who lack the resources or incentives to address their legal needs. Although this catalogue by no means exhausts the ethical problems facing the profession, it offers a representative array of the most commonly noted concerns. Discussion also focuses on some less commonly acknowledged difficulties in conceptualizing these problems, which have led to corresponding difficulties in identifying solutions.

I. Problems of Professionalism

Problems of professionalism arise from complex interrelationships among socioeconomic incentives, institutional structures, and professional ideologies. In some instances, these problems involve violations of existing rules; the difficulty lies in enforcement. In other instances, the conduct is at least arguably permissible; the difficulty lies in the content of the rules and in their economic and ideological foundations.

202

A. Overvaluing Client Interests

1. Neutral Partisanship

The central norm of contemporary American legal practice is one of neutral partisanship; the attorney's role is to advance client interests "zealously within the bounds of the law" regardless of the attorney's own assessment of their underlying merits. Although lawyers have certain obligations as officers of the court, these are quite limited and largely track the prohibitions on criminal and fraudulent conduct that govern all participants in the legal process.

This neutral partisanship model rests on two assumptions. The first is that an adversarial clash between two zealous advocates is the best way to discover truth and promote accurate legal decision making. A second assumption is that partisan advocacy provides the most effective protection for individual rights. Each of these assumptions has generated an extensive critique that is sufficiently familiar to require only a brief summary here.

The first assumption, that an adversarial clash yields accurate outcomes, is not self-evident. As many commentators have observed, this is not how most countries adjudicate disputes, how most professionals investigate facts, or even how most lawyers conduct inquiries outside the courtroom. In an adversarial model, the merits prevail only if the contest is a balanced one—that is, if each side has roughly equal access to relevant legal information, resources, and capabilities. Yet how often a fully balanced contest occurs in practice is open to doubt. American lawyers practice "in a social order that tolerates vast disparities in wealth, renders most litigation enormously expensive, and allocates civil legal assistance almost entirely through market mechanisms. Under these circumstances, one would expect that the 'haves' generally come out ahead."

Among defenders of current partisan norms, the conventional "solution" to the problem of unequal advocacy "is not to impose on counsel the burden of representing interests other than those of his client, but rather to take appropriate steps to ensure that all interests are effectively represented." What exactly those steps might be have never been satisfactorily elaborated. As subsequent discussion indicates, inequalities in access have been seriously confronted only at a rhetorical level.

A related problem involves the inadequacy of enforcement structures to ensure a fair adversarial contest. Conventional justifications for the neutral partisanship model assume that some neutral arbiter will sort out competing claims. Yet most lawyers work outside the oversight of any disinterested third party. Only a small part of legal practice involves litigation, and about 90 percent of litigated cases are resolved without trial. Even in cases involving neutral decision makers, we have no evidence about the relative effectiveness of partisanship in promoting justice. What we do have are substantial data suggesting that it falls short in too many circumstances.

Imbalances in representation, information, and resources are readily exploited under current procedural structures. The recent proliferation of civility codes and professionalism commissions testify to a widespread sense that partisanship norms are out of control. Surveys of discovery practices suggest the frequency of problems. In large, complex cases, lawyers report chronic abuses: the average litigant is "over-discovered ... overcharged, over-exposed, and over-wrought." In one in-depth study, 62 percent of Chicago litigators complained about overdiscovery, 45 percent complained about harassment, and 80 percent complained about incomplete or evasive responses to requests. Lawyers who handled large cases reported that in about half the matters that were settled and in about 30 percent of those that were tried, they had significant information that was not discovered by opposing parties. Similarly, in a survey of over 2500 litigators, about half of responding attorneys felt that unfair and inadequate pretrial disclosure of material information is a regular or frequent problem; three quarters believed that incomplete information presents such a problem. Responses by those attorneys to a hypothetical question illustrate the problems at issue. Where a witness admitted lying during a deposition, about 40 percent of survey lawyers saw no need to correct the record before settling the case if the client would not agree to the correction.

Smaller, more qualitative studies reveal a wide range of partisan practices that obstruct the search for truth. Common examples include: invoking technical defenses to defeat substantively meritorious claims; counseling destruction of inculpating documents before their retention is clearly required; presenting evidence or testimony that a lawyer reasonably believes but does not "know" is false; adopting strained interpretations of the attorney-client privilege; preparing witnesses by a "tour down memory lane with certain destinations clearly in view;" hiring experts based on the usefulness rather than the quality or likely accuracy of their testimony. Even in the absence of any abusive practices, accurate fact finding is at best an unintended byproduct, at worst an undesired outcome, of partisan efforts. The point of advocacy, as Socrates noted and subsequent experience confirms, is persuasion, not truth.

The unqualified pursuit of client interests carries obvious costs; it obstructs the decision-making process, imposes unnecessary delays and expense, and deters meritorious claims. Although aggregate estimates of the problem vary, some smaller scale studies are illuminating. The Rand Corporation's analysis of asbestos litigation, for example, found that over a third of total compensation went for legal fees and costs. The price of partisanship is borne not just by litigants, but also by the public generally in the form of higher costs, tax deductions for legal expenses, and governmental subsidies for adjudicative and administrative proceedings.

In response to such criticisms, proponents of neutral partisanship typically invoke a second line of defense. Whatever its effectiveness or efficiency in promoting truth, this partisan framework is an indispensable safeguard of individual rights. On this view, respect for clients' autonomy implies respect for clients' pursuit of legal claims and demands largely undivided loyalty from their legal advisors. By absolving attorneys from accountability for their clients' acts, the traditional advocacy role encourages representation of those most vulnerable to public prejudice and state oppression. The promise of non-judgmental advocacy may also encourage legal consultation by those most in need of ethical counseling. Any alternative system, it is argued, would threaten "rule by an oligarchy of lawyers." To demand that attorneys judge, rather than simply defend, their clients would be "equivalent to saying that saints must have a monopoly of lawsuits" and that lawyers should have a monopoly of deciding who qualifies for sainthood.

From an ethical standpoint, this justification for neutral partisanship presents two central difficulties. First, it conflates legal and moral entitlements; it assumes that society wishes to permit whatever lawmakers do not prohibit. Yet some conduct that is clearly antithetical to broader public interests may nonetheless remain legal—either because prohibitions appear too difficult or costly to enforce, or because decision makers are too uninformed, overworked, or pressured by special interests. Although lawyers may have no special moral expertise, they at least have a more disinterested perspective than clients on the ethical dimensions of certain practices. Attorneys can accept moral responsibility without necessarily imposing it. Unless the lawyer is the last in town, his or her refusal of the neutral partisan role may simply impose on clients the psychological and financial cost of finding alternative counsel.

A second problem with rights-based justifications for partisanship is that they fail to explain why the rights of clients should trump those of all other parties whose interests are inadequately represented. This failure is most apparent when the client is a well-heeled organization squaring off against an outmatched individual. Particularly where health and safety interests are at issue, partisanship on behalf of corporate profits has often ill-served values of human dignity and autonomy. The Dalkon shield and asbestos litigation offer illustrative case histories of the misery to which unqualified advocacy has contributed. In other less dramatic contexts, where clients view the risks of liability as small in relation to potential gains, zealous representation can readily frustrate regulatory objectives.

Much of the appeal of rights-based justifications for partisanship draws on the lawyer's role in criminal defense proceedings. Yet such proceedings are distinctive in their potential for governmental oppression and in their impact on individual life, liberty, and reputation. For the same reasons that our constitutional traditions impose special protections for criminal cases, most commentators suggest that the justifications for neutral partisanship are strongest in that context. To be sure, in some civil matters, the potential for state action or the constraints on fundamental rights raise concerns analogous to those at issue in criminal proceedings. Yet while zealous advocacy has been of enormous importance in such civil cases, they do not constitute the mainstay of legal work. Only a small portion of the bar is actively involved either in criminal defense or in civil rights, civil liberties, and public interest work. Professional norms that are appropriate in those cases can hardly serve as the paradigm for all legal practice.

2. Confidentiality

A corollary of the neutral partisanship principle is that of confidentiality, and the arguments supporting broad protection for client communications track the instrumental and rights-based justifications noted above. By encouraging individuals to seek legal advice and to disclose relevant information, the attorney-client privilege and related ethical rules facilitate compliance with legal norms and appropriate resolution of legal disputes. In addition, an assurance of confidentiality both enables individuals to assert legal rights and preserves specific entitlements such as those concerning privacy, effective assistance of counsel, and protections against self-incrimination.

Yet these arguments, however persuasive in the abstract, fail to justify the current scope of confidentiality protections. In general, bar ethical codes prohibit lawyers from revealing information related to client representation except under certain limited circumstances. Both the Code and the Model Rules permit lawyers to reveal confidences if required by law or court order and if necessary to collect a fee or defend themselves from accusations of wrongful conduct. The Code allows a lawyer to reveal "the intention of his client to commit a crime and the information necessary to prevent the crime." The Model Rules permit but do not require lawyers to disclose confidential information "to the extent the lawyer reasonably believes necessary . . . to prevent the client from committing a criminal act that the lawyer believes is likely to result in imminent death or substantial bodily harm." A small number of states have modified Code or Model Rule provisions by calling on lawyers to rectify frauds perpetrated during the course of representation or to disclose life-threatening conduct. In most jurisdictions, however, past crimes, torts, and non-criminal but life-threatening acts must remain confidential.

It is by no means obvious that such sweeping mandates are essential for adequate legal representation. Current rules have exceptions and indeterminacies that few clients comprehend; existing research leaves doubt that adding certain further qualifications would significantly alter client behavior. Moreover, whatever the rules, many individuals will be unwilling to trust their lawyers with compromising disclosures. In those cases, attorneys will often find independent sources for information, such as documentary evidence, corroboration by other witnesses, and so forth. Historical, cross-cultural, and cross-professional research makes clear that practitioners have long provided counseling on confidential matters without the sweeping protections from disclosure that the American bar has now obtained.

Although the costs of such protections are difficult to quantify, some indications emerge from reported cases, bar committee opinions, and survey data. Many innocent investors have suffered substantial losses as a result of attorneys' failure to disclose client fraud. The recent savings and loan debacles offer multiple examples; as one federal regulator noted, many of those disasters would not have occurred without the assistance of lawyers, who provided "little or no resistance to abusive activity."

Nor has the price of broad confidentiality protections been only financial. In some jurisdictions, attorneys have persuaded courts and bar ethics committees not to require disclosure of child abuse or kidnapping plans in contested custody cases. Even where identifiable individuals' lives have been at risk, many lawyers have felt that their confidentiality obligations trumped competing concerns. In one well-known Minnesota case, lawyers for an insurance company failed to reveal that their doctor had discovered a dangerous heart condition that plaintiffs' own medical experts had failed to discover.

Such cases suggest the extent to which bar ethical rules have lost touch with ordinary moral intuitions. In one of the few empirical studies on point, clients were much more likely than lawyers to believe that disclosure was, or should be required to protect third parties, and that such requirements would not discourage consultation with attorneys. This divergence between public and professional views has also been apparent in bar debates over appropriate confidentiality mandates. Concerns about lawyers' civil liability dominated discussion of the proposed Model Rules. Notably absent from the dialogue was any justification for disclosures to protect lawyers' own financial interests but not to preserve other individuals' health, safety, or economic security. Such provisions highlight more general problems with a regulatory process under exclusive control of the group to be regulated.

B. Undervaluing Client Interests

While clients' interests are overvalued in comparison with broader societal interests, they are undervalued in comparison with the profession's own interests. Inadequate representation often occurs where clients lack adequate information, financial resources, or bargaining leverage, or where attorneys' perceived relationships with other individuals are more critical than client satisfaction. Unlike the overvaluation of client concerns described above, underrepresentation is generally inconsistent with the profession's stated values. Problems typically arise because those values are inadequately specified or enforced under existing regulatory structures.

1. Resource Limitations

Underrepresentation is most chronic where neither the client nor a third party who is subsidizing legal services has sufficient resources for adequate assistance.... [T]he bar has sometimes exacerbated the difficulties by blocking efforts to reduce costs. In other settings, problems of underrepresentation arise from inherent conflicts of interest. For example, in contingent fee cases, attorneys' economic interest lies in maximizing the return on their work; clients' interest lies in gaining the highest possible settlement. Depending on the amount of effort and expense lawyers have invested in preparation, the alternative uses of their time, and their degree of risk adverseness, they may be more or less disposed to settle than their clients.

2. Lawyer–Client Relationships: Information and Bargaining Leverage

In cases where client resources are less constrained and lawyers are working for hourly fees, a converse set of problems arises. Undervaluing clients' interests leads to overpreparing their cases; meter running is a practice that lawyers frequently observe and, in some confidential surveys, acknowledge committing. Here, adversarial psychology and performance anxieties reinforce financial pressures. Lawyers will often prefer to "leave no stone unturned, provided, of course, they can charge by the stone." A related and reportedly widespread problem involves charging excessive fees because of unfamiliarity in the area, without disclosing that unusual preparation was required. Finally, some qualitative research suggests that lawyers' "creative billing" practices are often fraudulent or on the fringes of fraud: inflating hours, charging two clients for the same work or the same travel time, failing to disclose the basis of bills, and so forth. Although sophisticated corporate clients have become more adept at identifying such practices and have the leverage or expertise to avoid it, other individuals, particularly one-shot purchasers, are vulnerable to abuse.

These individuals often lack sufficient information to assess either the quality, competence, or cost-effectiveness of their representation. In an era of increasing specialty where lawyers know more and more about less and less, practitioners who do not routinely deliver particular services may have difficulty doing so efficiently. Yet bar ethical codes do not speak to this problem; they demand only skills "adequate" or "reasonably necessary" for representation. Nor have courts and disciplinary agencies been inclined to monitor the fairness of fee agreements except in cases of clear abuse.

Related problems arise where formal mechanisms of client accountability are weak and where inequalities of class, race, ethnicity, or gender reinforce professional dominance. So, for example, lawyers representing diffuse classes in public interest cases, or establishing priorities for scarce resources in legal service organizations, may lack incentives to remain adequately sensitive to client concerns. In other contexts, attorneys who have received little formal training in interpersonal skills end up talking past the concerns that are most central to the client. Studies of matrimonial practice reveal participants occupied with "two different divorces: lawyers with the financial and legal consequences of separation and clients with the social and emotional ones." Divorcing parties are often depressed, anxious, and unsure of what they want. Attorneys are often impatient, insensitive, and unresponsive in dealing with matters lacking direct legal relevance.

Other, more general research reveals a similar mismatch between professional and public concerns. Clients place highest value on lawyers' responsiveness to their needs as measured by "attentiveness, capacity and willingness to communicate, and respect for [their] intelligence and judgment." These considerations do not receive comparable priority in professional education and regulatory structures.

3. Collegial Relationships

Inadequate representation of client interests is also common where lawyers place priority on maintaining good relationships with other members of their community or participants in the legal process. If zealous pursuit of any single matter will antagonize individuals whose continuing cooperation or client referrals is important, attorneys may adjust their partisanship accordingly. For example, lawyers in surveyed consumer protection cases have often accommodated business opponents' concerns rather than maximized client objectives. Practitioners in small towns have similarly reported foregoing strategies that would generate ill will among opposing lawyers and established interests. Criminal defense attorneys have often found that retaining the good will of prosecutors and trial judges is more important than securing the best outcome for a particular client. There are, to be sure, limits on how far a lawyer can compromise fiduciary obligations and still maintain collegial respect. But there also are limits on what attorneys can do without jeopardizing their own workplace relationships and referral networks.

C. Nonrepresentation of Potential Client Interests

A final set of problems involves the lack of representation for a vast array of legal needs. Although methods for assessing such needs are inherently inexact, contemporary surveys give some sense of the general dimensions of the problem. About half the time lawyers devote to individual clients serves those with incomes in the top 15 percent of the population; only 10 percent of attorneys' time goes to those in the bottom third. By their own account, government-funded legal aid programs can handle only a small fraction of the needs of those eligible for assistance, and many other individuals of limited income cannot realistically afford such services. Studies of low-income households generally find that about 50–80 percent of their perceived legal problems remain unaddressed. A national study cutting across income groups found that individuals do not seek lawyers' help for between 30 and 40 percent of their personal legal needs.

There are, moreover, a wide range of unrepresented interests beyond those reflected in such studies. Surveys relying on self-reports exclude matters that individuals fail to identify as needs due to unawareness of legal rights and remedies. Also omitted are collective interests such as product safety, environmental protection, civil rights, and so forth. Given the extremely limited resources available to public interest organizations, these concerns remain chronically underrepresented. Finally, legal needs' studies typically leave out third party interests, such as those of children in divorce cases, whose welfare is implicated but generally not represented in legal proceedings.

Although delivery of legal services is not the focus of this paper, neither can any adequate discussion of legal ethics fail to acknowledge certain central distributional issues. First, in a society at least in principle committed to equal justice under law, the absence of adequate representation poses obvious dilemmas for lawyers in adversarial contexts. Second, the bar has itself compounded problems of inadequate assistance by invoking ethical concerns when resisting lay competition and procedural reforms. Such resistance has blocked changes that would minimize the need for lawyers in areas such as uncontested divorce, probate, immigration, residential real estate, and auto liability claims.

Finally, and most importantly, the bar collectively has been unable or unwilling to grapple with the full implications of these distributional issues. The ABA consistently has rejected proposals for mandatory pro bono service, and the vast majority of lawyers make no contributions to organized legal aid programs. Within some segments of the bar, a large part of the problem lies in the refusal to acknowledge that a significant problem exists. During the debates over a proposed Model Rules provision requiring pro bono assistance, opponents offered extensive variations on one commentator's theme: "I know of no person or worthy cause that has been refused legal service in [this] county, regardless of the ability to pay.... I have no reason to believe the same is not true of every other county of our [s]tate."

Moreover, even lawyers who acknowledge the problem of inadequate access typically ignore its connection to other issues of professional role. For example, in debates over another unsuccessful Model Rule proposal that would have required lawyers to avoid exploiting the ignorance of unrepresented opponents, commentators frequently expressed unwillingness to "coddl[e]" those "too cheap to hire an attorney." In the face of massive distributional inequalities, bar leaders typically have proposed only minor reforms, such as modest increases in voluntary pro bono contributions, legal services' subsidies, and nonlawyer services.

D. The Problem With the Problem

These critiques of professional norms have generated a corresponding body of criticisms, which inform the evaluation of possible responses set forth below. However, before addressing particular initiatives, several overarching observations are in order.

Claims about over- and under-valuing client interests typically rest on an unexpressed and unexplored vision of appropriate professional representation. Yet consensus on that vision exists only at the abstract level. The bar collectively has no shared understanding of what constitutes undue partisanship or ineffective assistance except in relatively egregious cases. In a professional context where either too much or too little client loyalty can result in ethical violations, it is often difficult to combat one dynamic without reinforcing the other.

Problems in addressing these problems are complicated by several factors. First, many ethical issues are inextricably linked to distributional issues and to limitations in resources available to clients, opponents, or third parties. It is, however, by no means clear what follows from that fact. Our nation's rhetorical commitment to equal justice under law is the kind of unexamined platitude that prompted Tawney's observation about equal opportunity. He wondered what would "horrify proponents most: the denial of the principle or the attempt to apply it?" Given the elasticity of legal needs and the disparity of financial resources among the public generally, equalizing access is an unrealistic aspiration. It would require not only massive government subsidies, but also the prohibition of private markets.

Yet once we acknowledge such inequality, some uncomfortable questions persist. What constitutes fairness in an adversarial structure? At what point does exploitation of resource advantages become ethically problematic? To what extent do definitions of competent assistance depend on ability and inclination to pay? How much claiming and blaming do we as a society wish to subsidize? Even modest calls to enhance if not equalize access leave most of these sticky points unaddressed. If we cannot reach agreement on these sorts of distributional issues at the societal level, it is unrealistic to expect consensus within a highly heterogeneous bar serving clientele of widely varying means.

A final complicating factor is that various psychological tendencies work against professionals' recognition of ethical problems. One such tendency is "cognitive conservatism." Individuals are more likely to register and retain information that is compatible with established beliefs or earlier decisions. A related phenomenon is reduction of "cognitive dissonance." After making a decision, individuals tend to suppress or reconstrue information that casts doubt on that decision. Accordingly, once lawyers have determined to represent a particular client, they become less sensitive to ethical problems arising from that choice.

Other cognitive processes push in similar directions. Individuals are more likely to retain information that reflects favorably on themselves and to form positive impressions of someone on whom their own success partly depends. So too, the very act of advocating a particular position increases the likelihood that proponents will themselves come to adopt that position. In many practice settings, these cognitive biases, together with financial self-interest, collegial pressure, and diffusion of responsibility inevitably skew ethical judgment. Such distortions can affect lawyers' sense of collective as well as personal responsibility. The more closely that individuals identify with their professional role, the less conscious they may become of problems in its normative foundations or practical consequences.

This insensitivity is exacerbated by common human tendencies to explain ethical misconduct in terms of individual deviance rather than institutional constraints. It is easier to attribute problems of professionalism to occasional lapses by aberrant practitioners than to acknowledge failures in market structures and regulatory design. Yet as the following discussion suggests, it is precisely those failures that require our attention if we are seriously committed to institutionalizing ethics.

[The omitted portion of the essay surveys possible responses. Part II explores changes in regulatory structures, such as admissions, discipline, and judicial oversight. Part III summarizes market initiatives that could increase consumer information and professional competition in the delivery of legal services. A final section considers strategies of professional socialization in law schools, law firms, and alternative forms of bar associations.]

. . .

B. ALTERNATIVE VISIONS

INTRODUCTION

Most alternative models of the advocate's role reject neutrality and partisanship as preeminent norms. These frameworks generally adopt the position that Deborah Rhode defends below: that lawyers should accept moral accountability for the consequences of their professional acts and that obligations to clients may need to be qualified by other values.

In other respects, such proposals vary considerably. Philosopher Gerald Postema proposes below that lawyers should view their profession as a "recourse role" in which their "duties and responsibilities are not fixed, but may expand or contract depending on the institutional objectives the role is designed to serve...."[1] Similarly, David Luban argues that lawyers should be allowed to forgo immoral tactics or the pursuit of unjust ends without withdrawing from a case. His model of advocacy would include four restrictions:

(1) on modes of practice that inflict morally unjustifiable damage on other people, especially innocent people;

(2) on deceit, i.e., actions that obscure truths or that lure people into doing business under misapprehensions, even if these are legally permissible;

(3) on manipulations of morally defensible law to achieve outcomes that negate its [purpose] or violate its spirit, and, in general,

(4) on the pursuit of substantively unjust results.[2]

William Simon, in the excerpt that follows, suggests a somewhat more circumscribed way for lawyers to exercise ethical discretion. Unlike other commentators, whose frameworks demand sensitivity to the full range of moral considerations implicated by a professional act, Simon proposes a decision-making structure grounded in the values of the system itself.

These alternative models of advocacy have been criticized as too demanding or not demanding enough, and as promising too significant or too insignificant a departure from existing standards. Defenders of current partisanship norms question whether clients would continue to place the same reliance on lawyers who had divided allegiance. Critics of existing standards wonder

1. Gerald J. Postema, Moral Responsibility in Professional Ethics, 55 *N.Y.U.L.Rev.* 63, 82–83 (1980).

2. David Luban, *Lawyers and Justice: An Ethical Study* 157 (1988).

whether significant change would come from attempting to alter the ideology of advocacy as long as social and economic pressures reinforce client loyalty. Demands that lawyers assume moral accountability for their actions may not significantly alter conduct where lawyers feel pressure to identify with client objectives. Questions have also been raised about proposals like Simon's, which rely on "plausible interpretations of the applicable law" as the benchmark for ethical decision making. How satisfactory will such proposals be where the law itself is unjust or indeterminate?

Consider the merits of these alternative frameworks. Are any of them more justifiable than the standard conception of neutral partisanship?

William Simon, "Ethical Discretion in Lawyering"
101 Harvard L.Rev. 1083–84, 1090–1109 (1988).

Lawyers should have an ethical discretion to refuse to assist in the pursuit of legally permissible courses of action and in the assertion of potentially enforceable legal claims. This discretion involves, not a personal privilege of arbitrary decision, but a professional duty of reflective judgment. One aspect of this judgment involves an assessment of the relative merits of the prospective client's goals and claims and those of other people who might benefit from the lawyer's services. Another is an attempt to reconcile the conflicting considerations that bear on the internal merits of the client's goals and claims. In both dimensions, the basic consideration should be whether assisting the client would further justice.

· · ·

II. The Discretionary Approach

The basic maxim of the approach I propose is this: The lawyer should take the actions that, considering the relevant circumstances of the particular case, seem most likely to promote justice. This "seek justice" maxim suggests a kind of non-categorical judgment that might be called pragmatist, ad hoc, or dialectical, but that I will call discretionary. "Discretionary" is not an entirely satisfactory term; I do not mean to invoke its connotations of arbitrariness or non-accountability, but rather its connotations of flexibility and complexity. Unlike the private norms of the *Code* and *Model Rules,* discretionary norms, as I define them, do not connote standardlessness and nonreviewability. I use the term in what Ronald Dworkin calls "a weak sense" to indicate that the relevant norms "cannot be applied mechanically but demand the use of judgment."

In the context of professional responsibility, lawyers tend to be skeptical that discretionary judgment based on the application of abstract ideals to particular cases could be anything but arbitrary. Lawyers also tend to regard discretionary judgment as plausible in the context of the judicial role. The kind of complex, flexible judgment proposed here has been extensively portrayed and defended against more categorical styles of decision in some of the best known literature of justice ... and legal theory in recent decades....

To propose a style of ethical judgment for private lawyers analogous to those familiarly associated with the judge's or prosecutor's role is not to say that lawyers should act as if they were judges or prosecutors. The analogy is to the style of judgment, not necessarily to the particular decisions that judges and prosecutors make. The discretionary approach incorporates much of the traditional lawyer role, including the notion that lawyers can serve justice through the zealous pursuit of clients' goals. Although it assumes a public dimension to the lawyer's role as well, that dimension is grounded in the lawyer's age-old claim to be an "officer of the court" and in notions about the most effective integration of the lawyering role with the other roles in the legal system.

The discretionary approach ... suggests that the lawyer should frame ethical issues in accordance with three general standards of relevance. First, a consideration is relevant if it is implicated by the most plausible interpretation of the applicable law. Issues would tend to be defined more narrowly under legal norms that regulate narrowly. For example, traffic laws suggest narrower framing than family laws. Second, a consideration is relevant if it is likely to have a substantial practical influence on the resolution. Issues tend to be defined more narrowly to the extent that the parties are situated so that substantively irrelevant factors are not likely to influence the resolution. Equality of resources and access to information will be among the more important factors weighing toward narrow definition under this second standard. Third, knowledge and institutional competence will affect the appropriate framing. More broadly framed issues tend to require more knowledge and more difficult judgments. When the lawyer lacks needed knowledge or competence, narrow framing becomes more appropriate.

. . .

Some may concede that lawyers have the capacity to make informal normative judgments but deny the legitimacy of their doing so. These critics would object that the discretionary approach enlarges lawyer power in a way that precludes effective checks. For them, the judicial analogy seems inappropriate because judges are subject to various power-legitimating public controls that do not apply to lawyers. With either a little cynicism about the ostensible public controls on judges or a little naivete about the bar's admissions and disciplinary procedures, one might argue that controls on lawyers are comparable to those on judges. But the case for ethical discretion does not require such an argument.

The basic objection is that discretion gives lawyers too much power, but the term "power" is rarely explicated in such complaints. What might it mean? Sometimes it seems to mean the capacity to be arbitrary or to impose purely personal goals, and the thrust of the complaint is that discretionary norms enlarge this capacity because they fail to yield clear answers in specific cases. This complaint conflates a norm that requires a more complex judgment with a norm that constrains decision less. But there is no reason to expect a lawyer who makes decisions in good faith to feel less constrained under discretionary norms than under categorical ones. Like a judge applying a norm such as "due process," the lawyer applying a discretionary norm may feel less confident about the answer she reaches, but so long as she is in good faith, she should not feel any more free to be arbitrary or to impose her own views.

Of course, lawyers will not always make decisions in good faith; hence in part the importance of disciplinary enforcement. Another possible meaning of the claim that ethical discretion gives lawyers too much power is that it increases practical immunity from disciplinary enforcement. Here the argument would be that applications of discretionary norms are more likely to be controversial among lawyers generally than comparable applications of categorical norms. If other lawyers are less likely to agree about what discretionary norms require in particular cases than they are about what categorical norms require, then disciplinary enforcement might constrain less under a discretionary regime.

This criticism confuses the ease with which a norm can be applied with the restrictiveness of a norm. A norm that says lawyers can do anything they want except steal from their clients is relatively easy to apply to particular cases, but it is not very restrictive. A norm that says lawyers must act loyally and competently toward clients may be more difficult to apply, but it is potentially far more restrictive. The great disadvantage of using categorical norms to avoid difficulties of application is that such norms tend to be both overinclusive and underinclusive relative to their purposes. Far more than discretionary norms, they tend to prohibit desirable conduct, permit undesirable conduct, or both.

. . .

Another meaning of "power" is the capacity to frustrate another person's goals. Thus opponents of the discretionary approach might complain that it increases lawyer power by requiring and legitimating greater intervention in opposition to client goals. We might respond that any such increased power would be justified to the extent that it served legal merit. But there is a more important response: the discretionary approach does not increase lawyer power because any increase in the lawyer's capacity to frustrate client goals is exactly balanced by a reduction in the lawyer's capacity to frustrate goals of third parties and the public. Lawyers serve client goals by using power against others. The discretionary approach puts the lawyer in opposition to clients by reducing her power to injure others for the sake of the client.

Still another meaning of "power" might be the capacity to fulfill one's own private goals. If the discretionary approach required decisions that coincided with the lawyer's private goals more frequently than did other approaches, one might argue that the discretionary approach extended lawyer power. To the extent that lawyers' private goals and ethical duties coincided simply because of their deep commitment to legality and justice, one might argue that any power arising from this fact should not be objectionable. However, it is not at all clear that the discretionary approach would in fact move ethical decisions closer to lawyers' private goals. Casual observation suggests that the private goals of many lawyers run overwhelmingly toward acquiescence in the goals of clients. These lawyers view increased responsibility to third parties and the public not as a form of empowerment, but at best as a demanding professional duty and at worst as an oppressive burden.

Furthermore, there are important indirect controls on the lawyer power under the discretionary regime. Two of the more important sources of the lawyer's power are her ability to refuse assistance and her ability to disclose information to third parties. But the lawyer's refusal usually will constrain the client only to the extent that other lawyers go along with her judgment, and disclosure will be harmful only to the extent that others, usually public officials, act on the information.

Finally, one of the basic sources of the lawyer's power—the ability to refuse assistance—is grounded in what most people would consider a fundamental right to control one's labor. To people not imbued with the ideologies of legal professionalism, it is bizarre to find lawyers responding to proposals for higher than minimal ethical standards by asking rhetorically why a lawyer should "arrogate to herself" the power to determine the justice of a client's goals. When the issue is whether the lawyer will lend her efforts to furthering the goals, this arrogation is nothing more than the right and responsibility of any person who aspires to ethical autonomy.

Deborah L. Rhode, "Ethical Perspectives on Legal Practice"

37 Stanford Law Review 589, 595–626, 643–647 (1985).*

III. Alternatives

. . .

Neither formalist nor individualist can sustain partisanship norms in their current largely unqualified scope. And the retreat into role fails even to confront, let alone resolve, the moral difficulties it raises.

A more ethically reflective form of legal practice will require different ideological foundations. In essence, lawyers must assume personal moral responsibility for the consequences of their professional actions. ... The rationale for [such] actions cannot depend on a reflexive retreat to role, which denies the need for reflection at the very point when reflection becomes most essential. To be convincing, professional judgments must withstand scrutiny by individuals seeking consistent, disinterested, and generalizable foundations for conduct. Within that framework, counsel can no longer categorically deflect responsibility to some governmental or private agent acting in a presumptively ideal regulatory system. Rather, attorneys must confront the consequences of their decisions against a realistic social backdrop, in which wealth, power, and information are unevenly distributed and democratic, adversarial, and market processes function imperfectly.

This reformulation of role in no sense contemplates that lawyers will become personally accountable for every adverse consequence that flows from client representation or collegial relationships. Under conventional ethical theories, moral responsibility depends on a variety of factors, including the significance of harm and the agent's degree of involvement, knowledge, and capacity to affect action. Nor does it follow that counsel must endorse every client's objectives or conduct before providing representation. Whether particular forms of assistance are defensible depends not only on the specific acts involved but also on their social and economic contexts, and the principles at issue.

What distinguishes this framework [from prevailing ideology] is the insistence on an ethical predicate, on an attempt systematically to justify the consequences of professional action. That a client may have a "legal right" to engage in certain conduct or invoke particular procedures is not conclusive of his moral right, or of the appropriateness of counsel's aid. ... This is by no means to imply that systematic reflection will yield determinate resolutions, or to overlook the [limitations of moral methodology]. But that concession need not invite paralysis. There may be no uncontrovertible answers, but there are better and worse ways of thinking about the questions. Thus, the attempt must be to create more channels within which serious normative dialogue can occur. Individuals must have ongoing occasions to confront ethical issues, to test their perceptions openly, and to raise concerns about client or collegial practices without professional risk. ... [To that end] the profession must fashion structures within and across employing institutions that can provide a sense of collective support and responsibility for normative concerns.

Gerald J. Postema, "Moral Responsibility in Professional Ethics"
55 New York University Law Review 63–64, 73–83 (1980).

Lawyers, like other professionals, acknowledge gravely that they shoulder special responsibilities, and believe that they should conform to "higher" ethical standards than laypersons. Yet, lawyers also claim special warrant for engaging in some activities which, were they performed by others, would be likely to draw moral censure. Skeptical of this claim to special license, Macaulay asked "[w]hether it be right that a man should, with a wig on his head, and a band round his neck, do for a guinea what, without these appendages, he would think it wicked and infamous to do for an empire." This conflict may trouble the layperson, but for the lawyer who must come to grips with his professional responsibilities it is especially problematic.

Montaigne offered one solution, the complete separation of personal and professional lives. "There's no reason why a lawyer

... should not recognize the knavery that is part of his vocation," he insisted. "An honest man is not responsible for the vices or the stupidity of his calling." The key to maintaining both profession-al and personal integrity in the face of professionally required "knavery" was, Montaigne thought, scrupulously to keep the two personalities apart: "I have been able to concern myself with public affairs without moving the length of my nail from myself. ... The mayor and Montaigne have always been two people, clearly separated."

Montaigne's solution is tempting. Maintaining a hermetically sealed professional personality promises to minimize internal con-flicts, to shift responsibility for professional "knavery" to broader institutional shoulders, and to enable a person to act consistently within each role he assumes. But for this strategy to succeed, the underlying values and concerns of important professional roles, and the characteristic activities they require, must themselves be easily segregated and compartmentalized. However, since there is good reason to doubt they can be easily segregated, Montaigne's strategy risks a dangerous simplification of moral reality. Fur-thermore, in compartmentalizing moral responses one blocks the cross-fertilization of moral experience necessary for personal and professional growth. This Article considers whether it is possible to follow Montaigne's suggestion and to separate one's private and professional personalities without jeopardizing one's ability to engage in professional activities in a morally and professionally responsible way. The central issue I address is not whether there is sufficient justification for a distinct professional code for law-yers, but whether, given the need for such a code, it is possible to preserve one's sense of responsibility. I argue that such preserva-tion is not possible when a professional must adopt Montaigne's strategy in order to function well in his professional role. I contend that a sense of responsibility and sound practical judg-ment depend not only on the quality of one's professional training, but also on one's ability to draw on the resources of a broader moral experience. This, in turn, requires that one seek to achieve a fully integrated moral personality. Because this is not possible under the present conception of the lawyer's role, as exemplified by the Code of Professional Responsibility, that conception must be abandoned, to be replaced by a conception that better allows the lawyer to bring his full moral sensibilities to play in his professional role.

III. Responsible Action Under the Standard Conception

The central problem I am concerned with is whether, given the fact of moral distance, it is possible to retain and act out of a mature sense of responsibility in a professional role. In this section, I argue that because of particular social and psychological features of professional roles, the pressures and tensions of acting and deliberating within such roles pose a serious threat to responsible professional behavior. In addition, I hope to show that the atrophy of the professional's sense of general moral responsibility is a serious and costly matter. If this argument is correct, we have discovered an important reason for radically rethinking the standard conception of the lawyer's role. This standard conception is marked by two central ideals:

(i) *Partisanship:* the lawyer's sole allegiance is to the client; the lawyer is the partisan of the client. *Within,* but all the way *up to,* the limits of the law, the lawyer is committed to the aggressive and single-minded pursuit of the client's objectives.

(ii) *Neutrality:* once he has accepted the client's case, the lawyer must represent the client, or pursue the client's objectives, regardless of the lawyer's opinion of the client's character and reputation, and the moral merits of the client's objectives. On this conception, the lawyer need not consider, nor may he be held responsible for, the consequences of his professional activities as long as he stays within the law and acts in pursuit of the client's legitimate aims. Thus, the proper range of the lawyer's concern— the boundaries of the lawyer's "moral universe"—is defined by two parameters: the law and the client's interests and objectives. These factors are the exclusive points of reference for professional deliberation and practical judgment. I contend that, far from encouraging the development and preservation of a mature sense of responsibility, the standard conception tends seriously to undermine it. To show why this is so I must sketch briefly what might be called "the problem of responsibility."

The problem is suggested in a rather grand way by Sartre in a familiar argument from his early existentialist period. Sartre insisted that to take role moralities seriously is to fail to take responsibility for oneself and one's actions. The essential property of human consciousness, according to Sartre, is its absolute freedom—the capacity to define oneself in action independently of one's role or roles. Roles, however, come "ready-made," packaged by society. When acting in a role, one simply acts as others expect one to act. Simply to identify with one's role is to ignore the fact that one is free to choose not to act in this way. In Sartre's view, it is therefore essential that one be capable of walking away from one's role. Furthermore, although it is psychologically possible to identify deeply with one's role, doing so is, in Sartre's view, morally unthinkable and a form of bad faith.

Identification is a strategy for evading one's freedom and, consequently, one's responsibility for who one is and what one does. By taking shelter in the role, the individual places the responsibility for all of his acts at the door of the institutional author of the role.

. . . The problem of responsibility lies in the fact that as the moral distance between private and professional moralities increases the temptation to adopt one or the other extreme strategy of identification also increases; one either increasingly identifies with the role or seeks resolutely to detach oneself from it. Under either extreme, however, one's practical judgment and sense of responsibility are cut off from their sources in ordinary moral experience. Yeats warned that "once one makes a thing subject to reason, as distinguished from impulse, one plays with it, even if it is a very serious thing." We might say, paraphrasing Yeats, that the artificial reason of professional morality, which rests on claims of specialized knowledge and specialized analytical technique, and which is removed from the rich resources of moral sentiment and shared moral experience in the community, tempts the professional to distort even the most serious of moral questions.

The problem of responsibility is especially troubling for the legal profession. The risk of severing professional judgment from its moral and psychological sources is particularly strong in a profession that serves a system of institutionalized justice.

. . .

To preserve his integrity, the lawyer must carefully distance himself from his activities. Publicly, he may sharply distinguish statements or arguments he makes for the client and statements on which he stakes his professional honor. The danger in this strategy is that a curious two-stage distancing may result. First, the lawyer distances himself from the argument: it is not his argument, but that of his client. His job is to construct the arguments; the task of evaluating and believing them is left to others. Second, after detaching himself from the argument, he is increasingly tempted to identify with this stance of detachment. What first offers itself as a device for distancing oneself from personally unacceptable positions becomes a defining feature of one's professional self-concept. This, in turn, encourages an uncritical, uncommitted state of mind, or worse, a deep moral skepticism. When such detachment is defined as a professional ideal, as it is by the standard conception, the lawyer is even more apt to adopt these attitudes.

The foregoing tensions and pressures have sources deep in the nature of the lawyer's characteristic activities. To eradicate them entirely would be to eliminate much of what is distinctive and socially valuable in these activities. Nevertheless, these tensions can be eased, and the most destructive tendencies avoided, if lawyers have a framework within which they can obtain an integrated view of their activities both within the role and outside it. The framework must provide the resources for responsible resolution of the conflicts that inevitably arise. The standard conception of the lawyer's role, however, fails notably on this score. Clearly, the standard conception calls for a sharp separation of private and professional morality in which, to quote Bellow and Kettleson, "the lawyer is asked to do 'as a professional' what he or she would not do 'as a person.'" The conception requires a public endorsement, as well as private adoption, of the extreme strategy of detachment. The good lawyer is one who is capable of drawing a tight circle around himself and his client, allowing no other considerations to interfere with his zealous and scrupulously loyal pursuit of the client's objectives. The good lawyer leaves behind his own family, religious, political, and moral concerns, and devotes himself entirely to the client. But since professional integrity is often taken to be the most important mark of personal integrity, a very likely result is often that a successful lawyer is one who can strictly identify with this professional strategy of detachment. That is, the standard conception both directly and indirectly *encourages* adoption of one or the other of the extreme strategies of identification. But, as we have seen, both strategies have in common the unwanted consequence that practical deliberation, judgment, and action *within* the role are effectively cut off from ordinary moral beliefs, attitudes, feelings, and relationships—resources on which responsible judgment and action depend. This consequence is very costly in both personal and social terms.

Consider first the personal costs the lawyer must pay to act in this detached manner. The maximal strategy yields a severe impoverishment of moral experience. The lawyer's moral experience is sharply constrained by the boundaries of the moral universe of the role. But the minimal strategy involves perhaps even higher personal costs. Since the characteristic activities of the lawyer require a large investment of his moral faculties, the lawyer must reconcile himself to a kind of moral prostitution. In a large portion of his daily experience, in which he is acting regularly in the moral arena, he is alienated from his own moral feelings and attitudes and indeed from his moral personality as a whole. Moreover, in light of the strong pressures for role identification, it is not unlikely that the explicit and conscious adoption of the minimal identification strategy involves a substantial element of self-deception.

The social costs of cutting off professional deliberation and action from their sources in ordinary moral experience are even more troubling. First, cut off from sound moral judgment, the lawyer's ability to do his job well—to determine the applicable law and effectively advise his clients—is likely to be seriously affected. Both positivist and natural law theorists agree that moral arguments have an important place in the determination of much of modern law. But the lawyer who must detach professional judgment from his own moral judgment is deprived of the resources from which arguments regarding his client's legal rights and duties can be fashioned. In effect, the ideal of neutrality and detachment wars against its companion ideal of zealous pursuit of client interests.

Second, the lawyer's practical judgment, in the Aristotelian sense, is rendered ineffective and unreliable. In section I, I argued that, because human values are diverse and complex, one is sometimes thrown back on the faculty of practical judgment to resolve moral dilemmas. This is as true within the professional context as outside of it. To cut off professional decisionmaking from the values and concerns which structure the moral situation, thereby blocking appeal to a more comprehensive point of view from which to weigh the validity of role morality, is to risk undermining practical judgment entirely.[46]

Third, and most importantly, when professional action is estranged from ordinary moral experience, the lawyer's sensitivity to the moral costs in both ordinary and extraordinary situations tends to atrophy. The ideal of neutrality permits, indeed requires, that the lawyer regard his professional activities and their consequences from the point of view of the uninvolved spectator. One may abstractly regret that the injury is done, but this regret is analogous to the regret one feels as a spectator to the traffic accident mentioned in an earlier example; one is in no way personally implicated. The responses likely from a mature sense of responsibility appear morally fastidious and unprofessional from the perspective of the present Code. This has troubling consequences: without a proper appreciation of the moral costs of one's actions one cannot make effective use of the faculty of

---

46. This may explain, in part, the attitude of "ethical minimalism" among lawyers which many, both within and outside the profession, deplore. This minimalism is an understandable reaction, in light of the fact that there are few fixed and settled rules in the Code and the lawyer is effectively cut off from the resources needed to resolve the indeterminacies unavoidably left by the Code.

practical judgment. In fact, a proper perspective of the moral costs of one's action has both intrinsic and instrumental value. The instrumental value lies in the added safeguard that important moral dilemmas will receive appropriate reflection. As Bernard Williams argued, "only those who are [by practice] reluctant or disinclined to do the morally disagreeable when it is really necessary have much chance of not doing it when it is not necessary. ... [A] habit of reluctance is an essential obstacle against the happy acceptance of the intolerance."

But this appreciation is also important for its own sake. To experience sincere reluctance, to feel the need to make restitution, to seek the other's pardon—these simply are appropriate responses to the actual feature of the moral situation. In this way, the status and integrity of important moral principles are maintained in compromising circumstances, and the moral relations between persons are respected or restored.

Finally, the moral detachment of the lawyer adversely affects the quality of the lawyer-client relationship. Unable to draw from the responses and relations of ordinary experience, the lawyer is capable of relating to the client only as a client. He puts his moral faculties of reason, argument, and persuasion wholly at the service of the client, but simultaneously disengages his moral personality. He views himself not as a moral actor but as a legal technician. In addition, he is barred from recognizing the client's moral personality. The moral responsibilities of the client are simply of no interest to him. Thus, paradoxically, the combination of partisanship and neutrality jeopardizes client autonomy and mutual respect (two publicly stated objectives of the standard conception), and yields instead a curious kind of *impersonal* relationship.

It is especially striking, then, that Charles Fried, the most sophisticated defender of these central ideals of the standard conception, should describe the lawyer as a "special purpose" friend. Indeed, it is the contrast between the standard conception of the lawyer-client relationship and the characteristics of a relationship between friends which, on reflection, is likely to make the deepest impression. The impersonalism and moral detachment characteristic of the lawyer's role under the standard conception are not found in relations between friends. Loyalty to one's friend does not call for disengagement of one's moral personality. When in nonprofessional contexts we enter special relationships and undertake special obligations which create duties of loyalty or special concern, these special considerations must nevertheless be integrated into a coherent picture of the moral life as a whole.

Often we must view our moral world from more than one perspective simultaneously.[50]   As Goffman points out, roles are often structured with the recognition that persons occupying the role fill other roles which are also important to them.   Room is left for the agent to integrate his responsibilities from each role into a more or less coherent scheme encompassing his entire moral life.

But it is precisely this integrated conception of the moral personality that is unavailable to the professional who adopts either the minimal or the maximal identification strategy.   Either the moral personality is entirely fragmented or compartmentalized, or it is shrunk to fit the moral universe defined by the role. Neither result is desirable.

IV.   Toward an Alternative Conception: The Recourse Role

The unavoidable social costs of the standard conception of professional legal behavior argue strongly for a radical rethinking of the lawyer's role.   One alternative is a "deprofessionalization" of legal practice so as to eliminate the distance between private and professional morality.   Deprofessionalization, however, would involve a radical restructuring of the entire legal system, reducing the complexity of the law as it currently exists so that individuals could exercise their rights without the assistance of highly specialized legal technicians.   But, setting aside obvious questions of feasibility, to discredit this proposal we need only recall that deprofessionalization ignores the significant social value in a division of moral and social labor produced by the variety of public and professional roles.

A second, more plausible alternative is to recognize the unavoidable discontinuities in the moral landscape and to bridge them with a unified conception of moral personality.   Achieving any sort of bridge, however, requires that lawyers significantly alter the way they view their own activities.   Each lawyer must have a conception of the role that allows him to serve the important functions of that role in the legal and political system while integrating his own sense of moral responsibility into the role itself.   Such a conception must improve upon the current one by allowing a broader scope for engaged moral judgment in day-to-

---

50. [Consider, for example, the epitaph on a Scottish gravestone: " 'Here lies Tammas Jones, who was born a man and died a grocer.'"   D. Emmet, Rules, Roles and Relations 154 (1966) (quoting W. Sperry, The Ethical Basis of Medical Practice 41 (1951)).] Tammas Jones ... was not just a grocer, he was also, *in'er alia,* a father, husband, friend, and neighbor.   It was possible for him to relate to his family, customers, neighbors, and friends, not as a role-agent, but as a person, because it could have been recognized that his moral personality penetrated through his activities in his roles, and that these roles did not exhaust that personality.

day professional activities while encouraging a keener sense of personal responsibility for the consequences of these activities.

The task of forging a concrete alternative conception is a formidable one. To begin, however, it may be useful to contrast two conceptions of social roles: the fixed role and the recourse role. In a fixed role, the professional perceives the defining characteristics of the role—its basic rules, duties, and responsibilities—as entirely predetermined. The characteristics may be altered gradually through social evolution or more quickly by profession-wide regulatory legislation, but as far as the individual practitioner is concerned, the moral universe of his role is an objective fact, to be reckoned with, but not for him to alter. Sartre, proponents of the standard conception, and advocates of deprofessionalization all rest their positions on the assumption that the defining features of each role remain fixed. But this assumption fits only some social roles. A bank clerk, for example, must follow set routines; little judgment is required, and he has no authority to set aside the rules under which he acts or alter these rules to fit new occasions. This is not troubling because the sorts of situations one is likely to face in such a job lend themselves to routine treatment.

In contrast, in a recourse role, one's duties and responsibilities are not fixed, but may expand or contract depending on the institutional objectives the role is designed to serve. The recourse role requires the agent not only to act according to what he perceives to be the explicit duties of the role in a narrow sense, but also to carry out those duties in keeping with the functional objectives of the role. The agent can meet these requirements only if he possesses a comprehensive and integrated concept of his activities both within and outside the role. Role morality, then, within a recourse role is not properly served by maximal identification with one's role. Nor can the role agent minimally identify with his role so as to abandon or disengage his personal morality or basic sense of responsibility. Indeed, responsible professional judgment will rely heavily on a sense of responsibility.

If we perceive the role of the lawyer in our legal system as a recourse role, a viable solution to the problem of responsibility may be available. A recourse role conception forces the lawyer to recognize that the exercise of his role duties must fully engage his rational and critical powers, and his sense of moral responsibility as well. Although not intended to obliterate the moral distance between professional and private moralities, a recourse role conception bridges that gap by integrating to a significant degree the moral personality of the individual with the performance of role responsibilities. Most significantly, this conception prevents the lawyer from escaping responsibility by relying on his status as an agent of the client or an instrument of the system. He cannot consider himself simply a legal technician, since his role essentially involves the exercise of his *engaged* moral judgment.

REFERENCES

For a general analysis of the tensions confronting professionals in bureaucracies see:

Bucher & Stelling, "Characteristics of Professional Organization" in *Colleagues in Organization: The Social Construction of Professional Work* 121–135 (R. Blankenship ed. 1977).

Dibble, "Occupations and Ideologies," 68 *Am.J.Soc.* 329 (1962).

Goodpaster, "Ethical Imperatives and Corporate Leadership," in *Ethics in Practice: Managing the Moral Corporation* (K. Andrews and D. David eds., 1989).

Hall, "Professionalization and Bureaucratization," 33 *Am.Soc. Rev.* 92 (1968).

Montagna, *Professionalization and Bureaucratization in Large Professional Organizations,* 74 *Am.J.Soc.* 138 (1968).

Murphy, "Creating Ethical Corporate Structures," *Sloan Mgmt. Rev.* (Winter 1989).

R. Pavalko, *Sociology of Occupations and Professions* 190–92 (1971).

Scott, "Professionals in Bureaucracies—Areas of Conflict," in *Professionalization* 265, 278–276 (H. Vollmer & D. Mills eds. 1966).

For analysis of the organizational pressures against reporting ethical abuses, see generally

Abel, "Comparative Sociology of Legal Professions; An Exploratory Essay," 1985 *A.B.F. Res.J.* 3, 54–56.

Boyle, "A Review of Whistle Blower Protections and Suggestions for Change," 41 *Labor L.J.* 821 (1990).

Dworkin and Callahan, "Internal Whistleblowing: Protecting the Interests of the Employee, the Organization, and Society," 29 *Am.Bus.L.J.* 267 (1991).

J. Fleishman, L. Liebman & M. Moore, eds. *Public Duties: The Moral Obligations of Officials* (1981).

E. Freidson, *Doctoring Together* 125–35 (1975).

Geller, "On the Irrelevance of Evil: The Organization and Individual Action," 34 *J.Soc.Issues* 125 (1978).

Kohn and Kohn, "An Overview of Federal and State Whistle-blowing Protections," 4 *Antioch L.J.* 99 (1986).

M. Glazer and P. Glazer, *The Whistleblowers: Exposing Corruption in Government and Industry* (1989).

Miceli and Near, "The Relationship Among Beliefs, Organizational Position, and Whistle–Blowing Status: A Discriminant Analysis," 27 *Acad. Mgmt. J.* 687 (1984).

Office of Merit Systems Review and Studies, U.S. Merit Systems Protection Board, *Blowing the Whistle in the Federal Government: A Comparative Analysis of 1980 and 1983 Survey Findings* (1984).

Office of Merit Systems Review and Studies, U.S. Merit Systems Protection Board, *Whistleblowing and the Federal Employee* (1981).

C. Peters & T. Branch, *Blowing the Whistle* (1972).

J. Rohr, *Ethics for Bureaucrats* (1978).

Soeken and Soeken, "A Survey of Whistleblowers: Their Stressors and Coping Strategies," in *Whistleblower Protection Act of 1987: Hearings Before the Subcommittee on Federal Services, Post Office, and Civil Service of the Senate Committee on Governmental Affairs*, 100th Cong., 1st Sess. (1987).

Trevino and Victor, "Peer Reporting of Unethical Behavior: A Social Context Perspective," 35 *Acad. Mgmt. J.* 38 (1992).

A. Westin, ed., *Whistle-blowing: Loyalty and Dissent in the Corporation* (1980).

For a useful bibliography on these issues see E. Gunn, *Ethics and the Public Service: An Annotated Bibliography and Overview Essay* (Bureau of Government Research, April 1980).

C. CONDUCT IN LITIGATION

INTRODUCTION

In 1906, in a celebrated report on "The Causes of Popular

Dissatisfaction With the Administration of Justice,"[1] Roscoe Pound observed:

> The sporting theory of justice, the "instinct of giving the game fair play," as Professor Wigmore has put it, is so rooted in the profession in America that most of us take it for a fundamental legal tenet. But it is probably only a survival of the days when a lawsuit was a fight between two clans in which change of venue had been taken to the forum. So far from being a fundamental fact of jurisprudence, it is peculiar to Anglo-American law; and it has been strongly curbed in modern English practice. With us, it is not merely in full acceptance, it has been developed and its collateral possibilities have been cultivated to the furthest extent. Hence in America we take it as a matter of course that a judge should be a mere umpire, to pass upon objections and hold counsel to the rules of the game, and that parties should fight out their own game in their own way without judicial interference.

The extent to which that "sporting theory of justice" in fact yields justice remains open to debate.

Marvin E. Frankel, "The Search for Truth: An Umpireal View"

123 University of Pennsylvania Law Review 1031,
1031–33, 1035–41, 1050–53, 1055–59 (1975).

I. The Judicial Perspective

My theme, to be elaborated at some length, is that our adversary system rates truth too low among the values that institutions of justice are meant to serve. Having worked for nine years at judging, and having evolved in that job the doubts and questions to be shared with you, I find it convenient to move into the subject with some initial reminders about our judges: who they are, how they come to be, and how their arena looks to them.
. . .

In any event, our more or less typical lawyer selected as a trial judge experiences a dramatic change in perspective as he moves to the other side of the bench. It is said, commonly by judges, that "[t]he basic purpose of a trial is the determination of truth." . . . Justice David W. Peck identified "truth and . . . the right result" as not merely "basic" but "the sole objective of the judge. . . ."

.   .   .

1. 20 *A.B.A.Rep.* 395, 404–05 (1906).

In a passage partially quoted above, Presiding Justice David W. Peck said:

> The object of a lawsuit is to get at the truth and arrive at the right result. That is the sole objective of the judge, and counsel should never lose sight of that objective in thinking that the end purpose is to win for his side. Counsel exclusively bent on winning may find that he and the umpire are not in the same game.

Earlier, stating his theme that court and counsel "complement" each other. Justice Peck said:

> Unfortunately, true understanding of the judicial process is not shared by all lawyers or judges. Instead of regarding themselves as occupying a reciprocal relationship in a common purpose, they are apt to think of themselves as representing opposite poles and exercising divergent functions. The lawyer is active, the judge passive. The lawyer partisan, the judge neutral. The lawyer imaginative, the judge reflective.

Perhaps unfortunately, and certainly with deference, I find myself leaning toward the camp the Justice criticized. The plainest thing about the advocate is that he is indeed partisan, and thus exercises a function sharply divergent from that of the judge. Whether or not the judge generally achieves or maintains neutrality, it is his assigned task to be nonpartisan and to promote through the trial an objective search for the truth. The advocate in the trial courtroom is not engaged much more than half the time—and then only coincidentally—in the search for truth. The advocate's prime loyalty is to his client, not to truth as such. All of us remember some stirring and defiant declarations by advocates of their heroic, selfless devotion to The Client—leaving the nation, all other men, and truth to fend for themselves. Recall Lord Brougham's familiar words:

> [A]n advocate, in the discharge of his duty, knows but one person in all the world, and that person is his client. To save that client by all means and expedients, and at all hazards and costs to other persons, and, among them, to himself, is his first and only duty; and in performing this duty he must not regard the alarm, the torments, the destruction which he may bring upon others. Separating the duty of a patriot from that of an advocate, he must go on reckless of consequences, though it should be his unhappy fate to involve his country in confusion.

Neither the sentiment nor even the words sound archaic after a century and a half. They were invoked not longer than a few months ago by a thoughtful and humane scholar answering criticisms that efforts of counsel for President Nixon might "involve his country in confusion." There are, I think, no comparable lyrics by lawyers to The Truth.

This is a topic on which our profession has practiced some self-deception. We proclaim to each other and to the world that the clash of adversaries is a powerful means for hammering out the truth. Sometimes, less guardedly, we say it is "best calculated to getting out all the facts. ..." That the adversary technique is useful within limits none will doubt. That it is "best" we should all doubt if we were able to be objective about the question. Despite our untested statements of self-congratulation, we know that others searching after facts—in history, geography, medicine, whatever—do not emulate our adversary system. We know that most countries of the world seek justice by different routes. What is much more to the point, we know that many of the rules and devices of adversary litigation as we conduct it are not geared for, but are often aptly suited to defeat, the development of the truth.

We are unlikely ever to know how effectively the adversary technique would work toward truth if that were the objective of the contestants. Employed by interested parties, the process often achieves truth only as a convenience, a byproduct, or an accidental approximation. The business of the advocate, simply stated, is to win if possible without violating the law. (The phrase "if possible" is meant to modify what precedes it, but the danger of slippage is well known.) His is not the search for truth as such. To put that thought more exactly, the truth and victory are mutually incompatible for some considerable percentage of the attorneys trying cases at any given time. ...

Whatever doctrine teaches, it is a fact of interest here that most criminal defense counsel are not at all bent upon full disclosure of the truth. To a lesser degree, but stemming from the same ethos, we know how fiercely prosecutors have resisted disclosure, how often they have winked at police lapses, how mixed has been their enthusiasm for the principle that they must seek justice, not merely convictions. While the patterns of civil cases are different, and variable, we may say that it is the rare case in which either side yearns to have the witnesses, or anyone, give *the whole truth*. And our techniques for developing evidence feature devices for blocking and limiting such unqualified revelations.

The devices are too familiar to warrant more than a fleeting reminder. To begin with, we leave most of the investigatory work to paid partisans, which is scarcely a guarantee of thorough and detached exploration. Our courts wait passively for what the parties will present, almost never knowing—often not suspecting—what the parties have chosen not to present. The ethical standards governing counsel command loyalty and zeal for the client, but no positive obligation at all to the truth. Counsel must not knowingly break the law or commit or countenance fraud. Within these unconfining limits, advocates freely employ time-honored tricks and stratagems to block or distort the truth. ...

That is the great release from effective ethical inhibitions. We are not to pass judgment, but only to marshal our skills to present and test the witnesses and other evidence—the skills being to make the most of these for our side and the least for the opposition. What will out, we sometimes tell ourselves and often tell others, is the truth. And, if worse comes to worst, in the end who really knows what is truth?

There is much in this of cant, hypocrisy, and convenient overlooking. As people, we know or powerfully suspect a good deal more than we are prepared as lawyers to admit or explore further. The clearest cases are those in which the advocate has been informed directly by a competent client, or has learned from evidence too clear to admit of genuine doubt, that the client's position rests upon falsehood. It is not possible to be certain, but I believe from recollection and conversation such cases are far from rare. Much more numerous are the cases in which we manage as counsel to avoid too much knowledge. The sharp eye of the cynical lawyer becomes at strategic moments a demurely averted and filmy gaze. It may be agreeable not to listen to the client's tape recordings of vital conversations that may contain embarrassments for the ultimate goal of vindicating the client. Unfettered by the clear prohibitions actual "knowledge" of the truth might impose, lawyers may be effective and exuberant in employing the familiar skills: techniques that make a witness look unreliable although the look stems only from counsel's artifice, cunning questions that stop short of discomfiting revelations, complaisant experts for whom some shopping may have been necessary. The credo that frees counsel for such arts is not a doctrine of truth-seeking.

The litigator's devices, let us be clear, have utility in testing dishonest witnesses, ferreting out falsehoods, and thus exposing the truth. But to a considerable degree these devices are like other potent weapons, equally lethal for heroes and villains. It is worth stressing, therefore, that the gladiator using the weapons in the courtroom is not primarily crusading after truth, but seeking to win. If this is banal, it is also overlooked too much and, in any event, basic to my thesis. ...

Our relatively low regard for truth-seeking is perhaps the chief reason for the dubious esteem in which the legal profession is held. The temptation to quote poetical diatribes is great. Before fighting it off altogether, let us recall only Macaulay on Francis Bacon, purporting not to

> inquire ... whether it be right that a man should, with a wig on his head, and a band round his neck, do for a guinea what, without those appendages, he would think it wicked and infamous to do for an empire: whether it be right that, not merely believing but knowing a statement to be true, he should do all that can be done by sophistry, by rhetoric, by solemn asseveration, by indignant exclamation, by gesture, by play of features, by terrifying one honest witness, by perplexing another, to cause a jury to think that statement false. ...

As for advocates specifically, the rule is essentially that they must not "knowingly" use "fraudulent, false, or perjured testimony" or "[k]nowingly engage in other illegal conduct. ..." These are not sufficient rules for charting a high road to justice. The lawyer's capacity for ignorance is large. The proscriptions defining the "illegal" are narrow. The prohibitions, ethical or disciplinary, are under a canon telling the lawyer to *"represent a client zealously within the bounds of the law."* And the proscription of fraud and illegality is under an italicized heading proclaiming the *"Duty of the Lawyer to the Adversary System of Justice,"* not to the Truth or to Justice *simpliciter.*

Let us by all means stress ethics and seek to uplift ourselves. But let us not build our hopes for the system on a breed of lawyers and judges much better or worse than mere human beings. If we limit our fantasies in this respect, we will not expect that better rules of warfare are apt to produce peace and cooperative crusades for justice.

IV. Some Proposals

Having argued that we are too much committed to contentiousness as a good in itself and too little devoted to truth, I proceed to some prescriptions of a general nature for remedying these flaws. Simply stated, these prescriptions are that we should:

(1) modify (not abandon) the adversary ideal,

(2) make truth a paramount objective, and

(3) impose upon the contestants a duty to pursue that objective.

A. Modifying the Adversary Ideal

We should begin, as a concerted professional task, to question the premise that adversariness is ultimately and invariably good. For most of us trained in American law, the superiority of the adversary process over any other is too plain to doubt or examine. The certainty is shared by people who are in other respects widely separated on the ideological spectrum. The august *Code of Professional Responsibility,* as has been mentioned, proclaims, in order, the *"Duty of the Lawyer to a Client,"* then the *"Duty of the Lawyer to the Adversary System of Justice."* There is no announced "Duty to the Truth" or "Duty to the Community." Public interest lawyers, while they otherwise test the law's bounds, profess a basic commitment "to the adversary system itself" as the means of giving "everyone affected by corporate and bureaucratic decisions . . . a voice in those decisions. . . ." We may note similarly the earnest and idealistic scholar who brought the fury of the (not necessarily consistent) establishment upon himself when he wrote, reflecting upon experience as devoted defense counsel for poor people, that as an advocate you must (a) try to destroy a witness "whom you know to be telling the truth," (b) "put a witness on the stand when you know he will commit perjury," and (c) "give your client legal advice when you have reason to believe that the knowledge you give him will tempt him to commit perjury." The "policies" he found to justify these views, included, as the first and most fundamental, the maintenance of "an adversary system based upon the presupposition that the most effective means of determining truth is to present to a judge and jury a clash between proponents of conflicting views."

Our commitment to the adversary or "accusatorial" mode is buttressed by a corollary certainty that other, alien systems are inferior. We contrast our form of criminal procedure with the "inquisitorial" system, conjuring up visions of torture, secrecy, and dictatorial government. Confident of our superiority, we do not bother to find out how others work. It is not common knowledge among us that purely inquisitorial systems exist scarcely anywhere; that elements of our adversary approach exist probably everywhere; and that the evolving procedures of criminal justice, in Europe and elsewhere, are better described as "mixed" than as strictly accusatorial or strictly inquisitorial.

In considering the possibility of change, we must open our minds to the variants and alternatives employed by other communities that also aspire to civilization. Without voting firmly, I raise the question whether the virginally ignorant judge is always to be preferred to one with an investigative file. We should be prepared to inquire whether our arts of examining and cross-examining, often geared to preventing excessive outpourings of facts, are inescapably preferable to safeguarded interrogation by an informed judicial officer. It is permissible to keep asking, because nobody has satisfactorily answered, why our present system of confessions in the police station versus no confessions at all is better than an open and orderly procedure of having a judicial official question suspects. ...

B. Making Truth the Paramount Objective

We should consider whether the paramount commitment of counsel concerning matters of fact should be to the discovery of truth rather than to the advancement of the client's interest. This topic heading contains for me the most debatable and the least thoroughly considered of the thoughts offered here. It is a brief suggestion for a revolution, but with no apparatus of doctrine or program.

We should face the fact that the quality of "hired gun" is close to the heart and substance of the litigating lawyer's role. As is true always of the mercenary warrior, the litigator has not won the highest esteem for his scars and his service. Apart from our image, we have had to reckon for ourselves in the dark hours with the knowledge that "selling" our stories rather than striving for the truth cannot always seem, because it is not, such noble work as befits the practitioner of a learned profession. The struggle to win, with its powerful pressures to subordinate the love of truth, is often only incidentally, or coincidentally, if at all, a service to the public interest.

We have been bemused through the ages by the hardy (and somewhat appealing) notion that we are to serve rather than judge the client. Among the implications of this theme is the idea that lawyers are not to place themselves above others and that the client must be equipped to decide for himself whether or not he will follow the path of truth and justice. This means quite specifically, whether in *Anatomy of a Murder* [66] or in Dean Freedman's altruistic sense of commitment,[67] that the client must be

---

66. R. Traver, Anatomy of a Murder (1958). For those who did read or have forgotten it, the novel, by a state supreme court justice, involved an eventually successful homicide defense of impaired mental capacity with the defendant supplying the requisite "facts" after having been told in advance by counsel what type of facts would constitute the defense.

67. *See* text accompanying note 58 *supra.* In M. Freedman, Lawyers' Ethics in an Adversary System, ch. 6 (forthcoming), Dean Freedman reports a changed view on this last of his "three hardest questions." He would under some circumstances (including the case in *Anatomy of a Murder*) condemn the lawyer's supplying of the legal knowl-

armed for effective perjury as well as he would be if he were himself legally trained. To offer anything less is arrogant, elitist, and undemocratic.

It is impossible to guess closely how prevalent this view may be as a practical matter. Nor am I clear to what degree, if any, received canons of legal ethics give it sanction. My submission is in any case that it is a crass and pernicious idea, unworthy of a public profession. It is true that legal training is a source of power, for evil as well as good, and that a wicked lawyer is capable of specially skilled wrongdoing. It is likewise true that a physician or pharmacist knows homicidal devices hidden from the rest of us. Our goals must include means for limiting the numbers of crooked and malevolent people trained in the vital professions. We may be certain, notwithstanding our best efforts, that some lawyers and judges will abuse their trust. But this is no reason to encourage or facilitate wrongdoing by everyone.

Professional standards that placed truth above the client's interests would raise more perplexing questions. The privilege for client's confidences might come in for reexamination and possible modification. We have all been trained to know without question that the privilege is indispensable for effective representation. The client must know his confidences are safe so that he can tell all and thus have fully knowledgeable advice. We may want to ask, nevertheless, whether it would be an excessive price for the client to be stuck with the truth rather than having counsel allied with him for concealment and distortion. The full development of this thought is beyond my studies to date. Its implications may be unacceptable. I urge only that it is among the premises in need of examination.

If the lawyer is to be more truth-seeker than combatant, troublesome questions of economics and professional organization may demand early confrontation. How and why should the client pay for loyalties divided between himself and the truth? Will we not stultify the energies and resources of the advocate by demanding that he judge the honesty of his cause along the way? Can we preserve the heroic lawyer shielding his client against all the world—and not least against the State—while demanding that he honor a paramount commitment to the elusive and ambiguous truth? It is strongly arguable, in short, that a simplistic preference for the truth may not comport with more fundamental ideals—including notably the ideal that generally values individu-

edge to promote perjury. Exploring whether the Dean's new position is workable would transcend even the wide leeway I arrogate in footnotes.

al freedom and dignity above order and efficiency in government.[68] Having stated such issues too broadly, I leave them in the hope that their refinement and study may seem worthy endeavors for the future.

C. A Duty to Pursue the Truth

The rules of professional responsibility should compel disclosures of material facts and forbid material omissions rather than merely proscribe positive frauds. This final suggestion is meant to implement the broad and general proposition that precedes it. In an effort to be still more specific, I submit a draft of a new disciplinary rule that would supplement or in large measure displace existing disciplinary rule 7–102 of the *Code of Professional Responsibility*.[69] The draft says:

(1) In his representation of a client, unless prevented from doing so by a privilege reasonably believed to apply, a lawyer shall:

(a) Report to the court and opposing counsel the existence of relevant evidence or witnesses where the lawyer does not intend to offer such evidence or witnesses.

(b) Prevent, or when prevention has proved unsuccessful, report to the court and opposing counsel the making of any untrue statement by client or witness or any omission to state a material fact necessary in order to make state-

---

68. Two previous Cardozo Lecturers have been among the line of careful thinkers cautioning against too single-minded a concern for truth. "While our adversary system of litigation may not prove to be the best means of ascertaining truth, its emphasis upon respect for human dignity at every step is not to be undermined lightly in a democratic state." Botein, *The Future of the Judicial Process*, 15 Record of N.Y.C.B.A. 152, 166 (1960). *See also* Shawcross, *The Functions and Responsibilities of an Advocate*, 13 Record of N.Y.C.B.A. 183, 198, 500 (1958).

69. The affected portions of DR 7–102 are:

(A) In his representation of a client, a lawyer shall not:

. . .

(3) Conceal or knowingly fail to disclose that which he is required by law to reveal.

(4) Knowingly use perjured testimony or false evidence.

(5) Knowingly make a false statement of law or fact.

(6) Participate in the creation or preservation of evidence when he knows or it is obvious that the evidence is false.

(7) Counsel or assist his client in conduct that the lawyer knows to be illegal or fraudulent.

. . .

(B) A lawyer who receives information clearly establishing that:

(1) His client has, in the course of the representation, perpetrated a fraud upon a person or tribunal shall promptly call upon his client to rectify the same, and if his client refuses or is unable to do so, he shall reveal the fraud to the affected person or tribunal.

(2) A person other than his client has perpetrated a fraud upon a tribunal shall promptly reveal the fraud to the tribunal.

ments made, in the light of the circumstances under which they were made, not misleading.

(c) Question witnesses with a purpose and design to elicit the whole truth, including particularly supplementary and qualifying matters that render evidence already given more accurate, intelligible, or fair than it otherwise would be.

(2) In the construction and application of the rules in subdivision (1), a lawyer will be held to possess knowledge he actually has or, in the exercise of reasonable diligence, should have.

Key words in the draft, namely, in (1)(b), have been plagiarized, of course, from the Securities and Exchange Commission's rule 10b–5. That should serve not only for respectability; it should also answer, at least to some extent, the complaint that the draft would impose impossibly stringent standards. The morals we have evolved for business clients cannot be deemed unattainable by the legal profession.

Harder questions suggest themselves. The draft provision for wholesale disclosure of evidence in litigation may be visionary or outrageous, or both. It certainly stretches out of existing shape our conception of the advocate retained to be partisan. As against the yielding up of everything, we are accustomed to strenuous debates about giving a supposedly laggard or less energetic party a share in his adversary's litigation property safeguarded as "work product." A lawyer must now surmount partisan loyalty and disclose "information clearly establishing" frauds by his client or others. But that is a far remove from any duty to turn over all the fruits of factual investigation, as the draft proffered here would direct. It has lately come to be required that some approach to helpful disclosures be made by prosecutors in criminal cases; "the suppression by the prosecution of evidence favorable to an accused upon request violates due process where the evidence is material either to guilt or to punishment, irrespective of the good faith or bad faith of the prosecution." One may be permitted as a respectful subordinate to note the awkward placement in the quoted passage of the words "upon request," and to imagine their careful insertion to keep the duty of disclosure within narrow bounds. But even that restricted rule is for the *public* lawyer. Can we, should we, adopt a far broader rule as a command to the bar generally?

That question touches once again the most sensitive nerve of all. A bar too tightly regulated, too conformist, too "governmental," is not acceptable to any of us. We speak often of lawyers as "officers of the court" and as "public" people. Yet our basic conception of the office is of one essentially private—private in political, economic, and ideological terms—congruent with a system of private ownership, enterprise, and competition, however modified the system has come to be. It is not necessary to recount here the contributions of a legal profession thus conceived to the creation and maintenance of a relatively free society. It *is* necessary to acknowledge those contributions and to consider squarely whether, or how much, they are endangered by proposed reforms.

If we must choose between truth and liberty, the decision is not in doubt. If the choice seemed to me that clear and that stark, this essay would never have reached even the tentative form of its present submission. But I think the picture is quite unclear. I lean to the view that we can hope to preserve the benefits of a free, skeptical, contentious bar while paying a lesser price in trickery and obfuscation.

NOTES

In *Partisan Justice,* Marvin Frankel amplifies his indictment of adversarial methods.

Marvin E. Frankel, Partisan Justice
13–17 (1980).

The quality of private initiative and private control is, in its degree, the hallmark of the American judicial process. ... But the contest by its very nature is not one in which the objective of either side, or of both together, is to expose "the truth, the whole truth, and nothing but the truth."

That the quoted words, from the witness's oath, are not meant quite literally may be seen from more than one perspective. Consider the lawyer's major work of interviewing and "preparing" witnesses, including the client who plans to take the stand. ... [e]very lawyer knows that the "preparing" of witnesses may embrace a multitude of other measures, including some ethical lapses believed to be more common than we would wish. ... Whatever word is used to describe it, the process often extends beyond helping organize what the witness knows, and moves in the direction of helping the witness to know new things. At its starkest, the effort is called subornation of perjury, which is a crime, and which we are permitted to hope is rare. Somewhat less stark, short of criminality but still to be condemned, is the device of telling the client "the law" before eliciting the facts—i.e., telling the client what facts would constitute a successful claim or defense, and only then asking the client what the facts happen perchance to be. The most famous recent instance is fictional but apt: *Anatomy of a Murder,* a 1958 novel by Robert Traver, was an account by a pseudonymous state supreme court justice of a murder defendant educated by his lawyer about a defense of impaired mental capacity and then, conveniently, but obviously not truthfully, recounting "facts" that fit the defense and won an acquittal. It is not unduly cynical to suspect that this, if not in such egregious forms, happens with some frequency.

Moving away from palpably unsavory manifestations, we all know that the preparation of our witnesses is calculated, one way and another, to mock the solemn promise of the whole truth and nothing but. To be sure, reputable lawyers admonish their clients and witnesses to be truthful. At the same time, they often take infinite pains to prepare questions designed to make certain that the controlled flow of truth does not swell to an embarrassing flood. "Don't volunteer anything," the witnesses are cautioned. The concern is not that the volunteered contribution may be false. The concern is to avoid an excess of truth, where the spillover may prove hurtful to the case. . . .

Cross-examination is likewise, if sometimes more dramatically, among the partisan arts of courtroom conquest. It undoubtedly happens, and with some frequency, that an untruthful witness, or one who exaggerates or colors what he knows, is exposed by effective cross-examination. But the skillful cross-examiner, whose assignment is to win, not merely or necessarily to arrive at truth, will undertake much more. He or she will employ ancient and modern tricks to make a truthful witness look like a liar. As on direct examination, the cross-examiner will attempt to stop short of complete narratives, the test of high art being to know the stopping point most likely to discomfit the witness and score points for the cross-examiner's side, not only without regard for the whole truth, but commonly through a triumphant perversion in the form of a partial truth. Lawyers' texts on cross-examination teach the classic wisdom of successful veterans concerning the disaster of asking one question too many on cross; that blundering next question may give the entrapped witness a chance to *explain,* heaven forfend, to tell how it really was, not to be left looking as if it was some other, damaging way.

. . .

The simple point to be stressed, here and throughout, is that many of us trained in the learned profession of the law spend much of our time subverting the law by blocking the way to the truth. The subversion is not for the most part viewed as a pathology; rather, if somewhat paradoxically, it follows from the assigned roles of counsel in the very system of law which thus finds its purposes thwarted.

D. THE USE AND ABUSE OF PRETRIAL PROCEDURES
Marvin E. Frankel, Partisan Justice
17–18 (1980).

The games we play about fact finding are, of course, an old story and an old source of professional worry and efforts toward reform. During the last half century or so, much has been done through rules of "discovery" to cut down on concealment and surprises at trial. The idea is to allow demands for information before trial and to require responses from the adverse party. The device has on the whole worked substantial improvements. Predictably, however, it has been turned—and twisted—to adversary uses. Lawyers react characteristically by demanding as much as possible and giving as little as possible. What is not demanded is not given. It remains as true as ever that if a lawyer fails to ask the right question, the adversary will cheerfully refrain from disclosing what might be vital or decisive information. The discovery process itself, with rules that frequently are (or are made to be) intricate and abstruse, becomes the occasion for expensive contests, producing libraries full of opinions. Where the object always is to beat every plowshare into a sword, the discovery procedure is employed variously as weaponry. A powerful litigant in a complex case may impose costly, even crushing, burdens by demands for files, pretrial testimony of witnesses, and other forms of discovery. An approximately converse ploy has also been evolved to make the procedure a morass rather than the revelatory blessing it was meant to be. A litigant may contrive to dump truckloads of unassorted files on the party demanding discovery, hoping, often not in vain, that the searcher will be so exhausted that the damaging items will be overlooked or never reached.

The key point at every stage, which will bear recalling from time to time, is that the single uniformity is always adversariness. There are other goods, but the greatest is winning. There are other evils, but scarcely any worse than losing. Every step of the process, and any attempt to reform it, must be viewed in this light until or unless the adversary ethic comes to be changed or subordinated. The lawyer's response to a tax is how to avoid or minimize its impact on the client. Every law is probed for its loopholes— unless the lawyer has done the job in advance by being placed strategically to sew them in during the legislative process. Every idea for improved procedures must be imaginatively pretested to foresee its evolving shapes under the fires of adversary zeal.

Because the route of a lawsuit is marked by a running battle all the way, the outcome is nothing like the assuredly right result imagined in our dream that "justice will out." In that dream, neither eloquence nor lawyers' techniques nor cunning has much place. The person who is "right" should win. But that is very far from assured in the kind of contest we've been considering. Where skill and trickery are so much involved, it must inevitably happen that the respective qualities of the professional champions will make a decisive difference. Where sheer power and endurance may count, the relative resources of clients become vital. Describing the tendency of the enterprise as the major forces propel it, two students of the American legal system were led to conclude: "In an ideal adversary system, the less skillful antagonist is expected to lose, which under the laissez-faire notion is the proper outcome."

Wayne D. Brazil, "Civil Discovery: How Bad Are the Problems?"

67 American Bar Association Journal, 450–52, 454–56 (1981).*

During the last few years many practicing lawyers, judges, and legal scholars have criticized the way pretrial discovery is working in civil litigation and have committed a great deal of time to drafting proposals for its improvement. ... In 1979 the American Bar Foundation began sponsoring a study whose purpose was to meet this need. ... The data show that there are great differences between the character of discovery in large cases and in smaller cases and that in larger lawsuits the system is plagued with severe problems that prevent it from effectively serving the purposes for which it was designed. The interviews also produced a dramatically intense and consistent chorus of criticism of the role the courts play in the discovery arena. An overwhelming majority of the lawyers we interviewed blame the judiciary for many of the discovery system's most severe problems. Four of every five respondents believe the courts should impose sanctions more frequently. And litigators who primarily handle larger matters call in loud and remarkably united voices for more help from the courts in controlling what appears to be a runaway system.

We should begin with an overview of what the data show about discovery in larger cases, which we define as those in which $1,000,000 or more is in dispute.

. . .

Early in each interview we asked for general impressions about how well the discovery system is working. Only 7 per cent of the big case litigators offered clearly positive assessments. By contrast 43 per cent of the lawyers in this category expressed aggressively negative views.

Responding to specific questions about obstacles to their discovery efforts, big case lawyers portrayed a system whose most salient characteristic is gross inefficiency. Among the sources of that inefficiency, none plays a more pervasive, troublesome role than evasion ... Doctrinal shields of information also are significant sources of friction and inefficiency in the discovery stage of major lawsuits. [Yet] even while acknowledging that assertions of [the attorney client] privilege provoke many discovery disputes, very few of the attorneys we interviewed objected to the policies and values on which the privileges are based. In fact, many went out of their way to affirm their belief in the legitimacy and importance of privilege doctrine.

. . .

[Nonetheless,] the big case litigators we interviewed made it quite clear that they spend considerable time and creative energy trying to increase the odds that opposing counsel will fail to discover damaging information from their clients.

. . .

Several lawyers admitted that only a small percentage of the information their own discovery efforts produce is really useful. Many also reported that to uncover key information they had to develop elaborate systems of discovery probes, employing different kinds of discovery devices in carefully orchestrated sequences, and that they had to commit substantial resources not only to sifting through immense amounts of material produced by their opponents but also to framing careful follow-up inquiries.

Some of this inefficiency is attributable, of course, to the complex legal theories on which some large cases turn and to the large data bases the theories sometimes require. The lawyers we interviewed, however, left us with no doubt that whatever inefficiency is inherent in the development of big cases is substantially

aggravated by adversarial maneuvering that intensifies through
cycles of mutual mistrust.

... The data provided by the litigators we interviewed indicate that in half of the larger, more complex lawsuits that are
closed by settlement, at least one of the attorneys believes he
knows something of significance about the case that counsel for
other parties have not discovered. Lawyers who typically handle
larger cases also reported that in half of the cases they settle they
believe that another party still has relevant information, including communications protected by privilege, that they have not
discovered.

. . .

The predominantly big-case litigators in our sample reported
that in approximately 30 per cent of the cases they had tried to
completion they "still had arguably significant information (including information protected by privilege) which ... another
party had not discovered." About 75 per cent of these lawyers
reported having had that experience in at least one case they had
tried to judgment. More than 80 per cent of the big-case litigators
also admitted having been surprised by new information produced
by an opponent in at least one trial, but surprises reportedly occur
only in about 15 per cent of the tried matters.

. . .

The data generated by our study suggest that discovery in
smaller cases, which we defined as those in which $25,000 or less
is in dispute, is a very different animal from that in larger cases
and that in the smaller matters it is afflicted by substantially less
debilitating abuses and problems. As a group, lawyers who primarily handle smaller cases are measurably less dissatisfied with
how the discovery system works than are their larger case counterparts. While 43 per cent of the big case litigators expressed
clearly negative assessments of the discovery system, this view
was shared by only 23 per cent of the smaller case lawyers.

. . .

In smaller matters there is less money available to support
elaborate tactical plans, there tends to be less data to process, and
the existence and sources of relevant evidence tend to be more
predictable. Not surprisingly, smaller case attorneys reportedly
exchange information with less friction, less tactical jockeying,
and less harassment. ... 62 per cent of the large-case litigators
volunteered complaints about overdiscovery, and 45 per cent complained about harassment, while the corresponding figures for the
smaller case group were only 38 per cent and 28 per cent. ...

Evasive or incomplete responses to requests for information reportedly impede discovery by smaller case attorneys in about 40 per cent of their cases—not an insignificant incidence but a far cry from the 80 per cent figure reported by the big case lawyers.

. . .

Some dilatoriness is the product of intentional tactical ploys, but the principal source of the problem appears to be the vacuum created by the five-year backlog in the civil trial docket of the state courts. ... This severe backlog apparently encourages attorneys to overcommit themselves—that is, to accept more cases than they can prepare adequately for trial—and sets in motion cycles of procrastination.

. . .

The lawyers interviewed readily acknowledged that lawyers and ways of lawyering are responsible for many of the defects of the discovery system. Despite these concessions, however, many lawyers feel that the principal culprits in the discovery system's failings are judges. The only partly articulated theory supporting this belief seems to be that irresistible economic and adversarial pressures will compel attorneys to adopt evasive and sometimes abusive tactics unless the courts impose a system of predictably tight and telling restraints. In this view, it is the judiciary's responsibility to create an environment that is sufficiently hostile to chicanery and incompetence to drive those forces from the discovery arena. ... More lawyers mentioned the negative impact of the judiciary than any other single problem: 71 per cent volunteered complaints about the performance of the courts. ... Eighty per cent of *all* the interviewed lawyers believe that the courts should more frequently sanction discovery abuse. ...

Given the widely shared perception among big case litigators that the discovery system is almost out of control, it is hardly surprising that many of them want more from the courts than more vigorous enforcement of the rules. Eighty-two per cent of the lawyers who primarily handle larger matters support the broader proposition that the judiciary should be more thoroughly involved in the discovery stage of litigation. While there undoubtedly would be disagreement about the precise form of the involvement, there is little disagreement among big case litigators about the underlying need for more external control over and a better informed monitoring of the discovery process. Among smaller case lawyers, by contrast, there are sharper differences of opinion about whether there is a need for the judiciary to do more than strictly enforce the rules. Only about half of them favored "greater judicial involvement" (generally).

We should report one additional result of our study that has important implications for reform efforts. Contrary to some assumptions, there is no broad support for the notion that the scope of discovery should be narrowed. While among all the lawyers we interviewed 30 per cent favored cutting back the scope of discovery, twice as many (60 per cent) favored leaving the scope as it is and 10 per cent favored broadening it.

. . .

At least according to the lawyers in our sample, it would be a mistake to focus efforts to reform discovery on the formal descriptions of its proper scope. Instead, litigators believe the real need is to devise a system of restraints and rewards that will combat the pervasive problem of evasion and curb misuse of the system's tools.

———

NOTES

Discovery Abuse

In his nineteenth century treatise on professional deportment, David Hoffman advised:

> Should my client be disposed to insist on captious requisitions, or frivolous and vexatious defences, they shall be neither enforced nor countenanced by me. And if still adhered to by him from a hope of pressing the other party into an unjust compromise, or with any other motive, he shall have the option to select other counsel.[1]

If practice ever conformed to that prescription, norms have changed somewhat over the intervening decades. Although the pervasiveness of discovery abuse is a matter of some dispute, recent surveys and case histories leave little doubt that such pretrial problems are too prominent a feature of our legal landscape.

The causes of such discovery abuse spring from a complex set of social and ideological as well as economic forces. Most obviously, a party's objectives, resources, and stakes in litigation may dictate various strategies designed to evade or exhaust his adver-

---

1. D. Hoffman, "Resolutions In Regard to Professional Deportment" in A *Course of Legal Study* 754 (1836).

sary. So too, the hourly fee structure of most private practice encourages production of services for which clients are willing and able to pay. At worst, the elongation of pretrial disputes may involve intentional meter running; at best it reflects a more subtle mix of adversarial psychologies. Attorneys' own desires for victory, retribution, or simply exhaustive preparation can result in highly expensive pretrial maneuvers. Advocates will often prefer to "leave no stone unturned, provided they can charge by the stone." [6]

However, as Rhode's overview in "Institutionalizing Ethics" concludes:

> Despite a cottage industry of committees, commissions, and commentary devoted to curtailing procedural abuse, most remedies to date have raised as many difficulties as they have solved. Courts have a variety of sanctioning powers; the most important is Rule 11 of the Federal Rules of Civil Procedure and its state court analogues. The rule provides that lawyers' signature on any filing signifies that "to the best of the signers' knowledge, information and belief formed after reasonably inquiry," the filing is "well grounded in fact and is warranted by existing law or a good faith argument for the extension, modification, or reversal of existing law, and that it is not interposed for any improper purpose, such as to harass or to cause unnecessary delay or needless increase in the cost of litigation." A court that finds a Rule 11 violation must impose an "appropriate sanction," which may include fines sufficient to cover the reasonable expenses of opposing parties as a result of the violation.
>
> Until its amendment in 1983, the Rule made sanctions discretionary rather than mandatory and imposed no requirement of reasonable inquiry. In effect, this earlier version demanded a finding of subjective bad faith, and that standard was almost never met. After the 1983 amendments, Rule 11 enforcement escalated rapidly. Motions for sanctions became a standard part of the advocate's arsenal and generated more of the harassing litigation it was meant to deter. The problem was exacerbated by the ambiguity of standards governing "reasonable inquiry," "good faith," and "well grounded in fact". In one study, almost 300 judges divided almost evenly about whether to impose sanctions in six out of ten hypothetical cases. According to some, although not all research,

---

6. Rhode, *supra* note 3. *See also* Rosenberg, "Discovery Abuse," *Litigation,* Spring 1981 at 8; Brazil, "Ethical Perspectives on Discovery Reform," 3 *Rev. of Litigation* 51 (1982).

courts have disproportionately exercised their discretion to penalize civil rights plaintiffs.

In response to these problems, the United States Judicial Conference has proposed further amendments to the rule. The most significant would make sanctions once again discretionary, and would create a 21 day "safe harbor" interval, during which a party notified of a Rule 11 motion could withdraw the offending papers without penalty. ...

For those concerned with institutionalizing ethics, this history is instructive in several respects. The first is that it helps to explain why bar ethical codes have been so ineffectual in response to procedural abuse. Both the Code and Model Rules enjoin lawyers from asserting frivolous positions or taking positions merely to harass, but exclude actions that can be supported by a "good faith argument for an extension, modification, or reversal of existing law." Like Rule 11 before its amendment, these provisions have proven largely unenforceable in practice. Not only is the burden of proving a violation unrealistically high, but litigants have little if anything to gain from referring the case to bar disciplinary agencies. Those agencies generally will not impose fines that compensate complainants. ...

[A]n alternative approach would be to strengthen penalty options to reach those most impervious to modest fines, while exempting those most vulnerable to arbitrary enforcement. For example, some commentators [including David Wilkins] have recommended making monetary sanctions unavailable against plaintiffs suing under one-way fee shifting statutes, such as civil rights or environmental legislation. Such an exemption would recognize the legislature's intent to encourage these claims, and the legal, factual, and economic hurdles that these claimants already face. For other categories of cases, appropriate responses could include publicizing sanctions more broadly, referring violations to disciplinary agencies, restructuring those agencies' responses to provide effective remedies, and requiring organizational offenders to institute educational and monitoring programs. More resources must also be available for judicial oversight, not only by trial courts but also magistrates and special masters.[1]

Disclosure Obligations to the Courts and Third Parties

As the preceding discussion suggested, partisan norms often skew dispute resolution processes by preventing appropriate infor-

---

1. Rhode, "Institutionalizing Ethics" *Case Western L.Rev.* (1993); Wilkins, "Who Should Regulate Lawyers," 105 *Harv.L.Rev.* 801 (1992).

mation from reaching courts and third parties. The challenge lies in structuring responses that will accommodate two primary concerns: "One is to preserve some measure of confidentiality, candor, and trust in lawyer-client relationships. A second concern is to prevent freeloading. Overreliance on disclosures from an adversary may result in inefficiency and injustice. One party could end up subsidizing both sides of a lawsuit, or neither party might prepare adequately." [2]

According to many commentators, however, these concerns do not justify the current absence of disclosure obligations in most practice contexts. Early drafts of the Model Rules suggest alternative approaches. Initial provisions would have prohibited lawyers from: offering evidence, without suitable exploration, that the lawyer knows is substantially misleading; and failing to disclose adverse facts to a tribunal when disclosure would probably have a substantial effect on the determination of a material issue. Early draft proposals also would have given lawyers discretion to disclose favorable evidence to an opposing party and would have obligated them to reveal confidences under certain limited circumstances (such as to prevent death or serious bodily injury and to correct manifest misapprehensions of fact resulting from their own or their clients' previous representations.) According to some commentators, such rules could help give the lawyer's role as an officer of the court greater practical content.

E. CROSS CULTURAL COMPARISONS

A final, more fundamental set of reform proposals build on comparative models. Civil law countries in Western Europe and Latin America employ an "inquisitorial system" with certain features that some American commentators would like to import.

Deborah L. Rhode, Ethics by the Pervasive Method (1994).

To many individuals, the term "inquisitorial procedure" evokes visions of state torture, reminiscent of the Spanish Inquisition. That image is highly misleading. In fact, the primary distinction between adversarial and inquisitorial systems lies in the distribution of authority between lawyers and judges. In an adversary system, parties develop the case and the judge is a largely passive umpire. In an inquisitorial system, the judge, or panel of judges acts as director as well as decisionmaker, and

2. Rhode, *supra* note 1.

attorneys play a far less central role.[1]

For example, in German civil cases, a lawyer begins a case through a complaint, which not only alleges the basis for a claim, but also proposes means of proving its central allegations. The complaint includes or identifies relevant documents and lists potential witnesses. The defendant's answer follows the same pattern. Typically, however, neither counsel will have conducted any significant investigation for evidence beyond what their client has provided.

The case will then be assigned to a presiding judge, who will review the findings, order relevant documents, and conduct a series of hearings with counsel, and sometimes with parties and witnesses. Depending on the circumstances of the case, the judge may succeed in promoting settlement. If the parties are unable to agree, the court establishes a sequence for taking proof and decides what witnesses should be called, what documents are necessary, and what experts, if any, to appoint. The court also takes responsibility for examining witnesses and summarizing their testimony for the record, although lawyers may occasionally ask supplemental questions or suggest changes in wording.

Unlike the American system, with its sharp division between trial and pretrial proceedings, the inquisitorial format involves a series of proceedings which seek to minimize overpreparation, inefficiency, and surprise. If, for example, a key issue involves the validity of an affirmative defense, the court can take evidence on that point first and, if it finds for the defendant, avoid the need for proof on other aspects of the case. If a new question unexpectedly surfaces, the judge can delay the proceedings to allow investigation. Civil cases are resolved without juries, generally by a panel of judges, and appellate review involves a de novo consideration of the record, supplemented if necessary by additional evidence.

The lawyers in such proceedings play a circumscribed role, and their partisanship is subject to certain important restrictions. Attorneys may comment on the court's decisions through oral or written submissions and may suggest additional lines of inquiry. However they may not influence witnesses and are discouraged

---

1. The material in this section draws on *Lawyers in Society* (Richard L. Abel & Philip S. Lewis, eds., 1988) (3 volumes): Vol. 1: *The Common Law World*; Vol. 2: *The Civil Law World*; Vol. 3: *Comparative Theories;* Dietrich Rueschemeyer, *Lawyers and Their Society: A Comparative Study of the Legal Profession in Germany and in the Unit-* ed States (1973); Edward A. Tomlinson, "Nonadversarial Justice: The French Experience," 42 *Md.L.Rev.* 131, 150–64 (1983); Deborah L. Rhode & David Luban, *Legal Ethics* 169–78 (1991); John H. Langbein, "The German Advantage in Civil Procedure," 52 *U.Chi.L.Rev.* 823, 826–31 (1985).

even from contacting them. Lawyers may not contradict an opponent's statement if they believe it to be true, and have some obligation to verify a client's representation before attesting to its validity. Fees are set by statute, based largely on the type of case and amount in controversy, irrespective of the hours involved. Contingent fees are not permissible.

Despite such constraints on partisanship, German lawyers generally believe that their primary loyalty is to their client rather than to the state. German and American attorneys often report similar economic pressures and distortions of the decision-making process. However, the structure of German proceedings and billing practices works against certain abuses that plague American adversarial processes. Lawyers who cannot charge by the hour, who have no chance for pretrial depositions, and who need not worry about surprise have fewer incentives for unnecessary preparation and meter running. Prohibitions on influencing witnesses and hiring experts minimize some of the distortions described ... [above]. Proceedings that resemble "routine business meetings" rather than sporting contests or theatrical performances make disparities in the quality of legal representation and attorneys' tactical maneuvers less relevant.[2]

There are, of course, countervailing disadvantages to a system that relies so heavily on judicial control. One continuing concern, developed more fully by the Joint Conference Report, is that the judge who "opens his mouth closes his mind," and de novo appellate review is an expensive and only partial corrective.[3] America has traditionally been wary about vesting too much power in centralized bureaucracies and career civil servants who are largely insulated from direct popular accountability. Some wariness may also stem from this nation's frequent practice of appointing or electing judges based on prior political connections rather than merit, experience, or training. Unless and until the appointment process changes, allocating greater authority to the judiciary poses obvious concerns.

Differences in procedural systems both reflect and reinforce differences in national temperament, and what is effective in one cultural context may prove unworkable or unacceptable in another. As comparativists often note, inquisitorial systems generally place less importance on protection of individual freedom and more on efficiency, uniformity, and equality of treatment. Our

2. J.H. Langbein, *supra* note 1.
3. W. Zeidler, "Evaluation of the Adversary System: As Comparison, Some
Remarks on the Investigatory System of Procedure," 55 *Aust.L.J.* 390, 395 (1981) (quoting Chief Baron Palles of Ireland).

priorities are reversed. Yet even granting these cultural variations, many American experts believe that some aspects of the
civil law system are worth emulating. As John Merryman notes:

For those who are concerned about the relative justice of the
two systems, a statement made by an eminent scholar after long
and careful study is instructive: he said that if he were innocent,
he would prefer to be tried by a civil law court, but that if he were
guilty, he would prefer to be tried by a common law court. This
is, in effect, a judgment that criminal proceedings in the civil law
world are more likely to distinguish accurately between the guilty
and the innocent.[4]

F. NEGOTIATION

Alvin B. Rubin, "A Causerie on Lawyers' Ethics in Negotiation"

35 Louisiana Law Review, 577–78, 580–86, 588–89, 591 (1975).

I asked him whether, as a moralist, he did not think that
the practice of the law, in some degree, hurt the nice feeling of
honesty. Johnson: "Why no, sir, if you act properly. You are
not to deceive your clients with false representations of your
opinion: you are not to tell lies to a judge." 2 Boswell's Life
of Johnson 47 (G.B. Hill ed. 1934).

The philosopher of Mermaid Tavern did not discuss the morality expected when lawyers deal with other lawyers or with laymen. When a lawyer buys or sells a house or a horse or a used
car, he is expected to bargain. When he becomes a Secretary of
State—like Dean Acheson or John Foster Dulles—or a Governor,
or a Senator, or a Congressman or a legislator, he will negotiate
and compromise.

In such activities lawyers may be acting for themselves as
principals, or they may be representing constituents. But they
are not practicing their profession as attorneys-at-law. It may be
assumed that the lawyer who is buying or selling a farm on his
own behalf is expected to behave no differently from any other
member of his society, that no special ethical principles command
his adherence or govern his conduct. And while the lawyer-
diplomat or lawyer-politician may conceive of himself as a profes-

---

4. J. Merryman, *The Civil Law Tradition* 139 (1969). *See also* G. Hazard
and M. Taruffo, *American Civil Procedure: An Introduction* (1993) (analysis
of American civil procedure compared
with European system under civil code,
particularly Italian and German).

sional, rather than as an amateur, he will not be practicing a profession, as that term is generally understood.

When the lawyer turns to his law practice and begins to represent his clients as attorney or advocate, he assumes the role of a professional. What constitutes a profession is difficult to define comprehensively, but all attempts include reference to a store of special training, knowledge, and skills and to the adoption of ethical standards governing the manner in which these should be employed. When acting as an advocate, the lawyer professes a complex set of ethical principles that regulate his conduct toward the courts, his own clients, other lawyers and their clients.

Litigation spawns compromise, and courtroom lawyers engage almost continually in settlement discussions in civil cases and plea bargains in criminal cases. We do not know what proportion of civil claims is settled by negotiation before the filing of suit, but it must be vastly greater than the number of cases actually filed. [In the Federal Courts, between 85 and 90 percent of cases are disposed of prior to trial, most involving regulation].

Although less than one fourth of the lawyers in practice today devote a majority of their time to litigation, and most spend none at all in the traditional courtroom, there are few lawyers who do not negotiate regularly, indeed daily, in their practice. Some lawyers who handle little conventional litigation persist in saying that they do not act as negotiators. If there are a few at the bar who do not, they are *rarae aves*. Patent lawyers, tax counsellors and securities specialists and all those who perform the myriad tasks of office law practice may not dicker about the value of a case—though some assuredly do; but they constantly negotiate the settlement of disputed items.

. . .

There are a few rules designed to apply to other relationships that touch peripherally the area we are discussing. A lawyer shall not:

- knowingly make a false statement of law or fact.
- participate in the creation or preservation of evidence when he knows or it is obvious that the evidence is false.
- counsel or assist his client in conduct that the lawyer knows to be illegal or fraudulent, or
- knowingly engage in *other illegal conduct* or conduct contrary to a Disciplinary Rule.
- conceal or knowingly fail to disclose that which he is *required by law* to reveal.

In addition, he "should be temperate and dignified and ... refrain from all illegal and morally reprehensible conduct." The lawyer is admonished "to treat with consideration all persons involved in the legal process and to avoid the infliction of needless harm."

Taken together, these rules, interpreted in the light of that old but ever useful candle, *ejusdem generis,* imply that a lawyer shall not himself engage in illegal conduct, since the meaning of assisting a client in fraudulent conduct is later indicated by the proscription of *other* illegal conduct. As we perceive, the lawyer is forbidden to make a false statement of law or fact *knowingly.* But nowhere is it ordained that the lawyer owes any general duty of candor or fairness to members of the bar or to laymen with whom he may deal as a negotiator, or of honesty or of good faith insofar as that term denotes generally scrupulous activity.

Is the lawyer-negotiator entitled, like Metternich, to depend on "cunning, precise calculation, and a willingness to employ whatever means justify the end of policy?" Few are so bold as to say so. Yet some whose personal integrity and reputation are scrupulous have instructed students in negotiating tactics that appear tacitly to countenance that kind of conduct. In fairness it must be added that they say they do not "endorse the *propriety*" of this kind of conduct and indeed even indicate "grave reservations" about such behavior; however, this sort of generalized disclaimer of sponsorship hardly appears forceful enough when the tactics suggested include:

- Use two negotiators who play different roles. (Illustrated by the "Mutt and Jeff" police technique; "Two lawyers for the same side feign an internal dispute. ...")
- Be tough—especially against a patsy.
- Appear irrational when it seems helpful.
- Raise some of your demands as the negotiations progress.
- *Claim* that you do not have authority to compromise. (Emphasis supplied.)
- After agreement has been reached, have your client reject it and raise his demands.

Another text used in training young lawyers commendably counsels sincerity, capability, preparation, courage and flexibility. But it also suggests "a sound set of tools or tactics and the know-how to use (or not to use) them." One such tactic is, "Make false demands, bluffs, threats; even use irrationality."

. . .

Let us consider the proper role for a lawyer engaged in negotiations when he knows that the opposing side, whether as a result of poor legal representation or otherwise, is assuming a state of affairs that is incorrect. Hypothesize: *L,* a lawyer, is negotiating the sale of his client's business to another businessman, who is likewise represented by counsel. Balance sheets and profit and loss statements prepared one month ago have been supplied. In the last month, sales have fallen dramatically. Counsel for the potential buyer has made no inquiry about current sales. Does *L* have a duty to disclose the change in sales volume?

Some lawyers say, "I would notify my client and advise him that *he* has a duty to disclose," not because of ethical considerations but because the client's failure to do so might render the transaction voidable if completed. If the client refused to sanction disclosure, some of these lawyers would withdraw from representing him *in this matter* on ethical grounds. As a practical matter, (*i.e.,* to induce the client to accept their advice) they say, in consulting with the client, the lawyer is obliged to present the problem as one of possible fraud in the transaction rather than of lawyers' ethics.

In typical law school fashion, let us consider another hypothet. *L,* the lawyer is representing *C,* a client, in a suit for personal injuries. There have been active settlement negotiations with *LD,* the defendant's lawyer. The physician who has been treating *C* rendered a written report, containing a prognosis stating that it is unlikely that *C* can return to work at his former occupation. This has been furnished to *LD. L* learns from *C* that he has consulted another doctor, who has given him a new medication. *C* states that he is now feeling fine and thinks he can return to work, but he is reluctant to do so until the case is settled or tried. The next day *L* and *LD* again discuss settlement. Does *L* have a duty either to guard his client's secret or to make a full disclosure? Does he satisfy or violate either duty if, instead of mentioning *C's* revelation he suggests that *D* require a new medical examination?

Some lawyers avoid this problem by saying that it is inconceivable that a competent *LD* would not ask again about *C's* health. But if the question as to whether *L* should be frank is persistently presented, few lawyers can assure that they would disclose the true facts.

.   .   .

Interesting answers are obtained if lawyers are asked whether it is proper to make false statements that concern negotiating strategy rather than the facts in litigation. Counsel for a plaintiff

appears quite comfortable in stating, when representing a plaintiff, "My client won't take a penny less than $25,000," when in
fact he knows that the client will happily settle for less; counsel
for the defendant appears to have no qualms in representing that
he has no authority to settle, or that a given figure exceeds his
authority, when these are untrue statements. Many say that, as a
matter of strategy, when they attend a pre-trial conference with a
judge known to press settlements, they disclaim any settlement
authority both to the judge and adversary although in fact they do
have settlement instructions; estimable members of the bar support the thesis that a lawyer may not misrepresent a fact in
controversy but may misrepresent matters that pertain to his
authority or negotiating strategy because this is expected by the
adversary.

To most practitioners it appears that anything sanctioned by
the rules of the game is appropriate. From this point of view,
negotiations are merely, as the social scientists have viewed it, a
form of game; observance of the expected rules, not professional
ethics, is the guiding precept. But gamesmanship is not ethics.

. . .

A lawyer should not be restrained only by the legal inhibitions on his client. He enjoys a monopoly on the practice of law
protected by sanctions against unauthorized practice. Through a
subpart of the profession, lawyer-educators, the lawyer controls
access to legal education. He licenses practitioners by exacting
bar examinations. He controls access to the courts save in those
limited instances when a litigant may appear *pro se,* and then he
aptly characterizes this litigant as being his own lawyer, hence
having a fool for his client.

The monopoly on the practice of law does not arise from the
presumed advantages of an attorney's education or social status:
it stems from the concept that, as professionals, lawyers serve
society's interests by participating in the process of achieving the
just termination of disputes. That an adversary system is the
basic means to this end does not crown it with supreme value. It
is means, not end.

If he is a professional and not merely a hired, albeit skilled
hand, the lawyer is not free to do anything his client might do in
the same circumstances. The corollary of that proposition does
set a minimum standard: the lawyer must be at least as candid
and honest as his client would be required to be. The agent of the
client, that is, his attorney-at-law, must not perpetrate the kind of
fraud or deception that would vitiate a bargain if practiced by his

principal. Beyond that, the profession should embrace an affirmative ethical standard for attorneys' professional relationships with courts, other lawyers and the public: *The lawyer must act honestly and in good faith.* Another lawyer, or a layman, who deals with a lawyer should not need to exercise the same degree of caution that he would if trading for reputedly antique copper jugs in an oriental bazaar. It is inherent in the concept of an ethic, as a principle of good conduct, that it is morally binding on the conscience of the professional, and not merely a rule of the game adopted because other players observe (or fail to adopt) the same rule. Good conduct exacts more than mere convenience. It is not sufficient to call on personal self-interest; this is the standard created by the thesis that the same adversary met today may be faced again tomorrow, and one had best not prejudice that future engagement.

Patterson and Cheatham correctly assert that the basic standard for the negotiator is honesty. "In terms of the standards of the profession, honesty is candor. ..." Candor is not inconsistent with striking a deal on terms favorable to the client, for it is known to all that, at least within limits, that is the purpose to be served. Substantial rules of law in some areas already exact of principals the duty to perform legal obligations honestly and in good faith. Equivalent standards should pervade the lawyer's professional environment.

. . .

While it might strain present concepts of the role of the lawyer in an adversary system, surely the professional standards must ultimately impose upon him a duty not to accept an unconscionable deal. While some difficulty in line-drawing is inevitable when such a distinction is sought to be made, there must be a point at which the lawyer cannot ethically accept an arrangement that is completely unfair to the other side, be that opponent a patsy or a tax collector. So I posit a second precept: *The lawyer may not accept a result that is unconscionably unfair to the other party.*

A settlement that is unconscionable may result from a variety of circumstances. There may be a vast difference in the bargaining power of the principals so that, regardless of the adequacy of representation by counsel, one party may simply not be able to withstand the expense and bear the delay and uncertainty inherent in a protracted suit. There may be a vast difference in the bargaining skill of counsel so that one is able to manipulate the other virtually at will despite the fact that their framed certificates of admission to the bar contain the same words.

The unconscionable result in these circumstances is in part created by the relative power, knowledge and skill of the principals and their negotiators. While it is the unconscionable result that is to be avoided, the question of whether the result is indeed intolerable depends in part on examination of the relative status of the parties. The imposition of a duty to tell the truth and to bargain in good faith would reduce their relative inequality, and tend to produce negotiation results that are within relatively tolerable bounds.

. . .

But, like other lawyers, judges hear not only of the low repute the public has for the bench but also of the even lower regard it has for the bar. We have been told so in innumerable speeches but, more important, our friends, neighbors and acquaintances tell us on every hand that they think little of the morality of our profession. They like us; indeed some of their best friends are lawyers. But they deplore the conduct of our colleagues. This is not merely an aftermath of Watergate: it is, in major part, because many members of the public, not without some support in the facts, view our profession as one that adopts ethics as cant, pays lip service to DR's and on behalf of clients stoops to almost any chicane that is not patently unlawful. We will not change that attitude by Law Days alone. It is to serve society's needs that professions are licensed and the unlicensed prohibited from performing professional functions. It is inherent in the concept of professionalism that the profession will regulate itself, adhering to an ethos that imposes standards higher than mere law observance. Client avarice and hostility neither control the lawyer's conscience nor measure his ethics. Surely if its practitioners are principled, a profession that dominates the legal process in our law-oriented society would not expect too much if it required its members to adhere to two simple principles when they negotiate as professionals: Negotiate honestly and in good faith; and do not take unfair advantage of another—regardless of his relative expertise or sophistication. This is inherent in the oath the ABA recommends be taken by all who are admitted to the bar: "I will employ for the purpose of maintaining the causes confided to me such means only as are consistent with truth and honor."

Steven D. Pepe, "Standards of Legal Negotiations: Interim Report for ABA Commission on Evaluation of Professional Standards and ABA House of Delegates"

251, 254–55 (1983).

Introduction

The following is a summary of preliminary findings of the Study on the Standards of Legal Negotiations. This research project explores the attitudes of litigation attorneys, judges, and law school teachers of professional responsibility regarding various ethical issues involved in pretrial negotiations. In addition, the study gathers information on professional ethics generally and factors in ethical decision-making. This study is being sponsored by the American Bar Foundation and is being undertaken in conjunction with the University of Michigan Law School and the Institute for Social Research.

These preliminary findings were drawn from responses by 1034 litigation attorneys from the State of Michigan [M] and 1513 from large law firm litigators throughout the country [N] as well as 256 state judges, 75 federal judges and 128 law professors. The survey instrument used a hypothetical negotiation problem to solicit attitudes on a number of ethical issues.

. . .

SURVEY FINDINGS ON PATTERNS OF CANDOR AND DECEPTION

a. Disclosures of Client Misrepresentation
and Settlement Without Disclosure

When an attorney receives information that his client has knowingly given false information on a material issue at a deposition, over half of both samples felt there was no need to disclose this to the other side if the client would not authorize such a correction (58% N, 55% M). When asked a similar question, 60% of the Federal Judges and 41% of the State Judges thought an attorney should disclose this change, whereas less than 30% of the litigators agreed (29% N, 27%   M).

The current DR7–102(B)(1) requires that when a client has committed a fraud, the attorney shall call upon the client to rectify the fraud and if the client refuses, the attorney shall make the disclosure. In 1974, the ABA added a proviso to DR7–102(B)(1) that does not require attorney disclosure if the information indicating that a fraud had been committed was gained through a privileged or confidential communication. In a comparison of all the attorneys in 14 states that have adopted some version of the

1974 proviso with attorneys from 29 states that have not adopted it, no significant difference in attitudes toward disclosure was found. However, a significant difference (.05) did exist among the largest firm lawyers in the proviso and non-proviso states. Large firm litigators (over 75 person firms) from the 29 non-proviso states were significantly more likely to feel that there was an obligation to disclose than their large firm counterparts in 14 states with the proviso. Thus, it may be that if the 1974 proviso to DR7–102(B) had any substantial effect on lawyers' attitudes, it was primarily in the largest firms.

While all states except two have a duty for an attorney to ask the client to rectify a fraudulent statement, only 57% of the Michigan litigators and 75% of the National litigators felt that an attorney had a duty to ask a client to correct his clearly false deposition testimony on a material issue in the case.[9] Fifty percent of the Michigan litigators and 31% of the National litigators thought you could enter into a settlement without disclosing the false deposition testimony. Thirty-eight percent of the Michigan litigators and 26% of the National litigators thought it was permissible for an attorney in negotiations to refer to deposition testimony known to be false. If asked during negotiation about the portion of the deposition testimony now known to be false, less than half the attorneys felt that if they answered the question, the response had to be truthful and complete (49% N, 44% M). Forty-six percent of the National litigators and 56% of Michigan litigators felt that they could give a partially true but incomplete answer that did not reveal the critical element upon which the deposition was false. While several attorneys thought it permissible to refer to a client's deposition knowing it to be false, or to avoid a question by a partially true but incomplete response, only a small percentage felt that an attorney could positively assert a known falsehood in response to an inquiry (5% N, 11% M).

While all but three states require an attorney to withdraw if continued representation will result in a violation of an ethical rule, only 57% of the National litigators and 37% of the Michigan litigators felt that an attorney must seek to withdraw if the client will neither correct his false deposition nor allow the attorney to do so prior to entering into a settlement. In the three states that have a separate withdrawal requirement in the ethical rule dealing with client fraud [DR7–102(B)] rather than the general mandatory withdrawal provision of DR2–110(B), attorneys were signifi-

---

9. Ninety-two percent of the federal judges and 94% of law school teachers in the field of legal ethics, felt the attorney should ask the client to correct the false testimony.

cantly (.04) more likely to feel that withdrawal was necessary in the above situation.

James J. White, "Machiavelli and the Bar: Ethical Limitations on Lying in Negotiation"

1980 American Bar Foundation Research Journal, 926–34.

The difficulty of proposing acceptable rules concerning truthfulness in negotiation is presented by several circumstances. First, negotiation is nonpublic behavior. If one negotiator lies to another, only by happenstance will the other discover the lie. If the settlement is concluded by negotiation, there will be no trial, no public testimony by conflicting witnesses, and thus no opportunity to examine the truthfulness of assertions made during the negotiation. Consequently, in negotiation, more than in other contexts, ethical norms can probably be violated with greater confidence that there will be no discovery and punishment. Whether one is likely to be caught for violating an ethical standard says nothing about the merit of the standard. However, if the low probability of punishment means that many lawyers will violate the standard, the standard becomes even more difficult for the honest lawyer to follow, for by doing so he may be forfeiting a significant advantage for his client to others who do not follow the rules.

The drafters appreciated, but perhaps not fully, a second difficulty in drafting ethical norms for negotiators. That is the almost galactic scope of disputes that are subject to resolution by negotiation. One who conceives of negotiation as an alternative to a lawsuit has only scratched the surface. Negotiation is also the process by which one deals with the opposing side in war, with terrorists, with labor or management in a labor agreement, with buyers and sellers of goods, services, and real estate, with lessors, with governmental agencies, and with one's clients, acquaintances, and family. By limiting his consideration to negotiations in which a lawyer is involved in his professional role, one eliminates some of the most difficult cases but is left with a rather large and irregular universe of disputes. Surely society would tolerate and indeed expect different forms of behavior on the one hand from one assigned to negotiate with terrorists and on the other from one who is negotiating with the citizens on behalf of a governmental agency. The difference between those two cases illustrates the less drastic distinctions that may be called for by differences between other negotiating situations. Performance that is standard in one negotiating arena may be gauche, conceivably unethical, in another.　More than almost any other form of lawyer behavior, the process of negotiation is varied; it differs from place to place and from subject matter to subject matter.　It calls, therefore, either for quite different rules in different contexts or for rules stated only at a very high level of generality.

A final complication in drafting rules about truthfulness arises out of the paradoxical nature of the negotiator's responsibility.　On the one hand the negotiator must be fair and truthful; on the other he must mislead his opponent.　Like the poker player, a negotiator hopes that his opponent will overestimate the value of his hand.　Like the poker player, in a variety of ways he must facilitate his opponent's inaccurate assessment.　The critical difference between those who are successful negotiators and those who are not lies in this capacity both to mislead and not to be misled.

Some experienced negotiators will deny the accuracy of this assertion, but they will be wrong.　I submit that a careful examination of the behavior of even the most forthright, honest, and trustworthy negotiators will show them actively engaged in misleading their opponents about their true positions.　That is true of both the plaintiff and the defendant in a lawsuit.　It is true of both labor and management in a collective bargaining agreement.　It is true as well of both the buyer and the seller in a wide variety of sales transactions.　To conceal one's true position, to mislead an opponent about one's true settling point, is the essence of negotiation.

Of course there are limits on acceptable deceptive behavior in negotiation, but there is the paradox.　How can one be "fair" but also mislead?　Can we ask the negotiator to mislead, but fairly, like the soldier who must kill, but humanely?

Truthtelling in General

The obligation to behave truthfully in negotiation is embodied in the requirement of [proposed Model] Rule 4.2(a) that directs the lawyer to "be fair in dealing with other participants."　Presumably the direction to be fair speaks to a variety of acts in addition to truthfulness and also different from it.　At a minimum it has something to say about the threats a negotiator may use, about the favors he may offer, and possibly about the extraneous factors other than threats and favors which can appropriately be used in negotiating.　As I have suggested elsewhere, each of these issues has important ramifications, and each merits independent consideration by the drafters of the Model Rules and by lawyers.　In this paper I ignore those questions and limit my consideration to the question of truth-telling.

The comment on fairness under Rule 4.2 makes explicit what is implicit in the rule itself by the following sentence: "Fairness in negotiation implies that representations by or on behalf of one party to the other party be truthful." Standing alone that statement is too broad. Even the Comments contemplate activities such as puffing which, in the broadest sense, are untruthful. It seems quite unlikely that the drafters intend or can realistically hope to outlaw a variety of other nontruthful behavior in negotiations. Below we will consider some examples, but for the time being we will consider the complexity of the task.

Pious and generalized assertions that the negotiator must be "honest" or that the lawyer must use "candor" are not helpful. They are at too high a level of generality, and they fail to appreciate the fact that truth and truthful behavior at one time in one set of circumstances with one set of negotiators may be untruthful in another circumstance with other negotiators. There is no general principle waiting somewhere to be discovered as Judge Alvin B. Rubin seems to suggest in his article on lawyer's ethics. Rather, mostly we are doing what he says we are not doing, namely, hunting for the rules of the game as the game is played in that particular circumstance.

. . .

[Another] case is related to puffing but different from it. This is the use of the so-called false demand. It is a standard negotiating technique in collective bargaining negotiation and in some other multiple-issue negotiations for one side to include a series of demands about which it cares little or not at all. The purpose of including these demands is to increase one's supply of negotiating currency. One hopes to convince the other party that one or more of these false demands is important and thus successfully to trade it for some significant concession. The assertion of and argument for a false demand involves the same kind of distortion that is involved in puffing or in arguing the merits of cases or statutes that are not really controlling. The proponent of a false demand implicitly or explicitly states his interest in the demand and his estimation of it. Such behavior is untruthful in the broadest sense; yet at least in collective bargaining negotiation its use is a standard part of the process and is not thought to be inappropriate by any experienced bargainer.

Two final examples may be more troublesome. The first involves the response of a lawyer to a question from the other side.

Assume that the defendant has instructed his lawyer to accept any settlement offer under $100,000. Having received that instruction, how does the defendant's lawyer respond to the plaintiff's question, "I think $90,000 will settle this case. Will your client give $90,000?" Do you see the dilemma that question poses for the defense lawyer? It calls for information that would not have to be disclosed. A truthful answer to it concludes the negotiation and dashes any possibility of negotiating a lower settlement even in circumstances in which the plaintiff might be willing to accept half of $90,000. Even a moment's hesitation in response to the question may be a nonverbal communication to a clever plaintiff's lawyer that the defendant has given such authority. Yet a negative response is a lie.

It is no answer that a clever lawyer will answer all such questions about authority by refusing to answer them, nor is it an answer that some lawyers will be clever enough to tell their clients not to grant them authority to accept a given sum until the final stages in negotiation. Most of us are not that careful or that clever. Few will routinely refuse to answer such questions in cases in which the client has granted a much lower limit than that discussed by the other party, for in that case an honest answer about the absence of authority is a quick and effective method of changing the opponent's settling point, and it is one that few of us will forego when our authority is far below that requested by the other party. Thus despite the fact that a clever negotiator can avoid having to lie or to reveal his settling point, many lawyers, perhaps most, will sometime be forced by such a question either to lie or to reveal that they have been granted such authority by saying so or by their silence in response to a direct question. Is it fair to lie in such a case?

Before one examines the possible justifications for a lie in that circumstance, consider a final example recently suggested to me by a lawyer in practice. There the lawyer represented three persons who had been charged with shoplifting. Having satisfied himself that there was no significant conflict of interest, the defense lawyer told the prosecutor that two of the three would plead guilty only if the case was dismissed against the third. Previously those two had told the defense counsel that they would plead guilty irrespective of what the third did, and the third had said that he wished to go to trial unless the charges were dropped. Thus the defense lawyer lied to the prosecutor by stating that the two would plead only if the third were allowed to go free. Can the lie be justified in this case?

How does one distinguish the cases where truthfulness is not required and those where it is required? ... [certain cases are easy] because the rules of the game are explicit and well developed in those areas. Everyone expects a lawyer to distort the value of his own case, of his own facts and arguments, and to deprecate those of his opponent. No one is surprised by that, and the system accepts and expects that behavior. To a lesser extent the same is true of the false demand procedure in labor-management negotiations where the ploy is sufficiently widely used to be explicitly identified in the literature. A layman might say that this behavior falls within the ambit of "exaggeration," a form of behavior that while not necessarily respected is not regarded as morally reprehensible in our society.

The last two cases are more difficult. In one the lawyer lies about his authority; in the other he lies about the intention of his clients. It would be more difficult to justify the lies in those cases by arguing that the rules of the game explicitly permit that sort of behavior. Some might say that the rules of the game provide for such distortion, but I suspect that many lawyers would say that such lies are out of bounds and are not part of the rules of the game. Can the lie about authority be justified on the ground that the question itself was improper? Put another way, if I have a right to keep certain information to myself, and if any behavior but a lie will reveal that information to the other side, am I justified in lying? I think not. Particularly in the case in which there are other avenues open to the respondent, should we not ask him to take those avenues? That is, the careful negotiator here can turn aside all such questions and by doing so avoid any inference from his failure to answer such questions.

What makes the last case a close one? Conceivably it is the idea that one accused by the state is entitled to greater leeway in making his case. Possibly one can argue that there is no injury to the state when such a person, particularly an innocent person, goes free. Is it conceivable that the act can be justified on the ground that it is part of the game in this context, that prosecutors as well as defense lawyers routinely misstate what they, their witnesses, and their clients can and will do? None of these arguments seems persuasive. Justice is not served by freeing a guilty person. The system does not necessarily achieve better results by trading two guilty pleas for a dismissal. Perhaps its justification has its roots in the same idea that formerly held that a misrepresentation of one's state of mind was not actionable for it was not a misrepresentation of fact.

In a sense rules governing these cases may simply arise from a recognition by the law of its limited power to shape human behavior. By tolerating exaggeration and puffing in the sales transaction, by refusing to make misstatement of one's intention actionable, the law may simply have recognized the bounds of its control over human behavior. Having said that, one is still left with the question, Are the lies permissible in the last two cases? My general conclusion is that they are not, but I am not nearly as comfortable with that conclusion as I am with the conclusion about [other] cases.

Geoffrey C. Hazard, Jr., "The Lawyer's Obligation to Be Trustworthy When Dealing With Opposing Parties"

33 South Carolina Law Review 181, 191–96 (1981).

Upon careful consideration, it thus is clear that the Kutak Commission's proposed rules on trustworthiness do little to alter the status quo as set forth in the Code of Professional Responsibility. Yet the Commission considered and ultimately rejected a more sweeping proposal. Its Discussion Draft of January 30, 1980, included the following formulation:

4.2 Fairness to Other Participants

(a) In conducting negotiations a lawyer shall be fair in dealing with other participants.

(b) A lawyer shall not make a knowing misrepresentation of fact or law, or fail to disclose a material fact known to the lawyer, even if adverse, when disclosure is:

(1) Required by law or the Rules of Professional Conduct; or

(2) Necessary to correct a manifest misapprehension of fact or law resulting from a previous representation made by the lawyer or known by the lawyer to have been made by the client. ...

Proposed paragraph (a) went well beyond the fraud standard, prescribing a general requirement that lawyers be "fair." This certainly encompasses a concept of truthful representations. On the other hand, paragraph (b) restates DR 7–102(A)(5) and subparagraph (b)(1) does not depart radically from the present Code. Subparagraph (b)(2) parallels the *Restatement (Second) of Agency*, which provides that under certain circumstances, if a lawyer does not correct a manifest misapprehension on the part of the opposing party, the lawyer could incur civil liability. Furthermore, the lawyer would probably be guilty, under existing legal principles, of the ethical offense of "assisting" the client in "illegal" conduct.

The idea underlying the Kutak Commission's original proposal was not very complicated: the lawyer, as the instrument of a transaction, should be the guardian of its integrity. The proposal did not purport to hold lawyers strictly liable for the integrity of transactions or even burden them with a duty of reasonable care. Their only duty was to disclose facts of which an opposing party was obviously ignorant and which might affect the integrity of the transaction.

Much more fundamental objections were leveled at the proposal, particularly at the requirement that lawyers be "fair." Many members of the Commission and certainly the Reporter were surprised at the vehemence of the objections. "Vehemence" is the correct word, since much more heat than light was forthcoming in the reaction to the proposal. The Commission's surprise was compounded because the proposal seemed appropriate to the lawyer's role and appeared to reflect one interpretation of the lawyer's duty as established in the decisional law.

Although the explanation of the bar's aversion to the January 1980 proposal is complex, some concerns can be identified. First, many members of the bar do not realize or are unwilling to accept the fact that the law at large applies to lawyers. Perhaps these members of the bar believe an immunity attaches to lawyers against the civil liabilities imposed by the law on other intermediaries such as real estate brokers or securities underwriters. More subtly, perhaps lawyers recognize that the law at large applies to them but do not wish to be accountable for that obligation in the context of professional discipline.

Still subtler concerns were involved. The fundamental difficulty appears to stem from the lack of a firm professional consensus regarding the standard of openness that should govern lawyers' dealings with others and the lack of settled and homogeneous standards of technique in the practice of law. This lack of consensus indicates that lawyers, at least nationally, do not share a common conception of fairness in the process of negotiation. The lack of this consensus means that lawyers lack the language to express norms of fairness in negotiation and the institutional means to give effect to these norms.

The underlying disagreement about standards of fairness is not difficult to understand. Lawyers' standards of fairness are necessarily derived from those of society as a whole, and subcultural variations are enormous. At one extreme lies the "rural

God-fearing standard," so exacting and tedious that it often excludes the use of lawyers. At the other extreme stands "New
York hardball," now played in most larger cities using the wall-to-
wall indenture for a playing surface. Between these extremes are
regional and local standards and further variations that depend on
the business involved, the identity of the participants, and other
circumstances. Against this kaleidoscopic background, it is difficult to specify a single standard that governs the parties and thus
a correlative standard that should govern their legal representatives.

The second area of disagreement concerns professional technique. Lawyers differ widely in the technical sophistication they
expect of themselves and of others with whom they deal. As a
result, their expectations regarding their own or their opponents'
knowledge in the context of a given transaction may vary widely
... Lawyers accustomed to less sophisticated techniques are
understandably fearful that they will be outmatched or even
hoodwinked, with the possibility of loss to their clients and humili-
ation or even worse for themselves.

Lawyers accustomed to more sophisticated techniques have a
correlative but perhaps less apparent dilemma. First, signs of
bumbling on the other side cannot necessarily be taken at face
value; there is such a thing as country-slickering and it occurs
even in the city. Second, sophisticated lawyers are at risk precisely because of their technical sophistication. High-level technicians recognize aspects of transactions that lawyers of lesser
sophistication may overlook. But what is to be done with that
knowledge? If it is withheld, the transaction becomes vulnerable
to rescission because of the lawyer's nondisclosure. The lawyer's
professional competence, if not fully deployed for the benefit of the
opposing party, thus becomes a potential infirmity for the transaction. Conversely, if the lawyer's competence is deployed for the
benefit of the opposing party, where does the deployment properly
stop, short of a takeover of the transaction and assumption of
responsibility for the interests of both parties? ...

This range of possibilities is difficult to govern by regulation.
A rule based on the premise that the legal profession is substantially homogeneous in technical sophistication would put the technically sophisticated lawyer in a hopeless dilemma when dealing
with an unsophisticated opposing counsel. Such a lawyer could
straightforwardly be a partisan of his own client unless it became
evident that the other side was inadequately represented. But in
that case, the superior technician would have to assist the other
side to guard against the risk of a subsequent charge of nondisclo-

sure or fraud. Yet until a transaction is well under way, a lawyer cannot know which course of action is required. At the same time, the lawyer who is unsophisticated or is simply acting according to his idea of the applicable conventions of openness would be in jeopardy of giving away his client's position. Thus, in a situation where the opposing lawyers differ substantially in technical sophistication, a rule requiring reciprocal disclosure could not yield genuine reciprocity.

On the other hand, it would be practically impossible to formulate a general rule that accounts for variations in technical sophistication. Consider the difficulties with the concept of specialization and with the definition of specialization once the concept was accepted, or with the problem of "incompetence" among the trial bar. Could we imagine rules of disclosure that were based on a distinction between Type A Lawyers and Type B Lawyers? Anyone who is sanguine about overcoming these difficulties should try drafting the criteria by which to differentiate the technically sophisticated practitioner from the bar at large.

In light of these constraints, legal regulation of trustworthiness cannot go much further than to proscribe fraud. That is disquieting but not necessarily occasion for despair. It simply indicates limitations on improving the bar by legal regulation.

NOTES

Proponents of greater honesty and fairness in negotiation conduct generally rest their arguments on both practical and normative grounds. As a practical matter, they invoke recent research that casts doubt on the usefulness of hard-nosed adversarial strategies. According to this research, the paradigm case for competitive frameworks involves a "zero-sum" situation in which parties lack a continuing relationship, and are unlikely to detect deception. These circumstances are less typical than is commonly assumed. Proponents of cooperative negotiation argue that most bargaining contexts present "value-creating" as well as "value-claiming" opportunities. Adversarial approaches may preempt the discovery of mutually advantageous solutions to joint problems. Recent work on game theory also verifies what common sense suggests. Negotiators who encounter each other repeatedly will penalize aggressive bargainers; cooperation works better over the long run.[1]

---

1. *See* Robert Axelrod, *The Evolution of Cooperation* (1984). For general arguments favoring cooperative styles, *see* Carrie Menkel–Meadow, "Toward Another View of Negotiation: The Structure of Legal Problem Solving," 31 *U.C.L.A. L. Rev.* 754 (1984).

Other commentators argue for cooperation, candor, and fairness on normative grounds. Some feminists maintain that aggressive partisanship undervalues concerns about preserving relationships, concerns that have been traditionally associated with women.[2] Many theorists also claim that individuals' own interests in preserving their honesty, integrity, and fairness deserve a central role in evaluating negotiating behavior. From this perspective, common excuses for deceptive or manipulative tactics are unpersuasive. To rely on rationalizations such as "everyone does it" or "the other side is doing it" presupposes an impoverished view of morality—a view generally rejected in other contexts. Moreover, if we know that our adversary is lying, then a retaliatory lie is not simply corrective justice; rather, it is an attempt to impose the kind of injury that we have avoided by discovering the deception.

Another common problem in the way that negotiators rationalize cutting ethical corners lies in the selective evaluation of the consequences. Consciously or unconsciously, individuals tend to overvalue the personal short-term benefits from unethical tactics, and to disregard the long-term systemic costs. Deception adversely affects both parties and the process. When misrepresentation is suspected or revealed, it compromises the perpetrator's credibility, and may provoke retaliatory or defensive responses. Even lies that remain undiscovered can have corrosive consequences. As commentators often note, there is much truth to the cliche that it is easy to tell one lie but difficult to tell only one. Deception that remains undetected encourages more deception and ultimately may diminish parties' level of trust, their capacity to reach fair agreements, their ability to exchange credible commitments, and their sense of personal integrity. Honesty and fairness are to some extent collective goods. The more that lawyers seek to become "free riders," the greater the difficulty in maintaining a climate of trust, credibility, and fair dealing.

So too, an unqualified willingness to exploit an opponent's ignorance or mistake carries broader costs. Disparities in talent, resources, and information inevitably skew negotiation results.

2. Some studies on negotiation suggest that women attach higher importance to social relations, process concerns, and cooperative interaction than do their male counterparts. By contrast, other surveys find that women do not respond differently than men to common negotiating dilemmas and that both sexes' styles depend heavily on context, substantive objectives, power disparities, and the sex of other participants. See sources cited in Deborah L. Rhode, "The No–Problem Problem: Feminist Challenges and Cultural Changes," 100 *Yale Law Rev.* 1731, 1788 (1991); Lloyd Burton et al., "Feminist Theory, Professional Ethics and Gender–Related Distinctions in Attorney Negotiating Styles," 1991 *J. Dispute Res.* 199, 227–47 (finding no substantial gender differences).

While it may be unrealistic to expect parties to forego all the advantages that arise from such inequalities, it may be reasonable to expect negotiators to forego some. Particularly where parties lack equal access to relevant facts, it will often be both equitable and efficient to impose minimal disclosure obligations. Thus, Gerald Wetlaufer argues that we need to accept

> the proposition that ethics and integrity are things for which a price may have to be paid ... [To that end] we might clearly define winning in a way that leaves room for ethics. It might, for instance, be understood not as "getting as much as we can" but as "winning as much as possible without engaging in unacceptable behavior," and "unacceptable behavior" might then be understood to exclude not just those things that are stupid or illegal but also those other things that are unethical. And finally ... [we must] do our best to understand and confront the choices between the harsh individualist reality or instrumental effectiveness and ... between the elusive possibilities of ethics, integrity, reciprocity and community.[3]

REFERENCES

A. Baier, "Trust and Antitrust," 96 *Ethics* 231 (1981).

L. Brown & E. Dauer, *Planning by Lawyers: Materials on a Nonadversarial Legal Process* (1978).

Carr, "Is Business Bluffing Ethical?" *Harv.Bus.Rev.* Jan.-Feb. 1968 at 143.

Eisenberg, "Private Ordering Through Negotiation: Dispute-Settlement and Rulemaking," 89 *Harv.L.Rev.* 637 (1976).

Menkel–Meadow, "Toward Another View of Negotiation: The Structure of Legal Problem Solving," 31 *UCLA L.Rev.* 754 (1984).

Menkel-Meadow, "Legal Negotiation: A Study of Strategies in Search of a Theory" (Review Essay), 1983 *Am.B.Found.Research J.* 905.

H. Ross, *Settled Out of Court: The Social Process of Insurance Claims Adjustments* (1970).

T. Schelling, "An Essay on Bargaining," in *The Strategy of Conflict* (1960).

Schwartz, "The Professionalism and Accountability of Lawyers," 66 *Calif.L.Rev.* 669 (1978).

---

3. Wetlaufer, "The Ethics of Lying in Negotiations," 75 *Iowa L.Rev.* 1219, 1272–73 (1990). *See also* S. Bok, *Lying: Moral Choice in Public and Private Life* 17–32 (1978).

____, "The Zeal of the Civil Advocate" in D. Luban ed., *The Good Lawyer* (D. Luban ed. 1983).

G. THE LAWYER AS COUNSELOR

Geoffrey C. Hazard, Jr., Ethics in the Practice of Law
136–37, 143–46 (1978).

Many courses of action taken by a client are "wrong" at least in the exacting sense that they are not what would be done by a supremely moral person unconcerned with costs. If this were the standard by which a lawyer should judge whether to continue his association with a client, there would be few of either clients or lawyers.

Ethically sensitive lawyers are very much concerned about clients who refuse to follow advice, particularly when it concerns a serious matter of right and wrong.

. . .

In considering this question, it should be kept in mind what a lawyer may include in the advice he gives a client. Legal advice takes the form of a suggestion concerning a course of action that might or should be pursued or avoided, with a supporting explanation. The explanation is the heart of the matter, for otherwise the advice amounts to nothing more than a Delphic pronouncement. A legal adviser's explanation can include one or more of the following elements:

• A report of the text of the law as it stands.

• An estimate of how key provisions of the law properly should be interpreted (if the advice is given within the government) or will likely be interpreted by the officials responsible for its administration (if the advice is given outside the government).

• An estimate of the likelihood that a serious effort will be made to invoke the rule in question.

• A projection of the best, worst, and intermediate situations that could result as a consequence of the rule's being invoked.

• An appraisal of the significant consequences of possible courses of action, whether they will provoke retaliation, etc.

• A judgment whether the recommended course of action is in some less pragmatic sense good or right.

. . .

The legal adviser in such a situation surely is not clothed with the immunity of a pure bystander. But what sort of responsibilities does he have? In recent years, some critics of the legal profession have suggested that a lawyer for a corporation is responsible for its conduct in at least two related respects: his advice to such a client should consist not merely of what the client legally might do but also of what the client morally ought to do; and he should not serve a client who is not disposed to follow advice of that character. According to this line of analysis, the probity of a lawyer can be deduced from the conduct of his clients. If the client has engaged in misconduct, his lawyer is prima facie guilty also, either because his advice was followed but was morally insufficient, or because his advice was not followed and he has shown himself willing to continue in the service of a morally deficient master. The same analysis could be applied to a lawyer for a government agency.

The attack is a difficult one to meet. The response conventionally made by the bar is to suggest that the same criticism would apply to a lawyer for a criminal accused. If it did, the argument runs, the consequence would be that an accused could not obtain representation by a lawyer of standing; since the latter is inadmissible, it must be that the criticism is invalid. Hence, a lawyer is not responsible for what his client does.

This seems to hold, however, only if the actual relationship between a corporation or agency and its general counsel corresponds to the Victorian model and the latter is limited to criminal cases. It is perfectly possible to think that the lawyer for the criminal accused is not "responsible" for him, while at the same time thinking that the general counsel for a corporation or agency is, in some sense of the word, "responsible" for it. The point is made by suggesting that it is one thing to represent a sometime murderer, quite another to be on retainer to the Mafia.

Thus, the question has to be faced: Is a lawyer responsible for the conduct of a regular client? This is a question that confronts others besides lawyers, a point that has double significance. In the first place, analysis of the lawyer's problem is applicable to other advisers, such as accountants, scientific consultants, and indeed members of the client's own administrative and technical staffs. In the second place, in advising people in important matters the lawyer does not stand in a unique situation. The legal profession often talks as though a legal counsellor bears some special burden because he is privy to especially deep secrets. From this it is thought to follow that he enjoys special immunity from the responsibility that might fall on one who is in some way

involved in another's conduct. But the accountant who knows of
fraud because he has access to the client's books, or the scientist
who knows of poisonous emissions because he has access to the
client's premises, is surely in a position that is different at most in
degree from a lawyer who has learned of such facts from a
consultation with a client.

The obvious answer for the adviser whose advice is ignored is
that he can resign. In some circumstances that is the only
honorable course to be followed, but it is impractical as a response
to all except fundamental disagreements. More important,
though not often recognized by the critics of legal and other
advisers to corporations, the sanction of resignation involves some
ethical problems of its own. If taken seriously, it should be
applicable only when any right-thinking adviser would resign.
But this is to say that such a client ought to have no right-
thinking adviser at all, at least until the client redirects his
conduct so that it would no longer be objectionable to a right-
thinking adviser. There are situations in which it seems proper
that the client should suffer that kind of penalty, for example if he
insists on fabricating evidence or carrying out a swindle. But if
the case is less extreme than this, the sanction of resignation is too
severe. It implies that the client should have to function without
proper guidance, or perhaps cease functioning at all, because its
managers do not see fit to follow the advice of its advisers.

If this were the consequence that should ensue from a client's
refusal to follow advice, it would mean that the advice was in
effect peremptory—not an informed suggestion but a command.
When an adviser's advice is in effect peremptory, however, the
result is a reversal of the underlying structure of responsibility for
the organization's conduct. The adviser becomes the ultimate
arbiter and the client a subordinate. If the reversal of responsibilities becomes permanent, as it must if the adviser is deemed
responsible for all critical decisions, the erstwhile adviser now
becomes principal and we are back at the beginning. Furthermore, in the meantime the nominal principal has the excuse that
he was merely following directions and so is not responsible for
action taken in his name. Putting the point differently, when
responsibility is transferred to an adviser, it is also transferred
from his principal.

It seems unlikely that such a transfer of responsibility is
contemplated by those who say that an adviser has some kind of
responsibility for what his principal does. Probably it is assumed
that the organization will not be left helpless for want of essential
assistance, but rather that some other adviser will come along to

take the place of the right-thinking adviser who resigns. This assumption, however, has some curious implications. It may mean that an equally highminded adviser can step in as successor because he was not involved before. As a result, that which is reprehensible when done by one adviser in continuous service becomes acceptable when done by multiple advisers acting in a relay. A lot of moral knots are cut this way but it surely is an Alexandrine technique. On the other hand, the assumption may be that a less high-minded successor can be expected to take over. If so, it reduces the significance of resignation to a merely personal matter and perhaps a case of narcissism. (It may also have the result of simply insulating the client from conscientious advisers in the future.) Still another possibility is that the client will figure out how to retain high-minded advisers without creating situations in which they will feel impelled to resign; the client will learn not to ask for advice in the cases that might put his counsel under that kind of pressure.

H. LAWYERS IN ORGANIZATIONAL SETTINGS

NOTES [1]

Although most of the basic theoretical work on legal ethics has focused on individual lawyer-client relationships, that paradigm cannot adequately capture the range of circumstances in which ethical questions arise. Approximately two-thirds of the bar now work in organizations, many of which display attributes Max Weber associated with bureaucracies: specialization, hierarchy, and an ethos mandating institutional loyalty.[2] Such structures coexist uneasily with a professional code that assumes individual moral autonomy and commitment to client rather than organizational objectives.[3]

The tensions between professional ideals and institutional imperatives can arise in a variety of contexts. Any bureaucratic setting encourages team players, and the incentives in certain

1. A more extended discussion of these issues appears in Rhode, "Ethical Perspectives in Legal Practice," 37 *Stan.L.Rev.* 589, 626–638 (1985).

2. *From Max Weber; Essays in Sociology* 196–99, 240 (H. Gerth & C. Mills eds. 1946).

3. The current ABA Code of Professional Responsibility makes almost no reference to the organizational context

of legal practice. The proposed Model Rules of Professional Conduct hold subordinate attorneys responsible for any ethical violation except where they act in accordance with a supervisory lawyer's reasonable resolution of an arguable question of professional duty. Model Rule 5.5. *See also* ABA Committee on Ethics and Professional Responsibility, Informal Opinion 1203.

forms of legal practice can be especially potent. For example, both the profit orientation and competitive structure of law firms may tend to constrict normative vision. For junior attorneys, passing moral judgment on a superior's choice of clients or tactics is rarely a costless enterprise. With greater seniority comes greater ability to decline cases or to challenge conduct, but also less mobility and a larger social, psychological, and economic investment in professional relationships. Over time, that can yield a normative as well as occupational inertia.

This problem is compounded by other institutional patholo-gies. Attorneys working on fragmented aspects of a substantial matter may feel little accountability for its ultimate consequences. Particularly in hierarchical organizations, the sources of rationali-zation multiply; lack of experience, certitude, or formal responsi-bility supply ready grounds for suspending judgment. And once habituated to fraternal norms and practices, a lawyer may have increased difficulty viewing them through moral lenses.

Moreover, even where other attorneys' misconduct is evident, the costs of informing can be substantial. Bar disciplinary statis-tics reflect only a tiny number of lawyers willing to incur the consequences of tattling.[4] Case studies such as the Berkey–Kodak antitrust litigation, the OPM computer leasing fraud, and Chicago Greylord investigations illustrate some of the organizational pres-sures that deter disclosure of collegial frailties.[5] In many institu-tional contexts, the path of least resistance is selective avoidance of moral tensions. Through that process, a "variant of Gresham's Law asserts itself, leaving those most in need of ethical confronta-tion least likely to receive it."[6]

Bar ethical standards traditionally have provided little guid-ance regarding lawyers' obligations within organizational settings.

---

4. The infrequency of complaints by attorneys against other attorneys is an-alyzed in Lynch, "The Lawyer as In-former," 1986 *Duke L.J.* 491. Ad Hoc Committee on Grievance Procedures, Ass'n of the Bar of the City of N.Y., *Report on the Grievance System* 41 (1976); Marks & Cathcart, "Discipline Within the Legal Profession: Is It Self–Regulation?", 1974 *U.Ill.L.F.* 193, 207; Thode, "The Duty of Lawyers and Judges to Report Other Lawyers' Breaches of the Standards of the Legal Profession", 1976 *Utah L.Rev.* 95; Note, "The Lawyer's Duty to Report Profes-sional Misconduct," 20 *Ariz.L.Rev.* 509 (1978).

5. For discussion of the Berkey–Ko-dak litigation, involving perjury and non-disclosures by Wall Street attor-neys, see J. Stewart, *The Partners* (1983) and Kiechel, "The Strange Case of Kodak's Lawyers," *Fortune* 188 (May 8, 1978). The 200 million dollar OPM leasing scandal, in which counsel played a reportedly crucial and unjusti-fiable role in consummating fraudulent financial agreements, is detailed in Re-port of the Trustees Concerning Fraud and Other Misconduct in the Manage-ment of the Affairs of the Debtor (Bankr.S.D.N.Y.1982).

6. Rhode, *supra* note 1.

The Code of Professional Conduct has almost no references to the issue, beyond the statement in its Ethical Considerations that lawyers representing organizational clients owe their allegiance "to the entity and not to a stockholder, director, officer, employee, representative, or other person connected with the entity." EC 5–18. The Model Rules, Rule 1.13, contain a similar provision about representing the entity. However the Rule also sets forth procedures for lawyers who become aware of decisions that may violate the law and impair an organizational client's interests. In essence, Rule 1.13 provides that lawyers may seek reconsideration, separate legal opinions, or referrals to the highest authority in the organization that can act on the organization's behalf. Once that authority has reviewed the issue, however, the only further action that the Model Rules authorize is withdrawal (including public notice of the withdrawal and disaffirmance of any prior opinion) (Model Rule 1.6).

The Model Rules, unlike the Code, also make explicit reference to the duties of supervisory and subordinate lawyers. Rule 5.1 provides that "[a] lawyer having direct supervisory authority over another lawyer shall make reasonable efforts to ensure that the other lawyer conforms to the rules of professional conduct." Rule 5.2 provides that a subordinate lawyer is bound by the rules of professional conduct "even if the lawyer acts at the direction of another person." However, the lawyer "does not violate the rules if that lawyer acts in accordance with a supervisory lawyer's reasonable resolution of an arguable question of professional duty."

Do these rules speak adequately to the ethical constraints that Jackall and MacIntyre describe? If not, what other initiatives, such as those identified by Rhode, would you support?

Deborah L. Rhode, "Ethical Perspectives on Legal Practice"
37 Stanford Law Review 589, 624 (1985).*

The bar's conventional view is that counsel ought not to second guess policy decisions of corporate officers and directors; absent evidence of financial self-dealing, a lawyer's arrogation of normative authority would displace the appropriate mechanism of corporate governance. Such arguments presuppose that organizational authorities are, by definition, more able than counsel to assess the full ethical dimensions of their policies. That supposition appears questionable on a number of grounds.

Corporate structures inevitably tend to fragment moral responsibility. The impersonal character of bureaucracies, their departmentalized concepts of accountability, their claims of personal loyalty, and their devaluation of concerns not readily translated into relatively short-term advantages all conspire to circumscribe ethical vision. Since prestige in the business world turns heavily on ability to maximize organizational sales and growth, less tangible values are often discounted. Indeed, within some constituencies, the perception remains that "the social responsibility of business is to make profits." [119]

Yet, given the frequent presence of market externalities and barriers to information, competition, legal redress, or political oversight, some divergence between private and public interests is inescapable. If corporate executives are convinced that "[s]afety doesn't sell," [120] or if third world nations lack capacity to regulate hazardous corporate conduct, the human costs of profit maximization can be substantial. To be sure, lawyers have no special expertise in assessing such costs. But their distance from organizational incentive structures may at least permit a more disinterested perspective than that of corporate officers. By exploring the moral consequences of clients' contemplated actions, counsel may broaden the agenda of decision-making. Conversely, by declining that role, lawyers may compound the deflection of responsibility that too often characterizes organizational behavior. Clients can justify asocial action on the ground that counsel have pronounced it not unlawful, while counsel can rationalize their participation by deferring to client autonomy.

Alasdair C. MacIntyre, "Utilitarianism and Cost-Benefit Analysis: An Essay on the Relevance of Moral Philosophy to Bureaucratic Theory"

in K. Sayre, ed., Values in the Electric Power Industry 219–237 (1977).

... The moral philosopher will at once recognize that the disclosure of bureaucracy thus conceived reproduces the argumentative forms of utilitarianism. Not perhaps those of utilitarianism largely conceived as a morality capable of dealing with every area of life, but those reflecting acceptance of J.S. Mill's judgment upon

---

119. L. Silk and D. Volk, *Ethics and Profits* 139 (1976).

120. Dowie, "Pinto Madness," *Mother Jones* Sept.–Oct. 1977 (quoting Lee Iacocca).

"what a philosophy like Bentham's can do. It can teach the means of organizing and regulating the merely *business* part of the social arrangements." Poetry, music, friendship, and family life, as Mill sees it may not be captured by the Benthamite calculus; but there is a part of life which may be so captured, and which therefore may be rendered calculable.

If it is correct that corporate activity embodies the argumentative forms of utilitarianism, then we ought to be able to identify the key features of utilitarianism, including its central errors and distortions, within corporate activity. The guide that I shall use to identify the argumentative forms of corporate activity will be the text-book versions of cost-benefit analysis, which not only form the mind of the corporate executive but provide paradigmatic examples from practice. The question is whether we discover in the texts the same lacunae and incoherences as in classical utilitarianism. First we must characterize these deficiencies.

UTILITARIANISM AND ITS DEFICIENCIES

The doctrines of classical utilitarianism appear to first sight simple and elegant. Every proposed course of action is to be subjected to the test: will it produce a greater balance of pleasure over pain, of happiness over unhappiness, of benefits over harms, than any alternative course of action? It is right to perform that action which will be productive of "the greatest happiness of the greatest number," which will have the greatest utility. In calculating the greatest happiness, everybody is to count for one and nobody for more than one. Utilitarianism sometimes has entangled itself, but perhaps need not entangle itself, in questions about the meaning of such words as "right" and "good". Bentham at least made no pretence that his doctrine was an analysis of what moral agents had hitherto meant in using such words; he proposed it instead as a rational substitute for the confusions and superstitions of earlier moral theory and it is as such that I shall examine it.

Two main versions of utilitarianism have been advanced: that which holds that the utilitarian test is a test of actions and that which holds that it is a test of rules. On the former view, generally known as act-utilitarianism, rules simply summarize our findings to date about what classes of action generally tend to produce the greatest happiness of the greatest number; they are rough and ready guides to action, but if it appears on a given occasion that an action which transgresses a rule hitherto employed will produce a greater balance of pleasure or pain than one which conforms to that rule then the former action ought to be preferred to the latter. On the other rule-utilitarian view, we perform those actions which the best moral rules we have prescribe; and we decide which moral rules are best by applying the "greatest happiness" test. But David Lyons has argued cogently that any case in which an act-utilitarian would have a good reason for breaking a rule would be a case in which a rule-utilitarian would have an equally good reason for amending his rule. Hence in practice they come to the same theory and our discussion can safely ignore their differences.

About any version of utilitarian doctrine five major questions arise. The first concerns the range of alternative courses of action which are to be subjected to the utilitarian test. For clearly at any moment an indefinitely large range of alternative courses of action are open to most agents. In practice I may consider a very limited set of alternatives: shall I use this money to paint my house or to educate my child? But perhaps I ought to weigh every proposed expenditure of energy, time or money against the benefit that might accrue from devoting it to the solution of world population problems or the invention of labor-saving devices or the discovery of new methods to teaching music to young children .... If I try to construct a list of this kind of indefinite length, all decision-making will in fact be paralyzed. I must therefore find some principle of restriction in the construction of my list of alternatives. But this principle cannot itself be utilitarian; for if it were to be justified by the test of beneficial and harmful consequences as against alternative proposed principles of restriction, we should have to find some principle of restriction in order to avoid paralysis by the construction of an indefinitely long list of principles of restriction. And so on.

Utilitarian tests therefore always presuppose the application of some prior non-utilitarian principle which sets limits upon the range of alternatives to be considered. But this is not all that they presuppose. Bentham believed that there was one single, simple concept of pleasure or of happiness. It did not matter what you called it.

... But Bentham's beliefs are of course false and were recognized as false even by his immediate utilitarian heirs.

... A politician has to decide whether to propose spending a given sum of money on a new clinic for aged patients or on a new infant school; a student has to decide between embarking on a career as a musician or becoming an engineer. Both wish to promote the greatest happiness of the greatest number, but they are being called upon to decide between incommensurables— unless they can provide some prior scheme of values by means of which goods and evils, pleasures and pains, benefits and harms are to be ranked in some particular way. Such a method of rank-ordering will however have to be non-utilitarian. For like the principle which specified the range of alternatives to be considered it has to be adopted before any utilitarian test can be applied.

Thirdly there is the question of whose assessment of harms and benefits is to be considered by the agent making his assessment. For it is clear not only that there are alternative methods of rank-ordering, but also that different types of people will adopt and argue for different methods. The old do not weigh harms and benefits in the same way as the young; the poor have a different perspective from the rich; the healthy and the sick often weigh pain and suffering differently. "Everybody is to count for one and nobody for more than one," declared Bentham; but others—Sir Karl Popper, for one—have suggested that the relief of pain or suffering always should take precedence over the promotion of pleasure or happiness. So we have at least two contingently incompatible proposals immediately, for the outcome of Bentham's rule clearly will often conflict with the results of applying Popper's maxim.

Fourthly there is the question of what is to count as a consequence of a given action. We might be tempted to suppose this a very straightforward question, but it is not. For the apparently straightforward answer "All the predictable effects of my action are to be counted as consequences of my action" at once raises the question, "What are reasonable standards of prediction?" How much care and effort am I required to exert before I make my decision? Once again certain maxims must be adopted prior to the utilitarian test. But this is not the only difficulty which arises over the notion of a consequence. In the Anglo-Saxon legal tradition chains of cause-and-effect arising from an action are often thought to be modified when they pass through another responsible agent in such a way that the later effects are no longer held to be consequences of my action. I am a teacher grading a student's examination. I give him a well-deserved C-. The student who has hoped for an A goes home and in his anger beats his wife. Suppose that I could somehow or other have reasonably predicted this outcome; ought I to have counted the wife-beating as a consequence of my action in grading the paper? Ought I to have weighed this consequence against others before deciding on what grade to give the paper? Classical utilitarianism appears to be committed to the answer "Yes", the Anglo-Saxon legal tradition by and large to the answer "No". About what are they disagreeing? Obviously it is about the range of effects of an action for which the agent can be held responsible. Thus it turns out that some particular theory of responsibility must be adopted before we can have a criterion for deciding what effects are to count as consequences.

Fifthly, a decision must be made about the time-scale which is to be used in assessing consequences. Clearly if we adopt a longer time-scale we have to reckon with a much less predictable future than if we adopt a shorter one. Our assessment of long-term risks and of long-term probabilities is generally more liable to error than our assessment of short-term risks and probabilities. Moreover, it is not clear how we ought to weigh short-term harms and benefits against long-term contingencies; are our responsibilities the same to future generations as they are to the present one or to our own children? How far ought the present to be sacrificed to the future? Here again we have a range of questions to which non-utilitarian answers have to be given or at least presupposed before any utilitarian test can be applied.

Utilitarianism thus requires a background of beliefs and of evaluative commitments, a fact that has usually gone unnoticed by utilitarians themselves. They are able to apply the test of utility only because they have already implicitly decided that the world ought to be viewed in one way rather than another, that experience ought to be structured and evaluated in one way rather than another. The world which they inhabit is one of discrete variables, of a reasonably high degree of predictability; it is one in which questions of value have become questions of fact and in which the aim and the vindication of theory is its success in increasing our manipulative powers. The utilitarian vision of the world and the bureaucratic vision of the world match each other closely.

Yet this is not just a matter of resemblance; the bureaucratic world contains a number of devices for ensuring that thought, perception and action are organized in a utilitarian way. The most important of such devices in contemporary bureaucracy is probably the cost-benefit analysis.

COST–BENEFIT ANALYSIS AND BUREAUCRATIC DECISION–MAKING

The cost-benefit analysis is an instrument of practical reason, and it is one of the central features of practical reason that it operates under time constraints in a way that theoretical reason does not. Nothing counts as a solution of a practical problem which does not meet a required deadline; it is no good achieving a perfect solution for defeating Wellington at Waterloo on June 19, if the battle had to be fought on June 18.   Hence problems cannot be left unsolved to await future solutions.   But problems of a cost-benefit kind—of a utilitarian kind in general—can only be solved when all the elements of the problems are treated as belonging to the realm of the calculable and the predictable.   Hence the executive is always under pressure to treat the social world as predictable and calculable and to ignore any arbitrariness involved in so doing.   This pressure may operate in either of two opposite ways.   It may appear in a tendency to restrict our operations to what is genuinely predictable and calculable; one manifestation of this will be a tendency to prefer short-term to long-term planning, since clearly the near future is generally more predictable than the more distant future.   But the same pressure may equally appear in an opposite tendency to try to present all that we encounter as calculable and predictable, a tendency to overcome apparent difficulties in calculation by adopting *ad hoc* devices of various kinds.   These conflicting pressures may appear in the way in which decisions are taken or evaluative commitments are made in any of the five areas which define the background of utilitarianism and which in a precisely parallel way define the background of cost-benefit analyses.

There is first of all the restriction of alternatives so that the benefits and the costs of doing this rather than that are weighed against one another, but neither alternative is assessed against an indeterminately large range of other alternatives.   Yet ever so often in corporate or governmental or private life the range of alternatives for which cost-benefit analyses are sought changes; and this change always signals a change in underlying evaluative commitments.   Up to a certain point in the history of a marriage, divorce remains an unthinkable alternative; up to a certain point in the history of a foreign policy, embarking on an aggressive war remains an unthinkable alternative; up to a certain point in the history of a war, truce or withdrawal remains unthinkable.   Corporate parallels are not difficult to think of.   The history of publishing or of automobile manufacture abound with them.   The one-volume novel or the cheap intellectually substantial paper-back were once unthinkable; so was the car which could be advertised primarily for safety factors.

Corporate executives may respond to this by saying that what restricts the range of alternatives which they consider is simply profitability.   They can attend only to those alternatives which in the shorter or longer run will yield their stockholders a competitive return in the market.   What this reply fails to notice is that what is profitable is partly determined by the range of evaluative commitments shared in the community. Sir Allen had to *make* the intellectual paperback profitable for the very first time and for that a firm conviction about intellectual values was required. What attitude both automobile manufacturers and the public take to death on the roads *changes* what is profitable. Consumer markets are *made,* not just given. Underlying the restricted range of alternatives considered by corporate executives we may therefore find both covert evaluative commitments and also un-spelled-out assumptions about human wants and needs.

. . .

Secondly, the use of cost-benefit analyses clearly presupposes a prior decision as to what is a cost and what a benefit; but more than that it presupposes some method of ordering costs and benefits so that what otherwise would be incommensurable becomes commensurable. How are we to weigh the benefits of slightly cheaper power against the loss forever of just one beautiful landscape? How are we to weigh the benefits of increased employment and lessened poverty in Detroit against a marginal increase in deaths from automobile accidents? Once somebody has to consider both factors within a cost-benefit analysis framework these questions have to be answered. Considerable ingenuity has in fact been exercised in answering them.

Writers on cost-benefit analysis techniques have devised four alternative methods for computing the cost of a person's life. One is that of discounting to the present the person's expected future earnings; a second is that of computing the losses to others from the person's death so as to calculate their present discounted value; a third is that of examining the value placed on an individual life by presently established social policies and practices, e.g. the benefits in increased motor traffic which society at the present moment is prepared to exchange for a higher fatal accident rate; and a fourth is to ask what value a person placed on his or her own life, by looking at the risks which that person is or was prepared to take and the insurance premiums which he or she was prepared to pay. Clearly, those four criteria will yield very different answers on occasion; the range of possible different answers to one and the same question that you can extract from the same techniques of cost-benefit analysis makes it clear that all the mathematical sophistication and rigor that may go into the modes of computation may be undermined by the arbitrariness (relative to the mathematics) of the choice to adopt one principle for quantifying rather than another. Thus there once more appears behind the ordered world of discrete, calculable, variable elements in which the cost-benefit analysis is at home, a range of relatively arbitrary decisions presupposed—and sometimes actually made—by the analyst himself.

Thirdly, once more as with utilitarianism in general, the application of cost-benefit analysis presupposes a decision as to *whose* values and preferences are to be taken into account in assessing costs and benefits. Indeed the choice of a method for weighing costs against benefits, the adoption of the type of principle discussed immediately above, will often involve equally a decision as to which voices are to be heard. Consider once again the different methods employed to estimate the cost of a human death. One of these considers the individual's own earnings, one the losses to others, one certain socially established norms, and one the individual's own risk-taking. The last is an attempt to give the individual the value which he sets on himself; the second gives him the value he has to others; the third the value he has in the eyes of "society;" the fourth perhaps the value that he has in the eyes of the taxation system. To adopt one of these methods rather than another is precisely to decide *who* is to decide what counts as a cost and what counts as a benefit.

Consider the range of possible decision-makers with whom a corporate executive might be concerned: his superiors, the consumers of his product, the stockholders, the labor force, the other members of his profession (if he is, say, a lawyer or an actuary), the community in which the corporation is cited, the government, and the public at large. What makes the question "Who decides?" so crucial is another feature of cost-benefit analyses.

. . .

It may be said that the author of a cost-benefit analysis simply cannot be expected to deal with unpredictability at all. If this were indeed so it would be equivalent to saying that he must exclude from his view a central feature of social reality—as in fact seems to happen with many studies of organization and management as well as with many conventional texts on the methodology of the social sciences. But of course this consciously or unconsciously willed blindness is not necessary. Reasoning of a cost-benefit analysis kind may include—often does include—some provision for unforseen contingencies. But once again how much and what types of unpredictability are allowed for will rest upon judgments independent of and prior to the cost-benefit analysis itself. Among these judgments will once again be those as to the length of time within which costs and benefits are to be reckoned; and once again there is, relative to the cost-benefit analysis, an element that seems purely arbitrary.

. . .

The moral structure underlying the corporate executive's thinking is one of which he remains almost entirely unaware. He does not recognize himself as a classical utilitarian; and he cannot therefore recognize that the presuppositions of classical utilitarianism which he shares—which the utilitarians themselves did not recognize—must go doubly unrecognized by himself and his colleagues. His vision of himself remains that of a man engaged in the exercise of a purely technical competence to whom moral concerns are at best marginal, engaging him rather *qua* citizen or *qua* consumer than *qua* executive. Does this false consciousness of the executive, whether in the private corporation or in government, itself have a function? It is plausible to suppose that it does. To consider what that function is, imagine what would occur if all these considerations became manifest rather than latent.

The executive would then be presented with a set of moral problems, or moral conflicts, on which he would have to make overt decisions, over which he would have to take sides in the course of his work.

. . .

Moral arguments are in our culture generally unsettleable. This is not just a matter of one party to a dispute generally being unable to find any natural method to convince other contending parties. It is also the case that we seem unable to settle these matters within ourselves without a certain arbitrary taking of sides.

It follows that to allow moral issues to become overt and explicit is to create at least the risk of and more probably the fact of open and rationally unmanageable conflict both between executives and within each executive.

. . .

But it is obvious at once that both these devices are central to the structures of life of the corporate executive, as I described them earlier. The morality of contract with the autonomous consumer and the morality of governmental regulation operate in carefully defined areas so that questions of their coherence or conflict with each other or with other moral considerations are prevented from arising. The moral considerations are prevented from arising. The moral considerations underlying cost-benefit analysis are simply suppressed.

Robert Jackall, Moral Mazes: The World of Corporate Managers

(Oxford University Press 122–123 (1988)).

... Drawing lines when information is scarce becomes doubly ambiguous, a problem that often emerges in shaping relationships with one's colleagues. For instance, Black, a lawyer at Covenant Corporation, received a call from a chemical plant manager who had just been served with an order from the local fire department to build retaining dikes around several storage tanks for toxic chemicals so that firemen would not be in danger of being drenched with the substance should the tanks burst if there were a fire at the plant. The plant manager indicated that meeting the order would cause him to miss his numbers badly that year and he wondered aloud if the fire chief might, for a consideration, be persuaded to forget the whole thing. Black pointed out that he could not countenance even a discussion of bribery; the plant manager laughed and said that he was only joking and would think things over and get back to Black in a few weeks. Black never heard from the plant manager about this issue again; when they met on different occasions after that, the conversation was always framed around other subjects. Black did inquire discreetly and found out that no dikes had been built; the plant manager had apparently gone shopping for a more flexible legal opinion. Should he, Black wondered, pursue the matter or in the absence of any firm evidence just let things drop, particularly since others, for their own purposes, could misconstrue the fact that he had not acted on his earlier marginal knowledge? Feeling that one is in the dark can be somewhat unnerving.

More unnerving, however, is the feeling that one is being kept in the dark. Reed, another lawyer at Covenant, was working on the legal issues of a chemical dumpsite that Alchemy Inc. [a subsidiary of Covenant] had sold. He suddenly received a call from a former employee who had been having trouble with the company on his pension payments; this man told Reed that unless things were straightened out in a hurry, he planned to talk to federal officials about all the pesticides buried in the site. This was alarming news. Reed had no documentation about pesticides in the site; if Alchemy had buried pesticides there, a whole new set of regulations might apply to the situation and to Covenant as the former owner. Reed went to the chemical company's director of personnel to get the former employee's file but was unable to obtain it. Reed's boss agreed to help, but still the director of personnel refused to release the file. After repeated calls, Reed was told that the file had been lost. Reed went back to his boss

and inquired whether it might be prudent for Covenant to repur-
chase the site to keep it under control. This was deemed a good
idea. However, the asking price for the site was now three times
what Covenant had sold it for. Everyone, of course, got hesitant;
another lawyer became involved and began working closely with
Reed's boss on the issue. Gradually, Reed found himself excluded
from discussions about the problem and unable to obtain information that he felt was important to his work. His anxiety was
heightened because he felt he was involved in a matter of some
legal gravity. But, like much else in the corporation, this problem
disappeared in the night. Eventually, Reed was assigned to other
cases and he knew that the doors to the issue were closed, locked,
and bolted.

Robert Jackall, Moral Mazes: The World of Corporate Managers

17, 19–21, 106–12 (1988).

The hierarchical authority structure that is the linchpin of bureaucracy dominates the way managers think about their world
and about themselves. Managers do not see or experience authority in any abstract way; instead, authority is embodied in their
personal relationships with their immediate bosses and in their
perceptions of similar links between other managers up and down
the hierarchy. When managers describe their work to an outsider, they almost always first say: "I work for [Bill James]" or "I
report to [Harry Mills]" or "I'm in [Joe Bell's] group," and only
then proceed to describe their actual work functions....

... [The] "management-by-objective" system, as it is usually
called, creates a chain of commitments from the CEO down to the
lowliest product manager or account executive. In practice, it also
shapes a patrimonial authority arrangement that is crucial to
defining both the immediate experiences and the long-run career
chances of individual managers. In this world, a subordinate owes
fealty principally to his immediate boss. This means that a
subordinate must not overcommit his boss, lest his boss "get on
the hook" for promises that cannot be kept. He must keep his
boss from making mistakes, particularly public ones; he must
keep his boss informed, lest his boss get "blindsided." ... A
subordinate must also not circumvent his boss nor ever give the
appearance of doing so. He must never contradict his boss's
judgment in public. To violate the last admonition is thought to
constitute a kind of death wish in business....

In return, [a subordinate] can hope for those perquisites that are in his boss's gift—the better, more attractive secretaries, or the nudging of a movable panel to enlarge his office, and perhaps a couch to fill the added space, one of the real distinctions in corporate bureaucracies. He can hope to be elevated when and if the boss is elevated, though other important criteria intervene here. He can also expect protection for mistakes made, up to a point. However, that point is never exactly defined and depends on the complicated politics of each situation. The general rule is that bosses are expected to protect those in their bailiwicks. Not to do so, or to be unable to do so, is taken as a sign of untrustworthiness or weakness. If, however, subordinates make mistakes that are thought to be dumb, or especially if they violate fealty obligations—for example, going around their boss—then abandonment of them to the vagaries of organizational forces is quite acceptable....

It is characteristic of this authority system that details are pushed down and credit is pulled up. Superiors do not like to give detailed instructions to subordinates. The official reason for this is to maximize subordinates' autonomy. The underlying reason is, first, to get rid of tedious details. Most hierarchically organized occupations follow this pattern; one of the privileges of authority is the divestment of humdrum intricacies. This also insulates higher bosses from the peculiar pressures that accompany managerial work at the middle levels and below.... Perhaps more important, pushing details down protects the privilege of authority to declare that a mistake has been made. A high-level executive in Alchemy Inc. explains:

> If I tell someone what to do—like do A, B, or C—the inference and implication is that he will succeed in accomplishing the objective. Now, if he doesn't succeed, that means that I have invested part of myself in his work and I lose any right I have to chew his ass out if he doesn't succeed. If I tell you what to do, I can't bawl you out if things don't work. And this is why a lot of bosses don't give explicit directions. They just give a statement of objectives, and then they can criticize subordinates who fail to make their goals.

Moreover, pushing down details relieves superiors of the burden of too much knowledge, particularly guilty knowledge.... This pushing down of details has important consequences.

First, because they are unfamiliar with—indeed deliberately distance themselves from—entangling details, corporate higher echelons tend to expect successful results without messy complications. This is central to top executives' well-known aversion to bad news and to the resulting tendency to kill the messenger who bears the news.

Second, the pushing down of details creates great pressure on middle managers not only to transmit good news but, precisely because they know the details, to act to protect their corporations, their bosses, and themselves in the process. They become the "point men" of a given strategy and the potential "fall guys" when things go wrong. . . .

The moral ethos of managerial circles emerges directly out of the social context that I have described. It is an ethos most notable for its lack of fixedness. In the welter of practical affairs in the corporate world, morality does not emerge from some set of internally held convictions or principles, but rather from ongoing albeit changing relationships with some person, some coterie, some social network, some clique that matters to a person. Since these relationships are always multiple, contingent, and in flux, managerial moralities are always situational, always relative. . . .

[A case involving financial self-dealing illustrates the dilemmas that arise in these contexts]. Brady [an accountant] was disturbed to discover, upon first taking office, that there were a number of financial irregularities occurring in his company, including sizable bribery payments to officials of developing countries. Brady immediately had himself and his staff examined by his company's internal auditors, sent them to Mexico and Venezuela to do detailed field investigations of the bribes, and had the auditors send copies of the report to the CEO. In effect, he "blew the whistle on himself" and was later glad he did since the U.S. Attorney's office subsequently came in to investigate the matter; with the aid of the federal investigation, Brady was able to eliminate the irregular payments. . . .

As it happened, however, he soon came across much more serious and potentially damaging information. Key people in the corporation—at this stage, Brady was not sure just who was involved—were using about $18 million from the employee pension fund as a profit slush fund. Essentially, there was too much money in the pension fund. Explicit rules govern such a contingency but these were being ignored. The money was not declared as an asset but concealed and moved in and out of the corporation's earning statements each year so that the corporation always came in exactly on target. In fact, each October key officials could predict earnings per share for the year to the penny even though one-third of all earnings were in foreign currency. This uncanny accuracy assured top executives, of course, of completely reliable bonus payments. These were tied to hitting profit targets and gave top managers in the company up to 100 percent of the annual salary in deferred income in stock on top of whatever benefits they had accrued in the pension plan. Whatever money was not needed to make the incentive program work to its maximum immediate benefit was set aside for a rainy day.

This knowledge deeply upset Brady. He feels that there are rules in accounting that one can break and rules that one cannot break. The key thing is to explain what one is doing at all times. In his view, the point of being an accountant is precisely to account, that is, to find out the facts—Brady uses the word "truth"—and report them accurately. When one deals with other people's money, one has to be especially careful and forthright. Brady saw the pension fund manipulation as a direct violation of fiduciary trust, as depriving stockholders not only of their rightful knowledge but also of material benefits and as a misuse of other people's money for personal gain. It was, he felt, a practice that could in hard times jeopardize the employees' pension fund. He now had no way of reporting the matter through normal channels. His boss, the corporate vice-president for finance, had been hostile to him ever since Brady came under his control, distrusting Brady, it seems, because of his attempted reporting of the doctored invoices; the vice-president was friends with Brady's old boss's boss, the divisional president. Brady felt, however, that if the CEO were informed about the manipulation of funds, he would act decisively to end the violation. The CEO was "the captain of the boat; the man who wanted a report on everything; [the man] who wanted perfection."

Brady discussed the matter with a close friend, a man who had no defined position but considerable influence in the company and access to the highest circles of the organization. He was Mr. Fixit—a lobbyist, a front man, an all-around factotum, a man who knew how to get things done. Most big corporations have such men, often stashed in their public relations division. He was rewarded for his adroitness with a company Cadillac, a regular table at the 21 Club, and a very sizable expense account. Brady's information alarmed this man, and, with a detailed memorandum written anonymously by Brady, he approached a key director of the corporation who chaired the directors' audit committee. The director took the memorandum into a meeting with the CEO and his top aides, including the corporate vice-president for finance. Immediately after the meeting, Brady's friend was fired and escorted from the building by armed guards.

Only at this point did Brady realize that it was the CEO himself who was fiddling with the numbers. The entire dual reporting system that the CEO had personally initiated was in part an elaborate spy network to guard against discovery of the slush fund manipulation, and perhaps other finagling, rather than a system to ensure financial honesty. The top people still did not know that Brady had written the memo, but he was under suspicion. In time, the pressure on him mounted, with adverse health effects, and Brady had had enough. While his boss, the corporate vice-president, was in Europe, Brady went to the chief lawyer in the whole corporation and laid out the case for him. The lawyer "did not want to touch the issue with a barge pole." He sent a friend of Brady's, yet another corporate vice-president, to Brady to cool things down. According to Brady, the vice-president argued: "Look, why don't you just forget the whole thing. Everyone does it. That's just part of the game in business today." When Brady persisted, the vice-president asked if Brady could not just go along with things even if he did not agree. Brady said that he could not. Brady mentioned the managerial bonus program and acknowledged that that too could be adversely affected by his action. The vice-president blanched and became quite upset. Right after Brady's boss returned from Europe, Brady was summarily fired and he and his belongings were literally thrown out of the company building.

It is important to note the sharp contrast between Brady's reasons for acting as he did and other corporate managers' analyses of his actions. For Brady, the kinds of issues he confronted at work were distinctly moral issues, seen through the prism of his professional code. He says:

> So what I'm saying is that at bottom, I was in jeopardy of violating my professional code. And I feel that you have to stick up for that. If your profession has standing, it has that standing because *someone stood up for it.* If the SEC [the Securities and Exchange Commission] had come in and did an analysis and then went into the details of the case and put me up on the stand and asked me—What is your profession? Was this action right or wrong? Why did you do it then? I would really be in trouble ... with myself most of all. I am frightened of losing respect, my self-respect in particular. And since that was tied with my respect for my profession, the two things were joined together. I had such a fear of losing that precisely because of my high respect for it.

He goes on to comment further about his relation to professional standards and how those standards contrast with the prevailing ethos of corporate life.

I have fears in a situation like that.... It's not exactly a fear of what could happen to me, although that certainly crossed my mind. What it is is a fear of being found out not to stand up to standards that I have claimed as my own. It is a fear of falling down in a place where you have stuck a flag in the ground and said: "This is where I stand." I mean, why is it in life today that we have to deny any morality at all? But this is exactly the situation here. I was just too honest for that company. What is right in the corporation is not what is right in a man's home or in his church. *What is right in the corporation is what the guy above you wants from you.* That's what morality is in the corporation.

The corporate managers to whom I presented this case see Brady's dilemma as devoid of moral or ethical content. In their view, the issues that Brady raises are, first of all, simply practical matters. His basic failing was, first, that he violated the fundamental rules of bureaucratic life. These are usually stated briefly as a series of admonitions. (1) You never go around your boss. (2) You tell your boss what he wants to hear, even when your boss claims that he wants dissenting views. (3) If your boss wants something dropped, you drop it. (4) You are sensitive to your boss's wishes so that you anticipate what he wants; you don't force him, in other words, to act as boss. (5) Your job is not to report something that your boss does not want reported, but rather to cover it up. You do what your job requires, and you keep your mouth shut.

Second, the managers that I interviewed feel that Brady had plenty of available legitimations to excuse or justify his not acting. Clearly, they feel, a great many other executives knew about the pension fund scam and did nothing; everybody, especially the top bosses, was playing the game. The problem fell into other people's areas, was their responsibility, and therefore their problem. Why, then, worry about it? Besides, Brady had a number of ways out of the situation if he found it intolerable, including resigning. Moreover, whatever action he took would be insignificant anyway so why bother to act at all and jeopardize himself? Even a fool should have known that the CEO was not likely to take whatever blame resulted from the whole affair.

Third, these managers see the violations that disturbed Brady—irregular payments, doctored invoices, shuffling numbers in accounts—as small potatoes indeed, commonplaces of corporate life. One cannot, for example, expect to do business abroad, particularly in the Third World, without recognizing that "one man's bribe is another man's commission." As long as one does not try to extort an unfair market advantage but rather simply facilitates or speeds along already assigned duties, bribes are really the grease that makes the world work. Moreover, as managers see it, playing sleight of hand with the monetary value of inventories, post- or predating memoranda or invoices, tucking or squirreling large sums of money away to pull them out of one's hat at an opportune moment are all part and parcel of managing in a large corporation where interpretations of performance, not necessarily performance itself, decide one's fate. Furthermore, the whole point of the corporation is precisely to put other people's money, rather than one's own resources, at risk.

Finally, the managers I interviewed feel that Brady's biggest error was in insisting on acting according to a moral code, his professional ethos, that had simply no relevance to his organizational situation. "When the rubber hits the road," they say, abstract ethical and moral principles are not of much use. Moreover, by insisting on his own personal moral purity, his feeling that if he did not expose things he himself would be drawn into a web of corruption, he was, they feel, being disingenuous; no one reaches his level of a hierarchy without being tainted. Even more to the point, Brady called others' organizational morality, their acceptance of the moral ethos of bureaucracy, into question, made them uncomfortable, and eroded the fundamental trust and understanding that make cooperative managerial work possible. One executive elaborates a general sentiment:

> What it comes down to is that his moral code made other people uncomfortable. He threatened their position. He made them uncomfortable with their moral standards and their ethics. If he pursued it, the exposé would threaten their livelihood and their way of life. So they fired him. I personally believe that people in high places in big companies at some stage lose sight of the objectives of their companies and begin to focus on their positions. That's the only way you can really rationalize the pension fund issue.
>
> But any time you begin to threaten a person's position ... make him *uncomfortable,* well, in that situation, confrontation is inevitable.
>
> The guy's an evangelist. Under the guise of honesty, he's going to get at the truth no matter what. And those guys are going to lose. Eventually, if the thing hits the newspapers, the big guys will lose. But, in the meantime, within the organization that guy is going to lose. And he will go through life feeling that he was honest and wasn't as crooked as the guys above him.

Brady refused to recognize, in the view of the managers that I interviewed, that "truth" is socially defined, not absolute, and that therefore compromise, about anything and everything, is not moral defeat, as Brady seems to feel, but simply an inevitable fact of organizational life. They see this as the key reason why Brady's bosses did him in. And they too would do him in without any qualms. Managers, they say, do not want evangelists working for them.

The finale to the story is worth recounting. After Brady was fired, the CEO retired and elevated to his position a man known throughout the company as "Loyal Sam." The latter had "tracked" the CEO throughout his career. The CEO went back to his old corner office on a middle floor, his home before he ascended to power, and took an emeritus position with the firm—chief of the internal audit department. He now travels around the world, writing scrutinizing reports about the same companies on which he worked his legerdemain when he was CEO. When the managers to whom I present the case hear the outcome, they laugh softly, nod their heads, and give even an outsider like myself one of the sharp, knowing looks that one imagines they usually reserve for trusted others in their world.

Karl Mannheim points out that bureaucracy turns all political issues into matters of administration. One can see a parallel alchemy in managers' responses to Brady's dilemma. Bureaucracy transforms all moral issues into immediately practical concerns. A moral judgment based on a professional ethic makes little sense in a world where the etiquette of authority relationships and the necessity for protecting and covering for one's boss, one's network, and oneself supercede all other considerations and where nonaccountability for action is the norm. As a matter of survival, not to mention advancement, corporate managers have to keep their eye fixed not on abstract principles but on the social framework of their world and its requirements. Thus, they simply do not see most issues that confront them as moral concerns even when problems might be posed in moral terms by others. Managers' essential pragmatism stems thus not only from the pervasive matter of factness engendered by the expertise so typical of bureaucracies, but from the priority that managers assign to the rules and social contexts of their bureaucratic world. . . .

Sissela Bok, "Blowing the Whistle," in *Public Duties: The Moral Obligations of Government Officials* (J. Fleishman, L. Liebman & M. Moore, eds.)
204, 205, 210–11, 213–14 (1981).

Given the indispensable services performed by so many whistleblowers—as during the Watergate period and after—strong public support is often merited. But the new climate of acceptance makes it easy to overlook the dangers of whistleblowing: of uses in error or in malice; of work and reputations unjustly lost for those falsely accused; of privacy invaded and trust undermined. There comes a level of internal prying and mutual suspicion at which no institution can function. And it is a fact that the disappointed, the incompetent, the malicious, and the paranoid all too often leap to accusations in public. Worst of all, ideological persecution throughout the world traditionally relies on insiders willing to inform on their colleagues or even on their family members, often through staged public denunciations or press campaigns.

. . .

INDIVIDUAL MORAL CHOICE

What questions might those who consider sounding an alarm in public ask themselves? How might they articulate the problem they see and weigh its injustice before deciding whether or not to reveal it? How can they best try to make sure their choice is the right one?

In thinking about these questions it helps to keep in mind the three elements mentioned earlier: dissent, breach of loyalty, and accusation. They impose certain requirements: of accuracy and judgment in dissent; of exploring alternative ways to cope with improprieties that minimize the breach of loyalty; and of fairness in accusation. For each, careful articulation and testing of arguments are needed to limit error and bias.

Dissent by whistleblowers, first of all, is expressly claimed to be intended to benefit the public. It carries with it, as a result, an obligation to consider the nature of this benefit and to consider also the possible harm that may come from speaking out: harm to persons or institutions, and ultimately to the public interest itself. Whistleblowers must therefore begin by making every effort to consider the effects of speaking out versus those of remaining silent. They must assure themselves of the accuracy of their reports, checking and rechecking the facts before speaking out; specify the degree to which there is genuine impropriety; and consider how imminent is the threat they see, how serious, and how closely linked to those accused of neglect or abuse.*

If the facts warrant whistleblowing, how can the second element—breach of loyalty—be minimized? The most important question here is whether the existing avenues for change within the organization have been explored. It is a waste of time for the public as well as harmful to the institution to sound the loudest alarm first. Whistleblowing has to remain a last alternative because of its destructive side effects: it must be chosen only when other alternatives have been considered and rejected. They may be rejected if they simply do not apply to the problem at hand, or when there is not time to go through routine channels, or when the institution is so corrupt or coercive that steps will be taken to silence the whistleblower should he try the regular channels first.

What weight should an oath or a promise of silence have in the conflict of loyalties? Those sworn to silence are doubtless under a stronger obligation because of the oath taken. They have bound themselves, assumed specific obligations beyond those assumed in merely taking a new position. But even such promises can be overridden when the public interest at issue is strong enough. They can be overridden if they were obtained under duress or through deceit. They can be overridden, too, if they promise something that is in itself wrong or unlawful. The fact that one has promised silence is no excuse for complicity in covering up a crime or a violation of the public's trust.

. . .

From the public's point of view, accusations that are openly made by identifiable individuals are more likely to be taken seriously. Since the open accusation is felt to be fairer to the accused, and since it makes the motives of the whistleblower open to inspection, the audience is more confident that the message may have a factual basis. As a result, if whistleblowers still choose to resort to surreptitious messages, they have a strong obligation to let the accused know of the accusation leveled, and to produce independent evidence that can be checked.

During this process of weighing the legitimacy of speaking out, the method used, and the degree of fairness needed, whistleblowers must try to compensate for the strong possibility of bias on their part. They should be scrupulously aware of any motive

---

* In dissent concerning policy differences rather than specific improprieties, moreover, whistleblowing, with its accusatory element, is often an inappropriate form of warning. It threatens the public interest in that it so easily derails into ideological persecution. Many other forms of dissent exist when there is reason to voice policy disagreement or ideological differences.

that might skew their message: a desire for self-defense in a difficult bureaucratic situation, perhaps, or the urge to seek revenge, or inflated expectations regarding the effect their message will have on the situation.*

Likewise, the possibility of personal gain from sounding the alarm ought to give pause. Once again there is then greater risk of a biased message. Even if whistleblowers regard themselves as incorruptible, their profiting from revelations of neglect or abuse will lead others to question their motives and to put less credence in their charges. If the publicity matters greatly to them, or if speaking out brings them greater benefits at work or a substantially increased income, such risks are present. If, for example, a government employee stands to make large profits from a book exposing the iniquities in his agency, there is danger that he will, perhaps even unconsciously, slant his report in order to cause more of a sensation. If he supports his revelation by referring to the Code of Ethics for Government Service urging that loyalty to the highest moral principles and to country be put above loyalty to persons, party, or government department, he cannot ignore another clause in the same Code, specifying that he "ought never to use any information coming to him confidentially in the performance of government duties as a means for making private profits." ...

To weigh all these factors is not easy. The ideal case of whistleblowing—where the cause is a just one, where all the less dramatic alternatives have been exhausted, where responsibility is openly accepted, and where the whistleblower is above reproach— is rare. The motives may be partly self-serving, the method questionable, and still we may judge that the act was in the public interest. In cases where the motives for sounding the alarm are highly suspect, for example, but where clear proof of wrongdoing and avoidable risk is adduced, the public may be grateful that the alarm was sounded, no matter how low its opinion of the whistleblower.

. . .

---

* Needless to say, bias affects the silent as well as the outspoken. The motive for *holding back* important information about abuses and injustice ought to give similar cause for soul-searching. Civil servants who collaborate in the iniquities of so many regimes; business executives who support them through bribes and silent complicity; and physicians the world over who examine the victims of torture and return them to their tormentors: all have as much reason to examine *their* motives as those who may be speaking out without sufficient reason.

Deborah L. Rhode, Ethics by the Pervasive Method
(1994).

From a societal standpoint, whistleblowing by lawyers, like other employees, can promote crucial interests. Most significantly, it can prevent future health, safety, environmental, or financial injuries. Such preventive action may also avert harms to the organization such as fines, liability judgments, and impaired reputation and morale. In cases of past or continuing misconduct, whistleblowing may mitigate or compensate injuries, as well as deter future abuse. From the standpoint of whistleblowers, putting their principles into practice carries obvious psychological rewards. Public objection may also serve less commendable objectives such as gaining personal recognition or settling personal grudges, although available research suggests that such motivations are less common than is often supposed. Most whistleblowers attempt internal review before going public, and the external rewards are rarely sufficient to outweigh the career costs.

Those costs can be substantial. Harassment, isolation, retaliatory dismissals, transfers, and blacklisting are well documented, although their frequency varies by context. In two major studies involving thousands of federal employees, whistleblowers suffered retaliation in less than 20% of all cases. In some smaller-scale studies including private-sector employees, the frequency of reprisals was considerably higher. Lawyers who pass judgment on a colleague or client may also find that their influence is greatly reduced; like the employees Robert Jackall describes, they fall "out of the loop" of information exchange and institutional leverage.

The personal price of whistleblowing, of course, depends heavily on contextual factors. Those who go outside the organization typically run greater risks, because the major beneficiaries of such action are also outsiders. For the organization itself, the costs of external whistleblowing in legal liability and adverse publicity generally outweigh any gains. The principal exception is where illegal or immoral actions would probably come to light eventually and early disclosure could prevent or significantly reduce their costs. However, in the most common cases of external whistleblowing, it is individual victims or society generally that benefits from disclosure, and organizations that do not. This asymmetry helps account for many well-documented instances of corrupt, illegal, and hazardous conduct in which whistles are never in use.

Fred Zacharias' study of New York lawyers and clients suggests an example. Under one hypothetical in his survey:

> The general counsel to a firm that produces a metal alloy used in the manufacture of airplanes learns of a company study that suggests that in some high altitude flight patterns the alloy might weaken and cause a plane to explode. The alloy does, however, meet the minimum safety standards set by the government. The lawyer urges the Board of Directors to recall the alloy or at a minimum to inform users of its potential danger. The Board decides that the study is too inclusive to warrant action in light of the dire financial consequences of disclosure to the company.

Over three-quarters of surveyed lawyers indicated that they would not disclose the information, a decision consistent with New York code provisions. Approximately half of the surveyed clients believed (incorrectly) that attorneys had discretion to disclose under current rules, 85% believed that attorneys should disclose, and only 15% indicated that disclosure would affect their willingness to use an attorney's services.

If such findings are indicative of broader patterns, do they suggest a need for different confidentiality norms within the bar?

In analyzing whistleblowing obligations, commentators on professional ethics generally focus on three basic considerations. Does the practice at issue result in serious harm? Has the individual taken reasonable steps to exhaust internal channels of review? Does the employee have documentation of the objectionable practice and a reasonable basis for believing that going public will bring about significant change? Should these be the primary considerations for lawyers? If not, what other factors would be crucial? If so, what changes in bar codes, legal doctrine, and organizational practices might encourage socially desirable whistleblowing?

Strategies for Change

1. Bar Codes

Proponents of greater whistleblowing by lawyers suggest changes in bar ethical rules along the lines of early Model Rule proposals. One such draft of the Model Rules would have required lawyers to report present or imminent violations of the law to shareholders or to the appropriate government agency. A somewhat later proposal would have allowed lawyers to take "remedial actions," including disclosure of confidential information to persons outside the organization if: (1) its highest authority had acted out of personal or financial interest that conflicted with the organization's interest, and (2) such disclosure was "necessary in the best interests of the organization." Several states, including Maryland, Michigan, New Hampshire and New Jersey have adopted this second version. Compare these proposals to the Code of Ethics for Engineers:

> Should the Engineer's professional judgment be overruled under circumstances where the safety, health, and welfare of the public are endangered, the Engineers shall inform their clients or employers of possible consequences and notify other proper authority of the situation, as may be appropriate.

[Which] formulation of professional responsibility [would] be appropriate for lawyers?

2. Legislation

Several legislative strategies are possible. One is to expand compulsory reporting obligations for employees who become aware of unsafe conditions or illegal activity. For example, under Nuclear Regulatory Commission mandates, employees who know of certain nuclear safety risks must inform government officials. In the highly publicized proceeding against the law firm of Kaye, Scholer, the Office of Thrift Supervision argued that under some circumstances, lawyers for regulated banking institutions assumed the same obligations as their clients to disclose material facts to regulatory agencies.

A second possibility is to provide greater safeguards against reprisal for internal and external whistleblowers. Over the last half century, Congress has extended protection for federal employees who disclose fraud, corruption, and waste, as well as for other individuals who report violations of certain federal safety and environmental statutes. Over the past decade, about two-thirds of the states have also passed legislation providing some similar safeguards. However, this protective patchwork still excludes most private-sector employees. Many state statutes cover only civil servants or reports to government agencies. For that reason, commentators have proposed model legislation that would extend protection more broadly or would codify certain common law doctrine that limits retaliatory discharges.

Common Law

In the absence of adequate legislative protections, there has been increasing support for changes in the law governing employment relations. By the early 1990s, about half of all jurisdictions recognized exceptions to employers' rights to fire at will in response to ethical resistance. Yet although most courts have allowed employees to sue for wrongful discharge if they are fired for refusing to do something illegal, similar protection has not been available where employees lose their jobs after aggressively reporting unethical or unlawful conduct to management. [Further common law or legislative initiatives could offer greater protection to whistleblowers who fear retaliation.]

Institutional Strategies

Changing the ethos against whistleblowing will require more than changes in formal rules; organizational norms must also change. Commentators have proposed a number of strategies:

creation of internal hotlines, ethics or audit committees, and inspector general/ombudsperson positions;

increased resources for enforcement of existing antireprisal regulations; creation of governmental review agencies; and

support for whistleblowers by professional organizations, such as legal funds to pursue wrongful discharge claims or awards for ethical resistance.

Which of these proposals strike you as most promising? What other strategies might be effective?

REFERENCES

For discussion of lawyers' ethical responsibilities in various counseling contexts, *see e.g.*

Annette Baier, "What Do Women Want in a Moral Theory?," 19 *Nous* 53 (1985).

B. Bitker ed., *Professional Responsibility in Federal Tax Practice* (1970).

Conference, "The Ethical Responsibilities of Corporate Lawyers," 22 *Bus.Law.* 1173 (1978).

Cornel, "Ethical Guidelines for Tax Practice," 28 *Tax L.Rev.* 1 (1972).

Darrell, "Conscience and Propriety in Tax Practice," 17 *Inst. on Fed.Tax'n* 1 (1959).

Donnell, "Reflections of Corporate Counsel in a Two-Way Mirror," 22 *Bus.Law.* 991 (1967).

J. Freund, Lawyering: A Realistic Approach to Legal Practice (1979).

Gillers, "Protecting Lawyers Who Just Say No" 5 *Geo.St. L.Rev.* 1 (1988).

Gordon, The Independence of Lawyers, 68 *B.C.L.Rev.* 1 (1988).

Gordon and Simon, "The Redemption of Professionalism?," in *Lawyers' Ideals/Lawyers' Practices: Transformations in the American Legal Profession* 230 (R. Nelson, D. Trubek, R. Solomon, eds., 1992).

D. Luban, *Lawyers and Justice* (1988).

Patterson, "Tax Shelters for the Client—Ethics Shelters for the Lawyer" (Book Review), 61 *Tex.L.Rev.* 1163 (1983).

Redlich, "Should a Lawyer Cross the Murky Divide?", 31 *Bus.Law.* 478 (1975).

Rhode, "Institutionalizing Ethics," *Case Western L.Rev.* (1993).

Rotunda, "Law Lawyers and Managers" in *The Ethics of Corporate Conduct* (C. Walton ed. 1977).

Schneyer, "Professionalism and Public Policy: The Case of House Counsel," 2 *Geo.J.Leg. Ethics* 449 (1988).

Williams, "Corporate Accountability and the Lawyer's Role," 34 *Bus.Law.* 7 (1978).

B. Wolfman & J. Holden, *Ethical Problems in Federal Tax Practice* (1981).

I. THE ROLE RECONSIDERED

Charles Fried, "The Lawyer as Friend: The Moral Foundations of the Lawyer-Client Relationship"

85 Yale Law Journal, 1060–62, 1065–72, 1067–89 (1976).[*]

Can a good lawyer be a good person? The question troubles lawyers and law students alike. They are troubled by the demands of loyalty to one's client and by the fact that one can win approval as a good, maybe even great, lawyer even though that loyalty is engrossed by over-privileged or positively distasteful clients. How, they ask, is such loyalty compatible with that devotion to the common good characteristic of high moral principles? And whatever their views of the common good, they are troubled because the willingness of lawyers to help their clients use the law to the prejudice of the weak or the innocent seems

[*] Reprinted by permission of The Yale Law Journal Company and Fred B. Rothman & Company from *The Yale Law Journal*, Vol. 85, pp. 1060–62, 1065–72, 1067–89.

morally corrupt. The lawyer is conventionally seen as a professional devoted to his client's interest and as authorized, if not in fact required, to do some things (though not anything) for that client which he would not do for himself. In this essay I consider the compatibility between this traditional conception of the lawyer's role and the ideal of moral purity—the ideal that one's life should be lived in fulfillment of the most demanding moral principles, and not just barely within the law. ... My inquiry is one of morals: Does the lawyer whose conduct and choices are governed only by the traditional conception of the lawyer's role, which [the profession's code] reflects, lead a professional life worthy of moral approbation, worthy of respect—ours and his own?

. . .

I will argue in this essay that it is not only legally but also morally right that a lawyer adopt as his dominant purpose the furthering of his client's interests—that it is right that a professional put the interests of his client above some idea, however valid, of the collective interest. I maintain that the traditional conception of the professional role expresses a morally valid conception of human conduct and human relationships, that one who acts according to that conception is to that extent a good person. Indeed, it is my view that, far from being a mere creature of positive law, the traditional conception is so far mandated by moral right that any advanced legal system which did not sanction this conception would be unjust.

The general problem raised by the two criticisms is this: How can it be that it is not only permissible, but indeed morally right, to favor the interests of a particular person in a way which we can be fairly sure is either harmful to another particular individual or not maximally conducive to the welfare of society as a whole?

. . .

B. The Utilitarian Explanation

I consider first an argument to account for fidelity to role, for obligation, made most elaborately by the classical utilitarians, Mill and Sidgwick. They argued that our propensity to prefer the interests of those who are close to us is in fact perfectly reasonable because we are more likely to be able to benefit those people. Thus, if everyone is mainly concerned with those closest to him, the distribution of social energies will be most efficient and the greatest good of the greatest number will be achieved. The idea is that the efforts I expend for my friend or my relative are more likely to be effective because I am more likely to know what needs to be done. I am more likely to be sure that the good I intend is in fact accomplished. One might say that there is less overhead, fewer administrative costs, in benefiting those nearest to us. I would not want to ridicule this argument, but it does not seem to me to go far enough. Because if that were the sole basis for the preference, then it would be my duty to determine whether my efforts might not be more efficiently spent on the collectivity, on the distant, anonymous beneficiary. But it is just my point that *this* is an inquiry we are not required, indeed sometimes not even authorized, to make. When we decide to care for our children, to assure our own comforts, to fulfill our obligations to our clients or patients, we do not do so as a result of a cost-benefit inquiry which takes into account the ease of producing a good result for our friends and relations.

Might it not be said, however, that the best means of favoring the abstract collectivity is in certain cases not to try to favor it directly but to concentrate on those to whom one has a special relation? This does not involve tricking oneself, but only recognizing the limitations of what an individual can do and know. But that, it seems to me, is just Mill's and Sidgwick's argument all over again. There is no trickery involved, but this is still a kind of deliberate limitation of our moral horizon which leaves us uncomfortable. Do I know in a particular case whether sticking to the narrow definition of my role will *in that case* further the good of all? If I know that it will not further the general good, then why am I acting as the role demands? Is it to avoid setting a bad example? But for whom? I need not tell others—whether I tell or not could enter into my calculation. For myself then? But that begs the question, since if short-circuiting the role-definition of my obligation and going straight for the general good is the best thing to do in that case, then the example I set myself is not a bad example, but a good example. In short, I do not see how one can at the same time admit that the general good is one's only moral standard, while steadfastly hewing to obligations to friends, family, and clients. What we must look for is an argument which shows that giving some degree of special consideration to myself, my friends, my clients is not merely instrumentally justified (as the utilitarians would argue) but to some degree intrinsically so.

I think such an argument can be made. Instead of speaking the language of maximization of value over all of humanity, it will speak the language of rights. The stubborn ethical datum affirming such a preference grows out of the profoundest springs of morality: the concepts of personality, identity, and liberty.

C. Self, Friendship, and Justice

Consider for a moment the picture of the human person that would emerge if the utilitarian claim were in fact correct. It would mean that in all my choices I must consider the well-being of all humanity—actual and potential—as the range of my concern. Moreover, every actual or potential human being is absolutely equal in his claims upon me. Indeed, I myself am to myself only as one of this innumerable multitude. And that is the clue to what is wrong with the utilitarian vision. Before there is morality there must be the person. We must attain and maintain in our morality a concept of personality such that it makes sense to posit choosing, valuing entities—free, moral beings. But the picture of the moral universe in which my own interests disappear and are merged into the interests of the totality of humanity is incompatible with that, because one wishes to develop a conception of a responsible, valuable, and valuing agent, and such an agent must first of all be dear to himself. It is from the kernel of individuality that the other things we value radiate. The Gospel says we must love our neighbor as ourselves, and this implies that any concern for others which is a *human* concern must presuppose a concern for ourselves. The human concern which we then show others is a concern which first of all recognizes the concrete individuality of that other person just as we recognize our own.

It might be objected that the picture I sketch does not show that each individual, in order to maintain the integral sense of himself as an individual, is justified in attributing a greater value to his most essential interests than he ascribes to the most essential interests of all other persons. Should not the individual generalize and attribute in equal degree to all persons the value which he naturally attributes to himself? I agree with those who hold that it is the essence of morality for reason to push us beyond inclination to the fair conclusion of our premises. It *is* a fair conclusion that as my experience as a judging, valuing, choosing entity is crucial to me, I must also conclude that for other persons their own lives and desires are the center of their universes. If morality is transcendent, it must somehow transcend particularity to take account of this general fact. I do not wish to deny this. On the contrary, my claim is that the kind of preference which an individual gives himself and concrete others is a preference which he would in exactly this universalizing spirit allow others to exhibit as well. It is not that I callously overlook the claim of the abstract individual, but indeed I would understand and approve were I myself to be prejudiced because some person to whom I stood in a similar situation of abstraction preferred his own concrete dimensions.

... Those who object to my thesis by saying that we must generalize it are not wholly wrong; they merely exaggerate. Truly I must be ready to generalize outward all the way. That is what justice consists of. But justice is not all of morality; there remains a circle of intensity which through its emphasis on the particular and the concrete continues to reflect what I have identified as the source of all sense of value—our sense of self.

Therefore, it is not only consonant with, but also required by, an ethics for human beings that one be entitled first of all to reserve an area of concern for oneself and then to move out freely from that area if one wishes to lavish that concern on others to whom one stands in concrete, personal relations. Similarly, a person is entitled to enjoy this extra measure of care from those who choose to bestow it upon him without having to justify this grace as either just or efficient. We may choose the individuals to whom we will stand in this special relation, or they may be thrust upon us, as in family ties. Perhaps we recognize family ties because, after all, there often has been an element of choice, but also because—by some kind of atavism or superstition—we identify with those who share a part of our biological natures.

In explicating the lawyer's relation to his client, my analogy shall be to friendship, where the freedom to choose and to be chosen expresses our freedom to hold something of ourselves in reserve, in reserve even from the universalizing claims of morality. These personal ties and the claims they engender may be all-consuming, as with a close friend or family member, or they may be limited, special-purpose claims, as in the case of the client or patient. The special-purpose claim is one in which the beneficiary, the client, is entitled to all the special consideration *within* the limits of the relationship which we accord to a friend or a loved one. It is not that the claims of the client are less intense or demanding; they are only more limited in their scope. After all, the ordinary concept of friendship provides only an analogy, and it is to the development of that analogy that I turn.

D. Special-Purpose Friends

How does a professional fit into the concept of personal relations at all? He is, I have suggested, a limited-purpose friend. A lawyer is a friend in regard to the legal system. He is someone who enters into a personal relation with you—not an abstract relation as under the concept of justice. That means that like a friend he acts in your interests, not his own; or rather he adopts your interests as his own. I would call that the classic definition of friendship. To be sure, the lawyer's range of concern is sharply limited. But within that limited domain the intensity of identification with the client's interests is the same. ...

III. The Two Criticisms and the Friendship Analogy

A. The Choice of Clients: The Question of Distribution

It is time to apply the concept of legal friendship to the first of the two criticisms with which this essay began: that the lawyer's ethic of loyalty to his client and his willingness to pick clients for any and every reason (usually, however, for money) result in a maldistribution of a scarce resource, the aid of counsel. It is this criticism which the lawyer shares with the doctor. The preceding sections demonstrated at least this much: that legal counsel—like medical care—must be considered a good, and that he who provides it does a useful thing. But this first criticism in no way questions that conclusion. On the contrary, precisely because medical care and legal counsel are benefits to those who receive them, the critic blames the individual doctor or lawyer for not bestowing his skills in the way which best meets the social need. The notion of legal friendship helps us respond to this criticism.

The lawyer-client relation is a personal relation, and legal counsel is a personal service. This explains directly why, *once the relation has been contracted,* considerations of efficiency or fair distribution cannot be allowed to weaken it. The relation itself is not a creature of social expediency (though social circumstances provide the occasion for it); it is the creature of moral right, and therefore expediency may not compromise the nature of the relation. This is true in medicine because the human need creates a relation of dependence which it would be a betrayal to compromise. In the lawyer-client relation, the argument is more complex but supports the same conclusion. The relation must exist in order to realize the client's rights against society, to preserve that measure of autonomy which social regulation must allow the individual. But to allow social considerations—even social regulations—to limit and compromise what by hypothesis is an entailment of the original grant of right to the individual is to take away with the left hand what was given with the right. Once the relation has been taken up, it is the client's needs which hold the reins—legally and morally.

So much for the integrity of the relation once it has taken hold. But what of the initial choice of client? Must we not give some thought to efficiency and relative need at least at the outset, and does this not run counter to the picture of purely discretionary choice implicit in the notion of friendship? The question is difficult, but before considering its difficulties we should note that the preceding argumentation has surely limited its impact. We can now affirm that whatever the answer to this question, the individual lawyer does a morally worthy thing whomever he serves and, moreover, is bound to follow through once he has begun to serve. In this he is like the doctor. So if there is fault here it is a limited fault. What would be required for a lawyer to immunize himself more fully from criticism that he is unjust in his allocation of care? Each lawyer would have to consider at the outset of his career and during that career where the greatest need for his particular legal talents lies. He would then have to allocate himself to that area of greatest need. Surely there is nothing wrong in doing this (so long as loyalty to relations already undertaken is not compromised); but is a lawyer morally at fault if he does not lead his life in this way? It is at this point too that the metaphor of friendship and the concept of self as developed above suggest the response. But this time they will be viewed from another perspective—the lawyer's as opposed to the client's rights and liberties.

Must the lawyer expend his efforts where they will do the most good, rather than where they will draw the largest fee, provide the most excitement, prove most flattering to his vanity, whatever? Why must he? If the answer is that he must because it will produce the most good, then we are saying to the lawyer that he is merely a scarce resource. But a person is not a resource. He is not bound to lead his life as if he were managing a business on behalf of an impersonal body of stockholders called human society. It is this monstrous conception against which I argued earlier. Justice is not all; we are entitled to reserve a portion of our concern and bestow it where we will. We may bestow it entirely at our discretion as in the case of friendship, or we may bestow it at what I would call "constrained discretion" in the choice and exercise of a profession. That every exercise of the profession is morally worthwhile is already a great deal to the lawyer's credit. Just as the principle of liberty leaves one morally free to choose a profession according to inclination, so within the profession it leaves one free to organize his life according to inclination. The lawyer's liberty—moral liberty—to take up what kind of practice he chooses and to take up or decline what clients he will is an aspect of the moral liberty of self to enter into personal relations freely.

I would not carry this idea through to the bitter end. It has always been accepted, for instance, that a court may appoint an available lawyer to represent a criminal defendant who cannot otherwise find counsel. Indeed, I would be happy to acknowledge the existence of some moral duty to represent any client whose needs fit one's particular capacities and who cannot otherwise find counsel. This is not a large qualification to the general liberty I proclaim. The obligation is, and must remain, exceptional; it cannot become a kind of general conscription of the particular lawyer involved. And the obligation cannot compromise duties to existing clients. Furthermore, I would argue that this kind of representation should always be compensated—the duty to the client who cannot afford representation is initially a duty of society, not of the individual lawyer. I go this far for a number of reasons. If the representation is properly compensated, then the very need to appoint a lawyer will be exceptional, an anomaly arising in one of two ways: a fortuitous perturbation in the law of supply and demand or a general, if not concerted, professional boycott of this particular client. If the first is the reason, then the lifetime imposition on any one lawyer will be slight indeed. If it is the second, then the assertion of a duty, oddly enough, serves to express and strengthen the principle of the lawyer's independence. For the moral position of the lawyer rests on the claim that he takes up his client's interests irrespective of their merits. By accepting from time to time the duty to represent the undesirable, he affirms this independence.

But surely I must admit that the need for legal representation far exceeds what such an unstructured, largely individualistic system could supply. Are there not vast numbers of needy people with a variety of legal problems who will never seek us out, but must be sought out? And what of the general responsibility that just laws be passed and justly administered? These are the obligations which the traditional conception of the lawyer, with his overriding loyalty to the paying client, is thought to leave unmet. At this point I yield no further. If the lawyer is really to be impressed to serve these admitted social needs, then his independence and discretion disappear, and he does indeed become a public resource cut up and disposed of by the public's needs. There would be no justice to such a conception. If there are really not enough lawyers to care for the needs of the poor, then it is grossly unfair to conscript the legal profession to fill those needs. If the obligation is one of justice, it is an obligation of society as a whole. It is cheap and hypocritical for society to be unwilling to pay the necessary lawyers from the tax revenues of all, and then to claim that individual lawyers are morally at fault for not choosing to work for free. In fact, as provision of legal services has come to be seen as necessary to ensure justice, society has indeed hired lawyers in an effort to meet that need.

Finally, I agree that the lawyer has a moral obligation to work for the establishment of just institutions generally, but entirely the wrong kind of conclusions have been drawn from this. Some of the more ecstatic critics have put forward the lawyer as some kind of anointed priest of justice—a high priest whose cleaving to the traditional conception of the lawyer's role opens him to the charge of apostasy. But this is wrong. In a democratic society, justice has no anointed priests. Every citizen has the same duty to work for the establishment of just institutions, and the lawyer has no special moral responsibilities in that regard. To be sure, the lawyer like any citizen must use all his knowledge and talent to fulfill that general duty of citizenship, and this may mean that there are special perspectives and opportunities for him.

. . .

2. Immoral Means

I come to what seems to me one of the most difficult dilemmas of the lawyer's role. It is illustrated by the lawyer who is asked to press the unfair claim, to humiliate a witness, to participate in a distasteful or dishonorable scheme. I am assuming that in none of these situations does the lawyer do anything which is illegal or which violates the ethical canons of his profession; the dilemma arises if he acts in a way which seems to him personally dishonorable, but there are no sanctions—legal or professional—which he need fear.

This set of issues is difficult because it calls on the same principles which provide the justification for the lawyer's or the friend's exertions on behalf of the person with whom he maintains a personal relation. Only now the personal relation is one not of benefit but of harm. In meeting the first criticism, I was able to insist on the right of the lawyer as friend to give this extra weight to the interests of his client when the only competing claims were the general claims of the abstract collectivity. But here we have a specific victim as well as a specific beneficiary. The relation to the person whom we deceive or abuse is just as concrete and human, just as personal, as to the friend whom we help.

It is not open to us to justify this kind of harm by claiming that personal relations must be chosen, not thrust upon us. Personal relations are indeed typically chosen. If mere proximity could place on us the obligations of friendship, then there would soon be nothing left of our freedom to bestow an extra measure of

care over and above what humanity can justly claim. But there is
a personal relation when we inflict intentional harm; the fact that
it is intentional reaches out and particularizes the victim. "Who
is my neighbor?" is a legitimate question when affirmative aid is
in question; it is quite out of order in respect to the injunction "Do
not harm your neighbor." Lying, stealing, degrading, inflicting
pain and injury are personal relations too. They are not like
failing to benefit, and for that reason they are laid under a
correspondingly stricter regime than abstract harms to the collectivity. If I claim respect for my own concrete particularity, I must
accord that respect to others. Therefore, what pinches here is the
fact that the lawyer's personal engagement with the client is
urging him to do that to his adversary which the very principles of
personal engagement urge that he not do to anyone.

It is not wrong but somewhat lame to argue that the lawyer
like the client has autonomy. From this argument it follows that
the lawyer who is asked to do something personally distasteful or
immoral (though perfectly legal) should be free either to decline to
enter into the relationship of "legal friendship" or to terminate it.
And if the client can find a lawyer to do the morally nasty but
legally permissible thing for him, then all is well—the complexities of the law have not succeeded in thwarting an exercise of
autonomy which the law was not entitled to thwart. So long as
the first lawyer is reasonably convinced that another lawyer can
be found, I cannot see why he is less free to decline the morally
repugnant case than he is the boring or poorly paid case. True,
but lame, for one wants to know not whether one *may* refuse to do
the dirty deed, but whether one is morally *bound* to refuse—bound
to refuse even if he is the last lawyer in town and no one else will
bail him out of his moral conundrum.

If personal integrity lies at the foundation of the lawyer's
right to treat his client as a friend, then surely consideration for
personal integrity—his own and others'—must limit what he can
do in friendship. Consideration for personal integrity forbids me
to lie, cheat, or humiliate, whether in my own interests or those of
a friend, so surely they prohibit such conduct on behalf of a client,
one's legal friend. This is the general truth, but it must be made
more particular if it is to do service here. For there is an opposing
consideration. Remember, the lawyer's special kind of friendship
is occasioned by the right of the client to exercise his full measure
of autonomy within the law. This suggests that one must not
transfer uncritically the whole range of personal moral scruples
into the arena of legal friendship. After all, not only would I not
lie or steal for myself or my friends, I probably also would not

pursue socially noxious schemes, foreclose on widows or orphans, or assist in the avoidance of just punishment. So we must be careful lest the whole argument unravel on us at this point.

Balance and structure are restored if we distinguish between kinds of moral scruples. Think of the soldier. If he is a citizen of a just state, where foreign policy decisions are made in a democratic way, he may well believe that it is not up to him to question whether the war he fights is a just war. But he is personally bound not to fire dum-dum bullets, not to inflict intentional injury on civilians, and not to abuse prisoners. These are personal wrongs, wrongs done by his person to the person of the victim. So also, the lawyer must distinguish between wrongs that a reasonably just legal system permits to be worked by its rules and wrongs which the lawyer personally commits. Now I do not offer this as a rule which is tight enough to resolve all borderline questions of judgment. We must recognize that the border is precisely the place of friction between competing moral principles. Indeed, it is unreasonable to expect moral arguments to dispense wholly with the need for prudence and judgment.

Consider the difference between humiliating a witness or lying to the judge on one hand, and, on the other hand, asserting the statute of limitations or the lack of a written memorandum to defeat what you know to be a just claim against your client. In the latter case, if an injustice is worked, it is worked because the legal system not only permits it, but also defines the terms and modes of operation. Legal institutions have created the occasion for your act. What you do is not personal; it is a formal, legally-defined act. But the moral quality of lying or abuse obtains both without and within the context of the law. Therefore, my general notion is that a lawyer is morally entitled to act in this formal, representative way even if the result is an injustice, because the legal system which authorizes both the injustice (*e.g.,* the result following the plea of the statute of limitations) and the formal gesture for working it insulates him from personal moral responsibility. I would distinguish between the lawyer's own wrong and the wrong of the system used to advantage by the client.

. . .

I do not imagine that what I have said provides an algorithm for resolving some of these perennial difficulties. Rather, what I am proposing is a general way of looking at the problem, a way of understanding not so much the difficult borderline cases as the central and clear ones, in the hope that the principles we can there discern will illuminate our necessarily approximate and prudential quest for resolution on the borderline. The notion of the lawyer as the client's legal friend, whatever its limitations and difficulties, does account for a kind of callousness toward society and exclusivity in the service of the client which otherwise seem quite mysterious. It justifies a kind of scheming which we would deplore on the part of a lay person dealing with another lay person—even if he were acting on behalf of a friend.

But these special indulgences apply only as a lawyer assists his client in his legal business. I do not owe my client my political assistance. I do not have to espouse his cause when I act as a citizen. Indeed, it is one of the most repellent features of the American legal profession—one against which the barrister-solicitor split has to some extent guarded the English profession—that many lawyers really feel that they are totally bought by their clients, that they must identify with their clients' interests far beyond the special purpose of advising them and operating the legal system for them. ...

There is a related point which cuts very much in the opposite direction. It is no part of my thesis that the *client* is not morally bound to avoid lying to the court, to pay a just debt even though it is barred by the statute of limitations, to treat an opposite party in a negotiation with humanity and consideration for his needs and vulnerability, or to help the effectuation of policies aimed at the common good. Further, it is no part of my argument to hold that a lawyer must assume that the client is not a decent, moral person, has no desire to fulfill his moral obligations, and is asking only what is the minimum that he must do to stay within the law. On the contrary, to assume this about anyone is itself a form of immorality because it is a form of disrespect between persons. Thus in very many situations a lawyer will be advising a client who wants to effectuate his purposes within the law, to be sure, but who also wants to behave as a decent, moral person. It would be absurd to contend that the lawyer must abstain from giving advice that takes account of the client's moral duties and his presumed desire to fulfill them. Indeed, in these situations the lawyer experiences the very special satisfaction of assisting the client not only to realize his autonomy within the law, but also to realize his status as a moral being. I want to make very clear that my conception of the lawyer's role in no way disentitles the lawyer from experiencing this satisfaction. Rather, it has been my purpose to explicate the less obvious point that there is a vocation and a satisfaction even in helping Shylock obtain his pound of flesh or in bringing about the acquittal of a guilty man.

... [When] we fulfill the office of friend—legal, medical, or friend *tout court*—we do right, and thus it would be a great wrong to place us under a general regime of always doing what will "do the most good." What I affirm, therefore, is the moral liberty of a lawyer to make his life out of what personal scraps and shards of motivation his inclination and character suggest: idealism, greed, curiosity, love of luxury, love of travel, a need for adventure or 'repose; only so long as these lead him to give wise and faithful counsel.

———

NOTES

A fundamental question raised by the preceding materials is whether norms of partisanship applicable in litigation settings should govern contexts lacking neutral arbiters and procedural safeguards. A related issue is the extent to which any single set of ethical standards can cope with the varied circumstances in which representation occurs. For example, what significance should attach to the following facts:

- the relationship between the parties: *e.g.*, are they engaged in a single or ongoing transaction?

- the relationship between the lawyers: how much professional or personal contact have they had or are they likely to have?

- the legal and social context of the dispute: are both parties voluntary participants, is their agreement subject to any oversight, and are they communicating with reference to commonly understood conventions and expectations?

- the conduct of one party during the course of the dispute: to what extent does one participant's bad faith alter the other party's obligations?

- the stakes and objectives: how much do the parties stand to lose and gain, and how significantly will the outcome affect their futures, the lives of third parties or the evolution of important principles?

- the relative bargaining strength of the parties and their counsel: how evenly are they matched in sophistication, resources, and access to material information?

The relevance of such factors, both in assessing individual attorneys' ethical responsibilities and in codifying ethical standards, remains the subject of considerable dispute.

In part, the controversy turns on underlying philosophical differences concerning the functions of legal advocacy and professional regulation. If, for example, one accepts the premium placed on client autonomy by commentators such as Charles Fried, then the range of lawyers' "moral scruples [that enter] the arena of legal friendship" narrows considerably, whatever the context of representation.[1] Partisan obligations become good in themselves, independent of their effect in furthering the just resolution of disputes. If, by contrast, one views the attorney as an independent moral agent who contracts to provide limited services, then the friendship paradigm appears more problematic. Thus, William Simon observes:

> Fried writes: "[L]ike a friend [the lawyer] acts in your interests, not his own; or rather he adopts your interests as his own. I would call that the classical definition of friendship." Now this is clearly an error. The classical definition of friendship emphasizes, not the adoption by one person of another's ends, but rather the sharing by two people of common ends. Moreover, the classical notion of friendship includes a number of other qualities foreign to the relation Fried describes. These missing qualities include affection, admiration, intimacy, and vulnerability. On the other hand, if Fried's definition is amplified to reflect the qualification, which Fried repeatedly acknowledges, that the lawyer adopts the client's interests *for money,* it becomes apparent that Fried has described the classical notion, not of friendship, but of prostitution .... [In essence,] Fried celebrates the frankly exploitative alliances of convenience between desperate, selfish little men. Fried explicitly strives to infuse with pathos and dignity the financial problems of the tax chiseler and the "disagreeable dowager". By collapsing traditional moral categories, this rhetoric reflects the homogenization of previously distinct personal characteristics. Fried can assert that the lawyer affirms the client's individuality because ... Fried's clients have almost no individuality. Any pretense to the contrary is abandoned by the middle of the article when Fried insists that corporations as well as natural persons are entitled to "legal friendship." After all, Fried argues, corporations are "only formal arrangements of real persons pursuing their real interests." Fried began his defense of the analogy by emphasizing that both friendship and the lawyer-client relation involve direct contact with a concrete individual. It

---

1. Fried, "The Lawyer as Friend: Client Relation," 85 *Yale L.J.* 1060,
The Moral Foundations of the Lawyer-   1084 (1976).

now appears that these concrete individuals have so little individuality that a lawyer's relation to a "formal arrangement" can manifest the same qualities. Fried's final example of legal friendship involves friendship with a "finance company." [2]

Other commentators, while more sympathetic to Fried's concerns for individual dignity and autonomy, emphasize that those values demand respect for the lawyer's as well as the client's personality. And ongoing involvement in deceptive or unjust conduct can prove highly corrosive. As Sissela Bok has emphasized, such involvement may result in "coarsened judgment and diminished credibility"; after a point, individuals can "lose some ability to discriminate among kinds and degrees of falsehood . . . ." [3]

A related issue involves the role of professional codes in minimizing such corrosive behavior. The premise of many commentators, reflected in the latest Model Rules, is that a code which "sets its moral sights too high will be routinely violated, thereby compromising the credibility of the entire regulatory structure." [4] A countervailing consideration, however, is that

> [w]here a threat of formal sanctions is remote, as is generally the case in professional contexts, the most significant albeit highly limited functions of official standards will be symbolic and pedagogic . . . . To the extent that codified precepts can affect behavior, an exclusively minimalist approach could prove misguided. The result may be socialization to the lowest common denominator of conduct that a highly self-interested constituency will publicly brand as deviant.[5]

Robert Gordon, "The Independence of Lawyers"
68 *Boston University L. Rev.* 1 (1988).

Probably the most common critique of the independence ideal is that it either conflicts with the ideal of client loyalty or

---

2. Simon, "The Ideology of Advocacy: Procedural Justice and Professional Ethics," 1978 *Wis.L.Rev.* 29, 108–09. *See also* Barry, "And Who Is My Neighbor?" (Book Review) 88 *Yale L.J.* 629 (1979); Dauer and Leff, *Correspondence*, 86 *Yale L.J.* 573, 581 (1977).

3. S. Bok, *Lying: Moral Choice in Public and Private Life* 132 (1978).

4. Rhode, "Ethical Perspective on Legal Practice," 37 *Stan.L.Rev.* ___ (1985) (summarizing commentary on the ABA's Proposed Model Rules of Professional Conduct, Discussion Draft, 1980).

5. *Id.*

arrogates to lawyers an improper role in political decisionmaking, or both....

Underlying the illegitimacy critique is the central belief that lawyers' roles begin and end with vigorously pursuing their clients' interests within the limits of the law. Rather than injecting any of their own political views into the lawyering process, they should simply function as an extension of their clients' interests, accepting those interests according to the terms the clients use to characterize them....

Although this position is *very* commonplace, I think it rests on incoherent premises and leads to indefensible conclusions.... [The] position appears to license an untempered adversarial advocacy which when aggregated could easily nullify the purposes of any and every legal regime. Take any simple case of compliance counseling: suppose the legal rule is clear, yet the chance of detecting violations low, the penalties small in relation to the gains from noncompliance, or the terrorizing of regulators into settlement by a deluge of paper predictably easy. The mass of lawyers who advise and then assist with noncompliance in such a situation could, in the vigorous pursuit of their clients' interests, effectively nullify the laws. The only justification for their doing so would have to be their confidence that the system was self-equilibrating, so that some countervailing force would operate to offset their efforts. But such confidence is unfounded. Examples of aggressive advocates virtually precluding the fulfillment of any conceivable purposes of a legal regime—except of course the purpose of enacting symbolic laws never intended to have any effect—are plentiful. Even when legislators prodded by mass opinion have moved to stiffen penalties and strengthen enforcement, lawyers have moved to nullify that too. It is at least questionable whether a social system maintained primarily through the internalization of legal norms rather than state terror can survive much of such behavior. Yes, lawyers must pursue clients' interests within the framework of the rules of the game. But the issue of lawyers' public responsibility is precisely that of what their position should be vis-à-vis those rules.

The principal fallacy implicit in the view of lawyering underlying the illegitimacy critique, is that lawyers must reconcile two sets of social purposes—clients' interests and the law's plain meaning—that arrive at their offices already fully formed and filled in with some definite determinate content. But in fact part of the lawyer's job is to interpret both sets of purposes. At the barest minimum lawyers have to translate clients' desires into something processable by the legal system, and investigate the various ways in which legal officials might, in turn, process them. Usually they must go well beyond that, translating clients' interests into a number of possible alternatives that until that moment might never have been thought of then asking for a ranking of alternatives, and then estimating the possible consequences of each. Through this back-and-forth dialectical interaction, both the client's "interests" and the "law" governing the situation will gradually take the shapes sculpted by the social agents who interpret and transmit them.

But the critic then says: all right, lawyers play legitimate roles in helping both to define the clients' interests and to predict the legal consequences likely to flow from various definitions. But in this capacity lawyers have no right to intrude their opinions, their influence, their political values. They are neither elected officials nor their agents; lawyers have no special authority to go around telling people how they should behave.

The traditional response to this is simple: lawyers do indeed have an official status as licensed fiduciaries for the public interest, charged with encouraging compliance with legal norms. In contexts like counseling, where there is no official third party like a judge to oversee the interaction between the client and the state, the lawyer is not only supposed to predict the empirical consequences of certain behavior, but also to represent the viewpoint of the legal system to the client. Lawyers can't coerce anyone; they can only advise and persuade, sometimes only under the threat of resignation rather than disclosure. Surely the right of the lawyer to encourage compliance with the law's purposes through persuasion is at least as clear as the client's right to demand the lawyer's help in exploiting the law's ambiguities and procedural opportunities and in engaging in strategic behavior designed to evade the law. The other and even better response to the critic is that even conceding that lawyers have no special authority to guide their clients, neither do they have any special immunity from responsibility for the things they help their clients do....

More fundamentally, it seems rather extreme to refrain from trying to develop and act on a commitment to a particular view of legal purposes simply because others may arrive at a different view. That may be a reason for caution, for avoiding dogmatism, for empathizing with and taking account of the views of opponents, but not for paralysis. After all, as William Simon points out, the legal system routinely grants judges and administrators discretionary authority to interpret legal purposes. Judges and administrators, in turn, routinely engage in such interpretive exercises, believing that they can do so reliably despite their

knowledge that other judges and officials are constantly disputing
them and reaching contrary views.

C. The Competence Critique. The position that lawyers
have no special competence to bring to counseling, nor any special
contribution to make to political life, makes sense as a critique of
the most pompously inflated view of political independence. According to that view, expressed in the nineteenth century, lawyers
belong to a distinct elevated estate uniquely endowed with political wisdom and insight into everybody's long-term best interests.
That was always ridiculous, and has become more so with the
specialization of the profession. We are bright technicians, for the
most part, not philosopher-kings (or queens).

Most of the arguments in favor of lawyers playing an independent role in counseling and politics, however, are much more
modest. One such argument concerns the nature of legal training
and experience. Legal education is to some extent an education in
applied political theory. Lawyers are articulate in one of the
major media of public discourse, legal language. They often have
diverse experience—government work, different kinds of clients,
different kinds of corruption and evil, all the myriad ways in
which plans can misfire and go askew. They are professionally
capable of detachment, able to see different sides of a problem and
analyze motivations. They know powerful people and something
about what makes them tick and what will move them. Thus
legal training and experience provide a firm foundation for the
exercise of independent judgment.

Arguments from good motivations also have some modest
force. The legal profession attracts, along with a lot of fairly
venal and opportunistic types, a large number of the most public-
regarding, socially-conscious people in our society. It's a total
waste to define a lawyer's role in a way that will deny such people
the chance to act on altruistic intentions. The lawyers too diffi-
dent to advise are probably the ones whose advice would be most
valuable.

Finally, there are arguments from opportunity. The main
idea is just that the chances to act independently are *there*.
Lawyers are scattered all over civil society in intermediary and
advisory positions from which they have opportunities to exercise
influence.

It's easy to say lawyering is not a club for superhumans, and
that especially in this century lawyers have been joined, and in
many areas of political life displaced, by rival interpreters and
articulators and mediators of social purposes. What's absurd is to

argue that because of this lawyers are uniquely *disqualified* as citizens or moral and political actors—the one group of individuals in the world who should conscientiously attempt to reduce themselves to ciphers, pure media of transmission. Why should everybody else around the corporation—the engineers, the financial people, the safety and health division—be permitted to deliberate upon and engage in the internal politics of the corporation to promote their views of its best interests, but not the lawyers?

Robert C. Post, "On the Popular Image of the Lawyer: Reflections in a Dark Glass"
75 *Calif.L.Rev.* 379 (1987).

[Public opinion data indicates] that lawyers are especially disliked because they manipulate the legal system in the interests of their particular clients, without regard to the common, universal values of right and wrong. [Such data also reflect] that lawyers are praised because their first priority is to the private perspective of their clients. Lawyers, in other words, bestride the following cultural contradiction: we both want and in some respects have a universal, common culture, and we simultaneously want that culture to be malleable and responsive to the particular and often incompatible interests of individual groups and citizens. We expect lawyers to fulfill both desires, and so they are a constant irritating reminder that we are neither a peaceable kingdom of harmony and order, nor a land of undiluted individual autonomy, but somewhere disorientingly in between. Lawyers, in the very exercise of their profession, are the necessary bearers of that bleak winter's tale, and we hate them for it.

We hate them, that is, because they are our own dark reflection. We use lawyers both to express our longing for a common good, and to express our distaste for collective discipline. When we recognize that the ambivalence is our own, and that the lawyer is merely our agent, we use the insight as yet another club with which to beat the profession. For then we dismiss the lawyer as a mere "hired gun," or "paid ... tool," or, worse yet, as an inveterate liar. The charge of insincerity strikes a particularly tender nerve in the modern sensibility, because the master of our many roles, rather than the reverse, but the persistent and unsettling example of the lawyer will not let us rest easy in this belief. If Goffman is correct, and if we are in fact constituted by our performances, the intensity of the animosity we bear toward lawyers may come precisely from the fact that they are so very threatening to our need to believe that we possess stable and coherent selves.

Analyzed in this way, the special hatred which popular culture holds for the lawyer can be an illuminating resource for understanding cultural contradictions of the deepest and most profound kind. The lawyer is the public and unavoidable embodiment of the tension we all experience between the desire for an embracing and common community and the urge toward individual independence and self-assertion, between the need for a stable and coherent self and the fragmented and disassociated roles we are forced to play in the theater of modern life. In popular imagery the lawyer is held to strict account for the discrepancy between our aspirations and our realities. But this discrepancy is not the lawyer's alone, and once we understand this we may also come to see that in popular culture the lawyer is so much our enemy, because he is so much like us.

REFERENCES

For amplification of ethical theories that may assist counsel in making normative judgements, *see e.g.*

D. Brink, *Moral Realism and the Foundations of Ethics* (1989).

A. Donogan, *The Theory of Morality* (1977).

R. Dworkin, *Taking Rights Seriously* (1977).

J. Feingberg ed., *Reason and Responsibility* (4th ed. 1978).

W. Jones, F. Sontag, M. Beckner & R. Fgelin eds., *Approaches to Ethics* (3rd ed. 1977).

C. Gilligan, *In a Different Voice: Psychological Theory and Womens' Development* (1982).

A. Goldman, *The Moral Foundations of Professional Ethics* (1981).

V. Grassian, *Moral Reasoning: Ethical Theory and Contemporary Moral Problems* (1981).

S. Hampshire, *Innocence and Experience* (1989).

G. Harman, *The Nature of Morality: An Introduction to Ethics* (1977).

H.L.A. Hart, "Between Utility and Rights," 79 *Columbia L. Rev.* 828 (1979).

A. Hirschman, *Exit, Voice, and Loyalty* (1970).

E. Kittey and D. Meyers, eds. *Women and Moral Theory* (1987).

A. MacIntyre, *After Virtue* (1980).

A. MacIntyre, *A Short History of Ethics* (1976).

J. Mackie, *Ethics* (1977).

H. Miller & W. Williams eds., *The Limits of Utilitarianism* (1982).

T. Nagel, "The Fragmentation of Value," in *Mortal Questions* (1979).

J. Rachels, *The Elements of Moral Philosophy* (1986).

J. Rawls, *A Theory of Justice* (1971).

P. Singer, *Practical Ethics* (1979).

J. Smart & B. Williams, *Utilitarianism: For and Against* (1973).

Dennis Thompson, "Moral Responsibility of Public Officials: The Problem of Many Hands," *American Political Science Review*, vol. 74, no. 4 (December, 1980): 905–16.

Michael Walzer, "Political Action: The Problem of Dirty Hands," in Marshall Cohen *et al.*, eds., *War and Moral Responsibility* (Princeton: Princeton University Press, 1974).

B. Williams, *Morality: An Introducing to Ethics* (1972).

H. Sidgwick, *The Methods of Ethics* (7th ed., reissued 1962).

IV. MULTIPLE INTERESTS

INTRODUCTION

Lawyers' representation of multiple or conflicting interests has attracted increasing professional attention over the last two decades. Much of that attention has focused on somewhat technical questions of simultaneous or successive client representation. Although such questions are of considerable practical importance, they do not generally present the theoretical issues that are at the core of this volume's concern. Accordingly, the following chapter focuses on other contexts involving representation of multiple interests that require departures from conventional partisanship norms.

One of the most common examples of such representation involves clients who are seeking to establish a new relationship or amicably modify an existing one. Launching a business venture for co-entrepreneurs, formulating a plan of reciprocal wills for married couples, or orchestrating a "no-fault" divorce all entail the kind of role Justice Louis Brandeis labeled as "lawyer for the situation." Until recently, that role received little attention in discussions of professional responsibility, and none in the bar's formal ethical codes. One distinctive feature of the new Model Rules of Professional Conduct is their recognition of such a role, under the heading "lawyer as intermediary."

By definition, any intermediary function requires adjustments in the lawyer's conventional partisan orientation. In essence, the lawyer must be moderate, disinterested, and concerned for all parties to the transaction. That role thus embodies the very features that critics have often found lacking in conventional adversarial representation. Yet, somewhat ironically, this has not shielded the intermediary function from equally strong criticisms. Rather, such representation is often thought to entail various conflicts of loyalty and responsibility.

Analogous tensions confront lawyers representing organized groups. In theory, the attorney owes duties to the membership in its entirety, but in practice, the content of those responsibilities can be difficult to determine. When representing a plaintiff class or a governmental agency, lawyers often enjoy considerable power to define the terms of their assistance; for practical purposes, the lawyer assumes the authority normally reposing in the client.

The more diffuse and divided the constituency, the greater the potential for departures from conventional partisanship norms.

Another context in which partisan premises have even less relevance concerns the lawyer's relationship with the client. The attorney's position of superior knowledge and power frequently opens opportunities for exploitation or paternalism. Thus, the necessity for self-restraint in the exercise of fiduciary obligations is central to any coherent concept of the lawyer's role. Yet difficulties in assessing those obligations can be significant, given the situational pressures of certain forms of practice and the natural temptation to perceive what the client actually wants in terms of what he "ought" to want.

The following excerpts explore certain recurring conflicts faced by attorneys when acting as fiduciaries, intermediaries, or counsel for collective interests. As is apparent, the obligations that such roles presuppose cannot be captured by any simple partisanship model of professional responsibility.

A. THE LAWYER FOR THE SITUATION

Deborah L. Rhode, Ethics by the Pervasive Method (1994)

Like other forms of alternative dispute resolution, mediation is thought to have certain advantages over traditional adversarial processes. Compared with conventional litigation structures, mediation is promoted as cheaper, quicker, more capable of focusing on the underlying sources of conflict, and more likely to increase party satisfaction and compliance with any agreement.

At an abstract level, the goals and structure of mediation command broad consensus: an impartial facilitator assists parties in identifying their interests, understanding their legal options, and reaching an acceptable agreement. At a more concrete level, disagreement centers on what constitutes impartiality and acceptability; ... how to deal with confidential disclosures; what cases are inappropriate for mediation; what training is essential for mediators; and how to respond to inequalities in the bargaining process and its outcomes. Because formal recognition of lawyers' mediation role is relatively recent, many of these questions remain unsettled under bar ethical codes and committee interpretations.

The Regulatory Framework

The Code of Professional Responsibility mentions mediation only in the ethical considerations, not the disciplinary rules, and provides little guidance to attorneys who function in that role. EC 5–20 notes:

> A lawyer is often asked to serve as an impartial arbitrator or mediator in matters which involve present or former clients. He may serve in either capacity if he first discloses such present or former relationships. After a lawyer has undertaken to act as an impartial arbitrator or mediator, he should not thereafter represent in the dispute any of the parties involved.

The only disciplinary rules governing mediators are the general provisions on conflicts of interest.

Model Rule 2.2 expressly deals with lawyers acting as intermediaries. It provides:

> (a) A lawyer may act as intermediary between clients if:

> (1) The lawyer consults with each client concerning the implications of the common representation, including the advantages and risks involved, and the effect on the attorney-client privileges, and obtains each client's consent to the common representation;

> (2) the lawyer reasonably believes that the matter can be resolved on terms compatible with the clients' best interests, that each client will be able to make adequately informed decisions in the matter and that there is little risk of material prejudice to the interest of any of the clients if the contemplated resolution is unsuccessful; and

> (3) the lawyer reasonably believes that the common representation can be undertaken impartially and without improper effect on other responsibilities the lawyer has to any of the clients....

> . . .

> (c) A lawyer shall withdraw as intermediary if any of the clients so request, or if any of the conditions stated in paragraph (a) is no longer satisfied. Upon withdrawal, the lawyer shall not continue to represent any of the clients in the matter that was the subject of the intermediation.

Whether this rule applies to some common mediation contexts, including divorce, is not entirely clear. Unlike earlier drafts, the final version of Rule 2.2 and its Comment does not mention divorce mediation as an example of the intermediary role. The Comment also advises that a "lawyer cannot undertake common representation of clients between whom contentious litigation is imminent or who contemplate contentious negotiations." For the many divorce mediations that are potentially acrimonious, this admonition raises doubts about the applicability of Rule 2.2 and the appropriateness of the intermediary role in general. Moreover, the Comment to Rule 2.2 indicates that the provision does not apply to a "lawyer acting as arbitrator or mediator between or among parties who are not clients of the lawyer, even where the lawyer has been appointed with the concurrence of the parties." Since some state bar ethics opinions have held that an attorney-mediator in divorce cases represents neither of the parties, Rule 2.2 would be inapplicable to mediation in those jurisdictions.

What a lawyer's role should be in such intermediary contexts is a matter of ongoing dispute. At one end of the spectrum are state bar committee opinions prohibiting conventional forms of divorce mediation; underlying these decisions are concerns about the inherent potential for conflicting interests and inadequate protection for confidentiality. Other bar committees have authorized divorce mediation on the theory that the lawyer represents neither party. By contrast, Rule 2.2 and many experts take the view that the lawyer-intermediary represents both parties.

Of these approaches, the flat ban seems unduly restrictive, while the practical differences between the permissive approaches remain unduly ambiguous. According to some recent data, at least one party is unrepresented in most uncontested divorces, and where resources are limited, joint access to counsel may be preferable to lopsided representation. Whether mediators are viewed as "representing" both or neither parties seems less critical than the concrete obligations that the relationship entails, such as requirements of informed consent, and rejection of cases involving excessive power disparities.

Independent Legal Advice

Some bar ethics committees, in an effort to minimize conflicts of interest, have prohibited mediators from drafting a final agreement or have required that they advise parties to obtain an independent attorney's assessment of any proposed settlement. Although such review may often be helpful, it can also create its own set of problems. If independent counsel intervenes after parties have become emotionally committed to an agreement, the advice may be futile, or it may require reopening the entire mediation process. For that reason, the American Bar Association's Standards of Practice for Family Mediators (1984) (Standard VI) advise consultation prior to agreement. Yet independent counsel's intervention during the mediation process can also risk duplicating or subverting mediators' own work. Lawyers who provide such outside review services need a clear understanding of what functions would be useful. Common examples include assistance in evaluating assets and/or provision of tax advice.

Professional Skills and Unauthorized Practice

Another area of controversy involves the appropriate training and scope of practice for mediators. In some areas, such as divorce mediation, the majority of practitioners are mental health professionals. Their ability to offer services on problems with legal consequences or to affiliate with attorneys has been constrained by prohibitions on unauthorized practice. Every state has some form of prohibition on nonlawyer practice that is reinforced by bar ethical codes. DR 3–101 and Model Rule 5.5 prohibit lawyers from aiding nonlawyers in the practice of law; DR 3–102 and Model Rule 5.4(a) prohibit lawyers from sharing fees with nonlawyers; and DR 3–103 and Model Rule 5.4(b) prohibit forming partnerships with nonlawyers if any of the activities of the partnership consist of the practice of law.

The application of these rules to divorce mediators is unclear, in part because prevailing definitions of unauthorized practice are unclear. As one commentator puts it, decisions regarding the permissible scope of lay services are "consistent only in their inconsistency." In theory, nonlawyer-mediators do not purport to give legal assistance; in practice, many of these individuals cannot provide competent services without considering legal issues. As bar leaders have themselves recognized, "all kinds of professional people are practicing the law almost out of necessity."

In response to that reality, some courts have carved out exceptions to broad unauthorized practice prohibitions. Exemptions are common for lay legal practice that is widespread in the community, that is incidental to another profession or business, or that serves the public interest. Many commentators believe that mediator services in areas such as divorce should fall under one of these exceptions. In their view, the primary justifications for prohibiting lay practice—protecting the public from unqualified or unscrupulous practitioners—do not support unqualified bans on mediation of legal disputes. Lawyers have not "cornered the market on morality." Many lay mediators are mental health experts who must already satisfy good moral character requirements. Other practitioners could be subject to comparable certification standards.

So too, while not all lay mediators have legal expertise, not all lawyer-mediators have therapeutic skills. The best answer for both groups may be to expand the training available, both in professional school and post-licensing programs. An increasing array of educational programs are starting to develop, ranging from a two-year postgraduate degree program to a five-day training course followed by 250 hours of practice with an experienced family mediator. More cross-professional collaboration between attorneys and other trained experts could also be desirable for many clients. Yet current restrictions on lawyer/nonlawyer affiliations discourage such cooperation. Although lawyers and therapists may be able to work together under existing rules by avoiding formal partnerships and billing separately for services, these constraints warrant rethinking. If mediation services continue to attract increasing public support, they should also have regulatory and educational structures carefully tailored to their use.

Fairness and Impartiality

The ethical issue arising most frequently in mediation involves the facilitator's dual responsibility to remain impartial and to insure a defensible process and result. The issue arises in varying forms: how to present options and their legal implications; how actively to intervene in the face of coercive techniques or disparities in bargaining skills; and how to handle inequities in a proposed settlement. On all of these issues, mediators vary widely. Debates within the professional community reveal four distinct positions, and practitioners generally fall somewhere on the spectrum among them.

The first perspective, dominant in commercial and labor contexts, assumes that impartiality requires neutrality; the mediator's role is to help parties reach a resolution that they find acceptable, whether or not it conforms to the mediator's own views of fairness. This role has the advantage of protecting parties' autonomy, preserving mediators' credibility, and maximizing the chances that those with superior bargaining leverage will agree to mediated solutions.

At the opposite end of the spectrum are those who define impartiality as fairness; in their view, the mediator's responsibility is to ensure a process and result that meet some minimum standards of justice. This role may require active intervention to maintain a "balanced dialogue," and a settlement that reasonably accommodates the concerns of the parties as well as unrepresented groups or broader societal interests. So, for example, some commentators believe that mediators in environmental disputes should take account of long-term spillover effects, and that mediators in divorce cases should consider children's interests as well as

those of more vulnerable spouses.[19] From this perspective, mediators' obligation of impartiality is satisfied if they avoid accepting
cases where prior loyalties distort their ability to be even-handed
and if they disclose any substantive commitments that might
affect their role.[20]

Between these two positions lies a third, intermediate alternative. This approach, reportedly the most common in divorce
mediation, seeks to balance concerns for fairness and autonomy.
The ABA's Task Force on Mediation for the Section on Family
Law attempts such a balance in its Divorce and Mediation Standards of Practice (1992). Other commentators and professional
groups have made similar proposals. Judith Maute suggests that
the Model Rules include a requirement that a lawyer may not
knowingly finalize an agreement reasonably believed to be illegal,
grossly inequitable, or based on false information.[22] Would you
support such a proposal? Would it be preferable to the approach
of the ABA Standards?

For cases falling short of grossly inequitable or misinformed
agreements, many mediators simply recommend that each party
seek review by separate outside counsel. How often such recommendations prevent unfairness is open to question. It is often
difficult or impossible for a reviewing attorney to know whether a
proposed settlement is in the client's best interest without engaging in precisely the process that the parties entered mediation to
avoid.

In recognition of this fact, some commentators, including
many feminists and critical race theorists, argue that mediation is
inappropriate for certain kinds of cases. This fourth position, one
not necessarily inconsistent with any of the preceding three,
opposes mediation for cases involving substantial power disparities. Critics also object to mandatory mediation programs, such as
those established by some jurisdictions for domestic violence or
child custody cases.[23] Because mediation places the parties on

---

19. Lawrence Susskind, "Environmental Mediation and the Accountability Problem," 6 *Vt.L.Rev.* 1, 46–47
(1981). Leonard L. Riskin, "Toward
New Standards for the Neutral Lawyer
in Mediation" 26 *Ariz.L.Rev.* 329, 354–
57 (1984); Sara Cobb & Janet Rifkin,
"Practice and Paradox: Deconstructing
Neutrality in Mediation," 16 *Law &
Soc'y Inquiry* 35 (1991).

20. Christopher Honeyman, "Bias
and Mediators' Ethics," 1986 *Negotiation J.* 175, 176–77. Joseph P. Folger &

Sydney E. Bernard, "Divorce Mediation:
When Mediators Challenge the Divorcing Parties," *Mediation Q.*, Dec. 1985, at
5, 19.

22. See Judith Maute, "Public Val-
ues and Private Judging: A Case for
Mediator Acceptability," 4 *Geo.J.Legal
Ethics* 503, 515 (1991).

23. Lisa G. Lerman, "Mediation of
Wife Abuse Cases: The Adverse Impact
of Informal Dispute Resolution on
Women," 7 *Harv.Women's L.J.* 57, 72
(1984); Trina Grillo, "The Mediation

equal footing and invites compromise, it may lead to inappropriate concessions from more vulnerable participants and may fail adequately to deter abusive conduct or coercive bargaining. Some evidence suggests that women as a group are less willing than men to assert their own needs, or to tolerate conflict, and that a conciliatory process may not provide adequate checks for racial, ethnic, and gender bias.[24]

By contrast, defenders of mediation note that women and subordinate groups do not necessarily fare better in more adversarial processes.... As Jay Folberg and Alison Taylor explain:

> The voiced concern about the fairness aspect of mediated agreements tends to compare mediation with a romanticized notion of formal justice. In considering whether mediated settlements will be fair and just, we must ask "compared to what?" ...
>
> Many disputes resolved outside of mediation are the result of unequal bargaining power due to different levels of experience, patterns of dominance, different propensities for risk avoidance, the greater emotional needs of one disputant, or psychological obstacles in the path to settlement. Should the matter proceed to litigation, the same items may skew the fairness of the outcome in court as in the bargaining phase— and in addition there may be unequal resources to bear the costs of litigation, different levels of sophistication in choosing the best attorneys, and just plain luck as to which judge is assigned to make a decision. These comments are not intended as unique criticisms of our adversarial or judicial systems; no dispute resolution mechanism is devoid of problems concerning fair outcomes, and none of the alternatives is the best for every dispute.[26]

From this perspective, the most productive strategy is not either to require or to remove the mediation option for a given set of cases, but rather to provide a choice of processes that seek to minimize unjust tactics and results.

Which of these preceding four positions would you find most appropriate....?

Alternative: Process Dangers for Women," 100 *Yale L.J.* 1545, 1599 (1991).

24. Jessica Pearson & Nancy Thoennes, "Divorce Mediation Research Results, Divorce Mediation" 429, 440–41 (Jay Folberg & Ann Milne eds., 1988); Richard Delgado, *et al.,* "Fairness and Formality: Minimizing the Risk of Prej-

udice in Alternative Dispute Resolution," 1985 *Wis.L.Rev.* 1359.

26. Jay Folberg & Alison Taylor, *Mediation: A Comprehensive Guide to Resolving Conflicts Without Litigation* 246–47 (1984). *See* Menkel–Meadow, *supra* note 10.

Eric Schnapper, "Legal Ethics and the Government Lawyer"
32 The Record 649–51, 656 (1977).

I

All litigation presents to some degree, real though not always perceived, a conflict between each attorney's responsibility as a representative of his or her client and as an officer of the court. Winning the case and seeing that justice is done must be inconsistent goals for counsel on at least one side in a case, if not on both. However substantial this problem may be regarded, it is certainly more complex for counsel for the government. Unlike a private attorney subject to dismissal for ignoring a client's wishes, counsel for the government often has, subject to the variables of intragovernmental relations, the power to take a course of action or accept a settlement contrary to the wishes of the agency officials involved. In addition, government counsel owes some arguable duty to the opposing party, not only as a citizen and taxpayer of the entity for which he or she works, but also because that party seeks to invoke the same laws as those which he or she is committed, in theory if not by oath, to enforce. The relationship of agency officials to government counsel is not that of client and attorney in any ordinary sense, for the identities and desires of those officials may vary with popular opinion, the vote of the electorate, or the whims of their superiors, while the law to which both officials and counsel owe their allegiance remains unaltered.

Although attitudes on this problem vary significantly among and within government law offices, the general practice of government counsel seems to be to refrain from making any independent judgment on the merits of the agency's position, or to argue for that position even when the lawyer believes it is wrong.

Three related explanations are commonly advanced by government attorneys for resolutely defending whatever conduct, or advancing whatever claim, the agency involved may prefer. It is urged that the agency is entitled to a lawyer, that the agency's theory or argument should be ruled on by a court rather than by government counsel, and that no harm can come of pressing the agency's case since the courts will ultimately resolve the matter correctly. While legitimate considerations underlie each of these contentions, none is sufficient to absolve counsel for the government from his or her responsibility to scrutinize the validity of the conduct or contention he or she is asked to defend in court.

The suggestion that government bodies are entitled to counsel has a heady Sixth Amendment ring to it, but there is less here than meets the eye. The issue at the outset is not a right to counsel, but a right to unlimited free representation by counsel with the prestige and resources of an attorney general's or corporation counsel's office. No one denies the right of a public employee to retain private counsel and litigate in his or her own name any legal theory, however fanciful, he or she may favor, subject to establishing the requisite standing. Whether such special counsel should be provided at public expense depends on whether, to use an admittedly troublesome phrase, the "real party" is the state or city or merely a whimsical or lawless public employee. ...

... The decision whether an agency or official is "entitled" to government counsel seems to turn on whether the disputed conduct in fact represents public policy, bearing in mind that even the policies of a high official are not public policies if in violation of public law, or the private whims of one or more government employees. Thus, this line of reasoning provides no foundation for a general obligation on the part of government counsel to represent the views of agency officials, but merely supports a duty to represent agency officials when they are right.

The second argument does have some independent weight. In our adversary system courts are created for resolving disputes of law and legally significant disputes of fact, and are frequently an optimal forum for doing so. Any action which cuts off such contentions from reaching the courts prevents the mode of resolution generally regarded as most fair and definitive.

. . .

The argument that litigation can be cavalierly and endlessly pursued on behalf of public agencies without social cost is manifestly unsound. Any litigation places burdens on the opposing side, which, unlike the state officials, usually is not receiving free representation, and that often irreparable burden seems progressively less conscionable as the state or city contention becomes less substantial. In many cases continued litigation will entail a delay in the awarding of necessary relief. If in these cases the private party prevails to the merits, the public policy and thus true state interest will have been found to be on its side, and thus to have suffered because of continued representation of the views of one or more public employees. ...

Finally, it must be noted that government counsel has alternatives to either arguing whatever position is preferred by agency

officials or asserting a view or agreeing to a settlement contrary to
their wishes. An attorney general believing a view erroneous but
entitled to consideration in court can seek to arrange for that view
to be presented by special outside counsel or agency house counsel;
in such a case the attorney general could take no position or
perhaps file an amicus brief against the agency. Government
counsel can choose to present an argument expressly explained to
be an agency contention on which counsel takes no position.
Where the agency has taken a position government counsel believes unsound, but there are other parties in the litigation prepared to defend it, counsel enjoys some freedom to decline to take
a stand on the issue. If the position of an attorney general's or
corporation counsel's office is subject to ultimate control by a
governor or mayor, an attorney who believes the position taken to
be erroneous can and usually should decline to have his or her
name placed on the brief involved. Each of these responses serves
to protect for other cases the independence and stature of an
attorney general's or corporation counsel's office and provides a
method short of the more drastic step of imposing a settlement for
putting pressure on agency officials to reconsider a questionable
stance.

REFERENCES

For analysis of analogous problems involving government lawyers
and the revolving door *see, e.g.:*

ABA Comm. on Professional Ethics and Grievances, Formal
Op. 342 (1975).

D.C. Bar Committee on Legal Ethics, "Tentative Draft Opinion Inquiry 19," *District Law.*, Fall 1976, at 39.

Fahy, "Special Ethical Problems of Counsel for the Government," 33 *Fed.Bar J.* 331 (1974).

C. Horsky, *The Government Lawyer* (1952).

L. Huston, A. Miller, S. Krislov & R. Dixon Jr., *Roles of the
Attorney General of the United States* (1968).

Kaufman, "The Former Government Attorney and the Canons of Professional Ethics," 70 *Harv.L.Rev.* 657 (1957).

Lacovara, "Restricting the Private Law Practice of Former
Government Lawyers," 20 *Ariz.L.Rev.* 369 (1978).

Lawry, "Who Is the Client of the Federal Government Lawyer? An Analysis of the Wrong Question," *Fed.Bar J.*,
Fall 1978, at 61.

Morgan, "Applicable Limits on Participation by a Former Agency Official in Matters Before an Agency," 1980 *Duke L.J.* 1.

Poirier, "The Federal Government Lawyer and Professional Ethics," 60 *A.B.A.J.* 1541 (1974).

Weinstein, "Some Ethical and Political Problems of a Government Attorney," 18 *Me.L.Rev.* 155 (1966).

Geoffrey C. Hazard, Jr., Ethics in the Practice of Law
58, 61–66 (1978).

Lawyer for the Situation

The problem of deciding who is the client arises when a lawyer supposes that a conflict of interest prevents him from acting for all the people involved in a situation. That is, if the interests of the potential clients were in harmony, or could be harmonized, no choice would have to be made between them and the lawyer could act for all. When the lawyer feels that he can act for all, it can be said simply that he has several clients at the same time. When the clients are all involved in a single transaction, however, the lawyer's responsibility is rather different from what it is when he represents several clients in transactions that have nothing to do with each other. This difference is suggested by the proposition that a lawyer serving more than one client in a single transaction represents "the situation." * . . .

- Acting for a partnership or corporation, not only as legal adviser but also as mediator, go-between, and balance wheel among the principals in the business.

- Acting as an informal trustee for second and third generation members of a family having various active and passive interests in inherited property holdings.

- Acting as counsel, board member, and business affairs advisor for charitable organizations such as hospitals, libraries, and foundations.

- Acting as intermediary between a business and its creditors in a period of financial difficulties.

- Acting as intermediary between a corporate chief executive and his board of directors in the face of fundamental differences of policy.

* The term was coined by Louis Brandeis in a hearing in which this ethics were questioned. For an account of the Brandeis case, see Frank, "The Legal Ethics of Louis D. Brandeis," 17 *Stan. L.Rev.* 683 (1965).

• Acting as something like a marriage broker between clients
wanting to settle a complex contract arrangement on terms that
would be "fair to everyone."

Similar functions are performed by lawyers on corporate legal
staffs regarding differences between divisions and levels in the
corporation, and by lawyers for government agencies that become
enmeshed in conflicts of policy. It is safe to say that "ordinary"
practitioners do the same sorts of things all the time for small
businesses, families, public bodies such as school boards, and local
civic and political organizations. ...

"Situations" can arise in different ways. Two or more people
who have not been clients may bring a "situation" to a lawyer.
Sometimes a client who has a lawyer will become involved in a
transaction with a third party who does not, and the transaction is
one that ought to be handled as a "situation." Most commonly,
perhaps, a lawyer may find himself in a "situation" involving
clients that he has previously served in separate transactions or
relationships. In this circumstance the lawyer, if he properly can,
will intercede before the transaction between his clients reaches
counterposed positions. Doing so is in his interest, because that
way he can retain both clients.

Having a lawyer act for the situation is also in the clients'
interests, if adjustment on fair terms is possible, because head-on
controversy is expensive and aggravating. A lawyer who failed to
avoid a head-on controversy, given reasonable opportunity to do
so, will have failed in what his clients generally regard as one of
his chief functions—"preventive" legal assistance. ... That is,
loyalty to client, like loyalty to country, may take different forms.

It is not easy to say exactly what a "lawyer for the situation"
does. Clearly, his functions vary with specific circumstances. But
there are common threads. The beginning point is that no other
lawyer is immediately involved. Hence, the lawyer is no one's
partisan and, at least up to a point, everyone's confidant. He can
be the only person who knows the whole situation. He is an
analyst of the relationship between the clients, in that he undertakes to discern the needs, fears, and expectations of each and to
discover the concordances among them. He is an interpreter,
translating inarticulate or exaggerated claims and forewarnings
into temperate and mutually intelligible terms of communication.
He can contribute historical perspective, objectivity, and foresight
into the parties' assessment of the situation. He can discourage
escalation of conflict and recruitment of outside allies. He can
articulate general principles and common custom as standards by
which the parties can examine their respective claims. He is

advocate, mediator, entrepreneur, and judge, all in one. He could be said to be playing God.

Playing God is a tricky business. It requires skill, nerve, detachment, compassion, ingenuity, and the capacity to sustain confidence. When mishandled, it generates the bitterness and recrimination that results when a deep trust has been betrayed. Perhaps above all, it requires good judgment as to when such intercession can be carried off without unfairly subordinating the interests of one of the parties or having later to abort the mission.

When a relationship between the clients is amenable to "situation" treatment, giving it that treatment is perhaps the best service a lawyer can render to anyone. It approximates the ideal forms of intercession suggested by the models of wise parent or village elder. It provides adjustment of difference upon a wholistic view of the situation rather than bilaterally opposing ones. It rests on implicit principles of decision that express commonly shared ideals in behavior rather than strict legal right. The basis of decision is mutual assent and not external compulsion. The orientation in time tends to be a hopeful view of the future rather than an angry view of the past. It avoids the loss of personal autonomy that results when each side commits his cause to his own advocate. It is the opposite of "going to law."

One would think that the role of "lawyer for the situation" would have been idealized by the bar in parity with the roles of partisan advocate and confidential advisor. The fact that it has not been may itself be worth exploring. ... [B]eyond saying that he will undertake to represent the best interests of all, a lawyer cannot say specifically what he will do or what each of the clients should do in the situation. (If the outcome of the situation were clearly foreseeable, presumably the lawyer's intercession would be unnecessary.) Moreover, he cannot define his role in the terms of the direction of his effort, for his effort will not be vectored outward toward third persons but will aim at an interaction among the clients. Hence, unlike advocacy or legal counselling involving a single client, lawyering for a situation is not provided with a structure of goals and constraints imposed from outside. The lawyer and the clients must create that structure for themselves, with the lawyer being an active participant. And like the other participants he cannot reveal all that is on his mind or all that he suspects the others may have on their minds, except as doing so aids movement of the situation along lines that seem productive.

A lawyer can proceed in this role only if the clients trust him and, equally important, he trusts himself. Trust is by definition ineffable. It is an acceptance of another's act without demanding that its bona fides be objectively provable; to demand its proof is to confess it does not exist. It is a relationship that is uncomfortable for the client but perhaps even more so for the lawyer. Experienced as he is with the meanness that people can display to each other, why should the lawyer not doubt his own susceptibility to the same failing? But trust is involved also in the role of confidential advisor and advocate. Why should lawyers regard their own trustworthiness as more vulnerable in those roles that in the role of "lawyer for the situation"?

Perhaps it is because the legal profession has succeeded in defining the roles of confidential advisor and advocate in ways that substantially reduce the burden of being trustworthy in these roles. The confidential advisor is told that he may not act to disclose anything about the client, except an announced intention to commit a crime. Short of this extremity, the rules of role have it that the counsellor has no choices to make between the interests of his client and the interests of others. His commitment is to the client alone. Correlatively, the advocate is told that he may assert any claim on behalf of a client except one based on fabricated evidence or one empty of any substance at all. Short of this extremity, the advocate also has no choices to make.

The "lawyer for the situation," on the other hand, has choices to make that obviously can go against the interest of one client or another, as the latter perceives it. A lawyer who assumes to act as intercessor has to evoke complete confidence that he will act justly in the circumstances. This is to perform the role of the administered justice itself, but without the constraints inherent in that process (such as the fact that the rules are written down, that they are administered by independent judges, and that outcomes have to be justified by references to reason and precedent). The role of lawyer for the situation therefore may be too prone to abuse to be explicitly sanctioned. A person may be entrusted with it only if he knows that in the event of miscarriage he will have no protection from the law. In this respect, acting as lawyer for the situation can be thought of as similar to a doctor's "authority" to terminate the life of a hopeless patient: It can properly be undertaken only if it will not be questioned afterwards. ...

Thomas L. Shaffer "The Legal Ethics of Radical Individualism"
65 Texas Law Review 963–71, 976–78 (1987).

There's a magnifying glass all cracked and broken, and when you look at broken things through the lens you'd swear they'd turned whole again.

—Anne Tyler

Most of what American lawyers and law teachers call legal ethics is not ethics. Most of what is called legal ethics is similar to rules made by administrative agencies. It is regulatory. Its appeal is not to conscience, but to sanction. It seeks mandate rather than insight. I argue here that what remains and appropriately is called ethics has been distorted by the weaker side of an old issue in academic moral philosophy. This "weaker side" rests on two doctrines: first, that fact and value are separate; and second, that the moral agent acts alone; as W.H. Auden put it, each of us is alone on a moral planet tamed by terror. The influence of this philosophical position deprives legal ethics of truthfulness and of depth....

I. The Ethical Context

Ethics properly defined is thinking about morals. It is an intellectual activity and an appropriate academic discipline, but it is valid only to the extent that it truthfully describes what is going on. Those in contemporary ethics who concentrate on the importance of the truthful account argue first that fact and value are not separate—that stating the facts is, as Iris Murdoch put it, a moral act, a moral skill, and a moral art; and second, that organic communities of persons are prior in life and in culture to individuals—in other words, that the moral agent is not alone....

In the practice of estate planning, for example, the facts that are available for moral description are death and property: property seen in the context of mortality, death seen in the context of owning things....

What reconciles death with the ownership of property is the family. The family is the lens through which we understand death as the death of an owner, and property as something owned by dead people. The family is the cracked magnifying glass that shows how things broken by discord and death are whole. The family is normally why people bother with estate planning— "normally" in the sense that, but for the family, estate planning would not be a legal subject. The family is the cultural focus for the realization that estate planning is a worthwhile thing for people to do, because it reflects the hope that none of us will die alone. The human fact that is prior to the moral agency of which moral philosophy usually speaks is the family; the moral art of description in the legal ethics of estate planning is the skill to describe a family....

II. The Case of the Unwanted Will

I use, in teaching legal ethics, a series of quandaries that were posed in the *American Bar Association Journal* in 1979.[15] One of these quandaries describes John and Mary, a middle-aged couple with adult children. John and Mary want their wills drafted before beginning a vacation trip abroad. Based on John's instructions, the lawyer prepares a set of parallel wills, each leaving all property to the surviving spouse, or, if both are dead, to their children in equal shares. On a second visit to the law office, the lawyer presents the prepared wills to the couple, and John executes his:

> [T]he lawyer [then] suggests to John that he would like to be alone with Mary before she signs. John withdraws to another office. The lawyer asks Mary if the will is as she would have made it had her husband not been present at the conference and if the will were to be secret from her husband. She says no, that the will as drawn contains several provisions that are contrary to her wishes, and that she would change if her husband were not to know the ultimate disposition of her estate. However, she says that she would not be willing to precipitate the domestic discord and confrontation that would occur if her husband were to learn that she had drawn a will contrary to his wishes and in accordance with her own desires.

You could say that the problem never would have arisen had the lawyer not talked to Mary alone. That description, of course, trivializes the problem, but many law students, and some ponderers of legal ethics, pose the quandary and the solution in just those terms. From that viewpoint, the immediately noticeable premises for the two judgments that there is a problem present, and that the problem is moral, are four. First, a lawyer's proper employment is by or for an individual. Second, employment by or for more than one individual is exceptional. Third, as a consequence, multiple party employment is necessarily superficial. Finally, the means for protecting the superficiality (or, if you like, the means for protecting the principle that employment is ordinarily and properly by or for individuals) is ignorance of any facts known to one of the individuals but not to the other.

It follows from this typical analysis that the lawyer's moral mistake was in talking to Mary alone. Otherwise, Mary's secret intention never would have come to his attention; her thoughts

---

15. *The Case of the Unwanted Will,* 65 A.B.A.J. 484 (1979). I included an abridged version of these quandaries in my textbook. *See* T. Shaffer, *American Legal Ethics* 313 (1985).

would be hidden, and that is appropriate because John's thoughts are hidden. Now that the lawyer *has* talked to Mary alone, he is in an impossible situation: he cannot allow John to board the plane with the mistaken belief that Mary agreed with what "they" had decided. Nor, for the same reason, can he help Mary to make a different will. And, of course, he cannot allow Mary to execute a will that does not do what she wants it to do.

This principled analysis of *The Case of the Unwanted Will* fails because of what is prior to analysis: the moral art of description. The failure is sad and, I think, corrupting. It is corrupting, first, because it rests on an untruthful account of what is going on. What is present in the law office is a family, and this one-lawyer-for-each-person way of first seeing a moral quandary in this situation and then resolving the quandary with the ethics of autonomy (the ethics of aloneness) leaves the family out of the account. The analysis looks on Mary as a collection of interests and rights that begin and end in radical individuality. Her affiliation with her husband, and with the children they have made and reared, is seen as a product of individuality(!), of contract and consent, of promises and the keeping of promises—all the consensual connections that lonely individuals use when they want circumstantial harmony. The employment of the lawyer is a result, then, of the links, the promises, the contract, the consent, and the need for circumstantial harmony. The family in the office is there only as the product of promise and consent. It is relevant to the legal business at hand only because the (radical) individuals, each in momentary and circumstantial harmony with one another, want it to be. The promise and the consent create the family.

This description is offered by the legal ethics of radical individualism. It is sad, corrupting, and untruthful. An alternative argument is that the *family* created the promises, the contract, the consent, and the circumstantial harmony—not the other way around. The family is not the harmony; it is where the harmony (and disharmony) comes from. A truthful description of *The Case of the Unwanted Will* is that the lawyer's employer is a family. I suspect that that proposition will sound unusual in legal ethics, but my argument would be ordinary in other contexts. It treats, sees, and describes the family the way families are treated, seen, and described in the stories we tell, in the television commercials we watch, in the comics, and in our religious tradition. * * * The lawyer in *The Case of the Unwanted Will,* for example, did not err in turning his attention to Mary, in John's absence. (Nor would it have been a mistake to turn his attention to John, in Mary's absence; if evenhandedness is important, it would have been more evenhanded to talk privately with each of them.) The deep things to be found out about John and Mary, in particular the deep things involved in their will making, are family things. Inquiring into deep family things is not only tolerated, but it is required by common representation, because *the client is the family.* Any other description is incomplete and, thus, untruthful and corrupting. If an adequate account of what is going on in the family (to the extent that it has to do with their will making) requires talking to either or both parents alone, then talking to them alone is appropriate. If the family is well represented, it (that is, each person in it) will learn how to take Mary's purposes into account, because Mary is in the family.... My argument is that [the lawyer] has begun to do a good thing. It is a good thing because it is a more truthful description of the reality that is the goal of the lawyer's work.... The estate planning issue, therefore, is whether this family is equal to the truth of what it is.

Suppose in *The Case of the Unwanted Will* some further facts about Mary's purposes. One of the couple's sons, Henry, was married for ten years to, and is now divorced from, a woman named Susan. Henry and Susan had children who now live with Susan, and Henry lives alone. John and Mary, however, remain fond of Susan and, despite the divorce, continue to be friendly with her. The lawyer's questions to John and Mary have brought this affection to the surface, but John, as is typical, thinks of property and family together, and Susan no longer is in the family. During the joint interview, Mary sits silent while John says that they want "Henry's share" to go to Henry and, if Henry is dead, to his children. In the cases of the other children of John and Mary, says John, the child's share is to go to the child's spouse. What Mary says to the lawyer when they are alone, however, is that she wants her will to provide for Susan. Mary wants some of her family's property to be available for Susan, after Mary dies, when what is left of Mary will be in her family. Mary will be there, not because of a fictional notion about ownership, but because Mary did not die alone.

It is interesting to note how the narrative force of that statement about Mary's property changes as the case is described differently. Does Mary dispose of *her* property, *her family's* property, *her husband's* property, or *her children's* property? The point is that seeing and saying are moral and legal acts, and moral and legal arts. The law is a language; legal authority will support any one of these ways of speaking of this property, and any of the statements is a moral judgment, as, indeed, the word "property" is a moral judgment.

NOTES

As a matter of the substantive law of property as it stands, each spouse is legally empowered to dispose of his or her own property (subject to limited constraints of community property law, nonbarrable shares in property of a deceased spouse, and so forth). As a matter of the substantive law, each spouse is legally empowered to make decisions in his or her own interest. When assisted by a lawyer in making such decisions, each spouse is legally entitled to sufficient information to make decisions as an autonomous individual. If this is the substantive legal context, is the lawyer required to shape representation of two spouses accordingly? Does Professor Shaffer's discussion take adequate account of the background of substantive law?

Derrick A. Bell, Jr., "Serving Two Masters: Integration Ideals and Client Interests in School Desegregation Litigation"

85 Yale Law Journal 470, 471–72, 485–87, 504–05 (1976).*

The espousal of educational improvement as the appropriate goal of school desegregation efforts is out of phase with the current state of the law. Largely through the efforts of civil rights lawyers, most courts have come to construe *Brown v. Board of Education* as mandating "equal educational opportunities" through school desegregation plans aimed at achieving racial balance, whether or not those plans will improve the education received by the children affected. To the extent that "instructional profit" accurately defines the school priorities of black parents in Boston and elsewhere, questions of professional responsibility are raised that can no longer be ignored:

How should the term "client" be defined in school desegregation cases that are litigated for decades, determine critically important constitutional rights for thousands of minority children, and usually involve major restructuring of a public school system? How should civil rights attorneys represent the often diverse interests of clients and class in school suits? Do they owe any special obligation to class members who emphasize educational quality and who probably cannot obtain counsel to advocate their

* Reprinted by permission of The Yale Law Journal Company and Fred B. Rothman & Company from *The Yale Law Journal*, Vol. 85, pp. 471–72, 485–87, 504–05.

divergent views? Do the political, organizational, and even philosophical complexities of school desegregation litigation justify a higher standard of professional responsibility on the part of civil rights lawyers to their clients, or more diligent oversight of the lawyer-client relationship by the bench and bar?

As is so often the case, a crisis of events motivates this long overdue inquiry. The great crusade to desegregate the public schools has faltered. There is increasing opposition to desegregation at both local and national levels (not all of which can now be simply condemned as "racist"), while the once vigorous support of federal courts is on the decline. New barriers have arisen— inflation makes the attainment of racial balance more expensive, the growth of black populations in urban areas renders it more difficult, an increasing number of social science studies question the validity of its educational assumptions.

Civil rights lawyers dismiss these new obstacles as legally irrelevant. Having achieved so much by courageous persistence, they have not waivered in their determination to implement *Brown* using racial balance measures developed in the hard-fought legal battles of the last two decades. This stance involves great risk for clients whose educational interests may no longer accord with the integration ideals of their attorneys. Indeed, muffled but increasing criticism of "unconditional integration" policies by vocal minorities in black communities is not limited to Boston. Now that traditional racial balance remedies are becoming increasingly difficult to achieve or maintain, there is tardy concern that racial balance may not be the relief actually desired by the victims of segregated schools.

This article will review the development of school desegregation litigation and the unique lawyer-client relationship that has evolved out of it. It will not be the first such inquiry. During the era of "massive resistance," Southern states charged that this relationship violated professional canons of conduct. A majority of the Supreme Court rejected those challenges, creating in the process constitutional protection for conduct that, under other circumstances, would contravene basic precepts of professional behavior. The potential for ethical problems in these constitutionally protected lawyer-client relationships was recognized by the American Bar Association *Code of Professional Responsibility,* but it is difficult to provide standards for the attorney and protection for the client where the source of the conflict is the attorney's ideals. The magnitude of the difficulty is more accurately gauged in a much older code that warns: "No servant can serve two masters: for either he will hate the one, and love the other; or else he will hold to one, and despise the other."

. . .

II. Lawyer-Client Conflicts: Sources and Rationale

. . .

3. *The Atlanta Case*

Prior to Detroit, the most open confrontation between NAACP views of school integration and those of local blacks who favored plans oriented toward improving educational quality occurred in Atlanta. There, a group of plaintiffs became discouraged by the difficulty of achieving meaningful desegregation in a district which had gone from 32 percent black in 1952 to 82 percent black in 1974. Lawyers for the local NAACP branch, who had gained control of the litigation, worked out a compromise plan with the Atlanta School Board that called for full faculty and employee desegregation but for only limited pupil desegregation. In exchange, the school board promised to hire a number of blacks in top administrative positions, including a black superintendent of schools.

The federal court approved the plan. The court's approval was apparently influenced by petitions favoring the plan's adoption signed by several thousand members of the plaintiffs' class. Nevertheless the national NAACP office and LDF lawyers were horrified by the compromise. The NAACP ousted the Atlanta branch president who had supported the compromise. Then, acting on behalf of some local blacks who shared their views, LDF lawyers filed an appeal in the Atlanta case. The appeal also raised a number of procedural issues concerning the lack of notice and the refusal of the district court to grant hearings on the Compromise Plan. These issues gave the Fifth Circuit an opportunity to remand the case to the district court without reaching the merits of the settlement agreement. Undaunted, LDF lawyers again attacked the plan for failing to require busing of whites into the predominantly black schools in which a majority of the students in the system were enrolled. But the district court's finding that the system had achieved unitary status was upheld by the same Fifth Circuit panel.

As in Detroit, NAACP opposition to the Atlanta Compromise Plan was not deterred by the fact that local leaders, including black school board members, supported the settlement. Defending the Compromise Plan, Dr. Benjamin E. Mays, one of the most respected black educators in the country, stated:

We have never argued that the Atlanta Compromise Plan is
the best plan, nor have we encouraged any other school system to
adopt it. This plan is the most viable plan for Atlanta—a city
school system that is 82 percent Black and 18 percent white and is
continuing to lose whites each year to five counties that are more
than 90 percent white.

. . .

More importantly, Black people must not resign themselves to
the pessimistic view that a non-integrated school cannot provide
Black children with an excellent educational setting. Instead,
Black people, while working to implement *Brown,* should recognize that integration alone does not provide a quality education,
and that much of the substance of quality education can be
provided to Black children in the interim.

. . .

Idealism, though perhaps rarer than greed, is harder to control. Justice Harlan accurately prophesied the excesses of de-
railed benevolence, but a retreat from the group representational
concepts set out in *N.A.A.C.P. v. Button* would be a disaster, not
an improvement. State legislatures are less likely than the ABA
to draft standards that effectively guide practitioners and protect
clients. Even well intentioned and carefully drawn standards
might hinder rather than facilitate the always difficult task of
achieving social change through legal action. And too stringent
rules could encourage officials in some states to institute ground-
less disciplinary proceedings against lawyers in school cases,
which in many areas are hardly more popular today than they
were during the massive resistance era.

Client involvement in school litigation is more likely to increase if civil rights lawyers themselves come to realize that the
special status accorded them by the courts and the bar demands in
return an extraordinary display of ethical sensitivity and self-
restraint. The "divided allegiance" between client and employer
which Justice Harlan feared would interfere with the civil rights
lawyer's "full compliance with his basic professional obligation"
has developed in a far more idealistic and thus a far more
dangerous form. For it is more the civil rights lawyers' commitment to an integrated society than any policy directives or pressures from their employers which leads to their assumptions of
client acceptance and their condemnations of all dissent.

Deborah L. Rhode, "Class Conflicts in Class Actions"

34 Stanford Law Review 1183–85, 1187–91, 1204–
07, 1209–12, 1258, 1261–62 (1982).*

A fundamental premise of American adjudicative structures is that clients, not their counsel, define litigation objectives. Thus, the American Bar Association's current and proposed ethical codes both emphasize that an attorney must defer to the client's wishes on matters affecting the merits of legal action. However, by presupposing an individual client with clearly identifiable views, these codes elide a frequent and fundamental difficulty in class action proceedings. In many such cases, the lawyer represents an aggregation of litigants with unstable, inchoate, or conflicting preferences. The more diffuse and divided the class, the greater the problems in defining its objectives.

This article examines those problems in one selected context: plaintiff class actions seeking structural reforms in public and private institutions. Such cases merit special attention on two grounds. First, the often indeterminate quality of relief available makes conflicts within plaintiff classes particularly likely. Most school desegregation, employment discrimination, prison reform, and related cases present no obvious single solution flowing ineluctably from the nature of the violation. Nor will all class members alleging unlawful conduct agree on what should be done about it. Moreover, the prominence of institutional reform litigation vests these intra-class cleavages with particular significance. Such cases account for a high percentage of all class suits and an even greater proportion of legal claims attracting widespread societal concern. Thus, institutional reform litigation provides a useful paradigm for analyzing some of the most vexing issues in class representation.

In exploring these issues, this article takes one central proposition for granted. On the whole, institutional reform class actions have made and continue to make an enormous contribution to the realization of fundamental constitutional values—a contribution that no other governmental construct has proven able to duplicate. That contention has been defended at length elsewhere, and the arguments need not be recounted here. Thus, the following discussion should not be taken to suggest that institutional reform class actions are misused or misconceived, or that there are preferable alternatives. The point, rather, is that the framework in which such actions proceed could benefit from both conceptual and mechanical refurbishing.

Much of the renovation required concerns our concept of class representation. In particular, we need a more coherent theory of class interests and of the role plaintiff preferences should play in defining class objectives. As a first cut at reconceptualization, this article posits a theory of representation mandating full disclosure of, although not necessarily deference to, class sentiment. A central premise is that the class as an entity has interests that may not be coextensive with the preferences of its current membership. Often those able to register views will be insufficiently disinterested or informed to speak for the entire constituency of present and future class members who will be affected by the court's decree. Nonetheless, preferences matter, not because they are conclusive of class interests, but because their disclosure is critical to the efficacy and legitimacy of judicial intervention.

. . .

I.   Intra-Class Conflicts and Disclosure Obligations
A.   A Taxonomy of Conflicts

. . .

The importance, complexity, and protracted character of structural reform lawsuits create opportunities for conflict at every stage of litigation. Class members who prefer the certainty of the status quo to the risks of judicial rearrangement may oppose litigation from the outset. For example, some parents who anticipate busing or closure of institutional facilities as a consequence of legal intervention will prefer to never initiate proceedings. So too, minority employees have feared retaliation by co-workers and management, or loss of job-related advantages in the aftermath of Title VII actions. ...

Far more common, however, are schisms that surface during settlement or remedial deliberations. Often when a suit is filed, plaintiffs will not have focused on issues of relief. The impetus for the action will be a general sense that rights have been infringed or needs ignored, rather than a shared conviction about the appropriate remedy. Thus, there may be consensus only on relatively abstract questions—that ghetto schools are bad, institutional conditions unbearable, or special education programs inadequate. During the liability phase of litigation, class members may not be sufficiently informed or interested to participate in decisionmaking. However, once it becomes clear that some relief will be forthcoming, factions emerge. Also, where proceedings are protracted, changes in legal doctrine, contested practices, or plain-tiff preferences can create new sources of dissension.

School desegregation cases provide the most well-documented instances of conflict. Both commentators and litigators have described in some detail the balkanization within minority com-munities over fundamental questions of educational policy. Dis-pute has centered on the relative importance of integration, finan-cial resources, minority control, and ethnic identification in en-riching school environments. Constituencies that support inte-gration in principle have disputed its value in particular settings where extended bus rides, racial tension, or white flight seem likely concomitants of judicial redistricting. ...

Comparable cleavages arise in various other institutional re-form contexts. Parents challenging the adequacy of existing bilin-gual or special education programs have differed over whether mainstreaming or upgrading separate classes represents the better solution. Suits involving rights of the disabled have divided their families over whether to demand institutional improvement or creation of community care alternatives. ... In employment cases, controversy has centered on tradeoffs between back-pay awards and prospective relief, the formula used to compute dam-ages, and the means chosen to restructure hiring, promotion, and transfer systems.

Moreover, as with any form of collective litigation, parties often differ in their amenability to compromise and their assess-ment of particular proposals. Given the uncertainty of outcome and indeterminacy of relief in many institutional reform class actions, risk-averse plaintiffs will often be prepared to make substantial concessions. Other class members will prefer to fight, if not to the death, at least until the Supreme Court denies certiorari. Particularly where the proffered settlement provides generously for a few named plaintiffs, or where some individuals have special reasons for wanting expeditious relief, dissension may arise within the ranks. And, as the following discussion will suggest, all of these problems are compounded by class counsels' own interests and by a doctrinal framework that fails to raise, let alone resolve, the most difficult issues. ...

II.   The Participants' Roles in Disclosing
Conflict: Rules and Realities

· · ·

B.   Class Counsel

A familiar refrain among courts and commentators is that lawyers assume special responsibilities in class litigation. Accord-

ing to one circuit court of appeals, the duty to ensure adequate
representation rests "primarily upon counsel for the class ... in
addition to the normal obligations of an officer of the court, and
... counsel to parties of the litigation, class action counsel
possess, in a very real sense, fiduciary obligations to those not
before the court." Principal among those duties is the responsibility to apprise the trial judge of conflicting interests that may
warrant separate representation or other corrective measures.

Although unobjectionable in concept, that role definition has
frequently proved unworkable in practice. To be sure, many
attorneys make considerable efforts to appreciate and accommodate the broadest possible spectrum of class sentiment. ... [But]
where the range and intensity of divergent preferences within the
class are unlikely to surface without counsel's assistance, he often
has strong prudential and ideological reasons not to provide it.
One need not be a raving realist to suppose that such motivations
play a more dominant role in shaping attorneys' conduct than
Rule 23's directives and the accompanying judicial gloss.

1. Prudential interests.

An attorney active in institutional reform class actions is
subject to a variety of financial, tactical, and professional pressures that constrain his response to class conflicts. Of course,
none of these constraints is unique to this form of litigation. And
the intensity of such pressures varies considerably depending,
inter alia, on the sources of funding and organizational support for
particular cases. Nonetheless, it is important to identify, in
generic form, the range of prudential interests that can affect
counsel's management of internecine disputes, and the inadequacy
of conventional correctives.

The most patent of these interests arises from the financial
underpinnings of institutional reform litigation. Support for such
cases derives largely from limited public interest funding and from
court-awarded counsel fees to prevailing parties. Among the
factors affecting the attorney's fee award are the relief obtained,
the costs of attaining it, and the number of other counsel who
have contributed to the result. Given the expense of institutional
reform class actions, few litigators can remain impervious to fee-
related considerations or organizational budget constraints. And
flushing out dissension among class members can prove costly in
several respects.

For example, opposing parties often seek to capitalize on class
dissension by filing motions for decertification. If such efforts
prove successful, class counsel may lose a substantial investment

that he cannot, as a practical matter, recoup from former class members. At a minimum, such motions result in expense, delay, and loss of bargaining leverage, and deflect resources from trial preparation. Certification disputes may also trigger involvement of additional lawyers, who would share the limelight, the control over litigation decisions and, under some circumstances, the resources available for attorneys' fees.

Exposing conflict can also impede settlement arrangements that are attractive to class counsel on a number of grounds. As in many other litigation contexts, attorneys often have a bias to settle not shared by their clients. Since institutional reform plaintiffs generally do not underwrite the costs of litigation, their primary interest is in the result attained; the time and effort necessary to attain it are of less concern. Yet from the attorney's perspective, a modest settlement may generate a result "bearing a higher ratio to the cost of the work than a much larger recovery obtained only after extensive discovery, a long trial and an appeal." For example, if the prospects for prevailing on the merits are uncertain, some plaintiffs will see little to lose and everything to gain from persistence. That viewpoint may be inadequately aired by class counsel, who has concerns for his reputation as well as competing claims on his time and his organization's resources to consider.

The potential for attorney-client conflicts is compounded when a proposed settlement makes extremely generous, or totally inadequate, provision for class counsel. Of course a lawyer may attempt to avoid compromising influences by refusing to discuss fees until agreement on all other issues is final. However, that strategy is not necessarily in anyone's interest if it inhibits favorable settlement offers, and many defendants are reluctant to compromise without some understanding of their total liability. Moreover, in an escalating number of civil rights cases, defendants have sought to make settlement on the merits conditional on counsel's waiver or curtailment of claims to statutory compensation. . . .

A final set of problems emerges in test-case litigation. In some instances, counsel may be reluctant to espouse positions that are at odds with those he has taken or intends to take in other proceedings or that could establish an unwelcome precedent. Moreover, test-case litigation often generates settlement biases directly converse to those discussed above. Once a lawyer has prepared a claim with potentially significant impact, he may be disinclined to settle. He almost certainly would not share some plaintiffs' enthusiasm for pre- or post-trial agreements promising generous terms for the litigants but little recognition and no

precedential value for similarly situated victims. Few professionals, class attorneys included, can make decisions wholly independent of concerns about their careers and reputations among peers,
potential clients, and funding sources. Litigating well-publicized
institutional reform cases can provide desirable trial experience,
generate attractive new cases, legitimate organizational objectives
in the eyes of private donors, and enhance attorneys' personal
standing in the legal community. Where such rewards are likely,
counsel may tend to discount preferences for a low-visibility settlement, particularly if it falls short of achieving ideological objectives to which he is strongly committed. ...

    2.   Ideological interests.

        . . .

    Relying on case histories from Boston, Atlanta, and Detroit,
Derek Bell submits that NAACP attorneys' "single-minded commitment" to maximum integration has led them to ignore a shift
in priorities among many black parents from racial balance to
quality education.

    Similar indictments have been leveled against attorneys in
other civil rights contexts. For example, in 1974, a number of
parents and guardians brought suit in behalf of all present and
future residents of Pennsylvania's Pennhurst facility for the re-
tarded. Class counsel took the position that his obligations ran
solely to the residents, and that their interests dictated Pennhurst's closure and replacement with community facilities. Accordingly, counsel made little effort to expose or espouse the views
of parents and guardians preferring institutionalization. Indeed,
according to one of the lawyers subsequently involved, class counsel sought to avoid "stir[ring] people up" by deemphasizing the
possibility of Pennhurst's closure in his out-of-court statements.
After the district judge ordered removal of Pennhurst residents to
community facilities, a systematic survey of their parents and
guardians revealed that only 19% of respondents favored deinstitutionalization. Accounts of other civil rights litigation suggest
that *Pennhurst* is not an isolated example.

    It does not follow, of course, that attorneys in these and
comparable cases failed to represent class interests. Much depends on who one views as appropriate spokesmen for the class
and how broadly one defines "interest." As the analysis in Part
III will suggest, parents are often poorly situated to speak for all
children who will be affected by judicial decree. But neither is an
attorney with strong prudential or ideological preferences well
positioned to decide which class members or guardians deserve a

hearing and which do not. And one critical problem with existing class action procedures is that they fail to assure adequate disclosure of counsel's own interests or of countervailing client concerns.

. . .

[Discussion is omitted concerning limitations in the two most common procedural approaches to class conflicts. The current pluralist approach—which is to rely on separate counsel for separate interests—may, in some instances, exacerbate problems of delay, expense, manageability, and accountability. In other contexts, that strategy can bias results toward those with the organizational acumen and financial resources to make themselves heard. The majoritarian alternative is to provide for direct class participation through plebiscites and public hearings. Yet that approach cannot adequately respond to circumstances where those registering preferences are uniformed, unrepresentative, or unresponsive to the needs of most current or future class members. For example, the complexity of remedial tradeoffs may be difficult to convey to large constituencies. And parents whose children will bear the short term costs of certain desegregation and deinstitutionalization remedies may be poorly situated to evaluate their long-range benefits.

However, granting these difficulties, the article considers various strategies to encourage more reflective resort to pluralist or majoritarian strategies in appropriate circumstances. Among other things, courts could be required to make a record concerning their responsiveness to class conflicts. To assist judicial determinations, class counsel could submit statements detailing contacts with class members, and attorneys' fee awards might be structured to create greater incentives for lawyer-client communication.]

IV. Alternatives and Apologia

C. The Bounded Potential of Procedural Solutions

The ultimate effect of procedural reforms is difficult to predict. There remains the possibility that greater reliance on separate counsel or court-appointed experts will simply increase the numbers of platonic guardians involved in institutional reform litigation. And requiring fact-finders to make more detailed records in support of their conclusions has had mixed success in other contexts. According to Joseph Sax, "emphasis on the redemptive quality of [such] procedural reform" in administrative decision-making is "about nine parts myth and one part coconut oil." Yet while systematic data are lacking, most commentators would probably agree with Richard Stewart's less dire assessment. In his view, forcing the decisionmaker to "direct attention to factors that may have been disregarded" has in some instances proved of real prophylactic value.

Moreover, clearer mandates to class counsel than those provided by existing procedural and ethical rules could serve important socialization functions. Concededly, asymmetrics between class interests and preferences will often force counsel to function more as a Burkean trustee than instructed delegate. Even so, it should be possible to recast that trusteeship role to encompass more explicit fiduciary obligations to dissenting constituencies. Requiring attorneys to record contacts with the class and perceptions of conflict would, if nothing else, narrow their capacity for self-delusion about whose views they were or were not representing. Explicit professional obligations, even those unlikely to trigger any formal sanction, often affect behavioral norms simply by sensitizing individuals to the full implications of their conduct.

. . .

To be sure, none of the proposals outlined here can guarantee better results in [institutional reform cases]. But that conclusion, if disconcerting, is not necessarily damning. Given the values at issue in institutional reform cases, conflicts are an ineradicable feature of the legal landscape. Virtually all of the pluralist and majoritarian deficiencies that impede judicial management of such conflicts would arise with equal force if the underlying issues were addressed in legislative or bureaucratic settings. Indeed, one of the strongest justifications for those governance structures is equally available to class actions: While we cannot depend on disinterested and informed judgment by any single group of decisionmakers, we can at least create sufficient procedural checks and balances to prevent the worst abuses.

Moreover, to acknowledge that the formal mandates governing class actions promise far more than they deliver is not to condemn the pretense. No hypothesized procedures can insure that all class interests will be "adequately represented" or that counsel will singlemindedly pursue his "client's" objectives. But the risks of abandoning either fiction may be too great.

No matter how faulty the enforcement mechanism, such mandates serve important legitimating functions. Broad injunctions concerning client autonomy and adequate representation allow us to affirm the individual's right to be heard without in fact paying the entire price. Giving overly fixed content to those terms could propel us toward some generic prescription that raises more difficulties than it resolves. An unqualified embrace of pluralism would entail problems of increased expense and diminished effectiveness. To totter towards majoritarianism would require confrontation with the awkward fact that paternalism is often offensive in principle but desirable in practice. Like other "white lies" of the law, those governing class adjudication have spared us such discomfitting choices by masking certain "weak spots in our intellectual structure."

[And, given the extraordinary achievements of this form of litigation, that is a useful, if sometimes unbecoming, role.]

REFERENCES

ABA Comm. on Professional Ethics and Grievances, Informal Op. 517 (1962).

Aronson, "Conflict of Interest," 52 *Wash.L.Rev.* 807 (1977).

Association of the Bar of the City of New York, Comm. on Professional and Judicial Ethics, Inquiry Ref. No. 80–23.

Coffee, "Balancing Fairness and Efficiency in the Large Class Action," 54 *U.Chi.L.Rev.* 877 (1987).

Coffee, "Rethinking the Class Action: A Policy Primer on Reform," 62 *Ind.L.Rev.* 625 (1987).

Crouch, "Mediation and Divorce: The Dark Side Is Still Unexplored," *Fam.Advoc.*, Winter 1982, at 27.

Cutler, "Conflicts of Interest," 30 *Emory L.J.* 1015 (1981).

Dam, "Class Actions: Efficiency, Compensation, Deterrence and Conflict of Interest," 4 *J. Legal Stud.* 47 (1975).

Developments, "Conflicts of Interest in the Legal Profession," 94 *Harv.L.Rev.* 1244 (1981).

Frank, "The Legal Ethics of Louis D. Brandeis," 17 *Stan. L.Rev.* 683 (1965).

Garth, "Conflict and Dissent in Class Actions: A Suggested Perspective," 77 *Nw.U.L.Rev.* 492 (1983).

Hovdesven, "The Model Rules: Conflict of Interest," 68 *A.B.A.J.* 812 (1982).

Kane, "Of Carrots and Sticks: Evaluating the Role of the Class Action Lawyer," 66 *Tex.L.Rev.* 385 (1987).

Legal Ethics Forum, "Representation of Multiple Clients," 62 *A.B.A.J.* 648 (1976).

Leubsdorf, "Pluralizing the Lawyer–Client Relationship," 77 *Cornell L.Rev.* 825 (1992).

Macey and Miller, "The Plaintiff's Role in Class Action and Derivative Litigation: Economic Analysis and Recommendations for Reform," 58 *U.Chi.L.Rev.* 1 (1991).

Morgan, "Conflicts of Interests and the Former Client in the Model Rules of Professional Conduct," 1980 *Am.Bar Found.Research J.* 993.

B. LAWYER–CLIENT CONFLICTS OF INTEREST AND PROBLEMS OF PATERNALISM

Douglas E. Rosenthal, Lawyer and Client: Who's In Charge?
96, 98–99, 106, 110, 111–12 (1974).*

THE LAWYER'S CONFLICT WITH HIS CLIENT

The single source of pressure upon the lawyer most likely to affect adversely the client's interest, and which can most easily be documented, is the strain of prolonged litigation and the economics of case preparation. Simply put, a quick settlement is often in the lawyer's financial interest, while waiting the insurer out is often in the client's financial interest. To understand how this can be, consider ... how a plaintiff attorney's time might plausibly be spent on a single medium-value claim, raising no special problems, where the attorney is experienced and very conscientious in case preparation. Two competing pressures affect the lawyer's motivation to terminate the case: on the one hand, the sooner he settles, the less effort expended pursuing the claim; on the other hand, given the reluctance of most insurers to make generous early settlements the longer he holds out the greater the recovery he can anticipate. If attorneys billed their clients on an hourly basis, the lawyer's motive for early settlement would be canceled. This, however, is almost never done. Instead, the client pays a fee contingent upon the eventual recovery. If there is no recovery, there is no fee; with some recovery, a large percentage of it goes to the attorney as a fee. ...

The widespread assumption that the contingent fee makes the lawyer a "partner" of the client in his claim with complete mutuality of interest in the ultimate case disposition is, in dollars and cents, simply not true. To see why, let us add some details to the hypothetical medium-sized claim, not unlike several made by the sampled clients. Let us value the attorney's work time at $40 an hour (a conservative figure since approximately $20 of this figure usually goes for office overhead) and assume that he is both efficient and hard working and puts in eight productive hours per work day. Assume further that the defendant's insurer's claims adjuster has formulated the following settlement policy: (1) to make an initial settlement offer of $2,000 during the first three months after the accident; (2) to raise it to $3,000 just prior to a scheduled examination before trial (about one year after the accident); and (3) to make a final offer of $4,000 during the final pretrial negotiation (about three years after the accident). Assume further that the plaintiff's lawyer is reasonably confident that he can get a jury verdict if the case goes to trial and that, if tried, the verdict would be for about $8,000. Finally, assume (as is frequently the situation) that the attorney charges the client the maximum fee permitted under the Appellate Division rules. Table 4.2 shows the relative returns that the attorney and his client will realize at each of the four termination stages. In the given case, the lawyer's financial interest lies in quick settlement at the discounted early offer of $2,000. The client's financial interest lies in going to trial. A lawyer who literally made his client's interest his own, in more than a few of these cases, would quickly be out of business.

Table 4.2

Relative Returns to Lawyer and Client at Each Recovery Stage

Time after Accident	Gross Recovery	Lawyer's Fee	Lawyer's Costs	Lawyer's Net	Client's Net
3 months	$2,000	$ 900	$ 160	$740	$1,100
1 year	3,000	1,300	1,120	180	1,700
3 years	4,000	1,650	2,400	−750	2,350
trial	8,000	3,050	4,480	−1,430	4,950

· · ·

Faced with an economic crunch, even after weeding out the thin cases and utilizing economies of specialization, the ethical and competent attorney has four realistic options for proceeding with the claim: (1) He can cut corners in preparing the case. (2) He can build his fee by charging disbursements to the client. (3) He can persuade the client that a discounted early settlement is in his best interest. (4) He can bring the existing interest conflict to

the client's attention and negotiate a compromise claims strategy.
Lawyers employ various combinations of these options in their
work, although the fourth is not used frequently. The first three
of these options for making the economics of representation feasible put the lawyer in direct conflict with his client's interest—
without making the client aware of the fact. ...

When faced with an economic interest that competes with the
client's, most attorneys employ the device of preparing the client
to accept less than he anticipates and persuading him that it is in
his best interest to do so—"cooling the client out." Cooling the
client out is not per se good or bad. Most lawyers justify the
practice because, they claim, most clients expect to become rich
out of their claims. Where this unrealistic expectation is indeed
held, the client must be disabused to forestall inevitable disappointment. However, interviews indicate that some clients have
lost the "pot of gold" mentality by the time they reach the lawyer.
For many of them, being cooled out by their attorney is less
justifiable as a reality principle. Instead, it makes sense only as a
way to make the case disposition economically feasible for the
attorney. If the lawyer can convince the client that holding out
for a trial or pretrial last-ditch settlement offer is dangerous, he
can manage the client into an early discounted settlement. This
may well be the main reason why a majority of clients receive a
smaller recovery than the panel evaluation of their case worth.

. . .

The inexorability of the economic conflict of interest between
lawyer and client in so many cases, raises a serious question about
the appropriateness of the traditional ideal that an ethical and
competent lawyer can and will make the client's interest his own.
Goffman puts the matter as follows:

> Performers often foster the impression that they have
> ideal motives ... and ideal qualifications for the role and
> that it was not necessary for them to suffer any indignities,
> insults, and humiliations, or make any tacitly understood
> "deals" in order to acquire the role. ... Reinforcing these
> ideal impressions there is a kind of "rhetoric of training"
> whereby ... licensing bodies require practitioners to absorb
> a mystical range and period of training, in part to maintain a
> monopoly, but in part to foster the impression that the li-
> censed practitioner is someone who has been reconstituted by
> his learning experience and is now set apart from other men.[27]

27. Goffman, *The Presentation of
Self in Everyday Life*, *p. 46.*

Richard Wasserstrom, "Lawyers as Professionals: Some Moral Issues"

5 Human Rights 1, 15–21, 23–24 (1975).

The role-differentiated behavior of the professional also lies at the heart of the second of the two moral issues I want to discuss, namely, the character of the interpersonal relationship that exists between the lawyer and the client. As I indicated at the outset, the charge that I want to examine here is that the relationship between the lawyer and the client is typically, if not inevitably, a morally defective one in which the client is not treated with the respect and dignity that he or she deserves.

. . .

One way to begin to explore the problem is to see that one pervasive, and I think necessary, feature of the relationship between any professional and the client or patient is that it is in some sense a relationship of inequality.

. . .

To begin with, there is the fact that one characteristic of professions is that the professional is the possessor of expert knowledge of a sort not readily or easily attainable by members of the community at large. Hence, in the most straightforward of all senses the client, typically, is dependent upon the professional's skill or knowledge because the client does not possess the same knowledge.

Moreover, virtually every profession has its own technical language, a private terminology which can only be fully understood by the members of the profession. The presence of such a language plays the dual role of creating and affirming the membership of the professionals within the profession and of preventing the client from fully discussing or understanding his or her concerns in the language of the profession.

These circumstances, together with others, produce the added consequence that the client is in a poor position effectively to evaluate how well or badly the professional performs. In the professions, the professional does not look primarily to the client to evaluate the professional's work. The assessment of ongoing professional competence is something that is largely a matter of self-assessment conducted by the practising professional. Where external assessment does occur, it is carried out not by clients or patients but by other members of the profession, themselves. It is

significant, and surely surprising to the outsider, to discover to
what degree the professions are self-regulating. They control who
shall be admitted to the professions and they determine (typically
only if there has been a serious complaint) whether the members
of the profession are performing in a minimally satisfactory way.
This leads professionals to have a powerful motive to be far more
concerned with the way they are viewed by their colleagues than
with the way they are viewed by their clients. This means, too,
that clients will necessarily lack the power to make effective
evaluations and criticisms of the way the professional is responding to the client's needs.

. . .

Finally, as I have indicated, to be a professional is to have
been acculturated in a certain way. It is to have satisfactorily
passed through a lengthy and allegedly difficult period of study
and training. It is to have done something hard. Something that
not everyone can do. Almost all professions encourage this way of
viewing oneself; as having joined an elect group by virtue of hard
work and mastery of the mysteries of the profession. In addition,
the society at large treats members of a profession as members of
an elite by paying them more than most people for the work they
do with their heads rather than their hands, and by according
them a substantial amount of social prestige and power by virtue
of their membership in a profession. It is hard, I think, if not
impossible, for a person to emerge from professional training and
participate in a profession without the belief that he or she is a
special kind of person, both different from and somewhat better
than those nonprofessional members of the social order. It is
equally hard for the other members of society not to hold an
analogous view of the professionals. And these beliefs surely
contribute, too, to the dominant role played by a professional in
any professional-client relationship . . . [One possible response is
to] "deprofessionalize" the law—to weaken, if not excise, those
features of legal professionalism that tend to produce these kinds
of interpersonal relationships. . . .

Without developing the claim at all adequately in terms of
scope or detail, I want finally to suggest the direction this might
take. Desirable change could be brought about in part by a
sustained effort to simplify legal language and to make the legal
processes less mysterious and more directly available to lay persons. The way the law works now, it is very hard for lay persons
either to understand it or to evaluate or solve legal problems more
on their own. But it is not at all clear that substantial revisions
could not occur along these lines. Divorce, probate, and personal

injury are only three fairly obvious areas where the lawyers' economic self-interest says a good deal more about resistance to change and simplification than does a consideration on the merits.

The more fundamental changes, though, would, I think, have to await an explicit effort to alter the ways in which lawyers are educated and acculturated to view themselves, their clients, and the relationships that ought to exist between them. It is, I believe, indicative of the state of legal education and of the profession that there has been to date extremely little self-conscious concern even with the possibility that these dimensions of the attorney-client relationship are worth examining—to say nothing of being capable of alteration. That awareness is, surely, the prerequisite to any serious assessment of the moral character of the attorney-client relationship as a relationship among adult human beings.

. . .

William L.F. Felstiner & Austin Sarat, "Enactments of Power: Negotiating Reality and Responsibility in Lawyer–Client Interactions"

77 Cornell Law Review 1447, 1147–1456, 1459–1464, 1466–71, 1497–98 (1992).

INTRODUCTION

The view that social relations are constructed and power is exercised through complex processes of negotiation is now widely shared.... [Yet] surprisingly, a review of the empirical literature on the lawyer-client relationship hardly suggests that lawyers and clients negotiate relationships, or that they enact the structure and meaning of professionalism and professional power through negotiation. The literature portrays professional practice as dominated by the lawyer or the client, depending on who has superior status or resources, or as split into rigidly defined spheres of influence, with clients autonomously defining goals and lawyers determining the means to achieve them.

In this paper we challenge these views. After studying the enactments of power in lawyer-client interactions in divorce, we find that these interactions run with the great tide of social life rather than counter to it. Power in these interactions is a complicated phenomenon that, over time, is constructed and reconstructed so that its possession is neither necessarily obvious nor rigidly determined. Indeed, it is probably more accurate to say that power is not possessed at all. Power is mobile and volatile, and it circulates such that both lawyer and client can be considered more or less powerful, even at the same time. Even to describe power as an "it" implies more of an independent existence than we intend. It is better, perhaps, to view it as a dimension of relationships rather than a resource under someone's control.

In the traditional ideology of professionalism, professionals maintain control over the production of services. But in the cases that we observed, the delivery of professional service instead involved complex processes of negotiation between lawyer and client; processes in which we saw resistance as well as acquiescence, contest as well as cooperation, suspicion as well as commitment. These cases indicate that the services provided by lawyers to clients are contested and negotiated in the stream of interactions that constitute the professional relationship, and that the content and contours of the interaction vary considerably from case to case, and from moment to moment within cases....

I

Conventional Views of Power in Lawyer-Client Relations

The predominant image of the lawyer-client relationship is one of professional dominance and lay passivity. The lawyer governs the relationship, defines the terms of the interaction, and is responsible for the service provided. The client, in contrast, is the consumer of a service whose quality is difficult to evaluate. Studies of a wide range of legal situations and types of legal practices bolster this image. For example, Hunting and Neuwirth, writing more than thirty years ago, found that the majority of litigants in automobile accident claims in New York City had no idea what their lawyers were doing in their cases and had no say in when to settle or how much to accept. Legal services lawyers studied by Hosticka rarely even asked their clients what they wanted them to do. Such lawyers habitually engage in maneuvers that "exploit and reinforce client dependency on the lawyer's specialized knowledge and technical skill." Kritzer's review of a national survey of lawyers and clients in litigated cases found low client involvement in case development and strategy. From these studies one might think that contemporary lawyers fulfill Bakunin's 19th century prediction about scientific intelligence, namely, that it would lead to an aristocratic, despotic, arrogant and elitist regime.

Indeed, even where clients are involved in the management of their own cases, their involvement often is limited. Thus, Rosenthal's notion of a high level of client participation in personal injury litigation is confined in its interactive dimensions to expressing special concerns and making follow-up demands for attention. Lawyers resent and resist the few clients who take an active role in their cases, considering them hostile and problematic rather than helpful and persistent. In the conventional wisdom, people have "problems" and experts have "solutions."

There is, however, a less polemical view, one that is more reliable as a general view of the profession because it is more sensitive to context. Spangler, for example, reports that private practitioners and corporate counsel are less likely to dictate action to their clients than are legal services lawyers. Heinz and Laumann recognize that there is considerable variation, by area of law, in the practice characteristic they term "freedom of action," a notion reflecting the lawyer's unilateral power to decide on strategy and operate free of close client supervision.

While these scholars see variation in enactments of power by area of practice, others have found it on a case-by-case basis. Still other researchers find power distributed between lawyer and client according to task. Finally, other analysts suggest that power in the professional relationship directly reflects control over resources. Thus Flood, having observed the history of two lawsuits in his ethnographic study of a large Chicago law firm, suggests that the allocation of power between lawyer and client depends on whether clients are likely to produce repeat business or pay fees that command attention. Abel is perhaps the strongest proponent of this view. He argues that corporate clients are typically the "dominant" actors in lawyer-client relationships, while solo and small-firm practitioners "dominate" their clients.

Two things should be noted about conventional views of power in lawyer-client relationships. First, these views are basically structural: they suggest that power varies by status, economic resources, field of law, or the vagaries of particular clients. Second, they treat power as a "thing" possessed at one time or another by one of the parties to a lawyer-client relationship. As we see it, power in lawyer-client interactions is less stable, predictable, and clear-cut than the conventional view holds. Power is not a "thing" to be possessed; it is continuously enacted and reenacted, constituted and reconstituted. The enactments and constitution are subtle and shifting; they can be observed only through close attention to the microdynamics of individual lawyer-client encounters.

II

ENACTMENTS OF POWER IN DIVORCE CASES

In the divorce lawyer's office two worlds come together: the legal world for which the lawyer speaks and to which he provides access and the social world of the client, beset with urgent emotional demands, complex and changing relationships, and unmet financial needs. Just as the legal world appears arcane and ritualized to the uninitiated, the world of the client is one to which the lawyer has access in only a limited, very mediated way. When lawyer and client interact, each confronts, in the world the other inhabits, something new and opaque, yet something of indisputable relevance to their relationship.

To each, the hidden world of the other becomes known mostly through reciprocal accounts. This means that lawyer-client interaction is a process of story-telling and interrogation in which lawyer and client seek to produce for each other a satisfying rendition of her distinctive world....

For both lawyer and client the stakes are high in what the other knows and reveals. While the client must rely on the lawyer's legal experience, the lawyer is largely dependent on the client's interpretations of her social world. For both, motives, goals and data may be suppressed by plan or inadvertence. Each may consciously adopt a narrative style and rules of relevance that limit what the other can assimilate. They may each say both more and less than they intend as they explain what they want the other to know.

Although lawyers and clients are highly dependent on each other, the stories they tell about their interactions are tales of suspicion and doubt. Clients are suspicious about the depth of commitment lawyers bring to their cases and their own ability to control the content and timing of their lawyers' actions. They worry about lawyers who are too busy to attend fully to the idiosyncracies of their cases, and about divided loyalties, competence, judgment and personality. Lawyers, on the other hand, are concerned because they have to deal with and depend on people who are likely to be emotionally agitated, in the midst of a profound personal crisis, ambivalent about divorce, determined to hurt their spouse, and misguided about what they can expect from the divorce process.

These concerns lead to responses that themselves produce secondary problems. Lawyers worried about the emotional instability of their clients often appear hyper-rational, detached, disloyal, and callous. Clients, put off and alienated by such appearances, appear even more unstable and unpredictable to their lawyers. Lawyers worry about distortions introduced into client accounts and attempt to test client stories without expressing overt skepticism. . . .

III

ENACTMENTS OF POWER AND THE NEGOTIATION OF REALITY

In the world of no-fault divorce, the legal process formally has limited functions—dividing assets and future income, fixing custody and visitation, and, occasionally, protecting physical safety and property. Lawyers must understand their client's objectives concerning these issues. But determination of clients' interests is a known quagmire. Clients may not know what they want or may not want what they ought to want. They may change their minds in unpredictable ways, or they may not change their minds when they ought to do so. Clients may be insufficiently self-conscious, or plagued by false consciousness. Moreover, they may find it difficult to distinguish between lawyers who are trying to impose their vision of client needs on clients and lawyers who are trying to get clients to share a vision of those needs that is not controlled by the power of the lawyer's professional position.

When it comes to defining goals, lawyers generally are permissive. That is, they are intensely concerned that the client adopt "reasonable" goals, but within the rather broad parameters of that notion, lawyers are not directive. For divorce lawyers and their clients, the realm of "reality" is the realm of the possible. Within that realm, the final choice is generally left to the client. However, before that choice can be made, considerable energy is devoted to the construction of a mutually acceptable account of the reality of divorce. Defining and identifying "realistic" goals, and orienting and reconciling clients to the world of the legally possible, occurs during complex negotiations in which struggle, if not overt conflict, is frequent.

The mutual construction of reality takes two forms in divorce cases. On the one hand, lawyer and client may develop, over time, a set of goals and tactics that capitalize on the lawyer's knowledge of the legal world and the client's knowledge of her own social world. The final version of what is real is not dictated by one or the other, but built by them together without the need for either to alter the other's view in many important respects. On the other hand, lawyer and client may not see reality in converging terms and each may seek to defend and/or advance his particular vision. Developing a mutually satisfying sense of what reasonably can be expected or achieved is at the heart of the complex lawyer-client interactions we observed. Yet that sense is

not so concrete and tangible that, once achieved, it can be taken
for granted and easily maintained. It is always in danger of
slipping away as events from the client's social world intrude into
the deliberations, and as lawyer and client together gather information about the goals, expectations and strategies of their adversaries.

In examining the ongoing and fragile negotiation of reality
between lawyers and clients, we focus first on the factors that
"distort" reality for lawyers and clients, and then on the strategies
and tactics employed to promote particular versions of reality.
Clients, of course, have greater difficulty than lawyers in becoming oriented to the world of the legally possible. Some of the
difficulty is obvious. Emotionally off-balance, angry, depressed,
anxious or agitated, they may have trouble understanding what
they are told, believing the information that they get and focusing
on the alternatives that are presented to them. They may be
impelled to strike at or "pay back" their spouse in ways that are
inconsistent with reality and even, by altering the posture of the
other side, make their goals more difficult to attain.

Second, clients may expect more of the legal system than it
can deliver under even the best of circumstances. Unrealistic
expectations may range from saving the marriage to transforming
the spouse, but they are most likely to be centered on financial
affairs. Clients tend to reason up from needs, rather than down
from resources, and they have great difficulty in dealing with the
gap between the two. Additionally, clients are slow to realize that
many legal entitlements are not self-executing. The judge at the
hearing on temporary support may say that the client is entitled
to $100 a week, but that does not guarantee that the client will
receive anything. Many clients are naive about their own financial needs, and may have to be patiently educated by their lawyers. Some clients have difficulty grasping the limits of what is
possible because they cannot believe that the law actually is as it
actually is. Finally, clients are slow to understand the costs of
achieving their objectives. Vindication, the last dollar of support,
meticulous estimates of property value, a neat and precise division
of property, a visitation scheme that covers a very wide range of
contingencies, and equitable arrangements that govern the future
as well as the present may be theoretically possible, but even
approximations require extensive services that middle-class clients
generally cannot afford.

Lawyers, of course, are less encumbered on the legal side in
developing a view of reality in particular cases. Nevertheless, it is
not all clear sailing for them. There are, for instance, three kinds

of information problems. In order to form a view of the possible they may need to know things that clients sometimes cannot tell them. These include client goals as well as things that clients sometimes will not tell them, such as their feelings. In addition, there are things that clients sometimes try to tell lawyers that lawyers do not recognize or understand. For example, in a case that we previously analyzed at some length, the client could not decide whether she wanted to settle or litigate, and could not make the lawyer understand that she had great difficulty in negotiating a settlement with her spouse because she could not trust him to fulfill any commitments that he made.

It would, however, be a mistake when thinking about divorce cases to assume that clients are emotional cripples and that the personalities, problems and politics of lawyers do not interfere with their ability to define reality and/or respond to their clients' definitions. Lawyers may not be astute, attentive or experienced enough to catch the client's message. In addition, they may be so overworked or so worn down by practice that they do not have the patience or stamina to negotiate effectively with their clients. . . .

Still, many divorce lawyers use their knowledge and experience in a manipulative way. The most common technique is to engage in what we call "law talk." Law talk consists of the conversations that lawyers and clients have about the legal system, legal process, rules, hearings, trials, judges, other lawyers and the other lawyer in the case. In general, we have found law talk to be a form of cynical realism through which the legal system and its actors are trashed on various accounts, frequently in an exaggerated fashion. The purpose of this rhetorical style is usually to convince the client that the legal process is risky business, that legal justice is different from social justice, and that clients can only achieve reasonable certainty at a reasonable cost, and maintain some control over a divorce, by negotiating a settlement with the other side.

Even when it takes the form of hyperbole, law talk is not commonly introduced into lawyer-client conversations in an aggressive way. Lawyers often join with their clients' positions and appear, at least initially, to be sympathetic. They introduce their clients to reality by invoking their own understanding of legal norms and their own expectations about what courts would do were they to go before a judge. Clients are told that it does not make sense to "insist on something that is far out of line from what a court would do."

Lawyers use delay and circular conversation to convey messages about what is legally realistic. They engage in a form of

passive resistance, maintaining the form of the agency relationship while subtly altering its substance. Rarely are expectations
overtly branded as unrealistic in a judgmental sense; instead,
most lawyers patiently, but insistently, remind their clients of the
constraints that the law imposes on both of them, that is, of law's
definition of reality. ...

In addition to deploying their knowledge of their own social
world, clients frequently assert their views, or resist their lawyers', through repetition and denial. Lawyers may talk about the
unreasonable or the unobtainable, they may predict this or that
outcome, but clients need not, and frequently do not, acquiesce.
Rather, clients may become quiet or change the subject, only to
reintroduce the same topic later. What may seem to the observer
to be wasted motion and circularity, may really be a tactic in an
ongoing negotiation. Finally, clients on occasion fight back by
withholding information, sometimes explicitly, sometimes not.
They use this tactic when they want to exclude the lawyer from
some field of inquiry, often because they consider an issue out of
bounds or would be embarrassed by some disclosure.

The negotiation of reality between lawyer and client is time-
consuming and repetitive, yet often incomplete or unclear in its
results. Whose definition of reality prevails is often impossible to
determine. Even as decisions are made and documents are filed,
how those decisions and documents relate to lawyer-client conversations about goals and expectations can be mysterious. It is,
however, precisely by attending to this mystery that one can
understand enactments of power and tactics of resistance.

IV

ENACTMENTS OF POWER AND THE NEGOTIATION OF RESPONSIBILITY

[D]ivorce cases are not self executing. It is not always clear
what needs to be done, who is going to do it and who is responsible
for assuring that it gets done.... In this context, enactments of
power, either in assuming or assigning responsibility, are, like
those in the negotiation of reality, often unclear or confused....

One of the surprising aspects of the lawyer-client relationship
in divorce proceedings is the rarity of the imperative mode. Put
quite starkly, clients almost never say to their lawyers something
on the order of "I am the client, I am paying the bill, now do this."
...

Lawyers are no more inclined to command than are their
clients. They may urge, cajole, flatter, use rhetorical tricks,
provide unqualified or contingent advice, predict harm, discomfort,

frustration or catastrophe, but they almost never say, "I am the professional, I am the expert, now do this." ... Both lawyers and clients apparently recognize that, were they to behave as if they were hierarchically empowered, they would undermine the legitimacy of what is generally considered to be a cooperative enterprise. But sound as the conventional forms may be for defining the limits of overt power, an unwillingness to issue commands opens a wide territory for subtle and latent maneuver....

As in many human endeavors in which progress is not externally imposed or organized, procrastination in divorce cases is frequently the weapon of choice.

. . .

Procrastination may be purposeful and self-conscious. It may also be structural, built into the way that lawyers organize their practice. Lawyers in small and medium-sized practices are extremely reluctant to turn prospective clients away. As a consequence, they frequently order their workloads in some form of queue. In the doctor's office one waits in line to see the doctor. In legal matters, the wait is not to see the lawyer, but once having seen him, to have him attend to your case. The outcome of such a regime is clients who press their lawyers to keep their cases moving, or clients who are frustrated and angry at the lack of progress.

Additionally, lawyers sometimes lose interest in cases, especially when the other side is intransigent over settlement and the client does not have the resources to pay for full-scale adjudication....

On many occasions, rationalizations for inaction are offered that may simply excuse poor organization, inattention or bad work habits. Matters do not receive attention because the lawyer is concerned about provoking the other side, is trying to conserve the client's money, or is trying to get the client to take more responsibility for his own life....

[M]any of these lawyers went to great lengths to stay on good terms with the lawyer on the other side, even if this meant not prosecuting their client's case to the extent they had promised.

However, procrastination can originate in sound strategy. Lawyers frequently do not do what they have agreed to do, or implied they would do, because they disapprove of their client's agenda, disagree over questions of timing, or are deterred by cost. In these circumstances divorce lawyers are especially affected by their view of their client's emotional situation. Are the client's emotions under control? Is he able to function as a reasonable litigant? Has the psychic divorce kept pace with the legal proceedings, or ought the latter be delayed until the client achieves a more stable emotional perspective?

Clients also may have sound reasons to procrastinate. While they frequently do not agree with their lawyers, they may not want to contest the issue with them directly. A client may be in this posture because of information she is unwilling to share with the lawyer, because she may be embarrassed by her own ambivalence, or because she may be inclined to trust her own, rather than her lawyer's, judgment or intuition. Client procrastination may relate to major as well as minor matters. We observed a client decline to tell his spouse that he intended to seek a divorce after he assured his lawyer that he would; another client refused, without explanation, to authorize service of a divorce petition on the spouse from whom she repeatedly claimed she wished to be divorced; and a third client successfully evaded her lawyer's entreaties to agree to a medical examination to determine whether she was fit to hold a job....

In addition, we encountered vacillation and indecision in three different sets of circumstances: first, when both negotiations and adjudication appeared seriously flawed; second, when either the lawyer or the client viewed the other as unstable or unpredictable; and third, when one or the other apparently lacked the ability to order and rank alternatives. These occasions do not involve overt assertions of power; rather, they are power drifts, instances where context or personality disables lawyers and/or their clients from grasping the reins of power....

Divorce clients are typically weaker parties in their relationship with their lawyers. The weaker party in a relationship that reflects a major disparity in power does not often directly confront the stronger. Slaves, prisoners, students, and wives subjected to patriarchal hegemony have realized that effective resistance, even effective symbolic resistance, must be indirect, subtle, elusive and ambiguous. In divorce, lawyer and client negotiate power, but they do so on uneven terms. We have pointed out the entrenched position of lawyers—their turf, their rules, their vernacular—and the enhanced vulnerability of clients—high stakes, high affect, and inadequate resources. Avoidance and exit become the ultimate recognition of legal hierarchy, the final expression of a structurally-inferior person who cannot fight, but will not surrender.

But what can we learn from the reluctance of lawyers to insist that clients accept their professional opinion, from their disinclination to insist on action that incorporates their professional judgment? We interpret this behavior as a signal that the relationship between lawyer and client is hierarchically complex; that although it is not symmetrical, it is two-sided. The lawyers' position reflects professional power, but clients have two sources of structural power of their own—they pay the bills and they make the ultimate decisions to settle or fight, to accept the deal or not. Lawyers almost always want to retain clients on whose cases they have worked, and they almost always want to be paid. Since clients who come into direct and explicit conflict with their lawyers may conclude that their only recourse is exit, lawyers who engage in explicit confrontation, who draw lines in the sand rather than maneuver around impasses, jeopardize both these objectives. Thus, our model, like any analysis of the negotiation of power in human interaction, must take structural realities as well as individual initiatives into consideration.

To what extent is our view of the enactment of power in the negotiation of reality and responsibility limited to the divorce cases from which it is derived? Divorce practice is different from most other legal practice. Divorce, more than most litigation, originates in personal failure and rejection. The number of clients in divorce who are experiencing some form of personal crisis is high, probably higher than in parallel fields such as criminal law, personal injury, worker compensation, landlord and tenant, consumer, and bankruptcy. As a consequence, the negotiation of reality may be more difficult and salient in divorce. And because divorce law lies at the discretion end of the rules-discretion continuum, the opportunity for creativity in interpreting the legally possible is greater than where rules narrow the scope of interim maneuvers and acceptable outcomes. Perhaps most importantly, the relative social status and economic power of divorce lawyers and their clients, rather than conforming to a single pattern, (as may be the case in fields as diverse as criminal and corporate law), is more varied, since the status of clients reflects the population at large. Thus, divorce lawyers tend to encounter clients of diverse social and economic status and, as a result, are less likely to develop patterns of domination and control than lawyers whose social position, relative to that of their clients, is more consistent.

On the other hand, many of the enactments of power in negotiations of reality and responsibility between divorce lawyers and their clients do occur in other areas of practice. Lawyers and clients must always negotiate a consistent version of events, an account of the client's situation and interactions with the other

side.   They must negotiate a fit between the client's goals and
expectations and the results achievable through legal process.
They must negotiate the timing of action to be taken in pursuit of
the client's goals, and the division of labor between them.   In each
of these areas, whether the area of law be commercial or criminal,
power is neither stable nor static.

NOTES

In "Lawyer Advice and Client Autonomy: Mrs. Jones's Case,"
50 *Maryland Law Review* 213 (1991), William Simon describes a
case he handled as a young inexperienced attorney.   His client,
Mrs. Jones, was a 65–year old black woman charged with leaving
the scene of an accident.   He obtained strong evidence that the
charge was unfounded.   The arresting officer's remarks also suggested that her arrest was racially motivated.   Given the strength
of that evidence, Simon believed that she would be acquitted at
trial.   However, concern about his own inexperience prompted
Simon to enlist the aid of an experienced criminal defense lawyer.
The lawyer negotiated a plea agreement that would have resulted
in six months probation for the client.   Simon was troubled by the
fact that the woman would lose her opportunity for vindication
and for exposure of the police conduct.   He presented the plea
agreement to his client and her minister, who had accompanied
her to the courthouse to serve as a character witness.

> I insisted that, because the decision was hers, I couldn't tell
> her what to do.   I then spelled out the pros and cons. . . .
> However, I mentioned the cons last, and the last thing I said
> was, "If you took their offer, there probably wouldn't be any
> bad practical consequences, but it wouldn't be total justice."
> Up to that point, Mrs. Jones and her minister seemed anxious-
> ly ambivalent, but that last phrase seemed to have a dramatic
> effect on them.   In unison, they said, "We want justice."
>
> I went back to my friend and said, "No deal.   She wants
> justice."   My friend stared in disbelief and then said, "What?
> Let me talk to her."   He then proceeded to give her his
> advice.   He didn't tell her what he thought she should do, and
> he went over the same considerations I did.   The main differ-
> ences in his presentation were that he discussed the disadvan-
> tages of trial last, while I had gone over them first; he
> described the remote possibility of jail in slightly more detail
> than I had, and he didn't conclude by saying, "It wouldn't be

total justice." At the end of his presentation, Mrs. Jones and her minister decided to accept the plea bargain, and as I said nothing further, that's what they did.

How would Richard Wasserstrom evaluate the conduct of Simon and his more experienced colleague? How would you?

––––––

REFERENCES

See also:

Alshuler, "The Defense Attorney's Role in Plea Bargaining," 84 *Yale L.J.* 1179, 1181–87 (1975).

Blumberg, "The Practice of Law as a Confidence Game," 1 *Law and Soc. Rev. Rev.* 15 (1967).

Brickman, "Contingent Fees Without Contingencies: Hamlet Without the Prince of Denmark?", 37 *UCLA L.Rev.* 29 (1989).

Burt, "Conflict and Trust Between Attorney and Client," 69 *Geo.L.J.* 1015 (1981).

J. Casper, *American Criminal Justice: The Defendant's Perspective* (1972).

Casper, "Did You Have a Lawyer When You Went to Court? No, I Had a Public Defender," *Yale Rev.L. & Soc. Action* (Spring 1971).

Fleming, "Client Games: Defense Attorney Perspectives on Their Relations with Criminal Clients," 1986 *Am. B.Found.Res.J.* 253.

Goffman, "Cooling the Mark Out; Some Aspects for Adaptation to Failure," reprinted in W. Bennis ed., *Interpersonal Dynamics: Essays and Readings on Human Interaction* 417–430 (1964).

Hosticka, "We Don't Care About What Happened, We Only Care About What Is Going to Happen: Lawyer-Client Negotiations of Reality," 26 *Soc.Probs.* 599 (1979).

Luban, "Paternalism and the Legal Profession," 1981 *Wis. L.Rev.* 454.

Macaulay, "Lawyers and Consumer Protection Laws," 14 *Law & Soc'y Rev.* 115 (1979).

Mazor, "Power and Responsibility in the Attorney-Client Relation," 20 *Stan.L.Rev.* 1120 (1968).

Patterson, "Legal Ethics and the Lawyer's Duty of Loyalty," 29 *Emory L.J.* 909 (1980).

Sarat and Felstiner, "Law and Social Relations: Vocabularies of Motive in Lawyer–Client Interaction," 22 *Law Soc'y Rev.* 737 (1988).

Schulhofer, "Plea Bargaining as Disaster," 101 *Yale L.J.* 1979 (1992).

Spiegel, "Lawyering and Client Decisionmaking: Informed Consent and the Legal Profession," 128 *U.Pa.L.Rev.* 41 (1979).

Part III

THE DELIVERY OF LEGAL SERVICES
I. REGULATING THE MARKET

INTRODUCTION

The standard justification for ethical restrictions concerning the market for legal services rests on two central assumptions. One involves the need for regulatory structures; the other involves the appropriateness of professional control over those structures.

The first assumption is that certain imperfections in the market for legal assistance justify external governance. Such imperfections include what economists variously describe as information barriers, free riders, and externalities.

An initial difficulty stems from many consumers' inability to make informed assessments about the services they receive, either before or after purchase. Most individual (as opposed to organizational) clients are one-shot purchasers; many will not consult an attorney more than once, and of those who do, a majority will select different lawyers.[1] This lack of experience, coupled with the expense and difficulties of comparative shopping for professional services, makes it hard for such consumers to identify cost-effective practice. In the absence of some external regulation, these clients may suffer significant losses from incompetent or unethical practitioners.

An additional difficulty involves "free riders"; i.e., those who gain benefits without contributing to collective goods. For example, the bar collectively has an interest in securing the public's trust, and in having lawyers conduct themselves as fiduciaries in such a way as to maintain that trust. However, absent effective regulatory structures, individual attorneys may have inadequate economic incentives to avoid cheating; they can benefit as free riders from the bar's general reputation without adhering to basic ethical mandates themselves.

1. *See* B. Curran, *The Legal Needs of the Public: The Final Report of a National Survey* 190 (1977).

377

A final category of problems calling for regulatory responses involves external costs to society and third parties from conduct that may be advantageous to particular clients and their lawyers. For example, the public generally has an interest in seeing just and expeditious resolution of disputes and discouraging non-meritorious claims, but in specific circumstances a litigant or attorneys' economic interests may be to the contrary.[2]

Although commentators on the legal profession generally agree that these problems call for regulatory intervention, there is considerable dispute about the forms it should take, and how much control the profession should exercise over the governance process. The following materials explore that dispute from various perspectives.

A. SOLICITATION

NOTES

The organized bar traditionally has been much concerned with self-promotion by its members. Studies of bar association activities during the first part of this century reflect that a high proportion of efforts were directed toward deterring competition.[1] Prevailing ethical canons and accompanying interpretations generally combined broad exhortations to righteousness with detailed prescriptions of etiquette; the use of Christmas cards, telephone book typeface, and embossed matchbooks were all matters of professional concern.[2] As Karl Lewellyn observed, those ethical constraints were fashioned with reference to small town practice where

> reputation speaks itself from mouth to mouth .... Turn these same canons loose on a great city and the results are

2. *See* generally McKean, "Some Economic Aspects of Ethical Behavioral Codes," 27 *Political Studies* 251 (1979); Leubsdorf, "Three Models of Professional Reform," 67 *Cornell L. Review* 1021 (1982); R. Blair and S. Rubin, eds., *Regulating the Professions* (1980).

1. *See, e.g.,* J. Hurst, *The Growth of American Law* 331 (1950) (finding that of the 150 opinions by the ABA between 1924 and 1936, almost half dealt with advertising, solicitation, fees (including minimum fee requirements) and relations between lawyers and lay competitors); Cappell and Halliday, "Professional Projects of Elite Chicago Lawyers, 1950–1974," 1983 *Am.B.Found.Research J.* 291, 328 (noting that the vast

majority of Chicago Bar Association disciplinary activity in the 1950's involved solicitation of personal injury cases).

2. ABA Comm. on Professional Ethics, Formal Op. 309 (1963) (Christmas cards mentioning profession deemed unethical; cards picturing scale of justice or lawyer dressed as Santa Claus held permissible); ABA Comm. on Professional Ethics, Formal Op. 284 (1951) (listing name in boldface type in alphabetical section of telephone directory held unethical); In re Maltby, 68 Ariz. 153, 202 P.2d 902 (1949) (matchbooks with name and profession warranted censure).

devastating in proportion to its size .... This means, in result, undone legal business. A-plenty. Or it means chancing it .... [T]he conditions of metropolitan legal business make it no simple thing to reach into the grab-bag and pull out a lawyer who is able, experienced in the case at hand, not too taken up with other matters, and also reasonable in fee.[3]

Beginning in the 1970s, the anachronism of the bar's traditional position came under increasing criticism, and Supreme Court decisions proved somewhat responsive to that sentiment. However, while liberalizing restrictions on advertising and targeted mailings, the Court essentially reaffirmed prohibitions against in-person solicitation except by attorneys with no financial stake in the representation. In the majority's view, the dangers of fraudulent, misleading, overreaching, or intrusive communications, and the risk of encouraging baseless litigation were sufficient to justify categorical restraints on solicitation.[4]

That reasoning has been questioned on a variety of grounds as the following readings reflect.

Jerold Auerbach, Unequal Justice: Lawyers and Social Change in Modern America
41–50 (1976).

The new canons drew heavily upon George Sharswood's *Essay on Professional Ethics,* published in 1854. Sharswood's *Essay* was, at best, antiquated; at worst, irrelevant. He had addressed it to a generation accustomed to moral exhortation and confident that its own definitions of character, honor, and duty were eternal verities. Warning even in the 1850's of "a horde of pettifogging, barratrous, money-making lawyers," Sharswood had urged "high moral principle" as the bedrock of professional dignity. Passivity and patience were his cardinal virtues. Like young maidens awaiting suitors, aspiring lawyers must await clients. "Let business seek the young attorney," Sharswood insisted. It might come too slowly for profit or fame (or never come at all), but if the lawyer cultivated "habits of neatness, accuracy, punctuality, and despatch, candor toward his client, and strict honor toward his adversary, it may be safely prophesied that his business will grow

---

3. Llewellyn, "The Bar's Troubles, and Poultices—and Cures?" 5 *L. & Contemp.Probs.* 104, 115–16 (1938).

4. *Compare* Bates v. State Bar of Arizona, 433 U.S. 350 (1977); and

Shapero v. Kentucky Bar Association, 486 U.S. 466 (1988) *with* In re Primus, 436 U.S. 412 (1978); Ohralik v. Ohio State Bar Association, 436 U.S. 447 (1978).

as fast as it is good for him that it should grow." Sharswood's safe prophecy may have comforted a young nineteenth-century attorney in a homogeneous small town, apprenticed to an established practitioner, known in his community, and without many competitors. It could hardly reassure his twentieth-century counterpart, the new-immigrant neophyte in a large city where restricted firms monopolized the most lucrative business and thousands of attorneys scrambled for a share of the remainder. He could draw scant comfort from Sharswood's confident assertion that some preordained rule determined that his practice grew no faster than was good for him. He either hustled or starved.

. . .

A cluster of canons pertaining to acquiring an interest in litigation, stirring litigation, and division of fees almost exclusively affected the activities of struggling metropolitan solo lawyers. They did not apply to the conduct of the firm members or securely established practitioners who formulated them.

. . .

The prohibition against advertising instructed lawyers that success flowed from their "character and conduct," not from aggressive solicitation. It thereby rewarded the lawyer whose law-firm partners and social contacts made advertising unnecessary at the same time that it attributed inferior character and unethical behavior to attorneys who could not afford to sit passively in their offices awaiting clients; it thus penalized both them and their potential clients, who might not know whether they had a valid legal claim or where, if they did, to obtain legal assistance. The canon prohibiting solicitation discriminated against those in personal injury practice, who bore the pejorative label "ambulance chasers." And although the fee-fixing canon reminded lawyers that their profession was "a branch of the administration of justice and not a mere money-getting trade," only the contingent fee (the hallmark of negligence lawyers) was explicitly subjected to judicial scrutiny. That distinction suggested that the decisive question was who earned the fee, not the size of the fee earned.

In tandem, these canons condemned the acquisitive urge (especially among lawyers who earned least), consigned the lawyer to his office to await a client who wandered by with a case that assured fame and fortune, and attributed success (hardly unrelated in American society to monetary accumulation) to good character. The lower the fee a lawyer earned, and the less discreet he was in pursuit of it, the more likely it was that his "money-getting" activities would be scrutinized and criticized. The Canons especially impeded those lawyers who worked in a highly competitive urban market with a transient clientele. . . . Legal doctrine [reduced] the opportunity of an accident victim to recover damages; furthermore, legal services were available only to those who could afford to purchase them.

The consequences were starkly exposed in Crystal Eastman's study *Work-Accidents and the Law,* conducted for the Russell Sage Foundation and published in 1910 as part of the landmark Pittsburgh Survey. In more than half of all work-accident fatalities in Allegheny County, widows and children bore the entire income loss. In fewer than one-third of these cases did an employer pay as much as five hundred dollars—the equivalent of a single year's income for the lowest-paid workers. Similarly, more than half of all injured workers received *no* compensation; only 5 percent were fully compensated for their lost working time while disabled. The result, Eastman concluded, was "not hardship alone, but hardship an outcome of injustice."

. . .

"Ambulance chasing" was never precisely defined. As a term of art it ostracized plaintiffs' lawyers who, representing outsiders to the economic system, solicited certain types of business. Once fee-hungry ambulance chasers were isolated, they could be excluded from professional respectability by a series of discriminatory ethical judgments. Their methods of solicitation were condemned, but nothing was said about company claim agents who visited hospitalized workers to urge a quick and inexpensive settlement. Their fees were isolated for judicial scrutiny, but larger corporate retainers were ignored by professional associations. Their pecuniary interest in the outcome of litigation was criticized, but the pecuniary interest of most lawyers in their cases (even when not ascertainable in advance) was disregarded. Not only were they criticized for professional malfeasance; their speech was mocked (many were recent immigrants) and their perseverance was denigrated as aggressiveness (many were Jewish). Commercialization, speculation, solicitation, and excessive litigation were decried, but there was no mention of the contribution of contingent fees to the enforcement of legitimate claims otherwise denied by the victim's poverty. Few lawyers complained about the Hobson's choice imposed upon an accident victim, who could either relinquish all hopes of recovery or merely relinquish (to his attorney) one-third of what he might recover if he overcame doctrinal impediments. Aggressive solicitation of personal injury litigation through a contingent fee arrangement doubtlessly produced its share of abuses. But when the sole alternative was the waiver of legitimate claims, one is compelled to agree with the conclusion that "the social advantage seems clearly on the side of the contingent fee."

The ethical crusade that produced the Canons concealed class and ethnic hostility. Jewish and Catholic new-immigrant lawyers of lower-class origin were concentrated among the urban solo practitioners whose behavior was unethical because established Protestant lawyers said it was. There were serious "social, economic and occupational differences between the rulemakers and others subject to the rules. ..." Elite practitioners insulated themselves from "ethically contaminating influences" while they compelled lawyers whose low status was attributable to their ethnic and class origins to bear the brunt of such pressures. Rules of ethical deviance were neither universal nor timeless. They were applied by particular lawyers to enhance their own status and prestige. Deviance was less an attribute of an act than a judgment by one group of lawyers about the inferiority of another.

Deborah L. Rhode, "Solicitation"

36 *Journal of Legal Education* 317, 317–321, 321–330 (1986).

.   .   .

How lawyers find clients has always been a matter of some interest to the legal profession. It has also aroused occasional concern [and criticism] among a broader constituency, most often in the wake of some mass disaster creating an obvious need for legal services and an obvious focus for public attention.

.   .   .

Yet [i]f solicitation continues to be the central scapegoat in such contexts, it may deflect attention from more basic problems in the structures by which we allocate legal services and resolve legal disputes.

The following discussion seeks to locate those problems in a broader context. Controversies surrounding solicitation should place in sharp relief issues both of individual motivation and institutional design. Underlying those controversies are questions not only of our professional ethics but also of our capitalist ethos. At least part of what is disturbing about personal injury solicitation is the spectacle of the invisible hand made visible, of lawyers making markets out of misery. If we find that image unpalatable, we need to give more searching attention to alternatives.

I.

Much of the commentary surrounding solicitation has had all the trappings of a medieval morality play. Lawyers generally emerge as either heroes or villains in plots that rarely thicken enough to admit any narrative complexity. All too often, the result has been a rhetorical standoff that fails to capture the competing values at issue.

To many commentators in both the press and the profession, recent experience with mass disasters provides ample justification for the bar's traditional view of solicitation.... Particular opprobrium [has been] .... reserved for "ambulance chasers," the "ghoulish" and "nefarious" souls who lurked about scenes of human distress where tort actions might be waiting to be born.... Except under certain limited circumstances, involving for example, *pro bono* representation or advice to friends and relatives, the bar's official codes have prohibited in-person solicitation. The stated rationale for such prohibitions has rested on concerns about underrepresentation and overreaching that have been historically associated with solicitation.

. . .

Underrepresentation in this context has generally assumed two forms. The most obvious has involved attempts to minimize risks and maximize profits through high volume caseloads. Surveys of personal injury lawyers in Chicago earlier in the century revealed lawyers with unmanageable backlogs, sometimes seven to eight hundred cases awaiting trial.

. . .

[More recently in Bhopal, India] some 80 to 100 American attorneys acquired record caseloads in record time. Working through local counsel and free of the brooding presence of bar disciplinary committees, United States lawyers completed retainer agreements with few of the customary preliminaries. One of the more industrious lawyers signed over 7,000 individual claimants in less than a week; according to reporters' calculations, that totaled about one victim per 60 seconds.

. . .

By all accounts, the circumstances under which such professional relationships were consummated scarcely made for informed dialogue. Most retainer contracts were printed on English forms, and observers recounted that relatively little effort was made to ensure that clients understood the nature of their agreements or that lawyers understood the nature of their clients' injuries. Some local counsel were offering between 50 and 1,000 rupees (roughly 4 to 85 American dollars) per signature, and under such inducements, some victims lost count of the number of agreements they signed. Many were unaware that they were granting multiple powers of attorney or that they were relinquishing one-third of their potential recoveries.

. . .

Another cluster of evils historically associated with solicitation has included [overreaching: e.g.] misrepresentation, overcharging, and intrusiveness. Although systematic evidence is lacking, ethical violations in pursuit of personal injury clients have unquestionably been coupled with ethical violations in pursuit of their claims. Jerome Carlin's study of Chicago solo practitioners in the 1960s revealed frequent informal practices of kickbacks or guarantees of inflated medical fees to those physicians who referred clients. Subsequent reported cases have disclosed similar abuses, including fraud, bribery, perjury, and fabricated evidence. More common problems have involved indelicate or exploitative forms of client contact. Enterprising attorneys with retainer agreements in tow have too often appeared in emergency wards and funeral parlors. For victims of mass disasters, the period following their release from the hospital has sometimes been anything but restful; on her first day home, one victim of the 1981 Hyatt Regency hotel fire received seven calls from local practitioners interested in her legal health. Relationships forged under many such circumstances are unlikely to reflect the kind of informed consideration of alternatives that the free market paradigm presupposes.

Nor do fee agreements reached even in less coercive contexts necessarily bear a fair relationship to the value of services performed or risks assumed. Standard contingency arrangements serve the obvious advantage of underwriting litigation by those otherwise unable to afford it. Such agreements also have the obvious disadvantage of permitting windfall compensation to attorneys who carefully screen their caseloads. By accepting only claims where liability appears reasonably certain and damages quite substantial, personal injury lawyers can recover exceptionally large judgments with exceptionally little risk or effort. Lucrative fee arrangements are not, of course, unique to contingent fee cases. Yet there remains something particularly disturbing about a system that routinely reallocates a large percentage of relief from severely disabled plaintiffs to their already affluent attorneys under circumstances requiring minimal legal assistance. ...

[It is also the case, however, that legal entrepreneurs have prevented as well as profited from exploitation. Bhopal is a case in point. The activities of American attorneys prompted unprecedented concern for disaster victims who routinely go uncompensated under Indian legal procedures. The government not only declared itself the representative of Indian claimants, it established special tribunals, legal aid programs, and disaster relief systems.]

. . . While the adequacy of these measures remains open to question, there is little dispute that the intervention of American attorneys has been critical in promoting progressive legal change. The presence of these attorneys has raised expectations and increased bargaining leverage among victims, and has helped goad the government into redesigning remedial structures that might prove useful for plaintiffs in future cases. However distasteful its other features, global ambulance chasing has also conveyed a message to multinational corporations about the costs of exporting high-risk or poorly supervised technology. It seems unlikely that most Third World tort victims will be worse off as a result.

The same has been true in countless other instances of indigenous solicitation. Aggressive recruitment by American personal injury and public interest lawyers has often made significant contributions to the quality of human life. It is, to be sure, impossible to calibrate those contributions with any degree of precision. Given the absence of systematic data on the frequency and consequences of solicitation, its virtues may seem less tangible than its vices. What little historical and anecdotal research is available, however, suggests that personal contact with potential clients has served interests repeatedly undervalued by the bar's ethical canons.

Prohibitions on advertising and solicitation developed in small town settings, where reputation was a matter of common knowledge and virtue was not its only reward. As the profession became increasingly urbanized, those prohibitions became increasingly anachronistic. Given the legal naivete and transient nature of their clientele, personal injury practitioners were often unable to attract a respectable caseload through what the organized bar defined as respectable conduct. The consequences were felt by potential clients as well as by struggling advocates. For example, a 1910 Russell Sage survey found that less than half of all work-related injuries and fatalities resulted in any legal recovery, and only 5 percent of workers were fully compensated. It has been, at least in part, the evolution of an ambulance-chasing personal injury bar that has contributed to more favorable liability doctrine and provided opportunities to invoke it.

So too, many civil rights attorneys during the last quarter century have found personal persuasion to be the most effective means of rousing relevant constituencies. To cite only the most notable example, the named plaintiff in *Brown v. Board of Education* was initially "anything but eager" to incur the risks of legal proceedings. As the facts in *Primus* similarly suggested, the retiring posture contemplated by conventional bar etiquette is ill-suited to the realities of much public interest litigation. Without personal contact, many victims of constitutional violations will remain unaware of potential remedies or means to pursue them.

Lawyers willing to skirt the official rules on decorum have made for a more humane social order in both public and private law contexts. By helping to redistribute the costs of accidents, the personal injury bar has increased incentives for reducing accidents while ameliorating the conditions of victims and their dependents. Similarly, by raising the costs and consciousness of various constitutional and statutory violations, entrepreneurial public interest attorneys have helped produce some of the most progressive social changes in this nation's history.

If those virtues have not always been adequately appreciated, at least part of the reason lies in the structures of professional governance and political influence. Many activist attorneys are understandably reluctant to endorse self-promotion by citing, from personal experience, examples that could provoke disciplinary sanctions. The clients who benefit most from such activism form a diffuse and relatively powerless constituency, with more pressing concerns than organizing to alter bar ethical codes.

By contrast, those with greatest political and professional influence have perceived little to gain from relaxing traditional rules against solicitation. A relatively small percentage of the bar is engaged in the kinds of personal injury, criminal defense, or public interest work where personal overtures to previously unknown parties is most useful. A large percentage of the profession, however, has a high stake in its social status. In bar opinion polls, poor public image consistently ranks as attorneys' chief concern, and solicitation is still viewed as a major contributor to that problem. During the recent debates over the new Model Rules of Professional Conduct, proposals to liberalize the bar's conventional position met with overwhelming opposition. The specter of lawyers overtly making markets for their services aroused animus in all quarters. Even direct mail appeals would, in the view of most *Model Rules* commentators, have disastrous effects on the profession's image. Yet to fair-minded observers, the transparent parochialism of much of the bar's opposition has scarcely enhanced that image.

II.

From an historical perspective, the recent debate over solicitation leaves a disquieting sense of deja vu. Little of the Bhopal coverage moved beyond the traditional rhetorical standoff. Most popular and scholarly comment has cast lawyers in the role of either scavenger or savior. Critics and defenders, equally imbued with a sense of moral complacency, have ended up speaking past each other on virtually all the critical issues.

. . .

What is needed, rather, are [approaches] that focus more systematically on issues of individual responsibility and institutional design. The abuses historically associated with solicitation should not be presented as isolated or inevitable byproducts of such direct client contact. In the kinds of cases that have generated the most serious misconduct, there is often plenty of guilt to go around. ... What little empirical evidence is available leaves doubt that abuses such as tampering with documents or filing frivolous claims are unusually prevalent in the areas of practice most often linked with solicitation.

So too, the intrusiveness of personal injury lawyers in the wake of mass disasters is frequently related to, and/or dwarfed by, the intrusiveness of insurance claims adjusters, who are not subject to the same professional prescriptions regarding decorum. [R]ecent mass disasters have witnessed industrious industry representatives waylaying family members en route from the funeral. Uninformed consent, while too often reflected in solicited lawyer-client agreements, is also too often evident in insurance adjusters' settlements. The conditions of legal ignorance and economic necessity that have permitted exploitation by plaintiffs' counsel have presented equal opportunities for their adversaries.

Nor should the visible ethical impropriety in some solicited cases obscure the less visible ethical abdications that often precede it. If health and safety litigation is to serve as a morality play of sorts, other dramatis personae deserve more than walk-on roles. Attention should also focus on counsel who help shape corporations' investments and remedial decisions. Certainly the defendant's normative posture in the aftermath of the Bhopal disaster warrants some scrutiny: its choice of certain hard-line litigation strategies, [and] its inadequate emergency relief measures. ...

As to problems of underrepresentation and overcharging, the question is always "compared to what?" As previously noted, the contingent fee agreements that generally accompany solicitation can create conflicts of interest leading to inadequate preparation or excessive charges. But the same can be true of hourly fee contracts. High volume caseloads and undue incentives to settle are endemic to much private criminal defense practice where contingent fees are unlawful. Standard hourly fee arrangements prevailing in insurance defense can create different incentive structures but comparable conflicts of interest. All too frequently, attorneys have been anxious to leave no stone unturned as long as they can charge by the stone. The result may be excessive work and excessive fees in relation to the claims at issue. While plaintiffs' attorneys in the asbestos litigation recovered from 34 to 39 cents out of every dollar paid to victims by insurance companies, fees to defense lawyers were even higher. Such figures give a somewhat ironic cast to invectives from the corporate bar against contingent fee lawyers who "are allegedly in it for the money." That is scarcely less true of their opponents, who often recover comparable fees without the contingency. There is, in short, no systematic evidence that the problems linked with attorney solicitation are unusually frequent in that context. Nor is there evidence that banning all such personal contacts prevents more exploitation than it permits.

The point of such a comparative approach is not, however, to minimize the seriousness of abuses that may accompany solicitation.

... That comparable abuses exist elsewhere is not a reason for complacency. The response rather should be to focus on common causes and institutional responses. In particular, that focus should extend to the structures under which we regulate the legal profession, allocate legal services, and extend legal remedies.

As a threshold matter, control over solicitation, like other regulatory issues, should be vested in a more disinterested constituency than the organized bar. The general rationale for transferring such authority has been set forth at length in other contexts and need not be rehearsed here. It is sufficient to note that the profession's attitudes toward solicitation have been demonstrably self-interested, and that its current regulatory approach fails to accommodate the competing interests at issue. Prevailing constitutional doctrine and codified standards, by focusing on attorneys' motives rather than conduct, have misconstrued the problem and misconceived the solution. The kind of pure eleemosynary intent ostensibly present in *Primus* has become increasingly unusual given recent legislation expanding the potential for fee recoveries in public interest litigation. Since unalloyed altruism is rare, to prohibit personal contact except in the highly atypical circumstances where lawyers have no conceivable financial interest in the outcome is both over- and underinclusive. Such an approach bans conduct that need not result in overreaching or underrepresentation, and it ignores the ways in which nonmonetary concerns can compromise counsels' fiduciary obligations. Attorneys' personal interests and ideologies are often implicated in pro bono contexts. ...

. . .

A constituency more concerned with the fact than the image of impropriety should seek a different regulatory framework. Exploration of alternatives ought to figure more prominently in law school curricula and scholarship. It should also be informed by a more systematic understanding of clients' preferences, and framed by a comparative analysis of regulatory strategies in related consumer contexts. One possible approach would be the kind of time, place, and manner restrictions suggested in an earlier draft of the ABA Model Rules and in other proposals submitted to state and national bar officials. Rather than imposing a categorical ban on personal contact, the profession could proscribe specific forms of abuse, such as coercive or harassing conduct, or communications where the lawyer reasonably should know that the client's physical or psychological state prevents informed deliberation. Curtailment of prohibitions on direct attorney-client contact could be coupled with expanded protections from other forms of abuse. We should exercise more stringent control over contingent fee agreements and inadequate representation. For example, courts or regulatory commissions could require more equitable graduated fee formulas that bear some relationship to the services performed and risks assumed. Such requirements could be monitored through well-publicized and low-cost fee arbitration systems. Attorney incompetence should be subject to more effective remedies, and overreaching by insurance claims agents should result in more stringent sanctions.

These regulatory strategies cannot, of course, provide wholly adequate protection against the cupidity and callousness that has accompanied some solicitation. But too much outrage has been directed at intractable individual frailties and too little at institutional failures. Ultimately, the most effective way to minimize attorney overreaching is to minimize the profit incentives that encourage it. To that end, we should be designing remedial structures that rely less on lawyers in general and on privately, subsidized lawyers in particular. Our present legal procedures, rather than focusing on restitution for victims, divert an inordinate percentage of compensation to attorneys. Yet there has been no lack of models for no-fault insurance schemes and alternative dispute resolution systems that promise some improvement. Nor has there been an absence of innovative pro bono models for delivering emergency legal aid for mass disaster victims. What has been notably lacking, however, is support from the bar.

. . .

[It is that constituency which must rethink the premises and processes by which we distribute legal services.]

REFERENCES

J. Bartlett, *The Law Business: A Tired Monopoly* 47–52 (1982).

Federal Trade Commission, *Improving Consumer Access to Legal Services: The Case for Removing Restrictions on Truthful Advertising* (1984).

Hill, "Solicitation by Lawyers: Piercing the First Amendment Veil," 42 *Me.L.Rev.* 369 (1990).

Llewellyn, "The Bar's Troubles, and Poultices—and Cures?" 5 *L. & Contemp.Probs.* 104 (1938).

Radin, "Maintenance by Champerty," 24 *Calif.L.Rev.* 48 (1935).

CASES

In re Primus, 436 U.S. 412, 98 S.Ct. 1893, 56 L.Ed.2d 417 (1978).

Ohralik v. Ohio State Bar Association, 436 U.S. 447, 98 S.Ct. 1912, 56 L.Ed.2d 444 (1978).

NAACP v. Button, 371 U.S. 415, 83 S.Ct. 328, 9 L.Ed.2d 405 (1963).

Koffler v. Joint Bar Association, 51 N.Y.2d 140, 432 N.Y.S.2d 872, 412 N.E.2d 927 (1980).

In re Teichner, 75 Ill.2d 88, 25 Ill.Dec. 609, 387 N.E.2d 265 (1979).

B. ADVERTISING

INTRODUCTION

Although many attorneys view advertising by their fellow professionals as a recent and lamentable development, in fact it is restrictions on advertising that are recent. Lawyers in ancient Greece and Rome were not shy about promoting their services; nor were distinguished eighteenth and nineteenth century attorneys, including Abraham Lincoln, who employed circulars or newspaper listings.[1] However, as earlier discussion indicated, after the turn of this century, bar leaders became increasingly concerned with promotional practices. Both the Canons of Ethics and the Code of Professional Responsibility as originally enacted banned most advertisements.

During the 1960s and early 1970s, a growing constituency both inside and outside the profession challenged traditional constraints on competition. The increasing heterogeneity of the bar, the rise of an organized consumer movement, and a widening concern about access to legal services all set the stage for legal challenges that eventually reached the Supreme Court.

The first of these suits, Bates v. State Bar of Arizona, 433 U.S. 350 (1977), involved a somewhat colorless advertisement for a legal clinic offering "legal services at very reasonable fees." The ad also listed charges for certain routine services such as uncontested divorces, adoptions, and simple personal bankruptcies. The Supreme Court held that lawyer advertising could not be subjected to blanket suppression, and that the advertisement at issue fell within First Amendment protections. In subsequent decisions, the Court struck down further restrictions on lawyers' commercial speech and summarized its approach as follows:

> Truthful advertising related to lawful activities is entitled to the protections of the First Amendment. But when the particular content or method of the advertising suggests that it is inherently misleading or when experience has proved that in fact such advertising is subject to abuse, the States may impose appropriate restrictions. Misleading advertising may be prohibited entirely.... Although the potential for deception and confusion is particularly strong in the context of advertising professional services, restrictions upon such advertising may be no broader than reasonably necessary to prevent the deception.

1. William Forsyth, *The History of Lawyers* (1873); Lori Andrews, *Birth of a Salesman: Lawyer Advertising and Solicitation* 1 (1980).

Even when a communication is not misleading, the State retains some authority to regulate. But the State must assert a substantial interest and the interference with speech must be in proportion to the interest served.... Restrictions must be narrowly drawn and the State lawfully may regulate only to the extent regulation furthers the State's substantial interest.[2]

All these decisions provoked strong dissension within the Court and widespread opposition within the bar. Surveys following the *Bates* opinion have generally found that most lawyers oppose mass media advertising and that a significant number of practitioners agree with former Chief Justice Burger that such self-promotion is one of the most "unethical things a lawyer can do." [3] By contrast, most nonlawyers believe that advertising is informative, the vast majority of consumers believe that it is professionally acceptable.[4]

Evidence of the effect of advertising on lawyers' image is mixed. In some studies, consumers who are aware of lawyers' ads rated the profession or lawyers who advertise lower on characteristics such as trustworthiness, professionalism, honesty, and integrity.[5] In another study, exposure to the advertisements "heightened pre-existing biases that jury awards are too high, [that] justice can be 'bought and sold,' [and] that most lawyers will help clients win 'even if they know they are lying.' " [6] However, other research, including a national study by the ABA, finds that "dignified" advertisements reflect favorably on the profession and on attorneys who advertise.[7]

2. In re RMJ, 455 U.S. 191, 203 (1982) (striking down provisions limiting advertising to certain categories of information). Subsequent cases held that states could not prohibit nondeceptive graphic illustrations or descriptions of ongoing litigation, Zauderer v. Office of Disciplinary Counsel, 471 U.S. 626 (1985); mailings targeted to a specific recipient rather than members of the general public, Shapero v. Kentucky Bar Association, 486 U.S. 466 (1988); or accurate identification of an attorney as a certified trial specialist, Peel v. Attorney Registration and Disciplinary Commission, 496 U.S. 91 (1990).

3. Archer W. Honeycutt and Elizabeth A. Wibker, *Consumers' Perceptions of Selected Issues Relating to Advertising by Lawyers*, 7 J. of Prof. Services Marketing 119, 120 (1991).

4. *Id.;* Milo Geyelin, *Debate Intensifies Over State Regulations that Restrict TV Advertising by Lawyers*, Wall St. J., Aug. 31, 1992, at B1, B4; Diane B. MacDonald & Mary Anne Raymond, *Attorney Advertising: Do Attorneys Know Their Clients?*, 7 J. of Prof.Services Marketing 99 (1991).

5. In one study, decline after exposure to ads was substantial: trustworthiness (71% to 14%), professionalism (71% to 21%), honesty (65% to 14%), and integrity (45% to 14%). W. Ward Reynaldson, *The Case Against Lawyer Advertising*, 75 A.B.A.J. 60 (January 1989).

6. Geyelin, *supra* note 4, at B4.

7. Honeycutt & Wibker, *supra* note 3, at 124; ABA Commission on Advertising, *Report on the Survey on the Image of Lawyers in Advertising* (Jan. 1990).

Controversy over commercial speech is reflected in continuing challenges to bar ethical rules and evaluated in the readings that follow.[8]

Geoffrey C. Hazard, Jr., Russell G. Pearce and Jeffrey W. Stempel, "Why Lawyers Should Be Allowed to Advertise: A Market Analysis of Legal Services"
58 New York University Law Review 1084, 1086, 1089–99, 1105–09 (1984).

. . .

I

Legal Services as a Market Commodity

Most commentators have assumed that all legal services are similar and thus have failed to recognize that advertising's impact, whether favorable or unfavorable, will not be the same for all legal services. The debate on lawyer advertising presupposes that if legal services could be categorized, complexity would be the only relevant determinant. Participants in this debate start from the premise that even a petty controversy can be complex, and implicitly conclude that individualized legal services are always preferable.

We believe that this analysis overlooks important considerations and think that legal services can be regarded as of two types: those that can be satisfactorily standardized, and those that require individualized treatment. We call these two categories "standardizable" services and "individualized" services, respectively. Conceivably, many individualized services could be delivered in standardized ways, while many routine services could be provided in an individualized manner. Whether a legal service is individualized or standardizable depends primarily on the degree of risk that the particular legal problem poses for the client. In this context, risk is a function of (1) the gravity of the consequences to life, liberty, or property that might ensue if the legal

---

8. Common observation of lawyer advertising in yellow pages, television, and other mass media indicates that the informational messages focus on personal injury (including workers' compensation), divorce, bankruptcy, and DWI (drunk driving criminal charges), much more than on civil rights, welfare rights, landlord-tenant relationships, and employment discrimination. One obvious distinction between the matters in the first category and those in the second is that the former hold prospect for substantial lawyer fees, while the latter as "social cause" cases usually do not. Does this development cast doubt on the policy premises under which the Supreme Court invalidated traditional restriction on solicitation and advertising, in cases such as NAACP v. Button, 371 U.S. 415 (1963) and Brotherhood of Railway Trainmen v. Virginia, 377 U.S. 1 (1964)?

service does not favorably resolve the matter in question, and (2) the probability that one or more of these consequences will actually occur. ...

Using complexity as the sole or primary determinant of legal services categorization is thus inappropriate. A complex legal matter does not necessarily require elaborate legal services when there is a low probability that serious adverse consequences will result if routine handling of the matter permits a mistake to be made. While a petty matter can be legally complex, not all legally complex matters involve substantial risk. ...

Because participants in the advertising debate have failed to recognize that legal services are delivered in a market, they have also presupposed that both production and consumption of legal services are static. For instance, opponents of lawyer advertising assume that because legal services are a necessity, advertising will stimulate demand only by encouraging frivolous, ill-spirited litigation. This view fails to recognize, however, that as legal services become more affordable, middle and low income consumers who currently do not purchase necessary legal services will be able to purchase such services. ... The demand for legal services is elastic. For example, if the price of legal services decreases, other factors remaining the same, the inclination to purchase them will increase. Similarly, supply is elastic in the legal services market. For instance, if the demand for legal services increases, suppliers will have more incentive to provide additional volume. This interdependence can be illustrated through example. If several law firms begin to advertise, demand for their legal services will increase, encouraging these firms to provide more services. As additional volume is produced, the supplier's cost of providing legal services may decline because fixed costs in the production process can be distributed over more units of service. These firms can achieve economies of scale through specialization, work force composition (e.g., the use of paralegals), or altering clients' expectations about the degree of personalized service to be provided. They can also structure their practices so as to focus on early diagnosis of risk—which can ordinarily be estimated very quickly by ascertaining the stakes involved in the matter—and to process low risk and high risk matters differently. This reduction in average costs in turn makes it possible to cut prices and to stimulate still additional demand. The additional demand will give producers incentive to increase the supply of legal services. Thus, opponents and supporters of advertising have not fully recognized that advertising, by enabling the dynamics of normal market forces to operate on the delivery of legal services, may alter methods of supplying, as well as delivering, legal services.

. . .

II

The Role of Advertising in the Legal Services Market

Individuals seeking to purchase legal services rely on the same sources of information that consumers rely on in other markets: personal knowledge, reputation, and advertising. It is essential to recognize that advertising is rarely, if ever, the only source of information about products and prices. ...

As a partial result of the general insufficiency of personal knowledge, a second source of information—reputation—becomes an important element of consumer decisions to purchase legal services. Reputation provides the potential buyer with a form of personal knowledge as it has been accumulated by others. Hence, the prospective purchaser will find reputation information both less complete and less trustworthy than his personal knowledge. Whenever possible, he will seek to confirm reputation information with personal knowledge, or will at least try to verify the reputation's accuracy.

Because some consumers have much greater access than others to reputation information, not all prospective purchasers of legal services are equally well equipped to verify reputation information. For example, one valuable source of reputation information, personal contact with a lawyer or with those who frequently use legal services, is concentrated most heavily among whites and property owners with high incomes and better education. ...

A third source of product information is advertising. Advertising consists of a message, usually short, that is relayed to a large group at the instance of the producer. Like reputation information, advertising allows consumers to compare goods or services without having repeated, broad-based personal experience. It enables them to gather, at little personal cost, information about a range of goods or services—information that may be indispensable for substantiated market comparisons and choices. Advertising has a number of characteristics that make its impact relatively ineffectual in comparison with either direct experience or reputation information. The brevity of its message constrains producers from communicating all of the information consumers need or desire. Because the advertising information comes from an impersonal source, consumers often pay little or no attention to it. Similarly, the obviously biased source of the message encourages them to seek corroboration through other available reputation information.

Advertising has advantages and disadvantages for producers as well. ... Advertising's primary advantage is that it enables the producer to reach and recruit a large number of consumers and thereby to increase revenue; the increased volume may permit the reduction of production costs through economies of scale and thereby generate further increases in profits. Advertising, however, also has drawbacks for the producer. Its chief drawback is its high cost; moreover, efficacy normally requires repetition. Advertising also incurs the costs associated with mass marketing, such as that of preparing for levels of production sufficient to meet the demand generated by advertising promotion. This increased demand may also require some form of standardized production, both to absorb marketing costs and to increase output, and standardized production, entails start-up costs such as expenditures for research and development. Thus, restrictions on advertising limit lawyers' exposure to entrepreneurial risk. If lawyers cannot advertise, and legal services are promoted through personal knowledge and reputation information, lawyers will not bear any of the direct costs of providing consumers with information. Furthermore, because without advertising demand is relatively stable, lawyers will lack incentives to incur the set-up costs associated with mass production.

Because advertising may fail to alter consumer choice, the producer who advertises is subject to considerable entrepreneurial risk. If he spends a great deal of money and fails to gain the consumers' attention, he has lost much. ...

If reputation and experience information are unfavorable, advertising can have the ironic effect of informing a much larger group of consumers about the poor quality of the producer's goods or services. Thus, while advertising offers the potential of attracting a high volume of business, it also carries with it the possibility of a significant loss of business. ...

III

The Effect of Market Forces on the
Utility of Lawyer Advertising

... Providers of primarily individualized services have little use for advertising of any kind and no use for mass advertising. Because purchasers of individualized legal services have a great deal at stake, they are likely to evaluate carefully information about legal services. Advertising provides little information useful to such consumers. Its brevity renders it relatively ineffective in communicating the complexity, reliability, and uniqueness of an individualized service. Furthermore, advertising originates from an obviously biased source. Simply put, advertising is not cost effective for the seller of individualized services because it cannot communicate information likely to influence potential purchasers of those services.

Other factors contribute to the ineffectiveness of individualized legal services advertising. Many individualized services clients are repeat users of legal services and accordingly have personal knowledge of particular firms' past work. Similarly, clients with sophisticated legal problems, business or personal, usually associate with other persons having similar legal problems. Reputation information about individualized firms, therefore, is often available to the client with a need for individualized services. The availability of alternative reliable information sources makes advertising largely irrelevant to patrons of individualized firms.

Firms offering primarily standardizable services, however, must appeal to a broader-based, less well-connected, and less well-informed clientele to generate the volume of business necessary to profit from their moderate prices. To generate this large client pool, these practices must stimulate the latent demand for legal services. They must reach those persons who, because of the relative infrequency of their legal problems, the high cost of legal services, or the mystique surrounding the legal profession, do not consult attorneys for any but the most pressing problems. For the potential client, even the minimal information that advertising provides about a primarily standardizable practice is useful. Standardizable service firms must provide consumers with this threshold of information; personal knowledge and reputation cannot reach such a wide audience efficiently.

Stewart MacCauley, "Lawyer Advertising: Yes But ..."
Working Papers/Institute for Legal Studies: 2 (Dispute Processing Research Program: Working Paper 7-3, Madison, Wisconsin, 1985) pp. 14-16, 22-24, 26-29, 30, 31, 33-43, 54-56, 58-59, 70-71, 72, 73, 75.

Opponents of lawyer advertising paint a gloomy but easy to recognize picture. Lawyers will advertise, and the relationship between lawyers and clients will be transformed from a professional to a commercial one. Instead of an ethic of service, lawyers will march to the drum of the market and self interest. Advertising will stress low prices for basic legal needs. Lawyers can offer these prices only by standardization. This prompts the growth of large organizations that can afford the staff and equipment necessary to process large numbers of routine cases. Once they lose opportunities for creativity and responsibility, bored lawyers[26] will only put in their hours. The quality of the work will then decline to a mediocre level.

Advertising legal services, in this gloomy picture, also leads to misrepresentation. It is hard to evaluate legal services. There is no thing called a will or a divorce that is always the same. Low prices will be quoted for basic services, and lawyers will have to meet the competition. In order to offer services at prices driven down by competitive advertising, lawyers will cut the quality of the work they deliver. Clients will be fooled into thinking that they need only a standardized product when actually they need work that takes account of their special situation. Other lawyers may engage in "bait and switch" tactics, luring clients to their offices by advertising low prices but persuading them to buy costly but unneeded personalized services once they are there. In all of this, good ethical lawyers will be driven out by the bad who can successfully win over a gullible public responding to advertising tricks.[27]

Those advocating broad freedom for lawyers to advertise tell a very different story.[28] Informed consumers will compare prices and make judgments about the likely quality of services offered by various attorneys. This will spark competition among lawyers who will lower prices and increase quality. Lawyers will lower costs by increasing efficiency, turning to new technology, and substituting less skilled for more skilled workers wherever possible. Competition will drive untalented and inefficient lawyers from the practice or they will change their ways. Firms will strive to establish valuable trade names as part of advertising their reputations, and this will induce them to avoid doing anything to harm their image. The market will thus police itself against misrepresentation and bait and switch tactics. In addi-

---

26. Routine and boredom already are part of practice. A survey of ABA members in 1983 showed that only 59% said they would choose law again if given a second chance. "Fourteen percent, including many lawyers 30 or younger, indicated they would like to be doing work that was less routine in nature." See Smith, "A Profile of Lawyer Lifestyles," 70 *A.B.A.J.* 50, 54 (1984). The mass processing involved in highly advertised legal clinics may make practice even more boring.

27. ... Mr. Justice Powell's dissenting opinion in the *Bates* case states most of the arguments against advertising, 433 U.S. at 389–404, and this opinion is relied on by the Royal Commission on Legal Services in the United Kingdom.

28. This morality play can be found in a number of places. For relatively pure versions, uncluttered with qualifications, see Staff of Federal Trade Commission, *supra* n. 9; Greene, "Lawyers versus the Marketplace," *Forbes*, Jan. 16, 1984, at 73.

tion, advertising will expand the market by attracting new clients who have never used lawyers in the past. Advertising opens access to the legal system. Greater access itself will allow efficient lawyers to exploit economies of scale and further reduce costs.

These morality plays, of course, are rhetorical ploys in a political battle among partisans. Both stories seem plausible, reflecting simple common sense. However, both contain elements of truth well mixed with overstatement. Neither side is much troubled by data and complexity. Claims about lawyer advertising are not put forward as part of a neutral exercise, and much is at stake. If we are to appraise the positions, we need to understand the context of the battle. ...

Scholars from various fields have written about lawyer advertising. We can distinguish three kinds of studies: (1) surveys of attitudes of potential clients and lawyers toward attorney advertising; (2) applications of economic analysis; and (3) the Federal Trade Commission's staff's research about the impact of various kinds of regulation of advertising on prices and quality. We have some data and analysis, although far less than we need to resolve the issues these writers raise. We will in turn consider these types of studies critically.

A number of articles report research concerning attitudes about lawyer advertising.[41] Questionnaires administered to more or less random samples of lawyers and consumers can tell us who likes and who dislikes advertising. However, they cannot tell us how much weight to give such things as a lawyer's judgment that it will confuse and mislead consumers. These attitude studies reach predictable conclusions, suggesting that consumers favor lawyer advertising while lawyers do not.

Kallis and Vanier report that 75% of those in a quota sample of 361 adults in Southern California thought lawyers should be free to advertise; 62% did not think that lawyers who advertised did inferior work; and 76% wanted advertisements containing information about specific fees. However, 40% said that advertis-

---

41. *See, e.g.,* Kallis & Vanier, "Consumer Perceptions of Attorney and Legal Service Advertising: A Managerial Approach to the Delivery of Legal Services," 14 *Akron Bus. & Econ.Rev.* 42 (1983); Linenberger & Murdock, "Legal Service Advertising: Wyoming Attorney Attitudes Compared with Consumer Attitudes, 17 *Land & Water L.Rev.* 209 (1982); Smith & Meyer, "Attorney Advertising: A Consumer Perspective," 44 *J. Marketing* 56 (1980); Dyer & Shimp, "Reactions to Legal Advertising, 20 J.Ad.Research 43 (1980); Shimp & Dyer, Now the Legal Profession Views Legal Service Advertising, 42 J. Marketing 74 (1978); Shimp, Ohio Lawyers' Attitudes Toward Legal Service Advertising," 4 *Ohio N.L.Rev.* 576 (1977).

ing would not influence their choice of a lawyer. Only 26%
thought that advertising would give them an opportunity to make
a better selection of one.

Linenberger and Murdock surveyed samples of Wyoming consumers and lawyers in 1981. They tell us that 66% of the lawyers
agreed that advertising created a bad public image for the profession while nearly 80% of the consumers disagreed. 70% of the
consumers thought that advertising would improve the quality of
legal services while 67% of the lawyers disagreed. [Most] lawyers
thought existing sources of information about attorneys were
adequate while 69% of the consumers thought they were inadequate.

Most of these surveys were conducted in the late 1970s or
early 1980s, before the *Bates* decision had much impact. We
cannot be sure of the continued validity of these earlier studies.
Research conducted today or in the future could tap reactions
based on actual experience.

Mitchell suggests that extensive mass media advertising
should be effective in densely populated markets for frequently
required services which can be supplied by low cost, high volume
production methods. Lawyers can advertise other kinds of services in relatively inexpensive telephone directory yellow pages or
newspaper classified sections. This approach is likely to have a
limited, but perhaps important, impact on practice. Some lawyers
may be able to gain clients they otherwise would not have seen.
Consumers who notice lawyer advertising will have some additional information. A potential client can discover, for example, that
a particular lawyer is willing to take bankruptcy or divorce cases.

However, once lawyers begin to advertise in the telephone
directory or newspapers, others are likely to match their efforts.
Consumers often face page after page of lawyer advertisements
that say almost the same thing. There are no meaningful statistics such as a won and lost record, and critics do not publish
reviews of lawyers as they review restaurants and films.[45] Those
who can pay large fees often have better sources of information

---

45. Law directories rate lawyers, but
the rating systems can offer only rough
indicators of quality such as time in
practice, representative clients, and
some suggestion of general reputation
in the local legal community. Sophisticated users of these directories often
use the ratings to exclude some attorneys. Then they consider those left after seeking recommendations from people who know the local bar. Existing
directories would be little help to individuals seeking legal assistance for personal matters. Consumer advocates
could produce directories that would be
helpful to individuals, but it is not clear
that individuals would pay to get this
information. Group legal services
plans, such as those sponsored by unions and cooperatives, may serve to rate
lawyers for members.

about lawyers than advertising. Hazard, Pearce and Stempel point out that advertising is relatively ineffective compared with personal knowledge and reputation. Advertising must be brief, and it comes from an impersonal source. Often readers or viewers pay little attention to it.

Mudec and Trebilcock note that some law firms have tried to establish national trade names. They hope these names will attract potential clients who rely on the firm's reputation as a way of getting quality service. If the trade name were promoted by advertising, it might enable the firm to market complex and costly services. People could rely on getting reasonable quality and price from a firm concerned with its reputation. However, this reputational sanction may work better in long-term continuing relationships than in one-shot deals.

On the other hand, Mudec and Trebilcock speculate that highly advertised second-class lawyering may drive out good lawyering where clients cannot tell what they are getting. "[C]lients will not be able to verify advertised quality claims and lawyers providing better quality will be unable to recoup the high cost of providing higher quality service since clients will not be willing to pay a higher price for a feature of the service which they cannot be sure that they are indeed receiving."[46] Attanasio suggests that the case for advertising usually assumes efforts at standardization so that a given product can be sold for a named price. He argues that the aggregate quality may increase, but standardization also "increases the potential to shortchange individuals whose problems stray far from the norm."[47]

These writers also theorize about the impact of advertising on the legal profession, an impact that ultimately could affect society as well. Mudec and Trebilcock think that the situation may be a zero sum game. Advertising "will principally have the effect of shifting around market shares amongst existing law firms."[48] Hazard, Pearce and Stempel disagree. They state that advertising will increase the total market for legal services by stimulating latent demand.[49] People will learn that they can afford a lawyer and that they need one in situations where they would not now use one. These people will talk about problems, lawyers and the quality of services they received in their social networks. Conversations at taverns or places of employment may pass along a new

---

46. Mudec & Trebilcock, *supra* n. 43, at 74.

47. Attanasio, *supra* n. 1, at 527.

48. Mudec & Trebilcock, *supra* n. 43, at 99.

49. See Becharov & Martle, "Here Come the Mediocre Lawyers," *Wall St. J.*, Feb. 22, 1985, at 26, cols. 3–5.

legal consciousness as well as suggestions about which lawyers to see.

[The] Federal Trade Commission ... measured the impact of restrictions on lawyer advertising imposed by different state laws on the prices charged for five routine legal services. The services were (1) a simple will, (2) a simple will with a trust provision, (3) a non-business bankruptcy, (4) an uncontested divorce, and (5) a personal injury where the driver of the other car admits responsibility and there is no permanent pain, disability or lost earning capacity. Lawyers in seventeen cities in different states were asked what they would charge for each service. The fees asked were transformed to reflect differences in the cost of living in each of the cities. The laws concerning lawyer advertising were classified for restrictiveness, and multiple linear regression analyses were applied to the data. The basic finding of the study was

> [g]enerally, ... restrictions on advertising raise prices. Attorneys in the more restrictive states, *on the average*, charged higher prices for most simple legal services than those in the less restrictive states. The fact that stronger restrictions on advertising are associated with higher prices suggests that, in this type of market, the dominant effect of advertising is to enhance price competition by lowering consumer search costs. (Emphasis added.) [54]

What are we to make of the FTC study? We should read it carefully because it is likely to play a role in debates about lawyer advertising. Its very title—"The Case For Removing Restrictions on Truthful Advertising"—suggests that it is a partisan brief in the form of a scientific study about the impact of restrictions on lawyer advertising on the price of basic legal services.[55] The study does offer evidence of the expected relationship between restriction and price. However, the case is not as clear as the study's conclusions and the press reports about them claim.[56] At the

---

54. *Id.* at 79.

55. We cannot treat the staff report as a scientific study in a referred journal. We must read it carefully, remembering that its authors are not neutrals. The American Bar Association has tried to gain legislation or judicial decisions which would stop the FTC from regulating lawyers. The FTC, in turn, is very critical of what its staff sees as the ABA's attempt to ward off competition in the delivery of legal services. Nevertheless, while the report is a partisan document, some or all of it may be right.

56. Linda Greenhouse reported in the *N.Y. Times*, Dec. 25, 1984, at 22, col. 1, "[a] Federal Trade Commission staff report issued earlier this month was only the latest of numerous studies to conclude that advertising by lawyers brings increased competition and lower prices for legal services.... The researchers found that legal fees for the same services were lower, by 5 to 13 percent, in states with the fewest restrictions on advertising." As we will see, this misreports what the study actually found and ignores many important qualifications. James J. Kilpa-

outset, the sample of cities studied seems strange. The largest cities in the country are omitted. The study does not deal with New York, Los Angeles, Chicago, Philadelphia, Dallas-Ft. Worth or Atlanta. The investigators wanted to match states with different kinds of restrictions on lawyer advertising. However, California is represented by Fresno and not San Francisco, Los Angeles or San Diego. Missouri is represented by Springfield and not St. Louis or Kansas City. A defender of the study could argue that we might expect freedom to advertise to have greater impact in the larger cities where there would be mass markets that could be reached. A critic could object that the study's sample is so far from ideal that its statistical results are suspect.[57]

With one exception,[58] less than a quarter of the lawyers in any city studied advertised at all.[59] Almost none of those who advertised used television or radio. Most used the yellow pages of the telephone directory, a means that is cheap but unlikely to have a powerful effect on fees. Very few of those who did advertise anything stated specific fees that would be charged for particular services. This casts doubt on whether, as the FTC report asserts, the "dominant effect of advertising is to enhance price competition by lowering consumer search costs." [60] Indeed, we can ask how the nature of the state's rules on advertising caused differences in the cost of the five types of legal services studied if so few of the lawyers exercised their freedom to advertise.

Most of the results stressed in the text of the FTC report were based on averages. However, averages can be misleading and difficult to interpret. We often think of an average as typical, but extreme cases can make an average misleading. When we read the FTC study's tables carefully, we see that the presence or absence of advertising restrictions often does not produce the effect predicted by the investigators' theory. At the very least, we must recognize that limiting advertising is not always associated with higher prices for all kinds of work. For example, Table D of

---

trick, the conservative columnist said that the "significant evidence turned up by the FTC study is that prices for five familiar legal services are lower in the less-restrictive states." Kilpatrick, "Lawyer Advertising Drives Prices Down," *Wis.St.J.*, Jan. 16, 1985, § 1, at 9, col. 5. Data reported in the tables of the FTC study do not show this. Kilpatrick was misled by the text of the report.

57. See Bork and Ray, "Selection Biases in Sociological Data," 11 *Soc.Sci. Research* 352 (1982).

58. 37% of the lawyers in Albuquerque advertised.

59. In all but five of the seventeen cities, less than 20% of the lawyers advertised. In the five cities where more lawyers advertised the percentages were Milwaukee 20%, Baltimore 20%, Columbus 21%, Fresno 23%, and Albuquerque 37%.

60. Staff of the Federal Trade Commission, *supra* n. 9, at 79.

the study shows there is a statistically significant relationship between barring direct mail advertising and a *lower* price for a simple will but *higher* prices for divorces and personal injury work.   There is also a statistically significant relationship between limiting the content of advertisements in any way and a *lower* price on simple wills but *higher* prices on personal injury work. Connecticut has very restrictive rules on lawyer advertising. However, the fees of Hartford lawyers for four out of the five services studied are lower than average while the fee for the fifth service is just average.

Furthermore, the lack of restrictions on advertising did not necessarily mean lower prices for all the legal services studied. This was true even where a relatively high percentage of the lawyers advertised.   California, Michigan and Wisconsin were classified by the FTC staff as the three least restrictive states. Fresno is the only California city included in the study.   23% of the lawyers surveyed in Fresno advertised, and this is the second highest percentage in the 17 cities surveyed.   Nonetheless, Fresno has *higher* than average rates for each of the five routine legal services except personal injury.   Also, in Detroit, Michigan, the average rates for wills with trusts, bankruptcy and divorces were lower than the average fees of the 17 cities in the study; however the average fees for simple wills and personal injury were higher. Milwaukee, Wisconsin has above average fees for simple wills and divorces but lower than average fees for a will with a trust and bankruptcy.   The percentage of the award taken under contingent fees in personal injury was 1% lower than average.

The study also compared fees of attorneys in all 17 cities who advertised and fees of those who did not.   Those who advertised a specific service provided it at a lower price than both those lawyers who did not advertise at all and those who advertised but did not mention that particular area of practice.   However, personal injury was the exception.   "In the three cities with statistically significant results for personal injury service, attorneys who advertised personal injury services appeared to charge about a 3 percent higher contingent fee if the case [was] settled before trial than those who did not advertise personal injury services." [61]   In a footnote, the report says

> we have been told by some legal clinics that they expect their other routine services to give them a client base for the more lucrative personal injury case. This would be consistent with

61. Staff of the Federal Trade Commission, *supra* n. 9, at 125.

advertising firms charging less for the other services to attract clients with personal injury cases.[62]

This statement, submerged below the text, undercuts much of the argument made in the body of the FTC report. Perhaps loss leaders do serve consumer interests, but this is a very different argument than that made in the report.

The FTC report argues that advertising allows informed consumers to compare prices and that this tends to push prices downward. However, exceptions to this axiom, found in the study's tables but not stressed in its text, show that it does not always work this way. The causal mechanism is not simple and direct. Competition and somewhat informed consumers may affect the behavior of those marketing any product or service, but suppliers have many options. For example, Americans came to believe that Japanese cars were of higher quality than American ones. American manufacturers could have responded by improving the quality of their cars or advertising so that the public would think that their quality was better. Of course, they did both, and some of us think they did more advertising than engineering. Lawyers, too, will be able to cope with more, but not fully, informed consumers in a number of ways. Lower prices for higher quality work is not necessarily the only option open to them. Indeed, it may be easier for lawyers to create the false impression of quality than it is for automobile manufacturers. Legal services are harder to judge than automobiles that will not operate.

The FTC study attempted to deal with the concern that lower prices would also lower the quality of service. The authors point out that quality is difficult to define since clients may be satisfied with poor service or unhappy with excellent technical lawyering. They speculate that advertising may compensate for any corner-cutting by pressing for new efficient techniques of delivering legal service. Then they rely on Muris and McChesney's[63] study of the Jacoby & Meyers Legal Clinic in Los Angeles.[64] The clinic advertised extensively, and took steps to control costs. The first part of the Muris and McChesney study compared clients' subjective reactions to Jacoby & Meyers' handling of several types of cases with the reactions of others who had used traditional firms for similar cases. Jacoby & Meyers did better than traditional firms on all seven ratings of lawyer quality used. Clients saw it as "more prompt, interested, and honest; as better at explaining matters,

---

62. *Id.* at 125, n. 267.

63. Muris & McChesney, *supra,* n. 43.

64. *See* Sullivan, "The Upstart Lawyers Who Market the Law," *N.Y. Times,* Aug. 26, 1979, § 3 at 1, cols. 1–2.

keeping clients informed, and paying attention to customers; and, finally, as more fair and reasonable in its charges." [65] However, Muris and McChesney sent out 650 questionnaires but only 74 (52 from the traditional firms and 22 from Jacoby & Meyers) were returned in a form that was usable. The authors tell us nothing about the 576 clients who did not respond. While Muris and McChesney's results support their position, clearly we must be cautious about using this part of their study.

The second part of Muris and McChesney's study involved comparing the results obtained by Jacoby & Meyers and by traditional firms in cases where monthly child support payments were at issue. They used multiple regression analysis to estimate the degree to which representation by the clinic influenced the amount of the award as compared with other factors. They thought this was an objective measure of the quality of service. " 'Better service' for the husband would be defined as a lower award of child support, all else being equal, and for the wife as a higher award of child support." [66] They found that clinic representation of the wife increased the per child award, a result significant at the .025 level. "Clinic representation of the husband reduced the monthly payment, though this figure is not significant at a level that statisticians would consider sufficient to conclude that the clinic provides better quality."[67]

The FTC staff recognized the limitations of Muris and McChesney's article. They point to the size of the data base, and they acknowledge that it is a case study of one clinic that had been in existence seven years. We cannot be sure that the positive outcomes were caused by the clinic form and its high volume approach based on advertising. Perhaps those who ran the clinic would have run a traditional law practice in such a way as to produce equally positive results. We do not know that Jacoby & Meyers continued what Muris and McChesney argue was its superior service when they conducted the study. We do not know whether other clinics or other lawyers who advertise but do not organize their practice in the clinic form would do as well. Some might want to debate the measures of quality. For example, we might want to appraise an entire divorce proceeding and not just child support. Child support often is but part of a total solution to the divorcing parties' and children's problems. Nonetheless, the FTC staff insist that the study shows at least that low prices and an elaborate advertising campaign do not necessarily reduce quality. They conclude "there are no other empirical studies of the

65. *Id.* at 198.
66. *Id.* at 202–203.
67. *Id.* at 205.

legal services market which contradict these results." However, since when the Report was written there were no other empirical studies at all, the absence of contradiction does not seem like overwhelming evidence of anything.

IV.   Lawyer Advertising and Problems of Access and Equality before the Law.

Up to this point, I have accepted the way leaders of the bar opposed to lawyer advertising and reformers who advocate it have framed the issues. However, their debate might divert our attention from important problems. Even if advertising leads to delivering conventional legal services that can be standardized to more clients at a reasonable price, major questions of access and equality before the law will remain.

Insofar as it is successful, lawyer advertising may bring the wrong people to attorneys. Some clients might better solve their problems in other ways. The studies talk about the simple will, the consent divorce where there are no children and no issues of property division, and routine personal injury work. But why should lawyers handle these problems in most instances? Advertising legal clinics or cut-rate lawyers may hinder the development of even cheaper kinds of solutions to standardized problems. Today one can buy do-it-yourself books and forms to handle wills and divorces. In a community where adjusters and lawyers settle automobile accidents on a routine basis, many victims could handle the negotiations themselves if information about the rules of the game were available.

If self-help is not appropriate, counselling from non-lawyers might be all that most literate people need. In many nations a person can buy help in filling out forms and taking them to the right place from people lacking the formal training of lawyers. These people charge far less. Legal advertising may work to keep simple matters in the hands of the bar rather than fostering the development of less highly trained people who could handle routine work more cheaply. Law firms and legal clinics delegate more and more work to paralegal workers. This suggests that they are cutting costs by moving problems out of the hands of lawyers and into those of people paid less. But even in these instances, clients probably are paying more than if lawyers were involved only minimally or not at all. Some of the "law store" approaches that have developed in the United States involve kits for such things as divorces or changes of names plus the chance to get advice from lawyers about how to fill out the papers and where to file them.

Advertising may have some impact on access to justice. People may learn just enough to tip the balance and send them to a lawyer. Potential clients can gain at least a little additional information about the kind of person they might hire from advertisements in the telephone directory yellow pages and a little more from television commercials. Sometimes they will sense that they should avoid the lawyer in question. They may learn that lawyers have different personalities and not all are stiff upper-class members of the elite. Advertising also may make the issue of legal advice salient and remind people there are many kinds of legal services available. Furthermore, if a simple divorce is widely advertised as available for $250, this may affect expectations and allow potential clients to make a rough estimate of what their more complex situation might cost. It could limit the fee for a complex divorce. At least, a lawyer who would charge a great deal more might have to convince a client that the increased price is justified by an added degree of complexity.

All of this is highly speculative because we do not know that much about naming, blaming and claiming and how advertising might affect the process.

Indeed, the debate about lawyer advertising may draw our attention from the larger question of access and vindication of rights. Advocates for unrestricted lawyer advertising claim it will lower the prices for lawyers' services in the market. This will solve the problems of access without requiring public subsidy. However, the services made available by increased demand created by advertising will not be the time-consuming counselling and "bargaining in the shadow of the law" that lower-income clients need to cope with public and private bureaucracies. Assuming that lawyer advertising succeeds in delivering low cost wills, uncontested divorces and name changes, we can also ask its advocates to show us what it will do for vindicating the rights found in constitutions and reform legislation.

Lawyer advertising may play some part in enlarging access to legal services. This may provoke more substantive equality in our society. We cannot be sure because we know so little about the transformations involved in processing disputes. We do not know how people decide they need a lawyer and which one to call. We are just beginning to study what happens between lawyer and client when they meet. Advertising may push lawyers to work cheaply rather than doing the job right. However, it is hard to see why advertising will add much to the pressures to cut corners that have long existed. Advertising alone is not likely to push the bar into crass commercialism or produce a nation of rational informed clients seeking to maximize utility. Recognizing this, we must be concerned that largely symbolic debates about lawyer advertising may divert us from concern with more pressing issues of access and equality.

———

REFERENCES

Andrews, "Lawyer Advertising and the First Amendment," 1981 *Am.Bar Found.Research J.* 967.

L. Andrews, *Birth of a Salesman: Lawyer Advertising and Solicitation* (1980).

Federal Trade Commission, *Improving Consumer Access to Legal Services: The Case for Removing Restrictions on Truthful Advertising* (1984).

Ladinsky, "The Traffic in Legal Services: Lawyer Seeking Behavior and the Channeling of Clients," 11 *Law & Soc'y Rev.* 207 (1976).

Moss, *"The Ethics of Law Practice Marketing,"* 61 Notre Dame L.Rev. 601 (1986).

Muris and McChesney, "Advertising and the Price and Quality of Legal Services: The Case for Legal Clinics," 1979 *Am.Bar Found.Research J.* 179.

M. Schwartz & R. Wydick, *Problems in Legal Ethics* 56–57 (1983).

D. Tuerck ed., *The Political Economy of Advertising* (American Enterprise Institute for Public Policy Research, 1978).

CASES

Bates v. State Bar of Arizona, 433 U.S. 350, 97 S.Ct. 2691, 53 L.Ed.2d 810 (1977).

In re R.M.J., 455 U.S. 191, 102 S.Ct. 929, 71 L.Ed.2d 64 (1982).

Princeton Community Phone Book, Inc. v. Bate, 582 F.2d 706 (3d Cir.1978).

In re Burgess, 279 S.C. 44, 302 S.E.2d 325 (1983).

In re Marcus, 107 Wis.2d 560, 320 N.W.2d 806 (1982).

In re Utah State Bar Petition for Approval of Changes in Disciplinary Rules on Advertising, 647 P.2d 991 (Utah 1982).

State ex rel. Oklahoma Bar Association v. Schaffer, 648 P.2d
   355 (Okl.1982).

C. LAY COMPETITION

Milton S. Friedman, Capitalism and Freedom
144–49 (1962).

POLICY ISSUES RAISED BY LICENSURE

It is important to distinguish three different levels of control:
first, registration; second, certification; third, licensing.

By registration, I mean an arrangement under which individuals are required to list their names in some official register if
they engage in certain kinds of activities. There is no provision
for denying the right to engage in the activity to anyone who is
willing to list his name. He may be charged a fee, either as a
registration fee or as a scheme of taxation.

The second level is certification. The governmental agency
may certify that an individual has certain skills but may not
prevent, in any way, the practice of any occupation using these
skills by people who do not have such a certificate. One example
is accountancy. In most states, anybody can be an accountant,
whether he is a certified public accountant or not, but only those
people who have passed a particular test can put the title CPA
after their names or can put a sign in their offices saying they are
certified public accountants. Certification is frequently only an
intermediate stage. In many states, there has been a tendency to
restrict an increasing range of activities to certified public accountants. With respect to such activities there is licensure, not
certification. In some states, "architect" is a title which can be
used only by those who have passed a specified examination. This
is certification. It does not prevent anyone else from going into
the business of advising people for a fee how to build houses.

The third stage is licensing proper. This is an arrangement
under which one must obtain a license from a recognized authority in order to engage in the occupation. The license is more than
a formality. It requires some demonstration of competence or the
meeting of some tests ostensibly designed to insure competence,
and anyone who does not have a license is not authorized to
practice and is subject to a fine or a jail sentence if he does engage
in practice. ...

... Certification [is more difficult than registration] to justify. The reason is that this is something the private market

generally can do for itself. This problem is the same for products as for people's services. There are private certification agencies in many areas that certify the competence of a person or the quality of a particular product. The *Good Housekeeping* seal is a private certification arrangement. For industrial products there are private testing laboratories that will certify to the quality of a particular product. For consumer products, there are consumer testing agencies of which Consumer's Union and Consumer's Research are the best known in the United States. Better Business Bureaus are voluntary organizations that certify the quality of particular dealers. Technical schools, colleges, and universities certify the quality of their graduates. One function of retailers and department stores is to certify the quality of the many items they sell. The consumer develops confidence in the store, and the store in turn has an incentive to earn this confidence by investigating the quality of the items it sells.

One can however argue that in some cases, or perhaps even in many, voluntary certification will not be carried as far as individuals would be willing to pay for carrying it because of the difficulty of keeping the certification confidential. The issue is essentially the one involved in patents and copyrights, namely, whether individuals are in a position to capture the value of the services that they render to others. If I go into the business of certifying people, there may be no efficient way in which I can require you to pay for my certification. If I sell my certification information to one person, how can I keep him from passing it on to others? Consequently, it may not be possible to get effective voluntary exchange with respect to certification, even though this is a service that people would be willing to pay for if they had to. One way to get around this problem, as we get around other kinds of neighborhood effects, is to have governmental certification. ...

Licensure seems to me still more difficult to justify. It goes still farther in the direction of trenching upon the rights of individuals to enter into voluntary contracts. Nonetheless, there are some justifications given for licensure that the liberal will have to recognize as within his own conception of appropriate government action, though, as always, the advantages have to be weighed against the disadvantages. The main argument that is relevant to a liberal is the existence of neighborhood effects. The simplest and most obvious example is the "incompetent" physician who produces an epidemic. Insofar as he harms only his patient, that is simply a question of voluntary contract and exchange between the patient and his physician. On this score, there is no ground for intervention. However, it can be argued that if the physician treats his patient badly, he may unleash an epidemic that will cause harm to third parties who are not involved in the immediate transaction. In such a case, it is conceivable that everybody, including even the potential patient and physician, would be willing to submit to the restriction of the practice of medicine to "competent" people in order to prevent such epidemics from occurring.

In practice, the major argument given for licensure by its proponents is not this one, which has some appeal to a liberal, but rather a strictly paternalistic argument that has little or no appeal. Individuals, it is said, are incapable of choosing their own servants adequately, their own physician or plumber or barber. In order for a man to choose a physician intelligently, he would have to be a physician himself. Most of us, it is said, are therefore incompetent and we must be protected against our own ignorance. This amounts to saying that we in our capacity as voters must protect ourselves in our capacity as consumers against our own ignorance, by seeing to it that people are not served by incompetent physicians or plumbers or barbers.

So far, I have been listing the arguments for registration, certification, and licensing. In all three cases, it is clear that there are also strong social costs to be set against any of these advantages. Some of these social costs have already been suggested and I shall illustrate them in more detail for medicine, but it may be worth recording them here in general form.

The most obvious social cost is that any one of these measures, whether it be registration, certification, or licensure, almost inevitably becomes a tool in the hands of a special producer group to obtain a monopoly position at the expense of the rest of the public. There is no way to avoid this result. One can devise one or another set of procedural controls designed to avert this outcome, but none is likely to overcome the problem that arises out of the greater concentration of producer than of consumer interest. The people who are most concerned with any such arrangement, who will press most for its enforcement and be most concerned with its administration, will be the people in the particular occupation or trade involved. They will inevitably press for the extension of registration to certification and of certification to licensure. Once licensure is attained, the people who might develop an interest in undermining the regulations are kept from exerting their influence. They don't get a license, must therefore go into other occupations, and will lose interest. The result is invariably control over entry by members of the occupation itself and hence the establishment of a monopoly position.

Certification is much less harmful in this respect. If the certified "abuse" their special certificates; if, in certifying new-comers, members of the trade impose unnecessarily stringent requirements and reduce the number of practitioners too much, the price differential between certified and non-certified will become sufficiently large to induce the public to use non-certified practitioners. In technical terms, the elasticity of demand for the services of certified practitioners, will be fairly large, and the limits within which they can exploit the rest of the public by taking advantage of their special position will be rather narrow.

In consequence, certification without licensure is a half-way house that maintains a good deal of protection against monopolization. It also has its disadvantages, but it is worth noting that the usual arguments for licensure, and in particular the paternalistic arguments, are satisfied almost entirely by certification alone. If the argument is that we are too ignorant to judge good practitioners, all that is needed is to make the relevant information available. If, in full knowledge, we still want to go to someone who is not certified, that is our business; we cannot complain that we did not have the information. Since arguments for licensure made by people who are not members of the occupation can be satisfied so fully by certification, I personally find it difficult to see any case for which licensure rather than certification can be justified.

Deborah L. Rhode "The Delivery of Legal Services by Non-lawyers"

4 Georgetown Journal of Legal Ethics 209 (1990).

The last half-century has witnessed a rapid growth in the lay practice of law and a gradual decline in the legal profession's campaign against it. While competition from non-lawyers has increased, the organized bar has become less willing and able to restrain their activities. Recent developments, particularly in California, open possibilities for new approaches toward the unauthorized practice of law that will better serve the public interest. The following discussion surveys these developments within a broader social, economic, and political context and identifies considerations that should guide policy in this area.

I. THE HISTORICAL BACKGROUND

Although the organized bar has always justified its campaign against lay competitors in terms of public protection, the historical record suggests that other, somewhat less altruistic forces have been at work. Before the Depression, little attention focused on the grave threat to consumers that unauthorized practice subsequently has been said to pose. . . .

During the Depression, the profession's concern with lay competitors grew dramatically, although available evidence discloses no corresponding consumer sentiment. The American Bar Association appointed its first Committee on Unauthorized Practice of Law in 1930. By the close of the decade, more than 400 state and local associations had established similar bodies with educational, legislative, and enforcement responsibilities. During this period, many jurisdictions enacted or broadened unauthorized practice statutes. In addition, bar associations at the national, state, and local levels entered into formal "statements of principles" with individuals in competing occupations, including accountants, bankers, claims adjustors, law book publishers, real estate agents, and insurance brokers. . . .

These principles became the bar's preferred method of reconciling conflicts between "professions on the prowl" for new markets. Jurisdictional agreements also served as a means of delimiting the broad and indeterminate reach of unauthorized practice prohibitions.

II. Doctrinal Frameworks

State supreme courts generally have asserted control over lay legal services under their "inherent" power to regulate the practice of law. However, the judiciary has usually permitted legislative initiatives that are consistent with its own authority.

Slightly more than two-thirds of the states have statutes specifying unauthorized practice as a misdemeanor; others regard it as contempt of court. About fifteen jurisdictions prohibit without defining legal practice. Others employ a circular definition: the practice of law is what lawyers do. A third approach is to list activities that constitute legal practice, such as legal advice, representation, and preparation of legal documents. This latter strategy does not significantly restrict coverage, given the inclusive reach of terms such as "legal advice."

The American Bar Association's ethical standards add little clarity to these provisions. The *ABA Model Code of Professional Responsibility* maintains that it is "neither necessary nor desirable to attempt the formulation of a single specific definition of the practice of law." *Model Code* provisions then confirm this admonition by offering a formulation that verges on tautology: "Functionally, the practice of law relates to the rendition of services that call for the professional judgment of a lawyer." The *ABA Model Rules of Professional Conduct* avoid definitional problems by avoiding definition. They note simply that the meaning of the "practice of law is established by law and varies from one jurisdiction to another. Whatever the definition, limiting the practice of law to members of the bar protects the public against the rendition of legal services by unqualified persons." How well, and at what cost, are questions that remain unacknowledged and unaddressed.

Prevailing unauthorized practice rules encompass a sweeping array of common commercial activity. Many individuals, including accountants, bankers, real estate brokers, insurance agents, and title and trust officers, cannot provide competent services without referring to legal concerns.

In response to these realities, some courts have carved out a series of exceptions to broad statutory prohibitions. Such exceptions are steps in a desirable direction; however, as the discussion in Part VI of this article will suggest, none are sufficiently extensive to serve the public interest. The most common approaches are to exempt lay legal practice that is widespread in the community, that is incidental to another established business, or that involves only routine tasks requiring knowledge of an average citizen. The first two exceptions, however, are not directly responsive to the concerns about lay competence that have traditionally served to justify unauthorized practice prohibitions. Rather, as one consumer advocate suggested, such approaches seem little more than a "rationalization for territorial truces between the warring professions." Although the exception for routine services is more obviously related to competence, it permits a regulatory structure that is both under- and over-inclusive. By focusing on the nature of the task rather than the skills of the provider, this approach fails adequately to acknowledge consumer concerns. Typically, courts determine what tasks are beyond an average individual's grasp without reference to any evidence that offending practitioners have only average knowledge or that the public has been harmed by their activities.

[However, certain recent trends in the market for legal services have prompted limited liberalization in traditional unauthorized practice doctrine....]

III. THE INCREASED MARKET FOR LAY LEGAL SERVICES

The judiciary's increasing tolerance for lay competition reflects and reinforces broader social trends. Over the last quarter century, a number of forces have converged to encourage such competition, especially by form-preparation services. The rise in consumer awareness and organization has expanded the market for self-help assistance in general and *pro se* legal services in particular. Simplification of various procedures, such as those involving uncontested divorces and uncomplicated estates, have provided further impetus for lay assistance. By the late 1980s in certain surveyed California counties, the proportion of *pro se* filings ranged from 39% to 62% of family law cases, 14% to 34% of landlord tenant cases, and 10% to 34% of bankruptcies. In one of these counties, an estimated 70% to 80% of *pro se* divorce cases relied on form-preparation services.

[Republican] administrations' dramatic curtailment of subsidized legal aid ... fueled the demand for low-cost providers. Despite increasing innovations by the bar—including high-volume clinics, group legal service programs, and *pro bono* support structures—substantial portions of the public have been priced out of the market for private practitioners and left ineligible for subsidized alternatives. As subsequent discussion will suggest, the high percentage of unmet civil legal needs is a matter of critical national concern.

Other trends have encouraged non-lawyers to respond to this unmet demand. An increasing specialization in legal work, coupled with a growing reliance on paralegals and routinized case-processing systems, undercuts some of the traditional competence-related justifications for banning lay competitors. Law school and bar exam requirements provide no guarantee of expertise in areas where the need for low-cost services is greatest: divorce, landlord/tenant disputes, bankruptcy, immigration, welfare claims, tax preparation, and real estate transactions. In many of these contexts, secretaries or paralegals working for a lawyer already perform a large share of routine services, and this experience has equipped a growing number of employees to branch out on their own.

Administrative agencies also increasingly support non-lawyer assistance. A 1984 ABA survey of 33 federal agencies found that the overwhelming majority permitted lay representatives in both adversarial and non-adversarial procedures. Although lay advocacy reportedly was infrequent, few agencies cited any problems with misconduct or inability to meet acceptable standards.

[Other forms of lay practice have become an increasingly divisive question because they arise within an increasingly divided bar.]

At issue are competing concerns about the profession's profits, public image, commitment to consumer protection, and desire to increase access to legal services. In this context, it is not surprising that different bars with different internal politics have developed different unauthorized practice policies, and that bar leaders have generally seen little to gain from open evaluation of those policies.

In the absence of systematic data, the effects of unauthorized practice enforcement patterns on lay practitioners are difficult to gauge. As long as criminal penalties remain on the books and bar committees or other agencies engage in some oversight, the market for non-lawyer providers will remain restricted. The question that the profession needs to confront is whether those restrictions effectively serve its own or the public's interests.

V. CALIFORNIA AS A CASE STUDY

The California Bar has recently begun to focus on lay legal services, and its experience may provide interesting lessons concerning the future of enforcement policy. The issue arose in the mid–1980s, after the state bar disbanded its unauthorized practice committee and began referring all complaints to local law enforcement agencies. In 1985, a committee of the Los Angeles Bar Association called on the state Board of Bar Governors to take "immediate and drastic action" against a rising trend of unauthorized practice. By a 10–9 vote, the board created a Public Protection Committee, composed of four lawyers and four non-lawyers. Its mission was to determine whether public harm would be likely to result from lay practice, whether such harm would be substantial enough to warrant regulation, and what form such regulation should take.

The Committee recommended a registration system for non-lawyer "legal technicians" in certain areas where demand for routine services was greatest. Opposition from bar membership prompted appointment of a new Commission on Legal Technicians consisting of three lawyers, two judges, two non-lawyer providers of law-related services, and one member of the Department of Consumer Affairs. The Commission's mandate was to determine "guidelines for legal technicians which will ensure the protection of the public, including standards for their training, licensing, and regulation, the entity which should be responsible for their regulation, and the areas of practice and scope of tasks, if any, which they may carry out."

While the Commission on Legal Technicians was deliberating, HALT, in consultation with the bar disciplinary monitor and other experts, drafted a legislative proposal. Under its provisions, an independent commission would establish a regulatory structure for legal technicians.

This Board would have authority to identify substantive practice areas in which legal technicians could perform services under a licensing or registration structure. The statute lists 14 areas for consideration and specifies certain factors to guide the Board's assessment: "the likelihood of irreparable harm to consumers, the ability of consumers to evaluate the quality of the legal technician's work, the ease with which mistakes can be corrected, and ... consumers' interest in affordable costs ... [balanced against] consumers' interest in competent services."

Under the proposed statute, applications for licensure or registration would be available to individuals over age 18 who had not been disbarred or had not resigned with charges pending from any state bar. Licenses would be granted on successful completion of a practice-oriented exam, and renewal would be predicated on compliance with any other periodic reexamination or recertification requirements. The legislation also includes various other consumer protections including disclosure requirements, mandatory written contract provisions, a customer compensation fund, and extensive procedures for identifying, conciliating, and adjudicating complaints.

The California State Bar Commission on Legal Technicians recommended more limited regulatory reforms. In formulating its proposal, the Commission collected information from various sources. Most of those responding to a survey of bar association sections and committees opposed any provision of legal services by non-lawyers. Advisory groups in bankruptcy, family law, and landlord-tenant law stressed the significant risk of injuries from lay practice and the difficulty of protecting consumers given the limitations of resources among both victims and government enforcement officials. However, the Commission also compiled data concerning significant unmet legal needs and substantial cost advantages for consumers. The average price for a lawyer-assisted bankruptcy or uncontested divorce ranged between $600 to $900, while non-lawyer practitioners charged an average of $200 for such services. Surveys of organizations providing assistance to low-income groups also disclosed that less than 10% of respondents were aware of injuries among individuals who had been referred to lay services.

The Commission proposed licensing technicians in three areas—family law, landlord-tenant law, and bankruptcy—and listed several other specialties as "worthy of study" in the future, such as estate and probate work, government benefits, small business incorporation, and adoption/guardianship/name change services. Under the Commission's scheme, regulatory authority would rest with the Director of the Department of Consumer Affairs, an executive administrator, and a seven-member committee consisting of two licensed paralegals, one member of the bar, and four members of the general public. Regulations for the licensing system would be promulgated by the Director and subject to approval by the California Supreme Court. Like its predecessor, that proposal also generated substantial controversy.

[After this article was published, the California Board of Bar Governors in August 1991 defeated a pilot program for a bar-controlled board that would license legal technicians in one area, landlord-tenant law. Unlike earlier actions, the vote was not accompanied by a recommendation for further study. Those voting against the proposal included proponents of licensure who had lost earlier battles to expand the pilot program and reduce bar control.]

VI. Policy Alternatives

Any evaluation of policy alternatives should begin with a recognition of the fundamental values at issue. Restricting lay legal services implicates free speech and due process interests. Such restrictions affect non-lawyers' ability to convey information and the public's opportunity to receive it. As the Supreme Court has long recognized in other contexts, the right to sue and defend "is the right conservative of all other rights," and would often be of little value if it did not encompass access to legal assistance. Such access is necessary to ensure governmental legitimacy, protect fundamental interests, promote procedural fairness, and [offer opportunities for parties to] "have their wills 'counted' in societal decisions."

Unauthorized practice prohibitions that restrict such opportunities are of special concern in this society, given the high cost and unequal distribution of legal services. The United States spends more on legal services per capita than any other nation, but provides less civil legal aid than other countries with comparable legal systems. According to one representative survey, half of the time lawyers devote to individual clients serves those with incomes in the top 15% of the population; only 10% of American attorneys' time is devoted to those in the bottom third.

Such distributional patterns leave a wide array of unmet legal needs. Although methods for assessing such needs are inherently inexact, several recent surveys give some sense of the dimensions of the problem. One national sample of low-income households found that 43% of respondents experienced legal difficulties in the last year. For about 50% of those problems, no legal services were available. Several state studies have reached similar conclusions. Major reasons for not consulting an attorney were cost and lack of knowledge about how to obtain assistance. Another national study cutting across all income groups also found that surveyed individuals do not seek lawyers' help for between 29% and 40% of their personal legal needs. Unsurprisingly, cost is the greatest barrier to use of legal services, and it disproportionately restricts access among individuals of limited means.

A significant proportion of unmet need falls into areas where lay practitioners have been active, such as divorce and estate work. For low-income populations, increased assistance is particularly necessary on issues involving medical services, public benefits, utilities, family concerns, discrimination, consumer affairs, and housing. Some of these areas hold potential for greater lay involvement, although modifying unauthorized practice prohibitions is not a substitute for adequate government subsidies, *pro bono* services, or simplification of legal procedures. Rather, restricting the profession's monopoly should be seen as part of an overall strategy for expanding access to legal assistance.

Given the strong constitutional and policy concerns at issue, restraints on lay practice should meet the test generally applicable to commercial speech: restrictions must serve substantial state interests that cannot be more narrowly achieved. Similarly, antitrust immunity should only be available for measures that reflect a specific judgment by the state's highest court that anti-competitive practices serve public interests.

To meet these standards, unauthorized practice policy should be guided by certain general considerations. Regulatory standards should vary in light of the complexity of tasks involved and the range of education, training, and experience necessary to complete them. The extent of regulation should bear a close relationship to the demonstrable harms of lay practice. Relevant considerations should include those set forth in the proposed California legislation, primarily cost and the risk of irreparable consumer harm. The less able clients are to assess that risk, the greater the need for some regulatory mechanism to insure minimum performance standards.

From this perspective, the traditional rationale for unauthorized practice constraints—protection of the public from incompetent and unethical services—cannot support the scope of current prohibitions. Although the risk to consumers should not be overlooked, it has been too often overstated. As noted earlier, in many contexts where lay services are prevalent, certification as a lawyer is neither a necessary nor sufficient guarantee of competence.

Attorneys who lack experience in a particular substantive area may be less able to provide cost-effective routine services than experienced legal technicians. For example, the limited research available in contexts such as real estate sales, administrative agency appearances, or *pro se* divorces does not reflect greater evidence of incompetence among non-lawyers than among lawyers. Not only are consumer complaints infrequent, the only survey on customer satisfaction found higher rates of satisfaction with assistance from lay specialists than from lawyers. So too, significant problems are not apparent in many foreign countries that permit non-attorneys to give legal advice and that relegate specialized legal tasks to occupational groups with less formal education than lawyers.

Concerns about incompetent or unethical assistance also can be addressed by measures short of prohibiting all lay practice. Simplification of legal procedures, more effective consumer complaint mechanisms, provision of special assistance in court clerks' offices, public legal education programs, and *pro se* clinics could facilitate self-representation and non-lawyer services. Lay practitioners also could be held to the same standards of ethical conduct as attorneys regarding competence, confidentiality, and conflicts of interest, and could be subject to licensing or registration requirements.

Analysis of alternative regulatory frameworks should distinguish between occupations that already are subject to licensing systems and occupations that are not. As to the bar's licensed competitors, it is time to recognize reality and modify current prohibitions in light of actual practices. Groups such as accountants, real estate brokers, and insurance agents are necessarily involved in legal work, and no evidence suggests that their performance has been less satisfactory than that of lawyers. For the most part, prohibitions against their out-of-court assistance could be eliminated with relatively little risk of public injury.

With respect to currently unlicensed occupations, states should permit greater opportunities for practice by non-lawyer specialists. If significant problems arise under such a framework, measures short of categorical bans on lay services bear consideration, such as mandatory malpractice insurance or minimum qualifications. Special safeguards may be appropriate for areas such as immigration services, where many clients are unfamiliar with legal norms, and are unable or unwilling to invoke official complaint procedures.

However, with the exception of immigration assistance, it makes sense to resolve doubts in favor of less restrictive requirements and to give registration systems an adequate test before instituting licensing systems. Existing certification procedures for paralegals and for lawyers under state or bar specialty programs have not attracted widespread support. Nor have they been systematically evaluated to determine whether their cost is justified by demonstrable improvements in quality. Experts on occupational licensure in other contexts also have generally concluded that most regulatory structures are too restrictive. Almost invariably, the impetus for licensing has come from the group to be licensed rather than aggrieved consumers, and too much protection from competing service providers has been available. In light of this experience, the rationale for anti-competitive constraints should be demonstrated, not merely asserted.

Finally, and most critically, control over regulatory structures should rest with groups other than those regulated or their direct competitors. No matter how well-intentioned, no vocational group can be sufficiently disinterested in areas where its own status is at issue. Although lawyers inevitably will be involved in the regulatory process as judges, legislators, or enforcement officials, the organized bar should neither dictate policy nor determine the membership of bodies that will. Again, the recently proposed California legislation offers a useful model of an independent oversight board. Such a structure could ensure broader representation of public interests than that possible under current regulatory systems. Such a board need not be subject to courts' supervision in order to respect their "inherent powers" to regulate legal practice. Defensible interpretations of the inherent-powers doctrine permit legislative and administrative initiatives that do not impair judicial functions. Courts have long tolerated statutory regulation of lay practice, and the reforms proposed here could further judicial interests by expanding access to justice and improving the quality of *pro se* filings. Since judges generally lack the time, expertise, and objectivity to provide appropriate oversight of lay practitioners, little would be gained by placing their regulation under nominal court supervision.

Historically, unauthorized practice enforcement has been dominated by the group least able to pass disinterested judgment on its merits. The point was recently illustrated after the ABA Commission on Professionalism advocated modest liberalization of unauthorized practice rules. With exceptional candor, the Chair of the ABA's General Practice Section Committee on Professionalism responded that "[i]n an era of significant lawyer unemployment and under employment, it makes no sense to turn the practice of law over to unsupervised paralegals, however limited their license may be." In an era of overwhelming public need for low-cost legal services, however, it makes even less sense for attorneys to police their own competitors under frameworks more responsive to professional self-interest than societal interests.

Throughout the bar's history, many lawyers have led campaigns to broaden the distribution of legal services. The challenge now is to make unauthorized practice policy responsive to the profession's most, not its least, distinguished traditions.

REFERENCES: UNAUTHORIZED PRACTICE

Apsan "Assisting the Pro Se Litigant: Unauthorized Practice of Law or Fulfillment of a Public Need?," 28 *N.Y.U.L.Rev.* 691 (1983).

California State Bar, *Report of the Public Protection Committee* (1988).

Cavanagh and Rhode, "The Unauthorized Practice of Law and Pro Se Divorce: An Empirical Analysis", 86 Yale L.J. 104 (1976).

Christensen, "The Unauthorized Practice of Law: Do Good Fences Really Make Good Neighbors—Or Even Good Sense?," 1980 *Am. Bar Found. Research J.* 159.

Halt, *Challenges to the Lawyer Monopoly* (1988).

J. Lieberman, *The Tyranny of the Experts* (1970).

Marden, "The American Bar and Unauthorized Practice," 33 *Unauthorized Practice News* 1 (1967).

Ostry, "Competition Policy and the Self-Regulating Professions," in *The Professions and Public Policy* 19 (P. Slayton & M. Trebicock, eds., 1978).

Rhode, "Policing the Professional Monopoly: A Constitutional and Empirical Analysis of Unauthorized Practice Prohibitions," 34 *Stan.L.Rev.* 1 (1989).

CASES

Florida Bar v. Brumbaugh, 355 So.2d 1186, 1189 (Fla.1978).

Florida Bar v. Furman, 376 So.2d 378 (Fla.1979).

State Bar v. Arizona Land Title and Trust Co., 90 Ariz. 76, 366 P.2d 1 (1961), supplemented 91 Ariz. 293, 371 P.2d 1020 (1962).

II. THE DISTRIBUTION AND REDISTRIBUTION OF LEGAL SERVICES

INTRODUCTION

Although there are widely reported laments that we have too much law and too little justice, there is considerably less agreement about what precisely we ought to do about it, and in particular, whether attorneys figure more in the problem or the solution. While general diagnoses of "the problem" abound, meaningful prescriptions are less forthcoming. Among serious scholars, most of the critical issues remain in dispute. Whether America is in fact experiencing a bout of hyperlexis is not entirely clear.[1] Nor is it evident that delegalization is a uniformly desirable response; much depends on the context and targets of alternative dispute resolution.[2]

To some critics, the crucial issue is not simply the amount of legal process but its distribution. While wealthier sectors of society complain of inundation by lawyers, the lower sectors are barely serviced. As Mark Galanter has noted, that allocation of legal assistance magnifies the advantages of the "haves" over the "have nots;" those who can afford counsel have greater latitude to pick their issues, shape their transactions, and exhaust their adversaries.[3] The costs and difficulties of equalizing access to justice remain substantial. Like other distributive issues, the form and extent of public subsidies for legal services have proved highly divisive.

Such subsidies raise issues not only of resource priorities but also of social ideals. To what extent should public policy encourage translation of social grievances into legal claims? Under what

1. *Compare* Ehrlich, "Legal Pollution," *New York Times Mag.* Feb. 2, 1976; Manning, "Hyperlexis: Our National Disease," 71 *Nw.U.L.Rev.* 767 (1977), *with* L. Friedman, *Total Justice* (Russell Sage, 1985) and M. Galanter, *infra.*

2. *Compare* J. Auerbach, *Justice Without Law?* (1983); Abel, "The Contradictions of Informal Justice" in 1 R. Abel, *The Politics of Informal Justice* 267 (1982), *with* Smith, "A Warmer Way of Disputing: Mediation and Conciliation," 26 *Am.J.Comp.L.* 205 (Supp. 1978); Rosenberg, "Let's Everybody Litigate?" 50 *Tex.L.Rev.* 1349 (1972). For an overview of these issues *see* D. Trubek, "Turning Away From Law," 1984 *Wis.L.Rev.* 824.

3. Galanter, "Why the Haves Come Out Ahead: Speculations on the Limits of Legal Change," 9 *Law & Soc'y Rev.* 95 (1974).

circumstances will that translation prove an efficient means of resolving disputes, protecting principles, or catalyzing collective action? In what contexts will it exacerbate conflict, impose excessive costs, or deflect attention from more fundamental structural problems?

A. THE NATURE OF "THE PROBLEM:" TOO MANY LAWYERS OR TOO LITTLE JUSTICE?

Derek C. Bok, "A Flawed System of Law Practice and Training"
33 Journal of Legal Education 570, 571–74, 577–80 (1983).

One-half of our difficulty lies in the burdens and costs of our tangle of laws and legal procedures. Contrary to popular belief, it is not clear that we are a madly litigious society. It is true that we have experienced a rapid growth in the number of complaints filed in our courts. But filings are often only a prelude to some kind of voluntary settlement. The number of disputes *actually litigated* in the United States does not appear to be rising much faster than the population as a whole. Our courts may *seem* crowded, since we have relatively few judges compared with many industrial nations. Nevertheless, our volume of litigated cases is not demonstrably larger in relation to our total population than that of other western nations.

At the same time, the complexity of litigation seems to be increasing. Even if a case is settled without trial, preliminary motions and discovery procedures may occupy much time of judges and attorneys. Moreover, the country has experienced a marked growth in statutes and administrative regulations; the number of federal agencies jumped from twenty to seventy in the last two decades while the pages of federal regulations tripled in the 1970s alone. Paralleling these trends, the supply of lawyers has doubled since 1960 so that the United States now boasts the largest number of attorneys per thousand population of any major industrialized nation—three times as many as in Germany, ten times the number in Sweden, and a whopping twenty times the figure in Japan. In sum, though there may not be more court cases, the country has more legal work to do and many more attorneys to do it. Just what society pays for this profusion of law is hard to guess. Lloyd Cutler has put the figure at $30 billion a year, but the truth is that no one has bothered to find out. Be that as it may, legal costs are primarily people costs, and if we mark the growth in the total number of lawyers and the average compensation of attorneys, it is clear that legal expenditures have been climbing more rapidly than the gross national product for many years.

Is it wrong to spend so much on legal services? After all, people pay a lot for underarm deodorants, television soap operas, liquor, and drugs. If rules are passed by elected representatives and legal expenses are voluntarily incurred, is it clear that the nation is spending "too much" on law?

The catch in this argument, of course, is the quiet assumption that rules and regulations are all freely chosen through something akin to a market process. In fact, that is far from being the case. All lawsuits are heavily subsidized by the government and are usually desired by only one party to the dispute. Many rules are the work of judges or bureaucrats over whom the general public has little control. Although the public may support the general outlines of a statute, its details and complexities are rarely understood, let alone endorsed, by the average voter. Most of our laws and administrative regulations have been complicated by the efforts of pressure groups and lobbyists. Even legislation widely approved when enacted often proves unexpectedly cumbersome and ineffective, yet efforts at reform quickly die from inertia or from the opposition of vested interests. ...

If these observations are even half true, our legal system leads to much waste of money that could be put to better purposes. But even greater costs result from the heavy use of human talent. Not only does the law absorb many more young people in America than in any other industrialized nation: it attracts an unusually large proportion of the exceptionally gifted. The average College Board scores of the top 2,000 or 3,000 law students easily exceed those of their counterparts entering other graduate schools and occupations, with the possible exception of medicine. ...

The net result of these trends is a massive diversion of exceptional talent into pursuits that often add little to the growth of the economy, the pursuit of culture, or the enhancement of the human spirit. I cannot press this point too strongly. As I travel around the country looking at different professions and institutions, I am constantly struck by how complicated many jobs have become, how difficult many institutions are to administer, how pressing are the demands for more creativity and intelligence. However aggressive our schools and colleges are in searching out able young people and giving them a good education, the supply of exceptional people is limited. Yet far too many of these rare individuals are becoming lawyers at a time when the country cries out for more talented business executives, more enlightened public servants, more inventive engineers, more able high school principals and teachers.

These points may seem carping or conjectural, but they are not without tangible effects. A nation's values and problems are mirrored in the ways in which it uses its ablest people. In Japan, a country only half our size, 30 percent more engineers graduate each year than in all the United States. But Japan boasts a total of less than 15,000 lawyers, while American universities graduate 35,000 *every year*. It would be hard to claim that these differences have no practical consequences. As the Japanese put it, "Engineers make the pie grow larger; lawyers only decide how to carve it up."

The elaborateness of our laws and the complexity of our procedures absorb the energies of this giant bar, raise the cost of legal services, and help produce the other great problem of our legal system—the lack of access for the poor and middle class. The results are embarrassing to behold. Criminal defendants are herded through the courts at a speed that precludes individual attention, leaving countless accused to the mercy of inexperienced counsel who determine their fate in hasty plea bargaining with the prosecution. On the civil side, the cost of hiring a lawyer and the mysteries of the legal process discourage most people of modest means from trying to enforce their rights. Every study of common forms of litigation, such as medical malpractice, tenant evictions, or debt collections, reveals that for each successful suit there are several others that could be won if the victims had the money and the will to secure a lawyer.

Congress has tried to address this problem by creating the Legal Services Corporation. But even in its palmiest days, the corporation was only empowered to help the poor and had money enough to address but a small fraction of the claims of this limited constituency. Since then, its budget has been cut severely. Middle-income plaintiffs often find that legal expenses eat up most of the amounts that they recover. In personal injury claims, contingent fees may help surmount the cost barrier, but legal expenses consume a third or more of the average settlement in most proceedings and can often rise to 50 percent in cases going to trial. As many observers have testified, the costs and delays of our system force countless victims to accept inadequate settlements or to give up any attempt to vindicate their legal rights.

This state of affairs has become so familiar that it evokes little concern from most of those who spend their lives in the profession. As I visit in different cities, however, and talk to laymen in other walks of life, these problems loom so large as virtually to blot out every other feature of the legal system. The blunt, inexcusable fact is that this nation, which prides itself on efficiency and justice, has developed a legal system that is the most expensive in the world, yet cannot manage to protect the rights of most of its citizens.

... The problems just described might be contained if our legal system authorized someone to keep watch and make sure that the process as a whole is meeting the needs of those whom it purportedly serves. Unfortunately, such oversight and coordination do not exist. In principle, the legislature could exercise this authority, but it does so only occasionally and in a political environment that severely limits what can be done. Thus, power is divided among countless jurisdictions and tribunals, each intent upon the isolated fragments of human conflict that come before it. No one feels responsible for the operation of the entire system or worries whether the different parts fit together in a coordinated whole.

This environment produces a special kind of justice. It leads officials to exaggerate the law's capacity to produce social change while underestimating the cost of establishing rules that can be enforced effectively throughout the society. Since laws seem deceptively potent and cheap, they multiply quickly. Though most of them may be plausible in isolation, they are often confusing and burdensome in the aggregate, at least to those who have to take them seriously. Contrary to the views of left-wing scholars, the results are not simply a form of exploitation to oppress poor, defenseless people, the wealthy and the powerful also chafe under the burden. For established institutions, in particular, the typical result is a stifling burden of regulations, delays, and legal uncertainties that inhibit progress and allow unscrupulous parties to misuse the law to harass and manipulate their victims. For those of modest means, however, the results are even more dispiriting. Laws and procedural safeguards may proliferate, but they are of scant use to those who cannot afford a lawyer. All too often the ultimate effect is to aggravate costs and delays that deny legal protection to large majorities of the population. ...

Devising adequate remedies for this predicament will be extremely difficult. But certain points seem clear. To begin with, there is no single solution for our problems. ...

An effective program will require not only multiple efforts but a mixture that involves attempts to simplify rules and procedures as well as measures that give greater access to the poor and middle class. Access without simplification will be wasteful and expensive; simplification without access will be unjust.

A program embodying these principles will include initiatives along a number of lines already described. Lawmakers will need to adopt no-fault car insurance everywhere and extend the no-fault concept to new fields of liability. Legislatures will have to take a hard look at provisions for treble damages and other artificial incentives that stimulate litigation. Agency officials will want to mount a broad review of existing laws to simplify rules and eliminate regulations that do not serve a demonstrable public purpose. These efforts at simplification must be accompanied by larger appropriations to make legal counsel available to the poor. But money alone will not suffice. In cases involving debtors and creditors, landlords and tenants, and other disputes that touch the lives of ordinary folk, judges will have to develop less costly ways of resolving disputes, since expensive adversary trials ultimately deny access, and therefore justice, to countless deserving people. Likewise, lawyers will need to devise new institutions to supply legal services more cheaply. Such changes, in turn, will undoubtedly force the organized bar to reexamine traditional attitudes toward fee-for-service and the unauthorized practice of law. ...

In addition, judges, lawmakers, scholars will all have to recognize that our conception of the role of law has fallen into disrepair. In its place, they will need to search for a new understanding that is no less sensitive to injustice but more realistic in accounting for the limits and costs of legal rules in ordering human affairs in such a world, the law may seem enlightened and humane, but its constant stream of rules will leave a wake strewn with the disappointed hopes of those who find the legal system too complicated to understand, too quixotic to command respect, and too expensive to be of much practical use.

Marc Galanter, "Law Abounding: Legislation Around the North Atlantic"
55 *Modern Law Review* 1 (1992).

A few years ago a New Yorker cartoon depicted a young woman, seated on a sofa, legs crossed, responding to a suitor on bended knee before her who had, we gather, just proposed marriage. Her reply was: 'Interesting. Have your lawyer call my lawyer.' This epitomises an uncomfortable sense that the world has been legalised—that our world of primal experience has been penetrated, permeated, colonised and somehow diminished by a derivative and unprofitable layer of the legal. This unease—and recoil—manifests itself in many ways, from the wry reflection of our New Yorker cartoon to the concerns about the legal explosion, excessive litigation, and the liability crisis to recondite anxieties about the 'bureaucratisation of the world,' the 'juridification of social spheres' and 'the colonisation of the life-world.'

Although the 'rule of law' is praised as a good and noble thing, this excess of law is thought to produce—or at least accompany—a host of bads: palpable bads like high insurance rates, inefficiency and discouragement of product innovation. And beyond that, larger and more diffuse bads: atomisation, fragmentation, the decline of community, homogenisation and the decline of diversity, the loss of spontaneity, dignity and self-reliance.

Enlargement of the Legal World

[The article begins by describing the growth in law, lawyers, legal studies and legal doctrine. For example, in the United States, between 1960 and 1985:

the amount of the Gross National Product derived from legal services more than doubled;

the number of pages added annually to the *Federal Register* increased from 14,477 to 53,480;

the space devoted to state judicial opinions in *West Reporters* grew from 63 volumes and 61,097 pages to 127 volumes with 151,863 pages (a 149% increase in pages);

the number of general law reviews grew from 65 to 185, and specialized reviews grew from 6 to 140.

Technological innovations have also made such legal materials more accessible and have increased the amount and pace of their circulation. Personal computers, fax machines, on-line data services, e mail, and overnight delivery services have significantly altered and accelerated the structure of practice.]

More Litigation

During this period there has been more litigation. Total civil filings in the US federal courts grew from 59,284 in 1960 to 273,670 in 1985. Comparable figures for the state courts are not available, but a sense of the growth of state judicial activity can be gathered from the increase in lawyers employed by state courts, from 7,581 in 1960 to 18,674 in 1985.

. . .

Close examination of available data suggests a moderate and modulated rather than a feverish and unrestrained use of litigation. Wary of risks, delays and costs, litigants do not act as if propelled by an unappeasable urge for contest or public vindication. The world of litigation is composed of varied populations of cases, whose rise and fall reflects not global changes in the proclivity to litigate, but such specific factors as the number, concentration or diffusion of the injuries or troubles in question, the presence or absence of other ways of dealing with these troubles, the availability of information about legal remedies, and the development of lawyer expertise. Specific types of litigation decline while others rise. Thus, Kagan shows that debt litigation in the United States has not kept pace with the increase in the underlying activity. In the midst of the vaunted litigation explosion, the world of product liability claims (apart from asbestos) has been shrinking steadily since the mid–1980s. The careers of these changing populations cumulate into major changes in the make-up of court caseloads.

The shifting patterns of filings seem to reflect a general but uneven spread of higher expectations of justice and the growth of a sense of entitlement to protection from, or recompense for, many kinds of injury. But this sense is not self-activating, and its growth does not in itself sufficiently account for the patterns of court use. Its translation into litigation depends on the values and resources of claimants, and on the remedial options available to them. These in turn reflect changes in the wider institutional context in which disputes arise.

. . .

Laments about the litigation explosion in the United States typically blame the excess of litigation on individual claimants, often egged on by aggressive plaintiffs' lawyers. Little notice is taken that an increasing portion of this litigation involves businesses and large law firms. More frequently than before, companies are targets of civil rights, wrongful discharge and product liability claims. Less visibly, but as importantly, they have become more frequent and more aggressive users of the legal system in disputes arising from their dealings with one another. This is marked in the surge of contract, intellectual property and other business cases in the US federal courts. An increasing number of business disputes are not being resolved among the parties in the informal style that Stewart Macaulay described in the early 1960s. It has become acceptable for corporations to be plaintiffs and sue other corporations; there is an increased use of litigation as part of business strategy. A significant portion of this larger total of litigation is more complex and involves higher stakes, calling forth larger amounts of lawyering.

. . .

More Modalities, More Voices

[At the same time that litigation has increased, so have the range of alternative dispute resolution techniques. ADR has moved from the periphery to the center of the legal landscape. More techniques such as arbitration, mediation and summary jury trials, and neutral evaluation devices are annexed to courts embedded in organizations and structured as free-standing alternatives to litigation.

More groups and interests are also active participants in the legal arena. Expanded funding for legal services and the bulk of public interest law organizations have greatly increased the strategic players in the law game].

The Extended Reach of the Law

Not only is there more law, but it is more pervasive. This is reflected in popular perception of the ubiquity of law and its intrusion into areas previously immune from its impingement— for example, in stories about suits by children against their parents. A cartoon portrays an incredulous father who asks his son across the table, 'You say if I make you drink your milk, you'll sue me?' This theme presents itself seriously in the quest for recoveries for damage from child abuse.

There has been an extension of judicial oversight and the consequent legalisation of whole areas of governmental activity that were not previously thought to be in need of close articulation with legal principles. These include large sections of the criminal justice system, including police, prisons and juvenile justice; and other institutions dealing with dependent clients such as schools, mental hospitals and welfare agencies. Our period has seen the extension of governmental concern into areas of life previously unregulated by the state (for example, in the great proliferation of environmental health and safety regulation), or in which regulation was not closely linked with the application of legal principles. Although health care is organised very differently in each of our three countries, in each it has been legalised in important ways. Regulation of entitlement to treatment and of provider compensation have proliferated. And increasingly, patients seek legal recourse for perceived failings of treatment. Similarly, the employment relationship has been legalised, through the welfare state's job and income security programmes or through civil rights acts and wrongful discharge litigation. Nor are our amusements exempt: much of the sports pages are devoted to reports of legal rulings and manoeuvres. In each of these areas—health care, employment, sports—regulation by legal institutions inspires answering legalisation by bodies within these social fields, who promulgate rules, hold hearings and give decisions in a legal manner. The penetration of public standards in associational life does not reduce the amount of indigenous private regulatory activity, but multiplies it.

Legal norms and institutions are invoked to regulate dealings with intimates and to exert leverage on remote entities. Modern society throws up more predicaments in which people find themselves affected by remote actors where there is no leverage to control those actors and hold them accountable. Modern technology increases the power of remote actions to impinge on us. A greater portion of our dealings and of our disputes are with remote actors. Increasingly, our transactions and disputes are not with other persons, but with corporate organisations. The growth of knowledge enables us to trace out these connections and establish responsibility for ramifying consequences. Education and wealth make us more competent in using institutions. Law is a way to control and hold accountable remote and overwhelming actors. As perceptions of problems and estimates of alternative solutions vary, we use law more, both in its wholesale and *ex ante* forms of legislation and administrative regulation and in its retail and *ex post* form of litigation.

The 'New Information Order' of the Law

This more ample and more ubiquitous law has changed in the process of expansion and dispersion. The single most striking change is the way that information within and about the law is organised and transmitted.

A generation ago, information about the working of legal institutions was limited in content and restricted in circulation. The practices of law firms were shrouded in confidentiality. When Erwin Smigel studied Wall Street lawyers in the late 1950s, he encountered a massive institutionalised reticence. Older and conservative lawyers, he reported, 'thought of their organisations in much the same manner as clergymen think of the church—as an institution that should not be studied.' The world of law practice was preferredly opaque. 'Talking about clients and fees just isn't done, not even when lawyers gather among themselves....' The taboo on information about partnership agreements, finances, relations with clients, even their identity, was mirrored in bans on advertising, solicitation and promotion. The turnabout in the US came quite abruptly in the late 1970s as a curious by-product of the Supreme Court's 1977 *Bates* decision, ruling that sweeping restrictions on lawyer advertising violated the First Amendment. *Bates* liberated lawyers to talk to the press about their practices, for they no longer feared being accused of advertising. This new access to lawyers combined with a new curiosity about law and lawyers make possible the new legal journalism. Reporting about lawyers in general publications like the *New York Times,* the *Wall Street Journal* and the news weeklies became more frequent, detailed and intrusive. In 1978, a new kind of trade press suddenly appeared within the legal world. Publications like the *National Law Journal, American Lawyer* and *Legal Times* provided a steady diet of detailed backstage information about law firm structure, hiring policies, marketing strategies, clients, fees and compensation. Contemporary observers noted that 'law and lawyers are becoming demystified. The rites of secrecy have passed.' Information that just a few years earlier would have been available only to a few insiders now circulated freely.

This was part of a wider change that we might call the 'new information order' of the law. Not only are law firms more open, but the operations of courts are less shrouded, and many core legal activities are more accessible. In the US, this openness is dramatised by the Freedom of Information Act, by open meeting laws, by courtroom television, and by interviewing of jurors. Another mark of the new openness of the law world is the turnabout in the willingness of prosecutors and police officials to discuss enforcement policies.

. . .

In the old regime of restricted information about the law in action, the legal order could be perceived in terms of its esteemed frontstage qualities—as formal, autonomous, rule-determined, certain, professional, learned, apolitical, and so forth. Everyone knew it was not exactly that way in his or her own corner, but private and fragmented knowledge of local deviations did not challenge the received picture of the system as a whole. Professionals could maintain cherished images of the legal world even while aware of much that the dominant paradigm labelled atypical and deviant. But the profusion of information about the workings of the law makes it more difficult to dismiss discretion, bargaining, improvisation and politics as extraneous to the law.

The relatively stable and comfortable consensus about law that prevailed in 1960 has been shattered. Schools and movements of legal thought displaying a variety and disagreement then unimaginable now flourish in the legal academy and through conferences and journals—socio-legal studies, law and economics, critical legal studies, alternative dispute resolution and feminist legal theory.   The world of law is far more intellectually diverse than it was in 1960.

In the US at least, the increased diversity of legal thought is manifest among judges and practitioners as well as in the legal academy.   More of the decisions of appellate courts, both federal and state, are accompanied by concurring and dissenting opinions. Within the organised bar, debates on central professional issues once involved a narrow and homogeneous group of elite lawyers, and controversy, though often vigorous, was among a restricted set of views.   Now, such debate involves a wide array of organised groups and a far greater range of views.

Conventional and celebratory views about law still command the allegiance of some lawyers all of the time and most lawyers some of the time.   But they co-exist with a host of views that challenge the received picture of the legal world.   Increasingly diverse legal elites must address the demands of more informed, more critical and less deferential publics.

. . .

As law expands and penetrates the world, it changes in the process.   Its institutions flourish but lose their autonomous, self-contained quality.   On every front we can observe the boundaries of the legal world becoming blurred and indefinite: legal argument incorporates more non-legal materials and adopts modes of analysis that are not so distinct from other discourses.   Law firms become more like businesses;   courts become more like other governmental bodies and their judgments increasingly resemble legal scholarship;   legal academics become more like other academics.   This de-differentiation of the legal is mirrored in the lament of a distinguished American lawyer, that 'Our courts have become the handymen of society.   The American public today perceives courts as jacks-of-all-trades, available to furnish the answer to whatever may trouble us....'   It reappears in a recent *New York Times* report entitled 'What Do Law Schools Teach? Almost Anything.'   Of course, the traffic is not uni-directional— other institutions and discourses absorb legal ideas and simulate legal forms.

. . .

As the law becomes more voluminous, more complex, and more uncertain, the costs of using it increase.   Virtually every 'improvement' in adjudication—refinements of due process that require more submissions, hearings and findings; elaborations of the law that require more research, investigation, evidence and use of experts—increases the need and opportunity for greater expenditures. As the society gets richer, the stakes in disputes become higher and more organisations and individuals can make greater investments in litigation and lobbying. Expenditures on one side produce costs on the other. Transaction costs—in time and resources, and uncertainty about recovery and its amount—rise.

These higher transaction costs change the character of the process. As the scale of the required inputs increases, large scale organizations enjoy an advantage because they are the right size to gather, process and store information, to bankroll cases and assume the risks that attend the process. Also, higher costs imply a wider 'settlement range' in which both parties are better off than in running the full course of adjudication. As settlement ranges are extended, actors face the problem of how to reach agreement within the settlement range. The recent proliferation of settlement brokers (judges, mediators, special masters) and devices (such as mini-trials, early neutral evaluation and summary jury trials) testifies to the increasing demand for signals to identify points of convergence within the broad settlement ranges created by higher transaction costs. Disputants are less likely to pursue the contest to a decisive conclusion. In these inconclusive battles, the roles of professionals change: the lawyer is deflected from heroic advocate to negotiator and the judge from detached arbiter to mediator.

Higher costs blur the law in another way, by widening the *de facto* zone of immunity granted to all behaviour by the costliness of invoking legal controls. Gross observes that 'as litigation becomes slower, more expensive and less predictable, a larger class of cases will not be brought because they are not worth the cost, the trouble, or the risk.' Thus, '[a] major consequence of inefficiency in the legal system is to increase the range of conduct that is, as a practical matter, beyond formal legal control.'

Curiously, as law becomes more contingent and more expensive, it becomes more accessible and more participative in the sense that there are more effective 'strategic' legal actors. More people can play the legal game—but the game changes. It no longer produces definitive and immutable rules and predictable outcomes. Instead it presents, in many instances, an arena of moral debate, of symbolic contest (anchored in material claims) between conflicting commitments that have to be combined and prioritised in specific concrete situations.

. . .

Let me briefly recapitulate my sense of the common elements that surround and infuse them. Within their richer, more informed, more diverse societies:

— There are more laws, more lawyers, more claims, more strategic players of the law game; societies spend more, absolutely and proportionately, on law.

— Legal institutions (including courts and law firms) increasingly operate in a rationalised, business-like way, concerned with cost effectiveness.

— Lawyers, administrators and judges are more entrepreneurial and innovative in designing and re-designing institutions and procedures.

— The law is plural, decentralised, issuing from multiple sources.

— More rules and standards being applied by more actors to more varied situations means that legal outcomes are contingent and changing: fixed rules are increasingly accompanied by shifting dialogic standards.

— Increasingly, outcomes are negotiated rather than decreed.

— Law is less autonomous, less self-contained, more absorbent, more open to methods and data from other disciplines.

— Because law is contingent, flexible and technically sophisticated, legal work is increasingly costly. Most people are priced out of the market for direct use of law in most matters.

— Law operates increasingly through indirect symbolic controls—by radiating messages rather than imposing physical coercion. Indirect participation through groups and through the media increases more rapidly than direct participation.

It is too easy to extrapolate these trends. But such predictions have a peculiar quality. We can be fairly confident about what these legal systems will be like five years from now. At the same time, we should be quite cautious about what they will look like in 20 years. Nothing goes up forever. Surely there will be surprises. Where might we expect some turning points? At what point will democratic industrial societies have enough of ubiquitous soft-edged law? Will they devise some equally serviceable and versatile substitutes? The answer will not yield to the most painstaking study of the law, for the deep fountains of change are outside it.

Deborah L. Rhode, "The Rhetoric of Professional Reform"
45 *Maryland L.Rev.* 274, 280 (1986).

Much reformist rhetoric has a curiously schizophrenic tone. It is often simultaneously assumed that Americans are "over-lawyered and underrepresented." Critics have variously depicted a populace beseiged by "hyperlexis," "legal pollution," and "judicial overload." Yet of equal concern is the cost, complexity, and concomitant inaccessibility of law for the majority of Americans. These competing diagnoses of "the problem" lead to obvious difficulties in prescription. Much reformist rhetoric envisions some halcyon era in which law plays a far less promiscuous role, as well as a legal system to which all citizens can readily resort in pursuit of individual rights.

Not only are such critiques normatively inconsistent, they are often empirically inexact. Much of the argument proceeds by anecdotes, analogies, or statistics that are demonstrably inadequate to the occasion. The anecdotal approach is to depict a legal landscape awash in petty grievances. The decline in religious and secular institutions has allegedly left a void too often filled by contentious claimants and an imperial judiciary. Suitors sue dates, football fans sue referees, children sue parents, and beauty contestants sue each other.

Of course, what counts as undue litigiousness depends largely on the eye of the beholder. Claims against sex-segregated Little Leagues have been viewed as frivolous in some but scarcely all circles, and the criteria guiding critics' characterizations are almost never disclosed.

To claim a distinctive problem of rising dimensions, reformist rhetoric requires a different tack, and the course often chosen involves some statistical slight of hand. ... Among the most popular evidence of a legal epidemic is the growth in federal caseloads ... What this account leaves out is that the rate of increase has leveled off, and that the progression looks rather less alarming in the state courts, which account for ninety-seven percent of all civil litigation. Although precise statistical information is impossible to obtain, the best available evidence demonstrates only a modest rise in the total number of claims filed per capita over the last century, and a declining percentage of cases proceeding to trial. Moreover, the number of filings gives only a partial perspective on court congestion. A large percentage of the recent increase involves pro se prisoner petitions and uncontested divorces, which do not entail time-consuming adjudication. As Wayne McIntosh's and Lawrence Friedman's research indicates, there have clearly been historical periods and jurisdictional pockets in which the statistical level of American litigiousness has been significantly greater than at present. . . .

Given the proliferation of special tribunals, administrative forums, and nonlawyers performing legal functions in many countries, reliance on litigation rates or numbers of licensed attorneys provides a highly imperfect comparative picture. Japan produces twice as many law graduates per capita as America, and many of these individuals provide assistance comparable to that of American attorneys; the low number of licensed Japanese lawyers is a function of bar examination pass rates of under two percent. So too, America's level of litigation, while significantly higher than Japan's, is in the same range as that of other countries such as England, Australia, and Denmark, which are not typically viewed as verging on "legal hypochondria" or adjudicative "paralysis." Nor is it clear that American investment in litigation has reached intolerable levels. What little data is available suggests that a quite small fraction of individual grievances end up in court. [The entire federal budget for the judiciary has been] about one-third the cost of a single Trident submarine.

That is not to deny the force of all statistical observations. The last quarter century has witnessed an unprecedented growth in the volume of law and lawyers. In certain respects we remain, as de Tocqueville noted, an exceptionally legalistic culture and our tolerance for lawyers' fees is not easily rivaled. America's annual investment in legal assistance reportedly totaled over thirty-eight billion dollars in 1983, and between 1972 and 1983 increased at a rate of about twelve percent annually. Quite apart from any historical and cross cultural comparisons, it is fair to question a system generating that level of expenditure on professional intermediaries. Overall, legal fees consume between a quarter and a third of the recoveries in litigated cases, and do not necessarily bear close relationship to the professional time expended or risks assumed. In the typical case, lawyers for plaintiff and defendant together recover as much or more than the prevailing party. Between forty to eighty percent of accident insurance premiums end up paying attorneys and court costs rather than compensating victims.

Of equal concern is the inaccessibility of legal services to middle and low income individuals. A vast number of legal claims are unperceived or unpursued because of the cost and complexity of legal processes. The most comprehensive surveys have estimated that Americans consult lawyers on less than a third of all matters that "reasonably could be called legal problems" and that about a third of the adult population has never had contact with an attorney. By its own estimates, the federally funded Legal Services Corporation can handle only a small percentage of the legal problems annually encountered by persons below the poverty line. The number of attorneys working for nonprofit public interest organizations is estimated at under 500. The consequence, according to conventional critiques, is that America has "far too much law for those who can afford it and far too little for those who cannot."

As an abstract matter, greater access to justice is difficult to oppose. In a more practical sense, however, there is considerable fuzziness to the concept. The "legal need" studies are problematic on several levels. From an empirical perspective, it is unclear precisely what is being measured. Any society generates a vast array of conflicts that could give rise to legal action. Whether they do is a function of the organization of the legal system and its broader cultural setting. Legal needs are a social construct, not some "Archimedean starting point against which we can measure the adequacy of legal services." From a normative perspective, most muttering about access finesses the fundamental questions. Almost by definition, the demand for greater participation proceeds on the assumption that the current legal system yields justice: Why else would one want entry? Generally absent from the analysis is any acknowledgment that the same social, economic, and political forces that have constrained access may also constrain the quality of justice available. Expanding participation without redistributing power may simply legitimate existing structures.

Moreover, crusades for access seem strangely oblivious to concerns about litigiousness. What forms of legal conflict are socially desirable? How much "naming, blaming, and claiming" do we want to encourage and what level of public resources are we prepared to invest in that enterprise? On those points, egalitarian exhortations have been utterly unilluminating. There is broad agreement that the "right" distribution of legal talent is not simply a function of what individuals are willing and able to pay, but little indication of what alternative allocative criteria are appropriate. Typically the critic rests with some categorical condemnation of market measures, and a vague genuflection to equality. According to then President Jimmy Carter, access to justice "must not depend on economic status," and former federal judge and law professor Marvin Frankel has concurred. Justice ought not to be for sale; "substantially equal access to the services of lawyers" should become a national priority.

Except as symbolic subtext, such rhetoric has a vacuous ring. As Tawney once observed about equal opportunity, one wonders what would horrify proponents most, "the denial of the principle or the attempt to apply it." Given the elasticity of legal needs and disparity of talent within the profession, any meaningful effort to equalize access would require not only massive public subsidies but the prohibition of private markets. More modest calls to enhance, if not fully equalize, access still leave all the sticky points unaddressed. What price are we prepared to pay for process? How do legal services compare with other claims on our collective resources? Do we share the concerns raised by the British Royal Commission on Legal Services: "A society in which all human and social problems were regarded as apt for legal remedy ... would not be one in which we would find it agreeable to live"? If that is our concensus, which sorts of problems call for nonlegal responses and how should that determination be made?

B. AN OVERVIEW OF POSSIBLE PRESCRIPTIONS

INTRODUCTION

There are three principal ways of approaching inequalities of legal position. One is to reduce barriers to competition that impede efficient delivery of legal assistance. These barriers include certain restrictions on lawyer advertising and solicitation, as well as non-lawyer provision of law-related services. A second approach is to subsidize various kinds of assistance for individuals of low or moderate income. Providing civil legal aid, court-appointed counsel for indigent criminal defendants, ombudsmen, "pro bono" representation, alternative forms of dispute resolution, and tax incentives for employer-subsidized legal insurance are common examples. A third possibility is to restructure substantive or procedural laws in directions that favor the relatively less affluent. Examples include simplifying legal processes, redistributing transaction costs or altering legal entitlements. For instance, no-fault divorce reforms assist pro se litigants and truth-in-lending acts reallocate transaction expenses, while rent control and minimum wage requirements seek to transfer real income.

All of these prescriptions are often politically controversial. Traditionally, lawyers have resisted eliminating barriers to compe-

tition. The amount and form of state subsidies for legal assistance
have proved equally divisive, particularly when they encompass
claims that are themselves matters of significant social conflict.
Dispute has also centered on the appropriate means of allocating
assistance and on the efficiency of using legal services to redistribute real income. Subsidizing civil legal services directly channels
resources to lawyers, and probably results in net increases of
transaction expenses for other sectors of society. How effectively
such subsidies divert real income to the nonaffluent will depend
on a variety of circumstances. Relevant considerations include
the costs of achieving, enforcing, and sustaining legal entitlements
to primary goods, as compared with the costs of directly transferring these goods. Yet the virtues of any redistributive alternative
cannot be assessed solely in terms of economic efficiency. Enhanced access to legal assistance implicates other societal values
on both an instrumental and symbolic level.

1. REDUCING THE COSTS AND INCREASING ACCESS TO THE LEGAL SSYTEM

**Thomas Ehrlich and Murray L. Schwartz, Reducing the
Costs of Legal Services: Possible Approaches by
the Federal Government**

A Report to the Subcommittee on Representation of Citizen
Interests of the Senate Committee on the Judiciary,
93d Congress, 2d Session 1–2, 6–8 (1974).

Introduction

The subcommittee is seeking ways to reduce the costs of legal
services to the public. The search is rooted in a basic concept of
distributive justice. That concept mandates a choice for all Americans of use or nonuse of legal services—a choice that realistically
is not now available to many citizens within the present price
structure. The purpose of this report is to suggest possible approaches by the Federal Government to meet the problem.

The subcommittee has made two basic judgments that are
followed in this report: (1) reducing the costs of an array of legal
services, traditionally provided by lawyers, would increase utilization of those services; and (2) such increased utilization would be a
social good.

Several considerations militate against these judgments, particularly the second. For example, the judicial system is now
overburdened in many ways. Adding more litigation will exacerbate this problem. It is not always desirable—because of premature polarization of social and business relations—to introduce the

realistic prospect of litigation as a vehicle for resolving disputes at an early stage; much can be said for keeping conflicts in nonvisible and amorphous states. Overall costs of transactions will likely increase as the costs of lawyers' services are added, no matter how much these costs may be reduced on a unit basis.

However forceful these considerations may seem, they are outweighed by the concept of distributive justice stated at the outset. With the two judgments as a starting point, therefore, this report explores categorical ways of reducing the costs of legal services with these points of emphasis: (1) the costs of legal services to the average, middle-income American; (2) the potential Federal role with respect to those costs; and (3) the relationship between the training of persons who provide the services and the costs of the services themselves.

These are the principal questions considered in this report:

(1) To what extent is deregulation of the legal-services industry a realistic and desirable method of reducing the costs of legal services?

(2) To what extent can the costs of legal services be reduced by lessening the needs for those services?

(3) To what extent can the costs of legal services be reduced by a major expansion of the use of legal assistants and machines to perform services traditionally reserved for members of the bar?

(4) To what extent can the training of members of the bar be altered to reduce the ultimate costs of legal services?

(5) What effect will reduction in costs have on the quality of legal services?

Each of the questions is considered in turn. There is, however, no attempt to develop a detailed blueprint for subcommittee proceedings. Rather, areas that seem worth exploration through research studies and hearings and the types of concrete proposals for Federal action that might emerge as a result of those inquiries are discussed. ...

II.   To What Extent Can the Cost of Legal Services Be Reduced by Lessening the Needs for Those Services?

By definition, the costs of legal services would be substantially reduced if the legal system were altered so that there was little or no need for those services. The previous section considered the possibility of lowering costs by permitting a more competitive market to operate in supplying the services. In this section are discussed the possibilities of eliminating the need for some legal services. "Legal services" here means those functions of counseling, advising, negotiating, and litigating that one person performs for another, either in a representative capacity or as a professional counselor.

There are two major avenues to be explored: Simplification of transactions and creation of alternative methods of dispute resolution.

(A) Simplification of transactions.—Inasmuch as the call for laws that are simple enough for the commonest of the citizenry to comprehend has rung through the centuries—to little avail if our present legal system represents the response—recommendations in this regard are perforce modest. They are limited to those transactions: (a) In which middle-income Americans frequently engage; and (b) which are the source of controversies that require resolution, but for which the services of a lawyer are frequently too expensive.

Current categories of these transactions are: family law; real estate, including landlord-tenant matters; consumer transactions; and probate and testamentary matters. Foreseeably on the increase are disputes about various Government benefit programs, as for example, social security; on the likely decrease is personal-injury litigation; a probable constant is criminal law. For many of these transactions a lawyer is retained, but in others is not, many times because of the expense.

(1) With respect to these categories, the principal prospect of simplifying transactions to eliminate or reduce the utilization of lawyers is through the development of uniform codes of transactions. The underlying hypotheses are that it is less expensive (in terms at least of lawyers' time and charges) to prevent a controversy than to resolve it, and that one significant method of preventing controversies is to develop uniform codes to define the terms of the transactions.

. . .

The aim here is to convert types of legal problems from an individualized (retail) basis to a standardized (wholesale) basis. In short, individual variations in common legal arrangements should to the maximum extent be eliminated by requiring uniform, officially approved approaches. ...

(2) Another approach to reducing the costs of legal services is to focus on substantive areas that affect citizens generally and that involve large total costs of lawyering. These are areas where "delawyering" could have the largest economic impact.

Surveys show that four fields involving the transactions of individuals produce major shares of total lawyer revenue: Personal injury litigation, family law, real estate transactions, and probate. Reforms have already occurred in the first two of these fields. Personal injury litigation accounts for some 20 percent of the revenue of the private bar. The advent of no-fault insurance, particularly on a nationwide basis, will inevitably lead to a substantial reduction in the costs of legal services. Enthusiasm for no-fault is clearly related to dissatisfaction with the costs of the prior system. The adoption of workmen's compensation systems and the elimination of defenses in Federal Employer's Liability Act litigation are illustrations of the same general development in an earlier era.

The de jure recognition of no-fault divorce and the ease and speed of divorce proceedings in many jurisdictions should also produce significant reductions in lawyering costs. Much more needs to be done in this field to reduce the costs of legal services, but important steps have already been taken in some States.

The subcommittee should sponsor studies on ways to reduce the costs of legal services in other areas. Residential real-estate transactions and probate matters are first-order research targets; subsequently, this type of examination can be expanded to other fields.

(3) A third area for study would be ways in which legal costs might be reduced through procedural changes in litigation arrangements. Shifting burdens of proof and eliminating defenses are prime examples. The no-fault concept has been adopted in some foreign countries on a much broader basis than automobile accidents. Judicial procedures should not, of course, be determined solely on the basis of costs. But many Americans are denied effective access to the legal system—are denied, literally, their day in court—because of high legal costs. The subcommittee should review common types of legal transactions that affect the average person to determine how economies might be effected and rights more fully vindicated by changes of this kind.

(B) *Creation of alternative forms of dispute resolution.*—A different technique to effect reduction of costs is to change the forum, rather than the transaction. This approach assumes that a transaction has been entered into, a controversy has arisen, and some form of dispute resolution is in order. It was suggested at the outset of this report that there is a value in structuring dispute resolution so that not every dispute is processed expeditiously. To the extent that present dispute resolution requires lawyers and traditional judicial tribunals or administrative agencies, that result is assured. There simply is too much business in these traditional institutions now.

Richard L. Abel, "Delegalization: A Critical Review of Its Ideology, Manifestations, and Social Consequences," in E. Blankenburg, E. Klausa, and H. Rottleuthner, eds., Alternative Rechtsformen und Alternativen zum Recht

6 Jahrbuch für Rechtssoziologie und Rechtstheorie 27, 29–31, 40, 42 (1979).

It would clarify this analysis if I could offer a working definition of the phenomenon under consideration. But though I have identified it by the shorthand phrases "delegalization" and "substantive justice," its content and contours are just as vague as those concepts may suggest. Since the movement itself is relatively new and unformed, and efforts to understand it are even less advanced, we will have to be content with an enumeration of examples, in the hope that these will help to reveal its boundaries. The ideological foundation of the movement for delegalization is composed of the most diverse, not to say inconsistent strands as the following preliminary, and clearly incomplete, listing quickly demonstrates.

For some, delegalization means a return to nineteenth century small town virtues. This yearning for the alleged simplicity, intimacy, equality, and security of pre-industrial rural America has been a recurrent theme through our intellectual history, attracting proponents as distant in time, space, and style as Mark Twain, Jimmy Carter, and the communards of the 1960s. ...

But the purity of the legal system is not the only concern of advocates of delegalization. They are also troubled that the demands placed upon the system are too great, and its material resources too limited. In other words, they claim to be interested in caseload, congestion, and delay. These problems, naturally, are not peculiar to courts, or even to legal institutions. They are felt by all public institutions as demand (fostered in part by the ideal of equality) increases without a corresponding growth in governmental revenues. Thus these problems are one manifestation of the fiscal crisis of the state. The response to material scarcity, like the response to threats of ideological impurity, is highly selective. The blame for congestion is placed upon those with the least political power: those who have recently begun to use the courts; those who are incarcerated in correctional institutions or mental hospitals. ...

In addition to the defense of legalism and the desire for fiscal economies, there is a third element in the ideology of delegalization—the widespread feeling that legal institutions have simply failed to fulfill their purposes. The transaction costs of "going to law" have become so high that civil litigation is avoided wherever possible. And in a time of widespread fear it is difficult to maintain the myth that the system of criminal justice has adequately controlled crime, or could conceivably do so.

Because it is not possible simply to exclude categories of people from legal institutions in a regime that asserts its belief in liberal legalism, one strand of the delegalization movement is devoted to finding alternative institutions that can handle the "legal needs" of those who are diverted from the formal system. The search for such alternatives is also supported by the widespread hostility to professionals—not just lawyers (*see, e.g.,* Nader and Green, 1976; Tisher et al., 1977; Auerbach, 1976; Lieberman, 1978) but also doctors, educators, engineers, scientists—as well as by the antipathy to size (*see* Illich, 1977; Lieberman, 1970; H. Henderson, 1977; Schumacher, 1973; Kohr, 1978). Yet here again it is noteworthy that those who advocate deprofessionalization and decentralization often advocate it for others; they themselves are likely to continue using professionals and centralized institutions. ...

Delegalization presupposes that the people or entities that interact outside formal legal institutions are roughly equal in political power, wealth, and social status. Such an assumption must be made if those interactions are not to result in the party with greater power, wealth, or status simply dominating his opposite. We can see the assumption operating in the recommendations that divorce and its accompanying conditions be decided by (equal) spouses, that contractual agreements be concluded by (equal) parties, and that state regulation be replaced by negotiation between (equal) adversaries. ...

Because delegalization assumes equality but is implemented in a capitalist society characterized by extreme inequities of wealth, power, and status, such reforms will always be partial. The brief overview of innovations affecting compensation systems, land transfers, contracts, and estates consistently revealed their limitations. As with any other partial reform under capitalism, those who possess an initial advantage tend to be able to recoup any temporary loss of advantage: the privileged can do better both within the delegalized institution or process and outside it. Furthermore, given the antecedent distribution of privilege, it is the rights and interests of the underprivileged that tend to be delegalized, not those of the privileged.

Frank E.A. Sander, "Varieties of Dispute Processing"
70 Federal Rules Decisions 111, 111–31 (1976).

[O]ne concern to which we ought to address ourselves here is how we might escape from the specter ... [of a litigation overload]. This might be accomplished in various ways. First, we can try to prevent disputes from arising in the first place through appropriate changes in the substantive law, such as the adoption of a no-fault principle for automobile injuries or the removal of a criminal sanction for certain conduct, ... [or] greater emphasis on preventative law. ... A second way of reducing the judicial caseload is to explore alternative ways of resolving disputes outside the courts, and it is to this topic that I wish to devote my primary attention. ...

1) What are the significant characteristics of various alternative dispute resolution mechanisms (such as adjudication by courts, arbitration, mediation, negotiation, and various blends of these and other devices)?

2) How can these characteristics be utilized so that, given the variety of disputes that presently arise, we can begin to develop some rational criteria for allocating various types of disputes to different dispute resolution processes? ...

1. Nature of Dispute

Lon Fuller has written at some length about "polycentric" problems that are not well suited to an adjudicatory approach since they are not amenable to an all-or-nothing solution. ...

At the other extreme is a highly repetitive and routinized task involving application of established principles to a large number of individual cases. Here adjudication may be appropriate, but in a form more efficient than litigation (e.g., an administrative agency). Particularly once the courts have established the basic principles in such areas, a speedier and less cumbersome procedure than litigation should be utilized. ...

With respect to many problems, there is a need for developing a flexible mechanism that serves to sort out the large general question from the repetitive application of settled principle. I do not believe that a court is the most effective way to perform this kind of sifting task. In Sweden, in the consumer field, there is a Public Complaints Board which receives individual consumer grievances. Initially the Board performs simply a mediative function, utilizing standards set up by the relevant trade organizations. If initial settlement is impossible, the Board issues a non-binding recommendation to both parties, which often leads to subsequent settlement. Failing that, the grievant can sue in the newly established Small Claims Court. But another aspect of its activities is to seek to discern certain recurring issues and problems that should be dealt with by legislation or regulation. ...

2. Relationship Between Disputants

A different situation is presented when disputes arise between individuals who are in a long-term relationship than is the case with respect to an isolated dispute. In the former situation, there is more potential for having the parties, at least initially, seek to work out their own solution, for such a solution is likely to be far more acceptable (and hence durable). Thus negotiation, or if necessary, mediation, appears to be a preferable approach in the first instance. Another advantage of such an approach is that it facilitates a probing of conflicts in the underlying relationship, rather than simply dealing with each surface symptom as an isolated event. ...

[One] relationship that may be amenable to this type of dispute resolution mechanism is the family. Japan has long had a successful system of family conciliation tribunals, and although one must be necessarily wary in looking to entirely different cultures, it may well be that as our courts are beginning to play less and less of a role in divorce, as a result of the pervasive adoption of no-fault statutes, a need arises for some new flexible instrument—clearly not a court—that will concern itself with the resolution of family conflicts.

. . .

[A]n internalized grievance procedure, with limited last resort recourse to outside agencies, would appear to hold great promise for many disputes within an ongoing institution, such as a school, a welfare department, or a housing development. In view of the multifaceted nature of this type of grievance process, one might hope that if a case following such a procedure subsequently came to court, the court would give great, if not conclusive, weight to the prior determinations.

3. Amount in Dispute

Although, generally speaking, we have acted to date in a fairly hit-or-miss fashion in determining what problems should be resolved by a particular dispute resolution mechanism, amount in controversy has been an item consistently looked to to determine the amount of process that is "due".   The Small Claims Court movement has taken as its premise that small cases are simple cases and that therefore a pared-down judicial procedure was what was called for.   Next to the juvenile court, there has probably been no legal institution that was more ballyhooed as a great legal innovation.   Yet the evidence now seems overwhelming that the Small Claims Court has failed its original purpose; that the individuals for whom it was designed have turned out to be its victims.   Small wonder when one considers the lack of rational connection between amount in controversy and appropriate process.   Quite obviously a small case may be complex, just as a large case may be simple.   The need, according to a persuasive recent study, is for a preliminary investigative-conciliational stage (which could well be administered by a lay individual or paraprofessional) with ultimate recourse to the court.   This individual could readily screen out those cases which need not take a court's time (e.g., where there is no dispute about liability but the defendant has no funds), and preserve the adjudicatory process for those cases where the issues have been properly joined and there is a genuine dispute of fact or law.   Obviously such a screening mechanism is not limited in its utility to the Small Claims Court.

4. Cost

There is a dearth of reliable data comparing the costs of different dispute resolution processes.   Undoubtedly this is due in part to the difficulty of determining what are the appropriate ingredients of such a computation. . . .

5. Speed

The deficiency of sophisticated data concerning the costs of different dispute resolution processes also extends to the factor of speed.   Although it is generally assumed—rightly, I believe—that arbitration is speedier than litigation, I am not aware of any studies that have reached such a conclusion on the basis of a controlled experiment that seeks to take account of such factors as the possibly differing complexity of the two classes of cases, the greater diversity of "judges" in the arbitration group, and the possibly greater cooperation of the litigants in the arbitration setting.

[Implications]

At one time perhaps the courts were the principal public dispute processors.   But that time is long gone.   With the development of administrative law, the delegation of certain problems to specialized bodies for initial resolution has become a commonplace. ...

These were essentially *substantive* diversions, that is, resort to agencies having substantive expertise. Perhaps the time is now ripe for greater resort to an alternate primary *process*. As I have indicated earlier, such a step would be particularly appropriate in situations involving disputing individuals who are engaged in a long-term relationship. The process ought to consist initially of a mediational phase, and then, if necessary, of an adjudicative one. Problems that would appear to be particularly amenable to such a two-stage process are disputes between neighbors, family members, supplier and distributor, landlord and tenant. ...

What I am thus advocating is a flexible and diverse panoply of dispute resolution processes, with particular types of cases being assigned to differing processes (or combinations of processes), according to some of the criteria previously mentioned. Conceivably such allocation might be accomplished for a particular class of cases at the outset by the legislature; that in effect is what was done by the Massachusetts legislature for malpractice cases. Alternatively one might envision by the year 2000 not simply a court house but a Dispute Resolution Center, where the grievant would first be channelled through a screening clerk who would then direct him to the process (or sequence of processes) most appropriate to his type of case.

Green, Getting Out of Court—Private Resolution of Civil Disputes
Boston Bar Journal 11 (May-June 1984) *

1. A Conceptual Framework for "ADR"

"Alternate dispute resolution" is best thought of as involving "hybrid" processes other than the two most-used "primary" processes—adjudication and negotiation....

All alternative processes aim to allow the parties to reach a faster, less expensive and more appropriate resolution of their dispute than they would reach if they relied on the traditional processes of adjudication and negotiation.

Some alternative processes—such as mediation and Mini-Trials—aim to help facilitate the process of voluntary settlement.

Mediation, for example, may help calm the emotionalism of a dispute. Other alternative processes—such as binding arbitration—aim to provide a faster and less expensive binding resolution than would be obtained through the traditional in-court process. These alternative processes and techniques range from the purely private to the fully public, with some processes employing both private and public parts. Although many of the processes were custom-tailored in response to a particular dispute, they tend to share common characteristics of:

1. *Re-translation* from a legalistic dispute into a problem to be dealt with on its own terms;

2. *Co-operative* rather than aggressively adversarial processes, at least to the extent of depending on the parties' willingness to discuss the dispute openly and in good faith;

3. Involvement of a *neutral third party* at least as a facilitator; and

4. The involvement of *representatives of the parties*—often non-lawyers—with authority to resolve the dispute.

The most widely used ADR processes include:

• Mini-Trial

• Private judging; use of masters

• Self-Regulation

• Ombudsman

• Mediation

• Regulatory bargaining; negotiated development

• Neutral expert fact-finding; joint fact-finding

• Tailored arbitration

• Neutral lawyering

• Voluntary settlement conferences

• Court-annexed arbitration

. . .

The Mini-Trial mixes characteristics of many processes. A Mini-Trial is like adjudication in that it provides the parties with an opportunity to present proofs and arguments, but it is like mediation in that this is done in a non-win/lose situation. As in arbitration, the parties set their own rules and procedure and select a third party to help them resolve the dispute by considering the proper outcome. But the third party has no binding decision-making capacity, which is like mediation. The procedure is private like arbitration and mediation, but it is carried on within the structure of an on-going adjudication, and the goal is agreement rather than consistency with substantive law, which is like negotiation. In contrast with a close relation to which the Mini-Trial is often compared, traditional arbitration is characterized by a final, binding result announced by a third party after more formal and complete presentation by attorneys for each side with little or no participation by the clients. To contrast a Mini-Trial with another close relation, traditional settlement negotiations are characterized by a compromise agreement usually formulated by the attorneys and approved by the parties on the basis of the parties' relative power and positions rather than on the merits of the case. . . .

III. *Private Judging Under a General Order of Reference Rent-a-Judge*

In contrast to the purely private, non-binding qualities of the Mini-Trial, use of a private judge or "referee" pursuant to a general reference statute permits disputants to obtain fast, private, efficient, and competent resolution of their dispute plus all the benefits of a final, binding adjudication. Not surprisingly, the general reference procedure has attracted the enthusiastic attention of many institutional disputants and the criticisms of others concerned about its combination of private and public processing systems.

At least 48 states permit reference of at least some issues of fact or law, or both, to an outside party, but provisions vary from jurisdiction to jurisdiction along many dimensions. In some states, private payment of the referee is allowed; in others, it is disallowed. In some jurisdictions, the loser pays the cost of the procedure; in others, the state pays. Some states limit the subject matter that may be tried by reference; other states allow reference for a broader range of issues, but limit the extent to which the process may substitute for trial by being binding on the trial court. Some states require the presence of "exceptional circumstances" before reference, others allow reference in any case. Approximately ten states permit reference of all issues of fact and law in all cases and give the referee's decision the weight of a jury verdict or trial court judgment. . . .

Proponents of the reference procedure point to many advantages that private judging has over traditional adjudication. First and most importantly, in the reference procedure the litigants choose the third party who will decide the dispute, rather than trusting to the luck of the draw in the assignment of a trial judge....

A second major advantage the reference procedure has over traditional adjudication is its speed and convenience....

A third major advantage which the reference procedure has over adjudication is its flexible rules and procedures....

A fourth feature of the reference procedure which attracts many disputants is its confidentiality....

Another advantage of the reference procedure over traditional litigation is the speed with which a decision is rendered after the trial....

The reference procedure has not been without its critics. Chief Justice Rose Bird of the California Supreme Court has criticized the reference process as "a quasi-private judicial system for the wealthy." Her criticism is that the rent-a-judge system allows those who can afford it to play by different rules and sanctions in closed trials in law offices or court rooms while employing the imprimatur of the public judicial system for legitimacy. In addition, Chief Justice Bird criticizes the reference procedure for allowing those who can afford to hire a private judge to cut in line to the appellate courts. Other commentators have criticized the reference process on equal protection and first amendment grounds....

IV. Special Courts and Self-Regulatory Dispute Resolution

Another strategy for avoiding or resolving institutional litigation is the development of specialized dispute resolution courts and processes within clearly defined industries or institutions. Examples of such programs include the American Stock Exchange's program for security disputes, the dispute resolution program of the Council of Better Business Bureau's Advertising Division, and insurance industry arbitration.

These programs tend to share certain characteristics. First, they provide for speedy arbitration before industry experts....

Another common feature of these programs is that they are custom-designed for relatively self-contained industries in which failure to abide by the procedure can result in banishment from the industry association or marketplace. This is a sufficiently severe sanction to assure compliance.

Another interesting attitude common to each of these industry-wide dispute resolution mechanisms is that virtually no discovery is permitted except perhaps for the voluntary exchange of documents. . . .

Menkel-Meadow, Review Essay
69 *Judicature* 300 (1986) *

. . . [A]lthough many forms of dispute resolution now popular (such as arbitration and negotiation), are not new, the late 1960s produced a "flowering of interest in alternative forms of dispute settlement." . . . This development arose because of the confluence of the increase in legal rights asserted through lawsuits in a time of legal and social activism with a decrease in the number or quality of social institutions (churches, families, communities, schools and local government units) able to deal with and resolve these new competing demands. Thus, the volume of cases increased and there was a need to "process" them.

At the same time, many of the "movements" of the 1960s also demanded not only more substantive rights, but greater procedural rights, flexibility, and participation in the determination of disputes. "Maximum feasible participation" was a phrase attached to many social programs of the '60s, and this theme is echoed in many of the attempts to return disputes to the communities in which they occurred. Intellectual developments in this period, such as the work of Laura Nader in dispute studies in other cultures and Lon Fuller in legal scholarship, suggested experimenting with other forms of resolving different types of disputes, leading to such concrete developments as the neighborhood justice centers. This period also saw the rise of anti-professionalism, or at least a demystification of professional work and a demand for lay or client participation in legal services as well as other professionally delivered help. It seems clear to us now that the themes of this period were participation, flexibility of both process and result and access to justice of those previously foreclosed, as well as extension of models of procedural justice into such other domains as the workplace, local community and family.

The conceptual material for looking at adjudication raises important questions about just what it is that courts . . . and adjudication offer that we have come to regard as central to our system of justice—why do we place so much trust in a third party decider? When do the parties know better than the neutral? When do we need public articulation of rules and publicly viewed processes? When are court results and procedures too rigid and

---

* Reprinted by permission.

limited for the problems presented? ... One could ask of each form, for example if it is an expression of the qualitative side of dispute resolution (the hope for better solutions, greater party participation) or quantitative dispute resolution (more disputes can be handled more easily, cheaper, faster this way).... What are the moralities of each form? Does mediation place a higher value on agreement and peace ... where adjudication and arbitration place a higher value on the rule of law and "justice?" My own view on this important question is that it is not a simple question of form—both forms express both values, depending on the nature of the dispute, who the parties are and who the third parties are....

... [T]he early euphoric advocacy for these "alternatives" has worn off; why hasn't ADR become the accepted core for dispute processing? Should particular forms of dispute resolution be made compulsory or does that destroy the essence of "alternative" dispute resolution? Can disputes be prospectively assigned to the appropriate form of dispute resolution? Will such dispute "tracking" result in class-based segregations where some forms will be available to those who can pay and others only to those who have few resources? Will the use of private dispute resolution with an emphasis on compromise and accommodation threaten our system of public accountability and rule-making? Will dispute resolution in "alternative" forms become as "bureaucratized" as the present court system? How should dispute resolution be managed? Should there be separately trained dispute resolvers, new professionals with new skills, or lay people assisting other lay people? How should dispute resolution forms other than court-managed litigation be financed? What are the implications of private or public financing?... Other issues [include] as the increased mobilization of the state against the poor, the historical developments that have decreased the community solidarity thought to be needed for community based dispute resolution programs, the cross-cultural fallacies which we import into our discussion of dispute resolution when we try to use forms from other cultures. All of these issues and more are essential to the consideration of the advantages of "alternative dispute resolution" in our society in its present form.... One very important issue facing all students of dispute resolution is what is the relation of the form of dispute resolution to the type of case or manner of dispute resolution?... [I]t may not be the subject matter of the dispute that affects the "mediator's capacity to produce positive results." Instead, it may have more to do with the morphology of the dispute—where issues of dispute lie close to the surface, resolution by one form may be different than where disputes reflect "personal scripts, psychic conditions or social conditions" and are deeply buried "underlying causes...." Thus, efforts to easily categorize cases for one form of dispute resolution or another may fail if done on the basis of easily assessed "external" or demographic variables, rather than the more complex "internal" dimensions of the dispute.... [W]e must evaluate empirically the claims made on behalf of ADR. Are disputants differentially satisifed with different processes? Do they comply better with the more voluntary processes? What new hybrid forms will emerge from the primary forms or "old" hybrid forms? Whose interests will they serve? Will ADR itself become so bureaucratized that there will soon be alternatives to ADR, or, as is already emerging, will there be a plea to return to the more standard forms of adjudication? How will a broader conception of what it is appropriate to teach students about dispute resolution effect our daily transactions and, perhaps more importantly, our international transactions?...

Deborah Rhode, "The Rhetoric of Professional Reform"
45 *Maryland L.Rev.* 274, 280 (1986).

The debate over alternative dispute resolution encompasses a broad range of strategies designed to reduce reliance on law, lawyers, and adjudicative procedures. Arbitration, deregulation, no-fault compensation systems, assistance for pro se litigants, media ombudsmen, neighborhood justice centers, expanded small claims courts, and rent-a-judge services are among the conventional proposals for more accessible and less adversarial means of dispute resolution. Few of these approaches are entirely recent innovations. A number of American colonies and early utopian settlements sought to dispense with licenced attorneys, while various ethnic, religious, and commercial communities functioned with alternative arbitration processes throughout the nineteenth and twentieth centuries. Norwegian courts of conciliation, established in the late eighteenth century to protect citizens from the "gluttony of lawyers," have had various American analogues, including a spate of small claims courts beginning in the early 1920s. What is, however, distinctive about the current climate is the intensity of support for alternative dispute resolution within powerful public, private, and professional constituencies. Foundation officers, government officials, legal academics, and bar association committees have all joined forces under an informalist banner.

Much of their enthusiasm has centered on community justice programs, which began generating a small cottage industry during the late 1970s. Since such programs have been the most intensively studied offshoots of the alternative dispute resolution campaign, they provide an interesting case study in the implementation of reformist rhetoric and the dangers of undifferentiated diagnoses, prescriptions, and denunciations.

As an abstract concept, neighborhood justice appeared to offer all things to all constituencies. Community-based conciliation programs promised to secure cheaper, speedier forums for resolving grievances; to reduce court congestion by diverting minor disputes; to enhance individual autonomy by expanding party control while encouraging consensual mediated settlements; to further equal justice by redressing and deterring exploitation of previously unrepresented individuals; and to empower disadvantaged communities while reducing social friction.

In practice, however, such objectives turned out to be overstated and to some extent incompatible. In order to divert a significant number of disputes from court calendars while achieving cost advantages over formal tribunals, conciliation programs could not afford time-consuming consensual processes and assistance by adequate trained personnel. Since powerful adversaries were often unwilling to submit to voluntary processes or to accept unsatisfactory outcomes, the centers could do little to assist have-nots against haves without abandoning consensual premises. Strategies for reconciling individual grievances did not appear well suited for encouraging collective responses to common problems. Measured against their original objectives, neighborhood justice centers have inevitably fallen short. According to numerous empirical studies, such programs have not proved cheaper or significantly quicker than formal adjudication; they have not appreciably reduced court congestion; and they have not materially altered the disadvantages of the disadvantaged. As has generally been the case with small claims courts, neighborhood justice has remained too remote and cumbersome for the least well-off disputants, and on occasion has lent itself to capture by those already advantaged in formal adjudicatory processes. All too often, mediation between unequal parties has simply ratified rather than redressed the inequalities that contributed to disputes.

Thus, many critics from the left have viewed informalism as a strategy for avoiding problems of court reform by simply avoiding courts. From their perspective, an individualized conciliatory approach deflects attention from strategies that might provide more enduring collective solutions. Yet if reformist rhetoric has been uncritical in its endorsement of informalism, much revisionist rhetoric has been equally undiscriminating in its condemnation. Many leftist critiques glide over differences in program objectives and experiences which suggest that some informalist strategies have produced significant gains for the poor. Other analyses rest with exposing contradictions while ignoring relevant comparisons. The spectre of second-class justice for the poor implies that first-class justice is the plausible alternative. Yet as critics of informalism have frequently acknowledged, a full panoply of process has typically functioned more to protect the haves than the have-nots.

Moreover, the facade of formalism masks a system already heavily reliant on informal resolutions. In the halls of justice, "justice" has been determined largely in the halls, through settlement negotiations heavily insulated from paper protections. While weaker parties can be "cooled out" or pressured into inadequate settlements in informal proceedings, the same pressures occur under more ostensibly adversary processes. We have no systematic evidence that alternative dispute mechanisms generally produce less defensible results; if anything, participants' perceptions are to the contrary. Those who have had experience with adjudication report less respect for courts than the public generally, and are less satisfied than participants in more informal modes of dispute resolution. Whatever its other inadequacies, the process of neighborhood conciliation has appeared to litigants as more humane than its alternative, and that of itself should suggest problems with any monochromatic critiques.

It should also point up the need for less categorical rhetoric and more contextual analysis. The choice between informal and formal alternatives cannot be resolved in the abstract, nor should it be determined by crude economic indices such as the amount in controversy or parties' ability to buy their way into more adversarial settings. Informed decisions about the appropriate structure of dispute resolution must depend on greater attention to the social, political, and legal culture in which they function. Analysis should center not only on the comparative efficiencies of available processes, but also on the collective values to be served. Where these values are not readily reconciled, we need a clearer sense of priorities. Reducing cost and delay might be crucial in some categories of cases (*e.g.*, collection of child support); deterring future abuses might be most critical in others (*e.g.*, domestic violence). The choice of process should be more attentive to the particular rights, responsibilities, and relationships at issue.

Similar lessons can be drawn about the implementation of other strategies on the informalist agenda. Invariably, the rhetoric promises far more than the reform delivers. To take only the most obvious examples, the watered-down no-fault insurance schemes that have survived bar lobbying have failed to attain many of their promised objectives. Attempts to simplify trial procedures and pretrial practices have in some cases produced greater efficiency for lawyers, but because of prevailing fee structures, have not [necessarily] resulted in lower costs for clients. Small claims courts and form preparation services designed for pro se litigants have proved inaccessible to large percentages of their clientele since courts are not staffed to provide such assistance and private services have been legally barred from offering it. Yet these strategies have also yielded some clear benefits in reducing costs or empowering pro se parties, and have promoted greater understanding about directions for further reform.

To make those reforms meaningful, however, we need a richer set of narratives about a richer range of alternatives. Among other things, we might undertake more serious examination and experimentation with various forms of subsidies, streamlined delivery systems, and fee-shifting arrangements. For example, a number of jurisdictions have some variant of a rule providing that parties who refuse a formal settlement offer and receive a less favorable judgment at trial must pay the fees and expenses that their opponents incur after the offer, subject to certain exceptions and limitations. Such a strategy might prove salutary in some contexts by promoting settlements, deterring nonmeritorious litigation, and providing redress for small or moderate claims that are now too expensive to pursue. We could also borrow from the approach of other industrialized nations that have established simplified administrative and pretrial discovery procedures, progressive governmental subsidies, and citizen advice bureaus for various routine legal matters. Although no single strategy is likely to prove transformative, the cumulative effect of a composite approach might yield significant progress. If, as critics maintain, we have "too much law and too little justice," surely part of the reason is that we have had too much vacuous rhetoric and too little interest in attempting significant reforms or in pursuing the empirical and normative analyses that would make such efforts fruitful.

Geoffrey Hazard, Jr., "Court Delay: Toward New Premises"
Civil Justice Quarterly 236 (1986).

The court systems of many countries these days suffer from "delay." "Delay" means that there is an excessive interval between the point when a case is commenced and when it can be adjudicated. The definition of "excessive" often is not articulated but the concept is clear enough. The grievance is that an unreasonably long time is required to obtain justice, taking into account a reasonable time for the parties to attempt private settlement, a normal period to prepare for trial, and other pauses that seem necessary or unavoidable. ... The idea of getting rid of lawyers is the essence of many proposals for simplifying and popularising administered justice, for example, "people's" courts and informal arbitration schemes.

There are less drastic conventional remedies for court delay. One is to create more courts and more judgeships. Another remedy is to simplify judicial procedure, by directly reforming procedure in the principal courts or by transferring jurisdiction of certain cases to tribunals that use less elaborate procedures than those courts. Another remedy is to modify substantive rights so that rights and obligations are less easily disputed, and therefore less frequently litigated.

On closer examination, all standard remedies for court delay necessarily reduce themselves to one of two basic measures. The first is to increase the supply of adjudicative resources by creating more courts, more judges, larger clerical staff, etc. The second is to decrease the demand on existing adjudicative resources by reducing either the number of cases received or the scope of the consideration given to the average case. The logic of these possibilities is obvious. Indeed, it is so obvious as to suggest that systemic delay in court is a manifestation of deeper social difficulties. ...

Such a broader frame of reference would recognise that major court reform entails major political change. This is readily apparent when we look retrospectively in the historical study of a court system, and comparatively in the study of other legal systems. Thus, in the study of German or English reforms, we should seek an understanding not merely of the technical changes that were effectuated but an understanding of the functional failures experienced in the pre-existing systems in those countries, the resulting social dissatisfactions, the political opportunities that unfolded, the protagonists who exploited the opportunities, the rhetoric and tactics of reform, and the interests that supported reform and thereby consolidated it. We would pursue such an interpretation whether the institution under examination was a court system, a university, a transportation system, or some other institution. ...

In short, when we seek to understand major institutional change in the past, or abroad, or in some other sector of our own contemporary society, we search for the political, economic, and ideational forces that we know must have been at work. When legal scholars think about major change in their own court system in their own time, however, there is a tendency to consider the reform process as a *deus ex machina.* Inquiry focuses on the purely technical aspects of reform, on the implicit assumption that reform results from the intrinsic merit of reform proposals, their superior efficiency, fairness, or other virtue. This view is congenial to legal scholars, because we cannot readily accept the fact that the judicial apparatus is a political, economic, and cultural phenomenon as well as one that is legal and intellectual. Correlatively, it is difficult to accept that the phenomenon of court delay reflects political and ideational factors as well as mere bureaucratic inefficiency.

. . .

The first standard reform mentioned earlier is stronger administrative control over the use of time by judges and court officials. This reform conflicts with the self-interest of judges and court officials in maintaining their autonomy. But this self-interest is supported by considerations of constitutional principle, the principle of judicial autonomy in decision-making. This principle is implicated because in operation autonomy in decision-making conflicts with the principle of subordination in administration. Judges who are self-indulgent, or merely incompetent, thus have a principled basis for resisting reform in administration.

Another standard reform is to recruit additional and more capable judges and court staff. To be effective, this requires substantial augmentation of the judiciary's budget. Such a reform is not politically neutral because it creates immediate budgetary problems and may destabilise the whole public payroll. Furthermore, if the salary increase is enough to make a quantum difference in the quality of personnel attracted to the judiciary, it will also have effects on the socio-political makeup of the judiciary. Those effects can be regarded as raising constitutional issues, and certainly would do so if the judiciary became an economic elite.

Another reform is to streamline existing procedures. Immediate resistance to such reforms of course emanates from the legal profession, for change radical enough to have much effect threatens the bar's intellectual capital, which is its specialised knowledge of present practice. There are also deeper difficulties entailed in radical procedural change. Streamlined procedures by definition involve more limited examination of individual cases and by necessity can yield different outcomes, as compared with preexisting procedures. ... Procedural change therefore necessarily raises issues of principle, often ones of constitutional significance. To this evil is added the fact that changes in procedure may result in differences in outcome. ... Obviously the same analysis applies to reforms that change party incentives to litigate.

The last in the list of standard reforms is adoption of substantive legal change. Here, general political issues are of course drawn into consideration, for substantive legal reform necessarily derogates from existing substantive rights and expectations. ...

Legal scholars and members of the legal profession have tended to regard court reform as politically and socially neutral in its significance and effects. Systematic delay is regarded as a technical and administrative phenomenon, the remedy for which is the introduction of technical and administrative improvements. In the language of classical sociology, it is a Weberian problem requiring a Weberian solution. From what has been said, however, we must recognise that reform, even reform addressed to such a universally condemned evil as delay of justice, is not politically and socially neutral.

Every organised political community of course professes to seek "equal justice for all." Nevertheless, the evidence is plain that many modern political communities are unable to realise this objective.

The fundamental reason is that already suggested: There is no definite interest group, or coalition of interest groups, that wants to pay the price and carry the burden of political struggle to assure that automobile accident cases and [contested] divorces and landlord-tenant disputes can be adjudicated within a year rather than after a five-year wait.

If this unpleasant proposition is true, what follows?

The Privatisation of Justice

By the "privatisation of justice," I mean simply that the resources by which justice can be rendered should be considered to include non-state conflict resolution processes, specifically ones that are already embedded in society's substructures or which can be granted onto it. There are many examples.

An obvious one is arbitration. .... Another example is the authority of private voluntary associations to regulate affairs among their members, including adjudication of disputes.

This concept of "privatised justice" puts in broader perspective the development of Alternative Dispute Resolution procedures, or "ADR" as it is now called. Alternative Dispute Resolution refers to various extra-judicial procedures to deal with such variant matters as matrimonial disputes and legal controversies between large corporations. Some of the procedures are essentially mediation, others are essentially arbitration or private adjudication. Some are directly linked to the court system and are designed to "divert" cases otherwise destined for the courts. Others are designed to preempt resort to litigation. Some are connected to the social setting out of which the disputes arise, others are more or less independent institutions like the courts. Some are proving successful in one way or another, others have been total failures.

Although there is now vigorous experimentation with these procedures in the United States, they usually are considered from the presupposition that the paradigmatic mode of dispute resolution is adjudication in a public court. That presupposition, which derives from the premises earlier described, entails that the public courts alone can do "true" justice and that private justice is sufficient only if it approximates the judicial model. As a corollary, resort to private justice is purely optional on the part of the disputants. Yet the premise that true justice is a state monopoly need not be taken as given. It could be recognised that a person's "due" can come in various social forms and modes, just as there can be various forms and modes of education, health care, religious observance and economic enterprise. On that premise, the question for the legal system when justice is needed ought to be whether it shall be provided by the public courts or not at all. The question would be whether the parties, particularly the stronger one, had tried seriously to bring about a just resolution of the dispute through available private sources under auspices that are entitled to be respected by the public system of justice.

Furthermore, could not resort to a mechanism of nonpublic justice be made a precondition of resorting to court in many types of controversies? Is such a requirement not specially appropriate in an era when the public courts are unable, owing to their own congestion, to provide the social service of which they claim to be uniquely capable?

NOTES

It is widely argued that American society is overly litigious and that the accompanying direct and secondary costs are too high. However, as the preceding essays suggest, any efforts to reduce those costs implicate interests far wider than those of the legal profession, and involve issues beyond the design of legal processes. To be sure, many members of the bar profit from pervasive and expensive litigation, and the profession as a whole traditionally has been disinclined to seek major reforms that might jeopardize lawyers' economic interests. Yet the bar's position on these issues is not only a cause but also an effect: Litigation remains costly and widespread in large part because other constituencies want it that way, or at least can veto any significant change.

It is often suggested that these constituencies are aligned on different boundaries of socio-economic interest. Thus, some critics from the left have argued that business and governmental organizations tolerate the costs and delays of litigation as a means of discouraging suits and avoiding legal accountability. At the same time, critics from the right maintain that activist interests use litigation to coerce concessions that could not be secured under a more streamlined adjudicatory process, or one in which users paid the full costs of court procedures. Both arguments obviously can be stated in more detailed and elaborate form, and contain substantial elements of truth. That may, in turn, help explain why there is considerable agreement that the system of justice is burdensome and ineffective, and little consensus on what to do about it. Designing alternative structures that will not institutionalize second-class justice remains a matter of some difficulty.

Moreover, with respect to some of society's most divisive issues, elaborate legal process may be a substitute for coherent public policy. For example, some environmental and civil rights questions are politically intractable in the present fragmented state of public opinion. But the substantive problems persist, the courts are "there", and legal arguments one way or the other on the relevant issues readily suggest themselves. A protracted legal struggle involving indeterminate standards and a full panoply of process is one way to muddle toward negotiated compromises, if not principled solutions.

REFERENCES

J. Adler, D. Hensley and C. Nelson, *Simple Justice: How Litigators Fare in the Pittsburgh Law Court Arbitration Program* (1983).

J. Auerbach, *Justice Without Law* (1983).

Banks, "Gender Bias in Law School Classrooms," *J. of Legal Educ.* (1988).

Burger, "Agenda for 2000 A.D.—A Need for Systematic Anticipation," 70 *F.R.D.* 83 (1976).

Carlin & Howard, "Legal Representation and Class Justice," 12 *U.C.L.A. L.Rev.* 381 (1965).

B. Christensen, *Lawyers for People of Moderate Means* (1970).

R. Conner & R. Surette, *The Citizen Dispute Settlement Program: Resolving Disputes Outside the Courts, Orlando, Florida* (1977).

Danzig, "Toward the Creation of a Complementary, Decentralized System of Criminal Justice," 26 *Stan.L.Rev.* 1 (1973).

Danzig & Lowy, "Everyday Disputes and Mediation in the United States: A Reply to Professor Felstiner," 9 *Law & Soc'y Rev.* 675 (1975).

Delgado *et al.*, "Fairness and Formality: Minimizing the Risk of Prejudice in Alternative Dispute Resolution," 1985 *Wis.L.Rev.* 1359.

Duryee, "Mandatory Court Mediation," 30 *Family and Conciliation Courts Review* 260 (1992).

Englade "LSC Under Siege," 73 *A.B.A.J.* 70 (1987).

Felstiner, "Influences of Social Organization on Dispute Processing," 9 *Law & Soc'y Rev.* 63 (1974).

Fiss, "Against Settlement", 93 *Yale L.J.* 1073 (1984).

Friedman, "Access to Justice: Social and Historical Context" in 2 M. Cappelletti & J. Weisner eds., *Access to Justice* 3 (1978).

S. Goldberg, E. Green and F. Sander, *Dispute Resolution* (1985).

Grillo, "The Mediation Alternative: Process Dangers for Women," 100 *Yale L.J.* 1545 (1991).

Halbach, "Toward a Simplified System of Law" in M. Schwartz ed., *Law and the American Future* (1976).

J. Handler, E. Hollingsworth & H. Erlanger, *Lawyers and the Pursuit of Legal Rights* (1978).

Lazarson, "In the Halls of Justice, the Only Justice is in the Halls," *The Politics of Informal Justice: The American Experience* (R. Abel ed., 1982).

Lerman, "Mediation of Wife Abuse Cases: The Adverse Impact of Informal Dispute Resolution on Women," 7 *Harv. Women's L.J.* 53 (1988).

Marks, "Some Research Perspectives for Looking at Legal Need and Legal Services Delivery Systems: Old Forms or New?" 11 *Law & Soc'y Rev.* 191 (1976).

Mayhew, "Institutions of Representation: Civil Justice and the Public," 9 *Law and Soc'y Rev.* 401, 405 (1975).

McEwen and Maiman, "Small Claims Mediation in Maine: An Empirical Assessment," 33 *Me.L.Rev.* 237 (1981).

Menkel–Meadow, "Pursuing Settlement in an Adversary Culture: A Tale of Innovation Coopted or the Law of ADR," 19 *Fla.St.U.L.Rev.* 1 (1992).

Project, "An Assessment of Alternative Strategies for Increasing Access to Legal Services," 90 *Yale L.J.* 122 (1980).

Rifkin, "Mediation from a Feminist Perspective: Promise and Problems," 2 *Law & Inequality* 21 (1984).

Rosenberg, "Devising Procedures That Are Civil to Promote Justice That Is Civilized," 69 *Mich.L.Rev.* 797 (1971).

Sander, "Varieties of Dispute Processing," 70 *F.R.D.* 111 (1976).

Sarat, "Alternatives in Dispute Processing: Litigation in Small Claims Court," 10 *Law & Soc'y Rev.* 339 (1976).

Simon, "Legal Informality and Redistributive Politics," *Clearinghouse Review* 384 (1985).

Singer, "Nonjudicial Dispute Resolution Mechanisms: The Effects on Justice for the Poor," 13 *Clearinghouse Rev.* 569 (1979).

Slater, "Client Satisfaction Survey," 30 *Family and Conciliation Courts Review* 252 (April 1992).

Small Claims Study Group, *Little Injustices* (1972).

R. Tomasic & M. Feeley eds., *Neighborhood Justice: An Assessment of an Emerging Idea* (1982).

For a bibliographic overview, see

2. PRO BONO REPRESENTATION: THE RHETORIC AND REALITY

"Professional Responsibility: Report of the Joint Conference"
44 American Bar Association Journal 1159, 1216 (1958).*

Making Legal Services Available to All

If there is any fundamental proposition of government on which all would agree, it is that one of the highest goals of society must be to achieve and maintain equality before the law. Yet this ideal remains an empty form of words unless the legal profession is ready to provide adequate representation for those unable to pay the usual fees.

At present this representation is being supplied in some measure through the spontaneous generosity of individual lawyers, through legal aid societies, and—increasingly—through the organized efforts of the Bar. If those who stand in need of this service know of its availability, and their need is in fact adequately met, the precise mechanism by which this service is provided becomes of secondary importance. It is of great importance, however, that both the impulse to render this service, and the plan for making that impulse effective, should arise within the legal profession itself.

The moral position of the advocate is here at stake. Partisan advocacy finds its justification in the contribution it makes to a sound and informed disposition of controversies. Where this contribution is lacking, the partisan position permitted to the advocate loses its reason for being. The legal profession has, therefore, a clear moral obligation to see to it that those already handicapped do not suffer the cumulative disadvantage of being without proper legal representation, for it is obvious that adjudication can neither be effective nor fair where only one side is represented by counsel.

In discharging this obligation, the legal profession can help to bring about a better understanding of the role of the advocate in our system of government. Popular misconceptions of the advocate's function disappear when the lawyer pleads without a fee, and the true value of his service to society is immediately per-

* Reprinted with permission from the
American Bar Association Journal.

ceived. The insight thus obtained by the public promotes a deeper understanding of the work of the legal profession as a whole.

The obligation to provide legal services for those actually caught up in litigation carries with it the obligation to make preventive legal advice accessible to all. It is among those unaccustomed to business affairs and fearful of the ways of the law that such advice is often most needed. If it is not received in time, the most valiant and skillful representation in court may come too late.

NOTES

Although the bar has long supported pro bono in principle, its commitment in practice has been less consistent. Surveys from the late 1980s and early 1990s indicated that more than two thirds of the nation's attorneys donate some free legal services, but that the amounts are quite modest and little of this activity goes to representation of indigents.[1] One ABA study found that only 17 percent of American lawyers participate in organized legal assistance programs for the poor.[2] Other research suggests that much of attorneys' non-paying work goes to friends, relatives, and organizations likely to attract paying clients.[3]

The bar's official pronouncements, such as the Report of the Joint Conference excerpted above, generally speak of lawyers' pro bono "obligations," and the ABA Code of Professional Responsibility states that "the rendition of free legal services to those unable to · pay reasonable fees continues to be an obligation of each lawyer." (EC 2–25) In fact, however, this reference to a pro bono

1. Miskiewicz, "Mandatory Pro Bono Won't Disappear," *National Law Journal,* March 23, 1987 at 1; Pressman, "Forgetting the Poor," *California Lawyer,* May, 1990 at 17–18 (only 18% of American lawyers and 10% of California lawyers participate in pro bono programs that aid the indigent); Alenna Sullivan & Arthur S. Hayes, "Pro Bono Work," *Wall St.J.,* Sept. 27, 1991 at b 10 (over half of New York lawyers performed pro bono work but only 39% reported that such work was for poor clients or organizations that serve their need and only 28% perform more than 20 hours per year); Timothy J. Linden and Susan M. Hoffman, Pro Bono,

Washington Laywer, 29, 61 (September/October 1990) (over 40% of surveyed lawyers at large Washington D.C. firms performed 20 or fewer pro bono hours of work per year and less than half went to indigent clients).

2. ABA Consortium on Legal Services and the Public, *The 1989 Directory of Private Bar Involvement Programs* 182–83 (1989).

3. *See* research summarized in Rhode, "Why the ABA Bothers: A Functional Perspective on Professional Codes," 59 *Tex.L.Rev.* 689, 697–701 (1981).

obligation in the "aspirational" Ethical Considerations finds no counterpart in the Code's Disciplinary Rules.

Over the last quarter century, various bar groups have made repeated efforts to institute pro bono requirements, but these have met with widespread resistance. An early draft of the Model Rules of Professional Conduct would have required 40 hours of pro bono activity per year from each lawyer. In the face of strong opposition, subsequent drafts removed the quantitative minimum and instead required an unspecified amount of pro bono services. In the end, this requirement was also abandoned. The draft approved by the ABA in 1983 provided that "a lawyer should render public interest legal service," a provision that the Comment explained is "not intended to be enforced through disciplinary process." (Rule 6.1) In 1993, the ABA adopted an amended rule that recommended 50 hours of service to "persons of limited means," but again rejected any mandatory commitment.[4] Similar compulsory pro bono proposals met similar fates in various states during the late 1980s and early 1990s, although courts in a few local jurisdictions required lawyers to accept unpaid appointments in a small category of cases.[5]

Arguments favoring pro bono service generally begin from the premise that access to legal services is a basic entitlement. As the Supreme Court has recognized in other contexts, the right to sue and defend is "the right conservative of all other rights" and would often be of little value if it did not encompass legal assis-

4. Model Rules, Rule 6.1 (amended Feb. 8, 1993). The new rule reads as follows:

A lawyer should aspire to render at least (50) hours of pro bono publico legal services per year. In fulfilling this responsibility, the lawyer should:

(a) provide a substantial majority of the (50) hours of legal services without fee or expectation of fee to:

(1) persons of limited means or

(2) charitable, religious, civic, community, governmental, and educational organizations in matters which are designed primarily to address the needs of persons of limited means; and

(b) provide any additional services through:

(1) delivery of legal services at no fee or substantially reduced fee to individuals, groups, or organizations seeking to secure or protect civil rights, civil liberties or public rights, or charitable, religious, civic, community, governmental and educational organizations in matters in furtherance of their organizational purposes, where the payment of standard legal fees would significantly deplete the organization's economic resources or would be otherwise inappropriate;

(2) delivery of legal services at a substantially reduced fee to persons of limited means; or

(3) participation in activities for improving the law, the legal system or the legal profession.

5. See D. Rhode and D. Luban, *Legal Ethics* 873–74 (1992).

tance.[6] Access to such assistance is necessary to ensure governmental legitimacy, protect fundamental interests, promote procedural fairness, and register expressive needs.[7] As discussion elsewhere in this chapter indicates, the legal needs of low-income groups are far from being met under existing programs.[8] Pro bono service by the private bar could help fill the gap. On this analysis, the profession's right to a monopoly over the provision of legal services should carry with it a corresponding obligation to make such services more available to groups that cannot afford them.

Opposition to pro bono obligations rests on several grounds. One line of criticism has emphasized the infringement of lawyers' own rights.[9] Other licensed professionals are not expected to provide free goods and services. Why then should lawyers bear distinctive burdens? From this perspective, conscripting attorneys undermines fundamental rights of due process and just compensation. If society wishes to expand access, society as a whole should pay the cost.

Other critics claim that pro bono obligations are not an efficient way of realizing the benefits of broadened access. Lawyers who lack expertise and motivation to serve underrepresented groups will not provide cost-effective representation. Requiring attorneys to provide a minimal level of services of largely unverifiable quality cannot begin to meet this nation's massive unmet legal needs. Worse still, such token responses to distributional inequalities may deflect attention from the fundamental problems that remain and from more productive ways of addressing them.[10] Preferable strategies might include simplification of legal procedures, expanded subsidies for poverty law programs, and restriction of the professional monopoly over routine legal services.

How would you respond to these arguments? What ethical rules would you support?

6. Chambers v. Baltimore & Ohio R.R., 207 U.S. 142, 148 (1907).

7. *See* David Luban, *Lawyers and Justice: An Ethical Study* 263–64 (1988); Frank Michelman, "The Supreme Court and Litigation Access Fees: The Right to Protect One's Rights—Part I," 1973 *Duke L.J.* 1153, 1172.

8. *See* discussion at pages 473–477 *infra.*

9. *See* commentators quoted in Rhode, "Ethical Perspectives on Legal Practice," 37 *Stan.L.Rev.* 589, 610 (1985) and cases reviewed in D. Rhode and D. Luban, *Legal Ethics* 886–91 (1992).

10. *See* Lardent, "Mandatory Pro Bono in Civil Cases: The Wrong Answer to the Right Question," 49 *Md. L.Rev.* 78, 100–01 (1990). See also the arguments reviewed in Rhode, *supra* note 3, at 689–701. For responses to these objections, *see* Rhode and Luban, *supra* note 9, at 874–83; Cramton, "Mandatory Pro Bono," 19 *Hofstra L.Rev.* 1113, 1121–24 (1991).

What, exactly, is the relationship between a mandate of *pro bono* legal service, whether compulsory or aspirational, and the needs of the poor for legal assistance? Would we regard increased *pro bono* medical services as the way to meet the medical needs of the 37 million Americans who now lack medical insurance? Or increased *pro bono* teacher service (for example, through a Federal Vista program) as the way to meet the gross deficiencies of millions of American youth in reading, writing, and arithmetic? An individual lawyer's *pro bono* service, voluntary or obligatory, can have profound moral and professional significance to the lawyer. But how far would such services go in ameliorating the underlying social problem of inadequate justice resources for the poor? What is at issue in the debate over mandatory *pro bono?*

———

REFERENCES

Abel, "Socializing the Legal Profession," 1 *Law & Pol'y Q.* 5 (1979).

Association of the Bar of the City of New York, Special Committee on the Lawyer's Pro Bono Obligations, *Toward a Mandatory Contribution of Public Service Practice by Every Lawyer* (1979).

Bodine and Lundberg, "50 Hours for the Poor," 73 *A.B.A.J.* 55 (1987).

M. Frankel, *Justice: Commodity or Public Service* (Essay on American Institutions, 1978).

J. Handler, E. Hollingsworth & H. Erlanger, *Lawyers and the Pursuit of Legal Rights* 92–101 (1978).

MacCrate, "Pro Bono: The Lawyer's Response to a Public Calling," 73 *A.B.A.J.* (1987).

F. Marks, "The Practice of Law Is a Public Utility," in *The Lawyer, the Public and Professional Responsibility* (1972).

D. Shapiro, *The Enigma of the Lawyer's Duty to Serve*, 55 N.Y.U.L.Rev. 735 (1981).

Wolfram, "A Lawyer's Duty to Represent Clients, Repugnant and Otherwise," in *The Good Lawyer* 214 (D. Luban, ed., 1984).

3. SUBSIDIZED LEGAL SERVICES:
PROBLEMS OF ALLOCATION

INTRODUCTION

The first American legal aid society formed in 1876 as part of an organization to assist German immigrants. Within the next several decades, legal services programs were established in various urban areas through private charity and municipal subsidies. In 1919, Reginald Heber Smith published *Justice and the Poor,* which reported a total of some 40 organizations throughout the country with woefully inadequate resources. The ABA subsequently appointed Smith to head its Standing Committee on Legal Aid, which began providing modest support to local offices. However, as late as 1963, there were only some 250 legal services offices with a combined annual budget of approximately 4 million dollars, about 12% of which came from bar association contributions.[1]

The War on Poverty brought a massive influx of federal aid and a new reformist ethos to civil legal aid programs. The consequences were quickly apparent, as poverty law offices achieved significant victories in consumer, welfare, housing, health, and related legal areas. To provide somewhat greater political insulation for those efforts, Congress in 1974 established the Legal Services Corporation, with board members appointed by the President and confirmed by the Senate. However, legal victories also resulted in political backlash, which translated into curtailment of funds and restrictions on lawyer activities.[2] At recent funding levels, legal aid programs remain a long distance from meeting the needs of low income populations. During the early 1990s, such programs annually received less than $10 per poor person in their service area.[3]

---

1. B. Garth, *Neighborhood Law Firms for the Poor* 19–20 (1980). For accounts of the earlier development of legal aid programs *see* Pipkin, "Legal Aid and Elitism in the American Legal Profession," in *Before the Law: An Introduction to the Legal Process* 185 (J. Bonsignore *et al.* 2d ed. 1979).

2. Legal aid lawyers may not engage in lobbying or political organizing and may not provide representation in certain cases such as school desegregation, homosexual rights, abortion, military service and immigration. *See* Legal Services Corporation Act, 42 U.S.C. Section 2996 et seq. (1982). Legal services'

annual funding under the Reagan Administration was cut from $321 million to $241 million. Abel, "Law Without Politics: Legal Aid Under Advanced Capitalism," 32 *U.C.L.A.L.Rev.* 474, 532 (1985).

3. *See* Legal Services Corporation, Annual Report 7 (1991). For studies finding that between 50–80 percent of the legal needs of low-income populations remain unmet, *see* The Spanenberg Group, "National Survey of the Civil Legal Needs of the Poor" 3 (May, 1989); *Illinois Legal Needs Study* 2 (October, 1989).

Critics of legal services have never been lacking, and indeed have emerged from all points on the ideological spectrum. Then Vice President Agnew denounced poverty lawyers as ideological vigilantes who sought, at public expense, to act as social engineers without any "public direction or public accountability." [5] Other commentators have questioned the effectiveness of legal services in redistributing income and power. In their view, the costs of legal proceedings may in some cases be passed on to other poor consumers in the form of higher prices.[6] Alternatively, recognition of formal rights may have little concrete effect, given the post-judgment power relations of the parties, the difficulties of enforcement, and the possibility of legislative reversal.[7] According to some critics, publicly subsidized legal assistance often works against fundamental change by channeling legal conflict into forms that exact minor concessions but do not challenge basic power relations.[8]. Even avid supporters of such assistance have questioned the quality of representation, the potentially autocratic paternalism by which resource priorities are established, and the pretense that "equal access to justice" is a realistic social aspiration under a market system for dispensing legal services.[9]

By contrast, defenders of civil legal aid view it as a crucial means of securing basic entitlements, checking public and private abuses, and empowering low income constituencies. To withhold

5. Agnew, "What's Wrong With the Legal Services Program," 58 *A.B.A.J.* 930, 931 (1972). *See also* Brill, "The Uses and Abuses of Legal Assistance," 31 *Public Interest* 38 (1973); Heritage Foundation October 1980 Report (denouncing most legal aid lawsuits as a leftist effort to "erode the free enterprise system"). *See* Englade, "LSC Under Siege," 73 *A.B.A.J.* 70 (1987).

6. Hazard, "Social Justice Through Civil Justice," 36 *U.Chi.L.Rev.* 699, 337 (1969); Brakel, "Styles of Delivery of Legal Services to the Poor: A Review Article," 1977 *Am.Bar Found.Research J.* 219, 219–238. See also F. Piven and R. Cloward, Poor Peoples' Movements: Why They Succeed, How They Fail, 303–37 (1977). Of course, whether such adverse redistributive effects will occur depends on a complex set of market factors. *See* Ackerman, "More on Slum Housing and Redistribution Policy: A Reply to Professor Komesar," 82 *Yale L.J.* 1194 (1973).

7. For example, Stuart Scheingold has critiqued the individualist client orientation that diverts lawyers from "di-

rect and coordinated political action and channels them instead into piecemeal legal responses to perceived injustices." S. Scheingold, *The Politics of Rights—Lawyers, Public Policy and Political Change* 117–23 (1974).

8. Abel, *supra* note 2, at 530–31.

9. *See* generally Bellow, *infra* at 371; Bellow and Kettleson, "From Ethics to Politics: Confronting Scarcity and Fairness in Public Interest Practice," 58 *B.U.L.Rev.* 337 (1978) (and sources cited); Katz, "Lawyers for the Poor in Transition: Involvement, Reform, and the Turnover Problem in the Legal Services Program," 12 *Law & Soc'y Rev.* 275 (1978) (and sources cited); Abel, "Socializing the Legal Profession," 1 *Law & Pol'y Q.* 5 (1979). For example, critics from both the right and left have claimed that "routine" family law issues traditionally have attracted too little attention. Besharov, *Legal Services for the Poor: Time for Reform* (1989); Woods, "Challenges Facing Legal Services in the 1990s: Perspectives of Women and Family Law Advocates," *Clearinghouse Rev.* 457 (Oct.1988).

aid in the hopes of channeling frustrations into more fundamental change seems to these commentators strategically dubious and morally objectionable. In the absence of broader redistributive policies, the legal services program can at least redress some injustices and offers the potential for empowering clients.[10]

Given the enormous, and to some extent elastic, demand for legal aid and the finite resources that society has been prepared to supply, those critiques admit of no easy resolution. They do, however, pose a continuing challenge to those concerned about the adequacy of legal services to the poor.

Richard L. Abel, "Legal Services," in
M. Micklin and M. Olsen, eds.
Handbook of Applied Sociology (1981).[*]

Legal services are qualitatively different from the other social services discussed in this section. Physical and mental health, education, and leisure are important roughly in proportion to their quality and quantity. In seeking to improve the educational, medical, and recreational services available to disadvantaged groups, the fact that these services are unequally distributed throughout the population does not diminish the quality of whatever services are enjoyed. Equality of services may also be a goal, but it is an independent goal. This is not true of legal services. The role of the lawyer is to mediate conflict: to avoid, prepare for, engage in, and resolve disputes. This role presupposes an adversary. Consequently, the services of a lawyer are valuable only if they are roughly equal, in quality and quantity, to the services possessed by adversaries. Indeed, legal services that are consistently inferior may be worse than no services at all, since both adversary and arbiter are often more solicitous toward an unrepresented party than they are toward one who is inadequately represented.

. . .

Achieving Legal Equality

Equality in the distribution of legal services has a value beyond that of enhancing the welfare of the unrepresented or underrepresented. The very integrity of the U.S. legal system as

---

10. Cramton, "Crisis in Legal Services for the Poor," 26 *Vill.L.Rev.* 521 (1981); Woods, *supra* note 9.

[*] From Handbook of Applied Sociology edited by Marvin Olsen and Michael

an adversary system depends upon equal representation of all parties. The legitimacy of contemporary law rests on the assumption that optimally efficient allocations of scarce resources are produced by parties who freely negotiate with each other on the basis of equal information about the law and equal competence to use it. The adversarial model of litigation—whether in a civil action or a criminal prosecution—is grounded upon the belief that factual truth and fidelity to substantive and procedural rules are best achieved by partisan struggle between equal opponents, which at a minimum means opponents who are equally represented. Moreover, the theory of democratic pluralism assumes that all citizens are equally able to influence the making and application of laws. Given the influence of lawyers in U.S. politics, that assumption requires equal representation by lawyers before both the legislature and the executive at all levels of government.

Virtually every problem in the area of legal services is related to this central issue of equality. To what extent does the existing distribution satisfy the fundamental criteria of justice? What reforms have been proposed or attempted to achieve that ideal? How successful have they been? To answer these questions it is necessary to specify more precisely what we mean by equality of legal services.

Barriers to Legal Equality

A preliminary question is whether the parties who confront each other—either in face-to-face negotiation or before a third party such as a judge, arbitrator, or mediator—represent all the interests affected by the controversy? If there are other interests, is their failure to participate a function of inadequate resources, lack of information, or insufficient organization, and how can these deficiencies be remedied? ...

Although the legal profession is relatively homogeneous when contrasted with the general population, internally it is highly stratified. ... [Lawyers] differ greatly in expertise, resources, and influence. Consequently, equality of representation is as much a question of who is representing the party as of whether the party is being represented at all. Differences in the quality of legal representation are equally important in evaluating reforms that consciously seek to achieve the adversarial ideal. Thus, it is essential to look at the backgrounds and training of lawyers, at the way in which they are organized, and at the sources and extent of their funding—in comparison to those of their adversaries—when assessing the adequacy of services provided to the unrepresented or underrepresented.

Finally, although these problems are posed most starkly in litigation, where the parties confront each other in the midst of controversy, they are even more important outside that context. Do the parties have, or can they be given, equal access to, and power within, those institutions that formulate the rules governing future controversies?

. . .

Governmental Action

The most substantial redistributive effort thus far is the Legal Services Corporation (formerly the OEO Legal Services Program), whose budget is now close to a quarter billion dollars a year. This program has pursued three potentially conflicting objectives: 1) providing the poor with representation in the kinds of problems for which middle-class people routinely use lawyers, 2) challenging substantive and procedural rules that operate to the disadvantage of the poor, and 3) organizing the poor to enhance their political, social, and economic power. There is considerable disagreement about whether each goal should be sought, the priority that should be assigned to it, and whether it is attainable. Legal services lawyers have argued that the "need" of the poor for routine representation (in uncontested divorces or landlord-tenant disputes, for example) can never be met with the available resources and that, in any case, to do so would not break the circle of poverty. Furthermore, many have observed that legal services lawyers "burn out" if restricted to routine matters and can only sustain their commitment to the hard and often frustrating task of representing the poor if they are able to transform individual problems into larger issues, thereby endowing the rare victory with greater significance (Katz, 1978). But there is debate whether litigation, the principal strategy of poverty lawyers, can ever result in substantial redistribution. It is also clear that the energetic efforts by poverty lawyers to promote legal change and organize the poor aroused vigorous opposition by conservative lawyers and politicians. This led to the Legal Services Corporation Act of 1974, which severely curtailed both the legal and the political activities of its lawyers. ...

Programs for delivering legal services to the unrepresented or underrepresented can be analyzed in terms of many variables, but one of the most significant is whether lawyers are full-time specialists in providing the redistributed service or are primarily engaged in other activities. Thus, we can contrast the public defender with the private attorney appointed by the court to provide criminal defense in a specific case, "closed-panel" prepaid legal service plans with "open-panel" plans ..., and public interest law firms with the pro bono activities of the private bar. The counterpart of the "staffed offices" of the Legal Services Corporation that provide legal aid to the poor is judicare (a neologism borrowed from medicare), which reimburses members of the private bar on a piecework basis for services rendered to qualified clients. Although judicare has only been tried as a pilot project in two states, it has considerable potential significance because: 1) that project was extensively described, 2) the Legal Services Corporation is required by law to choose some mix of staffed offices, judicare, and other alternatives, and 3) judicare is the prevailing form of legal aid in much of Europe.

Comparisons of staffed office with judicare delivery systems employ a number of criteria. First, the eligibility standards of the two systems are pushed in opposite directions. Staffed offices are under pressure from the private bar to keep their standards low and not accept clients who might possibly be able to afford a private attorney. Staffed office attorneys may share that inclination, both because their lawyers are ideologically committed to serving the very poor and because they operate under constant caseload pressures. Private attorneys reimbursed under judicare, on the other hand, tend to construe eligibility liberally to justify state payment for clients who could not otherwise retain them. Considerations of geographic accessibility favor judicare in rural areas where the poor are too few and too thinly scattered to justify a full-time attorney, whereas staffed offices are preferable in cities since private lawyers are rarely located in poor communities. And although data are not available on the kinds of problems handled, it seems plausible that private attorneys would assimilate the needs of their judicare clients to those of their paying clients, whereas staffed office specialists would focus on legal problems that are distinctive to the poor. One indication of such a bias may be the fact that only 5 to 10 percent of eligible families used judicare each year, whereas 20 percent of the eligible population used staffed offices in the comparison communities.

One of the primary advantages claimed for judicare is that it gives poor clients the same right to choose a lawyer that is enjoyed by those who can afford to pay. Yet, this argument is suspect on several grounds: First, it is advanced by lawyers, who have an interest in being chosen, and not by clients. Second, until very recently the organized bar systematically denied all potential clients the information they would need about cost and quality in order to make an intelligent choice. Third, legal services lawyers are selected—not by clients, it is true, but by the experienced directors of staffed offices from among the many highly qualified aspirants to those jobs. Furthermore, there is evidence that the choice judicare ostensibly offers poor people is significantly curtailed by the attorneys chosen. Of the 57 lawyers approached by judicare clients, 36 turned down at least one case for reasons that are inherent in the use of private practitioners to serve the poor: 1) conflict of interest (the private bar necessarily represents the principal adversaries of the poor), 2) too busy or fee too low (judicare clients invariably pay less than private clients), 3) the problem is diagnosed as not legal or beyond the lawyer's competence, or 4) the claim is seen as unmeritorious or unlikely to succeed (private lawyers often take a narrow, traditional, unsympathetic view of the legal problems of the poor and lack the necessary competence to deal with their problems). These same reasons explain why private lawyers who did accept poor clients engaged in virtually no appellate litigation directed toward changing the laws that disadvantage the poor, in sharp contrast to staffed office lawyers. The finding that judicare clients are substantially more satisfied with their attorneys than staffed office clients are with theirs must therefore be qualified by Brakel's failure to inquire about the responses of those clients who were turned down. It seems to reflect the form of the services provided rather than their substance. But perhaps most significant is the relative cost of the two systems: judicare attorneys are almost twice as expensive as their staffed office counterparts, by the most conservative estimates. Yet, because each system has advantages and disadvantages, a mix of the two might well be desirable and, indeed, allow them to compete, thus permitting a market test of the questions posed above. Furthermore, it would enable those staffed office lawyers, who no longer wish to make the financial and psychological sacrifices inherent in full-time representation of the poor, to serve some poor clients through judicare, thus using the expertise they acquired to fulfill the ideological commitment they developed.

Legal Services Corporation Act of 1974

§ 1001, 88 Stat. 378 (1974) (codified at 42 U.S.C.A. § 2996).

Statement of Findings and Declaration of Purpose

Sec. 1001. The Congress finds and declares that—

(1) there is a need to provide equal access to the system of justice in our Nation for individuals who seek redress of grievances;

(2) there is a need to provide high quality legal assistance to those who would be otherwise unable to afford adequate legal counsel and to continue the present vital legal services program;

(3) providing legal assistance to those who face an economic barrier to adequate legal counsel will serve best the ends of justice;

(4) for many of our citizens, the availability of legal services has reaffirmed faith in our government of laws;

(5) to preserve its strength, the legal services program must be kept free from the influence of or use by it of political pressures; and

(6) attorneys providing legal assistance must have full freedom to protect the best interests of their clients in keeping with the Code of Professional Responsibility, the Canons of Ethics, and the high standards of the legal profession.

Legal Services Corporation, 1976 Annual Report
29–31 (1976).

A confession that the Corporation is still struggling with the question "Why legal services?" may seem embarrassing from an organization whose job it is to support those services. The reality is, however, that the Legal Services Corporation was created with relatively little attention to that issue. For understandable reasons, it was assumed during the congressional debates on the 1974 Act that a legal services program was necessary, and primary attention was focused on the form of the organization that would support it. The Corporation must now attempt to develop fuller answers to the question "Why legal services?" and—even more important—a better understanding of the implications of those answers for the role of the Corporation.

"Because they are needed." Is that not a sufficient answer? Poor people have a disproportionate number of legal problems that involve basic issues of survival; they need help in handling them. But why is this need—as opposed to the other needs of society in general and poor people in particular—to be met by public funds? And is it to be met for all legal problems of all poor people, or only for some of those problems? In short, "Because they are needed," is undeniably true—but it does not answer the question of purpose. "Needed for what?" must be explained, as well as the rationale for using public funds.

A logical starting point for such an inquiry is the Act that created the Legal Services Corporation. The introductory section to that Act contains congressional findings regarding the need for a federally-funded legal services program.

Congress declared that "there is a need to provide equal access to the system of justice in our Nation for individuals who seek redress of grievances." This statement recognizes the reality that law weighs most heavily upon poor people, and legal assistance can help minimize that burden. The similarity of that language to the words of the First Amendment suggests a congressional determination that poor people should have access to *all* the institutions with primary responsibility for making laws.

Congress also declared that "providing legal assistance to those who face an economic barrier to adequate legal counsel will serve best the ends of justice." This provision expresses the judgment that society as a whole has a stake in all of its members having access to the legal system. Society's economic and other arrangements will work as they are intended to work only if everyone can enforce the rules.

This conclusion is reinforced by the declaration that "for many of our citizens, the availability of legal services has reaffirmed faith in our government of laws." This suggests that one purpose of the legal services program is to help keep public officials faithful to the laws they administer—to assure that the legislature's purposes are not frustrated by the bureaucratic maze—and underscores the need for the Corporation's independence from the Executive Branch. The importance of reaffirming faith in our government of laws also makes the point that citizens cannot be expected to live under the law unless they have access to the legal system and some opportunity to use it.

Another approach is to build upon the statutory framework, and to develop a set of basic responses to the question "Why legal services?" At the July meeting the Board discussed the four responses that have been most frequently advanced:

☐ Legal services are an effective means to ameliorate the effects of poverty. The issue is disputed, and it assumes that the questions of what causes poverty can be answered. A compelling case can be made, nonetheless, that over the past decade legal services lawyers have removed some of the deprivations and degradations of poverty by forcing the implementation of social welfare legislation and protecting the rights of the poor. In this basic sense, at least, legal services are a means to alleviate poverty.

☐ Legal services for the poor are essential because the hurdles imposed by the legal system should not be insurmountable because of poverty. The government requires everyone to use the legal system in some situations: When one is sued, for example, or when one wants a divorce, or receives an eviction notice. That requirement should carry with it the means— court fees and lawyers, if necessary—to ensure that the poor are not precluded from this use of the legal system.

☐ Many of the substantive rules of law and the institutions that apply them affect the poor unfairly. It may be that more empirical evidence is needed on the issue, but those who have considered the matter do not have any question about its validity. It is at least clear that many poor people must rely upon government to help obtain the basic necessities of life, and government generally acts through law. Substantive rules of law developed to govern commercial transactions in a market economy do not always take account of the thin economic margins and lack of bargaining power of poor people. In short, the legal system often places distinctive, heavier, and unfair burdens on the poor.

☐ Access to the legal system is an inherent right of citizenship. That system is the chief mechanism for ordering and adjusting the affairs of individuals and society. As part of government, it belongs to all citizens regardless of their means. A premise of this approach is that if political liberty means anything, it must mean the opportunity to use and influence the law. A related premise is that individuals can hardly be asked to live under and respect the law unless they have an opportunity to use it. Society as a whole has a substantial stake in making the legal system available to all citizens, not just to some.

Those four propositions are not the only ones that can be advanced as purposes of legal services, and they are by no means mutually exclusive. Each of the four, however, suggests a somewhat different ordering of priorities for allocating scarce resources.

Gary Bellow, "Turning Solutions Into Problems: The Legal Aid Experience"

34 N.L.A.D.A. Briefcase, August 1977 at 106, 106, 108–10, 117–22.

In the modern welfare state ... the following contradiction ... emerges sharply; the social services deny, frustrate and undermine the possibilities ... of a just society at the same time they work toward and, in part, achieve greater degrees of human well

*being .... They express concern for individual and social welfare,
but they do so in a form shaped by ... distorted values and
structures ... Operating within a political and economic context
... [which] organizes their role ... they support and reinforce
conformity, among both clients and workers, to the very institutions
and values that generate the problems to which they ... were
addressed in the first place.*

Galper, *The Politics of Social Services* (1975).

A. THE VIEW FROM ABOVE: THE EXPANSION OF FEDERAL SUBSIDIZED LEGAL SERVICES FOR THE POOR

The federal Legal Services Program has been considered by
many commentators the most successful of the poverty programs
of the sixties. Begun in 1965 as part of the efforts of the Office of
Economic Opportunity to generate community action in poverty
areas throughout the country, the program quickly gained support
from the national bar, explicit recognition (and legitimation) in
the Economic Opportunity Act of 1965, and increased appropriations through its first five years. When Sargent Shriver first
committed nineteen million dollars of OEO's discretionary funds
to legal services for the poor, less than two-tenths of one percent of
the money spent nationally for lawyers in civil cases was being
devoted to persons financially unable to hire their own attorney;
what service was available came from charitably endowed legal
aid societies or the volunteer efforts of private practitioners.

Today, the Legal Services Corporation Act, which places direction of the program under an independent non-profit corporation, supports the expenditure of over [three] hundred million
dollars yearly to finance a network of local agencies and programs
which hire attorneys to provide civil legal representation for the
indigent throughout the country. ...

. . .

B. THE VIEW FROM BELOW: THE EXPANSION OF PROFESSIONAL CONTROL IN THE LEGAL SERVICES SYSTEM

. . .

If one spent time in enough programs, on enough days, with
enough patience, common strands would soon emerge. Despite
their commitment to avoid the kind of cautious, detached, client
controlling service that so many public bureaucracies—public
housing authorities, welfare departments—seem to provide, my
guess is that, if one looked carefully, one would conclude that this
is precisely the kind of service our clients are receiving. What
research now exists suggests the following recurrent features:

Routine Processing of Cases

Problems presented by clients in legal services offices by and large are dealt with routinely and perfunctorily. If a case is not considered to be a "legal problem", a referral is suggested. There is no follow-up to see if the client actually got to the referral agency or any collaboration with the referral agency after the client is referred. If the case is considered appropriate for a lawyer, it is typically "slotted" into a standardized pattern, i.e., getting the client time to move out in an eviction case; working out a payment schedule in a debt case. Only rarely does such "representation" involve any research, investigation or courtroom work. Indeed, in most cases, the lawyers do not leave the office, making arrangements for resolving most cases over the phone. Only if a particular case raises an "interesting" issue, or the client is unusually attractive or demanding, will any unusual amount of time, effort or planning be expended in providing representation.

Low Client Autonomy

Relationships with clients are dominated by these routines. The definition of the client's problems and the "best" available solutions are not mutually explored and elaborated; they are imposed by the lawyer's view of the situation and what is possible within it. In most discussions between lawyer and client, the lawyer does almost all of the talking, gives little opportunity for the client to express feelings or concerns, and consistently controls the length, topics and character of the conversation. Insofar as the client must elaborate the facts, they are obtained by a series of pointed, standard questions rather than any process that resembles a dialogue. Clients take this as "all they can expect" and are rarely aware that a different relationship with a lawyer is possible.

Narrow Definitions of Client Concerns

The corollary of this limiting mode of inquiry is that the only problems handled by the lawyers are those actually presented by the clients. Thus, if a client seeking a divorce has been defrauded in purchasing consumer goods, or is not receiving the social security benefits to which (s)he is entitled (but is unaware that a lawyer might be of assistance with such difficulties) the lawyer will not initiate inquiry into such problems. There is no concept of a "legal check-up" in legal services practice. Indeed, many clients actually feel discouraged from discussing other possible legal difficulties.

"Inadequate" Outcomes

Not surprisingly the vast majority of cases handled in this way result in settlements. Clients "agree" to move out, or to accept a percentage of back benefits claimed from the welfare department, or to give up a damage action against a credit company in return for a reduction of an indebtedness. In any given case such results may or may not be desirable. That is, whether a settlement is a "good" one depends on (a) how much more could have been obtained if settlement were rejected and aggressive representation continued; (b) whether what is settled for is more than the discounted value to the clients of what would have been obtained if the case went to trial. The utility and probability calculations here are, to say the least, very difficult.

Nevertheless, when potential damage claims (for rat bite, lead paint poisoning, or clear violations of state protective legislation) are being "traded off" for insubstantial reductions of back rent or past debts, without any adequate discussion with the client of the possible recovery (as is the case in a number of legal services offices) because that's the "way we've been handling those cases here", one can say that such results are unacceptable. Although the research is still limited in scope, reviews of typical settlements in legal services programs by panels of experienced lawyers suggest that results are often lower than they need be. That is, despite the prevailing pattern (which generates its own expectations and makes a higher settlement more difficult to obtain), the cases should have been far more aggressively pursued.

Finally, a surprising number of clients are inappropriately "helped" to recognize that settlement is the best course to follow. That is, acquiescence in negotiated settlements by clients is secured by the lawyers overstating the risk of not settling, and systematically manipulating the client's perceptions of the benefits of the suggested resolution and the difficulties the lawyer encountered in obtaining it. To use Erving Coffman's phrase, the client is "cooled out" to guarantee that what (s)he gets is as much or more than (s)he has been led to expect. Some qualifications, however, should be kept in mind in reflecting on the meaning of this picture of legal aid practice. First, it's important to recognize that the legal aid attorney, as an individual, is sympathetic and concerned about the plight of clients. Most legal services lawyers are not aware of the patterns that have begun to emerge. Their actions are experienced as reasonable responses to client difficulties. Indeed, there appears to be relatively little of the "blaming the victim" syndrome in legal aid work which William Ryan found prevalent in government service to poor and minority-group clients. Although there is some stereotyping and a good deal of paternalism toward clients, the more common attitude among the lawyers is that the clients are victims of an unresponsive and essentially *unchangeable* system. Often the most a legal services lawyer feels he or she can do is to "ease" the burden a little, as efficiently as possible, for as long as possible. To do this over any period of time seems to require a good deal of detachment, "realism" and resistance to investing too much of one's time, energy (and credibility) in a particular case or controversy.

. . .

C. THE VIEW FROM WITHIN: THE NATURE OF THE LE-GAL SERVICES EXPERIENCE

. . .

Why, after all, should professional legal advice to the poor become shallow, cautious, and incomplete? Why should cases be handled passively, routinely, unaggressively? The lawyers who work in these programs are decent, committed human beings who have often given up better paying jobs and working conditions to do this sort of work. They come from a cross section of the nation's law schools as well as the upper stratum of the nation's successful students, and enter such poverty-type programs well aware of the dangers of bureaucratization and unresponsiveness in social services. Why are they not more cognizant of and resistant to influences which tend to undermine professional norms that support personal, partisan "legal care"?

Two related answers have often been advanced in response to these questions: (a) the high caseloads; and (b) the enormous need. Both correctly point to significant features of the availability of legal assistance in the United States. ...

The thesis is that these realities create enormous pressures for routinized, mass processing of cases. It is posited that, given the need, most recipients would rather receive a little help than none at all. The legal aid bar, which is subsidized, after all, to serve the community, feels it must respond to this need by taking many, many more cases than can be carefully, aggressively handled. The patterns of practice that emerge are the "best that can be done" under these circumstances.

The problem with this notion (which is widely articulated within programs) is that it functions far more as justification than explanation. Obviously, the service being offered does not simply reflect what clients "really want". Clients are not told they are receiving only minimal assistance, or that there may be approaches to some of their problems which are not being explored with them. They are also not afforded a choice between efforts which might more generally affect the conditions in the neighborhood or community in which they live, and some lesser attention to their immediate concerns. What people "want" is inevitably indeterminate, depending on their knowledge and what they consider possible and desirable. It's an unusual client who would know without being so advised, that a lawyer less committed to routine service might stimulate litigation and concerted action to control exclusions of their children from school, or might offer a way of doing something about the garbage on the street, or the rats in the walls.

Nor does the fact that some people with legal problems want some service rather than none answer the question of whether service should thereby be diminished to those who are already being helped. The legal profession's ethics insist that a lawyer not take more cases than he or she can reasonably handle, on the obvious ground that a client has very little ability to prevent the lawyer from cutting corners or otherwise compromising a case. A policy which ignored this mandate would seem to need more justification than "the greatest good for the greatest number", especially when the number is still so small. In circumstances ... in which available resources are grossly inadequate, it's a puzzling (and perhaps cynical) judgment that the small expansion of service that a "minimal help-maximum numbers" policy permits should essentially be paid for by limited attention to the program's existing clients.

Most important, such a policy reflects a choice by the lawyers of the priorities they pursue and the character of the service they offer. No program has ever been required by formal policy of either OEO or the Legal Services Program to process large numbers of clients in the routinized modes I've described. Indeed, the public pronouncements of the Legal Services Corporation embrace a far more partisan orientation in legal aid practice. The legal aid bar decides to handle the cases in the way they do, no matter how inevitable this course of conduct comes to be perceived and experienced. What is needed is to understand why the following may offer some clues to this puzzle.

1. The Demands for Accommodation

The most pervasive influence on the legal aid lawyer (and all lawyers in the United States) is the enormous pressure to settle. It is a given of the administration of justice in this country, whatever its performance in the show-case situation of a murder trial or other highly publicized hearing, that neither our judicial nor administrative machinery could function without primary reliance on, and powerful inducements to, agreed-upon outcomes.

The legal aid lawyer practices uncomfortably at the center of many of these pressures for settlement. Though the clients often have real potential claims and defenses, they are also highly vulnerable to loss and often unable to handle the uncertainties that lengthy legal procedures inevitably entail. Legal aid programs are in a similar situation. They have clear authority to aggressively assert the client's claims but are often vulnerable to political reprisal, including loss of funding, if they depart too dramatically from the "way things are done" in their communities. It's not surprising that the legal aid lawyer feels real pressure from clients and superiors not to take too many risks in the way cases are handled. This is compounded by further pressures from opposing lawyers and agency personnel, many of whom could not do their jobs or make a living unless large numbers of cases were smoothly processed and resolved, and judges and other "deciders" as well, who clearly recognize that they don't have the resources, time, or energy to hear every case on its merits. All have a very real stake in disputes being speedily and informally resolved.

The pressures created by clients and programs are very seductive. A negotiated settlement "satisfies" all interests with virtually no possibility of criticism. How, after all, is one to determine what is a "good" settlement? The client must rely on the lawyer's judgment about the risks of going to trial, or whether a settlement in a particular case is the best possible under the circumstances. An outsider can only compare the results in any given case with similar cases. Since most offices regularly settle for low value and rarely go to trial, there is usually no reasonable basis for saying that in any specific instance, a trial or different settlement was preferable to what was obtained.

The potential power of adversaries and judges over the lawyers and clients further adds to the settlement solutions. Opposing counsel or a court can bestow many benefits on lawyers willing to play by the bureaucratic rules of the game. This includes a break now and then for a client with a weak claim, accommodation to a busy schedule, or even being helped to "look good" when public performance slips a little. Law practice is an uncertain business; the need for some predictability in doing the "law job" essentially depends on good working relationships with other professionals engaged in it.

Indeed, to do otherwise, can invite very real sanctions. Most legal aid lawyers are well aware of the possibilities for retaliation available to the hostile social worker (initiating a fraud investigation against a client, for example) or the angry landlord's attorney (who can almost always serve the client with a "late rent" eviction notice). Few have not seen or known of judges who have punished clients for taking too much of the court's time, or for filing "frivolous motions". Bureaucratic imperatives speak loudly in the parts of the legal system in which legal aid lawyers work.

. . .

2. The Vulnerabilities of Inexperience

The foregoing pressures demand considerable skill and experience of any legal services attorney who would act more politically or aggressively than the norms of law-as-practiced generally permit. There is always the danger the opposing counsel or even the court will devote energy and resources to "teaching the lawyer a lesson", however legitimate the client's claim, or that settlement will be refused in cases when it is appropriate and necessary. Even when the lawyer has been relatively successful in obtaining his or her client's goals, there is never any assurance that these goals were not initially set too low, or that the lawyer has, by not pressing the particular case, severely limited his or her effectiveness in the future. Partisan representation of client interests in a highly bureaucratized legal system is always a source of considerable strain and uncertainty. These tensions are enormously exacerbated when the lawyer's client is poor.

Unfortunately, very little in the lawyer's training or education provides the skill, confidence, or orientations necessary to protect clients in such a system. Whatever his or her initial motives or politics, the attitudes and skills of a young lawyer are almost entirely shaped by the prevailing patterns of practice; that is, "rookie" lawyers, like their counterparts in welfare departments, police departments and baseball teams, tend to conform to established ways of doing things.

The legal aid lawyer is particularly vulnerable to these influences. Clients are usually not sufficiently knowledgeable and demanding to hold lawyers accountable to quality standards. The lawyers are unlikely to have had any law school instruction for a practice which, to be done well, requires knowledge of a large body of law and a complex panoply of skills. This is compounded by a turnover rate among experienced attorneys in legal aid work which is so high that there is virtually no training or supervision in the offices to supplement these deficiencies.

The massive caseloads perform complex functions in these circumstances. On the one hand, the number of cases confront the inexperienced lawyers with demands that prevent them from ever adequately developing their skills and knowledge.

Also the high caseloads afford a legitimate reason why particular cases cannot be thoroughly prepared and investigated, or linked to local efforts to organize or exert political pressure. To believe otherwise, would exacerbate the tensions of inadequate training for, at best, a very difficult job.

. . .

Systematic Self-Scrutiny of the Character and Quality of Practice

Critical to any steps to guarantee quality legal work within the legal services system are mechanisms for accurately and continuously assessing the representation being provided. Although the pressures of legal aid practices are quite real, we don't know how far and effectively they can be altered. The problem now is that most legal services lawyers are only dimly aware of the degree to which their work has become routinized, impersonal and controlling. What is needed are ways in which the prevailing patterns within offices can be exposed and discussed without generating resentment and defensiveness.

Such efforts would have to come largely from the lawyers themselves (but with the support of their programs and the Legal Services Corporation). Offices might experiment with (a) systematic review of case files; (b) case presentations (similar to post-mortems in medicine); (c) regularly circulating case files within the offices; (d) pairing lawyers in handling cases; (e) regular in-office testing of staff, on skills and information; (f) surveying clients to assess their reactions to the service; (g) review of the office's practices by outside consultants. Whatever method is used, its purpose must be to encourage the lawyers to articulate the implicit standards and attitudes they are bringing to the work and to systematically examine the ways cases are being handled.

. . .

Client Education and Participation

A related way to increase the accountability of lawyers to legal aid clients (and both lawyer and client awareness of the character of the service being provided) is to educate clients to evaluate the service themselves. Programs interested in this approach might encourage or institute: (a) written materials on what can be asked, expected, and obtained from/by lawyers in different kinds of cases (to be distributed in the waiting rooms and throughout the community served); (b) meetings and communications among clients and former clients interested in the work of the office; (c) more client participation in preparation of their cases; (d) regular legal "check-ups", benefit reviews and other directly beneficial educational programs designed to make clients more cognizant of their rights; (e) enlarged opportunities for paralegals and other office personnel to critique the quality and character of the service; (f) an effective procedure for receiving, investigating and deciding client grievances against the lawyers and the office; (g) regular public reports and meetings with the "client community" (through local press, travel and community groups, etc.); (h) inclusion of substantial numbers of clients on the Board of Directors.

None of these, of course, offer any kind of panacea. Several have been tried and have been more or less successful in given programs and communities. What they all have in common is the belief that there must be real attempts by the office to make itself accountable to the people it serves, both in individual cases and with respect to its overall operation. Whatever its limits, a real commitment by the programs' staff to explaining, disclosing and listening to criticism, not only from each other but from clients as well, is basic to altering the patterns that now dominate legal aid practice.

. . .

Focused Legal-Political Action

Finally, the offices and their staffs will have to be much more explicitly engaged in efforts to affect institutional practices and conditions than they are now. ... Specific discussion with clients about political choices in the handling of their cases is far more likely to empower and educate them than continuing the myth that their cases are being resolved by an apolitical body of rules in an apolitical legal system. Few lawyers who have been involved with clients in political activity (rent strikes, boycotts) have not been struck by the degree to which their ability to understand and "tell their lawyers what they wanted" increased in the course of the experience.

In addition to the foregoing is the real possibility that such an orientation in the day-to-day work of legal aid offices offers a way without re-introducing the test case-service case dichotomy of reconciling accountability to individual clients and the need for larger systemic changes in the private and public institutions that daily shape their lives. There is an enormous gap between existing laws and the practices of most public and private institutions.

1. *A sufficiently limited number of day-to-day cases so that* lawyers can coordinate and compare the way they handle cases;

2. *Selection of "target" institutions whose illegal practices* affect a significant number of the program's clients.

3. *Representation of large numbers of clients who have* been victims of these practices, through referrals, in-depth interviews, and solicitation. ...

4. *Service to clients that maximizes individual claims and* increases the office's knowledge of the personnel, practices and vulnerabilities of the target institutions.

5. *Coordination and communication within the office to* crystallize strategies and goals directed to the target institutions. This might include legislative efforts, support for community organization or class action litigation.

6. *Direct contact by the office with the target institutions to* seek change in the policies and practices documented in handling the cases.

7. *Coalitions with other community groups seeking similar* changes.

E. THE TROUBLING ALTERNATIVES

A massive expansion of minimal, routinized legal assistance throughout the low-income areas of the country, mediated by selective efforts at "law reform", is potentially a powerful system of social control, capable of defining and legitimating particular grievances and resolutions and ignoring others. Legal aid lawyers, unwilling or unable to respond to client concerns in ways which link them to a larger vision of social justice, can readily become purveyors of acquiescence and resignation among the people that they are seeking to help. Clients can be literally "taught" that their situations are natural, inevitable, or their own fault, and that dependence on professional advice and guidance is their only appropriate course of action; that is, legal assistance for the poor can become a bulwark of existing social arrangements. To echo a now familiar phrase, a profession that is not part of the solution can soon become part of the problem. The legal aid experience may soon be a troubling illustration of the modern homily.

W. Clark Durant, "Maximizing Access to Justice: A Challenge to the Legal Profession"

February 12, 1987—New Orleans, Louisiana

(This speech has been retyped by <u>Bar Leaders for the Preservation</u> <u>of Legal Services for the Poor</u> for the information of bar officials nationwide.)

. . .

Today I want to talk about maximizing access to justice and a challenge to our profession, a profession with a rich and glorious tradition. But it is a challenge that will require all of us to re-think some of our assumptions. Let us do it today with an open heart and in good faith for the demands of justice require no less.

The President, as he has since 1980, recommends zero funding for the Legal Services Corporation. As I said in Detroit, I welcome the courage of the President's proposal. It requires us to ask fundamental and basic questions, questions quite frankly that would not otherwise be asked. Senator Kennedy is correct when he stated that "the mere existence of a program is no excuse for its perpetuation . . . . the unexamined program is not worth keep-ing." Senator Moynihan, a fortnight ago, urged the replacement of the nation's current welfare system. "It cannot be reformed," he said. This was a follow-up to the President's courageous call for a new welfare strategy.

Today I am calling for the replacement of the Legal Services Corporation. It cannot be reformed in the present context. I am doing it because it is time to break out of the gridlock that restricts debate and more importantly denies maximum access to justice for poor people. Now is the time to go beyond the status quo. We must articulate a new vision, a vision that emphasizes client control, choice, and accountability; a vision that empowers all people to have more control over their own lives, a vision that broadens the neighborhood and community base of those who resolve disputes; and an idea that gives strength and dignity to advocates on behalf of the afflicted and oppressed.

I want to say at the outset that there are many good lawyers funded by LSC. I know, I have met many of them. ... But to achieve the broader vision of which I speak, there are at least three areas of reform: the debate about the Legal Services Corpo-ration itself, laws affecting the admission and practice of law, and the allocation of costs in litigation.

The ultimate empowerment for people to enforce their rights under law is to require, in some manner, the losing party to pay the litigation costs of a prevailing party. It is a rule that has need for much refinement. In its essence though the rule permits the claims of any person, no matter their income or status, to be evaluated by any lawyer and pursued or not primarily on their merits, not on one's ability to pay.

By expanding the base of lawyers to whom a poor person could and would go to pursue a claim, system overload on existing staff lawyers can be alleviated. It deserves study. Here though let us turn to the debate about LSC.

Whenever LSC is challenged, its champions insist that the poor deserve the same opportunities for high quality legal services as everyone else. The fact is the legal system does not work at all well for everyone else. Representation of the poor is not the primary root of this crisis. The problems are far broader and hence the scope of reform must be far broader.

The Legal Services Corporation debate is not a sudden, trivial, or transient debate. It is not a debate about whether there should be legal services for poor people. Of course there should be. The debate stems from two fundamentally different notions about federally funded legal services. One idea is essentially non-political. Lawyers represent people in individual cases to enforce their rights and to resolve any of the myriad of claims confronting individual people in dealing with the government, other individuals or institutions. Yes, even class actions are appropriate at times. It is not primarily about institutional or social reform. It is a dynamic relationship. The immediate need of the individual client is the focus.

The Legal Services Movement idea originated primarily in the OEO's effort in the Sixties to eradicate poverty and to bring about broad social reform through litigation. For many in the movement, then and now, social reform concerns the "meaningful redistribution of wealth and income in this country." Gary Bellow of Harvard says, changing America's "deeply stratified class system ... is [the] primary concern of most of us who do legal services work." In this idea of Legal Services, the poor are a class, a client community. According to Alan Houseman, their individual demand for legal services is considered uninformed.

This second idea of Legal Services is indeed a political movement to some extent. James Katz, the author of *Organizing for the Eighties*, notes that "future [law reform] success will depend upon the ability to develop the handles to mobilize the 'new unemployed' constituency into a potent political force." James D. Lorenz, Jr., a founder of California Rural Legal Aid, one of the oldest legal services organizations, said it very bluntly to *Newsweek* in 1981. "You can bankrupt the capitalist system through legal action ..."

Edgar Cahn, a former Law Dean at Antioch noted that Movement lawyers risk becoming unaccountable advocates imposing their own convictions as to what is best for a client rather than having a client-centered client-controlled relationship. Movement legal services focuses more on comprehensive strategies to implement policies said to be advantageous to the poor. Whether such policies are advantageous is a matter of much debate. That is why we have the political process though not free legal services.

Even within the Legal Services Movement the philosophic debate regarding LSC is overlapping. It results in, to quote Alan Houseman, "Much ... a blurring of principles and effects to the point that only pragmatism prevails." Pragmatism, glued together with lots of money, was what we had in 1980.

Pragmatism is hardly a program worthy of hard earned taxpayers' money. Pragmatism is hardly a vision to expand justice and open opportunities for the poor or any one else.

. . .

The greatest barrier to widely dispersed low cost dispute resolution services for the poor, and for all people, could very well be the laws protecting our profession. They make it a cartel. Like any such laws, they limit or distort supply; they increase prices; and they create dislocations in the marketplace.

. . .

The legal monopoly rests on two major pillars. The first are laws that set aside specific work exclusively for lawyers. Anyone else who performs "lawyer's work" may be prosecuted for the unauthorized practice of law [UPL statutes]. The second is a series of restrictions on how one may become a lawyer. These restrictions are really barriers to competition, not guardians of competence.

. . .

The question is really whether we truly want to maximize access to justice and in what ways. Shakespeare is wrong. We need not kill all the lawyers. We simply need to de-regulate them. Open up the profession. Broaden the base. Let more people, let more institutions deliver the services. Costs will come down, services will be expanded and alternatives in resolving disputes will be developed. Deregulation in the trucking, airline, and railroad industries, and even, to some extent the accounting profession, to name but a few, all reflect this positive development for consumers. Justice likewise is too important to be left bottled up by laws protecting the legal profession.

. . .

REFERENCES

R. Abel, *American Lawyers* (1988).

American Bar Association, *Civil Justice: An Agenda for the 1990s* (1990).

S. Brakel, *Judicare: Public Funds, Private Lawyers and Poor People* (1974).

Brakel, "Styles of Delivery of Legal Services to the Poor" (Book Review), 1977 *Am.Bar Found.Research J.* 219.

E. Brownell, *Legal Aid in the United States* (1951).

Buck, "The Legal Services Corporation: Finally Separate But Not Quite Equal," 27 *Syracuse L.Rev.* 611 (1976).

M. Cappelletti, J. Gordley, & E. Johnson, *Toward Equal Justice: A Comparative Study of Legal Aid in Modern Societies* (1975).

Carlin, Howard, & Messinger, "Civil Justice and the Poor: Issues for Sociological Research," 1 *Law & Soc'y Rev.* Nov. 1966.

Cole & Greenberger, "Staff Attorneys vs. Judicare: A Cost Analysis, 50 *J.Urb.L.* 705 (1973).

Cramton, "Crisis in Legal Services for the Poor," 26 *Vill. L.Rev.* 521 (1981).

Galanter, "The Duty *Not* to Deliver Legal Services," 30 *U.Miami L.Rev.* 929 (1976).

E. Johnson, *Justice and Reform: The Formative Years of the O.E.O. Legal Services Program* (1974).

Legal Services Corporation, *Delivery Systems Study: A Policy Report to the Congress and the President of the United States* (June 1980).

R. Marks, *The Legal Needs of the Poor: A Critical Analysis* (1971).

F. Marks, R. Hallauer & R. Clifton, *The Shreveport Plan: An Experiment in the Delivery of Legal Services* (1974).

Schlossberg and Weinberg, "The Role of Judicare in the American Legal System," 54 *A.B.A.J.* 1000, 1003–04 (1968).

Tunney, "Foreward: Financing the Cost of Enforcing Legal Rights," 122 *U.Pa.L.Rev.* 632 (1974).

Wexler, "Practicing Law for Poor People," 79 *Yale L.J.* 1049 (1970).

For related issues concerning public interest representation, see the bibliography in Part III.

Part IV

MAINTAINING PROFESSIONAL
STANDARDS

INTRODUCTION

A primary characteristic of any profession is its autonomy in defining qualifications of membership and standards of service. The nationale for such autonomy is that the profession is best situated to identify the ethical attributes and technical skills necessary for competent practice, and that such qualities can be assessed in educational, admissions, and disciplinary contexts. The following excerpts review the bar's attempts to make such assessments, and the premises from which they proceed.

James W. Hurst, The Growth of American Law
256, 277–84, 292–93 (1950).

Well past 1850, the chief method of legal education was the apprenticeship: The student read law in an older lawyer's office; he did much of the hand copying of legal instruments that had to be done before the day of the typewriter; and he did many small services in and about the office, including service of process. Sometimes the older man might take these incidental services as his pay for his preceptorship. But stiff fees were paid for the privilege of reading in the office of many a leader of the bar. Legal biography amply witnesses that such training was of widely varying thoroughness and quality; that it was typically not of great length of time; and that much of it, as in the interminable copying of documents, was of a rote character. ...

Even in the mid-nineteenth-century period of most nominal standards of admission, the states did not treat the practice of law as an activity that was an inherent, private right of any person who chose to follow it. There were early efforts in some colonies to forbid all law practice. But as the development of commerce and land speculation brought the first demand for full-time professional legal service, the colonial legislatures provided that the courts should control admission to the bar. Local procedures varied, but by the eve of the Revolution a relatively strong beginning had been made in creating some meaningful standards for admission to the practice. However, this beginning broke down during the Revolutionary years when a number of factors combined to turn public opinion against measures which might build up a strong legal profession. Many leading lawyers adhered to the Crown; English-based institutions, including the common law, were politically unpopular; debtors associated lawyers with the hardships of the depressed years after independence. The imperious demands of the democratic opinion which gathered force in the Jeffersonian years and came to full expression in the Jacksonian 1830's, brought extreme relaxation of professional standards.

As in so many other instances, so here the generation that began with the '70s was a turning point. It brought a new emphasis on the rationalization of private and then of public affairs, which showed itself in the matter of bar standards. Improvement in standards for admission to the bar was part of a general movement in which old callings regained professional status and new ones sought it.

Before the Civil War the only professions in this country that were not freely open to all comers were law and medicine (the latter category sometimes included dentistry), and in a few cities pharmacy. In all of these callings restrictions that earlier had some meaning wore very thin during the mid-nineteenth century. But between 1868 and 1878 the first State Board of Bar Examiners was set up (in New Hampshire).

... By the 1930's, "professional" licensing had so far extended as to suggest that there was more zeal to use this as a means to limit competition than to define areas that could be accurately described in required learning or standards as professions. A count in 1932 showed that 1 or more of 18 representative states had by then licensed a total of 210 occupations or businesses. ...

At no stage in this country was formal control of bar admissions given to the profession itself. This was the more notable because it departed from the strong contrary English tradition of guildlike organization of lawyers under their own discipline. On the other hand, we showed the English inheritance in the fact that control of the profession did not come to rest in the schools, as it did in large degree on the Continent. After 1750 in some Northern states, especially in Massachusetts and New York, the courts delegated their responsibility for admissions to county or other local bar organizations to such a degree as to make the bar the controlling authority. Such precedent might have broadened into general bar control. But this _de facto_ authority was exercised in so drastic a fashion as to spread the conviction that it was the instrument of a selfish monopoly. On the eve of the democratic revolution in standards, Massachusetts required, before complete privileges of law practice were granted, a course of training and practice that totaled eleven years for a man who had gone to college, or nine years for one who had not. New York required ten years in either case. Such terms of preparation fitted 1940 standards; plainly they were not justified by the available education of 1800. They quickly fell before the prevailing temper of relaxed standards. Not until the American Bar Association, in 1921, made its first firm assertion of recommended minimum admissions standards was there any substantial return to control of the situation by the organized bar. ...

Indeed, over most of our history there were no official standards of preparation for the bar, and such standards as existed in fact were largely the product of the schools' traditions. Of 19 states and organized territories in 1800, 14 required a definite preparatory period of professional study. But such a requirement was made by only 11 of the 30 states and territories that existed in 1830; and in 1860 only 9 of 39 states and territories had even nominal requirements of professional preparation. By 1890 nearly one half, by 1920 about three fourths, and by 1940 all states required some professional study preparatory to admission. The spread of this requirement was gradually attended by a lengthening of the period of professional preparation, up to the three-year requirement which by 1940 was fixed in forty states.

Naturally, through the years in which most states did not even set minimum requirements of professional training, they set no requirements for prelegal study. In 1921 the American Bar Association first committed itself to a substantial declaration in favor of higher standards. As late as this, only fourteen states had any requirements of preliminary general education, and only ten required the equivalent of graduation from high school as a condition of eligibility for admission to the bar. But advance was fast after the Association's action. By 1940 over two thirds of the states had adopted the requirement of at least two years of college preparation or its equivalent, as a prerequisite for admission.

Once a firm initiative was taken in 1921, progress toward higher preparatory requirements for the practice of law came with amazing speed. Twenty years saw change little short of a revolution. Of course this advance had more meaning for the future than for any immediate large-scale change in the background of the bar as a whole. Legal biography showed that, before he entered practice, the average lawyer of 1800 had a basic education a year or so short of finishing what the twentieth century would call grammar school, plus 6 to 14 months' training in law. A random sampling from over the country in 1931 showed an average basic education that reached through about one year of college and two and a quarter years in a law school or in office training. Clearly, during the whole period of 131 years the well-trained men from good law schools had been "a tiny stream—emptied into an ocean of inadequate preparation." Clearly, too, when one allowed for the comparative educational facilities of the times, and for the increased complexity of the society, the 1931 average of education was no startling degree beyond that of 1800.

The examination was throughout the main official instrument for enforcing standards of preparation for the bar. Before 1870 it was typically oral. In any case, oral or written, it was administered with casual leniency; the approach was characteristic of times and communities that were close enough to the frontier so that they had no awe of formality or specialized knowledge, and small enough so that personal acquaintance and relationships were a substantial check on conduct. ...

Jonathan Birch of Bloomington, Illinois, recalled the circumstances of his examination for the Illinois bar by Abraham Lincoln, a member of the board of examiners by appointment of the state supreme court. The candidate found the examiner in his hotel room, partly undressed, and so far as the facilities permitted, taking a bath, which proceeded during the examination. ...

The movement to lengthen the required period of professional study went on for a generation after the Civil War before it was accompanied by a substantial effort to improve the examining machinery. Before 1890 only four states had boards of bar examiners, and in no more than half a dozen had written examinations been used. However, when the leading law schools began to use the written examination, this encouraged adoption of the practice in the states, where it became the invariable method of examination after 1900. ...

Tighter examination standards involved important secondary issues. In the pattern typical of our legal growth, these questions were not squarely faced or planned for, but were allowed to work themselves out under the pressure of events. First was the problem of bringing the law curriculum and the bar examination requirements into reasonable relation. Second, and closely related, was the need to devise machinery which would make the examinations produce the selective result hoped of them. For forty years the schools and the state authorities had no regular channel of communication through which to seek agreement on the standards of legal education and of examinations. There was considerable friction. Until the 1930's, bar examinations tended to stress rote learning and details peculiar to the jurisdiction; both emphases were wholly foreign to what the leading schools and the American Bar Association standards envisaged as proper lines of professional training. This problem could not be separated from that of the organization of the bar examining machinery. Bar examiners were part-time workers at their task; they received no pay or inadequate pay; they were selected by no standard criteria; they served terms so limited as to prevent their building experience in the job. Although from 1900 on, the schools had their association, a National Conference of Bar Examiners was not created until 1931, to work to improve standards and to co-operate on a national basis with the bar and the schools.

We thus had a long history of easy access to the bar; applicants pressed eagerly forward; there was little organization or tradition to stiffen the administration of admissions requirements. It was not surprising, then, that the bar examinations worked directly to exclude only a small part of those who were willing and able to make repeated efforts to pass them. The examinations lacked the practical support to effect a quota system, if that was desired—as it was by a substantial opinion at the bar. In 1937, 81 per cent of the country's practitioners were in the 35 states which had adopted the American Bar Association standards for minimum qualifications for the bar.

As tests of professional preparation, examinations excluded impressive percentages of applicants on the first attempt—from 46 to 52 per cent the country over in the 1930's, for example. But the states invariably allowed persons who failed, to repeat the examination; only a few began ... to limit the number of attempts that might be made. When allowance was made for repeaters, survey in five states showed that about 90 per cent of all who applied from 1922 to 1925 eventually passed. ...

Even when admissions standards sank to their lowest point, eligibility was conditioned on the "good moral character" of the applicant. Though the states continuously insisted on this factor, up to mid-twentieth century they had not found adequate means to test "character." In their nature the bar examinations were not adapted to this end. ...

In the early 1920's several selective state bar associations campaigned successfully for laws establishing the "integrated bar." ... Among the rest, by 1940 over half had seen active promotion of the idea.

In origin, the "integrated bar" plan was advanced primarily as a means for better discipline of lawyers in their relations with clients. The inflexible remedy of disbarment was typically the only remedy theretofore provided to deal with professional misconduct. For it the integrated bar laws substituted a range of measures, from disbarment to suspension or reprimand. Old-style disbarment called for cumbersome proceedings in court; in place of these, the new type of law authorized proceedings by agencies of the bar itself, to apply the various remedies provided. Court proceedings inevitably meant publicity which might greatly damage the accused even if he were finally found innocent. In place of this the new laws provided unpublicized proceedings carried on within the organized bar. ...

Education, admissions policy, and organization wove together to form main strands in the character of the bar in the United States. The history of admissions policy and bar organization created a challenge to legal education. The decline in admissions standards, and the disappearance of dominant local bar associations, gave the law schools the opportunity to assert a leadership in regard to bar standards and law reform that was without parallel in the Anglo-American legal world.

I. LEGAL EDUCATION

**Robert Stevens, "Two Cheers for 1870:
The American Law School"**

5 Perspectives in American History 416–19, 426–
30 (D. Fleming & B. Bailyn eds. 1971).

Formalized apprenticeship, together with the severing of ties
with England, ... led to the establishment of private law
schools. They were generally outgrowths of the law offices of
practitioners who had shown themselves to be particularly skilled,
or popular, as teachers. The most famous of these schools was the
Litchfield Law School in Connecticut, formally established in 1784,
which grew out of the teaching activities of Tapping Reeve during
the Revolutionary War. There, under the guidance of Reeve and
James Gould, a course of studies based on Blackstone, but adapted
to the American scene, attracted students from every state in the
new nation—students who were to confirm the suspicion of many
that lawyers had an inside track in running for public office in
America. The school, in this sense, was singularly important in
developing an American legal culture. Other private schools—at
the height of their popularity at the beginning of the nineteenth
century there were a dozen such—also played a role, although
none rivalled Litchfield.

. . .

These mergers, which might be thought to have brought
together the best in "academic" and "practical" law, seemed to
bode well for establishment of institutions of legal education in
this country. The mergers coincided, however, with that general
undermining of established institutions known, conveniently, as
Jacksonian Democracy. For the next forty years the fledgling law
schools, like the fledgling medical schools, and, to a lesser extent
the universities themselves, were under a pressure which prevented what many were later to call "progress ...."

From the earliest times, and both before and after the Revolution, lawyers had been under various forms of attack, but such has
been the fate of the profession in many countries in many periods.
During the 1830's, however, the attack on "the class of lawyers"
reached a remarkable pitch, for many perceived the lawyer in
Tocqueville's terms—as the natural aristocrat in America.

. . .

504

Some states had abolished or reduced the requirements for apprenticeship even before 1830. But, as formal education increasingly fell into disrespect, the outward manifestations of professionalism appeared to collapse. ... The effect on legal education was in many ways predictable.

. . .

While a few new schools appeared both in the East and the Midwest, many also closed. In 1840 there were, in the nation, nine university-affiliated law schools with a total, including Harvard's, of 345 students. With a few possible exceptions in the South, the university base for all law schools was at most a holding operation in the decades before the Civil War.

. . .

[Developments after the Civil War were in large part influenced] by the rise of the Harvard Law School, a phenomenon attributable to two appointments: that of Charles Eliot, a scientist, as president in 1869 and that of Christopher Columbus Langdell to the newly created post of dean of the law school in 1870. There is no doubt that during Langdell's deanship, which lasted until 1895, Harvard became the preeminent law school in this country, and institutionalized legal training was clearly established as *de rigueur* for leaders of the profession. Moreover, finally and irrevocably, law was accepted as an appropriate study for university education.

It is from the Langdell period that many of the later characteristics of American legal education emerge. In addition to his contribution of the case class and the Socratic method, structurally it was Langdell's goal to turn the legal profession into a university educated one—and not at the undergraduate level, but through a three-year post-baccalaureate degree. The requirement of graduation from college as a prelude to law school was not finally achieved at Harvard until 1909, but the three-year degree was achieved somewhat sooner. In 1871 the LL.B. was extended from eighteen months to two years, and in 1899 the three-year goal was reached. In the meantime the increasingly strict entrance examination was supplemented by rigorous annual examinations.

While ... Eliot was planning his new school at Harvard, other forces were at work. Unwillingness to rely on law office training had affected not only those expecting to enter the elite levels of the profession. The Civil War saw the birth of the land grant college and thus the rapid expansion of state universities. Attendance at a university became possible for many who could not have considered it earlier. Iowa, in 1868, became the first state university west of the Mississippi to establish a law school, although a private university—Washington University in St. Louis—had established a law school the previous year.

. . .

The period also saw the beginning of training for black lawyers. Indeed, the growth of law schools of all types was so rapid that by 1917 only seven states did not have law schools within their borders. Perhaps more significant still was the urbanization of legal education. By 1917, fifty-nine percent of cities over 100,000 had law schools.

. . .

This latter development, in particular, was closely related to the rise of a whole new sector of the law school market. The first part-time schools were established in the 1860's with students who had full-time jobs—not by any means always in law offices. . . . In 1889–1890 there was one mixed day-and-night school with 134 students and nine night schools with 403 students (as contrasted with fifty-one "pure" day schools, with 3,949 students). By 1916 the emphasis had shifted dramatically. There were by then twenty-one day-and-night schools with 5,164 students and forty-three night schools with 5,570 students. . . . A class of students had arisen who saw, even more clearly than those with better qualifications, that law school was essentially the gateway to a professional career rather than predominantly an educational experience. The unannounced divisions and roles in the profession were now linked to the unacknowledged but obvious hierarchy among the law schools.

Barry B. Boyer and Roger C. Cramton, "American Legal Education: An Agenda for Research and Reform"
59 Cornell Law Review, 221–33 (1974).*

Introduction

American legal education is now enjoying unparalleled success. Each year many of the brightest college graduates choose to study law, . . . Curriculum offerings are expanding across the nation, both in the substantive content of courses and in the range of skills dealt with in the curriculum. A large and growing number of law schools have enriched their faculties by bringing in scholars from other disciplines such as economics, sociology, psychiatry, and history, and a new breed of law-trained teachers themselves possess more knowledge of related disciplines. Moreover, despite serious financial retrenchment in higher education, many law schools have suffered less than most other graduate schools from the squeeze of rising costs and diminished resources.

Yet even where law schools are financially healthy, there exists behind the facade of success a strong undercurrent of unease among those concerned about the future of legal education. Increasing selectivity in law school admissions, and greater dependence in admissions upon applicants' paper credentials, generate concerns whether the profession is drawing its recruits from too narrow a range of abilities and socioeconomic classes, and even whether the selection criteria are measuring the proper variables. The teaching method and first-year curriculum used by most law schools today antedate the present century. Yet innovations such as clinical law programs and interdisciplinary courses raise suspicions that law schools may only be responding to faddish demands for "relevance," which tend to diminish the quality of legal education, while avoiding needed reforms in legal education. Finally, the ostensible financial health of legal education may be only a reflection of a limited commitment to research and of student-faculty ratios that would be considered intolerable in most other disciplines. ...

What is the "state of the art" concerning our knowledge of the operation and effects of legal education? ...

A central historical datum is that law schools have monopolized the function of "gatekeepers" to the profession for a relatively short time. Fifty years ago, academic training for aspiring lawyers was an ideal rather than a requirement, and it is only within the past few years that the completion of three years of formal legal education has become virtually the universal method of entering the profession.

Although the law schools' control over entry into the profession has changed markedly, the basic techniques of legal education have proven remarkably stable and durable. The large-class, case method of instruction, usually in a "Socratic" question-and-answer format, has dominated law teaching since it was pioneered by Langdell nearly a century ago. The reasons for the longevity and popularity of the case method are several: its general pedagogical effectiveness, particularly in comparison to lectures; its adaptability to large classes, and thus its low cost; and, perhaps most important, its ability to accommodate differing intellectual currents and differing conceptions of the law. To Langdell, law was a science and its laboratory was the library; the case method extracted fundamental principles from the raw material of printed decisions in the logical manner of the physical sciences. Soon, however, doubts about the "scientific" nature of law and the existence of a manageable body of universally valid legal principles foreshadowed the pervasive skepticism of the Realist School that emerged during the 1930's. As this changing conception of the law evolved, the principal focus of the case method shifted from principles to process. But the case system continued to be the primary vehicle for instruction, even though conceptions of the nature of law changed radically. . . .

[One] aspect of this contemporary emphasis on the lawyer's many roles as manipulator and facilitator is the effort of many legal educators to develop in the student skills other than an ability to critically analyze presented cases. Concern for an understanding of legislative and administrative processes in earlier years has expanded to a broader interest in the totality of skills required for the many professional roles to be assumed by law graduates. Increasingly, training in these skills takes the form of role-playing experiences in clinical programs or simulated practice situations. Emphasis on the varied roles as investigator, counselor, negotiator, and advocate performed by lawyers is a major feature of current analysis of the law curriculum. It is both logical and a bit ironic that the case method of instruction, which was originally considered "clinical" in the sense of exposing students to "the living law" rather than abstract theory, is facing its strongest challenge from modern clinical methods of instruction.

II

Current Issues of Curriculum and Pedagogy

. . .

The effort to integrate law and the behavioral sciences has been going on for nearly half a century and that "[a]rticles could be lifted out of the Law School News of 1915 and passed off today as tolerably fresh ideas in the Journal of Legal Education." Major discussions of curricular reform published in the last few years, such as the Carrington Report and the Carnegie-sponsored monograph by Packer and Ehrlich, illustrate this phenomenon. Both works favor the encouragement of diversity in legal education, within and among law schools; both support experimentation with a "tracking" system that would provide substantially different educational experiences for those planning different careers in law. The recent proposals raise once again an issue which had been debated by the profession in the 1920's following Alfred Z.

Reed's landmark study, *Training for the Public Profession of the Law:*

> Reed described a wide range of kinds of legal education then common in this country .... The issue as Reed saw it was whether to try to force everyone into the image of the Harvard graduate or build a differentiated bar with some trained to do some things (he suggested that conveyancing, probate and trial practice might be possible), and others more broadly trained to be more widely competent.
>
> ... [A]s he viewed it, the "public" nature of the profession required part time legal education for those financially unable to attend college and full time law school. That being his prediction, it seemed to Reed more likely to be productive to work on redirecting the goals of part-time legal education. Classify the bar, either functionally or otherwise, with the part-time schools graduating men competent to perform the relatively routine tasks within the confines of a single jurisdiction.[26]

Moreover, the Carrington Report and the Packer-Ehrlich monograph attempt to reopen the question of whether three years of legal education, following four years of undergraduate college, is the appropriate length of schooling for a lawyer—a proposition which greatly concerned Langdell,[27] and which was formally endorsed by the American Bar Association in 1921. For nearly fifty years the trend in higher education has been in the direction of lengthening the period of education and increasing its cost. In the 1920's, admission to law school generally followed one, two, or three years of college. Today, when educational costs have advanced much faster than the rate of inflation in the economy, the bachelor's degree is generally required for admission to law school; and seven years of higher education is the norm for the law degree.

The increasing specialization of legal careers and the enormous range of abilities and skills required by a lawyer's activity have led to proposals for a two-year "generalist" curriculum followed by optional advanced or specialized programs of study.

. . .

26. Stolz, "Training for the Public Profession of the Law (1921): A Contemporary Review," in H. Packer & T. Ehrlich, *New Directions in Legal Education* 245–46 (1972).

27. *The American Law School* 430: From the beginning of his term as dean, Langdell had been anxious to return to the three-year model which Harvard had originally established in the 1820's; and eventually in 1878 Langdell achieved his goal. The requirement was slowly picked up by other schools. . . .

Another major characteristic of the law school curriculum in recent decades has been the proliferation of new courses.   ... New courses often are simply added on to the existing offerings rather than emerging from a shared faculty concept of how the educational process should be changed. A complementary and fairly recent phenomenon at most law schools is the lack of a recognized structure or theory for the elective curriculum that follows the required first-year courses. The sameness in course content and teaching methods throughout the law school experience, together with the absence of an orderly progression in the development of skills and substantive knowledge, have probably contributed to the frequently-noted boredom and withdrawal of some second- and third-year law students. ... Although these old curricular problems continue to elude solution. ...

Duncan Kennedy, Legal Education and the Reproduction of Hierarchy

i, ii, 3, 5–7, 16–17, 20–22, 58, 65, 68, 70, 101–03 (1983).

This is an essay about the role of legal education in American social life. It is a description of the ways in which legal education contributes to the reproduction of illegitimate hierarchy in the bar and in society. And it suggests ways in which left students and teachers who are determined not to let law school demobilize them can make the experience part of a left activist practice of social transformation.

The general thesis is that law schools are intensely *political* places, in spite of the fact that they seem intellectually unpretentious, barren of theoretical ambition or practical vision of what social life might be. The trade school mentality, the endless attention to trees at the expense of forests, the alternating grimness and chumminess of focus on the limited task at hand, all these are only a part of what is going on. The other part is ideological training for willing service in the hierarchies of the corporate welfare state.

To say that law school is ideological is to say that what teachers teach along with basic skills is wrong, is nonsense about what law is and how it works. It is to say that the message about the nature of legal competence, and its distribution among students, is wrong, is nonsense. It is to say that the ideas about the possibilities of life as a lawyer that students pick up from legal education are wrong, are nonsense. But all this is nonsense with a tilt, it is biassed and motivated rather than random error. What it says is that it is natural, efficient and fair for law firms, the bar as a whole, and the society the bar services to be organized in their actual patterns of hierarchy and domination.

. . .

The First Year Experience

. . .

The initial classroom experience sustains rather than dissipates ambivalence. The teachers are overwhelmingly white, male, and deadeningly straight and middle class in manner. The classroom is hierarchical with a vengeance, the teacher receiving a degree of deference and arousing fears that remind one of high school rather than college. The sense of autonomy one has in a lecture, with the rule that you must let teacher drone on without interruption balanced by the rule that teacher can't *do* anything to you, is gone. In its place is a demand for a pseudo-participation in which you struggle desperately, in front of a large audience, to read a mind determined to elude you.

. . .

The actual intellectual content of the law seems to consist of learning rules, what they are and why they have to be the way they are, while rooting for the occasional judge who seems willing to make them marginally more humane. The basic experience is of double surrender: to a passivizing classroom experience and to a passive attitude toward the content of the legal system.

The first step toward this sense of the irrelevance of liberal or left thinking is the opposition in the first year curriculum between the technical, boring, difficult, obscure legal case, and the occasional case with outrageous facts and a piggish judicial opinion endorsing or tolerating the outrage. The first kind of case—call it a cold case—is a challenge to interest, understanding, even to wakefulness. It can be on any subject, so long as it is of no political or moral or emotional significance. Just to understand what happened and what's being said about it, you have to learn a lot of new terms, a little potted legal history, and lots of rules, none of which is carefully explained by the casebook or the teacher. It is difficult to figure out why the case is there in the first place, difficult to figure out whether one has grasped it, and difficult to anticipate what the teacher will ask and what one should respond.

The other kind of case usually involves a sympathetic plaintiff, say an Appalachian farm family, and an unsympathetic defendant, say a coal company. On first reading, it appears that the coal company has screwed the farm family, say by renting their land for strip mining, with a promise to restore it to its original condition once the coal has been extracted, and then reneging on the promise. And the case should include a judicial opinion that does something like awarding a meaningless couple of hundred dollars to the farm family, rather than making the coal company do the restoration work.

The point of the class discussion will be that your initial reaction of outrage is naive, non-legal, irrelevant to what you're supposed to be learning, and maybe substantively wrong into the bargain. There are good reasons for the awful result, when you take a legal and logical view, as opposed to a knee-jerk passionate view, and if you can't muster those reasons, maybe you aren't cut out to be a lawyer.

. . .

The Ideological Content of Legal Education

... Law schools teach ... rather rudimentary, essentially instrumental skills in a way that almost completely mystifies them for almost all law students. The mystification has three parts. First, the schools teach skills through class discussions of cases in which it is asserted that law emerges from a rigorous analytical procedure called "legal reasoning," which is unintelligible to the layman, but somehow both explains and validates the great majority of the rules in force in our system. At the same time, the class context and the materials present every legal issue as distinct from every other, as a tub on its own bottom, so to speak, with no hope or even any reason to hope that from law study one might derive an integrating vision of what law is, how it works, or how it might be changed (other than in an incremental, case by case, reformist way).

Second, the teaching of skills in the mystified context of legal reasoning about utterly unconnected legal problems means that skills are taught badly, unselfconsciously, to be absorbed by osmosis as one picks up the knack of "thinking like a lawyer." Bad or only randomly good teaching generates and then accentuates real differences and imagined differences in student capabilities. But it does so in such a way that students don't know when they are learning and when they aren't, and have no way of improving or even understanding their own learning processes. They experience skills training as the gradual emergence of differences among themselves, as a process of ranking that reflects something that is just "there" inside them.

Third, the schools teach skills in isolation from actual lawyering experience. "Legal reasoning" is sharply distinguished from law practice, and one learns nothing about practice. This procedure disables students from any future role but that of apprentice in a law firm organized in the same manner as a law school, with older lawyers controlling the content and pace of depoliticized craft training in a setting of intense competition and no feedback.

. . .

This whole body of implicit messages is nonsense. Legal reasoning is not distinct, *as a method for reaching correct results,* from ethical and political discourse in general (i.e., from policy analysis). It is true that there is a distinctive lawyers' body of knowledge of the rules in force. It is true that there are distinctive lawyers' argumentative techniques for spotting gaps, conflicts and ambiguities in the rules, for arguing broad and narrow holdings of cases, and for generating pro and con policy arguments. But these are *only* argumentative techniques. There is never a "correct legal solution" that is other than the correct ethical and political solution to that legal problem.

Put another way, everything taught, except the formal rules themselves and the argumentative techniques for manipulating them, is policy and nothing more. It follows that the classroom distinction between the unproblematic legal case and the policy oriented case is a mere artifact: each could as well be taught in the opposite way. And the curricular distinction between the "nature" of contract law as highly legal and technical by contrast, say, with environmental law, is equally a mystification.

These errors have a bias in favor of the center-liberal program of limited reform of the market economy and pro forma gestures toward racial and sexual equality. The bias arises because law school teaching makes the choice of hierarchy and domination, which is implicit in the adoption of the rules of property, contract and tort, look as though it flows from legal reasoning, rather than from politics and economics. The bias is reenforced when the center-liberal reformist program of regulation is presented as equally authoritative, but somehow more policy oriented, and therefore less fundamental.

The message is that the system is basically OK, since we have patched up the few areas open to abuse, and that it has a limited but important place for value-oriented debate about further change and improvement. If there is to be more fundamental questioning, it is relegated to the periphery of history or philosophy. The real world is kept at bay by treating clinical legal education, which might bring in a lot of information threatening to the cosy liberal consensus, as free legal drudge work for the local bar or as mere skills training.

. . .

The Modeling of Hierarchical Relationships

Yet another way in which legal education contributes causally to the hierarchies of the bar is through ... law teachers that model for students how they are supposed to think, feel and act in their future professional roles. Some of this is a matter of teaching by example, some of it a matter of more active learning from interactions that are a kind of clinical education for lawyer-like behavior.

. . .

Often, it boils down to law review. At first, everyone claims they aren't interested, wouldn't want to put in the time, don't work hard enough to make it, can't stand the elitism of the whole thing. But most students give about equal time to fantasies of flunking out and fantasies of grabbing the brass ring. And even though the class has been together for a semester or a year, everything is still different after the lightning of grades. An instant converts jerks into statesmen; honored spokespeople retire to the margins, shamed. Try proposing that law review should be open to anyone who will do the work. Within a week or two, the new members have a dozen arguments for competitive selection. Likewise at the hour of partnership.

. . .

The culmination of law school as training for professional hierarchy is the placement process, with the form of the culmination depending on where your school fits in the pecking order.

. . .

By dangling the bait, making clear the rules of the game, and then subjecting almost everyone to intense anxiety about their acceptability, firms structure entry into the profession so as to maximize acceptance of hierarchy. If you feel you've succeeded, you're forever grateful, and you have a vested interest. If you feel you've failed, you blame yourself, when you aren't busy feeling envy. When you get to be the hiring partner, you'll have a visceral understanding of what's at stake, but it will be hard even to imagine why someone might want to change it.

. . .

Strategy

In the absence of a mass movement of the left, the way to organize a left intelligentsia is in the workplace, around ideas and around the concrete issues that arise within the bourgeois corporate institutions where the potential members of such an intelligentsia live their lives.

. . .

... Organizing around ideas means developing a practice of left study, left literature and left debate about philosophy, social theory, and public policy that would give professional, technical and managerial workers the sense of participating in a left community.

Along with workplace organization around ideas there goes organization around the specific issues of hierarchy that are important in the experience of people in these institutions. This has to do with the authoritarian character of day-to-day work organization—with the use of supervisory power. ... Selection, promotion and pay policies, along with a whole universe of smaller interventions, many of which are merely "social," maintain class/ sex/race and also generational and meritocratic stratification within the cells of the hierarchy, while at the same time disciplining everyone to participate in the complex of hierarchical attitudes and behaviors.

. . .

What this means is that lawyers can have and should have workplace struggles, no matter where they are situated in the hierarchy of the bar, and whether or not they are actively engaged in political law practice. For law students, it means that it is important to have a law school struggle, even if they are spending most of their time on extra-curricular activities that support oppressed people.

NOTES: RACE, ETHNICITY, AND GENDER

Contemporary critics of legal education also have identified problems related to race, ethnicity, and gender. Such problems are by no means a recent phenomena. As discussion in chapter 2 reflected, bias against these groups was long apparent in law school policies. Throughout the late 19th and early 20th centuries, most institutions excluded nonwhite and female applicants, and many actively discriminated against ethnic and religious minorities. In the mid 20th century, large numbers of institutions voluntarily altered their formal policies and litigation forced others to take comparable action. However, the lack of financial aid, affirmative action, or supportive academic environments kept the numbers of minority applicants at under 2% until the 1960s.[1]

Women's proportional representation was even lower; it never exceeded 3% throughout the first half of the 20th century. Part of the problem involved discrimination by law schools. Unlike the policies directed against other underrepresented groups, which were generally fueled by racial or ethnic prejudice, certain justifications for excluding women were more complicated. Some administrators were convinced that women lacked a "legal mind" and that exposure to masculine education and pursuits would lead to infertility, frigidity and "race suicide". Others were concerned about the dangers of unchaperoned intellectual intercourse in the library and distractions for male students in the classroom.[2] Many women who managed to gain admission found the atmosphere anything but welcoming. Their contributions were often discouraged, devalued, or restricted to certain specified "Ladies Days." [3]

During the 1960s, law school policies toward female and minority applicants improved dramatically. The change reflected a variety of developments including the civil rights and women's movements, an expansion in the market for young lawyers, and short-term declines in male applicants during the Vietnam War. A series of meetings under the auspices of the Office of Economic Opportunity led to the formation of a National Council on Legal Education Opportunity for Minorities, with representatives from the AALS, ABA, and LSAT Council. The Council's efforts, together with other governmental and social pressures, contributed to various initiatives. Expanded recruitment strategies, increased

1. C. Wolfram, *Modern Legal Ethics* 9–10 (1986); G. Segal, *Blacks in the Law* (1973); J. Auerbach, *Unequal Justice: Lawyers and Social Change in Modern America* (1976); Parker and Stebman, "Legal Education for Blacks," 403 *Annals of the American Academy* 144 (1973); Krauss, "Development of a Representative Legal Profession," 62 *A.B.A.J.* 591 (1976). *See* chapter 2.

2. K. Morrello, *The Invisible Bar: The Woman Lawyer in America 1638 to the Present 5 (1986);* O. Shuck, *History of the Bench and Bar of California* 831–32 (1901); R. Stevens, *Law Schools: Legal Education in America From the 1850s to the Present* 82–83 (1983); Lockwood, "My Efforts to Become a Lawyer," in *Women and the American Economy: A Documentary History*, 1675–1929, 298 (W. Brownlee and M. Brownlee eds., 1976). *See generally*, Rhode, "Perspectives on Professional Women," 40 *Stan.L.Rev.* 1163 (1988).

3. C. Epstein, *Women in Law* 61, 66–68 (1981); Fossum, "Law and Sexual Integration of Institutions: The Case of American Law Schools," VII *ALSA Forum* 222 (1983).

financial aid packages, prelaw institutes for talented minorities and supportive student organizations resulted in modest progress. By the mid-1980s, when blacks, Hispanics and Native Americans accounted for about a quarter of the nation's general population, they constituted about 10% of law schools' student population, 6% of the faculty and 6% of the practicing bar.[4]

For women, progress was more dramatic. Between the early 1960s and mid-1980s, the percentage of female law students grew from 3% to 40%. However, despite that rapid numerical growth, and the more gradual demise of overtly sexist practices such as Ladies Days, many women have felt that subtle barriers to equality remain. During the mid-1980s, a growing number of commentators began elaborating these perspectives. Not only has their work sought to improve the law school environment for women and minorities, it has raised more fundamental questions about legal institutions and ideologies.

Carrie Menkel-Meadow, "Women in Law? A Review of Cynthia Fuch Epstein's *Women in Law*"

1983 *Am.B.F.Res.J.* 192, 202.

A Postscript

In the conclusion of her book Epstein states:

[I]t would be unwise and unfair to delegate to women the responsibility for changing the legal profession. The law will become more responsive to all members of society only when those in power concede that is the proper thing to do, and it will be accomplished only if the powerful are drawn from a broader pool than before—one that includes not only women but also men with ideals and talent. Furthermore, in the matter of simple justice, no one group ought to be burdened with the expectation of unilateral altruism. [P. 385]

I agree that women should not bear this burden alone, but I also think they should not wait for men to join them before they begin their work of influencing law and legal practice toward becoming more fair and just.

What are the ways in which women might affect the practice and content of the law? Let me suggest a few: Women may force us to have a more sincere concern for the quality of our work, our personal lives, and their relationship to each other so that unnec-

---

4. C. Wolfram, *supra* note 1, at 10;
Parker and Stebman, *supra* note 1, at
147.

essary hard work will not interfere with important human relationships. Women may remind us to pay more sincere attention
to those with whom we work; if we cannot have a truly egalitarian workplace, then we should at least treat our fellow workers as
human beings and not as mere instrumentalities for the accom-
plishment of our work. Women may help us to appreciate the
purpose, meaning, and effects of the product of our work and to
become sincerely committed to work toward what we think is best
in our work and world. Women lawyers may provide us with
ways of practicing law that are less combative and dehumanizing,
less damaging to others and ourselves. Finally, women may, out
of their memory of being a disenfranchised and unequal group in
our society, forge a commitment to make better laws that promote
fair and equal treatment of all human beings. This does not need
to be a "women in the law" agenda, but *some* groups and individuals have to keep working toward the goal or we will all fall into
the trap of self-interested individualism in the practice of law.

Deborah L. Rhode, "Missing Questions: Feminist Perspectives on Legal Education"
45 Stanford Law Review 1547 (1993).

Feminist critiques of legal education generally proceed on two
levels. The first involves inadequacies that directly concern gender, including: the under-representation of women, particularly
women of color, in positions of greatest academic reward, security,
and influence; the inattention to issues of gender in standard
courses and texts; the persistence of sexually harassing and demeaning conduct; and the devaluation of women's classroom
participation. These problems have been discussed at length
elsewhere, and the appropriate responses are sufficiently obvious
to require little elaboration here.

A second level of critique, however, poses more fundamental
although related challenges to the structure of legal education.
These are the challenges I wish to examine, but not in the terms
usually presented. Feminists' structural critiques have drawn
heavily on one strand of feminist theory, popularized by Carol
Gilligan. This theoretical framework claims that women reason
in a "different voice": they are less likely than men to privilege
abstract rights over concrete relationships, and are more attentive
to values of care, connection, and context. Building on this
"relational" or "cultural" feminist approach, some theorists argue
that women bring a distinctive perspective to the resolution of

human problems, one that is silenced by the competitive, combative, and acontextual structure of legal education.

Such claims draw on a variety of narrative accounts and empirical research. For example, some small-scale studies have found that women rank competitiveness lower than men; that women in certain decision-making contexts are more likely than men to prefer collaborative, interactive leader-interpersonal client relationships, public service work, and empathetic reasoning processes.

The strength of such analyses lies in their demand that values traditionally associated with women be valued and that we focus on transforming social institutions, not just assimilating women within them. Yet efforts to claim an authentic female voice illustrate the difficulty of theorizing from experience without homogenizing it. To divide the world solely along gender lines is to ignore the ways in which biological status is experienced differently by different groups under different circumstances. There is no "generic woman," and relational feminism has ... failed adequately to address variations across culture, class, race, ethnicity, age, and sexual orientation.

The celebration of gender difference risks not only oversimplifying, but also overclaiming. Recent research raises substantial questions about how different women's voice in fact is. Psychological surveys generally find few attributes that consistently vary along gender lines. Even for these attributes, gender typically accounts for only about 5% of the variance. In contemporary American society, the similarities between men and women are far greater than the differences: small statistical distinctions do not support sweeping sex-based dichotomies. Most empirical studies of moral development or altruistic behavior do not disclose significant gender distinctions. Nor does research on occupational behavior reveal the strong sex-linked variations that relational feminism would suggest. Men and women who confront similar work-related pressures tend to have similar work-related responses. In general, recent studies underscore the importance of context in eliciting traits traditionally associated with women.

What little systematic information is available about gender differences in legal education reinforces the need for such contextual analysis. For example, recent surveys suggest that the motivations and experiences of women currently in law school differ in substantial ways from men's. Women law students demonstrate greater commitment to public interest, are substantially less likely to speak in class, and report higher levels of dissatisfaction, disengagement, and self-doubt than men. In research where race

is a variable, similar patterns are apparent or even more pronounced. Women of color differ most significantly from white
men, but also from men of color and white women. We also know
that female faculty are overrepresented in substantive areas involving personal rather than business needs and in non-tenure
track positions that stress teaching and clinical supervision rather
than research. By contrast, strong gender differences do not
emerge in various studies of negotiating conduct and legal decisionmaking, even on issues that involve interests traditionally
associated with women. Moreover, some research indicates that
gender may be less influential than other factors, such as preexisting ideological commitments and career goals, in explaining how
women experience legal education. In a recent study of Harvard
students, women who entered law school primarily for reasons
such as status, income, and job security were generally satisfied
with their training, while women who entered with predominantly
social justice motivations found the institution sexist and dehumanizing.

Taken together, these different accounts of gender difference
highlight a longstanding paradox in feminist theory. By definition, feminism claims to speak from the experience of women.
Yet that experience counsels attention to its own diversity, and to
the role of contextual variations and multiple identities in mediating gender differences. For feminists concerned with legal education, the point is to ground critiques in normative principles, not
essentialist premises. We can avoid sweeping claims about woman's essential nature while noting that particular groups of wom-
en under particular social conditions come to law with expectations and experiences different from those of men. We can also
observe that values traditionally associated with women have been
undervalued in legal education, and that their absence has impoverished the professional socialization of both sexes. In short, we
can affirm concerns that resonate with women's experiences, but
on the basis of feminist commitments, not biological categories.
The educational vision implicit in those commitments has much in
common with other critical perspectives, which should enrich our
theoretical analysis and expand our political alliances.

II.

At its most basic level, the feminist critique of professional
education parallels the feminist critique of professional roles.
What is troubling in the structure and substance of law school
pedagogy has much to do with what is troubling in lawyer-client
relationships. By tracing some of these connections, I do not
mean to overstate their causal relationship. Legal practice re-

sponds to a complex interplay of forces; law school socialization is only one, and in many arenas, hardly the most influential. But it is also the single factor over which academics have direct control, and most of us assume that some of what happens in law school affects law, lawyers, and lawyering. On that assumption, my argument here is that values central to feminist analysis—care, collaboration, and context—should also become more central to legal education and legal practice. The following analysis centers on two aspects of pedagogy. To paraphrase Fred Rodell's critique of legal scholarship, there are two things wrong with conventional law school teaching: one is style; the other is content.

A. *Educational Structure*

The dominant paradigm for legal education remains the quasi-Socratic lecture focusing on doctrinal analysis. While the abusive interrogations traditionally associated with this format unquestionably have declined, that increase in civility may have deflected attention from more fundamental questions. Is this method an effective way of teaching skills that are most essential to effective legal practice? What values concerning interpersonal interaction does it reinforce? Are certain traditionally disadvantaged groups likely to be further disadvantaged by these methods? From feminists' perspective, these questions highlight some of the most problematic aspects of law school pedagogy: the hierarchical, authoritarian relationship between students and professors; the competitive ethos of class participation and evaluation; and the effects of these dynamics when other status inequalities such as race and gender are also present.

All too often, a watered-down Socratic method offers only enough "freedom to roam in an intellectual cage." The professor controls the dialogue, invites the inhabitants to "guess what I'm thinking," and then finds the response inevitably lacking. The result is a climate in which "never is heard an encouraging word and the thoughts remain cloudy all day." For many students, the clouds never really lift until after graduation, when a commercial bar review cram course fills in what professional educators missed or mystified.

Although much of standard law school instruction is neither necessary nor sufficient to pass the state licensing exam, most institutions have managed to construe this as a virtue. We present ourselves as somehow "above trade," and insist that our conventional quasi-Socratic teaching styles build valuable, if immeasurable, capabilities. In theory, our reliance on controlled dialogue encourages careful preparation and rigorous analysis; in practice it often substitutes for both.

. . .

This authoritarian structure carries other costs. Legal education models a professional hierarchy that readily spills over to other relationships. Knowledge always carries power, but the forms of dominance that law schools validate offer a disturbing paradigm. Relationships between partners and associates, lawyers and clients, and professionals and support staff too frequently replicate the overbearing dynamics . . . of classroom settings.

These debilitating effects are compounded by other status differentials, such as class, race, and gender. Women, particularly women of color, consistently report a substantial incidence of demeaning or harassing conduct across a wide variety of legal settings. So too, studies involving relatively unsophisticated or economically subordinate clients reveal patterns of professional dominance that impede effective lawyering. Attorneys who constantly interrupt and redirect the conversations of those they purport to serve are replaying patterns inculcated in legal education; they are also losing opportunities to connect their skills with real human needs. Authoritarian styles often obscure an important part of what a client is seeking to address. They also perpetuate patterns of submission that effective advocacy should challenge.

The competitive climate of law school classrooms creates related problems. All too often, participants vie with each other to impress rather than to inform. Many students, particularly women and people of color, feel more alienated than challenged by the demand for "pseudo-participation," in which they "struggle desperately, in front of a large audience, to reach a mind determined to elude [them]." Groups that have internalized stereotypes of inadequacy or that have been socialized to avoid self-promotion are particularly likely to drop out of discussion. The conventional law school "search for knowledge," which so often becomes a scramble for status, runs counter to feminism's most basic insights, which stress learning through empathetic and collaborative interchange. In a sense, the individualistic ethos of legal education is also in tension with the needs of legal practice, where teamwork and an understanding of cooperative process is often critical.

The point of this analysis is not to suggest that conventional approaches have no value in legal education. In its most benign forms, Socratic exchange can cultivate skills that are useful in certain professional contexts, such as defending a position in the face of aggressive challenge, and arguing dispassionately about emotionally freighted issues. Given current patterns of gender socialization, women as a group have had less opportunity than men to develop some of these capacities. For many students, some exposure to conventional law school pedagogy offers a useful (if sometimes necessarily stressful) way to acquire important professional skills. The problem, however, is that the educational structure at most law schools reinforces competitive, confrontational capacities to the exclusion of other, equally significant relational skills. Even at its best, the large-class format offers inherently limited opportunities for participation by any individual, and the students most in need of such opportunities are least likely to exercise them.

The competitive dynamic of classroom culture is exacerbated by grading practices calculated more to rank than to instruct. Students receive little formal feedback aside from examinations, which often provide few constructive comments and test only a small fraction of skills relevant to lawyering.

. . .

We socialize students to compete, not collaborate. We offer little training in alternative dispute resolution. We enshrine client loyalty at the expense of broader societal interests. And we provide few occasions for systematic reflection about the price of unqualified partisanship for real people with real problems and resource constraints.

B. *Educational Priorities*

In fact, these real people rarely figure in legal education. The dominant texts are casebooks, which are generally "just that . . . — books of cases." Relatively little effort is made to explain the factual circumstances, legal choices, and ultimate consequences for litigants. Nor do conventional approaches adequately situate formal doctrine in social or historical context. The level of abstraction in most classrooms is both too theoretical and not theoretical enough; it neither probes the underlying foundations of legal doctrine nor offers practical assistance about how to use that doctrine in particular cases. In effect, students often get the legal analogue of "geology without the rocks . . . 'dry, arid logic, divorced from society. . . .'" What is missing from this picture is the context necessary to understand how law interacts with life.

Also absent is any sustained effort to address the emotional and interpersonal dimensions of legal practice. Thinking like a lawyer, typically presented as the functional equivalent of thinking like a law professor, is rational, distanced, and detached. The effective dimensions of lawyering are largely relegated to clinical courses, which are still treated as poor relations in most academic communities. It is thinking about thinking (or Theory as we prefer to call it) that brings greatest professional rewards. Prestige in scholarship often seems inversely related to relevance for practice, just as prestige in lawyering appears inversely related to individual client assistance.

Without adequate resources, status, or class hours, clinical courses barely begin to compensate for the neglect of practical and empathic skills throughout the standard curricula. According to the most comprehensive survey of practitioners to date, the abilities that legal education overlooks are those "most important to the actual practice of law." Although increasing numbers of clinical programs have improved the situation since that survey, training remains inadequate for many important interpersonal skills. Law school, as Gerald López notes, "is still almost entirely about law and is only incidentally and superficially about lawyering."

The inattention to practical and interpersonal skills carries a price for all graduates, but it is highest for those who predominantly serve individuals rather than businesses. Most corporate firms are able and willing (though sometimes grudgingly) to supply the practical training that law school neglects. Attorneys who work for less affluent clients and organizations find such assistance harder to come by. And the greater the distance between clients and counsel—across class, race, ethnicity, gender and education—the greater the potential barriers to effective representation.

Legal education teaches little about dealing with people who are "different," or in situations of stress, and the cost of this neglect is borne by those least able to absorb it. Many problems for which individuals seek assistance are "not primarily legal problems; they are deep human problems in which the law is enmeshed." Lawyers trained only to respond to legal issues may often end up talking past the concerns that are most central to the client. Divorce practice offers a case in point. The portrait emerging from various studies shows participants occupied with "two different divorces: lawyers with a legal divorce, clients with a social and emotional divorce." This mismatch is apparent in many dialogues that Austin Sarat and William Felstiner observed in divorce lawyers' offices. For example:

Client: There was harassment and verbal degradation. No interest at all in my furthering my education. None whatsoever. Sexual harassment. If there was ever any time when I did not want or need sex, I was subject to, you know, these long verbal whiplashings. Then the Bible would be put out on the counter with passages underlined as to what a poor wife I was. Just constant harassment from him.

Lawyer: Mmn uh.

Client: .... I could lock myself in the bathroom and he would break in. And I was just to listen, whether I wanted to or not.... There was no escaping him, short of getting in a car and driving away. But then he would stand outside in the driveway and yell, anyhow. The man was not well.

Lawyer: Okay. Now how about any courses you took?

As the researchers add, "[c]lient and lawyer are like performer and bored, but dutiful, audience—the lawyer will not interrupt the aria, but she will not applaud much either for fear of an encore."

. . .

For many clients, the legal process is "at best a distraction and at worst an additional trauma." To be sure, attorneys are not therapists, but skills of empathetic listening are not the unique preserve of psychoanalysis. As Sarat frames the issue, "Is dealing with the emotionally insensitive ... divorce lawyer beneath the dignity or beyond the competence of legal education?" One hopes that the question is rhetorical.

C. *Professional Education and Professional Ethics*

Although law schools have long proclaimed their commitment to public service and professional responsibility, most of this enthusiasm has remained at the symbolic level. Ethical issues are largely relegated to a single required course, which students typically perceive as the "dog of the law school" curriculum, taught to "vacant seats or vacant minds." Professional responsibility courses replicate in pronounced form the inadequacies of legal education in general. Most approaches are excessively doctrinal. By focusing on bar codes as vehicles for statutory analysis, these courses collapse legal ethics and ethical rules. As traditionally conceived, professional responsibility instruction offers too little theory and too little practice. It is too removed from the actual context of lawyering, and too uninformed by interdisciplinary frameworks from history, philosophy, psychology, sociology, economics, and so forth. Under conventional approaches a student may learn the rules, but will lack a foundation to challenge their premises and to explore their limitations.

More fundamentally, the failure to treat ethical issues as they arise throughout the curriculum undermines and trivializes the message of any required course. Casebooks outside the field of professional responsibility rarely address ethical issues in any detail. My recent survey of some 130 texts in 14 subjects found that the median amount of coverage in each volume was 1.4 percent of total pages, much of which involved simply reprinting relevant rules. Yet faculty who decline, implicitly or explicitly, to discuss ethical matters as they arise in each substantive area encourage future practitioners to do the same. Professional priorities are apparent in subtexts as well as texts, in what is left unsaid as well as said. Every educational institution teaches some form of ethics by the pervasive method, and pervasive silence speaks louder than formal policies or commencement platitudes.

Most law schools convey a similar message about pro bono commitments. Requirements of public interest work are notable largely in their absence, and even institutions that mandate service from students exempt faculty. Such double standards, however personally convenient, are pedagogically perverse. Treating pro bono as something we preach but do not practice subverts the point of the requirement.

Our failure to make professional ethics more central to professional education ill serves values that are central to feminist analysis. The normative questions missing from our curricula are missed opportunities; we are losing chances to enlarge students' capacities for reflective judgment and for understanding the ways that professional norms shape human relationships.

That is not to overstate the effects of educational socialization on professional conduct. We are unlikely to alter in a few classroom hours what students absorb over long periods from family, friends, schools, churches, and popular media. As skeptics have often noted, certain core values are matters, like "politeness on subways ... or fidelity in marriage," that cannot be acquired in professional schools. Moreover, as a wide variety of clinical and empirical studies make clear, ethical conduct is highly situational: collegial attitudes and workplace pressures often dwarf the importance of other influences.

For feminists as well as other theorists committed to contextual analysis, that insight is unsurprising and somewhat beside the point. Our influence as educators may be highly limited, but that is not an argument for declining to exercise it; the fact that we can do little does not mean we should do nothing. Most recent psychological research indicates that well-designed curricula can significantly improve capacities for moral reasoning, and that moral judgment bears some modest relationship to moral behavior. Through interactive and experiential learning, students can enhance skills in ethical analysis and build awareness of the situational factors that skew judgment. While professional education cannot fully simulate or insulate individuals from the pressures of practice, it can provide a setting to explore their causes and the regulatory structure best able to address them. In areas where professionals' personal or collective concerns do not coincide with those of the public, students can benefit from analyzing the gap before they have practical reasons to discount its existence.

. . .

Most of what feminists want is not unique to feminist agendas and does not require extended elaboration here. Law schools committed to more cooperative, collaborative, and empathetic lawyering would recast academic priorities along several dimensions. In terms of academic structure, far less reliance would be placed on large lectures or quasi-Socratic discussion; much greater emphasis would be given to legal clinics, simulations, pro bono programs, and other settings for interactive, experiential learning. Even large classes would break down patterns of overly authoritarian, abstract interchange by making greater use of out-of-class exercises, in-class role playing, and small discussion sections. Students would receive feedback on a more regular basis and on a more diverse range of abilities than simply issue spotting under exam pressures. Collaborative projects and development of interpersonal skills would occupy a more central role in standard courses and evaluation processes.

Corresponding changes would be necessary in educational substance as well as structure. Less focus would center on doctrinal analysis, and more on the social context of legal decisionmaking. Through "thick description" and narrative accounts, students would have more opportunities to see the legal world through a different lens.... Interdisciplinary and ethical materials would become integral parts of a sequential program, rather than occasional unsystematic digressions from the core curriculum. Dimensions such as gender, race, class, ethnicity, and sexual orientation would become more central categories in analyzing legal institutions and lawyer-client relationships. Such analysis would move beyond the kind of "add woman and stir" approach that often passes for curricular diversity: an occasional case or reference to gender, race, or similar issues. We would demand not simply acknowledgment of difference, but an exploration of the processes that give rise to its social meaning and consequences.

. . .

Clinical and pro bono programs offer particularly important opportunities, in part because clients' life experiences are so different from those of students. In these settings, individuals can confront issues of racial, class, and gender bias, develop strategies for reflective listening, and model lawyer-client relationships of mutual integrity and respect. For some students, such programs provide one of their only opportunities to see the legal world inhabited by the have-nots. An educational experience missing that dimension leaves future practitioners missing questions, let alone answers, about the "equal justice" that our system so often affirms and so rarely delivers.

There is, of course, a danger that in seeking to revalue traditionally undervalued dimensions of legal education, we will simply invert rather than dismantle its current hierarchy. For the same reasons that we should avoid categorical celebrations of women's difference, we should also avoid categorical complacency about particular legal methods. What works in any given law school will to some extent depend on context, on the distinctive strengths and commitments of its faculty, and the resources available to the institution from its graduates and the surrounding community. The preceding analysis is not meant to imply that clinical teaching or integration of ethical material is always effective, that quasi-Socratic methods are always counterproductive, or that focus on interpersonal dimensions of practice should always take precedence over more abstract theoretical analysis. In this, as in other contexts, we cannot dispense with contextual analysis. Inadequate interest, experience, and expertise can lead to superficial coverage of ethical issues that is worse than no coverage at all. Cursory treatment reinforces student skepticism and implies that value discussions are necessarily indeterminate and relatively unimportant. As clinicians have themselves emphasized, competitive and domineering styles of lawyering can be modeled in clinical as well as other classroom settings. And excessive psychologizing of legal practice can deflect necessary attention from its social and economic underpinnings.

Moreover, talk is cheap and many educationally desirable initiatives are not. There are obvious limits to how much time-intensive training we can provide without increasing costs, which may further restrict access or raise student debt burdens to intolerable levels.

Yet neither have we reached those limits. Not all the initiatives proposed earlier, such as role simulations, discussion sections, or clinical experiences, require extensive additional resources or excessive faculty involvement. Too little effort has centered on effective use of practitioners, teaching assistants, media programs, and students themselves in structured out-of-class learning. Many of us have been equally laggard in our obligation as educators to educate ourselves about effective teaching. Our "Lone Ranger" model of classroom performer gets in the way of learning from each other and from the increasing instructional literature available. Many conventional courses could benefit from research on how to foster interpersonal skills, ethical decisionmaking, and altruistic commitments.

Finally, as has been argued extensively elsewhere, the current structure of legal education requires reassessment. An inflexible requirement of three years in law school and passage of a general-knowledge exam may not be the best way to serve broader societal interests. Such admission criteria are neither necessary nor sufficient to secure cost-effective services in many substantive areas, particularly those involving routine form preparation. In an era of increasing specialization and substantial unmet legal needs among low and middle income consumers, a less rigid licensing structure makes sense. If individuals with varying degrees of training competed in the market for legal services, the result might be a less costly, more accessible legal system.

Robert Hutchens's characterization of universities as discrete substantive fields tied together by a central heating system has obvious parallels in many law schools' approach to teaching. We do relatively little to coordinate coverage, explore inadequacies, and reward innovation. Yet if we are seriously committed to developing the professionalism that we so often affirm, we need to translate more of our rhetorical commitments into educational priorities.

Kimberlé Williams Crenshaw, "Foreword: Toward a Race–Conscious Pedagogy in Legal Education"
National Black Law Journal, Winter 1989, at 1.

RACE IN THE LAW SCHOOL CLASSROOM

Minority students across the country have waged a series of protests to draw attention to problems of diversity in the nation's law schools. Although the students' bottom line demand is often for the recruitment of more minority faculty and students, the anger and frustration apparent in these protests indicate that the disappointment is not simply over the lack of "color" in the hallways. The dissatisfaction goes much deeper—to the substantive dynamics of the classroom and their particular impact on minority students. In many instances, minority students' values, beliefs, and experiences clash not only with those of their classmates but also with those of their professors. Yet because of the dominant view in academe that legal analysis can be taught without directly addressing conflicts of individual values, experiences, and world views, these conflicts seldom, if ever, reach the surface of the classroom discussion. Dominant beliefs in the objectivity of legal discourse serve to suppress the conflict by discounting the relevance of any particular perspective in legal analysis and by positing an analytical stance that has no specific cultural, political, or class characteristics. I call this dominant mode "perspectivelessness."

This norm of perspectivelessness is problematic in general, and particularly burdensome on minority students. While it seems relatively straightforward that objects, issues, and other phenomena are interpreted from the vantage point of the observer, many law classes are conducted as though it is possible to create, weigh, and evaluate rules and arguments in ways that neither reflect nor privilege any particular perspective or world view. Thus, law school discourse proceeds with the expectation that students will learn to perform the standard mode of legal reasoning and embrace its presumption of perspectivelessness. When this expectation is combined with the fact that what is understood as objective or neutral is often the embodiment of a white middle-class world view, minority students are placed in a difficult situation. To assume the air of perspectivelessness that is expected in the classroom, minority students must participate in the discussion as though they were not African–American or Latino, but colorless legal analysts. The consequence of adopting this colorless mode is that when the discussion involves racial minorities, minority students are expected to stand apart from their history, their identity, and sometimes their own immediate circumstances and discuss issues without making reference to the reality that the "they" or "them" being discussed is from their perspective "we" or "us." Conversely, on the few occasions when minority students are invited to incorporate their racial identity and experiences into their comments, they often feel as though they have been put on the spot. Moreover, their comments are frequently disregarded by other students who believe that since race figures prominently in such comments, the minority students—unlike themselves—are expressing biased, self-interested, or subjective opinions. The result is that minority students can seldom ground their analysis in their own racial experiences without risking some kind of formal or informal sanction. Minority students escape the twin problems of objectification and subjectification in discussions when minority experiences are deemed to be completely irrelevant, or are obscured by the centering of the discussion elsewhere. The price of this sometimes welcomed invisibility, however, can be intense alienation. I will elaborate on these dilemmas below.

The Problem of Objectification

Instructors create the conditions that lead to the objectification of minority students by narrowly framing classroom discussions as simple exercises in rule application and by not giving students permission to step outside the doctrinal boundaries to comment on or critique the rules.

In each of these cases minority students confront difficult choices. To play the game right, they have to assume a stance that denies their own identity and requires them to adopt an apparently objective stance as the given starting point of analysis. Should they step outside the doctrinal constraints, not only have they failed in their efforts to "think like a lawyer," they have committed an even more stigmatizing *faux pas:* they have taken the discussion far afield by revealing their emotional preoccupation with their racial identity.

Given the infrequency with which most law teachers create the space for and legitimize responses that acknowledge the significance of a racially-informed perspective, it is not surprising that minority students often choose the role of "good student" rather than run the risk of appearing to be incapable of exercising the proper decorum and engagement in legal analysis. Such experiences teach minority students that in law school discourse, their cultural and experiential knowledge is not important or relevant. Indeed, they learn that any failure to observe the constructed dichotomy between the rational—read non-racial and non-personal—and the emotional—read racial and experiential—may elicit derision or disregard....

Many of these problems could be averted if professors framed discussions so that the boundaries of acceptable responses were not so narrowly constructed. This would give students permission to drop the air of perspectivelessness, to stand within their own identity, and to critique the doctrine or rule directly. Yet instructors often fail to broaden the parameters of the discussion, perhaps believing that to do so would legitimize the inclusion of racial perspectives where none had existed before. Some may assert that since white students do not feel the need to fall back on personal, racialized views of the world, neither should minorities. This belief, however, is predicated on an erroneous view that white students—and indeed the instructors themselves—are not also reflecting racialized views when they frame and discuss issues. They accept the absence of an explicitly racial referent as evidence that the doctrinal or substantive framework being discussed is objective and race-neutral. However, majority as well as minority students view the world through a consciousness constructed in part through race. The appearance of perspectivelessness is simply the illusion by which the dominant perspective is made to appear neutral, ordinary, and beyond question. As a result, while the perspectives of minority students are often identified as racial, the perspectives of their majority classmates are not. . . .

An equally stressful, but conceptually more obscure experience is what I call subjectification. This is experienced by minority students when, after learning to leave their race at the door, their racial identities are unexpectedly dragged into the classroom by their instructor to illustrate a point or to provide the basis for a command performance of "show and tell." The eyes of the class are suddenly fixed upon the minority student who is then expected to offer some sort of minority "testimony". . . . Usually, the effort to illicit the minority perspective is a cue that the discussion is a policy—as opposed to a doctrinal—discussion. The racial conflict, if any, is seen as occurring outside of the classroom while the objective of the discussion is apparently to determine how best to address the problem. To the extent that the minority student can participate in this debate, she is viewed as a biased or specially interested party and thus, her perspectives are probably regarded as being too subjective to have a significant bearing on the ultimate solution.

This pattern of pigeon-holing minority student responses into a "special testimony" category occurs when their comments are essentially limited to providing information on how it feels to live in a ghetto, to go to segregated schools, to be harassed by police, or to risk being stigmatized by affirmative action. Instructors who until that startling moment have made no effort to create space for discussing how race shapes experiences or the role of law in maintaining racial subordination are sometimes surprised that minority students resent this episodic expression of interest. Instructors may believe that they have made a good faith attempt to include minority students in classroom discussions by offering them an opportunity to speak about something within their area of expertise. Yet to raise race in this way imposes multiple burdens upon minority students. First, it reinforces the view that racial differences and minority students' distinct racial experiences are essentially peripheral to the main course of law. Such efforts to compartmentalize racial experiences present racism as a series of individualized anomalous occurrences rather than systematically connected to larger institutional practices and values which are reflected in and reinforced by law. Presenting minority viewpoints in such narrowly-framed and marginalized discussions ignores the possibility that these insights might have some bearing on larger issues involving the role of law in constructing societal relationships and on the appropriateness of discussing those relationships in law school classrooms....

Some of these dilemmas can be addressed by altering the way racial issues are framed, by presenting racism as a serious societal problem, and by explicitly deprivileging dominant perspectives. Instructors wishing to explore racial issues without contributing to the anxiety of minority students should resist framing minority experiences in ways that make such experiences appear to be disconnected to broader issues and that can be easily forgotten as soon as the policy discussion is over. Instead, the frame should be shifted so as to illuminate the connection between racial subordination and the values and interests that appear to be race-neutral or that are simply taken for granted. This would provide space for minority students to contribute to discussions in ways that value their perspectives and do not put them on the spot. Thus, rather than asking how it feels to live in the ghetto, instructors wishing to explore, for example, the legal aspects of segregation might shift the frame to discuss how landlord-tenant law or banking practices perpetuate the maintenance of sub-standard dwellings in minority communities.

NOTES: THEORY MEETS PRACTICE

All law schools, whatever their status or focus, are educational institutions more or less isolated from practice. The degree of isolation has diminished in recent years through clinical and simulation training in law school curricula and, perhaps more significantly, through part-time practice by law students during school terms and summer vacations. Nevertheless, the predominant character of law schools remains that of either a bar cram shop, placement center, academic seminary, or some confused combination of all three. Law schools only partially reflect the technical, psychological, and moral climate of law practice. This discontinuity is a chronic source of conflict between the practicing bar and legal academia, and has been such since law schools became established.

A recurring complaint is that legal education is poorly integrated with practice. This critique generates continual controversy. Some reformers, chiefly in the bar, want the technique and ethos of legal education to teach practical skills. This line of argument usually assumes that practice is more or less homogenous, corresponding essentially to small firm general business practice. Other reformers, chiefly in academia, want the technique and ethos of legal education to become more fully differentiated from practice, in the direction of greater theoretical depth and interdisciplinary insight. This line of argument typically assumes that such a reform of legal education will improve law practice and thereby the state of social justice.[1]

In attempting to respond to both critiques, legal education inevitably risks satisfying neither. Current curricula can be charged with offering too little theory *and* too little practice—too little training in lawyering skills and too little grounding in other disciplines relevant to the law.

The resulting debates over legal education are often intense and sometimes interesting. The manifest agenda is the purpose and efficiency of legal education, but the latent agenda is of course the future of the law and of society.

REFERENCES

In addition to the references cited above, *see*

Auerbach, "Enmity and Amity: Law Teachers and Practitioners 1900–22" in D. Fleming & B. Bailyn eds., 5 *Perspectives in American History (Law in American History)* (1971).

Banks, "Gender Bias in the Classroom," 38 *J. Legal Educ.* 137 (1988).

Black, "Some Notes on Law Schools in the Present Day," 79 *Yale L.J.* 505 (1970).

Carrington and Conley "The Alienation of Law Students," 75 *Mich.L.Rev.* 887 (1977).

Chused, "The Hiring and Retention of Minorities and Women on American Law School Faculties," 137 *U.Pa.L.Rev.* 537 (1988).

---

1. The debate is not unique to American legal educators. See Twining, "Pericles and the Plumber," 83 Law Quarterly Rev. 396 (1967).

Cramton, "The Ordinary Religion of the Law School Classroom," 29 *J.Legal Educ.* 247 (1978).

Condlin, The Moral Failure of Clinical Legal Education, in *The Good Lawyer: Lawyers Roles & Lawyers Ethics* (D. Luban ed., 1984).

Coombs, "Crime in the Stacks, or a Tale of a Text: A Feminist Response to a Criminal Law Textbook," 38 *J. Legal Educ.* 117 (1988).

Czapansky and Singer, "Women in the Law School: It's Time for More Change," 7 *Law & Ineq. J.* 135 (1988).

Dworkin *et al., On Becoming a Lawyer* (1933).

Elkins, "Worlds of Silence: Women in Law School," 8 *A.L.S.A. Forum* (1984).

Erickson, "Final Report: 'Sex Bias in the Teaching of Criminal Law,'" 42 *Rutgers L.Rev.* 309 (1990).

Erlanger & Klegon, "Socialization Effects of Professional School: The Law School Experience and Student Orientations to Public Interest Concerns," 13 *Law & Soc'y Rev.* 11 (1978).

Gee and Jackson, "Current Studies of Legal Education: Findings and Recommendations," 32 *J. Legal Educ.* 471 (1982).

R. Granville, *The Making of Elite Lawyers* (1992).

R. Hall and B. Sandler, *The Classroom Climate: A Chilly One for Women* (1984).

Halperin, "On the Politics and Pathology of Legal Education," 32 *J. Legal Educ.* 383 (1983).

J. Hedegard, "The Impact of Legal Education," 1979 *A.B.F.Res.J.* 791.

Himmelstein, "Reassessing Law Schooling: An Inquiry into the Application of Humanistic Educational Psychology to the Teaching of Law," 53 *N.Y.U.L.Rev.* 514 (1978).

Homer and Schwartz, "Admitted But Not Accepted: Outsiders Take an Inside Look at Law School," 5 *Berkeley Women's L.J.* 1 (1989–90).

M. Kelly, *Legal Ethics and Legal Education* (1979).

D. Kennedy, *Legal Education and the Reproduction of Hierarchy: A Polemic Against the System* (1983).

Kennedy, "First Year Law Teaching as Political Action" 1 *Law & Soc.Probs.* 47 (1980).

——, "How the Law School Fails: A Polemic," 1 *Yale Rev.L. & Soc.Action* 71 (1970).

Klare, "The Law Curriculum of the 1980s: What's Left," 32 *J. Legal Educ.* 336 (1982).

Konefsky & Schlegel, "Mirror, Mirror on the Wall: Histories of American Law Schools," 95 *Harv.L.Rev.* 833 (1982).

Kronman, "Foreward: Legal Scholarship and Moral Education," 90 *Yale L.J.* 955 (1981).

Kronman, "Legal Scholarship and Moral Education," 90 *Yale L.J.* 955 (1981).

Lasswell & McDougal, "Legal Education and Public Policy: Professional Training in the Public Interest," 52 *Yale L.J.* 203 (1943).

Lesnick, "Legal Education's Concern with Justice; A Conversation With a Critic" 35 *J. Legal Educ.* 414 (1985).

G. Lopez, "Training Future Lawyers to Work with the Politically and Socially Subordinated: Anti–Generic Legal Education," *W. Va.L.Rev.* 305 (1988–89).

Luban, "Against Autarky," 34 *J. Legal Educ.* 346 (1984).

Luban, "Epistemology and Moral Education," 33 *J. Legal Educ.* 636 (1983).

Macaulay, "Law Schools and the World Outside Their Doors: Notes on the Margins of 'Professional Training in the Public Interest' ", 54 *Va.L.Rev.* 617 (1968).

Macauley, "Law Schools and the World Outside Their Doors II: Some Notes on Two Recent Studies of the Chicago Bar," 32 *J. Legal Educ.* 506 (1982).

Menkel–Meadow, "Feminist Legal Theory, Critical Legal Studies, and Legal Education or 'The Fem–Crits Go to Law School,'" 38 *J. Legal Educ.* 61 (1988).

Menkel–Meadow, "Women as Law Teachers: Toward the 'Feminization' of Legal Education," in *Essays on the Application of a Humanistic Perspective to Law Teaching*, Monograph III.

H. Packer & T. Ehrlich, *New Directions in Legal Education* 33 (1972).

Richards, "Moral Theory, the Development of Ethical Autonomy, and Professionalization," 31 *J.Legal Educ.* 359 (1981).

Rhode, "Ethics by the Pervasive Method," 42 *J. Legal Educ.* 31 (1992).

Simon, "The Trouble with Legal Ethics," 41 *Legal Educ.* 65 (1991).

R. Stevens, *Law School: Legal Education in America from the 1850s to the 1980s* (1983).

Stolz, "The Two-Year Law School: The Day the Music Died," 25 *J.Legal Educ.* 37 (1973).

Stone, "Legal Education on the Couch," 85 *Harv.L.Rev.* 392 (1971).

"Symposium: Legal Education in an Era of Change" 1987, *Duke L.J.* 1.

Weiss and Melling, "The Legal Education of Twenty Women," 40 *Stan.L.Rev.* 1299 (1988).

F. Zemans and V. Rosenblum, *The Making of a Public Profession* (1981).

II. ADMISSION TO THE BAR
A. COMPETENCE

INTRODUCTION

As the preceding excerpts reflect, training in professional schools, followed by standardized examinations, ultimately replaced apprenticeship as the primary method of regulating admission to the bar. The modern law school and the bar examination have had a symbiotic relationship since the turn of the century.

Formal examination exists to assure "the public" that lawyers are adequately trained, whatever their academic backgrounds may be. Law schools in turn are variously oriented to the bar examination. Some institutions teach to the exam, on the theory that it is the crucial obstacle their graduates face, and that their students can acquire practice skills on their own. Other law schools teach above the bar examination, on the assumption that their graduates can pass by intensive cramming and that the school's primary role is broadening students' academic backgrounds.

Law schools vary in orientation and status along a continuum defined by the foregoing extremes. The range of the continuum is different in different parts of the country. It is largest among the law schools feeding professional labor markets in large metropolitan regions and smallest in areas that are homogenous socioeconomically and in which the state university law school has a predominant local position. The structure of legal education thus to an important extent mirrors and reinforces the structure of the profession itself. On the other hand, the examination requirement is the same for all applicants in every state, and one state's bar examination is much the same as another's. Indeed, most jurisdictions now administer a single multistate test as a major component of their own examinations, adding a day of short essays for local flavor and assessment of writing skills.

Bar examinations evaluate only some of the forms of competence required for practicing law, such as elementary problem recognition, basic analytic and writing skills, knowledge of common legal information and vocabulary, and ability to function under a certain kind of intense pressure. However, in most phases of law practice, other forms of competence are also required, such as the ability to negotiate, to ask productive questions, to research unfamiliar areas and to relate well to other individuals under stressful circumstances. Hence, bar examinations are inevitably incomplete and inevitably discriminate against applicants whose portfolio of skills does not correspond to that tested by the examination. Thus, over 80 percent of surveyed lawyers believe that bar exams should be retained, although 70% also agree that the exams don't effectively measure ability to practice law.[1] This problem will prove intractable as long as other forms of screening are thought to involve equally serious difficulties, and open admission to practice is regarded as unacceptable. Thus, debates over competence seem destined to continue, with everyone agreeing that we need more of it, but no one knowing precisely how it can be tested or assessed.

David M. White, "The Definition of Legal Competence: Will the Circle Be Unbroken?"

18 Santa Clara Law Review 641, 644–46, 648–49, 681, 683, 685 (1978).

Introduction

The definition of legal competence in America is facing unprecedented challenge, aimed both at the standards for entry into the legal profession and the professional conduct of attorneys. Challenges to law school admissions criteria, law school attendance requirements, and bar examinations have emerged, as have movements advocating the relicensing of lawyers and the certification of specialists. ...

The Bar Examination

The bar examination has been challenged more frequently and more openly than any other element in the process of becoming a lawyer. Only four states allow graduates of certain law schools to join the bar without passing a bar examination, and for all other prospective lawyers the bar examination remains a barrier to practicing law. In at least ten states within recent years, lawsuits challenging the bar examination have been filed. The thrust of each suit is similar; the examination has a considerable discriminatory impact upon minority candidates, does not reflect the actual requirements of legal practice, and is administered in an arbitrary fashion. These suits reflect the more widespread discontent with the examination which has been expressed in both private conversations and public demonstrations.

---

1. Reidinger, "Law Poll: Bar Exam Blues," *A.B.A.J.* 34 (1987); Law Poll, 68 *A.B.A.J.* 544 (1982).

Challenges to bar examinations have met with universal defeat in the courts, although some suits are still pending. ... In these cases, the rigorous standards which have been applied to other employment tests were declared irrelevant to the bar examination, and only a rational relationship between the examination and the practice of law was required. This standard was met by bar examiners' testimony that they had met this standard based upon their own professional experience in practicing law and grading bar examinations. In addition, statistical proof was offered to demonstrate that bar examination results closely reflected law school examination results. Further proof that the bar examination reflected the practice of law was considered both impossible to produce and unnecessary to the result. ...

The various challenges to the examinations, admission criteria, and attendance are met with a circle of justifications. The LSAT is justified on the basis of its correlation with law school grades, and with the results on the bar examination as well. Law school attendance is justified because graduates tend to pass the bar examination in greater numbers. The bar examination itself is defended by a comparison of its pass rate with those who are successful in law school.

The result of this circular pattern has been the perpetuation of a bar composed largely of affluent, white males. These are the individuals who must pass on the challenges of minorities and women. These individuals also enjoy an advantage in entering law school, pursuing legal studies and passing the bar. These are the individuals who possess two assets essential to enduring the entry experience, but not available to all candidates and potential candidates—time and money. ...

The Standardized Tests

. . .

The Multistate Bar Examination

... The MBE yields scores which reflect the relative success of candidates on the test. No passing score is established for the nation; instead, each state chooses its own passing score. Since each score reflects relative performance rather than an independently established standard of performance, each state is actually opting for a probable pass rate on the bar when it chooses a passing score. Thus, although there is a theoretical opportunity for all who take the bar examination to pass, the introduction of the MBE makes it virtually impossible for all to pass. Scarcity is introduced where once there was opportunity.

Whatever the chosen passing score, the choice is unfortunate since candidates whose abilities are virtually indistinguishable will pass or fail the test because of blind luck. This is due to an "error of measurement" on the MBE which results in almost one-third of the candidates clustering around the average grade of 140 out of 200 questions with scores that are essentially the same. Some will cluster above the typical passing score of 70, others will fail.

While the MBE shares infirmities which infect the LSAT, solutions available to law school admission officials are not appropriate for bar examiners. First, scores on the LSAT which are so close that differences between them could occur by chance due to errors of measurement are supposed to be treated as reflecting no difference. Second, where the LSAT score is inconsistent with other data in a candidate's file, the score can be disregarded. These safeguards, necessary to correct the common faults of the LSAT and MBE, are unavailable for a licensing examination. First, since a single passing score must be chosen for all candidates, scores which are so close to the passing score that error of measurement could have caused the candidate to fail must nonetheless be considered failing scores. ...

If Title VII standards of job-relatedness are imposed on the bar examination and prerequisites to taking the examination, several major revisions are possible. As this article has argued, the most fundamental challenge possible to current legal licensing arrangements is the requirement that candidates attend law school. ... At the same time, the typical justification offered for current bar examinations—that they accurately reflect law school grades—would be suspect. Instead, the bar examination would necessarily be compared to the actual practice of law. ... Turning outward to study the actual work of lawyers and the actual needs of unserved but potential clients is a necessary beginning. The legal framework for scrutinizing requirements for admission to the bar exists. It remains the profession's responsibility to begin the scrutiny. ...

B. CHARACTER

Deborah L. Rhode, "Moral Character as a Professional Credential"

94 Yale Law Journal 491 (1985).*

INTRODUCTION

Moral character as a professional credential has an extended historical lineage. For lawyers, the requirement dates to the Roman Theodesian Code, and its Anglo-American roots reach to thirteenth century England. In this country, every state bar currently makes certification of character a prerequisite for practice, and most other nations and licensed professions impose a similar mandate. Yet despite the pervasiveness of these requirements, their content and implementation have attracted remarkably little serious scholarly interest. ...

The following analysis seeks to reopen that dialogue. It begins with a brief historical overview of character mandates in both admission and disciplinary contexts. Drawing on a variety of secondary source materials as well as primary empirical research, subsequent discussion focuses on the more recent implementation of those requirements. Through interviews with bar examiners in all fifty states, surveys of reported cases and character application forms, and interviews with selected law school administrators, the study presents the first comprehensive profile of the certification process. In addition, analysis of disciplinary actions for misconduct occurring within and outside lawyer-client professional relationships offers some insight into prevailing double standards for aspiring and admitted attorneys. ...

By focusing in depth on the administration of bar character mandates, this study raises certain fundamental questions about the premises and practices of our licensing structures. ... Although the number of applicants formally denied admission has always been quite small, the number deterred, delayed, or harrassed, has been more substantial. In the absence of meaningful standards or professional consensus, the filtering process has proved inconsistent, idiosyncratic, and needlessly intrusive. We have developed neither a coherent concept of professional character nor effective procedures to predict it. Rather, we have maintained a licensing ritual that too often has debased the ideals it seeks to sustain.

. . .

* This essay is excerpted from Rhode, *Moral Character as a Professional Credential*, 94 YALE L.J. 491 (1985). Reprinted by permission of The Yale Law Journal Company and Fred B. Rothman & Company.

[I.]   The Certification Process Reconsidered

A.   The Central Premises of Character Review

   . . . [C]ourts and commentators have traditionally identified two prophylactic objectives for the certification process. The first is safeguarding clients [and the administration of justice] from potential abuses, such as misrepresentation, misappropriation of funds, betrayal of confidences, . . . subornation of perjury, bribery, or the like. . . .

   A second, although less frequently articulated, rationale for character screening rests on the bar's own interest in maintaining a professional community and public image. In both its instrumental and symbolic dimensions, the certification process provides an opportunity for affirming shared values. As sociologists since Durkheim have argued, the concept of a profession presupposes some sense of common identity. Excluding certain candidates on character grounds serves to designate deviance, thus establishing the boundaries of a moral community. . . .

   [Moreover,] certification appears an integral part of the general effort to legitimate the profession's regulatory autonomy and economic monopoly. The appearance of moral oversight may help both to preempt the call for external involvement in bar governance processes, and to buttress justifications for banning unregulated (and hence potentially unethical) competitors. . . .

   Even as a theoretical matter, however, this [second] rationale for character screening remains problematic. While these professional interests help explain, they fail adequately to justify the bar's attachment to character screening. To prevent or deter individuals from entering a profession in order to promote the reputation, autonomy, or monopoly of existing members is troubling on constitutional as well as public policy grounds. . . . [I]t is difficult to construe the bar's parochial concerns as the kind of legitimate state interest normally required to restrain vocational choice.

   [In any event,] as an empirical matter, it is questionable whether the certification process as presently administered inspires public confidence and whether the system defines a moral community consistent with the profession's most enlightened instincts and ideals. As the following sections suggest, both structural and substantive constraints render current character screening procedures a dubious means of either protecting the public or preserving professionalism.

B.   Structural Problems in Current Procedures

   Among surveyed bar examiners, the most commonly cited problem in the certification process is the absence of adequate time, resources, staff, and sources of information to conduct meaningful character inquiries. ...

An inherent inadequacy in the certification process stems from the point at which oversight occurs. In essence, the current process is both too early and too late. Screening occurs before most applicants have faced situational pressures comparable to those in practice, yet after candidates have made such a significant investment in legal training that denying admission becomes extremely problematic. ... Once individuals have invested three years and thousands of dollars in their legal education, many examiners are reluctant to withhold certification. That reluctance undoubtedly helps account for the low incidence of applications denied on character grounds. In 1981, in the jurisdictions for which statistics were available, about 6.5% of all eligible candidates, [slightly under 2000] individuals, were subject to nonroutine character investigation. ...

In the 41 states which could supply 1982 information, bar examiners declined to certify the character of approximately .2% of all eligible applicants, an estimated 50-odd individuals. The only other empirical data available suggest that this percentage has remained relatively constant over the last quarter century. ...

These figures cannot, however, be taken as a measure of the screening process's overall effect. Statistics on denials afford no indication of the deterrent impact of licensing procedures, an impact compounded by other structural features of the certification process. ...

... [A]s some examiners pointed out, a substantial group of individuals may be deterred from applying to law school or to a particular state bar out of concern that they will not be certified. This deterrent effect is enhanced by the general lack of information concerning certification criteria and administration. Only one state has published policies or guidelines on the specific types of conduct that prompt investigation, and no jurisdiction issues statistics on the number of character investigations or denials of certification. With relatively few exceptions, definitive advance rulings by character committees are also unavailable. ...

C. Substantive Problems in Character Assessment

1. The Subjectivity of Admission Standards

As the most recent Bar Examiners' Handbook candidly concedes, "no definition of what constitutes grounds for denial of admission on the basis of faulty character exists." On the whole, judicial attempts to give content to the standard have been infrequent and unilluminating. ... [For example] in *Konigsberg v. California State Bar*, the Supreme Court focused on whether a "reasonable person could fairly find that there were substantial doubts about [the applicant's] honesty, fairness, and respect for the rights of others and for the laws of the state and nation." ... The difficulty, of course, is that reasonable men can readily disagree about what conduct would raise substantial doubts, a point amply demonstrated by the divergence in views among judges, bar examiners, and law school administrators. ...

2. The Idiosyncracies of Implementation

[Data from bar screening authorities in all 50 states revealed little consensus as to what forms of conduct were most likely to prove disabling].

Criminal Conduct and Abuse of Legal Processes

A threshold difficulty in applying character standards stems from the inclusiveness of "disrespect for law" as a ground for excluding applicants. The conventional view has been that certain illegal acts—irrespective of the likelihood of their repetition in a lawyer-client relationship—evidence attitudes toward law that cannot be countenanced among its practitioners; to hold otherwise would demean the profession's reputation and reduce the character requirement to a meaningless pretense. The difficulty, of course, is that this logic licenses inquiry into any illegal activity, no matter how remote or minor, and could justify excluding individuals convicted of any offense that affronted the sensibilities of a particular court or character committee. In fact, bar inquiry frequently extends to juvenile offenses, ... parking violations, and [civil disobedience, while] conduct warranting exclusion has been thought to include traffic convictions and cohabitation. ... Violation of a fishing license statute ten years earlier was sufficient to cause one local Michigan committee to decline certification. But, in the same state, at about the same time, other examiners sitting on the central board admitted individuals convicted of child molesting and conspiring to bomb a public building.

Decisions concerning drug and alcohol offenses have proved particularly inconsistent. Convictions for marijuana are taken seriously in some jurisdictions and overlooked in others; much may depend on whether the examiner has, as one put it, grown more "mellow" toward "kids smoking pot." ...

Not only does the "disrespect for law" standard invite inconsistencies in application, it permits a hierarchy of concerns that seems at best tenuously related to the primary justification of character review—protecting the public. It bears note that the conduct generating the greatest likelihood of investigation was unauthorized practice of law: eighty-four per cent of all jurisdictions would inquire into such activity, and it was the second most likely offense to preempt admission. Yet, by definition, as some examiners implicitly acknowledged, such misconduct would not recur after certification. And it is doubtful that the general public would view most lay assistance as evidencing serious and generalizable moral deficiencies. ...

Noncriminal Conduct

Other major areas of concern to courts and bar committees have been psychological instability, financial irresponsibility, and radical political involvement, although again attitudes vary widely as to the significance of particular conduct. For example, ... the bar applications of some jurisdictions make no inquiries as to mental health; others require a psychiatrist's certificate and in some cases an examination for candidates who have a history of treatment. ... The Nevada Supreme Court does not consider mental illness a ground for denial, while Wyoming, Arizona, and Illinois have excluded applicants evidencing "religious fanaticism", and personality disorders involving "hypersensitivity, unwarranted suspicion, and excessive self-importance," or a "propensity to unreasonably react" to perceived opposition.

Attitudes toward sexual conduct such as cohabitation or homosexuality reflect similar diversity. Some bar examiners do not regard that activity as "within their purview," unless it becomes a "public nuisance" or results in criminal charges. ... [In other jurisdictions] cohabitation and homosexuality can trigger extensive inquiry and delay, and some slight possibility of denial. In the remaining states, examiners reported few applications presenting evidence of "living in sin" or homosexuality. According to one Board of Bar Examiners president, "Thank God we don't have much of that [in Missouri]." How these individuals would view such conduct if brought to their attention remains unclear. ...

Financial mismanagement provokes comparable disagreement. Most jurisdictions make no inquiries concerning debts past due (73%), while others demand detailed information ranging from parking fines to child support obligations. ...

Remorse, Rehabilitation, and Cooperation with the Committee

A final context in which decisionmaking has proven [highly subjective] concerns candidates' apparent attitudes toward their

prior conduct and committee oversight. Arrogance, "argumenta-
tiveness", "rudeness", "excessive immatur[ity]]", "lackadaisical"
responses, or intimations that a candidate is "not interested in
correcting himself" can significantly color character assessments.
... Invocations of a "higher personal ethic" or a "protestations of
innocence" are generally inadvisable. Accordingly, Michigan's
repentant bomber was admitted to the bar despite several years in
a maximum security facility, while North Carolina's unconfessed
"peeping Tom" was thought too great a public threat to be
certified. ...

[Some] courts and committees appear to assume that "a leop-
ard never changes his spots;" neither civic involvements nor "self-
serving statements of remorse" will adequately atone for certain
sins. But whichever position they adopt on this point, bar decisionmakers are all operating on one shared empirical premise.
Their common assumption is that certain attitudes and actions are
sufficiently predictive of subsequent misconduct to justify the costs
of certification procedures. Yet as the following sections suggest,
that premise is empirically dubious and flatly at odds with the
disciplinary process as currently administered.

[II.] The Disciplinary Process

The inadequacies of bar disciplinary processes have been
documented extensively elsewhere and need not be rehearsed at
length here. However, some brief comparative observations are in
order. [From a public policy perspective, the rationale for disciplinary oversight is stronger for abuses committed within a lawyer-client relationship than for offenses occurring prior to the
point of licensure.] Yet as a practical matter, the bar's administration of admission and disciplinary processes has yielded precisely [the reverse] double standard; both substantive and procedural
requirements are more solicitous of practitioners than applicants.
... Except in the most egregious cases, the bar has always been
disinclined to cast out a colleague for abuses within a lawyer-client
relationship. Every major analysis of the disciplinary structures
has found them grossly insensitive both to serious professional
misconduct and to garden variety problems of delay, neglect,
incompetence and overcharging. ...

The disparity between entry and exclusion standards raises a
number of awkward questions about the current scope of certification procedures. If certain nonprofessional conduct is sufficiently
probative to withhold a license, why is it not also grounds for
license revocation? As long as bar members are unwilling to
monitor their colleagues' parking violations, psychiatric treat-

ment, and alimony payments, what justifies their reliance on such evidence in screening applicants? Insofar as the profession is truly committed to public rather than self-protection, the incongruity between disciplinary and certification procedures is untenable.

That is not, however, to imply that more serious proctoring of [attorneys'] nonprofessional offenses would be desirable. ... The central premise of moral oversight—that courts and committees can predict future misconduct from the prior offenses generally at issue in character proceedings—bears closer scrutiny. ...

[III.] The Predictive Power of Prior Conduct

. . .

Over the past half century, a vast array of social science research has failed to find evidence of consistent character traits. Hartshorn and May's seminal *Studies in the Nature of Character* found so little relationship between conduct reflecting children's honesty, integrity, and self-control that the authors concluded that moral behavior was more a function of specific habits and contexts than of any general attributes. Lying and cheating were essentially uncorrelated, and even the slightest change in situational variables dramatically altered tendencies toward deceit; one could not predict cheaters in one class on the basis of cheating in another. While subsequent studies have not been entirely conclusive, most have yielded similar results; their findings suggest that the person with a "truly generalized conscience ... is a statistical rarity." Although individuals clearly differ in their responses to temptation, contextual pressures have a substantial effect on moral conduct independent of any generalized predisposition. ...

Although systematic empirical evidence on lawyers' ethics is fragmentary, it also suggests that situational pressures play a critical role in shaping normative commitments and conduct. As Jerome Carlin's study of the Manhattan bar and Joel Handler's research on small town practitioners make clear, an attorney's willingness to violate legal or professional rules depends heavily on the exposures to temptation, client pressures, and collegial attitudes in his practice setting. ...

The situational nature of moral conduct makes predictions of behavior uncertain under any circumstances, and the context of bar decisionmaking presents particular difficulties. A threshold problem springs from the inherent limitations of clinical predictive techniques, *i.e.*, those based on non-statistical information. Even trained psychiatrists, psychologists, and mental health workers have been notably unsuccessful in projecting future dishonesty or other misconduct on the basis of similar prior acts. ...

[Moreover, n]ot only do examiners and judges generally lack clinical expertise, they are dealing with highly circumscribed data. Decisionmakers are frequently drawing inferences about how individuals will cope with the pressures and temptations of uncertain future practice contexts based on one or two prior acts, committed under vastly different circumstances. Yet, as just noted, a half century of behavioral research underscores the variability and contextual nature of moral behavior: a single incident or small number of acts committed in dissimilar social settings affords no basis for reliable generalization. Neither common sense nor common experience suggest that those who have violated drug laws or avoided military service are likely to commit professional abuses, or that applicants who on occasion have mismanaged their own financial affairs are destined to become comminglers. Indeed, if we cannot with reasonable accuracy predict cheaters in French from cheaters in math, it is difficult to entertain the far more attenuated inferences implicit in much bar decisionmaking. ... Thus, the inherent limitations in predicting moral behavior, coupled with the subjectivity of bar standards, leave substantial room for error. [And, these errors are by no means the sole costs of current licensing structures.] ...

[IV.] The Costs of Moral Oversight

A. The Misdirection of Resources

Taken as a whole, the current certification process is an extraordinarily expensive means of providing a dubious level of public protection. ... For the vast majority of candidates, the certification process is a highly burdensome mechanism for identifying the tiny number of individuals with serious offenses. ... [B]ar applications generally demand an extended array of personal information, supplemental documentary submissions, [and personal references]. ... Such requirements generate an enormous paper flow, which is time consuming for all concerned and ill-designed to generate useful information. ... [So too] each year, over 11,000 individuals—more than a quarter of those admitted to practice—submit to character interviews. ... Particularly in less urban areas, applicants may be required to travel substantial distances at inconvenient times in order to confirm their residency or make small talk about life as a lawyer. ...

A critical question ... is whether resources now directed toward predicting future misconduct would be better expended in identifying and responding to the abuses that actually occur. The merits of that alternative focus must also be evaluated in light of certain other costs of moral oversight. To the extent that prevailing certification procedures legitimate the bar's regulatory autonomy or deflect attention from its sorry record in policing practitioners, the system ill serves its primary objectives. And insofar as pursuit of those objectives compromises fundamental constitutional values, its necessity warrants reexamination.

B. First Amendment Concerns

Throughout this century, the moral character requirement has placed a price on nonconformist political commitments. Conscientious objectors, religious "fanatics," suspected subversives, and student radicals have been exhaustively investigated, frequently delayed, and occasionally denied admission. ... [S]ince most state bars demand disclosure of all arrests and criminal charges, and protesters frequently run the risk of unlawful arrest, the chilling effects of certification may extend to protected political activity. ...

By penalizing a show of character in proceedings nominally designed to detect it, the bar has enshrined a morality *manque*. To view subservience to authority as a requisite for virtue is to ignore a history rich in counterexamples. American ideals of liberty, equality and dignity have sometimes found their highest expression in peaceful defiance of legal mandates. Abolitionists, civil rights activists, suffragists and labor organizers—indeed, the architects of our constitutional framework—all were guilty of "disrespect for law" in precisely the sense that bar examiners employ it. As long as that criterion remains an indice of moral merit, the certification process will exemplify a commitment to conformity that makes mockery of the bar's highest traditions.

C. Due Process Values

As the Supreme Court has long recognized, pursuit of a chosen vocation is one of the core liberties protected by the due process clause of the Fifth and Fourteenth amendments. Accordingly, certification and disciplinary procedures must satisfy the requirements of specificity and regularity that give content to those constitutional guarantees. In addition, the scope of bar inquiry into personal affairs implicates concerns of privacy and substantive rationality that are also subject to due process constraints. The significance of these constitutional issues cannot be assessed solely or even primarily in doctrinal terms. As a policy matter, the societal values from which due process mandates draw should inform any judgments about the legitimacy of current character proceedings.

1. Vagueness

. . .

On its face, the bar's character requirement is—in Justice Black's phrase—"unusually ambiguous," and court and committee amplification have done little to refine analysis. Prevailing definitions of virtue are circular or conclusory, and there is broad disagreement regarding particular conduct within and across jurisdictions. ... Given such inconsistencies in application, the standard scarcely affords adequate notice of "conduct to avoid" or of the professional consequences of prior activities. ...

Moreover, current certification structures have proven largely unresponsive to these indeterminacies. Only a tiny percentage of disputed cases generate written opinions by either courts or bar examiners and not all bar decisions are readily available. Only three states have published policies regarding the types of conduct that would prompt investigation; the general assumption, as the California Board candidly concedes, is that no "meaningful guidelines can be stated." ... [So, too, most] certification processes operate without any formal boundaries on their scope of inquiry. Only about a fifth of the sampled states apply rules of evidence or formal constraints on questions examiners are authorized to ask. In general, committee inquiry ranges as broadly as members wish, and hearings may last anywhere from fifteen minutes to ten days. In all but one sampled jurisdiction, these hearings are not necessarily restricted to the areas that triggered review. ... [This] undisciplined scope of inquiry opens opportunities ... for capricious and prejudicial inferences from [information regarding highly private matters such as divorce, homosexuality, cohabitation, or mental health counseling.] ...

VI. Alternatives

... The current administration of moral character criteria is, in effect, a form of Khadi Justice with a procedural overlay. Politically non-accountable decisionmakers render intuitive judgments, largely unconstrained by formal standards and uninformed by a vast array of research that controverts the premises on which such adjudication proceeds. This process is a costly as well as empirically dubious means of securing public protection. Substantial resources are consumed in vacuous formalities for routine applications, and non-routine cases yield intrusive, inconsistent, and idiosyncratic decisionmaking. Examiners generally lack the resources, information, and techniques to predict subsequent abuses with any degree of accuracy. Only a minimal number of applicants are permanently excluded from practice, and the rationale for many of those exclusions is highly questionable. ...

[Discussion is omitted concerning various procedural and substantive restrictions designed to minimize the intrusiveness and increase the consistency, rationality, and predictability of character decisionmaking. The benefits of a more rule-bound system are then assessed against the risk that such structural renovation will simply help legitimate a fundamentally illegitimate system. Preserving the pretense of character review could simply buttress the profession's claims to social status, economic monopoly, and regulatory autonomy while deflecting attention from more meaningful forms of oversight. Given that possibility, increased attention should be given to abandoning character assessment or limiting disqualification to a few clearly specified offenses, and diverting resources to regulation of professional misconduct.]

As currently implemented, the moral fitness requirement both subverts and trivializes the professional ideals it purports to sustain. In seeking to express our aspirations, such rituals succeed only in exposing our pretenses. While hypocrisy is often the bow vice pays to virtue, better forms of tribute may be available.

REFERENCES

Carothers, "Character and Fitness: A Need for Increased Perception," *B. Examiner*, August 1982 at 25.

Dershowitz, "Preventive Disbarment: The Numbers Are Against It," 58 *A.B.A.J.* 815 (1972).

Elliston, "Character and Fitness Tests: An Ethical Perspective," *B. Examiner*, August 1982 at 8.

Garth, "Rethinking the Legal Profession's Approach to Collective Self-Improvement: Competence and the Consumer Perspective," 1983 *Wis.L.Rev.* 639.

J. Julin, "The Legal Profession: Education and Entry," in R. Blair & S. Rubin eds., *Regulating the Professions: A Public Policy Symposium* (1980).

Project, "Admission to the Bar: A Constitutional Analysis," 34 *Vand.L.Rev.* 655 (1981).

Rhode, "Moral Character: The Personal and the Political," *Loyola L.Rev.* (1988).

Reidinger, "Bar Exam Blues," *A.B.A.J.* July 1, 1987 p. 34.

Rosenhan, "Moral Character," 27 *Stan.L.Rev.* 925 (1974).

Special Comm. on Professional Education and Admissions of the Association of the Bar of the City of New York and the Comm. on Legal Education and Admissions to the Bar of the New York State Bar Association, "Committee Report: the Character and Fitness Committees in New York State," 33 *Rec.A.B.City N.Y.* 20 (1978).

III. POLICING PROFESSIONAL CONDUCT

INTRODUCTION [1]

Although the following articles focus on discipline for acts occurring within a lawyer-client relationship, the bar has also asserted regulatory jurisdiction over some forms of nonprofessional misconduct. Acts by an attorney in his personal capacity that reflect unfitness to manage a client's legal affairs, or that might subject the profession to public "derision or distrust", are thought to be appropriate grounds for disciplinary intervention.[2]

Except for felonies, nonprofessional misconduct of individuals already admitted to practice rarely triggers disciplinary sanctions.[3] Although admission to the bar has been delayed or denied for offenses such as traffic violations, nonpayment of debts, bankruptcy, consensual sexual activity, personality disorders, and petty drug violations, similar conduct almost never has comparable consequences for practicing attorneys.[4]

From the standpoint of maximizing public protection and confidence, this double standard is difficult to justify. Acts committed by an individual obligated to function as an officer of the court are at least as probative of future conduct in that office than acts committed prior to the point of licensure. While practicing attorneys may have a greater vested interest in their professional license than applicants to the bar, the time and money candidates invest in legal education is hardly insubstantial. Moreover, from a policy perspective, the bar's own interests cannot justify a less rigorous moral standard for those granted a public trust than for those seeking one. That is not to imply, however, that greater oversight of nonprofessional misconduct would necessarily prove desirable. Indeed, the bar's past involvement in such moral

---

1. A more extended discussion of these issues appears in Rhode, Moral Character as a Professional Credential, 94 Yale Law Journal 491 (1985); and Rhode, "Moral Character: The Personal and the Political," *Loyola L.Rev.* (1988).

2. In re Higbie, 6 Cal.3d 562, 99 Cal. Rptr. 865, 493 P.2d 97 (1972); In re Goldstein, 411 Ill. 360, 367, 104 N.E.2d 227, 280 (1952).

3. Except in the few states that automatically decertify attorneys convict-

ed of a felony, nonprofessional misconduct typically accounts for only 0–3% of all disbarments, suspensions, and resignations. A survey of reported disbarments found that most nonprofessional abuses concerned felonies such as tax evasion, mail fraud, racketeering, bribery, perjury, narcotics violations, and rape. Rhode, *supra* note 1.

4. *Id.*

oversight raises serious questions about the appropriate scope of disciplinary regulation.

In most jurisdictions, attorneys' misconduct is disabling only if it involves "moral turpitude," a requirement open to inconsistent and idiosyncratic interpretations. Throughout this century, the ebb and flow of concern for national security has led to disparate sanctions for allegedly subversive practitioners.[5] Sexual promiscuity has been a perennial concern, although the focus of inquiry has shifted somewhat. Early twentieth century cases centered on prostitution and fornication, and generated a set of somewhat "murky moral mandates." Commercial relationships with fallen women were permissible to a point; those who paid money for sexual favors were often forgiven while those who accepted money for abetting such activities were purged from the profession.[6] Seduction provoked varying responses; much depended on the notoriety of the victim.[7]

Although current definitions of deviance are less inclusive, more recent cases still reflect a broad spectrum in views. Embracing and fondling an incarcerated client shocked the sensibilities of Iowa's 1979 disciplinary committee,[8] and marijuana offenses have met with mixed results.[9] State courts are currently split as to whether wilful evasion of taxes or failure to file a return constitutes moral turpitude.[10]

---

5. *Compare* In re Burch, 73 Ohio App. 97, 54 N.E.2d 803 (1943) (no disbarment for political offense); In re Clifton, 33 Idaho 614, 196 P. 670 (1921) (no disbarment for disloyal statement); Lotto v. State, 208 S.W. 563 (Tex.Civ. App.1919) (statement "Germany is going to win the war and I hope she will" held not grounds for disbarment) *with* In re Smith, 133 Wash. 145, 233 P. 288 (1925) (disbarment for sympathetically addressing I.W.W.); In re Margolis, 269 Pa. 206, 112 A. 478 (1921) (disbarment for advocating anarchism and avoiding the draft); In re Arctander, 110 Wash. 296, 188 P. 380 (1920) (disbarment for charging a fee to fill out Selective Service questionnaires).

6. Rhode, *supra* note 1, comparing People ex rel. Black v. Smith, 290 Ill. 241, 124 N.E. 807 (1919) with In re Kosher, 61 Wn.2d 206, 377 P.2d 988 (1963); In re Okin, 272 App.Div. 607, 73 N.Y.2d 861 (1947); In re Wilson, 76 Ariz. 49, 258 P.2d 433 (1953).

7. *See* Rhode, *supra* note 1. Seducing one's secretary has been thought discreditable but not disabling; seduc-

ing the wife of a World War I hero was unforgiveable. *Compare* State *ex rel.* v. Byrkett, 4 Ohio Dec. 89, 3 Ohio N.P. 28 (1894) *with* Grievance Committee v. Broder, 112 Conn. 263, 152 A. 292 (1930). To a 1929 Missouri court, seduction by an unfulfilled promise to marry constituted "baseness, vileness and depravity" mandating disbarment. In re Wallace, 323 Mo. 203, 19 S.W.2d 625 (1929).

8. Committee on Professional Ethics v. Durham, 279 N.W.2d 280 (Iowa 1979). Although the state bar committee recommended a five year suspension from practice, the Supreme Court imposed only a reprimand, in light of the isolated nature of Ms. Durham's "indiscretion."

9. *Compare* Matter of Moore, 453 N.E.2d 971 (1983) *with* Matter of Rabideau, 102 Wis.2d 16, 306 N.W.2d 1 (1981).

10. *Compare* cases cited in In re Fahey, 8 Cal.3d 842, 853 nn. 7–10, 106 Cal.Rptr. 313, 319 nn. 7–10, 505 P.2d

There has been equally little consensus concerning the level of appropriate sanctions. Clearly the relationship between personal offenses and legal practice has not of itself been a controlling factor. Thus, an Indiana lawyer in 1983 lost his license after a conviction for growing marijuana, while Richard Kleindeinst received only a thirty day suspension for committing perjury in his confirmation hearings for Attorney General.[11]

These cases, although relatively infrequent, nonetheless raise broader questions about the bar's disciplinary processes. To what extent should professional regulation replicate the functions of criminal law? How should limited disciplinary resources be allocated? Given the inadequacy of prevailing responses to professional misconduct, the rationale for policing certain personal activities is not self-evident. It remains somewhat anomalous that most bar disciplinary authorities do not exercise jurisdiction over common client grievances, such as fee disputes and "mere" negligence, although such bodies retain authority to revoke licenses for a variety of matters much more tangentially related to practice.

American Bar Association, Commission on Evaluation of Disciplinary Enforcement, *Lawyer Regulation for a New Century*

xiv-xx, 1–5, 7, 11–14, 16–17, 21, 33–35, 38, 42–43, 70, 75 (1992).

The Clark Committee warned of a "scandalous situation" in professional discipline and called for "the immediate attention of the profession." Today this Commission can report that most states have resolved many of the problems identified by the Clark Committee.

. . .

It is no exaggeration to say that revolutionary changes have occurred. Twenty years ago, most states conducted lawyer discipline at the local level with no professional staff. Lawyer discipline was a secretive procedural labyrinth of multiple hearings and reviews. At the national level, there was the ABA's Model

1369 (1973) *with* In re O'Hallaren, 64 Ill.2d 426, 64 Ill.Dec. 332, 356 N.E.2d 520 (1976); Ohio State Bar Association v. Stimmel, 61 Ohio St.2d 316, 401 N.E.2d 926 (1980); Matter of Wines, 135 Ariz. 203, 660 P.2d 454 (1983). *See also* Kelly, "Lawyer Sanctions: Looking Through the Looking Glass," 1 *Georgetown J. of Legal Ethics* 469, 471 (1988); Selinger & Schoen, " 'To Purify the

Bar': A Constitutional Approach to Non-Professional Misconduct," 5 *Nat.Resources J.* 299, 355–56 (1965).

11. *Compare* Matter of Moore, 453 N.E.2d 971 (1983) *with* In the Matter of Kleindeinst, No. 5–37–75, slip op. (D.C.C.A. Jan. Term 1975). *See* Kelly, *supra* note 10.

Code of Professional Responsibility, but little coordination, guidance or research.

Today almost all states have professional disciplinary staff with statewide jurisdiction.

. . .

[C]ooperation among local, state, and national bar associations and state high courts has resulted in constant improvement and refining of disciplinary procedures. The most recent product of this ongoing process was the establishment of this Commission.

*The Need to Expand Regulation to Protect the Public and Assist
Lawyers*

Times, however, have changed. The expectations of the public and the client have changed. The existing system of regulating the profession is narrowly focused on violations of professional ethics. It provides no mechanisms to handle other types of clients' complaints. The system does not address complaints that the lawyer's service was overpriced or unreasonably slow. The system does not usually address complaints of incompetence or negligence except where the conduct was egregious or repeated. It does not address complaints that the lawyer promised services that were not performed or billed for services that were not authorized.

Some jurisdictions dismiss up to ninety percent of all complaints. Most are dismissed because the conduct alleged does not violate the rules of professional conduct. The Commission has gathered much information about these dismissed complaints. It convinces us that many of them do state legitimate grounds for client dissatisfaction. The disciplinary system does not address these tens of thousands of complaints annually. The public is left with no practical remedy. While some states have created fee arbitration and other programs, additional avenues should be created in all states to resolve these complaints.

The disciplinary process also does nothing to improve the inadequate legal or office management skills that cause many of these complaints. Many state bar associations have mandatory continuing legal education, substance abuse counseling, and other programs. However, these programs usually are not coordinated with the disciplinary process. Lawyers with substandard skills often need more help than these programs can provide. The judiciary and profession should create new programs and coordinate all such programs with the disciplinary system.

The Need to Strengthen Regulation of the Profession by the Judiciary

Neither the profession nor the judiciary can permit this situation to continue. Clients, the public, the justice system, and the profession are suffering harm from this state of affairs. If it does continue, the public may remove the authority of the judiciary to regulate lawyers. There have been several attempts to do so in the last twenty years. The failure of the profession and the judiciary to act imperils the inherent power of the court to regulate its officers. It threatens the independence of counsel. The judiciary must expand the regulatory structure and improve the disciplinary system. This is necessary to protect the public and to insure the judiciary's power to regulate the profession. No system will satisfy every client, but the system should strive to right wrong conduct.

The Need for Direct and Exclusive Judicial Control of Lawyer Discipline

To strengthen judicial regulation of the profession, it must be distinguished from *self*-regulation. Control of the lawyer discipline system by elected officials of bar associations is self-regulation. It creates an appearance of conflicts of interest and of impropriety. In many states, bar officials still investigate, prosecute, and adjudicate disciplinary cases. The state high court should control the disciplinary process *exclusively*. It should appoint disciplinary officials who are independent of the organized bar. The Court should oversee the disciplinary system with as much care and attention as it devotes to deciding cases.

The Need to Increase Public Confidence in the Disciplinary System

Secret disciplinary proceedings generate the most criticism of the system. It is ironic that this attempt to shield honest lawyers' reputations has made the profession look so bad. What does the public think of hearings held behind closed doors? What does the public think when the disciplinary agency threatens the complaining party with imprisonment for speaking publicly about the complaint? These do not sound like the judicial proceedings of a free society. Indeed, several federal and state courts have held that such provisions violate federal or state constitutional provisions. The public will never accept the claim that lawyers must protect their reputations by gag rules and secret proceedings.

In many states, not only does the disciplinary agency threaten the complainant, the respondent lawyer can file a libel suit. Disciplinary counsel summarily dismiss complaints with no explanation of the decision. Complainants have no right to have the decision reviewed. The way many disciplinary systems treat complainants does not inspire confidence in the process.

The Need to Expedite the Disciplinary Process

Most complaints allege minor incompetence, minor neglect, or other minor misconduct. Most disciplinary agencies do not consider single instances of incompetence or neglect to be grounds for disciplinary action, although technically these do violate the rules of professional conduct. *See* Model Rules of Professional Conduct 1.1, 1.3. Disciplinary counsel routinely dismiss these complaints.

When a lawyer shows a *pattern* of incompetence, neglect or minor misconduct, most disciplinary agencies have only two options. They can (1) negotiate a private admonition or public reprimand with the respondent's consent, or (2) hold a formal hearing.

Dismissing valid complaints does nothing to correct the lawyer's behavior or compensate the client. Dismissing so many complaints casts suspicion on the disciplinary process. An admonition or reprimand may motivate the lawyer to change, but provides no guidance on *how* to change. Formal disciplinary proceedings cost time and money out of proportion to the minor nature of the offense. They divert resources from serious cases.

In these cases, the complainant needs a remedy and the lawyer needs additional skills and guidance. Programs should be created to provide them. When discipline is appropriate, the system needs expedited procedures commensurate with the sanctions (admonition or reprimand) involved.

The Need to Provide Adequate Resources

In the last twenty years, lawyers have volunteered hundreds of thousands of hours to carry out Clark Committee reforms. Lawyers also have paid millions of dollars to fund disciplinary agencies. Still, funding and staffing have not kept pace with the growth of the profession. Most agencies handle cases of serious misconduct effectively, but some agencies are so underfunded and understaffed that they offer little protection against unethical lawyers. The highest courts in these states should provide the funds needed to operate their disciplinary systems effectively.

The Need for Preventive Measures

Every year, millions of dollars of clients' money are stolen by a relatively few lawyers. Yet, most disciplinary systems lack authority to take basic preventive measures such as auditing trust account records or monitoring trust account overdrafts.

Another area calling for preventive measures is fee disputes. Fee disputes generate many disciplinary complaints. These complaints clog the disciplinary process. Most are summarily dismissed, because the lawyers' conduct did not violate the rules of professional conduct. This is a continuing source of the public's dissatisfaction with the profession. Written fee agreements could prevent many fee disputes, or at least simplify resolution of them.

. . .

The Need for Immediate Action

During the Commission's investigations, we heard much criticism of the profession. Some of the public's dissatisfaction is a misunderstanding of the lawyer's role. Some is misplaced unhappiness with the results of legal proceedings. Many negative perceptions about the profession are out of proportion to reality. Most lawyers are honest and skillful, and their clients respect them.

Unlike other professionals, lawyers are more likely to be criticized because of the nature of their work. In litigation, fifty percent of the clients lose their cases. In domestic relations, almost everyone leaves the proceedings with some sense of dissatisfaction. Some clients who are unhappy with the results of litigation will continue to complain about their lawyers, and no amount of reform will eliminate that criticism.

However, much of the criticism we heard is justified and accurate. Some practices must change immediately if regulation is to remain under the judiciary. The public views lawyer discipline as too slow, too secret, too soft, and too self-regulated. The Commission can report that most states discipline serious misconduct effectively. This is not enough. The profession and judiciary must face the problems we have identified. They must make necessary reforms to improve both the practice of law and the system of regulating the profession. While no system will satisfy all complainants, these improvements will demonstrate to the public that judicial regulation is effective.

. . .

Recommendation 1
Regulation of the Profession by the Judiciary

Regulation of the legal profession should remain under the authority of the judicial branch of government.

Comments

Exclusive judicial regulation of lawyers has developed since colonial times. In the nineteenth century, both the judiciary and the legislature exercised some control over the profession. Disputes between the two usually arose over bar admissions. By the end of the nineteenth century, however, state courts were asserting an exclusive right to regulate lawyers. They based this right on the constitutional doctrines of inherent power and separation of powers.

This assertion of judicial power resulted from two circumstances. First, the number of law schools and graduates increased. Courts became concerned about the quality of these schools and graduates. They created the bar examination and later character and fitness inquiries as additional admission requirements. Second, neither state legislatures nor state executives were taking action against unethical lawyers. The courts did so, claiming the inherent power to discipline lawyers as officers of the court.

Today, judicial regulation of lawyers is a principle firmly established in every state. A 1987 study by The National Center for State Courts found that thirteen state constitutions expressly grant the judiciary authority to regulate lawyers. The study found state high courts' opinions unanimous that regulation of lawyers is an inherent judicial function.

Judicial regulation of the profession has been challenged repeatedly during the last decade. In 1984, the Florida Legislature considered legislation for legislative regulation of the bar. The California Legislature created a Bar Monitor to conduct an ongoing evaluation of the judiciary's disciplinary function and to report to the legislature. National legal consumer groups have lobbied several state legislatures to regulate lawyers. The Federal Trade Commission unsuccessfully sought Congressional approval to regulate aspects of the lawyer-client relationship.

. . .

Supporters of legislative regulation argue that the practice of law affects the public more than it affects the courts. They argue that the legislature, as an elected body, is more likely to regulate in the public interest. They argue that the inherent power and separation of powers doctrines do not require exclusive regulation by the judiciary. Legislatures, they claim, could still regulate to the extent necessary to protect the public interest. They argue that the practice of law is not so technical that it requires lawyers to regulate it. Informed nonlawyers, they claim, could regulate effectively.

Supporters of legislative regulation emphasize the fact that judges are lawyers. They argue it is a conflict of interest for lawyers to regulate themselves because their own economic interests and social status are at stake. When the courts delegate regulation to bar associations, they argue, the conflict is greater.

Finally, supporters of legislative regulation deny that legislative regulation would impair the independence of lawyers. Exclusive judicial regulation is a recent development. They argue that lawyers were challenging government decisions long before it developed. They believe that a lawyer regulatory system created by the legislature could be insulated from political pressure.

The Commission carefully examined these arguments and considered two basic questions. Does judicial regulation of lawyer discipline fail to treat complainants fairly or fail to protect the public because of an inherent conflict of interest? Does legislative regulation of other professions result in better protection of complainants and the public?

To answer these questions, the Commission surveyed nonlawyer adjudicators of lawyer disciplinary agencies. More than thirty lawyer discipline agencies have nonlawyer adjudicators. We asked them if the system was fair. The Commission also studied several agencies established by state legislatures to regulate other professions. We examined their power to protect the public compared to that of lawyer disciplinary agencies. The Commission also heard many witnesses on the issue during our regional hearings. Finally, the Commission discussed the issue for several hours with the President of the National Clearinghouse on Licensure, Enforcement, and Regulation, an interstate association of legislatively created regulatory agencies.

The Commission found no persuasive evidence that legislative regulation of other professions has resulted in better protection of the public. In general, legislatively created regulatory bodies suffer from the same problems as do judicially created lawyer disciplinary agencies. Public representation is no higher on most other professional regulatory bodies than on lawyer disciplinary boards. In this regard, other professions are as "self-regulating" as the legal profession or more so. Legislatively created regulatory agencies suffer from understaffing, underfunding, and delays in adjudication as much as do some lawyer disciplinary agencies. Most legislatively created agencies' ability to redress complaints is similarly limited to suspending or removing the respondent's license.

In at least one aspect, judicial regulation of the legal profession offers better protection to the public. Almost all state high courts have created client protection funds to compensate victims of lawyer misconduct. Lawyers pay to create these funds. There is no cost to the taxpayer. No legislatively created regulatory mechanisms match lawyer client protection funds in amount of reimbursement, funding by the members of the profession, or nationwide scope.

Finally, a large majority of nonlawyer disciplinary officials believe the system is fair and unbiased. These nonlawyers adjudicate discipline cases and are intimately familiar with the system.

. . .

The Commission finds no basis to believe that legislative regulation of lawyers *per se* would be an improvement over judicial regulation. We find no persuasive evidence that legislative regulation of other professions has addressed similar problems more successfully. We find no persuasive evidence that other professions are better regulated or the public better protected because of legislative control. Most important, we find no persuasive evidence that a system regulated by the judiciary is biased for respondent lawyers against complainants. To the contrary, we find strong evidence from those nonlawyers most familiar with judicial regulation that it is fair.

. . .

History offers no comfort that active legislative regulation would protect the independence of counsel. The legislature responds to the political will of the people. From the Alien and Sedition Acts of 1798 to the McCarthy era of the 1950s, history has shown that the people's respect for individual rights can sink dangerously low. Legislatures act accordingly. During such times, an independent judiciary and legal profession are necessary to protect those rights.

It is easy to forget how fragile our liberties are. Beyond our borders are myriad examples of the need for an independent legal profession. Around the world, suppression of the legal profession is a basic tool of authoritarian governments. Amnesty International and the Lawyers Committee for Human Rights have units that specialize in monitoring political arrests of lawyers.

Proponents insist, however, that procedures could be devised to shield lawyers from political pressure under legislative regula-

tion.   Since the Commission finds no advantages in legislative
regulation, there is no reason to take such a risk.   This Commission finds a need to expand the scope and efficiency of regulation.
These changes can be accomplished under judicial regulation.

. . .

EXPANDING REGULATION TO PROTECT
THE PUBLIC AND ASSIST LAWYERS

Existing regulation, while generally effective in disciplining
serious misconduct, does not adequately protect the public from
lawyer incompetence and neglect.   This failure is having severe
repercussions for the legal profession.

In 1988, over forty-four thousand disciplinary complaints were
summarily dismissed.   In some jurisdictions up to ninety per cent
of all complaints filed were summarily dismissed.   Most of these
were dismissed for failing to allege unethical conduct.   Some of
these complaints fail to allege grounds for any type of response,
even under the expanded system proposed here, but many others
do allege facts that should be addressed.   The thousands of dismissed complaints in this second category show a gap exists
between reasonable client expectations and existing regulation.   It
is clear that tens of thousands of clients alleging legitimate
grounds for dissatisfaction with their lawyer's conduct are being
turned away because the conduct alleged would not be a violation
of disciplinary rules.   The disciplinary system was not designed to
address complaints about the quality of lawyers' services or fee
disputes.   Yet in all but a few states it is the only regulatory body
available to complainants.

The incompetence and neglect of relatively few lawyers must
not continue to sully the image of the rest.   We cannot afford to
let legitimate disagreements between lawyers and clients go unresolved.   Without a mechanism to resolve these complaints and
disputes, clients are harmed and the profession's reputation unnecessarily suffers.

The consequences of continuing to ignore these problems are
clear.   The Federal Trade Commission has made several attempts
to gain jurisdiction over some complaints against lawyers.   State
legislatures have made forays into lawyer regulation with increasing frequency.   Legal consumer organizations have grown in membership and in political activism.

Disciplinary proceedings, reimbursement from client protection funds, and civil suits for legal malpractice are all that exists

in most jurisdictions to redress client injury. These are insufficient in several respects.

Discipline primarily offers prospective protection to the public. It either removes the lawyer from practice or seeks to change the lawyer's future behavior. Protection of clients already harmed is minimal. Respondents are sometimes ordered to pay restitution in disciplinary cases. However, in many states, the failure of a lawyer to make restitution ordered in a disciplinary proceeding will not bar subsequent readmission to practice.

Clients can seek restitution from client protection funds in those states that have them. Client protection funds are an innovation of the legal profession unmatched by any other profession. Every year lawyers, through payments into the funds, reimburse millions of dollars to clients harmed by unethical lawyers. The profession can truly be proud of this achievement.

However, the ability of client protection funds to compensate clients is limited. Restitution is generally available only when a lawyer has stolen client funds. Many client protection funds have limitations on the amounts that will be paid on any one claim. Many client protection funds require a finding of misconduct by the disciplinary agency before a claim will be considered, delaying reimbursement sometimes for years.

Not only are disciplinary agencies and client protection funds limited in the types of remedies they provide but, except for the most egregious cases, they do not address lawyer incompetence and neglect. Most jurisdictions treat individual instances of incompetence and neglect as not violative of the rules of professional conduct or as a minimal violation not worthy of disciplinary action. Yet these types of cases constitute a large proportion of all complaints filed with disciplinary agencies against lawyers.

Other lawyer conduct not regulated by discipline mechanisms is that which generates fee disputes. Fee disputes may arise because a lawyer fails to provide services in the manner promised, delays performance, fails to clarify the computation of the fee, gives an unrealistic initial estimate of the fee, or behaves in other ways that are unfair to the client and unprofessional. This behavior, while perhaps not a violation of the rules of professional conduct, is clearly a legitimate ground for complaint from a client's perspective. Only a handful of jurisdictions mandate that the lawyer submit to arbitration when there is a prima facie legitimate fee dispute. In all other jurisdictions, most clients who have a legitimate dispute are without an economically feasible remedy. Their only options are to sue or to not pay the fee and be sued by the lawyer. The sum involved may be substantial to the client, but often the cost to litigate will be more than the amount in dispute. The client often files a complaint with the disciplinary agency, but the claim is dismissed. The National Organization of Bar Counsel reports that fee dispute issues constitute the second largest category of complaints dismissed for lack of jurisdiction. The profession can no longer afford to ignore these complaints. For every such complaint filed and dismissed, undoubtedly many more clients simply give up without filing a complaint and then blame the profession.

In most jurisdictions, the only option for aggrieved clients other than the disciplinary agency or the client protection fund is a malpractice suit. While the Commission has heard claims that lawyers are unwilling to sue other lawyers, there is ample evidence to suggest that a client with a reasonable claim for large enough damages will be able to find representation. The problem is not the willingness of lawyers to handle malpractice cases but that the time and expense of a civil suit make only large claims economically feasible. Even when the claim is for a large sum, full civil proceedings are a slow and expensive method of resolving the dispute. Also, many types of lawyer conduct that are legitimate grounds for client dissatisfaction and dispute may not constitute malpractice.

The profession's attempts to deal with substandard practice have not worked. The "code of professionalism" is valuable only to those predisposed to improve their practice. Peer review programs have not been accepted. Mandatory continuing legal education programs may keep lawyers' legal skills current, but they were not designed to remedy substandard skills. While legal malpractice is a growing specialization, it must surely be the least desirable means of self-regulation. What is required is a variety of methods to address the different types of problems and circumstances that create disputes between lawyers and clients.

Recommendation 3

Expanding the Scope of Public Protection

The Court should establish a system of regulation of the legal profession that consists of:

> **3.1 component agencies, including but not limited to:**
>
> > **(a) lawyer discipline,**
> >
> > **(b) a client protection fund,**
> >
> > **(c) mandatory arbitration of fee disputes,**

(d) **voluntary arbitration of lawyer malpractice claims and other disputes,**

(e) **mediation,**

(f) **lawyer practice assistance,**

(g) **lawyer substance abuse counseling; and**

3.2 a central intake office for the receipt of all complaints about lawyers, whose functions should include: (a) providing assistance to complainants in stating their complaints; (b) making a preliminary determination as to the validity of the complaint; (c) dismissing the complaint or determining the appropriate component agency or agencies to which the complaint should be directed and forwarding the complaint; (d) providing information to complainants about available remedies, operations and procedures, and the status of their complaints; and (e) coordinating among agencies and tracking the handling and disposition of each complaint.

Comments

The availability of more than one mechanism to resolve disputes can backfire and result in increased public dissatisfaction unless a simple and direct procedure exists for making a complaint. Complainants should not be expected to know the distinctions among component agencies. They need a central intake office—one clearly designated agency to which to take any type of complaint. The state's highest court and its agency should provide the expertise needed to determine where prima facie valid complaints should be directed.

Detecting unethical behavior should remain the highest priority of the judicial branch. The central intake agency should screen all complaints for allegations of conduct that violates ethics rules. It should forward those complaints to the disciplinary agency and to any other relevant agency, to insure misconduct is not overlooked.

Lawyer discipline should be directly and exclusively controlled by the highest court in the jurisdiction. *See* Recommendation 5. However, it may be appropriate for bar associations to administer other components of the system, such as arbitration, mediation, lawyer practice assistance, *etc.,* under the court's authority. Therefore, the disciplinary agency should not be the administrative entity for other component agencies.

A fee dispute arbitration system that is mandatory for the lawyer eliminates the overwhelming advantage lawyers have over the majority of clients who are of modest means and have only the most rudimentary knowledge of the law. The experience of those states that provide mandatory fee arbitration demonstrates that these programs can work without being unduly burdensome on the profession. As is done in disciplinary matters, complaints that do not state legitimate grounds for dispute should be screened out. In cases of valid disputes, mandated fee adjustments can provide the incentive to reform for lawyers who do substandard work. Fee dispute arbitrators should therefore consider the competence and promptness of the lawyer's services in determining whether the fee was appropriate. In many cases involving substandard services, fee adjustments are sufficient to compensate injured clients. When a legitimate fee dispute arises and the lawyer enters arbitration in good faith, the client's opinion of both the lawyer and the profession can be improved. Fee arbitration decisions should follow applicable precedent. Decisions should be in writing and should be provided to both parties.

Providing an additional, voluntary arbitration mechanism for lawyers and clients can greatly benefit both the bar and clients. The ABA Standing Committee on Dispute Resolution reports that these programs have been tested successfully in settings such as bar associations, courts, prosecutors' offices, and neighborhood centers. Disputes to be considered could include contractual, non-disciplinary, and inadequate representation claims that today go unresolved and result in harm to the lawyer's reputation.

Mediation services are useful in preserving ongoing lawyer-client relationships when disputes arise or in matters where a lawyer has placed a lien on a client's file. When handled by a skilled mediator, the process can be simple and efficient, saving time and money for both parties. The lawyer's willingness to have a third party assist in resolving the dispute can demonstrate to the client that the lawyer's intention is to act in the client's best interest.

. . .

Recommendation 4

Lawyer Practice Assistance Committee

4.1 The Court should establish a Lawyer Practice Assistance Committee. At least one third of the members should be non-lawyers. The Lawyer Practice Assistance Committee should consider cases referred to it by the disciplinary counsel and the Court and should assist lawyers voluntarily seeking assistance. The Committee should provide guidance to the lawyer including, when appropriate: (a) review of the

lawyer's office and case management practices and recommendations for improvement; and (b) review of the lawyer's substantive knowledge of the law and recommendations for further study.

4.2 In cases in which the lawyer has agreed with disciplinary counsel to submit to practice assistance, the Committee may require the lawyer to attend continuing legal education classes, to attend and successfully complete law school courses or office management courses, to participate in substance abuse recovery programs or in psychological counseling, or to take other actions necessary to improve the lawyer's fitness to practice law.

. . .

INCREASING PUBLIC CONFIDENCE IN THE DISCIPLINARY SYSTEM

The Commission is convinced that secrecy in discipline proceedings continues to be the greatest single source of public distrust of lawyer disciplinary systems. Because it engenders such distrust, secrecy does great harm to the reputation of the profession. The public's expectation of government and especially of judicial proceedings is that they will be open to the public, on the public record, and that the public and media will be able to freely comment on the proceedings. The public does not accept the profession's claims that lawyers' reputations are so fragile that they must be shielded from false complaints by special secret proceedings. The irony that lawyers are protected by secret proceedings while earning their livelihoods in an open system of justice is not lost on the public. On the contrary it is a source of great antipathy toward the profession.

Recommendation 7

Access to Disciplinary Information

All records of the lawyer disciplinary agency except the work product of disciplinary counsel should be available to the public after a determination has been made that probable cause exists to believe misconduct occurred, unless the complainant or respondent obtains a protective order from the highest court or its designee for specific testimony, documents or records. All proceedings except adjudicative deliberations should be public after a determination that probable cause exists to believe that misconduct occurred.

Comments

Prior to the Clark Report, in most jurisdictions all proceedings were secret until the state high court issued an order finding misconduct. In 1979 the ABA adopted a policy recommending that disciplinary proceedings should be public upon the filing of formal charges. *See* MRLDE 16. Recommendation 7, as amended by the House of Delegates above, reaffirms MRLDE 16. Today, proceedings are public upon the filing of formal charges in over half of the states.

. . .

Both complainant and respondent may seek a protective order to seal records. The Commission has not specified grounds for issuing a protective order. That is best left to the highest courts and disciplinary agencies in each jurisdiction. In general, the Commission believes that a complainant should not be forced to choose between having confidences or secrets revealed or filing a complaint; a respondent should not have to chose between presenting a defense or protecting secrets and confidences of other clients. The respondent has no right to assert the complaining client's privilege if the complaining client does not assert it.

Disciplinary counsel should advise all complainants and respondents of the availability of protective orders. Any testimony, documents, or records, including the complainant's initial communication with the agency, for which a protective order is being sought should be confidential until the determination of the Court.

Legislative History of Recommendations 7 and 8

The Commission's original Recommendation 7 stated:

Recommendation 7

Fully Public Discipline Process

All records of the lawyer disciplinary agency except the work product of disciplinary counsel should be available to the public from the time of the complainant's initial communication with the agency, unless the complainant or respondent obtains a protective order from the highest court or its designee for specific testimony, documents or records. All proceedings except adjudicative deliberations should be public.

. . .

The Commission has carefully considered the need for secrecy to protect innocent lawyers from false complaints. All members of the Commission understand that a lawyer's reputation is not only the basis for his or her livelihood, it is a cherished and integral part of the lawyer's life. The lawyer's reputation defines the value of the lawyer's service to clients and the community.

However, we find in Oregon, Florida and West Virginia ample experience to demonstrate that public proceedings or public records of dismissed complaints do no harm to innocent lawyers' reputations. On the contrary, secrecy does great harm to the reputation of the profession as a whole.

If public interest in a particular lawyer's case is high, the public will learn the essential allegations through other sources. The disciplinary agency is then left in the embarrassing position of "neither confirming nor denying" the existence of an investigation, further damaging the profession's credibility. Secrecy rules do nothing to protect individual lawyers in these situations. In matters of little public interest, there is obviously little possibility that actual damage to a lawyer's practice will occur. Under a fully public and open disciplinary system, lawyers accused of misconduct as well as complainants are free to comment on the proceedings. In many states, respondent lawyers may not publicly reply to information leaked to the media.

An open disciplinary system demonstrates its fairness to the public. Secret records and secret proceedings create public suspicion regardless of how fair the system actually is. A fully open disciplinary system will preclude the possibility of disciplinary officials committing improprieties such as destroying evidence, shredding files, or covering up complaints against influential lawyers. Disciplinary officials in Florida, West Virginia and Oregon state that public scrutiny of their disciplinary systems motivates staff to do better work.

Making disciplinary records and proceedings public will avoid further constitutional challenges, sparing the profession additional negative publicity. Finally, a fully open disciplinary system eliminates special procedures for sanctions such as "private reprimands" or "admonitions" that were formerly confidential.

. . .

Recommendation 8

Complainant's Rights

8.1 Complainants should receive notice of the status of disciplinary proceedings at all stages of the proceedings. In general, a complainant should receive, contemporaneously, the same notices and orders the respondent receives as well as copies of respondent's communications to the agency,

except information that is subject to another client's privilege.

8.2 Complainants should be permitted a reasonable opportunity to rebut statements of the respondent before a complaint is summarily dismissed.

8.3 Complainants should be notified in writing when the complaint has been dismissed. The notice should include a concise recitation of the specific facts and reasoning upon which the decision to dismiss was made.

8.4 Disciplinary counsel should issue written guidelines for determining which cases will be dismissed for failure to allege facts that, if true, would constitute grounds for disciplinary action. These guidelines should be sent to complainants whose cases are dismissed.

8.5 Complainants should be notified of the date, time, and location of the hearing. Complainants should have the right to personally appear and testify at the hearing.

8.6 All jurisdictions should afford a right of review to complainants whose complaints are dismissed prior to a full hearing on the merits, consistent with ABA MRLDE 11B(3) and 31.

.   .   .

Recommendation 13

Funding and Staffing

The Court should insure that adequate funding and staffing are provided for the disciplinary agency so that: (a) disciplinary cases are screened, investigated, prosecuted and adjudicated promptly; (b) the work load per staff person permits careful and thorough performance of duties; (c) professional and support staff are compensated at a level sufficient to attract and retain competent personnel; (d) sufficient office and data processing equipment exist to efficiently and quickly process the work load and manage the agency; (e) adequate office space exists to provide a productive working environment; and (f) staff and volunteers are adequately trained in disciplinary law and procedure.

The Court should insure that adequate funding and staffing are provided for client protection funds, mandatory fee arbitration, voluntary arbitration, mediation, lawyer practice assistance, lawyer substance abuse counseling, and all other programs of the expanded regulatory system proposed under Recommendation 3.

. . .

Recommendation 16

Random Audit of Trust Accounts

The Court should adopt a rule providing that lawyer trust accounts selected at random may be audited without having grounds to believe misconduct has occurred and also providing appropriate procedural safeguards.

Deborah L. Rhode, "Institutionalizing Ethics"

Case Western Law Review (1993).

Unlike governance structures in other nations and professions, regulation of the American bar has remained under almost exclusive control of the group to be regulated. Courts in this country have asserted inherent authority to oversee the practice of law, and generally have permitted legislative initiatives only if consistent with judicial standards. Nonlawyers generally have obtained token representation on disciplinary bodies and lawyers have controlled the selection process. Few of these lay representatives have had the backgrounds, resources, or sense of accountability to consumers that would create a significant counterweight to professional power. Nonlawyer members who lack independent sources of information or ties to organized interest groups have difficulty maintaining the "[external] viewpoint they are supposed to bring."

The point is not to question the good faith of the attorneys and judges who control bar regulatory processes. Without doubt, most members of the profession are committed to improving the system in which they work. What is open to doubt is whether the bar as a whole can rise above self-interest on issues that place its income or status at risk. ...

The problem is compounded by attorneys' unwillingness to consider it a problem. The American bar's traditional position is that "[w]hile superficially there may appear to be a tension between professional responsibility and self-interest, in fact, broadly viewed, there is none." Among bar leaders, debates about professional regulation uniformly assume that professional autonomy is essential. According to the Model Rules' Preamble, self-regulation serves the public interest because it "helps maintain the legal profession's independence from government domination."

Such independence is, in turn, considered "an important force in preserving government under law, for abuse of legal authority is more readily challenged by a profession whose members are not dependent on government for the right to practice."

Majoritarian governmental control and total professional autonomy are not, however, the only alternatives. Other countries have established more hybrid regulatory structures. And in at least some instances, most recently in Great Britain, such structures have resulted in more consumer-oriented reforms than their professionally-dominated counterparts. So too, some state legislators have proposed oversight structures that would remain independent of both elected government and the organized bar. One California statute would have established a board under state supreme court auspices with members appointed by different decision makers and representing diverse constituencies. Of course, as subsequent discussion acknowledges, such a shift in oversight authority is no guarantee of effective oversight. Yet it is also plausible to suppose that a more publicly accountable body could generate a more socially responsive set of governance standards and structures.

. . .

In 1970, a special American Bar Association commission identified a "scandalous situation" in lawyer discipline. Some two decades later, much in that situation had remained unchanged, as yet another ABA Commission reported. Fundamental inadequacies in the disciplinary process have persisted in part because of one central problem that neither Commission acknowledged: the profession's almost exclusive control over its own regulation. Lawyers have interests that overlap but are not coextensive with those of the public. Most attorneys want a process that is sufficiently responsive to clear abuses to forestall more intrusive state regulation. But few have supported a system that would require major increases in their own bar dues, that would significantly expand oversight of their own conduct, or that would impose substantial risks of serious sanctions.

The result is a regulatory structure that rests on inconsistent premises. Standards governing admission and competition assume that a free market in legal services is inappropriate; clients are not in a position to make informed judgments about the quality and cost of services received. Yet bar disciplinary processes have worked on the opposite assumption. They rely almost exclusively on client grievances (together with felony convictions) as sources of information about attorney misconduct.

Lawyers and judges rarely report professional abuses, and little effort has focused on counteracting the obvious economic and psychological barriers to reporting. Many attorneys do not feel sufficiently blameless to cast the first stone unless they are sure of a fellow practitioner's serious misconduct, and the incentives to gather relevant information are almost nonexistent. Prosecution of disciplinary charges poses classic free rider problems. As one practitioner put it when explaining why he had not filed a grievance, "I represent Ford Motor Company, not the next guy.... I have a very narrow balance sheet." Even lawyers and judges who are willing to take a broader view of their professional obligations are often unwilling to file charges with agencies that have proved ineffective in responding.

As a consequence, most ethical violations never reach regulatory agencies. Many clients and injured third parties lack information about attorneys' misconduct or bar grievance processes; others are deterred by the cost, complexity, or seeming futility of reporting. Misconduct from which clients benefit, such as discovery abuse or misrepresentation in negotiations, is also unlikely to reach oversight agencies.

The system is similarly ineffective in responding to the grievances that are in fact reported. Resource constraints have led disciplinary agencies to decline jurisdiction over certain abuses for which an adequate civil remedy is theoretically available, such as "mere" negligence or excessive fees. The result is a mismatch between client needs and regulatory responses. The problems that consumers are most likely to experience such as neglect and overcharging are least likely to fall within agency jurisdiction. . . .

Even cases that fall squarely within bar disciplinary jurisdiction often fare no better. State agencies are generally underfunded and understaffed, and over 90 percent of complaints are dismissed without investigation. Although some significant percentage of these complaints are inherently implausible or reflect dissatisfaction with outcomes rather than attorney performance, the high dismissal rate is at least partly attributable to inadequate resources. Funding constraints also prevent agencies from undertaking proactive, independent investigations and limit their capacity to assist clients who need help in filing grievances. In most jurisdictions, the confidentiality of the process unless some public sanction is issued means that attorneys with large numbers of pending or dismissed complaints receive a "clean bill of health" from disciplinary authorities. Bar decision makers have nonetheless rejected proposals for greater public disclosure out of concern for lawyers who might be unjustly accused.

Concern for clients unjustly exploited has not met with similar solicitude. Even cases that satisfy the stringent "clear and convincing" standard applicable in disciplinary proceedings often conclude without adequate remedies. In principle, the objective is protection of the public, not punishment of the lawyer. In practice, the system accomplishes neither. Lawyers inevitably experience sanctions as punitive, and decision makers' reluctance to impose them prevents adequate protection. Less than 2 percent of complaints result in public sanctions, and they are rarely directed at practitioners from mainstream firms and organizations. Here again the mismatch between client expectations and regulatory outcomes is apparent, as two cases decided by the same state Supreme Court in the same year attest. An Indiana lawyer who knowingly allowed marijuana to grow on his premises was disbarred; a lawyer who "deceived his clients, ... neglected his clients' cases and abused his clients' trust" was suspended for forty-five days.

In part, this lenient sanctioning structure reflects a "there but for the grace of God go I" attitude among regulators. Most offenders have stress-related problems linked to family difficulties, substance abuse, financial strain, or other work related pressures; most decision makers appear more able to empathize with fellow professionals than with clients. Although many regulatory boards have lay representatives, these individuals never constitute a majority, are selected by the profession, do not represent organized public interest groups, and generally do not push for more stringent sanctions than their lawyer colleagues.

Although clients may find more sympathy from jurors in malpractice cases, the cost of those proceedings and the difficulties of proof make them inadequate remedies for most grievances. So too, many valid civil liability claims go unredressed because the lawyer has insufficient insurance or personal assets, and the bar's client security funds are woefully inadequate.

A more effective regulatory system will require a fundamental rethinking of self-regulatory premises. As previous discussion indicated, some improvement is likely to occur from removing professional control over the disciplinary process. That is not, however, to suggest that formal reallocation of authority is an all-purpose prescription for regulatory pathologies. As experience with administrative agencies makes clear, such bodies are often vulnerable to capture by the groups to be regulated. Such groups not only have incentives and resources for influence beyond those of a diffuse public, their cooperation may be critical to agency performance. The result is often a "friendly" relationship that constrains administrative oversight. Yet where such relationships are absent, the targets of regulation typically mobilize to alter personnel and policies or else circumvent their impact. Lawyers, who often successfully pursue such strategies for clients, are likely to be equally adept in their own behalf.

Moreover, in a context where professional performance is difficult to monitor and a high degree of professional discretion is essential, some ethic of self-regulation is important to maintain. The danger of overly intrusive, bureaucratized external structures is that they may erode the very sense of personal responsibility for professional regulation that is most central to its effectiveness.

Yet not all forms of external oversight present equal risks of co-optation or subversion of regulatory objectives. Agencies can minimize some of those risks by relying on long-term career employees and building public interest representation and accountability into the regulatory process. Moreover, some loss of [professional] control does not necessarily imply a corresponding loss of professional responsibility. To the contrary, most experts on occupational licensure advocate external checks as a means of prodding professionals to live up to their own aspirations.

Even without such a reallocation of control, strategies that increase public accountability are also likely to increase effectiveness. The California legislature greatly improved state disciplinary processes by using its power over bar dues to promote essential reforms and by appointing a state bar monitor to evaluate their implementation. Experience in other regulatory contexts suggests the usefulness of tripartite frameworks, in which organized public interest groups assume an official role in overseeing the oversight structure. Where no adequate organizations exist, the government can encourage their creation through financial support and the assurance of a significant regulatory function. Such groups could both create pressure for reforms and monitor their effectiveness in two areas: in regulatory agencies' capacity to identify misconduct and in their ability to provide adequate deterrent and remedial structures.

Expanding regulators' monitoring capacities will require expansion of resources and of proactive strategies. For example, the bar could improve disciplinary outreach efforts by increasing publicity, by requiring disclosure of grievance channels in lawyer-client retainer agreements, and by providing assistance to complainants. Regulatory authorities could also initiate investigations based on malpractice complaints, court-imposed sanctions, and random checks of trust funds. Increased accountability of disciplinary responses could occur if records and proceedings were publicly accessible. Greater efforts could be made to enforce rules requiring lawyers to report misconduct and greater pressure could be placed on judges to forward similar information. A recent Illinois decision imposing attorney discipline under such circumstances reportedly has increased practitioners' willingness to file complaints.

At the remedial level, the bar needs more accessible and less self-protective enforcement structures. Alternative forms of dispute resolution and mandatory arbitration under neutral panels should be available for performance ... as well as fee-related disputes. Serious misconduct should elicit serious sanctions. License revocations, extended suspensions, and probation should be routine responses. They should also be accompanied by conditions for reinstatement that are likely to provide both client remedies and societal protection (*e.g.*, restitution, completion of office management programs or substance abuse treatment, and so forth). A centralized directory or toll-free phone bank should supply information about lawyers' disciplinary records, and regulatory agencies should make greater use of publicity to reinforce sanctions. Client security funds should be dramatically increased, and adequate malpractice insurance should be required.

B.   Internal Oversight

Attention also needs to focus on the organizational context of ethical violations. A growing body of work on corporate compliance structures yields a useful and largely untapped resource for rethinking bar regulatory structures. In general, this work makes clear that internal methods of securing compliance work more effectively than external oversight structures. Organizations generally are in a better position to secure information and cooperation than regulatory agencies. Most people respond better to sanctions from peers than from more distant authorities, and restructuring institutional incentives is more likely to secure compliance than occasionally imposing sanctions. Organizations employing lawyers could substantially increase the likelihood of ethical conduct through monitoring and reward structures giving priority to that objective. Obvious examples include restructured billing incentives, firm-specific ethical guidelines, explicit reporting channels, internal education programs, and ethics committees concerned with more than conflicts of interest.

Such initiatives could be required for all employers over a certain size, or for those whose lawyers have received civil, judicial, or disciplinary sanctions. Where rule violations involve organizational failures, such as inadequate supervision or skewed incentive structures, the organization should be accountable. More innovative penalties and remedial directives, such as those developed for corporate misconduct, should become standard tools in professional regulation. For example, courts or disciplinary agencies could require that lawyers who committed malpractice or discovery abuse submit a regulatory plan to prevent subsequent misconduct by other members of their organization. Such a plan might include new educational programs, oversight committees, reporting channels, and so forth. Research on white-collar offenses also suggests that community service or publicity of organizational sanctions might have greater deterrent effect than prevailing approaches. Current strategies of low visibility reprimands for most disciplinary violations and modest fines for most procedural violations do not impose the reputational costs or convey the lasting message that more innovative sanctions might provide.

. . .

Susan R. Martyn, "Lawyer Competence and Lawyer Discipline: Beyond the Bar?"

69 Georgetown Law Journal 705, 725–29, 730–32, 736–43 (1981).*

In addition to law school screening and bar examinations, various methods designed to ensure the competence of practicing attorneys could be implemented as a means of improving the performance of the bar. Rather than using entry standards to project levels of performance, these methods attempt to measure or control competence by focusing on what a lawyer does or fails to do in rendering legal service. The bar has expressed a strong preference for continuing legal education, which is designed to provide a continual update of knowledge necessary to the ongoing process of legal representation. Voluntary continuing legal education programs have been adopted in about two-thirds of the states. Although these programs have been helpful to the bar, their major benefit appears to be skill enhancement of already motivated and relatively competent practitioners. This conclusion is buttressed by a recent empirical study that found no correlation between competent appellate advocacy and prior participation in relevant continuing legal education courses.

Nine states have made some form of continuing legal education mandatory. Mere attendance at educational seminars, however, will not ensure the internalization of their content. For that reason, some commentators have argued that continuing legal education unaccompanied by testing mechanisms is probably of little value. Like all process measures, continuing legal education is not a client complaint response mechanism. Furthermore, the bar's reliance on continuing legal education as a means of ensuring competence probably hinders efforts to define standards of lawyer proficiency. In fact, like the bar grievance process and the ABA Code of Professional Responsibility, continuing legal education may mislead the public. Although all these mechanisms purport to provide a measure of competence in return for a grant of monopoly, most focus primarily on the intellectual skill of the lawyer and thus ignore client concerns about the process of representation.

Another type of process measure, peer review, is far more developed in medicine than in law, in part because the particular institutional setting nurtures such review. Peer review functions best in institutional environments such as hospitals and joint practice medical centers, which require interdependent interactions among professionals. Opportunities for effective peer review in the legal profession, however, are limited by the lack of such interdependent collective enterprises. Lawyers have far fewer opportunities than doctors to observe and evaluate the performance of their colleagues. ... Furthermore, peer review cannot assess professional service adequately unless it considers consumer response to that service. Thus, although peer review offers some aid to professionals, it promises little hope to aggrieved consumers who have no input into the process.

The American Law Institute-American Bar Association's Committee on Continuing Professional Education has recently attempted to respond to these criticisms in its proposed Model Peer Review System (Model Peer Review System). Recognizing that grievance boards lack the resources, willingness, and experience to remedy most attorney incompetence, the Model Peer Review System offers both voluntary and referral peer review as remedial alternatives to the current disciplinary process.

Referral peer review is the most important of the suggested innovations. The Model Peer Review System proposes establishment of Lawyer Competence Review Boards that would formulate general competence criteria, remedial programs for individual lawyers, and evaluative and training materials for competence appraisal. Referrals from the lay public, other attorneys, or judges would initiate an initial screening in which the referred attorney might be asked to participate by the board's professional staff. ... A disciplinary committee could order an attorney who violated the ABA Code to undergo remedial competence training administered by the board and also could require board certification of the attorney's competence as a prerequisite to bar reinstatement. ...

The Model Peer Review System, however, is likely to suffer from historical prejudices ... [T]hough the Model Peer Review System suggests that board composition reflect a diversity of background and relevant experience and does not rule out lay participation, the proposal also suggests that the judiciary may delegate to state or local bar associations the authority, subject to judicial supervision, to determine board size and composition. It is thus possible and perhaps probable that a review board would be composed largely of professionals and would therefore develop patterns of response that reflect the traditional laissez-faire attitude of the bar. ...

A new forum armed with specific definitions of competence and broad remedial powers might be increasingly willing to act upon allegations of attorney incompetence. A board's willingness to act, however, does not overcome the probable reluctance of referred attorneys to participate in remedial activities. Referral peer review is theoretically directed at the marginal practitioner. This attorney is perhaps more likely than others to view participation as a waste of time as long as it appears that no other sanction will be forthcoming. Thus, to be truly effective, referral peer review must be supported by the disciplinary process. The Model Peer Review System recognizes this need but makes no attempt to detail the manner by which disciplinary committees should handle competence matters.

Most process measures can, at best, only be indirect indicators of proficiency. Because neither continuing legal education nor peer review seriously addresses consumer needs, they will be unlikely to change the bar's overall attitude toward competency disputes. At the same time, a change in attitude is necessary to encourage voluntary cooperation with and benefit from both programs. To the extent the public relies on these offerings as a mechanism for ensuring professional competency, it will continue to be misled.

A separate competency review proposal, relying on both professional standards and client input, could be modeled after Minnesota's attorney-client fee disputes arbitration system. Clients who use this system have the right to bring a fee dispute before a bar-appointed panel, even if the lawyer is not willing to submit to binding arbitration. The panel then holds a hearing to determine a fair fee, and panel members may offer expert testimony on behalf of the client if the matter is subsequently taken to court. As some commentators have suggested, this system could also be used to resolve complaints alleging incompetence. Such a system would serve both to establish competence standards through the interaction of the profession and clients and to establish an enforcement mechanism that would meet client needs.

NOTES *

Three decades ago, malpractice claims against attorneys were so rare and practitioners were so unconcerned about liability that insurance coverage was generally not available on the domestic market. By 1980, the situation had dramatically changed; 85% of practicing attorneys had some form of coverage and the number of claims was escalating rapidly. Estimates from the mid–1980s suggested that 10% of the nation's lawyers were facing malpractice charges.[1]

Nor was the legal profession unique. A rise in consumers' sense of entitlement helped account for increases in claims against other professionals as well; even clergy have felt the effects.[2] So too, increasing competition and stratification within the legal community made colleagues less hesitant to testify against each other in malpractice suits. Finally, financial speculation in the 1980's catalyzed more civil liability claims. Individuals who lost money in risky ventures looked for deep pockets to sue and often lighted on prosperous law firms that had brokered the transaction. In many cases, attorneys had written opinion letters that investors had relied upon (or claimed to have relied upon), and these documents formed the basis of legal malpractice actions.

Yet despite the escalation of malpractice claims, the barriers to successful actions have remained considerable. Many individuals with grievances against a lawyer are unwilling to incur the costs in time, money, and acrimony involved in filing charges. Unless liability looks clear, damages are substantial, and the

---

* This material is adapted from D. Rhode and D. Luban *Legal Ethics* 756–57 (1992).

1. Pfennigstorf, "Types and Causes of Lawyers' Professional Liability Claims: The Search for Facts," *A.B.F.Res.J.* 253 (1980); Lawscope, "Suing Lawyers," 72 *A.B.A.J.* 25 (April 1986).

2. *See, e.g.,* P. Danzon, *Medical Malpractice* (1986); Robinson, "The Medical Malpractice Crisis of the 1970s: A Retrospective," 49 *Law and Contemp.Probs.* 6 (1986); "CPA Suits Are Adding Up," *Nat'l,* May 16, 1983, at 1; Note, "Clergy Malpractice: Making Clergy Accountable to a Lower Power," 14 *Pepperdine L.Rev.* 137 (1986). *See generally* L. Friedman, *Total Justice* (1985).

defendant has sufficient assets to make a judgment collectible, attorneys who specialize in malpractice litigation will generally decline the case.

The burden of proof necessary to establish attorney liability is often difficult to meet. Data available in the mid–1980s indicated that over two-thirds of all malpractice claims result in no payment. Of those claims that are successful, 70% provide recoveries of under $1,000, and most involve fairly obvious errors, such as missing deadlines, neglecting to file documents, or failing to consult clients and follow their instructions.[3] In cases presenting less objective proof of error, clients will often have difficulty establishing what exactly the attorney did or didn't do, and how that conduct fell below average performance standards within the relevant legal community.

Despite such difficulties attorneys are facing increased pressure to prevent disputes that might trigger malpractice claims. One critical preventive technique involves time management systems that enable lawyers to meet important deadlines; such systems are more effective if they allocate responsibility for ensuring compliance with someone other than the person responsible for performance. An equally important strategy involves communication. Attorneys should provide realistic assessments of a client's chances of success as well as probable delays and costs. Disputes can also be preempted by detailed written retainer agreements and by ongoing reports concerning the status of the case (such as copies of major filings, notice of significant developments, etc.).[4]

3. R. Abel, *American Lawyers* 154 (1989); Gates, "Charting the Shoals of Malpractice," *A.B.A.J.* July 1, 1987 at 62; "Suing Lawyers," 72 *A.B.A.J.* 25 (April 1986); Standing Committee on Lawyer's Professional Liability, *Characteristics of Legal Malpractice: Report of the National Malpractice Data Center* 2–3 (1989). *See* Peters, Nord & Woodson, "An Empirical Analysis of the Medical and Legal Profession's Experiences and Perceptions of Medical and Legal Malpractice," 19 *U.Mich.J.Law Rev.* 601, 610 (1986) (half of all respondents were aware of competent colleague's deviation from accepted standards of care in past five years that resulted in an injury for which no claim was filed). Substantive areas giving rise to the highest number of claims are personal injury (plaintiff) (26%), real estate (23%), bankruptcy and collection (11%), and family law (8%) Standing Committee, *supra*. The most frequent errors involve substantive mistakes (43.-6%), such as failure to know or properly apply the law (9.4%); inadequate discovery or investigation (8.9%); failure to know or ascertain the relevant deadlines (6.8%); planning errors or procedure choice (7.6%); administrative and calendaring errors (25.76%); client relations (16.2%); and intentional wrongs (11.5%) such as fraud (4.1%) and malicious prosecution or abuse of process (4.1%). *Id.* at 6–7.

4. D. Stern and J. Felix–Retzhke, *A Practical Guide to Preventing Legal Malpractice* 177–78, 181–82 (1983); Mallen, "How to Avoid Becoming a Legal Malpractice Statistic," 1 *Legal Malpractice Rep.* 1 (1989); Harmon, "Protect Yourself: Develop a Malpractice Prevention Program for Your Law Prac-

Contrary to popular assumption, it is not young, inexperienced attorneys who experience most malpractice claims. Lawyers practicing less than 4 years account for 13% of the profession but only 4% of claims; lawyers practicing over 10 years account for 66% of malpractice filings.[5] The same financial and psychological factors that help lead to disciplinary charges are also contributors to malpractice: unrealistic caseloads, drug and alcohol abuse, and personal stresses such as divorce and burnout. The best protection for both lawyers and their clients is professional help when such problems arise, together with comprehensive malpractice coverage.[6]

REFERENCES

I. Ayres and J. Braithwaite, *Responsive Regulation: Transcending the Deregulation Debate* (1992).

ALI–ABA Comm. on Continuing Professional Education, *A Model Peer Review System* (Discussion Draft, 1980).

ALI–ABA Comm. on Continuing Professional Education, *Enhancing the Competence of Lawyers* (1981) (Report of the Houston Conference).

Arthurs, "Public Accountability of the Legal Profession," in P. Thomas & P. Lewis eds., *Law in the Balance: Legal Services in the Eighties* (1981).

Burger, "The Special Skills of Advocacy: Are Specialized Training and Certification of Advocates Essential to Our System of Justice?," 42 *Fordham L.Rev.* 227 (1973).

Carlson, "Measuring the Quality of Legal Services: An Idea Whose Time Has Not Come", 11 *Law & Soc'y Rev.* 287 (1976).

Eisenberg, "Attorney Negligence and Third Parties," 57 *N.Y.U.L.Rev.* 126 (1982).

Final Report of the Committee to Consider Standards for Admission to Practice in the Federal Courts to the Judicial Conference of the United States (Devitt Committee Report) (1979).

tice," *Legal Econ.*, September, 1987, at 20; Blumberg, "Risk Management: Preventing Malpractice Claims," *Legal Econ.*, September, 1987, at 52; Johnson, "Tips on Reducing Malpractice Exposure," *Wis.B.Bull.*, February, 1986, at 23.

5. Mallen, *supra* note 13; *Characteristics of Legal Malpractice, supra* note 3 at 44.

6. "Uninsured and Insecure," California Law, June, 1987 at 59; Schneyer, "Mandatory Malpractice Insurance for Lawyers in Wisconsin and Elsewhere," 1979 *Wis.L.Rev.* 1019.

Frankel, "Curing Lawyers' Incompetence: Primum Non Nocere," 10 *Creighton L.Rev.* 613 (1977).

Garth, "Rethinking the Legal Profession's Approach to Collective Self Improvement: Competence and the Consumer Perspective," 1983 *Wisc.L.Rev.* 639.

Kelly, "Lawyer Sanctions: Looking through the Looking Glass," I *Georgetown J.Legal Ethics* 469 (1988).

Leubsdorf, "Three Models of Professional Reform," 67 *Cornell L.Rev.* 1021 (1982).

Olley, "The Future of Self–Regulation: A Consumer Economist's Viewpoint," in *The Professions and Public Policy* (P. Slayton and M. Trebidock eds., 1978).

K. Ostberg, *HALT, Attorney Discipline: National Survey and Report* (1990).

Standing Committee on Lawyers' Professional Liability, American Bar Association, *Characteristics of Legal Malpractice: Report of the National Legal Malpractice Data Center* (1989).

Steel and Nimmer, "Lawyers, Clients, and Professional Regulation," 1976 *Am.B.Found.Res.J.* 917.

L. Trakman ed., *Professional Competence and the Law* (1981).

Wilkins, "Who Should Regulate Lawyers?", 105 *Harv.L.Rev.* 799 (1992).

Wilson, "The Politics of Regulation," in *The Politics of Regulation* (J. Wilson ed., 1980).

F. Zemans & V. Rosenblum, *The Making of a Public Profession* (1981).

✝